UNDERSTANDING
ORGANISATIONAL CONTEXT

We work with leading authors to develop the strongest educational materials in business and finance, bringing cutting-edge thinking and best learning practice to a global market.

Under a range of well-known imprints, including Financial Times Prentice Hall, we craft high quality print and electronic publications which help readers to understand and apply their content, whether studying or at work.

To find out more about the complete range of our publishing please visit us on the World Wide Web at: **www.pearsoned.co.uk**

UNDERSTANDING
ORGANISATIONAL CONTEXT

Inside and outside organisations

Second Edition

CLAIRE CAPON

Business School
Staffordshire University

FT Prentice Hall
FINANCIAL TIMES

An imprint of **Pearson Education**
Harlow, England • London • New York • Boston • San Francisco • Toronto • Sydney • Singapore • Hong Kong
Tokyo • Seoul • Taipei • New Delhi • Cape Town • Madrid • Mexico City • Amsterdam • Munich • Paris • Milan

Pearson Education Limited

Edinburgh Gate
Harlow
Essex CM20 2JE
England

and Associated Companies throughout the world

Visit us on the World Wide Web at:
www.pearsoned.co.uk

First published 2000
Second edition published 2004

© Pearson Education Limited 2000, 2004

ISBN 0 273 67660 1

British Library Cataloguing-in-Publication Data
A catalogue record for this book is available from the British Library

10 9 8 7 6 5 4 3 2 1
08 07 06 05 04

Typeset in 9.5/13pt Stone by 35
Printed by Ashford Colour Press Ltd., Gosport

The publisher's policy is to use paper manufactured from sustainable forests.

Contents

3 Organisational behaviour   81

4 Marketing   107

5 Operations management   151

8 The external environment   275

9 The composition of the external environment   293

List of case studies

Preface

The response to the first edition of *Understanding Organisational Context* has been excellent. Hence the approach of the first edition has been maintained, while revising and updating the text for this new edition. Facts and figures have been updated, with new data and information being included where it has been appropriate to do so, including a new chapter on organisational behaviour. In addition each chapter now contains 'Check your understanding' activities throughout and concludes with a full chapter summary. The learning outcomes have been specifically linked to appropriate activities at the end of each chapter, namely the case studies and assignment questions. The short-answer questions remain, the case studies have been updated to provide contemporary material, and a glossary has been added.

Overall, the desire remains to provide students studying broad-based business modules with a useful and appealing textbook covering both the external and internal environments of organisations, unlike the many business environment textbooks currently on the market.

A *Lecturer's Guide* is available at **www.booksites.net/capon** for lecturers adopting this book.

Claire Capon
May 2003

Teaching with this book

This textbook is designed to be used on level 1 modules on courses in business studies or on courses with a significant element of business in them. Examples of such courses would be BA Business Studies, BA Business Administration, HND/HNC Business Studies or courses such as BSc/HND Business and Technology. Additionally this book can be used successfully with postgraduate and post-experience students studying business for the first time.

This book is suitable for modules that examine the context in which organisations operate. The organisational context model, shown at the start of each chapter, summarises all that is covered in this book and provides a useful diagrammatic overview of all that organisations have to consider.

This edition of *Understanding Organisational Context* introduces organisations before going on to examine organisations and their environments more closely. The inside of organisations and what they consist of is considered in Chapter 1 by looking at organisations as resource converters, which organise or structure themselves to best use the resources and succeed in their external environment. The idea of organisational culture linked to structure is also explored briefly in Chapter 1. Correspondingly, Chapter 2 examines the influence of personal and national culture on doing business. Chapter 3 covers organisational behaviour by looking at the individual, groups and leadership in organisations.

The four key functions or areas of activity for organisations are covered in Chapters 4 to 7 (marketing, operations management, finance, and human resource management). Chapter 4 looks at the development of marketing, the discipline as it is today and some marketing tools. Chapter 5 presents an overview of the operations management activities that both manufacturing and service providers will undertake. Chapter 6 covers finance by looking at the key areas of financial management and management accounting, along with financial reporting and financial stakeholders (for more on stakeholders, *see* Chapter 11). Human resource (HR) management is examined in Chapter 7, covering the impact of the external environment on the HR function and the recruitment process.

Chapter 8 examines why organisations analyse their external environment and how such analysis may be undertaken. Chapter 9 builds on Chapter 8 and explores in great detail the elements that could go to make up the external environment of an organisation. Chapter 10 continues with the theme of the external environment, but considers an extremely important constituent of any organisation's external environment, namely competition.

The later part of the book examines tools and techniques for organisations to analyse and manage their position with respect to both their internal and external environments. Chapter 11 is devoted to stakeholder and SWOT analysis. The material on stakeholder analysis examines how an organisation can identify and manage those other organisations and people, both external and internal, that may have a role to play in the future of the organisation. The pages on SWOT analysis examine different approaches to analysing the internal strengths and weaknesses and external opportunities and threats of organisations. In common with Chapter 11, Chapter 12 considers tools and techniques for analysing organisations with the aim of gaining an improved understanding of the organisation's situation when managing a changing external or internal environment.

Designing a schedule of study

In modules designed to cover both the internal and external environments of organisations, there are several ways in which this book can be used. The most common semester length is 12 weeks and the most obvious programme of study using this book would be to cover one chapter per week. However, there are many possible combinations in which the chapters of this book could be studied during a 12-week teaching semester.

A possible schedule of study for an organisational context-type module is shown below. This schedule of study takes two weeks to cover Chapter 9, due to its length.

In considering the four key functional areas, tutors may choose to omit one as it is covered elsewhere on the students' course. For example, many business studies students will cover finance and accounting in a separate module. This is illustrated in the design of the schedule of study shown below.

Alternatively, if an area is not covered anywhere else on the first year of a business studies programme, it may be that more than one week will be spent on it in the organisational context-type module. The example used in the schedule of study shown below is operations management, which takes two weeks.

The remaining weeks of such a module may be used to cover the chapters presenting a variety of tools and techniques (Chapters 11 and 12).

Possible schedule of study for an organisational context-type module

Week 1	Chapter 1	Inside organisations
Week 2	Chapter 2	Culture and organisations
Week 3	Chapter 3	Organisational behaviour
Week 4	Chapter 4	Marketing
Week 5	Chapter 5	Operations management
Week 6	Chapter 5	Operations management
Week 7	Chapter 7	Human resource management
Week 8	Chapter 8	The external environment
Week 9	Chapter 9	The composition of the external environment
Week 10	Chapter 9	The composition of the external environment
Week 11	Chapter 10	The competitive environment
Week 12	Chapter 12	Managing a changing environment

Module delivery
To aid the tutor in delivering organisational context-type modules, a number of features appear in each chapter.

Clear chapter structure
Each chapter has the same layout: the organisational context model; entry case study; introduction; main text, including 'Check your understanding' activities throughout; full chapter summary; ethical issues case study with learning outcomes and questions; exit case study with learning outcomes and questions; short-answer questions; assignment questions with learning outcomes; weblinks; further reading; and references.

Organisational context model
The organisational context model at the start of each chapter shows by shading the areas examined in that particular chapter. This allows readers to see at a glance what is covered in a chapter.

Learning outcomes
Detailed learning outcomes allow tutors to check that they have covered everything they intended with a class and they also allow students to check that they have achieved the knowledge and skills covered by a particular chapter.

Case studies
There are three case studies in each chapter. Most of the case studies are copyright extracts from the *Financial Times* and are reproduced with its kind permission.

The entry case studies provide an example of the topic(s) covered in a chapter and are often referred to in the main text of the chapter by way of a real-life example. Therefore students should be encouraged to read the entry case study before starting to read the chapter in detail. Students should also be encouraged to refer back to the entry case study, if necessary, when it is discussed or referred to in the main text.

The ethical issues case studies appear at the end of chapters and have been included to provide a vehicle for discussion of some of the ethical or less clear-cut issues surrounding a topic. In contrast, the exit case studies have been chosen to allow students to apply the knowledge and skills gained to a real-life situation. In addition the ethical and exit case studies now have learning outcomes linked to them, making it easier to use them for coursework assessments.

Questions at end of chapter
The short-answer questions found at the end of each chapter have several uses. They could constitute a quick testing mechanism with students to see whether they have learned basic facts about a topic. This could be done in the form of an in-class quiz. Alternatively, if the formal examination for the organisational context-type module contains a section of short-answer questions, those provided in the book allow students an opportunity to practise answering short-answer questions.

Finally, the assignment questions are intended to be used for formal assessed coursework. The normal length of report or essay that a student should be able to produce in response to such questions is around 2000 words.

Lecturer's Guide
A *Lecturer's Guide* is available to lecturers adopting this book and can be found at **www.booksites.net/capon**.

About the author Claire Capon teaches strategy in the Business School at Staffordshire University. She previously taught in the Business School at Sheffield Hallam University. She has worked as a researcher at Huddersfield Polytechnic, and at UMIST as a researcher in the areas of strategic management and the use of design by SMEs.

A Companion Website accompanies
Understanding Organisational Context, 2nd edition
by Claire Capon

Visit the *Understanding Organisational Context* Companion Website at **www.booksites.net/capon** to find valuable teaching and learning material including:

For Students:
- Learning objectives for each chapter
- Multiple choice questions to help test your learning
- Links to relevant sites on the web
- An online glossary to explain key terms

For Lecturers:
- A secure, password protected site with teaching material
- Complete, downloadable Instructor's Manual including additional FT case studies
- PowerPoint slides that can be downloaded and used as OHTs

Also: This site has a syllabus manager, search functions, and email results functions.

Guided tour of the book

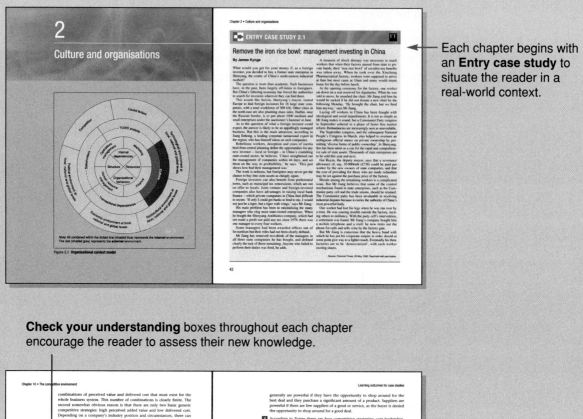

Each chapter begins with an **Entry case study** to situate the reader in a real-world context.

Check your understanding boxes throughout each chapter encourage the reader to assess their new knowledge.

Specific **Learning outcomes for case studies** enable students to focus on the most important concepts being illustrated.

A **Summary** at the end of each chapter reviews the key themes and ensures that these are understood.

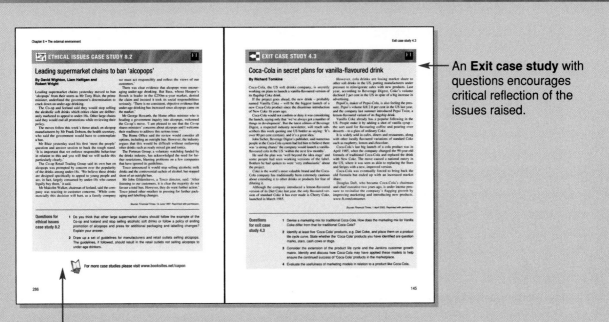

An **Exit case study** with questions encourages critical reflection of the issues raised.

In every chapter, an **Ethical case study** requires students to examine and gain an understanding of the role of ethics in business.

Weblinks, **Further reading** and **References** at the end of each chapter recommend reliable sources for further research and study.

Assignment questions provides activities for seminar and out-of-class use. These are preceded by **Learning outcomes** to indicate the objectives of these tasks.

Acknowledgements

I would like to thank my new friends and colleagues in the Business School at Staffordshire University who have enthused at the prospect of a second edition. This was invaluable while the manuscript was in preparation. Thanks also go to Brian Capon, Julia Capon and Ruth Capon. Finally, but by no means least, thanks go to Andrew Taylor, my development editor at Pearson Education, for his work and ideas on developing the text.

Publisher's acknowledgements

We are grateful to the Financial Times Limited for permission to reprint the following material:

Virtuous circle of a two-wheeled wonder, © *Financial Times*, 17 October 2002; Syngenta tries rice in fight for GM approval, © *Financial Times*, 20 August 2002; Remove the iron rice bowl: management investing in China, © *Financial Times*, 26 May 1998; Hewitt to call time on culture of long working hours, © *Financial Times*, 4 February 2002; Long-hours culture 'stalls better work-life balance, © *Financial Times*, 26 April 2002; US sets the pace in 'the culture of learning': View from the top: Stephen Kelly of Chordiant, © *Financial Times*, 3 April 2002; A man of strategic vision, © *Financial Times*, 30 June 2003; Delivering first-class leadership, © *Financial Times*, 20 February 2003; The Pearl River delta is attracting $1bn of investment a month amid one of the fastest bursts of economic development in history, © *Financial Times*, 4 February 2003; China's urban cool develop a thirst for a cappuccino, © *Financial Times*, 21 May 1998; Tobacco advertising, © *Financial Times*, 1 September 2001; Coca-Cola in secret plans for vanilla-flavoured drink, © *Financial Times*, 1 April 2002; Lessons in improvement, © *Financial Times*, 23 February 1998; The war of the weeds, © *Financial Times*, 4 July 2001; Boeing, boeing, bong, © *Financial Times*, 6 February, 1998; SmithKline's well-sugared pill, © *Financial Times*, 22 February 1997; PFI Vanishing trick, © *Financial Times*, 8 March 2002; TUC calls for up to 29% rise in minimum wage, © *Financial Times*, 12 August 2002; Alternative to poaching, © *Financial Times*, 13 February 1997; There's no accounting for magic, © *Financial Times*, 29 January 1997; Flexible friends, © *Financial Times*, 29 January 1997; US airlines: Big carriers unlikely to find much relief, © *Financial Times*, 30 January 2003; Leading supermarket chains to ban 'alcopops', © *Financial Times*, 14 June 1997; As annual sales near $270bn, can Wal-Mart conquer markets outside the US?, © *Financial Times*, 8 January 2003; Peugeot to build new plant in Slovakia, © *Financial Times*, 16 January 2003; 'People, plagues and prosperity', © *Financial Times*, 26 February 2003; Nike weighs return to Cambodia, © *Financial Times*, 18 June 2003; The holiday package undone by the internet, © *Financial Times*, 21 May 2003; Return to the wild frontier, © *Financial Times*, 1 April 1997; Ja! Organic wins fans, © *Financial Times*, 29 October 2001; Business keeps rolling, © *Financial*

Times, 25 October 1997; How Monsanto got bruised in a food fight, © *Financial Times*, 8 March 2002; The museum locked in the past, © *Financial Times*, 15 February 2002; Tata looks to MG Rover and the future, © *Financial Times*, 18 March 2003.

We are grateful to the following for permission to use copyright material:

Relative advantages of a personal passion from *The Financial Times Limited*, 19 September 2002, © Clare Gascoigne; Cruising: Sea change required on security from *The Financial Times Limited*, 7 September 2002, © Bill Glenton.

Exhibit 2.3 from *International Business: Competing in the Global Marketplace*, The McGraw-Hill Companies (Hill, Charles W.L., 1999 (2nd edn); Exhibits 2.4 and 11.4 from *Exploring Corporate Strategy*, Prentice Hall (Johnson, G. and Scholes, K., 1999); Exhibit 7.6 from *Personnel Management: HRM in Action* (Torrington, D. and Hill, L. 1995 (3rd edn); Exhibit 9.5 from http://bizednet.bris.ac.uk/compfact/tuc/tuc25.htm, the Trades Union Congress; Exhibit 9.12 from www.nato.int/welcome/home.htm, the North Atlantic Treaty Organization; Exhibit 9.18 from www.oecd.org/about/whats.htm, the Organisation for Economic Co-operation and Development; Exhibits 10.3 and 10.4, Reprinted with the permission of The Free Press, a Division of Simon & Schuster Adult Publishing Group, from *Competitive Advantage: Creating and Sustaining Superior Performance* by Michael E. Porter. Copyright C 1985, 1998 by Michael E. Porter. All rights reserved.

In some instances we have been unable to trace the owners of copyright material, and we would appreciate any information that would enable us to do so.

1

Inside organisations

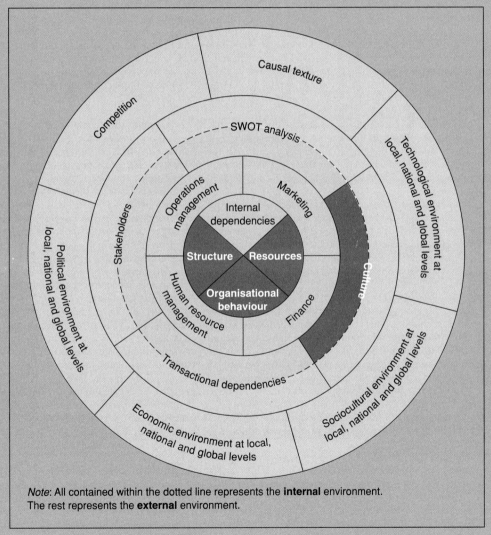

Note: All contained within the dotted line represents the **internal** environment.
The rest represents the **external** environment.

Figure 1.1 Organisational context model

ENTRY CASE STUDY 1.1

FT

Virtuous circle of a two-wheeled wonder

By Richard Donkin

Do the qualities that mark out a great employer fit with those that make a great company? What is a great company anyway? Is it one that has staying power or – to quote the buzz phrase of the moment – sustainability? Or is it one that makes a lot of money this year and next in a headlong rush for growth? Or has it nothing to do with money and everything to do with the products or services?

All these questions were prompted by a visit last week to the Oxford-based headquarters of Harley-Davidson Europe. More than any other company I have encountered in the past few years, Harley-Davidson appears to have cracked the 'great company' formula, producing a virtuous circle of desirable product, customer adoration and attentive employees.

How did the people at Harley do it with a motorcycle that in the 1970s had a reputation for unreliability and which could not hope to compete for speed with the Japanese best of breeds? Can there really be much mileage in a niche product that appeals to middle-aged rockers?

I don't ride motorcycles and know that only the most menopausal of 40-something men traverse their mid-life crises with visions of *Easy Rider* motoring on an open road. But the Harley offices all have motorbikes in their meeting rooms so it seemed churlish to refuse when John Russell, the managing director, relieved me of my bag and said: 'Go on, why not sit on it?'

Mr Russell is a Harley rider. He regularly rides out to places where other Harley owners meet. It's what bikers do. And this way he gets to know what they're saying about the bikes and about those of the competition. Harley is constantly drawing on feedback from the 700,000-strong Harley Owners Group – what Mr Russell calls 'connecting with the marketplace'. It also helps that about a quarter of the company's 9,000 employees owns Harley motorcycles.

It's tempting to think that the company relies on serendipity for its success. But *More Than a Motorcycle* (Harvard Business School Press, $24.95) by Rich Teerlink, retired chairman and chief executive, and Lee Ozley, an organisational consultant and coach, demonstrates that the company's resurgence after its struggle for survival in the early 1980s was underpinned by a fundamental restructuring of its management-employee relations. As the authors point out, this wasn't achieved overnight, or without a great deal of discussion and more than a few mistakes.

The result, however, is a strongly participative management style based on union involvement in decision-making and the encouragement of cross-functional collaboration. 'If you strip it all back,' says Mr Russell, 'We're behaving like human beings. If you treat people the way you want to be treated, you become a team.'

Genuine employee involvement seems to be a common feature among many of those companies that tend to be mentioned or listed repeatedly as exceptional employers. Whether it's the partnership structure of John Lewis in the UK or the deliberately egalitarian atmosphere of the Asda supermarket chain, which has driven out all the trappings of status that differentiate hierarchies from rank and file employees, there is a recognised productivity dividend in securing employee commitment.

An important conclusion of the Teerlink/Ozley research was that motivation could be defined as 'the drive within people that causes them to behave as they do'. If all human behaviour is 'motivated', they argued, it did not have to be the job of managers to motivate others but to ensure that employee motivation was aligned with the needs and priorities of the company.

Many of the ideas for achieving this came from a leadership training and development session. Most of the suggestions were quite simple and painless, such as 'keep people informed' and 'be courteous'. Some were straightforward perks such as providing a company bike for department use by employees, or forms of recognition, such as incentives for cross-functional training and offering stock options.

Another feature of great employers is that they work out how they should be doing things, often in close consultation with the people in the front line. Then they do things in an even-handed way from top to bottom. In *Great to Good* (Random House Business Books, £20), Jim Collins points out how Carl Reichardt started at the top when he decided to cut down waste after taking over as chief executive at Wells Fargo bank. Out went the executive dining room, the corporate jets and exotic plants from the executive suite and in came a two-year freeze on executive salaries.

Ken Iverson attacked hierarchical differences with an almost fanatical zeal when he became chief executive of Nucor, the steel company, reducing layers of management and cramming the tiny headquarters staff into a cheaply furnished rented office 'the size of a small dental practice'. Executives ended up with fewer perks than other employees. Visiting executives lunched in a sandwich shop across the street.

▶

Another widely celebrated example of this focus on the way that work is undertaken and the way that managers and employees relate to each other is Dallas-based Southwest Airlines where employees are given the information they need to 'think like owners' and take their own decisions. Chief executive Herb Kelleher has stressed the need for people to enjoy the work that they do. The idea that 'work should be fun' is built into the philosophy of the company.

At Happy Computers, a London-based IT training company, the concept is included in the name. As Henry Stewart, managing director, explains. 'You can't pick up the phone and say "Happy Computers" with a grumpy voice.'

A common misunderstanding by those who try to emulate the management style of these companies, is that securing workplace commitment is simply a matter of installing certain procedures. It is not. A great workplace is sustained only by a shared belief in the product or service and a constant attention to employee concerns. What all these businesses have in common is a deep understanding of people. They don't see employees as a necessary expense but as part of the community as people who like to be around each other.

They know how people react. Like John Russell when he asked me to sit on the bike. Motorbikes don't make sense. If you list the pros and cons, the reasons for not having one begin to run off the page. But then you sit on a Harley and begin to salivate. So why do people ride these bikes? Simple, says Mr Russell, 'It's cool.' It is, and I want one.

Source: *Financial Times*, 17 October 2002. Reprinted with permission.

Introduction

We all live in an increasingly complex and dynamic world in which organisations feature significantly. We work for organisations, we shop at them, we spend our leisure time in them and use them to improve the quality of our life (e.g. schools, doctors and dentists). Some of us even choose to teach about organisations or to study them at college or university.

This introductory chapter looks at **public-sector** and private-sector organisations and some of their elements and features, such as the use of resources, legal structures and organisational cultures and structures. The entry case study for this chapter on Harley-Davidson demonstrates the importance of people and organisational culture in the decision making process for a successful organisation.

The culture at Harley-Davidson, and other successful companies such as John Lewis, is often underpinned by good staff and their extensive involvement in the organisation, its management and development. Successful companies not only depend on staff, but also on correctly configuring resources such that they are used efficiently and effectively. For organisations such as the steel company Nucor, mentioned in the entry case study, this meant delayering the management structure and reducing costs. Equally Carl Reichardt of Wells Fargo bank (*see* entry case study) also cut costs and removed executive 'perks' such as corporate jets, exotic plants and the executive dining room. Both these corporate leaders sought to reduce the use of tangible resources and associated costs in their respective organisations with the clear aim of improving the efficiency with which resources were used.

Organisations may also seek to shape intangible resources. The company Happy Computers has its image deeply embedded in its name, 'You can't pick up the phone and say "Happy Computers" with a grumpy voice' (*see* entry case study). Good managers use resources, including people, money, facilities, buildings, image and reputation to develop successful organisations.

The public and private sectors

■ Characteristics of the public sector

The public sector consists of enterprises in which the whole or a majority stake is owned by either local or national government, or another publicly owned body established by government. Table 1.1 gives some examples of the more important organisations in the UK that remain in the public sector.

State schools deliver compulsory education free to children in the local area. Traditionally, local schools have been funded from and run by local government. However, in an effort to promote higher standards and to circumvent local authorities where the party in power was opposed to that in central government, the Conservatives introduced a system to allow for schools to opt out of local control and be funded directly by central government.

Some organisations that have been part of the public sector have had a mixed history. Some companies were private, then were nationalised, i.e. taken into public ownership, by previous Labour governments, and are now privately owned again. The largest wave of nationalisations occurred under the first post-war administration when Labour swept into power in the 1945 general election. The railway system in Britain was nationalised after the Second World War and British Rail was formed. This was followed about 40 years later by the privatisation of the railway system in the early 1990s under a Conservative government. This privatisation saw the formation of Railtrack (since replaced by Network Rail) and many train operating companies. Railtrack was responsible for running and maintaining track, signals and stations. The train operating companies, of which there are many (e.g. Midland Mainline and Virgin), run train services. The right to operate a train service on a particular route is determined by the train operating company purchasing the franchise to do so. For example, Midland Mainline runs services between London and Sheffield, while services from London to Glasgow are operated by Virgin on the west coast and GNER on the east coast.

As the public sector is owned and regulated by government itself, it operates in markedly different ways from the private sector. Public-sector organisations

**Table 1.1
Public-sector
organisations**

● National government	● NTVLRO	● Fire and rescue services
– ministries and departments	● Local government	● Universities and colleges
– agencies	● National Health Service	● State schools
– civil service	● Armed services	● Royal Mail
● DVLA	● Police forces	● Post Office

**Table 1.2
Privatised
organisations**

● Deregulated regional and local bus companies	● British Airways
● Regional electricity boards	● British Aerospace
● Regional water boards	● British Rail
● British Telecom	● British Steel
● British Gas	● British Coal

tend to provide a service over which they have a monopoly, or certainly most of the responsibility for provision. Public-sector organisations tend to be large and bureaucratic entities, governed by strict rules and procedures that are often prescribed in law.

■ Market forces

The Conservative governments between 1979 and 1997 believed strongly that the private sector, and competition in particular, had certain advantages over the monopolistic public sector. They believed that market forces and competition could bring better value for money in terms of public expenditure and for private individuals. Many organisations that had been in the public sector since nationalisation were privatised, i.e. sold off to the mass public, in what prime minister Margaret Thatcher referred to as the creation of a 'shareholder democracy'. It was felt that a deregulated private sector operating in a free market would be able to provide all the services and products needed at the market price. Examples of privatised organisations are shown in Table 1.2. This also led to considerable one-off cash revenues for the government, which were used in other parts of the government's fiscal policy.

An internal market was introduced to the NHS by the Conservative government in the late 1980s in an attempt to introduce some of the perceived benefits of private-sector operation, such as flexibility of decision making and market forces' effects on cost and pricing strategy. This allowed for general practitioners to become fundholders, deploying funds along with their referral of patients to hospitals, so that the number of referrals to a certain hospital became a key source of revenue. Hospitals, previously run by locally appointed boards on which locally elected councillors held a majority of seats, were able to opt out of this system and establish themselves as independent NHS trusts, directly funded by central government.

Public-sector organisations are sometimes run at a loss to government or are sometimes required to recoup their operating costs through income generation. However, public-sector enterprises rarely operate in order to make a profit.

■ Characteristics of the private sector

The private sector consists of privately owned companies and businesses. These may be owned by individuals, families or groups, or they may be large organisations that are quoted publicly on the Stock Exchange, with ownership residing in the hands of shareholders. The differences between limited companies and public limited companies are discussed later in this chapter, but for now it is enough to understand that a 'public limited company' has nothing to do with the public sector. Private-sector companies are regulated by laws and regulations introduced by the local, national and global levels of the external political environment.

Some services provided by the public sector also have private-sector providers, including hospitals and schools. Just as 'plcs' are not in the public sector, the term 'public school' refers to privately owned and run schools for which parents pay tuition fees, and not the free state-run counterparts.

As mentioned above, public-sector organisations are sometimes funded partly through their own income-generation activities, but their main source of income is budgets awarded by government from its tax revenues. For example, Strathclyde Passenger Transport Authority receives £35 million per annum from council tax, collected by local government, to subsidise rail services. Therefore, private-sector organisations making money and paying taxes in fact fund activities in the public sector. Private-sector organisations look to recoup their costs and make profits from their business activities.

■ Public and private partnership

The election of the Labour government in 1997 did not see the reversal of privatisation policies or a commitment to renationalise already privatised industries. Further privatisations, such as attempts to privatise the Post Office or the Royal Mail – which had been split into two for this purpose by the Conservatives – have, to date, not been pursued. Instead, the message became the formation of direct partnerships between the public and private sectors. The Conservatives began this idea with 'Private Finance Initiatives', enabling public-sector organisations to raise money for projects in private money markets, and it has been continued by Labour. For example, private monies continue to be available for public bridge and road-building schemes, schools, hospitals and prisons.

✓ Check your understanding

Do you understand the differences between a private-sector and public-sector organisation?

Check your understanding by describing and giving an example (not mentioned in this text) of both a public and private-sector organisation. Can you identify any type of organisation which operates in both the public and private sector?

Organisational resource conversion

One characteristic that all organisations share, irrespective of sector or activity, is the fact that they take in resources, process them, then deliver outputs which have greater value than the original inputs. The processes to which the inputs are subjected is known as organisational resource conversion, and all organisations engage in it to a greater or lesser extent. This is as true of public-sector organisations as it is of private-sector companies, and can be observed in both service and manufacturing sectors. A consumer appliance factory buys steel, motors and components, passes them through its machines and the hands of its workers, and sends out refrigerators that sell for more than the cost of the steel, components and labour. A university recruits school or college leavers, submits them to several years' teaching, learning and assessments, and passes out graduates who command higher salaries than they could have done without their higher education experience. Further examples are given later in this section.

In examining the resource conversion process, the organisation can be depicted as a chart containing a sequential list of inputs, conversion processes and consequent outputs (*see* Table 1.3). There are also three kinds of inputs, processes and outputs: human, tangible and intangible. These are discussed in detail later in this chapter.

Table 1.3 Organisational resource conversion chart

	Resource inputs	Processes	Outputs
Human	● Owners/ shareholders ● Managers ● Employees ● Part-timers ● Contractors	● Goal setting ● Decision making ● Planning products and services ● Managing functions (including HRM) ● Assembling parts ● Manufacturing goods ● Dealing with customers	● Job satisfaction or dissatisfaction ● Salaries and wages ● Bonuses ● Satisfied or dissatisfied customers
Tangibles	● Money (loans, overdrafts, profits, private capital) ● Buildings ● Machines and equipment ● Raw materials ● Components ● Energy (gas, water, electricity) ● Market research data	● Assembly ● Manufacture ● Service delivery ● Supply ● Quality control ● Accounting ● Distribution ● Formal communication systems ● Formal information systems	● Products ● Services ● Waste materials ● Waste energy ● Effluent ● Profit or loss
Intangibles	● Systems ● Design ● Information ● Innovation	● Informal communication ● Culture ● Corporate memory ● Informal information flow	● Professionalism ● Happiness ● Image and reputation ● Innovation

A generic organisational resource conversion chart delineates those activities that all organisations share. The generic chart can be adapted and applied to individual organisations according to their particular context. Following this generic chart, the model is applied to four fictional organisational examples.

The chart for any specific organisation contains those elements that are generically applicable to any organisation, such as buildings, as well as elements that apply specifically to an individual organisation's particular sector, activities or other contextual factors, e.g. a bakery needs flour and yeast as its raw materials in order to bake bread. Therefore, when using the organisational resource conversion chart to examine closely what any given organisation actually does, an exact model of its resource conversion process must contain generic inputs, processes and outputs as well as the specific elements, which are those inputs, processes and outputs found only in the individual organisational context.

It must also be recognised that while inputs, processes and outputs can be shown separately in the conversion model, they should not be considered as independent of each other. In the same way that organisations cannot be considered as independent of their external contexts, clear transactional dependencies can be identified between the various cause-and-effect stages of the resource conversion process, i.e. there can be no outputs if there are no conversion processes, and the processes cannot operate without inputs. Initially, however, each stage of the process is considered separately here.

As previously mentioned, resource inputs can be grouped into three categories: human resources (the people in the organisation); **tangible resources** (e.g. machines and money); and **intangible resources** (e.g. information). Both financial and human resources are covered in detail in this book (Chapters 6 and 7 respectively) as internal functional departments of the organisation, each interacting independently and together with elements of the external environment. However, in this chapter money and people are considered as inputs to the organisational resource conversion process.

■ Human resources

Human resource inputs are obviously key to organisational success, as without people there can be no organisational activity. Despite hierarchical definitions of roles and responsibilities within organisations, which differentiate employer and employee, manager and worker, all make fundamental contributions to the organisation's activity through their efforts. These efforts must be as effective and efficient as possible in order for operational costs to be minimised, while outputs and profits are maximised. Human resources, once input to the organisation, obviously contribute to the conversion processes themselves, regardless of their roles, responsibilities or level in the organisation. Without the right people in the right roles there is little or no possibility of the organisation being able to achieve its goals. Employers or managers have specific roles and responsibilities, which usually include recruiting, managing and supervising the human resources inputs of the organisation. Employees also have specified roles and responsibilities, which usually become more and more defined according to how low down the hierarchy the human resource input is made.

Organisations have to consider what human resource inputs they need to begin, maintain and develop their operations, and how many people are necessary in order to achieve a critical mass for operational efficiency and effectiveness. People in organisations then need to be managed on an ongoing basis in order to ensure that they have the relevant skills at the appropriate level to fulfil the responsibilities their roles require. The numbers of human resources input to the organisation then need to be monitored in order to respond to the changing needs of the operations, i.e. is it growing, shrinking or maintaining its size as a reaction to changes in the marketplace? Human resource management, then, is concerned with getting people into the organisation, making sure they can do the jobs they need to do while they are there, and planning for getting them out of the organisation when necessary. Human resource management is covered in Chapter 7.

■ Tangible resources – finance

Perhaps the most important tangible resource input is money. As in the case of human resources, without money the organisation is totally inoperable. Whether in the private or public sector, all organisations must raise money in order to survive. Financial inputs come from a variety of sources, such as shareholders, banks, profits, budget allocations from head office or reallocation of retained profits. Public sources of financial inputs include grants or allocated budgets from different levels of the state, including local government, or from supra-national bodies such as the European Union.

Financial inputs contribute to the organisational resource conversion process in three main ways. First, financial resources fund the acquisition of all other inputs. Money is needed to fund the human resources via their salaries or wages. How much the organisation can afford to pay its employees affects its ability to recruit and retain the people it needs to accomplish its tasks. Motivation is also directly linked to the amount of financial resource devoted to rewarding the efforts of its human resources. In the case of a manufacturing or assembly operation, money purchases the raw materials or component parts necessary to be able to manufacture the organisation's portfolio of products. Additional key inputs to the resource conversion process in a manufacturing organisation include machinery, equipment, and the energy required to operate it, along with the spare parts needed for repair and maintenance. In the service sector, money still funds all other inputs in terms of the service design, physical location of the service delivery and paying for the operation of customer service departments. It also funds the purchasing of external market information, which informs the internal operations of the organisation.

Second, financial resources fund the conversion processes themselves, not only by having paid for the inputs the organisation needs but also by providing the money the conversion processes themselves need. A factory that has purchased its machines needs a healthy cashflow to be able to run them on a daily basis, pay weekly wages or monthly salaries, and provide the money to fund all aspects of operations management, marketing, accounting and quality control that enable it to function. Equally, in the public-sector example of a hospital, money must be found to fund the daily activities of routine surgery, accident and emergency departments, organ transplants and the space for patients to recuperate.

Finally, financial resources are needed in the output stage, to fund the delivery and distribution of the organisation's services or products to its customers in the marketplace, at an appropriate time or location. In addition, sufficient financial resources are required to fund the advertising, sales promotion and marketing of the organisation's products and services, such that the organisation's external image is maintained and developed effectively. Even the disposal of waste products has a financial implication for the organisation.

■ Tangible resources

The next category of tangible resources to be considered are raw materials or component parts and these are obviously necessary for organisations to make the products or provide the services they offer to the marketplace. Key issues when considering raw materials or component parts are costs and quality, as organisations seek to maximise profits by minimising the cost of inputs, without compromising the quality of the resultant output products and services.

All organisations need premises or buildings, and they must have sufficient equipment in those premises for manufacturing, communications and health and safety requirements. There are issues here in relation to size of premises, their location – are they near to population centres, motorway networks, sea ports? – and their appropriateness for the required function – are there conversion costs or is it a purpose-built greenfield site?

Slightly less obvious tangible inputs are the resources purchased from the utility companies, e.g. water (including sewage and effluent treatment), gas and electricity, as well as local authority services such as transport infrastructure and refuse collection. These are inevitably key, as organisations cannot function without the input of energy to fuel their machines and light and heat their offices. In addition, roads providing access to the organisation for cars and lorries, convenient bus routes, bus stops and other connections for public transport as well as the regular collection and disposal of its waste are vital to ensure the organisation can function efficiently and effectively.

■ Intangible resources

Finally, there are intangible inputs to organisations, which consist of information and design. Information is essential, enabling an organisation to understand, analyse and react to events in its external environment. The key information inputs that organisations use for this purpose concern the marketplace and competitors. In terms of market information, an organisation needs to know how big the market is, what potential customers are likely to need or want, and how it could provide products or services that meet those needs. In terms of competitor information, an organisation needs to monitor what products or services competitor organisations provide, how much they are charging for these and what share of the market they currently serve. Marketing is considered in more detail in Chapter 4.

Information about the external political and economic environment is equally key for organisations, especially at times of impending significant change such as a general election or national budget, as such information must be used in attempting to predict or anticipate changes in the external environment, hence allowing the organisation to adapt to anything that is likely to have a major effect on it. How well this resource input of information is gathered, analysed and disseminated within the organisation – sending the right information to the right department at the right time – is both a symptom and a cause of operational effectiveness. A good information flow demonstrates that an organisation understands and analyses its external environment and ensures that it continues to be able to do so.

The design of an organisation's systems and processes can also be considered as an input to its resource conversion process. The efficient and effective design of the organisation, its internal communication systems, its accounting procedures, the factory layout or the positioning and decoration of its reception area, are all manifestations of its interaction with its external environment. The particular conversion processes that add value to the resource inputs vary according to the organisation and the business it is in. Perhaps the most easily understandable resource conversion process is manufacturing, where raw materials such as steel are turned physically into products such as automobiles. Some materials may be subassembled elsewhere, and these components may later be used by another organisation as part of its resource conversion process. In the service sector, planning and executing the delivery of a service counts as a resource conversion process, as this is also concerned with adding value to inputs in order to produce outputs.

In order to contextualise the resource conversion process, four different fictional contexts are given below, showing organisational resource conversion charts for public- and private-sector contexts, in manufacturing and services, and at varying levels of the external context.

**Table 1.4
Organisational
resource conversion
chart: Little Mester
Ltd, surgical steel
instrument maker**

	Resource inputs	Processes	Outputs
Human	• The owner/ manufacturer (Little Mester) • Suppliers	• All aspects of the business, including planning, manufacturing and selling done by the owner • Providing raw metal and small components	• Job satisfaction • Development of the toolmaker's craft • Wages and profits for the business • Satisfied customers
Tangibles	• Loans, mortgages, overdrafts, sales income, profits • Workshop and home • Machinery • Raw metals • Component parts • Energy	• Supplying metal and components • Manufacture and assembly of tools • Quality control (probably informal – throwing away or recycling mistakes) • Accounting • Delivering products to hospitals • Letters and adverts	• Surgical tools • Waste metal (maybe re-input as recycled raw metal) • Profit or losses
Intangibles	• Very informal systems for monitoring customer needs and reacting to them	• Everything is in the owner's head and hands	• Professionalism • Happiness • Image and reputation • Specialisation

---

✓ Check your understanding

Do you understand the term 'organisational resource conversion chart'?

Check your understanding by explaining how an organisation is represented by an organisational resource conversion chart.

■ Little Mester Ltd, surgical steel instrument maker

The example of a self-employed steel instrument maker (or 'Little Mester') in Sheffield shows a very different resource conversion process chart from the generic model (*see* Table 1.4). The context level is largely local, with some quite specific inputs (raw metals), processes (informal quality control) and outputs (development of the toolmaker's craft).

■ Natpower Ltd, electricity generator

The case of 'Natpower' concerns a private-sector service provider, in this case an electricity generator, in a predominantly national context. Its particular resource conversion chart (*see* Table 1.5) also contains generically applicable elements as well as context-specific items, such as electricity generator plants

**Table 1.5
Organisational
resource conversion
chart: Natpower Ltd,
electricity generator**

	Resource inputs	Processes	Outputs
Human	• Owners/shareholders • Managers • Full- and part-time workers in electricity generation • Contractors supplying services (e.g. repairs)	• Goal setting • Decision making • Planning for meeting electricity needs • Managing functions • Generating electricity from gas or coal • Dealing with electricity distribution companies	• Job satisfaction or dissatisfaction • Salaries and wages • Bonuses • Satisfied or dissatisfied customers
Tangibles	• Income, profits • Electricity generation plants • Generators and the supply grid • Coal or gas to convert and to power the plant • Data to plan electricity needs • Additional energy from overseas • Legal regulation	• Generating electricity • Quality control • Accounting • Supplying electricity via the grid to electricity supply companies • Formal internal communication systems • Formal internal information systems	• Electricity • Waste (pollution)
Intangibles	• Systems • Design • Information • Innovation	• Informal communication • Culture • Corporate memory • Informal information flow	• Professionalism • Happiness • Image and reputation • Innovation • Safety

(input), dealing with electricity distribution companies (process) and the intangible output of safety.

■ China National State Steel Corporation

Although economic reforms in the late 1980s and 1990s have led to the establishment of both a new private sector and newly privatised industries in China, much of the large-scale means of production remain under state control. Thus the example of the China National State Steel Corporation allows resource conversion at the global level of the external environment to be examined in the context of a public-sector manufacturing environment. Again, there are generic and specific elements in its resource conversion process chart (*see* Table 1.6). A huge, state-owned steel corporation in a country governed by a Communist Party has responsibilities far beyond those of private companies in capitalist countries. The organisation not only has to fulfil the demands of the government's plan for production but also has to provide for all the social welfare needs of its employees and their families, including healthcare, schooling, daily provisions and housing. The environment level would be national, although there are global implications for competition and the international political arena.

**Table 1.6
Organisational
resource conversion
chart: China National
State Steel
Corporation**

	Resource inputs	Processes	Outputs
Human	• Managers • Employees • Families	• Liaising with government departments regarding the five-year economic plan • Operational decision making • Planning products • Managing functions • Manufacturing steel and goods • Dealing with other organisations which use the steel	• Meeting the needs of employees and their families in terms of wages and social welfare needs
Tangibles	• State funding, sales income • Steel plants all over China • Machines and equipment • Raw materials • Components • Energy (generated on site) • Five-year plan	• Assembly • Manufacture • Supply • Quality control • Budget management • Distribution • Chinese Communist Party (CCP) organisation • Formal communication systems, including propaganda radio • Formal information systems (CCP)	• Fulfilling the five-year plan • Products • Social services (housing, hospitals, schools, shops) • Waste materials • Waste energy • Effluent and pollution • Profit or loss
Intangibles	• Planning, manufacturing and control systems • Product design • State and party information	• Informal communication between workers and families • Culture • Corporate memory • Informal information flows	• Basic standard of living for all • Party control of workers and families

■ Superbuys

A large, privately owned supermarket's resource conversion chart would, again, be fairly standard (*see* Table 1.7). The context would be global and national: global since many products are imported and there are branches overseas; and national as its largest customer base is in the UK. Specific inputs include suppliers of branded and own-label goods, with specific processes including shelf stacking and specific outputs including the image and reputation of the supermarket.

✓ Check your understanding

Do you understand how to construct an organisational resource conversion chart for an organisation with which you are familiar?

Check your understanding by producing an organisational resource conversion chart for your university, college or employer. Remember to include generic and specific items.

**Table 1.7
Organisational
resource conversion
chart: Superbuys**

	Resource inputs	Processes	Outputs
Human	• Owning family • Managers • Shop workers • Warehouse workers • Truck drivers • Suppliers of branded and own-label goods	• Goal setting • Decision making (e.g. loyalty cards, banking) • Planning products, services and new stores • Managing functions • Manufacturing own-brand goods • Dealing with customers	• Job satisfaction or dissatisfaction • Salaries and wages • Bonuses • Satisfied customers
Tangibles	• Capital, investment • Stores, warehouses • Equipment (checkouts, computers, shelving, lighting) • Imports and domestic goods • Energy • Market research data	• Manufacture • Shelf stacking • Supply and distribution • Quality control • Accounting • Formal communication systems • Formal information systems • Enhanced services (loyalty cards, banking, cafés, petrol stations)	• Products • Services • Waste materials • Waste energy • Effluent • Profit or loss
Intangibles	• Systems • Design • Information • Innovation	• Informal communication • Culture • Corporate memory • Informal information flow	• Professionalism • Happiness • Image and reputation • Innovation

The legal structures of business

■ The sole trader

A **sole trader** business is owned and administered by one person who is personally liable for all the debts of the business, this being the primary disadvantage of this type of legal structure.[1] The sole trader is the owner of the business, having raised the capital for it from personal funds. The sole trader has direct control over the business and takes all the decisions relating to products and services, customers and markets, staff employed and future development. The principal advantage of the sole trader legal structure is that all profits appertain to the owner.[2]

■ Partnership

A **partnership** is where two or more individuals join together in a business venture with each partner having unlimited liability.[3] Therefore, should the partnership result in debt or bankruptcy, each partner can be held liable for the full amount owed by the partnership. Creditors can either sue each partner in turn or all of the partners jointly for as many of the partners' assets as will pay off their debts. The other option is for the partnership to have limited liability, but limited partnerships are uncommon because only some of the partners can have limited liability, so therefore limited liability is usually established by creating a **limited company** instead of a partnership.[4]

■ The limited company

A limited company exists as a legal entity in itself, separately from its owners or managers. Therefore, liability for debts is limited to the amount of issued share capital, whether the shares have been sold or not.[5] The shareholders' personal assets cannot be claimed for the payment of business debts to creditors. The creation of a limited company requires the lodging of various documents with the Registrar of Companies, which must include a Memorandum of Association and Articles of Association. If all documentation is satisfactory, a certificate of incorporation is issued, bringing the company into existence as a legal entity.[6]

☑ Check your understanding

Do you understand the different legal structures a business may adopt?

Check your understanding by comparing and contrasting different legal structures which businesses may adopt.

Organisational structures

The structures that organisations adopt are usually aligned to one of the five generic organisational structures. These are the **simple structure**; the **functional structure**; the **divisional structure**; the **holding company structure**; and the **matrix structure**.

The simple and functional organisational structures are centralised structures where all the important and long-term decisions are taken by top management. Top management will determine the rules and procedures that closely govern and direct the jobs and tasks of managers further down the organisation and are responsible for the departments, products, services and markets on a day-to-day basis.

In contrast the divisional, holding and matrix organisational structures are decentralised, containing divisions/subsidiaries/project teams that have a significant amount of decision-making power and responsibility of their own. Co-operation and co-ordination between the divisions/subsidiaries/project teams and the board of directors are crucial if the spreading of power and responsibility throughout the structure is to work for the organisation as a whole.

**Figure 1.2
The simple structure**

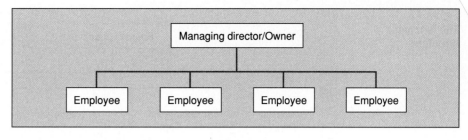

■ The simple structure

A company that adopts a simple structure (*see* Figure 1.2) is likely to be a small business in the private sector or one in the very early stages of its growth and development. The simple structure is centralised, with all short-, medium- and long-term power and decision-making responsibility resting with the managing director, who is also likely to be the owner of the business. The managing director/owner controls and oversees all aspects of the company's operations. Therefore, the simple structure is suitable for a small business in the early stages of growth and development, allowing the managing director/owner to have control over the future growth and development of the business, as s/he has a financial stake in the business, along with expertise relating to the product or service sold by the business and the markets to which it sells.

The simple structure becomes less suitable as the business grows. The managing director/owner finds it more and more difficult to control and oversee the greater number of tasks and activities undertaken by a larger and growing business. However, the likelihood also exists that the managing director/owner has the skills, knowledge and abilities to run a small business, but may be lacking some of those necessary to run a larger and growing business. This situation usually requires the business to restructure if it is to survive its growth and increase further in size. Simple structure businesses that grow in size commonly develop **functional structures**.

■ The functional structure

The functional structure (*see* Figure 1.3) is rigid and centralised with efficient management control systems, and is common both in companies that have outgrown the simple structure and in well-established public-sector organisations. Such organisations are medium sized and have a limited range of related products and services delivered to clearly defined and clearly segmented markets. The functional structure also sees the introduction of specialist functional managers who head the different departments, e.g. marketing manager, operations manager, finance manager and human resource manager. In the case of growing private companies, these new managers provide the specialist skills, knowledge and abilities that may have been missing under the simple structure.

**Figure 1.3
The functional
structure**

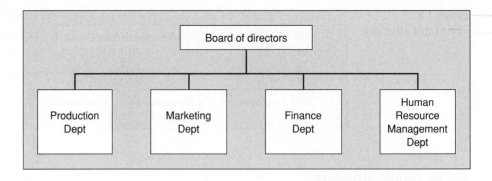

The managing director or board of directors will be in close contact with the new departmental heads who run the different departments on a day-to-day basis, hence the lines of communication and information flow within the functional structure are short and vertical. The structuring of the organisation around the different functions or tasks that have to be carried out by its employees results in job roles that are clearly defined and understood by everyone in the organisation. Short-term decision-making power and responsibility tend to rest with the departmental heads, who have to work together with the board of directors to ensure that what is happening at an operational level also reflects and feeds back into the long-term and medium-term decision-making process. Long- and medium-term decision-making power and responsibility, however, rest very much with the board of directors.

One of the reasons why organisations move on from the functional structure is that the organisation starts to diversify its product or service range and no longer has a limited range of related products or services for a clearly defined and clearly segmented market. An organisation that is outgrowing the functional structure is likely to have developed a wider range of products or services that are not so closely related and that sell to more diverse markets. The growth that has led to the need to restructure could have resulted from selling to markets that are more geographically diverse than was the case previously, e.g. the organisation has engaged in international business where before it dealt purely domestically. Another cause of growth could be selling to a wider customer base with more varied needs and wants than the traditional market segment.

When this type of situation arises, the functional structure becomes very stretched and cannot cope well with the increased diversity. The production and marketing managers now have to deal with a diverse range of products and services in a diverse marketplace, but in the functional structure there is only one marketing department and one production department to do everything. They are used to dealing with a limited range of closely related products or services and do not necessarily have the resources to service wider ranges or market segments. Thus, in essence, the functional structure has to change in order to cope with growth and diversification. It is the centralised and rigid nature of the functional structure that prevents it from adopting the decentralised and flexible practices needed to deal with more diverse markets and product ranges.

The rigid and centralised nature of the functional structure may also make it difficult to operate activities requiring cross-functional teams. Since the organisation is structured in the form of vertical and hierarchical functions, its different departments have clear views on their operational responsibilities and find it difficult to act outside their perceived remit. A classic example of the need for cross-functional teams is product development, which requires inputs from the marketing, operations management and finance departments in order to research what customers want, develop products or services accordingly, cost their delivery and determine their price. It may be difficult to make this work within the confines of a vertical and hierarchical functional structure, with its clearly defined and understood job roles.

■ The divisional structure

A company that has adopted a divisional structure (*see* Figure 1.4) contains separate divisions based around individual product lines or services, e.g. a motor manufacturer may have a car division, a truck and van division, and a passenger service vehicle (bus) division. Alternatively, divisions can be based on the geographic areas of the markets served, e.g. Europe, Asia and North America. Organisations may contain a mixture of different types of divisions, with some based on product or service lines and others geographically allocated, e.g. cars, buses, trucks and overseas sales. However, one single division would not usually be based on both product and location, so it is rare to find divisions called 'cars North America' or 'buses Asia'.

The divisional structure is decentralised and, as such, a company with a divisional structure usually offers a wide and diverse range of products and services compared with a company operating with the more rigid and centralised functional structure. The key benefit of a wide and diverse portfolio is the ability to spread either the general profitability of each division or

**Figure 1.4
The divisional
structure**

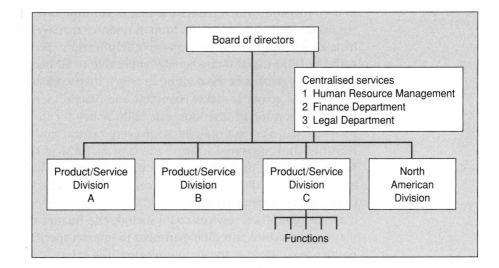

the burden of the poor performance of one of the divisions by subsidising it from the profits of the others.

Management of this diversity requires the divisional heads or managers to have short-term and medium-term decision-making power and responsibility for the division they manage. This allows the managing director and his/her board of directors to concentrate on long-term planning for the organisation as a whole. However, good communication and working relationships must exist between the divisional heads or managers and the board of directors, as short-, medium- and long-term decision making must all relate to each other and link together if the whole company is to move forward in the same coherent direction.

The divisions in a divisionalised company will be cost centres or profit centres in their own right, having to manage budgets, meet budgetary targets and operate within budgetary constraints. Divisions must also satisfy performance criteria relating to profitability and asset use, with profit margins and return on assets likely to be the key measures applied to individual divisions. The company will aggregate the financial information on each division's performance to produce the overall annual company report and accounts.

The separate divisions within the same organisation have an internal structure of their own. A common structure for individual divisions to adopt is the functional structure because it is suitable for the size and range of activities of a discrete division under the larger divisionalised organisation.

The potential difficulties with the divisional structure relate to the allocation of resources, overall co-ordination of activities and the cost of running separate divisions. The existence of an element of competition between separate divisions and a very limited resource base may lead to conflict between the divisions, as each separate division vies for the best possible allocation of resources and wants to perform well in the eyes of head office. The diverse range of divisions in a company may also make company-wide co-ordination demanding. This may be exacerbated if there is duplication of key activities in each division, which makes the cost of running individual divisions high. For example, the presence of a human resource management (HRM) function in each division would be expensive duplication. The activities associated with the HRM function are equally applicable to all people who work for the company, regardless of the division in which they work and, as such, centralisation of HRM activities makes economic and practical sense. With a centralised HRM function for all divisions, one HRM policy for the whole company can be developed and maintained, and every central and divisional employee recruited and measured against the central HRM policy. A different HRM function in each division risks resulting not only in wasteful duplication of effort but also in different HR practices being adopted, thus diluting corporate culture and corporate control.

Other centralised services could include the finance department and there may also be a discrete legal department to interact specifically with the various politico-legal issues at the various levels of the external environment.

■ The holding company structure

The holding company structure (*see* Figure 1.5) is usually found in large industrial conglomerates with a parent company acting mainly as an investment company acquiring and divesting smaller subsidiary companies. A company operating as a holding company will usually have a small corporate headquarters from which the parent company will conduct business. This means that central overheads will be low because of the economies of scale that this company-wide co-ordination achieves. The finance and legal sections are part of the parent company and their purpose is to provide the expertise needed centrally in the acquisition and divestment of subsidiary companies.

The subsidiary companies continue to trade under their own names, with the parent company either wholly owning its subsidiaries or acting as a majority shareholder in them. Subsidiary companies will operate fairly independently of the head office, with all decision-making power and responsibility for their own performance resting with their management. Industrial conglomerates adopting the holding company structure are therefore very decentralised. However, the control systems implemented by head office will tend to centre on the subsidiary companies meeting tight financial targets with regard to profit forecasts, profit margins and return on assets, or risking swift divestment by the holding company.

The ownership of a large number of subsidiary companies in a variety of industries spreads the risk and profit for the parent company as a whole. The

**Figure 1.5
The holding
company structure**

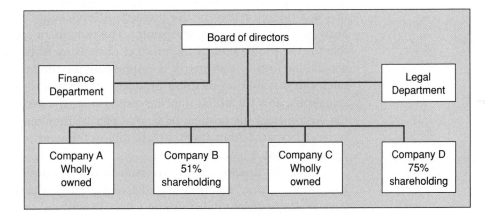

use of subsidiary companies to obtain diversity may ease divestment, especially in the light of poor performance, as that performance can be viewed as being ring-fenced in one or more companies and therefore contained.

The main potential disadvantage of the holding company structure relates to the subsidiary companies, which may view themselves as continuously up for sale. This type of situation invokes a high degree of uncertainty, and the likelihood of change can be difficult for the subsidiary companies to manage on a permanent basis. The other potential disadvantage relates to the general fact that diversity is more difficult to co-ordinate and manage overall than simplicity, and so the holding company management faces a more complex task.

Hanson plc was a diversified conglomerate built up over 30 years by James Hanson and Gordon White. It acquired a variety of subsidiary companies over the years, covering the areas of chemicals, tobacco, energy, building materials and building equipment. Given the variety of its acquisitions, Hanson became a holding company. Following the under-performance of the group in the early 1990s, when it lost 35 per cent of its stock-market value, the decision was taken in 1996[7] to demerge the Hanson group. The demerger resulted in four separately listed companies: Hanson, Imperial Tobacco, Millennium Chemicals and US Industries. Each has a turnover of more than £2 billion and shareholders received shares in each of the resulting four companies[8] after the demerger.

■ The matrix structure

The matrix structure attempts to merge the benefits of **decentralisation** with co-ordination across all areas of the business. **Matrix structures** are often used in organisations where there are two distinct and important areas of operation needing to be managed and co-ordinated in order to deliver the full product or service range. Matrix structures are often found in large multinational companies, educational establishments and small sophisticated service companies.

In a large multinational company (*see* Figure 1.6), the two arms of the matrix structure represent the product or services areas and the geographic areas in which the company operates. The product or service arm is responsible for the production of the product or delivery of the service, while each geographic arm of the matrix is responsible for the advertising, marketing, sales and distribution of those products or services to the end users in the geographic area for which they are responsible. The geographic arm becomes the customer of the product or service arm, as they purchase the product or service they need from them, before selling these on to their geographically defined customer base.

The matrix structure in a university business school (*see* Figure 1.7) also has two arms, one responsible for delivering the products – higher education courses – to their internal customer – the other arm of the matrix. This second

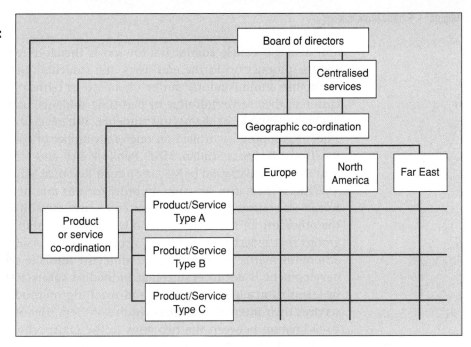

Figure 1.6
The matrix structure: multinational company

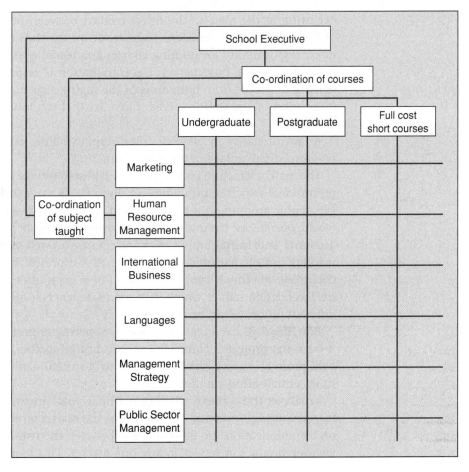

Figure 1.7
The matrix structure: educational establishment – university business school

arm manages course administration and is therefore responsible for delivering the product on to the end users, the students. The internal customers, the course administrators, can be organised in terms of the type of external customer they serve: full-time or part-time students; undergraduates or postgraduates; funded or fee-paying students. Whatever their provenance, each student grouping is enrolled on one of a number of courses or products, e.g. BA (Hons) Business Studies, HND Public Policy and Management, Master of Business Administration or MSc in Human Resource Management.

Within the matrix structure, in order for this arm of the matrix to be able to run its courses and satisfy its external customers, it needs the services of the other arm of the matrix, which represents the staff, usually organised in groups that reflect their academic expertise and the subject they teach. This arm of the matrix is responsible for supplying tutors to classes and for all staff development issues to ensure that individual tutors are competent enough in terms of academic expertise and teaching methodology to deliver the services their internal customers require of them. Hence communication and co-ordination between the two arms of the matrix should centre on subject groups and the course leaders reaching agreement over who will teach which subject to which classes on which courses, teaching being the main activity occurring in the matrix. The direct contact between people from both arms of the matrix allows decisions to be made by the staff at the sharp end with direct responsibility for running courses and teaching students, which should avoid hierarchical bureaucracy. Decentralisation of responsibility for decision making to people from both arms of the matrix structure should increase the motivation of the staff involved, provided that job tasks and responsibilities are clear.

A lack of clarity in people's roles, responsibilities and accountability is a potential disadvantage of the matrix structure.

The matrix structure for a small sophisticated service company will contain professional expertise groupings on one arm of the matrix and may contain geographic groupings on the other arm. A design consultancy (*see* Figure 1.8) would operate by having offices in various regions of Britain to handle the accounts and initial enquiries from clients, as well as having design staff working out of that office. The nature of the project from the client would determine whether it could be handled by a team of designers available from the local design staff or whether a team of designers from across the company's different offices would be required.

Bringing together a team to work on a specific project and then disbanding it once the project is complete, only to bring together another team for the next project, is a key feature of the matrix structure and is able to occur due its decentralisation and flexibility.

Whatever the context, whether multinational, private sector, public sector, manufacturing or service, the success of the matrix structure depends heavily on communication and co-ordination between the two arms of the matrix for any one product or service in any one market. This requires teams consisting

**Figure 1.8
The matrix structure:
sophisticated service
company – design
consultancy**

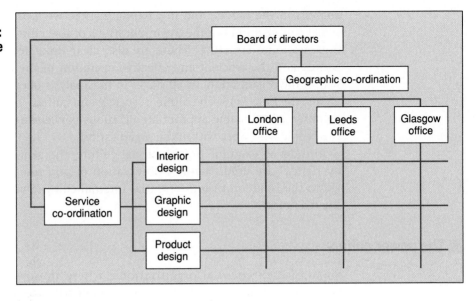

of people from both arms of the matrix to work together well at the points where they meet in the matrix and engage in their internal customer relationship. The quality of the end user or external customer experience depends heavily on the quality of this internal customer relationship between arms of the matrix. Therefore, the main potential difficulty with implementing the matrix structure occurs when people from both arms of the matrix fail to work together and co-ordination and communication between the two break down, thus impeding decision-making processes and adversely affecting the experience of the external customer or end user of the product or service.

☑ Check your understanding

Do you understand the characteristics of the holding company structure and the matrix structure?

Check your understanding by stating in what type of organisation the holding company and matrix structures may occur. Explain how they may be applied in the stated type of organisation.

Organisational culture and behaviour

The study of culture is a fascinating but complex topic. It is important, since organisations are necessarily filled with people who bring with them the culture they have acquired in society. Culture exists in both the external and internal environments of organisations. Culture in the external environment is dealt with in Chapter 9, as the sociocultural context or the 'S' of LoNGPEST analysis in the model, and in Chapter 2. Here we look at internal organisational culture and examine the implications of the 'chicken and egg' link with organisational structure. There are also clear links between organisational culture and the efficient and effective operation of the four functional areas within the organisation. At all stages in the analysis of organisational environments, the links between culture in society and culture in organisations should be observed to enable appropriate decisions concerning the management of the people who work within the organisation.

In order to examine organisational culture, the generic models developed by Handy[9] are used. Handy's observation of and research in organisations led to the isolation of four essential internal cultural models which are considered here.

■ The power culture

Small, entrepreneurial organisations, where the owner works with few employees, are likely to exhibit the **power culture**. This organisation is a club of intimates, where the colleagues or employees have been chosen by the owner/manager for their similarity to him/herself. The centre of power, and all crucial decision making, rests with the owner/manager, who either is in personal charge of every aspect of the work or can trust colleagues and employees to do things instinctively the way the owner/manager would have done them him/herself. This is depicted by the model (*see* Figure 1.9), which resembles a spider at the centre of its web.

Figure 1.9
The power culture

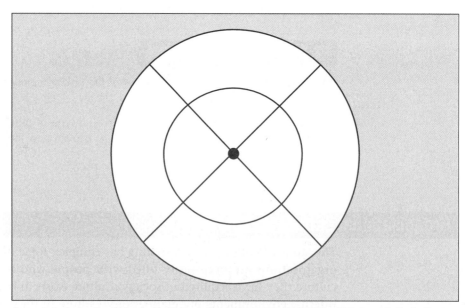

Source: *Understanding Organizations* by Charles Handy (Penguin Books 1976, Fourth Edition 1993). Copyright Charles Handy 1976, 1981, 1985, 1993. Reproduced by kind permission of Penguin Books Ltd.

The formal structure that most closely echoes the power culture is the simple structure, discussed earlier in this chapter.

The choice of 'cloned' employees can be deliberate or subconscious on the part of the entrepreneur. Whether explicitly sought or not, an internal culture develops that is intimate and comfortable for those on the inside. This creates further issues for anyone different who tries to enter the organisation, and this is possibly the culture that is least open to equal opportunities issues, as the club members do not wish to admit new members not in their likeness. The power culture is exciting because of the risks involved in its operation, as colleagues at the centre of power make decisions in an unauthorised but implicitly supportive environment. They operate the way they think the entrepreneur should, are rewarded and congratulated when they are correct, but risk censure when they inadvertently make a mistake.

Without the leader, the power centre is lost and the club can break down. Should the leader become ill or die, the organisation grieves and can recover from its loss only with difficulty. This illustrates a danger of the club culture, in that the organisation becomes too reliant on the originator and entrepreneur who is all too literally the heart and soul of the organisation.

When the organisation grows, the club becomes too big for all the members to retain their intimacy. Just as the structure changes with growth, developing from simple to functional structure, the culture also alters. The next of Handy's cultures is the **role culture**.

■ The role culture

The role culture (*see* Figure 1.10) mirrors the functional and **divisional structures** and is evident within more mature and larger organisations with

**Figure 1.10
The role culture**

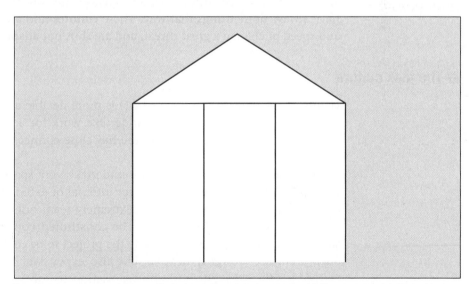

Source: *Understanding Organizations* by Charles Handy (Penguin Books 1976, Fourth Edition 1993). Copyright Charles Handy 1976, 1981, 1985, 1993. Reproduced by kind permission of Penguin Books Ltd.

Figure 1.11
The task culture

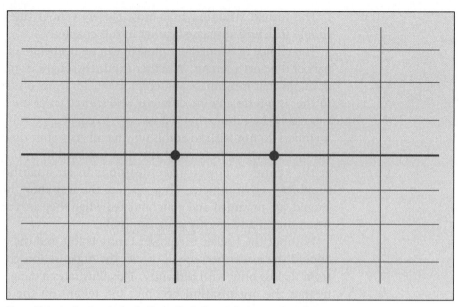

Source: *Understanding Organizations* by Charles Handy (Penguin Books 1976, Fourth Edition 1993). Copyright Charles Handy 1976, 1981, 1985, 1993. Reproduced by kind permission of Penguin Books Ltd.

departments, divisions and different geographic areas. The symptoms of the role culture are based on everyone in the organisation having a specific job title and description and knowing what it is they are expected to do in their contribution to the organisational mission. Role culture organisations are functional, bureaucratic and highly systematised, with clearly documented, routine procedures and well-organised and efficient operations. Because of their size and the routine nature of their operations, these organisations develop into solid and predictable institutions, which operate the way they do because they have always done things that way. These cultures find an increase in the rate and speed of change a great threat, and are thus not adaptive to change.

■ The task culture

Handy's **task culture** (*see* Figure 1.11) is more flexible and is often displayed in organisations that frequently undertake work for a variety of customers in a variety of fields. The task culture has close connections with the matrix structure.

Organisations with a task culture undertake very specific problem-solving or troubleshooting tasks as projects for internal or external clients, usually on a consultancy basis. The culture is extremely team oriented, since each task or project requires a fresh team to be constituted containing the required skills and knowledge that will enable the project to be completed successfully. Such a culture is highly flexible, but also expensive. This troubleshooting culture is often brought into an organisation to solve problems that others have found intractable. Members of the project team will exhibit their skills and competence through an extravagant use of resources, as they are used to being able to command anything that they need to get the job done.

The person culture

The fourth of Handy's organisational cultures is the **person culture**, where a set of professionals agree to collaborate to perform a specific service (*see* Figure 1.12). These people could be self-employed, or at least would have little notion of being employees of the organisation in the traditional sense. Rather, they grant the organisation the benefit of their services for which they accept monetary gratitude. They may even avoid the word 'organisation', preferring, as Handy states, terms such as 'practice' to describe the collective activities in which they engage. The person culture centres on the particular professional skills that the individuals possess and without which the organisation could not operate. The individuals consider themselves to be highly valued, unique, creative and ultimately unaccountable. Examples of these person culture professionals would be academics, doctors, solicitors and management consultants.

Figure 1.12
The person culture

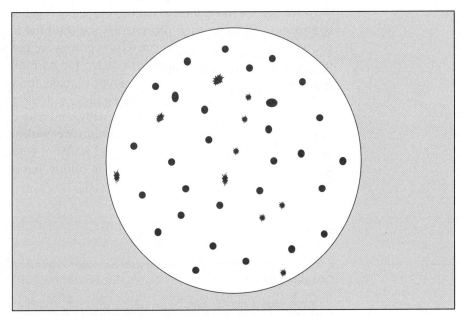

Source: Understanding Organizations by Charles Handy (Penguin Books 1976, Fourth Edition 1993). Copyright Charles Handy 1976, 1981, 1985, 1993. Reproduced by kind permission of Penguin Books Ltd.

✓ Check your understanding

Do you understand Handy's definitions of culture?

Check your understanding by defining Handy's four 'cultures' and describing the type of organisation in which each one occurs.

Culture and structure

There is undoubtedly a close link between culture internally and other elements of the internal environment as well as elements of the external environment. The size and structure of the organisation dictate the ways in which the people within it are able to operate. A small, entrepreneurial organisation with a simple structure will inevitably see and hear the leader regularly, and so have close contact with the original entrepreneur whom they are expected to emulate. A larger organisation with clearly defined departments and jobs will exhibit the role culture, so new recruits will be expected to learn their particular job and tasks quickly for two reasons: to enable them to fit into their position or role, and so that they can transmit the required behaviour to any new people they meet connected with the organisation. The task culture has a cause–effect link with the matrix structure, as both are linked with the provision of goods and services in a task or project-based environment. The person culture is, perhaps, less tightly knit to one of the particular structures, but the service offered by an organisation employing such individualistic stars is definitely linked to the behaviour of the people delivering that service.

As we will see in Chapter 2, culture in society is generated by us and it also controls us. Whatever their provenance, sociocultural impacts on the human resource inputs to the resource conversion process are key to that organisation's operational abilities. Organisations strive for harmony between the work they have to do, the structure they adopt to make the work possible and the culture of the human resources they employ, so their goals can be achieved. Organisations can be multicultural internally, and may need to be both global in their outlook on business, operating in many markets simultaneously, and local in their sensitivity to the needs and wants of employees and customers in a particular environment. Everyone lives culture, but only the clever are able to manage it.

☑ Check your understanding

Do you understand the relationship between organisational structures and Handy's cultures?

Check your understanding by identifying which structures and cultures most commonly go together.

Summary

This chapter examined different types of organisations, the use of resources by organisations, and the structure and culture of organisations. The following summary covers all aspects of this chapter.

1 Public-sector organisations are owned by local or national government or another publicly owned body. Examples of public-sector organisations include the police, the NHS, colleges and universities.

2 Private-sector organisations are owned by individuals, families or shareholders. Examples of private-sector organisations include Marks and Spencer, Marconi and Royal Doulton.

3 All organisations take in resources, process them and then deliver outputs which have greater value than the original inputs. This is known as 'organisational resource conversion'.

4 The inputs or resources of an organisation can be grouped into three categories, namely human, tangible and intangible.

5 All organisations have generic or general inputs, processes and outputs. General inputs include employees (human), money (tangible) and information (intangible). Additionally organisations will have specific inputs, e.g. for a university they include lecturers (human), overhead projectors (tangible) and specialist subject knowledge (intangible).

6 There are three basic legal structures which businesses can adopt. These are the sole trader, a partnership and a limited company. The sole trader business is owned and administered by one person who is personally liable for all the debts of the business. A partnership is where two or more individuals join together in a business venture with each partner having unlimited liability. Therefore, should the partnership result in debt or bankruptcy, each partner can be held liable for the full amount owed by the partnership. The limited company exists as a legal entity in its own right, therefore liability for debts is limited to the amount of issued share capital.

7 There are five generic organisational structures: the simple, functional, divisional, holding and matrix. The simple structure is centralised, with all short-, medium-, and long-term power and decision-making responsibility resting with the managing director. The functional structure is found in organisations which offer a range of related products and services to clearly defined and clearly segmented markets. The divisional structure is decentralised and as such is used by companies offering a wide and diverse range of products and services, compared with companies operating with the more rigid and centralised functional structure. The holding company structure is usually found in large industrialised conglomerates with a parent company acquiring and divesting subsidiary companies. Matrix structures are used in organisations where there are two distinct and important areas of operation needing to be managed and co-ordinated. Hence matrix structures are often found in large multinational companies, educational establishments and small sophisticated service companies.

8 Culture can be examined by looking at Handy's organisational cultures. The power culture is found in small entrepreneurial organisations, where the owner and employees are members of the 'club', with the owner being the centre of power. In the power culture organisation the simple structure usually occurs. The role culture is found in organisations where everyone has a specific job title and description and knows what it is they are expected to contribute to the organisational mission. The commonly used structures in role culture organisations are the functional and divisional structures. The task culture is commonly found in organisations which undertake team-based problem-solving work. In the task culture organisation the organisational structure is the matrix structure. Finally, the person culture is found in organisations in which a set of professionals agree to collaborate to provide specific services for their clients or customers, i.e. a dentists' practice. Little in the way of a recognised formal structure will exist in such an organisation.

Learning outcomes for case studies

While reading this chapter and engaging in the activities, you should have learned how to apply theory and models, analyse situations, and evaluate the application and analysis you undertake. The learning outcomes specified below outline the type of application, analysis and evaluation of which you should be capable in relation to organisations. The case studies and the questions which follow provide an opportunity for you to test how well you have achieved the learning outcomes for the ethical issues and exit case studies for this chapter.

Application	Check you have achieved this by	
1 Demonstrate the use of different legal structures by businesses	understanding the characteristics, pros and cons of different legal structures	answering exit case study questions 1 & 2
Analysis	**Check you have achieved this by**	
1 Analyse different types of business ownership	comparing and contrasting private and public ownership	answering exit case study question 3
2 Identify different views on GM foods	exploring the views of different stakeholder groups on GM foods	answering ethical case study questions 1 & 2
Evaluation	**Check you have achieved this by**	
1 Evaluate the success of tight regulation of the GM food industry and market	defending or attacking the GM food industry and the foodstuffs it produces	answering ethical case study question 3

ETHICAL ISSUES CASE STUDY 1.2

FT

Syngenta tries rice in fight for GM approval

By David Firn

In a new tack for its controversial genetically modified products, Syngenta, the world's largest agrochemicals group, is seeking marketing approval for a genetically engineered rice designed to improve the diet of kidney dialysis patients.

The new strain of rice has been altered to remove a protein responsible for allergic reactions. Aimed at the Asian market, it promises to improve the lives of kidney dialysis patients, who cannot eat rice because of an intolerance to the cereal's high protein content.

Although the sales potential is not significant, approval by Japanese regulators would mark a new strategy for Syngenta – formed last year by the merger of AstraZeneca's agrochemical concerns with those of its Swiss rival Novartis. As with its US rival, Monsanto, it has been forced to scale back its ambitions for GM crops in the face of widespread opposition in Europe and Brazil.

Syngenta has learned from Monsanto's climb-down after it failed to persuade European consumers that crops altered to produce their own insecticides, or to become resistant to weedkillers, were safe.

The company is spearheading its GM effort outside the US with crops that have clear benefits to customers.

Michael Pragnell, Syngenta chief executive, believes such crops will force regulators and customers to change the way they look at the GM issue, focusing on the risk–benefit ratio of individual products rather than the technology as a whole.

'It's a niche market, but it's a latch-lifter, the regulators either have to become less fastidious or deny benefits to patients,' Mr Pragnell said in an interview with the *Financial Times*.

'We are pursuing these markets not because we will make a fortune but because it will introduce some regulatory tension.'

David Evans, head of research, is under no illusion about the difficulty of winning over European consumers to the benefits of GM. 'The challenge is convincing the consumer it's safe. The second rung of the ladder is demonstrating real consumer benefits,' he said. 'But we need to be able to do the trials and you can't do trials in Europe right now.'

Syngenta's $2.5bn revenues from GM seeds are just a tenth of those of Monsanto, but analysts say Syngenta has one of the most impressive technology platforms in the industry.

Last year, Syngenta beat Monsanto and the public-sector International Rice Sequencing Project in the race to decode the genome of rice, the world's most important cereal crop. Larger than the human genome, and sharing much in common with other cereal crops, rice will provide a map for altering the genome of a wide variety of staple foods.

Source: *Financial Times*, 19 August 2002. Reprinted with permission.

Questions for ethical issues case study 1.2

1 In your opinion should the Japanese regulators approve the new GM protein-free rice? Justify your answer.

2 Should the regulators attach any conditions to sale and distribution of the protein-free rice? If so, what should they be?

3 Tight regulation of the production, distribution and sale of GM foodstuffs increases suspicion and doubt in the minds of consumers rather than ensuring consumer confidence in GM foods. Evaluate and comment on this statement.

Relative advantages of a personal passion

By Clare Gascoigne

A family business is often seen by outsiders as having particular drawbacks, such as family members who hang on to the business to support their lifestyle. But being family-owned can bring benefits beyond the thrill of having your name over the door.

'There are some good business reasons why a family-owned company might want to stay family-owned,' says Peter Leach of the Stoy Centre for Family Business. 'A family business can use its "family-ness" to create competitive advantage and differentiate itself from its rivals.'

For many families, the values embedded in the business keep them from selling out to a much bigger company that would swallow them up. 'Pride in their family's achievement is strong and there is often an overall sense of stewardship. The last thing most owners want is to be seen as the generation that sold the family silver,' says Grant Gordon, director-general of the Institute for Family Business, an independent association of family businesses.

But, as Mr Leach warns, the emotional ties must not be allowed to override commercial realities. 'Families often want a legacy with their name on it, or they argue that they have to keep going because their business creates local employment. These are emotional reasons and can be dangerous. The business must be run on proper lines.'

Deciding whether you are maintaining your family business for the 'right' reasons is not always simple. Mr Leach recommends that families constantly challenge why they are there, what family ownership brings to the company and whether it has a long-term future. 'You have to free yourself of the emotional stuff and challenge the status quo. It is about the constant updating and articulation of why you have a family business,' he says.

Staff employment is one issue. 'It is really important to a lot of families that they are seen to be promoting progressive employment and they see the family ownership paying off in terms of motivation and enterprise,' says Mr Gordon. He says family firms have a commitment to their staff that goes beyond what is expected of, say, a multinational, and can reap rewards from that.

A potential benefit of family ownership to the business is 'patient capital': shareholders who do not demand an ever-increasing monetary return. However, family business advisers warn that paying a decent return on family holdings may be necessary to avoid damaging family arguments.

'Many family businesses are able to take a much longer-term view than publicly quoted companies,' says Mr Gordon. 'The stock market can be an unfriendly place. Family businesses can take unorthodox business decisions with a view to building a business that might not make money for years to come but has lasting value.'

But taking the long view requires agreement and commitment from all the owners: in a family business there is a danger of failure because a fragmented ownership cannot agree on the purpose of the business, or the best means of achieving it. If the business has a large number of minority shareholders, a common vision may be difficult to formulate and the business may need to work hard to build a family creed to bring owners together. 'You need inspired leadership, a family leader who has fire in his belly,' says Mr Gordon.

But this may be a problem, Mr Leach says. 'To be honest, it's the minority of family businesses that have a good gene pool. Later generations are usually not as good as the first and you should bite the bullet if you believe you should sell.'

Succeeding generations may find the necessary drive by changing the nature of the business, which can anyway be an important factor in maintaining it. William Jackson & Son, the Hull-based food company, which makes products such as Yorkshire pudding under the brand name Aunt Bessie's, is now in the fifth generation; it started as a corner shop and the company moved into insurance and motor dealership before returning to its roots.

Another family concern, Timpson, has likewise changed, moving from shoe manufacturer to shoe retailer to shoe repairer and most recently diversifying into watch repairs.

John Timpson, chairman and chief executive of the Timpson's chain of 330 shoe repair, key-cutting and watch repair shops, feels passionately about the company started by his great-grandfather. 'Never a day goes by but I think about something to do with the business,' he says. 'It is my number one hobby – I have to be careful not to drive the rest of the family mad.'

Alexander Hoare, the first so far among the 11th generation of the family to join the privately owned bank C. Hoare, is also motivated by emotional ties. 'There is a sentimental attachment. The family business does generate some quite powerful forces and those forces can be good for the business – they can be a useful recruitment and retention tool among family members. A lot of people are motivated by more than money.'

But he also sees direct advantages for customers. The bank keeps customer numbers at a level that allows decisions to be taken on the basis of personal knowledge. ▶

'We were recently able to lend a customer £1m at 24 hours' notice, without having to go through several layers of credit checks. That would have been very difficult to arrange in a publicly owned bank – the controls and bureaucracies wouldn't allow it.'

The personal touch in family businesses extends to managing staff. Mr Timpson plans a big party for staff next year, to celebrate the business's centenary, which will be held at his home. 'People have met me and my son [James, managing director], they feel they know us and they like that,' he says. 'They know who is running the business and who is going to run it. That continuity is tremendously powerful. How can a business run well if the CEO is changed every three years?'

But he also cites other reasons why family ownership is beneficial. 'We can make terribly quick decisions. We just do it – and don't have to worry about calling a board meeting. And there is a lot less politics. There's no one breathing down my neck.'

A larger number of family owners at C. Hoare (eight family members are involved in management) ensures that strategy decisions are a group affair. But family ownership allows that strategy to follow an unusual path.

Mr Hoare says: 'It is nice to be able to offer something that the other banks cannot. We are deliberately positioned somewhere completely different to our competitors. There is an exceptional level of service and that is one of our specialities.'

The enthusiasm and emotion that drives a family business can overcome problems that would cause other companies to go under and extract a level of commitment for which multinationals would pay a lot of money. But it must be tempered with commercial and practical sense.

Source: Financial Times, 19 September 2002. Reprinted with permission.

Questions for exit case study 1.3

1 List the advantages and disadvantages of private family ownership of a business.

2 List the characteristics of public ownership of a company by shareholders.

3 Compare and contrast private and public ownership.

 For more case studies please visit www.booksites.net/capon

Short-answer questions

1   Explain the term 'a centralised organisation'.

2   Explain the term 'a decentralised organisation'.

3   What are the differences between organic and external growth?

4   List the five generic organisational structures.

5   Is the functional structure centralised or decentralised?

6   Summarise the key features, strengths and weaknesses of the matrix structure.

7   Is the divisional structure centralised or decentralised?

8   Define the term 'organisational resource conversion'.

9   What are the three stages of a resource conversion process chart?

10   What are the three main types of resource inputs? Give one example of each.

11   Name Handy's four organisational culture types.

12   What is the main danger for the organisation of the power culture?

13   Which two structures are likely to develop a role culture?

14   What sort of work are task culture organisations likely to be involved in?

15   In what type of organisation is the person culture found?

Learning outcomes for assignment questions

While reading this chapter and engaging in the activities, you should have learned how to apply theory and models, analyse situations, and evaluate the application and analysis you undertake. The learning outcomes specified below outline what you should be able to do and the assignment questions provide an opportunity for you to test how well you have achieved the learning outcomes for this chapter.

Application	Check you have achieved this by	
1 Apply the resource conversion chart to a specific organisation	drawing up a resource conversion chart for an organisation with which you are familiar	answering assignment question 1
2 Apply the generic organisational structures to a range of organisations	applying the organisational strutures to an organisation of your choice	answering assignment questions 2 & 3
Analysis	**Check you have achieved this by**	
1 Analyse a resource conversion chart for a specific organisation	commenting on an organisation's resource conversion chart	answering assignment question 1
2 Discuss possible structures for an organisation	identifying the most likely structures for an organisation	answering assignment questions 2 & 3
3 Discuss different organisational cultures	identifying the culture most likely to exist in a specific organisation	answering assignment question 4
Evaluation	**Check you have achieved this by**	
1 Choose an organisational structure for a specific organisation	comparing and evaluating different possible structures	answering assignment questions 2 & 3
2 Choose which organisational culture dominates in a specific organisation	comparing and evaluating different possible cultures	answering assignment question 4

Assignment questions

1 Identify and examine the relationships between the three stages of the organisational resource conversion chart. Use examples from the private or public sector to illustrate your answer. In what ways is it possible to ensure that outputs are of the highest possible quality?

2 Illustrate the structure of each of the following organisations in diagrammatic form. Name the type of generic organisational structure on which you have based your structure and explain your choice for each organisation:

■ A newsagent's shop in London run by the owner, and employing a morning paper boy, an evening paper girl and two shop assistants.

■ A garden centre on the outskirts of Glasgow selling a range of plants and gardening equipment to the general public. The garden centre is supplied with plants by a commercial nursery attached to it, which also supplies other shops and garden centres in the west of Scotland. The other gardening equipment is bought in wholesale from a number of suppliers.

The garden centre employs 30 people, including a nursery manager, a marketing manager, an accountant and a human resource manager.

■ A market research company operating across the UK, with offices in Aberdeen, Leeds, Southampton, Edinburgh, Manchester, Cardiff, Swansea, Nottingham, Glasgow and two offices in London.

3 Apply two of the five generic organisational structures to each of the following organisations. Compare and contrast the two structures you have chosen and comment on which is the more appropriate for each organisation:

■ A science department in a university with undergraduate BSc students doing full-time three-year degrees and some MSc and PhD students undertaking postgraduate research qualifications.

■ A management consultancy operating throughout the UK, Hong Kong, Singapore and Malaysia and which has recently opened a large office in Johannesburg, South Africa. The company offers consultancy services and expertise in the areas of auditing, taxation and business planning.

4 Compare and contrast the power culture with the role culture. Identify the advantages and disadvantages of both the power and role cultures. Comment on the link between culture and structure, and also on the effects of culture on the organisation's operational abilities.

Weblinks available online at www.booksites.net/capon

1 This website is for Harley-Davidson, the company looked at in the entry case study.
www.harley-davidson.co.uk

2 This website is for Syngenta, the company in the ethical case study.
http://www.syngenta.com/

Further reading

Brocklesby, J and Cummings, S (1996) 'Designing a viable organization structure', *Long Range Planning*, 29 (1), January.

Burack, E H (1990) 'Changing the company culture – the role of human resource development', *Long Range Planning*, 24 (1), February.

Carmichael, J (1992) 'Managing inputs', *Long Range Planning*, 25 (1), February.

Crush, P (2000) 'Out to get you', *Management Today*, November.

Curteis, H (1997) 'Entrepreneurship in a growth culture', *Long Range Planning*, 30 (2), April.

Deal, T and Kennedy, A (1988) *Corporate Cultures*, London: Penguin.

Foster, G (1996) 'Three over thirty', *Management Today*, May.

Greiner, L (1998) 'Evolution and revolution as organizations grow', *Harvard Business Review*, July/August 1972, reprinted May/June 1998.

Humble, J, Jackson, D and Thomson, A (1994) 'The strategic power of corporate values', *Long Range Planning*, 27 (6), December.

Johnson, G (1992) 'Managing strategic change – strategy, culture and action', *Long Range Planning*, 25 (1), February.

Johnson, G and Scholes, K (2002) *Exploring Corporate Strategy*, 6th edn, Chapter 9, Harlow: Financial Times Prentice Hall.

Karabadse, A, Ludlow, R and Vinnicombe, S (1988) *Working in Organizations*, Chapter 11, London: Penguin.

Kennedy, C (1993) 'The ICI demerger: unlocking shareholder value', *Long Range Planning*, 26 (2), April.

Kono, T (1990) 'Corporate culture and long range planning', *Long Range Planning*, 23 (4), August.

Lynch, R (2003) *Corporate Strategy*, 3rd edn, Chapter 18, Harlow: Financial Times Prentice Hall.

Thompson, J L (2001) *Strategic Management*, 4th edn, Chapter 21, London: Thomson Learning.

van de Vliet, A (1997) 'Are they being served?', *Management Today*, February.

References

1 Gore, C, Murray, K and Richardson, B (1992) *Strategic Decision Making*, London: Cassell.

2 Worthington, I and Britton, C (1997) *The Business Environment*, 2nd edn, Harlow: Financial Times Pitman Publishing.

3 Gore et al., op. cit.

4 Worthington and Britton, op. cit.

5 Gore et al., op. cit.

6 Worthington and Britton, op. cit.

7 Stevenson, T (1995) 'Hanson to break up into four companies', *Independent*.

8 Tieman, R (1997) 'Evolution plays its part in Hanson's big bang', *Financial Times*, 21 February.

9 Handy, C B (1993) *Understanding Organisations*, 4th edn, London: Penguin.

2

Culture and organisations

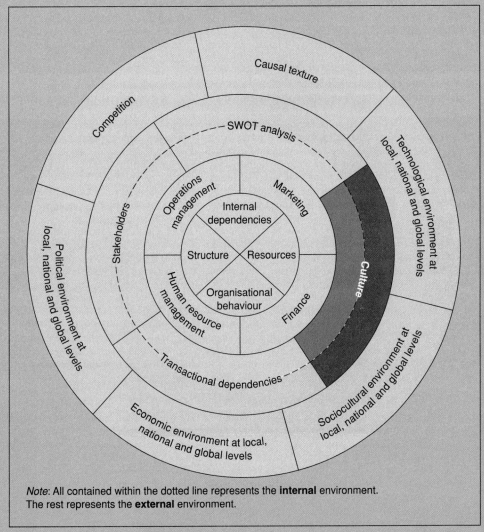

Note: All contained within the dotted line represents the **internal** environment.
The rest represents the **external** environment.

Figure 2.1 Organisational context model

➡ ENTRY CASE STUDY 2.1   FT

Remove the iron rice bowl: management investing in China

By James Kynge

What would you get for your money if, as a foreign investor, you decided to buy a former state enterprise in Shenyang, the centre of China's north-eastern industrial rustbelt?

The question is more than academic. Such businesses have, in the past, been largely off-limits to foreigners. But China's faltering economy has forced the authorities to search for investors wherever they can find them.

This month Mu Suixin, Shenyang's mayor, toured Europe to find foreign investors for 18 large state companies, with a total workforce of 309 436. Other cities in the north-east are also planning mass sales; Harbin, near the Russian border, is to put about 1000 medium and small enterprises under the auctioneer's hammer in June.

As to the question of what a foreign investor could expect, the answer is likely to be an appallingly managed business. But this is the main attraction, according to Jiang Enhong, a leading corporate turnaround expert in the region, who has himself taken on such companies.

Rebellious workers, deception and years of inertia bred from central planning define the opportunities for any new investor – local or foreign – in China's crumbling state-owned sector, he believes. 'I have straightened out the management of companies within 44 days, and set them on the way to profitability,' he says. 'This just shows how bad their management was.'

The work is arduous, but foreigners may never get the chance to buy into state assets as cheaply again.

Foreign investors can also benefit from preferential terms, such as municipal tax concessions, which are not on offer to locals. Joint venture and foreign-invested companies also have advantages in raising local bank finance – which private companies in China find difficult to secure. 'If only I could get banks to lend to me, I would not just be a tiger, but a tiger with wings,' says Mr Jiang.

His main problem has been in rationalising the many managers who clog most state-owned enterprises. When he bought the Shenyang Antibiotics company, which had not made a profit nor paid any tax since 1979, there was one manager to every four workers.

Some managers had been awarded offices out of favouritism but their roles had not been clearly defined.

Mr Jiang has removed two-thirds of the managers in all three state companies he has bought, and defined clearly the task of those remaining. Anyone who failed to perform their duties was fired, he adds.

A measure of shock therapy was necessary to teach workers that when their factory passed from state to private hands, their 'iron rice bowl' of socialist-era benefits was taken away. When he took over the Xincheng Pharmaceutical factory, workers were supposed to arrive at 8am but most came at 10am and many would return home for the day before lunch.

At the opening ceremony for the factory, one worker sat down on a seat reserved for dignitaries. When he was told to move, he smashed the chair. Mr Jiang told him he would be sacked if he did not donate a new chair by the following Monday. 'He brought the chair, but we fired him anyway,' says Mr Jiang.

Laying off workers in China has been fraught with ideological and social impediments. It is not as simple as Mr Jiang makes it sound, but a Communist Party congress in September ushered in a phase of faster free market reform. Redundancies are increasingly seen as unavoidable.

The September congress, and the subsequent National People's Congress in March, also helped to overturn an ambiguous official stance on private ownership by permitting 'diverse forms of public ownership'. In Shenyang, this has been taken as a cue for the rapid and comprehensive sale of state assets. Thousands of state enterprises are to be sold this year and next.

Gai Ruyin, the deputy mayor, says that a severance allowance of, say, 10 000rmb (£738) could be paid per worker by the new owners of state companies, and that the cost of providing for those who are made redundant may be set against the purchase price of the factory.

Morale among the remaining workers is a complicated issue. But Mr Jiang believes that some of the control mechanisms found in state enterprises, such as the Communist party cell and the trade unions, should be retained. The Communist party has been invaluable in resolving industrial disputes because it carries the authority of China's most powerful body.

One worker had lost his legs when he was run over by a train. He was causing trouble outside the factory, inciting others to militancy. With the party cell's intervention, a settlement was found. Mr Jiang's company bought him a mobile telephone and a stall: he now rents out the phone for calls and sells wine by the factory gate.

But Mr Jiang is conscious that the heavy hand with which he has put his corporate empire in order should at some point give way to a lighter touch. Eventually his three factories are to be 'democratised', with each worker owning shares.

Source: Financial Times, 26 May 1998. Reprinted with permission.

Introduction

The aim of this chapter is to introduce the complex issue of **culture** and its effects on organisational as well as personal efficiency and effectiveness in the workplace. This chapter necessarily combines aspects of a variety of specialisms, each with its own vast literature: sociology, psychology, management development and international business. Here some of the main strands are brought together and interwoven to form a useful framework for the business studies student wanting to examine the impact of culture on the way organisations work.

Culture at different levels of the external environment

■ Culture at the global level of the external environment

At the global level of the external environment, issues emerge with the interaction of more than one **national culture**. When one leaves one's home country to work, live or even visit abroad, one is faced with different ways of doing things. In Chapter 9, it is mentioned that changes in lifestyle and behaviour can lead to feelings of culture shock, where individuals have to recognise and cope with experiences that are different from those to which they are accustomed. Transferring one's life from Milton Keynes to Tokyo when one is sent off to work in Japan, having grown up in Milton Keynes and never left, is likely to include dealing with culture shock. However, with such a dramatic move we expect things to be different in Tokyo but anticipate we will be able to cope. This may not be the case. The thorough pre-departure orientation of executives posted overseas is one of the key issues in the management of international business operations that can contribute greatly to the success of overseas postings. Nevertheless, it is often overlooked.

■ Culture at the national level of the external environment

The chapter begins with an illustration of culture in society that aims to explain the concept of culture predominantly at the national level of the external environment. Once an individual's cultural influences from the national level of culture have been identified and analysed, the individual is then furnished with a vocabulary and consciousness that allows them to make coherent comparisons with other nations' cultures, giving that global-level view of cross-cultural issues. National cultural characteristics are adopted by one national grouping and attributed by one nation to others, leading to stereotype and prejudice. National culture, however, belies the fact that within it are local differences between communities, providing a more local perspective to cultural influences on organisations.

■ Culture at the local level of the external environment

Local cultural issues in the community are complex. The national and local levels of the sociocultural external environment can often intertwine, due to the fact that some people's national characteristics make them the people they are in their local communities. Although we recognise cross-cultural issues between nations, we sometimes do not recognise that equivalent culture shock can occur within the same country. This might have a particular resonance for a full-time student who, at a relatively young age, has left the family for the first time and is attending a higher education course in another part of the country far from home.

As communications, transport and technology have developed in western industrialised societies in the last 200 years, the provenance of this personal and social identity has changed. A sense of identity used to come from home, family and village, all elements of the local external environment. As society has developed, these local-level sociocultural influences emerge less importantly from influences located at the local level, since personal movement and individual horizons are no longer as limited as they once were. Now, because of the access to travel and communications media, an individual's cultural identity could be said to be much more strongly located at the national level, or has possibly emerged from more global influences, with the strong lifestyle messages emanating from global brands such as Coca-Cola and McDonald's.

✓ Check your understanding

Do you understand the difference between culture at the global, national and local levels of the external environment?

Check your understanding by giving an example of culture at the global, national and local levels of the external enviornment.

Culture inside organisations

It can be seen from the organisational context model at the start of this chapter that as well as forming part of the external environment, culture can be identified as existing in the internal environment of the organisation. This chapter therefore also presents models for identifying and analysing internal organisational or corporate culture. Organisations can and do develop their own culture. **Organisational culture** can emerge as a result of the internal structure of the organisation (*see* Chapter 1) and/or the type of people employed by the organisation.

Where managers identify cultural problems, they may make structural or personnel changes in an attempt to alter the organisational culture and ensure the desired organisational objectives are achieved. Culture can be as explicit or implicit within an organisation as it is in society. Whatever the case, it is vital for the newly recruited employee to understand an organisation's culture if he or she is to learn 'the way we do things around here'. Culture shock can occur within organisations when two whole organisations or sections of organisations are merged and two completely different sets of working practices and behaviours are expected to operate together.

The issues of culture within organisations and culture external to the organisation or in society are brought together in this chapter.

✓ Check your understanding

Do you understand where organisational or corporate culture comes from?

Check your understanding by briefly explaining what may shape organisational culture.

Personal cultural provenance

The topic of culture can begin at the individual level. **Personal cultural provenance** is the origins of individuals' culture. It is another way of saying, 'Where do I get my culture from?' (*see* Figure 2.2). External cultural influences can be identified at a basic level as being the system for understanding and expressing our identity.

Identity is a key concept from a sociological perspective, but here we will examine its influence on our sense of who we are, where we come from and how we do things. A first-year university student might identify themselves

Figure 2.2 Determinants of personal cultural provenance

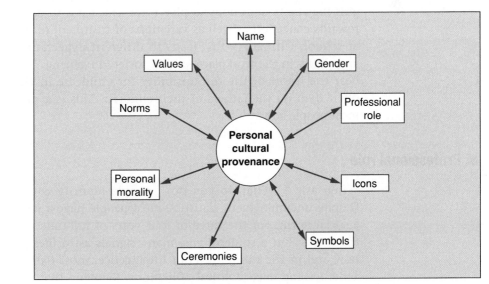

in all or some of the following ways. These could all be said to be expressions of culture that have their location in sources outside the individual. They are all facets of individual identity that can provide a useful insight to personal cultural provenance.

■ Name

People respond differently to the question 'Who are you?' according to context. With young people one's own age in an informal setting, it is most probable that the answer would be one of the names given by one's parents, and that the surname or family name would not be given unless specifically asked for later. If people do not use the full name their parents gave them, they use a version of it that they have chosen themselves, e.g. Chris instead of the full Christine or Christopher. Some people prefer to use a new and individual name that they have chosen for themselves. Others have a new name chosen for them by their peers and contemporaries, like a nickname that is a shortened version of their original name, or one based on a particular skill or habit they have, their appearance or their preferences.

■ Gender

Our gender is a fundamental element of our nature that also determines the cultural experience we have throughout our lives. In whatever ethnic culture we are born, the raising of children conveys clear gender identities and roles, and instils stereotypes and role models from an early age. The simple attribution of qualities or skills to either gender dictates the way a child interacts in society: boys may be discouraged from crying if they are hurt; girls may be taught to cook; boys may learn that fighting in self-defence is 'manly'; girls may be bought dolls to play with. This leads to differences in attitudes towards education as well as variations of treatment of the different genders at school. Ultimately this leads to different expectations of performance and ability in the workplace, and in society in general. Women, for example, bear the brunt of the responsibility for childcare in UK society far more often than do the fathers of their children. This is a social norm to which most people adhere.

■ Professional role

When asked 'What do you do?', people identify with their occupation. Despite unemployment statistics, most people have a job and, again, that is a social norm. For the three or four years of full-time undergraduate study, the words 'I'm a student' give many signals as to lifestyle, income bracket now and in the future, level of intelligence, most likely habits and leisure activities and even political affiliations. Replying that one does not have a job can again have many automatic connotations, depending on context: a woman with children who does not work may be praised for having devoted her time to raising the family; a man who has children and no job may be criticised for not providing for them and expecting the state to do it for him.

■ Icons

A first-year undergraduate who is just beginning to realise how much effort is involved in gaining their higher or further education qualification may respect someone who has already gained the qualification or is at least in the final year. At the same time, many national icons will have resonance. These come in the form of pop and rock stars, actors, television personalities, sports stars and supermodels, with good examples being David and Victoria Beckham. All such icons have influence over culture, as they have a bearing on what we wear, where and how we spend our leisure time, and our attitudes to religion, drugs, politics and a whole host of issues.

■ Symbols

For many people, an obvious and visible symbol of culture is the clothes they choose to wear. These often make a statement concerning their cultural identity. For example, many students choose to wear jeans and trainers, which are casual and acceptable attire for their relatively informal lifestyle. Other people, including students, may choose to identify more closely with their ethnic background and wear clothing that identifies them as belonging to a particular ethnic culture. In the UK this is often found among people whose families originate from India or Pakistan. Alternatively, people may view their values and professional role as an important part of their cultural identity and choose to symbolise this by wearing smart clothes to work.

Some employers require their employees to identify with the organisation they work for by virtue of the job they do and/or the organisation. For example, hospitals require nursing staff to wear uniforms. This is for two reasons: first, so nursing staff can be easily identified as such; second, because the work nursing staff undertake is sometimes messy and dirty, so a clean, easily washable uniform helps prevent the spread of infection and is preferable to getting one's own clothes dirty. The requirement on nurses to wear uniforms is a longstanding historical example of staff being required to wear clothes that identify them with a particular profession and hospital, since different hospitals often have different coloured uniforms for different types of nurse. Since the 1980s, the idea of a corporate uniform in the UK has caught on with banks, building societies, shops and some restaurants requiring staff to wear corporate uniforms, which identify the individual as working for an organisation with its own organisational culture.

■ Ceremonies

Most students will attend their graduation ceremony on being awarded their qualification and will enjoy the formal occasion with its mortar board, academic gown and procession before the chancellor of the university to collect the piece of paper bearing the university seal and stamp as proof of the studies they have undertaken. The graduation ceremony marks, in a formal manner, the successful completion of higher education studies, which will in turn influence the professional role one adopts throughout life and hence also an individual's personal cultural provenance.

■ Personal morality

Cultural influences also give us our innate sense of right and wrong. Thus in our culture it may be wrong to murder, to steal, or for adults to have sex with children. We all agree with this, and those who do not adhere to the code contradict our moral code and our laws, which are the political expression of our moral code. Culture may also express itself in those whom we respect. Therefore in a free-market or mixed economy, where self-reliance and providing for one's family's material well-being are considered admirable, people who are prudent and work hard all their life are admired. Those who do well for themselves and become 'self-made' by enriching themselves and their families through their own efforts are considered worthy of our respect. Entrepreneurs are admired and ennobled via political honours as people who created wealth for themselves and for the country, and thus have done a public service. Linked to religion, this is embodied in the 'work ethic', where it is seen as a good thing in northern European society to work hard for a living and provide for one's dependants.

Culture also emerges in our system of faith or beliefs, usually through the expression of formal religious belief. Once we have a common system for what we think is right or normal, we then have a language for expressing what we consider to be abnormal. Once we can identify people the same as us, who share our **norms** and **values**, we can then identify those who differ and so do not fit in with our norms and values. This gives rise to another key aspect that culture dictates, which is our moral standards. As we grow we learn society's norms and values, and with this embedded sense of normal and abnormal, right and wrong, we begin to judge the correctness of our own and others' behaviour. Thus the group becomes judgemental, dictating that certain modes of personal action are acceptable while others are not.

An example of this in many societies is the emphasis placed on the family. It is considered the norm, and thus deemed valued and morally correct by the group, for people to form lifelong heterosexual partnerships and to have children within that context. Thus the religious and politico-legal systems are designed to support this notion, and marriage, with its accompanying wedding ceremony, marriage certificate and wedding reception, has become the traditional as well as the normal way of demonstrating that this desired legal and social state has been entered into.

Social welfare systems, including pensions, sickness and unemployment benefit, and taxation systems, are also designed around the notion of a single breadwinner, a dependent adult and dependent children. Backed up by religion, this notion of the nuclear family becomes the moral as well as social and legal norm. Refer to Chapter 9 for the changing position of the nuclear family in society.

■ Norms

It is from all the elements in society that affect us as we develop that we obtain our cultural norms and values. Norms are literally ways of behaving or attitudes that are considered to be normal. Norms can be defined as the social rules and guidelines that prescribe behaviour. Furthermore, norms not only affect how an individual behaves but are the shared sense of what a group of individuals thinks is the normal way to behave. Parents begin by teaching them to babies, and children learn them as soon as they come into contact with other children. Thus to behave against the group's norms is abnormal, leading to ostracisation.

For many students a key element to take into account when choosing a university is its location and night life. Socialising thus becomes the first-year norm, with the vast majority of first years going out frequently to pubs, clubs and the students' union with new-found friends and peers. Many town or city-centre pubs and clubs aim to maximise income by cutting entrance and drinks prices on otherwise unpopular nights of the week. They introduce 'student nights', normalising socialising during the week instead of staying in and studying. Late nights and excessive intake of alcohol lead to the inability to rise early the following morning, so missing lectures or seminars becomes a social student norm.

■ Values

Values are things, people or attitudes that groups of individuals think are important or to be revered or respected. Thus many people might consider that loyalty and honesty between friends, not letting a friend down, not cheating on a boy- or girlfriend or trying to conform to the norms of the peer group are all values that the group would share. Values indicate what society sees as important collectively. While norms may be ways of behaving, values could be qualities that society looks up to.

Thus cultural norms and values contain a variety of elements and attitudes that can be said to come from external influences in society on the individuals who form the group of people constituting that society. These external influences can be formal and explicit, such as the teacher in the classroom rewarding good standards with public praise and a gold star, or punishing bad behaviour with public criticism and humiliation. Or external influences can be informal and implicit, such as the ways in which children observe adults' behaviour and then imitate that, taking their cues from what they perceive around them for the right and wrong way to behave either in the family context or in public.

☑ Check your understanding

Do you understand the determinants of an individual's culture?

Check your understanding by listing the determinants of personal culture and providing an example to illustrate each determinant.

Identifying British culture

The first thing to declare about defining British culture via Hill's[1] determinants of culture (*see* Figure 2.3) is that Britain is not a homogeneous society. It is recognised that there are many cultural groupings populating the British Isles. The United Kingdom of Great Britain and Northern Ireland comprises three countries and one province: England, Wales, Scotland and Northern Ireland. Arguably the Celts in Wales, Scotland and Ireland form the indigenous population of these islands, who suffered Anglo-Saxon, Roman and Norman invasion and conquering as history unfolded. In the twentieth century, there was large-scale immigration from territories within the former Empire and current Commonwealth, making the UK a multiracial society, with large

**Figure 2.3
The determinants
of culture**

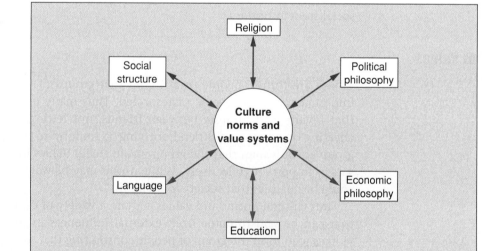

Source: Charles W L Hill, *International Business: Competing in the Global Marketplace*, 2nd edition, 1994. Irwin, reproduced with the kind permission of The McGraw-Hill Companies.

populations whose families originated from the Caribbean, the Indian sub-continent and Hong Kong. Thus any attempt to apply a model such as Hill's to 'British society' is liable to be relevant to some British people and irrelevant to others. This supports the notion that the study of culture in society and organisations is extremely complex.[2] Certain elements included in Hill's model (*see* Figure 2.3) may be irrelevant to the individual reader; however, it is expected that one can consider each determinant in relation to one's own personal cultural provenance and arrive at an individual conclusion about how one has been influenced during the acquisition of culture from external influences.

■ Religion

Many people have some kind of religious faith or have been brought up following the edicts of one of the world's major religions, be it Christianity, Islam, Judaism, Hinduism or Buddhism. The UK has a formal, state religion built into its constitutional monarchy, referred to as an established religion. It is a Protestant Christian religion, divided into churches representing the countries of the Union: England, Scotland, Wales and Northern Ireland. There are many other religions, and a long history of political struggle between the dominant Protestant faith and the previous historically dominant Catholic faith. In addition there are Methodists, Baptists and all the religions of the UK's immigrant communities. However, neither multiculturalism nor ecumenicalism is reflected in the country's political institutions, as the current Queen, who is head of state as well as head of the Anglican churches, has the formal title 'Defender of the Faith', meaning the established church, and not of all the faiths within the country. Prince Charles, heir to the throne, has stated that it is his intention to be enthroned 'Defender of Faith' in an effort to be more inclusive of all Britain's many religions.

Because of the establishment of the church, it is the norm for religion to play a part in all major state occasions. At the coronation of a new monarch, oaths are sworn before God to undertake the duties of sovereign. At the State Opening of Parliament the Queen gives the Queen's Speech, where she reads aloud the intended legislative programme of the government elected to govern in her name, and prayers are said. Royal weddings and state funerals take place in religious locations, such as Westminster Abbey or St Paul's Cathedral. Indeed, these major religious buildings are part of the country's cultural heritage and tourist landscape, linking state and church ever more tightly. There is at least one church in most towns or villages in the country.

At the local and more personal level, the norm for many families (though not all) is to mark the significant events of life, birth, marriage and death with ceremonies that are religious in nature. For the majority of these people the religion in question will be a form of Christianity. In this tradition, a baby's birth is celebrated with a christening, whereby the new infant is formally inducted into the church through a ceremony representative of the Biblical ritual wash-ing known as baptism. Godparents are appointed to offer spiritual and moral guidance, as well as having the functional role of caring for the children should the parents die. Other religions have their own similar ceremonies to welcome newly born family members, including, in many cultures, ritual circumcision of male babies. Even those who have grown up in a religious tradition but have rejected it still feel the need to celebrate the birth of a child with family and friends through some kind of secular naming ceremony following a recognised pattern, even though the mention of any God is omitted.

Similarly, the pair bonding that marks human relationships is institutionalised in celebrating the joining together of couples through legal marriage and wedding ceremonies. The Christian image of this religious ceremony has become the international symbol for marriage: the white dress of the bride and the church building as a backdrop. In the UK until recently there were only two places licensed to hold legal marriage ceremonies: registry offices and churches. This changed in the early 1990s to allow marriages to take place in any suitable venue holding a licence to hold weddings, which includes venues such as hotels and stately homes.

Finally, it is unusual in the UK to mark the passing of a relative or friend without the involvement of Christianity. Funerals, even if they do not consist of ritual burial of the corpse within consecrated ground such as a churchyard, are 'normally' presided over by a priest who invokes the care of God for the individual who has entered Heaven. This is the case even at municipal crematoria. It should be noted that in the UK at the end of the twentieth century, participation in organised religion on a regular basis was low. Religion also has a significant influence on language, as outlined below.

■ Politics

The link between culture and nationalism, and by implication politics, has been mentioned above. However, the political system under which we grow up has explicit and implicit effects on our personal cultural norms and values. The UK is a liberal democracy with a largely conservative tradition. While the monarchy's power has been limited over the centuries, and universal suffrage and the rule of Parliament have emerged, this has been achieved with the agreement and deference of the people and not as a result of large-scale popular revolt, apart from the Civil War of 1642–52. Following Oliver Cromwell's short-lived republic, the monarchy was restored in 1660 but severely restricted and subjugated to Parliament from 1688 onwards.

There are traditions that instil in the UK's citizens certain standards of civic behaviour and conduct. We consider democracy to be the norm, and that political life should be conducted with fairness and justice, decisions being made on a majority basis. We expect fair play, equity of access to power and that everyone's views will be taken into account.[3]

Nevertheless, there are some differences in approach to the state's institutions, with particular activist or terrorist factions taking more direct and undemocratic action in an attempt to achieve their goals, for example the terrorist groups in

Northern Ireland. On the surface, it seems that the UK's political culture is largely homogeneous and respectful of power and authority. It could be said that the national consensus started to break down at the end of the twentieth century, with votes in favour of devolution from central government in Westminster to regional Parliaments for Scotland, Wales and Northern Ireland. Kingdom writes: 'The geographical, class, gender and racial cracks in the social fascia are only smoothed over with political Polyfilla and concealed beneath unwritten constitutional wallpaper.'[4]

■ Economics

The UK is a regulated free market, as discussed in Chapter 9. This provides a set of economic norms and values that affect the way people behave and what they consider to be right or wrong behaviour. This was particularly evident in the western media reporting of the changes in Eastern Europe when the Communist governments lost power and former planned economies introduced free-market reforms. This was reported in many media as the 'normalisation' of their economies, rather than changing from one economic system to another, because now these countries were beginning to do things the way 'we' do and so were now deemed to be normal.

■ Education

The way in which we are educated (or, in some societies, whether we are educated) affects our comprehension and synthesis of the world around us. The word 'educate' originates from the Latin meaning 'to lead or draw out', and in western societies the focus for education is to draw out intelligence and understanding that are deemed to be inherent in all. The western tradition, founded in that of ancient Greece, is to teach people how to think, question, debate and argue their point with philosophical underpinning and supporting individual freedom to differ.

■ Language

When considering the effects of language on the development of culture,[5] there is a fundamental philosophical aspect to consider that cannot be resolved in this text: does language control thought or does thought control language? If language controls thought, then the way we use our language has some sort of control over the attitudes we hold and the norms and values that underpin our culture. If thought controls language, then the language we use is a symbol of our cultural norms and values.

In fact, when examining British culture it is possible to identify both. Aspects of its historical, political and religious development are evident everywhere in its language. First, the fact that until recent decades all British languages other than English were suppressed is evidence of English colonisation (Wales is now bi-lingual). Nevertheless, English is itself an impure language, having origins as it does in the Scandinavian languages spoken by the Angles, German spoken by the Saxons, Latin spoken by the Romans and French spoken by the Norman conquerors. So we have a formal, high-register language full of poly-syllabic words of Latin or French origin, reflecting the language of our rulers, while we have more Anglo-Saxon[6] monosyllabic slang and swear words, reflecting the social position of the indigenous peasants. Even the language of food contains class distinctions: beef, mutton and pork for the meat eaten by Norman aristocrats, but ox, sheep and swine for the animals tended by the Anglo-Saxon serfs. Due to this heritage, when inventing words for new technologies English reverts to scholarly words of Latin or Greek origins, while German or Chinese simply use words to describe the function of the new invention. Thus television (which caused a scandal at its coinage for being a hybrid of Greek and Latin) comes from tele ('far') and vision ('sight'), while in German the original word was simply *Fernsehen* ('far seer') and in Chinese it is *dianshi* ('electric sight'). Either of these would seem ridiculous in English.

In UK society, however, it is the way in which an individual uses the English language that says more about them than the mere words being used. As Britain remains a class-oriented society, dialect and accent can be a social advantage or disadvantage, depending on the context. There are different types of English that are taken as the standard or benchmark language: the Queen's English, Oxford English or BBC English. These are in fact not the standard lan-guage but are particular class or regional accents that are considered to reflect 'received pronunciation' (RP), or the way we ought to speak. The Queen's English is an aristocratic accent that evolved from her German ancestors, the Hanoverian Georges (I, II, III and IV), whose German accents the English courtiers imitated in order that their sovereign did not feel alien when in England. Oxford English refers to the English exhibited in the dictionaries and grammars written by scholars at one of the UK's oldest universities, a seat of learning that by definition has been invested with the authority to set the national standard. The national broadcaster, the British Broadcasting Corporation (BBC), has changed in its attitude towards accent over its 75 years of broadcasting. In the early days, only the King's English was broadcast across the nation and Empire. In fact, the King was one of the early broadcasters, using the new technology to send messages to his subjects around the world. During the Second World War, broadcaster Wilfred Pickles read the news bulletins and was deemed to have a strong Yorkshire accent for the time, although to the modern listener he sounds as 'posh' as all of his contemporaries. Today, regional accents are commonplace among presenters.

Nevertheless, accent is a passport giving access to different milieux in UK society. If you speak in an accent that sounds upper class, you are immediately accepted by 'posh' people into their society. If you speak colloquially and with a strong regional accent, you are accepted in that part of the country as 'one of us' but may be shunned elsewhere. Some accents have national reputations: Scottish or Yorkshire people sound trustworthy and reassuring; people from

Birmingham are widely deemed to be amusing and less intelligent. These language and culture relationships are being used by large companies when selecting locations for national call centres for their direct telephone services. Thus as soon as an individual opens their mouth to speak, those around them make immediate value judgements about social class, profession, education, status, ability and personality.

■ Social structure

British social structure has changed vastly over the last century. It is now a more fluid, dynamic and **meritocratic** society, with possibilities for social mobility through the classes depending on effort and ability. Up to the end of the Second World War, the British population knew its place in society and did not expect to undergo social change: once an aristocrat, always an aristocrat; once a manual labourer, always a manual labourer. As post-war social attitudes changed, so did traditional attitudes to authority, the family, our elders, and the more disadvantaged members of society such as the poor or the ill.

An aspect of social structure that has changed considerably is the family. Grown-up children move away from home and settle down in other parts of the country or even the world, following economic trends and the necessity to work. This means that they have no help with childcare from their parents, and the parents have no family members to care for them in their old age. This puts pressure on society in terms of providing healthcare for the elderly and childcare for pre-school toddlers. As divorce increases and people marry for the first time later in life, the number of single-person households is growing (29 per cent of all households in England in 1996 compared with 18 per cent in 1971;[7] for further detail *see* Chapter 9), which affects both the way social structures operate and government reaction to taxation, healthcare provision and education. In addition, the UK at the end of the twentieth century was a far more informal place than ever before. Attitudes on the part of young people towards their peers and their elders were more **egalitarian** and tolerant than at any time in the past.

Applying Hill's model in a Chinese context

The value of Hill's model (*see* Figure 2.3) is as a framework to help us consider what our culture is and how it affects who we are and how we behave as individuals in society. To aid in this understanding, it is now re-applied to a generic Chinese cultural context.

As part of this it is necessary to examine the issue of what it means to be Chinese and what being foreign means to a Chinese person. In the standard Chinese language the most common name for China is *zhong guo*, meaning 'middle country'. Thus China is the country at the centre of its universe, which equates with many cultures' own view of the world. Logically, everything that is not inside the middle country is outside it, hence the Chinese term for foreigner is *wai guo ren*, literally 'outside country person'. This can be compared to traditional Chinese life, especially in the countryside, where people are immobile and generations live and die in one locale. Anyone not from the same village or town is known as *wai ren* or 'outsider'. It can further be observed that *wa guo ren* is habitually used to mean 'white people'. The traditional image of foreigners for Chinese, often seen in the media, is of a *wai guo ren* with white skin, blond hair and blue eyes. When referring to other races, Chinese will usually specify for example 'Japanese', 'black people' or 'Arabs'. In the wider Chinese diaspora the term *wai guo ren* is used to refer to non-Chinese (and specifically white people), irrespective of whether the latter are in China or not.

Chinese remain Chinese and *wa guo ren* (white people) are *wai guo ren* (foreigners) even when nationality is shared or the white people in question are the indigenous population. Chinese never refer to themselves as *wai guo ren*. In contrast, English native speakers use nationality as a determinant, and are comfortable with referring to themselves as 'foreigners' when they are in another country.

After 'Liberation' (the Communist Party takeover in 1949), most foreigners left China, apart from some committed to the revolution's aims. From 1949 to the mid-1980s any foreigners visiting for business or pleasure were closely supervised by cadres of the Foreign Affairs Office to maintain an official filter between the bourgeois, capitalist outsiders and any Chinese people with whom they had contact. Interactions between foreigners and Chinese became carefully crafted and scripted events designed to put both parties as little at ease as possible. During the Cultural Revolution (1966–76), Chinese were persecuted to death for having had contact with foreigners or even for having relatives abroad, thus being culpable in the eyes of the Red Guards of bourgeois rightism and counter-revolution. While recent years have seen the normalisation and humanisation of Sino-foreign relationships, with many Sino-foreign marriages resulting, there is still to some extent a psychological hangover from the fervently anti-foreign dogma of the post-Liberation years that can affect the operational effectiveness of foreign workers in China.

■ Religion

The main religions affecting social and economic behaviour are Confucianism, Buddhism, Islam and Christianity. Attitudes towards issues of crime and punishment, sex and the family, the position and respect for the aged and how society cares for them can be set by ideological dictate. Buddhism, with its belief in reincarnation, leads the Chinese to be quite fatalistic in their view of the individual's importance in the grand scheme of things. Religious influences are stronger in Chinese societies outside China than within it, where religion has been banned and punished heavily in certain periods since 1949.

■ Politics

Irrespective of political colour, political systems in most Chinese societies are largely authoritarian, non-democratic or oligopolistic. In mainland China there is no aspect of life on which politics has not had a huge impact at some time during the second half of the twentieth century. It is hard, looking from the perspective of the West, to imagine a society where even the morning delivery of milk could depend on your having demonstrated the correct ideological stance at the workplace's weekly political study meetings. Indeed, the idea of a political study meeting at all in the workplace would seem inappropriate.

■ Economics

Early entrepreneurs tackled the problem of business with the People's Republic of China (PRC) or 'New China' unaided by source materials, secondary data or effective diplomatic relations. Doing business with the Chinese was a very unfamiliar process and experience, for two main reasons. First the system, with its interminable bureaucracy, vertical integration and complete lack of flexibility, interspersed with periods of complete economic breakdown due to the supremacy of political dogma, made coping with officialdom difficult for a western businessperson. Second, the culture, with the uniformly and impossibly inscrutable Chinese people and their unwritten, impregnable, yet unbreakable rules of engagement, led to paralysis through analysis on the part of foreigners interacting with them. Old China hands learned their way around through trial, error, good luck and good judgement.

The Deng era, with burgeoning official foreign trade organs at central and local levels, saw the rapid growth of the number of organisations empowered to deal directly with overseas organisations. Hence new entrants to the market-place in China have been able to use the services of consultants, 'how to' guides, agencies, information bureaux and government departments to seek the appropriate Chinese opposite number. While the system grows ever more complex as the volume of trade increases and hurdles are undoubtedly still numerous, there are now mechanisms in place to help foreigners understand and manipulate the system in order to meet corporate and individual needs on both sides. Even though there is increasing economic liberalisation, the economic systems in China and elsewhere in Confucian societies have featured interventionist government macro-economic policies to promote stable and rapid economic growth. It was only after the economic crises of late 1997/early 1998 that this interventionist stance was beginning to be questioned.

■ Education

Education is highly valued and greatly prized. Parents spend a large amount on ensuring the education of their offspring and their advancement to professional success and social security. This is a legacy from imperial days, where the Mandarins ruling China on the Emperor's behalf were all scholars who had passed rigorous entrance examinations. Confucian teaching also respects and values education and intelligence. The teachings of the ancient Chinese philosopher Confucius left a huge legacy in China, Japan and Korea as well as in Chinese societies in other countries. The tradition of master and pupil is much more didactic, in that the teacher is always right and should be copied and emulated by the student at all times.

The role of and respect for formal education, training and qualifications remains strong in most countries of the Far East. There are clear expectations that families will provide the funding and support for education and the student will put in the hard work necessary to succeed.

■ Language

Chinese is one language where the written form is not only a tool for communication but an art form as well. Chinese is an ideographic not an alphabetic language, meaning that each word is a picture. Having a good handwriting or calligraphic style is the sign of a good scholar and thus the sign of a good ruler. Otherwise, Chinese is a language of simple structure and ambiguous meaning. Unlike English, the fewer the number of words, the more formal the language being expressed. Thus each word has many meanings and is open to the interpretation of the individual and many nuances.

■ Social structure

The regional socialisation process in the Far East is strong and dominant, perhaps much more so than in Europe and North America. Social structures are still rigid and well defined, giving everyone a clear picture of their position and role in society. This fixed view of outsiders, described earlier in this chapter, comes from a cultural source as well as from the fact that the Chinese state classifies the nationality and ethnicity of its citizens automatically at birth. China's 1.2 billion citizens are categorised officially into 56 ethnic groups,[8] 96 per cent of the population being Han Chinese and 4 per cent divided into 55 official ethnic minorities. This is of key importance to the people themselves,[9] as Han Chinese are bound by the 'one child only' population control policy, while ethnic minorities may have two children.

✓ Check your understanding

Do you understand the determinants of national culture?

Check your understanding by listing the determinants of national culture and providing an example to illustrate each determinant.

The determinants of organisational culture

We now move from personal to organisational culture. The Johnson and Scholes cultural web[10] identifies and draws together many aspects of organisational culture: 'The cultural web is a representation of the taken-for-granted assumptions or paradigm of an organisation and the physical manifestations of organisational culture.'[11] In other words, organisational culture is determined by the entities taken for granted by the people in an organisation. If an organisation is to function effectively it must develop a coherent culture. This is supported by Deal and Kennedy,[12] who identify two types of culture: strong and weak. The strong culture is highly cohesive and coherent and has a system of informal rules, which indicates to people exactly what is expected of them, so that employees will know how to react and what to do in given situations. In contrast, people operating in a weak culture, one lacking in cohesiveness and coherence, will waste time working out what to do and how to do it.

The entry case study for this chapter showed how changing the determinants of organisational culture in the Shenyang Antibiotics company resulted in a stronger organisational culture. The changes in culture are illustrated by changes in the organisational and power structures: for example, the new owner Mr Jiang sacked two-thirds of managers and clearly defined the roles of those remaining. He also changed routines and **rituals**, with consequent alterations to the workers' behaviour. Workers were now required to arrive at 8am and do a full day's work, in contrast to the past when they turned up at 10am and went home at lunchtime. Those failing to work proper hours and perform their duties correctly were sacked. There was also the symbolic sacking of an employee who smashed a chair reserved for a dignitary at an opening ceremony, which sent a clear message to remaining employees as to what behaviour was and was not going to be tolerated by the new order.

■ Routines and rituals

Routines (*see* Figure 2.4) are the scheduled and deliberate practices carried out as a matter of course and forming the habits of day-to-day life in an organisation. In normal circumstances routines ensure the smooth running and operation of the organisation. In organisations with a strong culture, routine behaviour is clearly spelt out and allows employees, particularly new employees, to know and understand 'the way we do things around here'. A good example of an organisation where routine is important is a fast-food restaurant such as Burger King and/or a chain restaurant such as Pizza Hut. Here the actions employees have to take in preparing the food and taking orders are explicitly laid down, e.g. frying the french fries for exactly seven minutes or always asking the customer if they would like side orders of garlic bread or salad with their pizza.

Rituals in organisational life are used to reinforce the routines and 'the way things are done around here'. Rituals can be formal events that employees are subjected to such as induction courses, training courses or periodic assessments

Figure 2.4
The cultural web

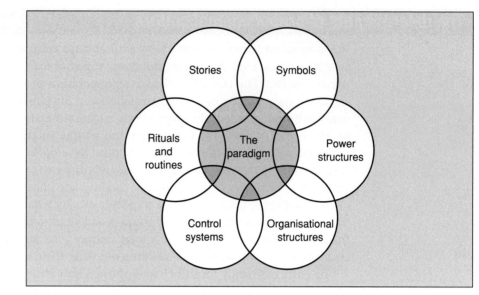

Source: Johnson, G and Scholes, K (1999) *Exploring Corporate Strategy*, 5th edn, Prentice Hall Europe.

to ensure an employee's performance is up to scratch and conforming to the routine way of doing things. Rituals may also be more informal in nature, for example the office Christmas party, drinks in the pub on Friday at the end of the working week, or gossiping around the office coffee machine. However, they still promote the common routine of the 'way we do things around here'.

■ Stories

In any organisation, **stories** will be told by employees to each other, to new recruits who join them and to others outside the organisation. The stories represent the organisation's history and typically highlight significant events and characters in its past. They characteristically focus on the achievements and failures of the organisation and the individuals involved, be they heros or villains. Stories summarise the meaningful and key aspects of an organisation's past and tell people what counts as acceptable conduct today.

■ Symbols

The **symbols** present in an organisation can be many and varied and often symbolise someone's position in the organisation or how much that individual is valued by the organisation. Symbols can include titles, office size, company car and salary scales, all indicating the power and value that an individual possesses with respect to an organisation. In long-established organisations like the Civil Service, many symbols will exist and indicate the power and importance of employees. In such organisations there will be a rigid structure, comprising different jobs at different grades with different salaries, with office accommodation directly dependent on job, grade and salary. Individuals with better offices, higher salaries and further up the hierarchy will have greater power and may be perceived to be of greater value to the organisation. In contrast, a newer organisation, such as an architects' practice which has all staff on performance-related pay, all working in an open-plan office, displays a different culture by virtue of the symbols that do or don't exist. The message in such an organisation is that all employees are equally valued and succeed on merit.

■ Power structures

Power structures evolve in organisations over time and consist of individuals with power, who all share a common set of beliefs and values that underpins the way they work together. Membership of the power structure is often determined by seniority and/or length of service in an organisation. Alternatively, power may be based on expertise, with a common source of power being technical expertise that is in short supply and highly valued in the organisation. This may occur particularly in firms where innovation is a key success factor (*see* Chapter 7). This type of power base will be strengthened if there are many valued experts who group together to promote or resist particular issues in the workplace.

■ Organisational structure

The structure that an organisation adopts will determine where the power exists within it (*see* Chapter 1). The location of power in an organisation will define the power relationships and designate the fundamental linkages between the seats of power and control. Nevertheless, in any formal organisational structure there will exist smaller, more informal structures and networks, which are equally important to the culture of the organisation.

■ Control systems

The term 'control systems' denotes systems for control, measurement and reward within the organisation. The systems that an organisation puts in place and monitors indicate what is important to it. Control systems include financial control and accounting systems such as cashflow and budgeting, which are systems for regulating expenditure. Measurement systems examine the output of organisations and their efficiency and effectiveness. The output of an organisation can be the amount of product manufactured or the throughput of customers. Efficiency and effectiveness relate to the aspects of time and resources used to produce the final output/throughput. In some organisations the control of expenditure will be more important than the measurement of output, in others both will be equally important.

The reward system in an organisation will determine how employees behave with respect to their work and jobs. A reward system that pays for a large volume of work will elicit very different behaviour to a reward system that pays for high-quality work.

✓ Check your understanding

Do you understand the determinants of organisational culture?

Check your understanding by listing the determinants of organisational culture and providing an example to illustrate each determinant.

Deal and Kennedy's organisational cultures

Deal and Kennedy[13] examined hundreds of companies and claim to have identified four generic cultures: **tough-guy macho**, **work hard/play hard**, **bet your company** and **process**. These cultures are defined by two factors in the marketplace: the degree of risk associated with the organisation's activities and the speed at which the organisation and its employees receive feedback on their performance. These cultures are summarised in Figure 2.5. Deal and Kennedy also acknowledge that no organisation will exactly fit one of their four generic cultures and some may not fit any at all.[14] However, they maintain that such a framework is a useful initial step in assisting managers to recognise the culture of their organisation.

■ Tough-guy macho culture

In organisations exhibiting the tough-guy macho culture, it is customary for staff to take high risks and receive rapid feedback on the effectiveness of their actions. Deal and Kennedy indicate that police departments, surgeons,

**Figure 2.5
Deal and Kennedy's organisational cultures**

		Risk	
		Low	High
Feedback	Slow	Process culture	Bet your company culture
	Rapid	Work hard/play hard culture	Tough-guy macho culture

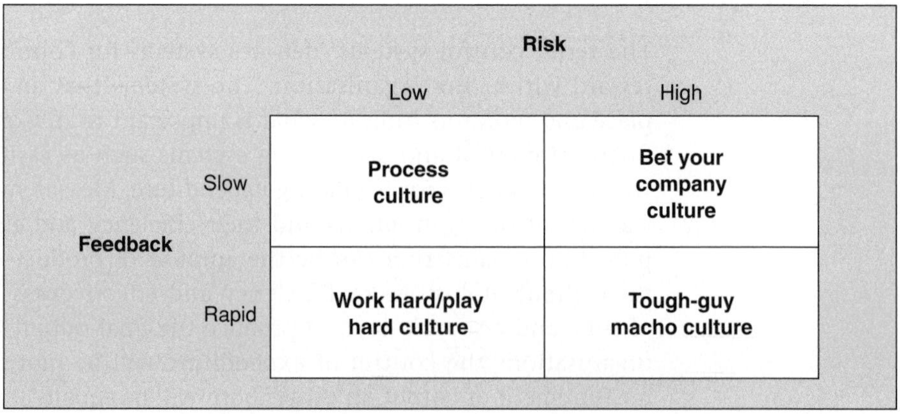

management consultants and the entertainment industry may all exhibit a tough-guy macho culture.[15] The key characteristics of this culture are rapid speed and the short-term nature of actions. This results in great pressure being placed on the individual culture to achieve success in the short term. This is often illustrated by such organisations having young staff achieving financial rewards early in life if they are successful.

The consequences of this type of culture are that burnout is common and failure is harshly condemned, often by dismissal. Those who do succeed and avoid burnout often do so by taking a tough stance with regard to their work and their colleagues, and pace themselves accordingly. This results in internal rivalries occurring, which in turn produce tension and conflict between staff, which is normally expected in these organisations. An organisation with this type of culture achieves quick returns from its high-risk environment, but it finds it difficult to achieve success via long-term investment. This is due to rapid staff turnover, along with very limited co-operation and tolerance between staff. Hence the creation of an organisation with a strong and cohesive culture is almost impossible if the predominating culture is tough-guy macho.

◼ Work hard/play hard culture

Organisations for which there is low risk and quick feedback on performance are those with a work hard/play hard culture. Sales along with a sense of fun and action are key characteristics of this culture. Typical work hard/play hard organisations include both manufacturing and service companies, such as fast food and computer companies. In both types of organisation the risks are small; in a service provision organisation failing to sell a single item will not severely damage the salesperson, and in a manufacturing organisation examinations and inspections will ensure that departures from the normal standard of product are minimised.

Quick feedback on performance is easily obtainable in such an organisation, e.g. whether staff have achieved sales or production targets. Hence organisations with a focus on sales and meeting targets are often customer oriented. This may be reinforced by the use of contests, games and rallies that focus on the achievement of individuals and teams of employees and are meant to motivate staff to succeed. There may be an inclination to focus on the sales volume achieved by individuals or teams, at the expense of service/product quality, and thus there is a focus on the short-term rather than the long-term future.

◼ Bet your company culture

The bet your company culture organisation takes high risks and waits a long time for the response to actions and decisions. This is because the investment is huge and long term and the outcome is seen in the long-term future. Examples include the manufacture of aircraft as undertaken by Boeing, or the finding and refining of oil as in British Petroleum. Hence there is an enormous amount of detailed planning that has to take place, evidenced in the ritualistic business meetings that occur. Decision making in this culture focuses on the future and is top down, reinforcing the hierarchical nature of the culture. The person who fares best and survives in this type of culture is the mature worker with a respect for authority and technical ability. They will also possess the skills to operate effectively in a team with similar-minded people and to cope under pressure.

The result of this type of working environment is that many high-quality innovations and scientific discoveries are made. However, innovation and scientific breakthroughs are long-term goals and this makes such companies vulnerable in an economy and to a stock market that are more interested in short-term profit and success. Nevertheless, it could be that companies that innovate are those most needed by western economies.

■ Process culture

The process culture is a low-risk and slow-feedback culture. The response to actions and decisions seems to take for ever. This type of culture is typically seen in the Civil Service, public-sector organisations, banks and insurance companies. The lengthy feedback time means that employees focus on how something is done, i.e. the process, rather than the reason for doing it or the outcome. The employees who survive best in such a culture are methodical and punctual. In the process culture there will be significant emphasis on job titles and roles and this will be symbolised by the size of someone's office and the style of office furniture that the rigid, strict and hierarchical organisation will allow that individual. This illustrates one further point concerning the process culture: the position that a person occupies deter-mines the amount of power that individual wields. This is the type of culture in which remaining with the organisation and enduring will be rewarded by long-service awards.

The process culture is most successful if the organisation operates in a predictable and stable environment and is perhaps likely to struggle if asked to react quickly to rapidly changing circumstances, as the organisation lacks the creativity and vision to do so. An alternative view is that such a culture offers a balance to the other three cultures, which all have either high risk and/or rapid feedback.

☑ Check your understanding

Do you understand the different types of culture which may exist in organisations?

Check your understanding naming the four Deal and Kennedy cultures and briefly summarising their key characteristics.

Understanding and managing culture

An understanding of personal cultural provenance and national culture is important, as it allows managers to develop the cultural awareness that is needed in the world of work at the beginning of the twenty-first century. This understanding of personal and national culture allows today's employee to appreciate the differing personal and national cultures of employees in a firm in a foreign country or individual consumers in a foreign country. They may have different expectations and different needs and wants (*see* Chapter 4) to those in the home market. In contrast, the entry case study for this chapter clearly demonstrates that overseas managers in China are faced with different organisational cultures resulting from a different national culture with regard to work – the 'iron rice bowl'.

Differences in national culture will be reflected in the way that organisations collaborate with one another in the international arena and evaluate the outcome of their activities. The compatibility of national cultures may influence an organisation as to the nationality of a collaborating partner company. For example, British companies least like to partner Japanese companies, primarily because of language difficulties.[16] The management of corporate or organisational culture is as important as that of individual and national culture and hence has a role to play in the overall management of culture. This is looked at on pages 68 to 70.

Managing culture in the international arena

■ Evaluating success

The way in which organisations evaluate their success or failure can reflect their home country and culture – *see* Figure 2.6. Companies with the USA as their home country are most likely to measure performance on the basis of key quantitative measures such as profit, market share and other key financial

Figure 2.6
Issues for managing culture in the international arena

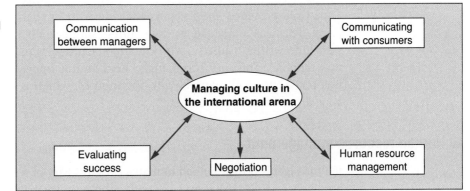

benefits. In contrast, Japanese companies evaluate success or failure via skills improvement and how that has strengthened the organisation's strategic position. In European companies a balance between profit and the meeting of social objectives is more often sought.[17] The existence of such variations in the way performance is evaluated can produce difficulties if two collaborating companies have very different expectations as to how success or failure is measured. The most extreme situation would be if one partner viewed the collaboration as a success and the other partner a complete failure.

Problems may also arise from differences in the corporate cultures of collaborating organisations. A collaboration between two companies is unlikely to be successful if the organisations involved have very different corporate cultures and neither is prepared to change. Referring back to Deal and Kennedy's organisational culture types discussed earlier in this chapter, merging an organisation with a tough-guy macho culture (high risk and rapid feedback) with a process culture organisation (low risk and slow feedback) is clearly unlikely to be successful. Hence organisations may agree to collaborate on large long-term projects with each other only once the water has been thoroughly tested by working together successfully on smaller projects, over a significant period of time. Therefore cultural compatibility is critical to ensuring the consolidation of business relationships.

■ Communicating with consumers

Consumer buying behaviour is complex and in the international arena there are many potential constraints that the marketer has to overcome to be successful in a foreign country. These include differences in language, taste and attitudes of the target market, as well as variations in government control, media availability and local distribution networks. Hence it is difficult to determine in advance whether new or different products will be accepted by an international or overseas market.

At the start of the twenty-first century there exists a large number of global brands that are familiar to people in many different cultures, such as McDonald's, Kodak and Levi's. However, even successful global brands have experienced difficulties in being accepted. For example on entering China, Coca-Cola provided shopkeepers with signs in English to advertise the soft drink. This was a mistake, as the Chinese shopkeepers translated the English signs into written Chinese, with the literal Chinese translation being 'Bite the wax tadpole'. This, not surprisingly, held limited appeal for the Chinese and was revised to read 'happiness in the mouth', which is more acceptable and appealing to the target market.[18]

■ Human resource management

If a manager is posted abroad to manage a subsidiary of a parent company, they are likely to find that they have wide-ranging responsibility for all functions of the business and relations with external stakeholders such as government, the local community, suppliers and customers. Selecting a manager (*see* Chapter 7) to fulfil such a role needs to be done with care. This is because managers with similar profit or cost responsibility at home in the larger parent company are only middle-level management and lack the skills and abilities to perform as a top manager in a foreign environment.[19]

The other type of foreign experience that a manager may encounter is as an international manager who finds him/herself frequently interacting with very high-level authorities in foreign countries. For example, this may occur when a construction company negotiates with a foreign government for a contract to build major infrastructure projects such as new roads or bridges, or if a company is negotiating to expand current facilities in a foreign country or selling a new, innovative technology. The tasks of an international manager are even more complex than those of subsidiary managers based in one foreign country, as an international manager has to gain trust and build relationships with officials in many foreign countries. Therefore the international manager will have to deal with the cultures of many countries. Appreciation and understanding of one's personal cultural provenance and national culture are good starting points from which to build a comprehension of the different cultures in which one may work.

■ Communication between managers

International managers or those interacting on a regular basis with cultures different from that of their home country must ensure that messages between headquarters and subsidiary operations are clearly understood. The advent of technology such as e-mail and faxes makes written communication with people almost anywhere in the world possible in an instant. However, there may be instances when direct contact and verbal communication are preferable to ensure a complex message or idea is correctly understood by its overseas recipients. This is achieved either by international travel, careful use of the telephone (take account of time difference) or video conferencing.

It should also be noted that the language of communication may influence how it is received and understood. A manager receiving a message in a non-native language is likely to take longer to read and comprehend it. Equally, a manager working abroad and having to carry out at least some of their work in a second language will take longer for the same reasons and have to work harder than when at home to produce the same quality of work.[20] Therefore in recruiting overseas managers and international managers, the language part of one's personal cultural provenance is important.

■ Negotiation

A country's national culture is likely to influence the way managers from that country behave in negotiating contracts with managers from a different national culture. For example, negotiations between the Saudi government and a British company wishing to secure defence contracts will be very different in nature to negotiations between a US and British firm wanting to merge. Hence the type of issue under negotiation and the national culture of negotiators are both likely to influence the nature of the negotiations. In some national cultures it will be normal for individual negotiators to have the power to make decisions, in contrast to other national cultures where referring back to those behind the scenes and head office will all be seen as part of the negotiating process. In some cultures negotiators are required to go through every line of a contract and every possible contingency, in comparison with other negotiators who will be satisfied with a holistic view and understanding of the contract.

The behaviour of the individual negotiators is based on their national culture and this can influence social behaviour in the negotiating process. For example, in some cultures eating and drinking will form part of the negotiating process, in others it will not, or will occur only once a contract has been settled. Equally, some cultures place great importance on punctuality and others do not. Therefore understanding the national cultures of the different parties involved in negotiations will help those involved discern whether the negotiations are based on their own culture, another party's culture or some hybrid of the different cultures involved.

Managing organisational culture

If the relevance of personal and national culture to business today has been understood, then the same level of perception regarding organisational or corporate culture is required if an individual manager is to work and manage within the context of an organisational culture. The human resource management function is the most powerful of all the four key business functions in influencing the management of organisational culture. For example, the human resource management function will help determine organisational rituals, such as induction courses, training courses and appraisal (*see* earlier in this chapter), as well as cultural symbols such as the allocation of offices, furniture, company cars, job grades, salaries, promotions and dismissals. Hence human resource policies and procedures can have a great influence on an organisation's culture. The outcomes of an attempt to manage culture using the complex influence of human resource policies and procedures are difficult to predict.

If a culture emphasises the importance of teamwork and innovation (*see* the bet your company culture earlier in this chapter) as crucial for success, the managers responsible for culture will want to create one that rewards imaginative and inventive technical behaviour and co-operation and collaboration with others in the workplace. This will mean that rewards, salaries, promotions and bonuses will have to reflect this focus. This may appear to be simple and straightforward, but it is not necessarily so. The lack of simplicity is due to the difficulty in foreseeing the full implications of a specific reward system or promotions policy. There are two main reasons for this: first, the full workings of any policy or procedure are often not determined in enough detail prior to implementation; second, those implementing the system and procedures do not always follow directions to the letter, putting a different interpretation on the policy and procedures and hence producing unexpected outcomes. This variation in interpretation of the policy and procedures compounds the complexities of managing culture in this way.[21]

The role of leadership

The successful management of organisational culture requires the support of top managers, as they play a key role in setting the vision (ideal culture) that the organisation is aiming to adopt. Top management also has responsibility for allocating tasks, activities and resources, and determining the organisational structure, which affects the power structures and control systems in the organisation. Therefore if human resource policies and procedures, as discussed in the previous section, are to be used in the management of culture, it is essential that top management is involved in the design of human resource policies and procedures, as part of its leadership responsibilities.[22]

The role of symbols

Peters[23] recognises a variety of characteristic practices that can enable an executive to influence the culture of their organisation. These include how top executives spend their time, their use of communication and their use of meetings (see Figure 2.7). The dominant theme in all these is personal enactment. Managing directors who seek to model an organisation's culture should individually personify the beliefs, values and assumptions that they seek to inspire in others. The same applies to all managers endeavouring to influence employees in the departments or divisions they manage. People generally comprehend a remarkable amount from modelling the conduct of those they respect, particularly if other benefits are derived from doing so. Leaders should seek to maximise the

**Figure 2.7
Issues for managing
organisational
culture**

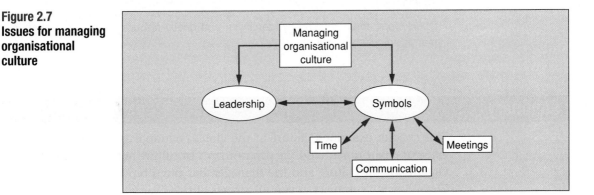

impact of such symbolic actions continually and regularly. Symbolic actions need to be positively reinforced in the shape of praise, money, status and other rewards to champion behaviours in line with the desired culture.

The use of time

Senior and middle managers are generally perceptive and sensitive to the activities of their leader and will spend time determining the consequences of what is seen and heard for their current and future careers. Hence a chief executive is able to communicate influential messages to employees through his/her actions.

The use of communication

A good managing director seeks to understand employees and their views on all elements of organisational life, including work activities, colleagues and the marketplace. If a managing director makes a public announcement that quality is the organisation's most pressing problem, employees will listen. If the managing director raises the issue on an ongoing basis and in a memorable fashion by the use of anecdotes and stories, in time people may begin to alter their view of the organisation and the key issues affecting it.

The use of meetings

Organisational leaders enjoy significant authority in determining the key issues, quality, innovation and marketing, which are vital to an organisation and its success. For example, a top manager can communicate the relative importance of an event or meeting by simply turning up or by turning down an invitation to attend. If a managing director always attends quality meetings but virtually never attends a meeting of the marketing team, the relative importance of quality over marketing is clearly indicated. Accordingly, leaders have the power to convene, postpone and cancel meetings, fashion agendas and the manner in which minutes are written up. These devices have a part to play in moulding employees' understanding of what is required of them, what beliefs it is deemed acceptable to hold, and how they are expected to perform their work activities.

✓ Check your understanding

Do you understand which issues are key in managing culture in an international setting?

Check your understanding by identifying and briefly discussing the key issues in managing culture internationally.

Summary

This chapter examined culture at the global, national and local levels of the external environment and the determinants of culture at these different levels. Organisational culture and the management of culture were also examined. The following summary covers all aspects of this chapter.

1 Culture at the global level of the external environment relates to the inter-action of at least one national culture with another. Culture at the national level can result from one nation attributing characteristics to another, which can result in stereotyping and prejudice. The national and local levels of culture can be intertwined, as for some people their national characteristics make them the people they are in their local communities.

2 The determinants of personal cultural provenance are name, gender, professional role, icons, symbols, ceremonies, personal morality, norms, values. It is these determinants which define an individual's culture, which in turn makes them the person they are.

3 National culture is determined by religion, politics, economies, education, language, social structure. It is these determinants, their variations and how they are viewed by other nationalities which define a country's national culture.

4 Organisational culture can result from the internal structure of an organisation and from the type of people it employs.

5 The determinants of organisational culture are presented in the cultural web, which includes routines and ritual, stories, symbols, power structures, organisational structures, control systems. All these determinants will have an impact on they type of place an organisation is to work in.

6 Deal and Kennedy identified four possible organisational types. The tough-guy macho culture is where staff take high-risk decisions and receive rapid feedback on the effectiveness of their actions. The work hard/play hard culture is found in organisations in which decisions are routinely low risk and feedback quick, which is often the case in sales-orientated companies. The bet your company culture organisation takes big risks and feedback takes a long time. This is typical of companies which build aircraft or undertake oil exploration. Finally the process culture is low risk with slow feedback, which is typically found in the civil service and public-sector organisations.

7 How a company manages and behaves in the international arena can be influenced by many factors. The key issues which need to be examined as they are influenced by differing global, national and local cultures include how success is measured, communications with consumers and the marketplace, human resource management, communication with overseas managers (locally based and international managers), and contract negotiations.

8 Managing culture and understanding its relevance to business requires a number of issues to be addressed. These include leadership, the role of symbols, and the use of time, communications and meetings in day-to-day organisational life.

While reading this chapter and engaging in the activities, you should have learned how to apply theory and models, analyse situations, and evaluate the application and analysis you undertake. The learning outcomes specified below outline the type of application, analysis and evaluation of which you should be capable in relation to organisations. The case studies and the questions which follow provide an opportunity for you to test how well you have achieved the learning outcomes for the ethical issues and exit case studies for this chapter.

Application	Check you have achieved this by	
1 Identify the different levels at which culture exists and may be changed	indicating possible changes to culture at different levels	answering ethical case studies question 1
2 Devise a plan for changing a particular determinant of culture in an organisation	specifying which actions should be implemented to alter an aspect of culture in an organisation	answering ethical case studies question 2
Analysis	**Check you have achieved this by**	
1 Analyse organisational culture	comparing and contrasting different possible cultures which may exist in an organisation	answering exit case study question 1

ETHICAL ISSUES CASE STUDY 2.2A

FT

Hewitt to call time on culture of long working hours

By Christopher Adams

Patricia Hewitt, trade and industry secretary, will this week commit the government to end Britain's long working hours culture in the next five years, as figures show one in six people puts in more than 48 hours a week. Speaking to unions and employers at a conference tomorrow, she is expected to say the government will have failed if excessive hours are not cut.

Unions demanding that the government drop its opt-out to European laws setting a limit on working hours may be disappointed, however. Ministers want to keep it. Nearly 4m employees, some 16 per cent of the labour force, work more than 48 hours a week, according to a report published today by the Trades Union Congress. That is a third of a million more than a decade ago.

The report shows that UK employees are the worst off in the European Union, spending an average of 43.6 hours a week at work, compared with an EU-wide average of 40.3 hours.

Britain is the only member state that allows staff to opt out of the EU directive setting the 48-hour maximum.

The TUC is urging the government not to extend the opt-out beyond 2003, when it is due for review.

However, the Confederation of British Industry is resisting.

Ministers want to retain the opt-out and support a 'partnership' approach between employers and unions to cut over-working.

'The long-hours culture is a national disgrace. It leads to stress, ill-health and family strains,' said John Monks, TUC general secretary.

The report shows that up to 1.5m people are working more than 55 hours a week. Men are more likely than women to be working beyond the EU maximum, with a quarter of males in this group. Long hours are most prevalent among men in manufacturing, construction and aviation.

'The government must not argue for the extension of the individual opt-out,' the TUC said. 'It should instead use 2003 as an end-date for a national campaign that promotes agreements to reduce excessive hours and extend the use of flexible working time arrangements.'

The CBI said workers had the right to choose the number of extra hours they worked and the directive gave them the power to refuse. 'Reducing long hours should be a matter of individual choice,' said John Cridland, deputy director-general.

Source: Financial Times, 4 February 2002. Reprinted with permission.

ETHICAL ISSUES CASE STUDY 2.2B

FT

Long-hours culture 'stalls better work-life balance'

By Nicholas Timmins

The 'long hours' culture, managers' lack of experience handling different working patterns, and lack of leadership are holding up progress in giving employees a better work–life balance, according to a study published yesterday.

The government and employers said they wanted to give employees more flexibility over working hours, said the report from the Institute for Employment Studies.

Many employers were offering that without being compelled to by legislation. But a big gap remained between the demand for greater flexibility and take-up, even in companies that had taken the issue seriously, the institute said.

'Rights to time off and flexible working practices are rarely enough,' said Sally Dench, a senior fellow at the institute. 'A change in culture and attitudes within the organisation is necessary for success.'

People were deterred because, even in companies that provided flexibility, a culture of long hours could remain entrenched. People worried about their career prospects, and heavy workloads could make the idea of flexibility seem impossible.

Managers and employees needed good information on what flexibilities a company would allow – and managers needed support to help them handle teams working different patterns while still meeting deadlines.

Leadership from senior managers was essential, said Richard Pearson, the report's co-author. 'Work-life policies don't just kick in automatically. There are significant management and cultural issues to resolve.'

Meanwhile, companies are spending large sums on perks such as subsidised canteens and free medicals when staff would rather have personal fitness trainers or an on-site hairdresser, according to a Norwich Union healthcare survey.

Source: Financial Times, 26 April 2002. Reprinted with permission.

Questions for ethical issues case studies 2.2a and 2.2b

1 How and at what levels does culture need to change if UK employees are to cease working the longest hours in Europe?

2 As a senior manager in a private-sector organisation with responsibility for instilling a culture of 'good work–life balance' in the company, identify the actions you would take, with timescales, over the next year to achieve this.

 **EXIT CASE STUDY 2.3**   FT

US sets the pace in 'the culture of learning'

View From The Top: Stephen Kelly of Chordiant

By Fiona Harvey

Englishmen are still sufficiently rare in Silicon Valley for Stephen Kelly to turn heads when he speaks.

'There's an expectation that the chief executive of an American company will be an American citizen, and my accent immediately gives me away,' he says. But the reaction is always welcoming: 'I've never had anything but a positive reception, which is very encouraging.'

Being a chief executive in the US is a very different to doing the same job in the UK, Mr Kelly believes. 'People tend to be much more gung-ho and effusive in the US, while English CEOs behave with more reserve. And even though they may be passionate about their companies, they usually speak about them with greater modesty in public.'

The culture is also much more open than in the UK, where heads of companies are usually fiercely guarded by secretaries. 'In the US, you are not screened so heavily: you get calls from everyone – ranging from advertising sales people to junior executives from clients.' But in the UK, senior executives can be too protected from the real world, and even from their customers.

While most chiefs only have to worry about their own customers, Mr Kelly has to think a step beyond, to his customers' customers – his business is customer relationship management software.

Chordiant was set up in May 1997, in Silicon Valley, and now numbers more than 400 employees, with sales of $76m last year, though the company recorded a loss. Chordiant floated in 2000, and is now valued at about $360m. Its customers include several British household names, such as British Telecommunications and Lloyds TSB, as well as US companies that include UPS and First USA Bank.

Mr Kelly helped to start Chordiant's UK operations in 1997, before taking on responsibility for Chordiant's field operations in early 2000, which meant a move to the US. He enjoys living in California, though his family remains behind in England until they join him later this year. He became Chordiant's chief executive at the start of this year.

As companies struggle to find new sources of revenue and to cut costs in the midst of the economic slowdown, Mr Kelly believes CRM software will assume greater importance for all organisations.

'You can save up to 30 to 40 per cent of the costs of managing your customers with CRM software, and that's something that speaks directly to CEOs in this climate. Add to that the fact that keeping a customer is always cheaper than finding a new one,' he says.

At its simplest, CRM means having a whole view of the customer, rather than the partial view most companies have. Consider, for example, a bank customer with a current account, mortgage and credit card: each of these may be dealt with by a different part of the bank, and the information about each may be kept on a different computer system. In order to deal effectively with that customer, however, customer service employees should have access to all of these areas. The integration of back-end systems takes time and is technologically complex, so CRM software can be hard to implement.

For some organisations, the phrase 'customer relationship management' is loaded with negative overtones. CRM projects have a reputation for being lengthy, costly and prone to failure. Companies weary from business process engineering projects, enterprise resource planning implementations, supply chain management software, just do not want to hear another three-letter acronym.

Many CRM projects do fail, Mr Kelly acknowledges. Managers should not lose faith as a result, however. Instead, they should examine the reasons why the project has failed.

Is it to do with the technology, or with the process of implementation? Has CRM really been tried, or found hard and left untried? Did the company whole-heartedly commit itself to make the project work, or did internal opposition, politicking or reluctance to change put a spanner in the work? Have business processes been changed in step with the new technology, or have the two been left out of synch?

Unless processes are aligned with technology, there can be no hope of success, Mr Kelly maintains. And for business processes to be aligned properly with a CRM system, a company must be fully committed to a sometimes painful regime of change. In many cases, companies simply find that their courage fails them, and the difficult project is shelved.

Take a closer look at the role of the chief executive. 'If the head of the company decides to throw his backing behind a CRM project, that's the best guarantee of success,' says Mr Kelly. Even if at points it looks as though the project is doomed because it is 'too difficult', hard driving from the top management will see it through.

▶

The differences between the UK and the US can be thrown sharply into relief during such projects. 'It's a stereotype, but often true, that lots of UK companies have a culture of blame and fear. The US, on the other hand, has a culture of learning,' observes Mr Kelly.

That extends to learning from failures – and rewarding successes. Companies in the UK would do well to adopt a similar attitude, he believes, instead of a negative culture that makes people afraid to take risks or try anything new, and too ready to block change.

Contrasts

UK companies are also too ready to undermine and ridicule 'the obsession with the customer that characterises American businesses', he says. 'You find people stand by the coffee machine making snide remarks (about your own company and your customers), which you don't find in the US.'

Only by reforming their attitudes to the customer will UK companies be able to compete with their US counterparts. This approach must come from the very top and be passed down to all levels of the organisation.

In leading his own company, Mr Kelly says, 'I don't pretend to be a genius. I never claim to be anything special, but I do simple things very well. Most of the things I say, my way of working, I have plagiarised from other companies that have been successful.'

He tells his own employees: 'Never be afraid.' People should be happy to seek advice, coaching and supervision internally, without feeling they will lose face. They should accept that failures can happen but instead of finding someone to blame, try to learn the lessons. They should not be anxious about questioning existing processes but should be open to change. And above all, he concludes, remember that the one thing crucial to success in business is the quality of relationship with the customer.

Source: *Financial Times*, 3 April 2002. Reprinted with permission.

| **Question for exit case study 2.3** | 1 | Identify the characteristics of successful CRM. Compare and contrast the characteristics of organisational culture which may lead to successful CRM with those which could lead to poor CRM. |

 For more case studies please visit www.booksites.net/capon

Short-answer questions

1 Define culture at the global level of the external environment.

2 Define culture at the national level of the external environment.

3 Define culture at the local level of the external environment.

4 Define organisational culture.

5 Summarise the impact of symbols on personal cultural provenance.

6 Explain, briefly, the role of norms in determining personal cultural provenance.

7 Name Hill's six determinants of culture.

8 Explain, briefly, the role of religion in determining national culture in your home country.

9 Identify the type of organisation in which a process culture is found.

10 Identify the type of organisation in which a bet your company culture is found.

11 Identify the type of organisation in which a work hard/play hard culture is found.

12 Identify the type of organisation in which a tough-guy macho culture is found.

13 Name six determinants of culture which constitute the cultural web.

14 In determining organisational culture, explain the role of 'stories'.

15 In the cultural web, what do routines and ritual represent?

Learning outcomes for assignment questions

While reading this chapter and engaging in the activities, you should have learned how to apply theory and models, analyse situations, and evaluate the application and analysis you undertake. The learning outcomes specified below outline what you should be able to do and the assignment questions provide an opportunity for you to test how well you have achieved the learning outcomes for this chapter.

Application	Check you have achieved this by	
1 Apply the personal cultural provenance factors to yourself	discussing the influence of your own cultural background on determining the sort of person you are today	answering assignment question 1
2 Apply the personal cultural provenance factors to a colleague with a different background to yours	discussing, with your colleague, your understanding of the influence of your colleague's cultural background on determining the sort of person s/he is today	answering assignment question 1
3 Apply Hill's determinants of culture to your home country	demonstrating how your home culture has evolved	answering assignment question 1
4 Apply Hill's determinants of culture to a foreign country (not your home country, Britain or China)	researching data and demonstrating how a foreign culture has evolved	answering assignment question 1
5 Apply Deal and Kennedy's organisational cultures to organisations you know well	employing the Deal and Kennedy cultures to examine the culture of organisations	answering assignment question 2
6 Apply the cultural web to an organisation with which you are familiar	discussing the determinants of an organisation's culture	answering assignment question 3
Analysis	**Check you have achieved this by**	
1 Assess the impact of personal and national culture on an individual's ability to suceed in the workplace	employing the Deal and Kennedy cultures to examine the culture of organisations	answering assignment question 1
2 Analyse an organisation's cultural web	identifying which determinants of an organisation's culture need to change if its culture is also to be changed	answering assignment question 3
Evaluation	**Check you have achieved this by**	
1 Evaluate the usefulness of organisational cultural models	determining the relevance of models of culture to working life for both the individual and the organisation	answering assignment question 2
2 Comment on the impact of organisational culture on efficiency and effectiveness	appraising the efficiency and effectiveness of organisations with different organisational cultures	answering assignment question 2

Assignment questions

1 Write a 2000-word essay that compares and contrasts the relative importance of personal cultural provenance and national culture to the successful performance of the individual in the workplace.

2 Compare and contrast Handy's cultures (end of Chapter 1) and Deal and Kennedy's organisational cultures. In your opinion, which is a more realistic representation of organisational culture? Justify and explain your answer. Present your response in a 2000-word essay.

3 The university or college you attend is to be privatised and students charged the full fees of around £5000 per annum. Apply Johnson and Scholes' cultural web before and after privatisation. Summarise how the culture of the university or college would have to change if it were to be successful and maintain student quality and numbers in the face of competition. Present your findings in a 2000-word report.

Weblinks available online at www.booksites.net/capon

1 This is the Business Open Learning Archive (BOLA). The page on this website about organisational culture looks briefly at definitions and approaches to organisational culture. The BOLA site is maintained by Brunel University.
http://sol.brunel.ac.uk/bola/

2 This business search engine can provide good articles and information about a range of business and organisational topics, including corporate culture.
http://www.business.com/

3 This is the web page of a US consulting company. Select the page 'Building a culture of choice', which looks at developing corporate or organisational culture.
http://w3.hcgnet.com/

Further reading

Black, S J and Gregersen, H B (1999) 'The right way to manage expats', *Harvard Business Review*, March/April.

Brown, A (1998) *Organisational Culture*, 2nd edn, London: Financial Times Prentice Hall.

Burnes, B (2000) *Managing Change*, 3rd edn, Harlow: Financial Times Prentice Hall.

Deal, T and Kennedy, A (1988) *Corporate Cultures*, London: Penguin Business.

Foster, M J and Minkes, A L (1999) 'East and west: business culture as divergence', *Journal of General Management*, 25 (1), Autumn.

Gracie, S (1998) 'In the company of women', *Management Today*, June.

Johnson, G and Scholes, K (2002) *Exploring Corporate Strategy*, 6th edn, Chapter 5, Harlow: Financial Times Prentice Hall.

Lewis, C (2001) 'Telling stories', *Management Today*, February.

Lynch, R (2003) *Corporate Strategy*, 3rd edn, Chapter 7, Harlow: Financial Times Prentice Hall.

Mitchell, A (1998) 'The dawn of a cultural revolution', *Management Today*, March.

Ogbonna, E and Harris, L C (1998) 'Organizational culture: It's not what you think . . .', *Journal of General Management*, 23 (3), Spring.

Senior, B (2002) *Organisational Change*, 2nd edn, London: Financial Times Prentice Hall.

Sparrow, P (1999) 'Abroad minded', *People Management*, 20 May.

Thompson, J L (2001) *Strategic Management*, 4th edn, Chapter 5, London: Thomson Learning.

Trompenaars, F and Woolliams, P (1999) 'First-class accommodation', *People Management*, 29 July.

Warner, M (1996) 'Managing China's enterprise reforms', *Journal of General Management*, 21 (3), Spring.

Wickens, P (1999) 'Values added', *People Management*, 20 May.

Wright, N J (1996) 'Creating a quality culture', *Journal of General Management*, 21 (3), Spring.

Yan, R (1998) 'Short-term results: the litmus test for success in China', *Harvard Business Review*, September/October.

References

1 Hill, C W L (1994) *International Business*, Burr Ridge, IL: Irwin.

2 Hofstede, G (1984) *Culture's Consequences: International Differences in Work Related Values*, London: Sage.

3 Hofstede, G (1980) 'Motivation, leadership and organisation: do American theories apply abroad?', *Organisational Dynamics*, Summer.

4 Kingdom, J (1991) *Government and Politics in Britain*, Cambridge: Polity Press.

5 Hill, op. cit.

6 Ibid.

7 Mintel Special Report (1996) *Single Person Households*.

8 Hill, op. cit.

9 Ibid.

10 Johnson, G and Scholes, K (2002) *Exploring Corporate Strategy*, 6th edn, Harlow: Financial Times Prentice Hall.

11 Ibid.

12 Deal, T and Kennedy, A (1988) *Corporate Cultures*, London: Penguin Business.

13 Ibid.

14 Ibid.

15 Ibid.

16 Cartwright, S and Cooper, C (1998) 'Why suitors should consider culture', *Financial Times*, 1 September, quoted in Daniels, J D and Radebaugh, L (1998) *International Business*, 8th edn, Reading, MA: Addison Wesley Longman.

17 Bleeke, J and Ernst, D (1991) 'The way to win in cross-border alliances', *Harvard Business Review*, quoted in Daniels and Radebaugh, op. cit.

18 Kotler, P, Armstrong, G, Saunders, J and Wong, V (1996) *Principles of Marketing: the European Edition*, Upper Saddle River, NJ: Prentice Hall.

19 Daniels and Radebaugh, op. cit.

20 Ibid.

21 Brown, A (1998) *Organisational Culture*, 2nd edn, London: Financial Times Pitman Publishing.

22 Ibid.

23 Peters, T J (1978) 'Symbols, patterns and settings: an optimistic case for getting things done', *Organizational Dynamics*, 3 (23), Autumn, quoted in Brown, op. cit.

3

Organisational behaviour

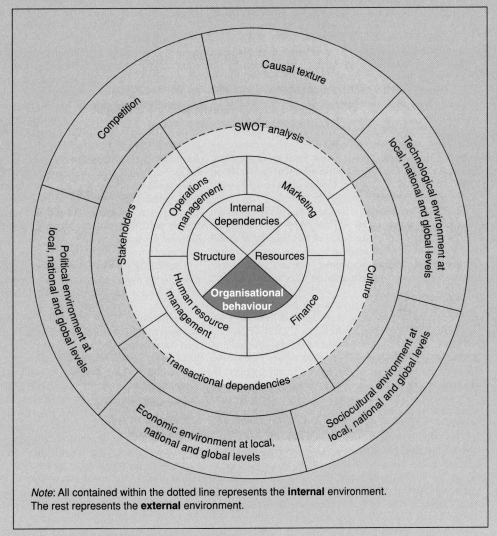

Note: All contained within the dotted line represents the **internal** environment.
The rest represents the **external** environment.

Figure 3.1 **Organisational context model**

A man of strategic vision

By Philip Coggan

Winston Churchill would not have lasted long in a modern office. His heavy drinking, cigar smoking, unusual hours and bullying of subordinates would probably have made him a regular defendant at industrial tribunals.

Indeed, just four years before he assumed the UK premiership, few Britons would have thought him a suitable leader. He was widely viewed as a Victorian anachronism, an adventurer associated with military failure (the Gallipoli campaign in the first world war), economic incompetence (the return to the Gold Standard in the 1920s) and political lost causes (the fight against Indian home rule, the monarchy of Edward VIII).

But Churchill had two great qualities that enabled him both to ascend to political leadership and to carry Britain to victory in the second world war. These key characteristics outweighed his many faults – indeed, they made the latter seem trivial by comparison.

First and foremost, Churchill had great strategic vision. In a sense, he was like a company chairman, whose grasp of detail is sometimes erratic, but who can see clearly the direction the company should take. Such vision enabled, for example, Nokia to recognise that the future lay in mobile phone manufacturing, turning an obscure Finnish company into one of the great global brands.

Churchill's great strategic insight in the 1930s was to see the potential threat posed to Europe by the emergence of Adolf Hitler, and to understand that this threat could be countered only by resistance, not by appeasement. Although that view was unpopular for many years, it was proved right by Hitler's attacks on Czechoslovakia and Poland.

When the apostle of appeasement, Neville Chamberlain, resigned, it was clear that Churchill was the only serious candidate for war leader.

Once Churchill had taken office, he quickly grasped that Britain's only serious chance for success was to draw the US into war as an ally, or at least as a major supplier. In a sense, he spotted the ideal joint venture candidate necessary to turn his business into a success. Churchill spent much effort in flattering Franklin Roosevelt, the US President, and in building a close relationship with him.

This effort bore fruit when, having been drawn into the war by the Japanese attack on Pearl Harbour, Roosevelt agreed with Churchill that the main coalition effort should be devoted to defeating Germany, the UK's prime opponent. After the war, even though he was in opposition, Churchill was the first to enunciate the threat posed by the Soviet Union's occupation of eastern Europe. His 'iron curtain' speech helped the dawning realisation that Stalin's regime, an ally during the Second World War, had turned into a potential enemy.

The phrase 'iron curtain' duly entered the English language, pointing to Churchill's other great gift, his eloquence. During the dark days of the war, his defiant speeches gave courage to the British people, convincing them that their leaders were ready for the fight.

Churchill's ringing phrases – 'We shall fight them on the beaches' . . . 'their finest hour' . . . 'Never has so much been owed by so many to so few' – have become clichés, so often have they been repeated. But at the time they had real power. For Churchill, the speeches also furnished his authority. He came to office without being elected and in the face of the hostility of his party, many of whom were either loyal to Chamberlain or suspicious of Churchill because of his record. Thanks to his speeches, his critics could quickly see the qualities that Churchill was bringing to the job.

Churchill's words also proved a great motivational tool for the British public. We are all familiar with managerial pep talks, often of dubious practical use or literary merit. Churchill showed how such things could be done. He spoke at the lowest possible moment for national morale, after German victories had left Britain facing a Europe dominated by the Nazis. Not only were his words inspiring, his message was clear; his rhetoric, while flowery, could be understood by all who heard it. Few executives could ever hope to match the power or succinctness of his words on taking office. 'You ask "What is our aim?" I can answer in one word. It is victory; victory at all costs, victory, in spite of all terror; victory, however hard and long the road may be, for without victory, there is no survival.'

The ability to make the correct strategic decisions, allied to the ability to express those opinions in a manner that all under his command could understand and be inspired by – these are great gifts in a leader.

Oddly enough, Churchill's faults are also instructive to any manager. He was a poor delegator, driving his generals mad with his meddling with military strategy. Here his tactical ideas, such as the Gallipoli raid or the assault on Italy, while honestly intended (he was looking for a way to avoid the heavy casualties involved on the Western front or the D-day landings), proved failures. Executives should remember his example – if they have the right 'big picture', then they should be willing to let others handle the details.

That, of course, depends on whether executives trust their subordinates. Here was another failing of Churchill. He hung on the premiership far too long, while he was in failing health. He seemed unwilling to give way to his successor, Sir Anthony Eden, whose premiership duly proved disastrous when it came. Arguably, the long wait to replace Churchill had affected his judgement.

However great the leader, his or her powers will eventually decline. A wise leader will retire, and appoint a vigorous successor, well before that moment comes.

Source: Financial Times, 30 June 2003. Reprinted with permission.

Introduction

This chapter introduces some of the different aspects of **organisational behaviour** which have been developed over the years, from Frederick Taylor through to Rosabeth Moss Kanter. The influences on individual **behaviour** in organisations are explored by looking at the impact of values, attitudes and perception. The types of groups individuals may find themselves in while working for an organisation are looked at, along with the process of group development. The final section looks at different types of leadership which are commonly found in organisations.

Approaches to organisational behaviour

There are many approaches to organisational behaviour and this section will look at some of the key contributions to organisational behaviour in the twentieth century.

■ Frederick Winslow Taylor

One of the first pioneers to study employees and their management was Frederick Winslow Taylor, who was born in Pennsylvania in 1856, trained as an engineer and died in 1917.[1] Taylor's approach is known as scientific management and he sought to study the performance of individuals in the workplace. Underpinning Taylor's approach was the basic assumption that people dislike work but will undertake it in order to earn a living. Taylor went on to argue that due to this assumed dislike of work, staff need very close supervision as they are not capable of self-management and motivation. Taylor expected that close and fair supervision would be respected and that people would perform their job of repetitive tasks at the required rate and standard, with extra effort gaining greater reward.

Taylor's studies of employees, their management and approach to work took place in factories in the US, such as Midvale Steel works, Johnson Company and the Bethlehem Iron Company in Pennsylvania. Taylor's approach underpins working practices in organisations today. Think about the approach to work taken by fast-food companies and call centres. It could be argued that Taylor took advantage of people and assumed they were unable to bargain or negotiate on their own behalf. However, in situations where piece-work systems were introduced due to Taylor's approach, staff were able to receive more take-home pay for increased productivity. The counter argument is that any pay increase was not in proportion to the productivity increase.

■ Elton Mayo

The human relations school came after scientific management and Taylor. Elton Mayo was born in Adelaide in Australia in 1880 and died in England in 1949. Unlike Taylor, who was an engineer by training, Mayo was a social psychologist. Mayo worked at the University of Queensland from 1911 to 1923, when he left for the US, where finally he worked at Harvard University for over 20 years until 1947.

Mayo's approach contrasted to Taylor's in at least one key way. Unlike Taylor, Mayo took the view that the financial incentive to work was relatively unimportant. Mayo's most well-known study into the workplace was conducted at the Western Electric Company's Hawthorne Works in Chicago, starting in 1927. The project covered around 20 000 people, and used between 75 and 100 researchers over a ten-year period.[2] The Hawthorne studies showed that social factors, such as the relationship between management and in particular the social grouping between staff, can influence the behaviour of employees in an organisation. In a study carried out at Hawthorne, called the Relay Assembly Room Study,[3] a group of women employees were moved to a room which resembled their normal place of work, where they undertook their normal work of assembling small telephone relays. The researchers wanted to examine the impact of the introduction of more rest periods on productivity, e.g. a mid-morning break, a reduction of half an hour in the working day, a move to a five-day working week. The expectation was that some changes, such as the mid-morning break, would help increase productivity and that the move to a five-day working week would reduce productivity. However, the surprising findings were that productivity continued in a gradual upward trend, regardless of the conditions applied to the staff being observed, along with a lower-than-expected rate of absenteeism.

The findings led to the consideration of psychological aspects of the work, as well as the objective alterations to the working environment, such as working hours and lunch breaks. The Hawthorne researchers reached the conclusion that the continued increase in productivity was in part due to the attention paid to the employees by the researchers. The response of the employees to favourable treatment, more breaks, shorter working week and attention from the researchers was to reciprocate by providing the researchers with results the employees perceived they were seeking. This phenomenon was termed the 'Hawthorne effect'.

■ Peter Drucker

Peter Drucker was born in Vienna in 1909, trained as a lawyer, then worked as a journalist in London between 1933 and 1936, before emigrating to the US in 1937. In 1942 Drucker undertook his first consultancy job for General Motors – where his direct approach to consultancy was not well received. However, Drucker continued to both work as a consultant and look at what

**Table 3.1
Drucker's
management tasks**

Drucker's seven tasks of tomorrow's manager
He or she should:
● manage by objectives
● take more risks, over a longer time period, and also allow this to happen further down the organisation
● take strategic decisions
● build an integrated team, in which members are capable of assessing their own performance in relation to common objectives
● communicate quickly and clearly and have a motivating influence on staff at all levels such that their participation, in a responsible manner, is obtained
● see the organisation as a whole and understand his/her role within it
● understand the external environment and the significant factors which impact on the organisation, its products and services, and the sector as a whole.

Source: summarised from Clutterbuck, D and Crainer, S (1990) *Makers of Management*, London, Papermac Macmillan.

constituted a modern organisation and what the managers should do. Drucker's consultancy work grew and in 1954 his book, the *Practice of Management*, was published, which resulted in management by objectives being high profile in the 1950s and 1960s.[4] In this work Drucker identifies the seven tasks of a manager of 'tomorrow' – *see* Table 3.1.

■ Douglas McGregor

Douglas McGregor was born in Detroit in 1906 and died in 1964. Like Elton Mayo he was a social psychologist. McGregor was professor of management at Massachusetts Institute of Technology between 1954 and 1964 and is best known for his work *The Human Side of Enterprise*, which presented the arguments for Theory X and Theory Y, which are polar opposites concerning the assumptions managers may make about employees.

Theory X assumes that people dislike work and seek to avoid it at all costs. Hence people need to be controlled, coerced, threatened and punished to achieve an adequate individual contribution to organisational goals. This also supports the assumptions that people prefer to be tightly supervised, with no responsibility and virtually no ambition. A manager making these assumptions about his or her staff will be autocratic, controlling and obsessed with seeking to make unco-operative employees perform. The likelihood is that staff will resent this approach and seek to do as little work as possible, hence reinforcing the original opinion of the manager.

The other extreme is theory Y in which people regard work as normal activity and are hence committed to objectives and self-motivated towards their achievement and the associated rewards. Additionally people will accept and seek out responsibility, and take the opportunity to behave creatively while resolving problems in organisations and developing organisations. Managers adopting such assumptions and views concerning their employees will develop a much more co-operative relationship with their employees.

■ Rosabeth Moss Kanter

Rosabeth Moss Kanter was born in Cleveland, Ohio in 1943 and is best known for her 1983 book *The Change Masters*, defined in the quote below:

> literally – the right people in the right place at the right time. The right people are the ones with ideas that move beyond the organisation's established practice, ideas they can form into visions. The right places are the integrative environments that support innovation, encourage the building of coalitions and teams to support and implement visions. The right times are those moments in the flow of organisational history when it is possible to reconstruct reality on the basis of accumulated innovations to shape a more productive and successful future.
>
> *Source*: Kanter, R M (1983) *The Change Masters*, New York, Simon & Schuster.

The Change Masters examined 115 cases of significant innovation within US companies with the aim of discovering the structures required for change and innovation. According to Kanter, this research showed that organisations have to first put in place systems, practices, cultures and rewards that will encourage and allow people to be enterprising and innovative. In such a culture, the structure must be one of small working teams which are functionally complete for the task being undertaken, and have autonomy at an operational level to allow the team to get things done. Finally Kanter's research showed that *The Change Masters* companies viewed people's problem solving, enterprise skills and ability to innovate as a great strength in which pride was taken.

✓ Check your understanding

Do you understand the key points of some approaches to organisational behaviour?

Check your understanding by matching the statements below with the person whose work they relate to: Rosabeth Moss Kanter, Peter Drucker, Douglas McGregor, Frederick Taylor and Elton Mayo.

(a) People dislike work but will undertake it in order to earn a living.

(b) The continued increase in productivity was in part due to the attention paid to the employees by the researchers.

(c) Managers should take more risks, over a longer time period, and also allow this to happen further down the organisation.

(d) People regard work as a normal activity and are committed to self-motivation and the achievement of objectives.

(e) Companies view people's problem solving, enterprise skills and ability to innovate as strengths in which pride should be taken.

Individuals in organisations

■ Values

Values are guiding principles which individuals, groups, organisations and society use to determine whether behaviour is acceptable or unacceptable. An understanding of the individual's values will provide a strong indication of their attitudes. Organisations should seek to employ staff whose values correspond with the dominant values of the organisation – if an appropriate match is obtained, the employee's levels of satisfaction and performance are more likely to be high. There are two types of values: terminal and instrumental.[5] Terminal values are desired outcomes, which people and/or organisations seek to achieve. Instrumental values are the types of behaviour preferred by the organisation – *see* Table 3.2.

Terminal values are often indicated in the mission statements which organisations issue, and these in turn inform stakeholders (e.g. customers, employees, suppliers, bankers) of the organisation's stance on, for example, quality, service, innovation and ethics. The aim of this is to ensure that organisational members – staff and managers – understand the standard and type of behaviour required of them in the workplace, which in turn helps determine the organisation's culture. This also helps ensure that external stakeholders understand the nature of the relationship they can expect with the organisation. For example, customers will expect quality and service in terms of goods, and suppliers will want prompt payment and clear contracts with the organisation.

However, often the most powerful values in an organisation are not written down but are the result of shared norms, beliefs, assumptions and thoughts which staff use to relate to each other and external stakeholders. These shared values inform the response of staff to particular workplace situations or organisational problems. In cultures where terminal and instrumental values are strong and clearly understood by the staff, the behaviour and response of staff will be that which the organisation desires. In contrast, in weak-culture organisations there is greater likelihood that clouded and misunderstood terminal and instrumental values will lead to staff not being able to respond to difficult situations or responding in an inappropriate manner. Hence the

Table 3.2
Values in organisations

Organisational values	
Terminal values	**Instrumental values**
● high quality ● excellence ● innovation ● profitability ● social responsibility	● being helpful and friendly ● hard working ● clean and tidy ● capable ● accurate ● creative

role of management and leadership needs to include the shaping and clear communication of organisational terminal and instrumental values.

■ Attitudes

Organisational behaviour includes the study of individuals and their attitudes to their employment. Attitudes to jobs cover a number of areas: job satisfaction, job involvement and organisational commitment.[6] Job involvement is the extent to which an individual identifies with and is involved in their job, while organisational commitment covers the degree to which an employee identifies with the organisation and is loyal to it. Job satisfaction reflects an individual's attitude to their job. A person with a high level of job satisfaction will hold positive views concerning their employment and vice versa.

Job satisfaction is determined by pay, challenges, other rewards, level of support from colleagues and working conditions. People tend to prefer jobs which include a variety of tasks, the opportunity to use and develop skills and abilities, the freedom to manage one's own workload, and the opportunity to receive constructive feedback on job performance. Hence jobs which provide these challenges and opportunities are those most likely to give a high level of job satisfaction.

The US psychologist Frederick Herzberg undertook work on job satisfaction and job dissatisfaction in the 1960s.[7] Herzberg interviewed around 200 Pittsburgh accountants and engineers and asked them to identify occasions on which they felt good about work and occasions on which they felt bad about work. Analysis of the research interviews showed that motivating factors associated with job satisfaction were quite separate from those linked to job dissatisfaction which Herzberg termed 'hygiene factors'. Attention by a company to ensuring the hygiene factors are of a suitable standard to reduce dissatisfaction will not lead to motivation, just an absence of frustration or dissatisfaction. Hence job satisfaction and job dissatisfaction are not exact opposites. Job satisfaction requires the motivating factors or the opportunity to achieve them to be embedded in the organisation.

Job dissatisfaction or frustration can take four major forms: fixation, regression, withdrawal or aggression.[8] Fixation occurs when an individual continually seeks to present the same arguments as discussion or seeks to solve problems using solutions which are known to be inadequate for the current situation. Regression is defined as immature or childish behaviour, including sulking and tantrums, although it can also present as an individual feeling exceptionally low or depressed. Withdrawal occurs when an individual seeks to remove him or herself from the organisation and can include absenteeism, extended breaks and ultimately success in seeking alternative employment. Hence organisations with high levels of job dissatisfaction or frustration often experience high levels of labour turnover. Finally the most severe form of behaviour which expresses frustration is aggression, which can range from nasty, unfounded gossip and rumour about the organisation or individuals who are seen as having caused the frustration through to acts of physical aggression – punching a senior manager – or sabotage, e.g. removing computer records or deliberately introducing a virus into the company's computer system.

■ Perception

Perception is an individual's personal view of the world and definition of reality. Other individuals will hold different views and perceptions concerning the same person, item or situation. Differences in perception can arise from a number of factors which can exist in the perceiver, in the item or individual being perceived, or in the situation in which the perception occurs. The perceiver is influenced by their personal characteristics, which include attitudes, personality, interests, motives, experiences and expectations. Equally, the personal characteristics of individuals being observed will influence what is perceived. A group of very drunk, noisy students in a pub on a Saturday night is likely to be perceived as more disruptive than two drunk old men sitting in the corner of the pub. This example also makes the point that the background or situation in which individuals are observed and their relative relationship to one another influences perception. The same two drunk old men in a pub serving Sunday lunches to mainly family groups would be more likely to be viewed as undesirable in this situation than in the previous one.

People have beliefs, motives and intentions and as a result when observing others will develop explanations for their behaviour. Attribution theory seeks to explain how people judge one another and depends on the meaning attributed to particular behaviour.[9] Judgement is dependent on whether an individual's behaviour is viewed as being internally or externally caused. Internally caused behaviour is seen as being under the control of the individual. The student who misses a 9am lecture on Thursday could have this behaviour attributed to him/her being out clubbing on Wednesday night, which is student night in the local nightclubs, and oversleeping the following morning. This late behaviour has an internal attribution. However, if the lateness was attributed to the student being caught in an unexpected traffic jam, due to a rush-hour traffic accident, this would be an external attribution. Generally people tend to view the behaviour of others as internally controlled and their own as externally controlled.

The understanding of whether behaviour is caused internally or externally is dependent on three factors: distinctiveness, consensus and consistency. Distinctiveness refers to the degree to which an individual behaves differently in different situations. Is the student who is late for today's 9am lecture also late for their group project meetings? If the student who was late for the lecture is otherwise normally on time for classes and meetings, then the late behaviour will normally be classed as having high distinctiveness (i.e. the late behaviour is unusual or distinctive for this student) and an external attribution. Alternatively, if the same student is nearly always late for classes and meetings, the late behaviour will more likely be given internal attribution and low distinctiveness – there is nothing unusual or distinctive about this student being late.

Consensus occurs when everyone who is faced with the same or similar situation responds or behaves in the same way. If all students who took the same route to the university missed or were late for the 9am Thursday lecture, the behaviour shows consensus and would normally be given an external attribution, e.g. the road traffic accident. In contrast, if all students made the 9am lecture and only our missing student didn't, there is not a consensus of behaviour and the behaviour will likely be given an internal attribution.

Finally, consistency in an individual's behaviour tends to be given an internal attribution, i.e. the missing student always stops out late and oversleeps. In contrast, an individual's actions which are not consistent tend to be given an external attribution, i.e. a student who has not been late for the first ten weeks of the semester but is missing in week 11 is more likely to have this behaviour given an external attribution, e.g. the traffic accident or a late train.

In summary, agreement is low if, for example, a student complains about their lecturer's teaching style and no one else in the class makes the same complaint. Consistency is high if the student has complained about the lecturer and their teaching style throughout the year and distinctiveness is low if the same student has always complained about their lecturers and their teaching styles. The combination of low agreement, high consistency and low distinctiveness leads to an internal attribution of the complaining behaviour. In contrast, agreement is high if many students make the same complaint, as it agrees with or supports the original complaining student's behaviour. Frequent complaints by the original student about this lecturer makes consistency high, and having never complained about a lecturer before, distinctiveness is also high. The combination of high agreement, high consistency and high distinctiveness means the resulting conclusion would most likely be an external attribution of student behaviour, which points to the lecturer being a poor teacher.

Finally, it should be noted that errors of judgement and bias occur with attribution theory, and in general people tend to over-estimate the impact of internal factors on behaviour and under-estimate the influence of external factors.

✓ Check your understanding

Do you understand the difference between internal and external attribution of behaviour?

Check your understanding by reading the passage below and decide whether Mr and Mrs Smith's behaviour has an internal or external attribution.

Mr and Mrs Smith eat out about once a week at their local Italian restaurant where the chef always receives lots of compliments from the diners when he comes into the front of the restaurant. Mr and Mrs Smith always compliment the chef if they particularly enjoy his style of cooking and variety of dishes. This is the first time Mr and Mrs Smith have genuinely felt like this about a restaurant's food and they complimented the chef accordingly.

Groups in organisations

A group is two or more people who come together to achieve objectives. Groups can be formal or informal in nature. A formal group is, for example, a department, team or division which is defined by an organisation (e.g. a company, a football team, a charity) and the group will have specific activities and tasks to undertake. The objectives of the formal group will be determined by the organisational goals. Formal groups can be command and/or task groups which are determined by the organisation.[10] Command groups are determined by an organisation's structure, for example a supervisor and his/her team of assembly workers in a TV factory. Task groups are determined by the organisation, but do not depend on the obvious hierarchical relationships which are present in command groups. Task groups come together, like a cross-functional team, to complete a particular job, task or project, and will contain employees from different departments or divisions in the organisation. It should also be noted that command groups are task groups, but task groups are not necessarily command groups as task groups cut across levels and departments in the organisation.

Informal groups are interest groups and friendship groups. People in an interest group may or may not belong to a particular command or task group, but may band together to achieve a common goal. Friendship groupings are formed from people who have a social allegiance. Staff in a friendship group may lunch together in the middle of the working day. Additionally, friendship groups may extend beyond the workplace and be based on a shared or social activity which is not related to work, e.g. gardening, going to the theatre, supporting a particular football team. Friendship and interest groups serve members' social needs and although informal do affect the behaviour and performance of individuals in the workplace.

✓ Check your understanding

Do you understand the different types of groups which may exist in organisations?

Check your understanding by matching the groups below with group type (group types are command, task, interest and friendship):

(a) A weekend hill walking group.

(b) A managing director and his/her team of senior managers and directors.

(c) A product development team.

(d) A group of workers who are trying to persuade their employer to substitute fringe benefits for extra holidays.

■ Reasons for group membership

People join groups for a variety of reasons, such as security, affiliation, esteem and task achievement. Group membership can provide individuals with a sense of security and a degree of protection from threats. This underpins the trade union movement, which seeks to give its members protection in the workplace and power in negotiations with employers. In becoming a group member individuals may gain a sense of security concerning their position. However, it is also possible for an individual to feel lost and insecure if the group is large and the individual does not understand their position or role within the group.

People enjoy the interactions which come with group membership and the emotional support it can provide. This interaction and acceptance by the group fulfils an important social need, which can in turn enhance an individual's feeling of esteem and self-worth. Esteem and self-worth provided by group membership also bring recognition by colleagues in the group, important if the nature of the work and achievement is not well understood by those outside the group. Additionally, of course, recognition by those both inside and outside the group can enhance individual and group status.

■ Group development

Task achievement is one of the key reasons for creating groups. A group may collectively have greater knowledge, skills and abilities to complete the job than any individual acting alone. Hence in organisations the use of formal groups to achieve goals can be effective. However, it needs to be recognised that groups and the associated behaviours change over time and this is shown by the five stages of development suggested by Tuckman and Jensen.[11]

The first stage is one of 'forming' in which group members are finding out about each other, making an impression on each other, seeking structure and direction from a leader, and orientating themselves in relation to the task. At this stage there will be a degree of uncertainty while relationships within the group and ground rules are established. There may also be confusion surrounding the tasks and goals facing the group. Stage 2, storming, is one of conflict in which individuals will jockey for position in the group in terms of leadership, control, priorities, and goal difference between members. Not surprisingly hostility and conflict will rise to the surface. If the group is to move on to the next stage of 'norming', then the management and resolution of conflict and differences of opinion is critical.

Stage 3, norming, is a much more cohesive stage than stage 2. By stage 3, groups will have moved on to a consensus over leadership, rules, behaviour and tasks. Allocation of tasks will be undertaken with co-operation, as the group has 'gelled' and the conflict of stage 2 has been successfully resolved. Stage 4, performing, builds upon the cohesiveness and co-operation established in stage 3. In a successful group, effective structures, flexibility, openness and a clear understanding of goals and successful performance required to meet those goals all ensure that stage 4 is completed. Less successful groups can become bogged down in the earlier stages and, for example, remain in continual conflict (stage 2) or remain in stage 3, fulfilling roles, but never moving on to completing the tasks and final achievement of objectives (stage 4). Finally, stage 5 is the disbanding of the group because the task is complete and/or individual members move on to different projects.

> ### ✓ Check your understanding
>
> *Do you understand the different stages of group development?*
>
> Check your understanding by naming Tuckman and Jensen's stages of group development and matching the behaviours below with the stages you have named:
>
> (a) Group members undertake tasks and activities harmoniously.
> (b) Group members tell each other about themselves and their role in the organisation.
> (c) Group members talk about the different projects they are going to work on next.
> (d) Group members complete tasks and finish the project.
> (e) Group members argue about what it is the group should achieve.

■ Group performance

Group size impacts on the performance of both the individual and the group. In large groups the total resource and effort is greater, but the impact and contribution of an individual is diluted. There are a number of characteristics of large groups and the behaviour of their members. Individuals are most tolerant of authority and very direct leadership in a large group, as group members recognise the difficulties in supervising a large team. Hence usually more formal rules and procedures are used to manage large groups. However, even with clear rules and procedures, large groups usually take longer than small ones to make decisions. It is also likely that job satisfaction in a large group will be less, as individuals have fewer opportunities to participate and receive less attention from the group and its leader. In contrast, in smaller groups individuals are more likely to view their participation as critical and are therefore more likely to involve themselves in the group and its activities. Finally, with large groups, a level of diminishing return is reached in terms of the outcomes of the group, due to the greater difficulties of co-ordinating and managing a larger group.

The quality of the work undertaken by a group is directly related to the relevance and diversity of members' characteristics, knowledge, skills and abilities. Teams which are composed of members with very similar traits and skills are likely to view a task or problem from a single perspective. This can result in the group being both efficient and effective in terms of completing the task or solving the problem. However, it is also the case that a single-perspective approach lacks critical awareness of the task, problem and possible solutions. Therefore this leads to the argument that groups with diversity in characteristics, knowledge, skills and abilities are more likely to consider a wider and more innovative range of approaches. This, however, does require that the more diversified characteristics, knowledge, skills and abilities are relevant to the group task – merely increasing the size of the group alone will not improve the group performance.

Roles

The role of a group member can be defined as their expected behaviour in the group. In formal groups in organisations the expected roles can be formally defined via a written job description and via how existing members perform similar roles or jobs. The tasks and activities an individual believes they are required to undertake are known as the perceived role. The expected role and perceived role may overlap or the two roles can diverge greatly. Finally, the enacted role is defined by actual conduct or behaviour of the individual in carrying out their tasks and activities. It is usual for the enacted role to more closely reflect the perceived role than the expected role.

Status

Status is the social worth conferred on an individual due to the position they occupy in the group. Status may be conferred by many factors, either separately or collectively, including title, salary, achievement, seniority and power. Higher status may be conferred on the most experienced or senior member of a group and equally this individual may feel they deserve higher status. However, if it is not also perceived by other group members, the higher status will not be conferred.

Norms

Norms are the rules which define acceptable behaviour, with behaviour not conforming to the norms being unacceptable. Norms help establish consistent behaviour and conduct among the group and can be formal and written or informal and unwritten. Professionals such as doctors and lawyers operate to formal and written codes of conduct, with those who do not conform to the code being 'struck off'.

Hackman defines norms as relating to the actions and situations perceived as important by the group and also as a reflection of the individual personalities in the group and the means by which they regulate behaviour within the group.[12] Norms will usually develop slowly over time, but should the group be under pressure, norms can develop quickly. Norms will apply differently to individual group members, with newer and more junior members expected to conform very closely to all the norms. In contrast, more senior and established group members, who likely enjoy higher status, may be 'exempt' from conforming to particular norms. It is key for group members to publicly comply to norms and adhere to this behaviour. However, group members do not need to privately accept the norms or group behaviour.

Cohesiveness

Cohesiveness is defined as the extent to which group members are attracted to and wish to remain in a group, i.e. how the group sticks together. Group cohesiveness increases if members share goals and the approach to achieving them, with any competition existing outside the group. Hence members of cohesive groups experience higher levels of job satisfaction, with greater and better communications, as the members share values, goals, and an approach to achieving goals. Therefore hostile and aggressive behaviour by members of cohesive groups is more commonly directed towards those outside the group. This type of behaviour can arise from a feeling of superiority among group members, which leads to the group seeking to reject outsiders.

Generally small groups, with less diversity and more opportunity to interact with all members, are more cohesive. In contrast, large groups with greater diversity, competition between members, dissimilar values and formal rules, will experience less cohesion. Cohesive groups, which are strong in terms of value and culture, are likely to be more resistant to change than less cohesive groups. Change which threatens a group's position and existence will be strongly resisted.

Leadership in organisations

Leadership is the ability to influence a group towards the achievement of goals.[13] A person may occupy a leadership role due to their position in the organisation. Normally leadership is associated with the role of manager. However, a leader and manager are not necessarily equivalent, as providing a manager with position and certain rights in an organisation is no guarantee that they will be an effective leader.

Formal leaders are appointed and exist within the formal structure of the organisation. Equally, informal leaders can emerge from outside the formal procedures and structure of the organisation. Both are important and can make a difference in the performance of groups and organisations. A change in leader can enhance the performance of under-achieving groups or organisations, while equally rapid turnover of leaders can be detrimental to performance.

■ Charismatic leadership

Transactional leaders clarify tasks and roles while motivating their followers or subordinates towards achievement of the group or organisational goals.[14] In contrast, transformational or charismatic leaders will create an organisational culture in which staff will be self-motivating and seek to contribute to the organisation. To achieve this a transformational or charismatic leader will need to be positive and self-confident in their own ability and judgement. The charismatic leader will present a clear vision offering a better future for the group or organisation than the status quo. The charismatic leader also needs to be strongly committed to the vision and prepared to bear personal risk and cost to achieve the vision. It therefore normally follows that charismatic leaders are perceived as initiators and managers of change rather than custodians of the status quo.

■ Visionary leadership

Visionary leadership goes beyond charisma.[15] Visionary leadership is the ability to develop the organisation beyond its current situation and to communicate a credible vision for the development in an articulate manner such that it is clearly understood by all relevant stakeholders.

A successful vision needs to offer the organisation and its members an outlook on the future that is a clear and significant improvement on that currently facing the organisation. The organisation and its members need to perceive the vision as challenging yet achievable to retain any motivation to pursue the vision. Effective visionary leaders need to communicate their vision, its objectives and the associated plan of action via oral and written communication such that it can be clearly understood by organisational members at different levels. Additionally the visionary leader will need to support the vision via their own behaviour in the organisation and be able to extend the vision, its objectives and plan of action beyond the organisation's current situation. This is key as the environments and situations in which organisations find themselves change continually.

■ Team leadership

Managers who are effective team leaders will trust their team, share information with them and understand intuitively when to intervene and when to withdraw and leave the team to control and manage a situation. Team leaders also have a role to play in developing and managing the team's relationship with the department or organisation in which it is based and with stakeholders, such as other teams in the organisation, customers and suppliers. Additionally team leaders have a role to play in helping their team resolve problems and conflicts. This includes asking questions which enable the team to structure or talk through problems and conflicts such that there is understanding of the difficulty, and generation, evaluation and implementation of solutions. If third parties, more or different resources are needed to help resolve the difficulties, the leader has a role to play in negotiating for these with other stakeholders.

Summary

This chapter examined approaches to organisational behaviour, individuals, groups and leadership in organisations. The following summary covers all aspects of this chapter.

1 Taylor's basic assumption was that people dislike work but will undertake it in order to earn a living. Close and fair supervision would be required if people were to contribute at the required level to the organisation, although extra effort could be rewarded.

2 Mayo undertook the 'Hawthorne' studies and reached the conclusion that increases in the productivity of a workforce may in part be due to the attention paid to the workers by researchers observing them.

3 Drucker developed the idea of managing by objectives and thought additionally that managers should be strategic, risk takers, delegators, team builders, effective communicators, and should understand the organisation and its environment.

4 McGregor is known for Theory X and Theory Y. Theory X assumes that people cannot be trusted and need to be very highly controlled, hence managers who believe in Theory X will be autocratic. Theory Y assumes people are self-motivated towards achieving objectives and hence managers who believe Theory Y will develop co-operative relationships with their employees.

5 Rosabeth Moss Kanter undertook research which showed that companies which were good at innovation and changing direction greatly value people's problem-solving skills, enterprise and creativity.

6 Values, attitudes and perception all impact on an individual's behaviour in an organisation. Values are guiding principles which individuals, groups, organisations and society use to determine whether behaviour is acceptable or unacceptable. An understanding of the individual's values will provide a strong indication of their attitudes. Attitudes to jobs cover a number of areas: job satisfaction, job involvement and organisational commitment. Job involvement is the extent to which an individual identifies with and is involved in their job, while organisational commitment covers the degree to which an employee identifies with the organisation and is loyal to it. Job satisfaction reflects an individual's attitude to their job. A person holding a high level of job satisfaction will have positive views concerning their employment and vice versa. Perception is an individual's personal view of the world and definition of reality. Other individuals will hold different views and perceptions concerning the same person, item or situation. Differences in perception can arise from a number of factors which can exist in the perceiver, the item or individual being perceived, or in the situation in which the perception occurs.

7 Groups can be formal or informal. Formal groups can be command or task groups. Command groups depend on a hierarchical relationship in the organisation, i.e. a manager and his/her subordinates. Task groups do not, and will cut across departments and levels in the organisation. Informal groups include interest groups in which members have a common goal and friendship groups are based on social groups.

8 Groups develop through five stages: forming (coming together), storming (roles are established), norming (tasks are undertaken), performing (tasks and the project are completed), and mourning (group disbands and members move on to new projects).

9 Group performance is affected by size, norms, cohesiveness, roles and status of group members. It is likely that job satisfaction is greater in small groups due to more opportunity to contribute. Norms define acceptable behaviour in the group and cohesiveness is the attraction that holds the members together as a group. An individual's expected role in a group may differ from their enacted role and more closely match their perceived role. Status is conferred on individuals in the group by other group members.

10 Leadership is the ability to influence a team towards the achievement of goals. Charismatic leaders create organisational culture in which staff are self-motivating and seek to contribute to the organisation. Visionary leaders have the ability to develop a vision which takes the organisation beyond its current position and to clearly communicate that vision to all stakeholders in the organisations. Effective team leaders are those who trust their team, share information with them and know how to develop the team.

Learning outcomes for case studies

While reading this chapter and engaging in the activities, you should have learned how to apply theory and models, analyse situations, and evaluate the application and analysis you undertake. The learning outcomes specified below outline the type of application, analysis and evaluation of which you should be capable in relation to organisations. The case studies and the questions which follow provide an opportunity for you to test how well you have achieved the learning outcomes for the ethical issues and exit case studies for this chapter.

Application	Check you have achieved this by	
1 Identify and discuss approaches to organisational behaviour	indicating differing views of organisational behaviour	answering exit case study question 1
2 Identify and discuss approaches to leadership	indicating your views of leadership	answering ethical case study question 1
Analysis	**Check you have achieved this by**	
1 Consider a particular approach to leadership in an organisation	specifying which actions a leader undertakes and should undertake	answering ethical case study question 2

ETHICAL ISSUES CASE STUDY 3.2   **FT**

Delivering first-class leadership

By Alison Maitland

Allan Leighton is never far from the headlines. As the man charged with turning round the loss-making Royal Mail, he has frequent robust exchanges over competition with Postcomm, the regulator. The former chief executive of Asda/Wal-Mart is also involved in the prospective battle for Safeway as adviser to Philip Green, the entrepreneur who owns BHS.

In the eyes of the government, the Royal Mail chairman is the ideal boss. Britain needs more 'really good managers' like him, according to Patricia Hewitt, trade and industry secretary.

Mr Leighton, who is one year into a three-year renewal plan at Royal Mail, holds nine other directorships and has no plans to give any up in the wake of the government-commissioned Higgs report, saying this is a matter for shareholders. He is chairman of BHS, Cannons, Lastminute.com, Wilson Connolly and the Race for Opportunity campaign. He is seen as the power-broker at Leeds United football club, where he is deputy chairman. He is a non-executive director of BSkyB, Dyson and George Weston. He also has a business advice website, www.going-plural.com.

Mr Leighton, who turns 50 in April, says the biggest influence on his career was his 18 years at Mars, where he learned the importance of talking directly to employees and customers. He is married with three grown-up children.

I probably manage things differently from most people. Everybody I talk to always [asks]: 'How do you manage your time? How do you go to meetings?' The most important thing about meetings is not having very many of them. I haven't been to many meetings where anything constructive has come out.

I don't manage time, I manage issues. I believe very strongly that if you lead companies, you have to be very visible. I've never been in a head office yet that takes any money. All the money is taken somewhere else, all the service is provided somewhere else, and you've got to be where it is.

The other day, I was working with a postman who said to me that to put mail through a letterbox you need it to come with large envelopes at the bottom so you can fold them round the small ones. We're not getting our machines to sort like that. It shows that you can put in a load of automation that you think is very efficient but all it's doing is passing the inefficiency down the line. It's blindingly obvious, but I'd never have picked that up if I hadn't spoken to that guy.

I get 300–400 e-mails a week from postmen and women and people in the company. Sometimes I phone them when I'm in the car. That's a great use of what others think is dead time. You've got to be accessible, but in control. I have my mobile but I never have it switched on.

I've always been in companies where I've had to manage thousands of people. I don't manage the top management team. I think I'm responsible for everybody.

You can build on your strengths, but all you can do about your weaknesses is be wary of them. I sometimes get impatient. Because I listen so much at grassroots level, sometimes I don't listen as well at the top end.

People think I'm the Scarlet Pimpernel because I'm all over the place. I'm out on the road early in the morning, any time between 6am and 6.30am, and I probably don't get home much before 8pm. I'm very organised about travelling. There isn't a post office, a delivery office, a mail centre, a building site, a retail shop, a Cannons leisure centre that I don't pass. Sometimes you only have to stick your head round the door for 10 minutes [and ask]: 'How are you doing, what's going on, what are the issues?'

Ordinary people are very important. They are the mass and if you don't understand that, you're missing out.

I've always been energetic. I go home at 8pm and go running. I sleep like a log. You've got to worry about things, but if you just worry and don't fix them you're probably in the wrong job.

I've always been able to focus on a particular issue or a particular business, and switch from one to the other. I've always tried to keep things very simple. You've got to be able to distil what you do succinctly. If you can't write it on a flip chart in five minutes, the chances of anybody doing it are pretty slim.

I like trying to make broken companies better and good companies great. I'm probably not very good at running steady-state businesses. I've turned lots of things down. I don't ever do things that I can't commit to. When people don't turn up to boards, that really hacks me off. If you're in, you're in, you understand the business and you participate.

I used to be [an avid reader of management books], but the problem is that they're all the same now. Everybody is on this leadership trip. You don't need that many great leaders, but you need some really good managers. Just being a very good manager in my book is right up there.

The difference between the average manager and the excellent manager is that great managers get things done through other people, willingly and well.

▶

I don't see myself as any sort of guru. I really don't get a buzz from [having a high profile]. This stuff is always a roller-coaster – you're up and you're down. People think you're good, people think you're bad. My friends think I'm still the same person.

I got quite a bit of stick from the press for setting up the website. You have to take the rough with the smooth. People write things like '[he is a] serial director'. It's like 'serial killer', it's not a term of endearment! That's life. If the website has helped some people, terrific.

I've been very fortunate in the people I've worked with. Philip [Green] is unique. I'm pretty focused, but he makes me look like a shrinking violet of focus! I've got Rupert [Murdoch] and Tony Ball at BSkyB, I've worked with Archie [Norman], I've got James Dyson. I always watch and learn from people. I copy shamelessly.

I learned a lot from Archie but we had some very good people in Asda. The thing that pleases me the most is how well Asda has done since I left. Archie had it and it did well; I had it and it did better; I've gone and it's done even better, because we put in some very good people. Everybody thought that when Sam [Walton] went at Wal-Mart that would be the end. It's got stronger, because he created a very good group of people to run it.

What really worked at Asda was that there were two of us. In big turnarounds you sometimes need that. That's why I've gone with Adam [Crozier] and Elmar [Toime] here. The combination works better than any one of them individually.

I'm going to see the three years through [at Royal Mail]. A lot of people feel for the first time that we'll [turn it round]. Me walking away from it would be letting them down. I think we've made a lot of progress, but it's still just scratching the surface. I think it's slow, but everybody else thinks it's fast.

Source: *Financial Times*, 20 February 2003. Reprinted with permission.

Questions for ethical issues case study 3.2

1 Do you think leaders are born or developed?

2 Which of Drucker's 'seven tasks of tomorrow's manager' does Allan Leighton undertake? Are there any he doesn't undertake and should?

◀◼ EXIT CASE STUDY 3.3   FT

The Pearl river delta is attracting $1bn of investment a month amid one of the fastest bursts of economic development in history

By James Kynge and Dan Roberts

Dr Martens, boot-maker to generations of punks, skinheads and factory workers, will this month quietly end centuries of volume shoe manufacturing in Britain by moving its production to a dusty plain in southern China.

Northampton, where Dr Martens is based, used to be synonymous with footwear, just as other Midlands towns were known around the world for their exports: pottery from Stoke, carpets from Kidderminster, hats from Luton.

Today, the booming cities of China's Pearl river delta have become the new workshops of the world.

Shunde styles itself as the microwave oven capital, with 40 per cent of global production emerging from just one of its giant factories. Shenzhen, the special economic zone, claims to make 70 per cent of the world's photocopiers and 80 per cent of its artificial Christmas trees. Dongguan has 80 000 people working in a single factory making running shoes for the world's teenagers. Zhongshan is the home of the world's electric lighting industry. Zhuhai, until recently a seaside town surrounded by paddy fields, is reclaiming land from the ocean to make more room for factories that already dominate global supply of everything from computer game consoles to golf clubs.

The Pearl river delta – an area the size of Belgium that winds inland from Hong Kong through a series of tightly packed islands – produces $10bn worth of exports and attracts $1bn of foreign investment a month. Already, 30m people work in manufacturing here; every day thousands more pour off trains from farms further north.

Just as Friedrich Engels wrote of the 'modern art of manufacture reaching its perfection' in Manchester in

1845, so the world's multinationals are bringing over their advanced production techniques to take advantage of cheap labour and low costs in the world's last great communist state. The gleaming outposts of Microsoft, BP, Honda or General Electric make a nonsense of the stereotype that China exports little more than plastic toys.

Many countries have experienced rapid, export-led industrialisation. But the speed and scale of this region's transformation is unprecedented. Last year, more goods were exported from China's Guangdong province, which encompasses the Pearl river delta, than during the entire 13-year period from 1978 to 1990. Total Chinese exports grew 21 per cent in 2002 to \$322bn and have doubled in just over five years. In contrast, British exports took 12 years to double after 1838. It took Germany 10 years to double exports in the 1960s and seven for Japan in the 1970s. While past booms eventually stoked inflation, the inexhaustable supply of land, labour and government encouragement has kept costs down and exported price deflation around the world. The Cantonese work ethic that built Hong Kong has created a culture where overtime is endemic and the sound of construction can be heard throughout the night.

The catalyst for the delta's explosive export growth is globalisation. China joined the World Trade Organisation last year. Increasing competition, falling transport costs and flagging consumer demand are forcing multinational manufacturing companies to flock to the region with the lowest production costs.

In Dr Martens' case, fierce price competition from rival US brands already produced in China forced the company's hand. 'It was absolutely obvious from the moment I arrived that we had to move to China like everyone else,' says David Suddens, managing director. Dr Martens will outsource production to factories owned by Pou Chen and Golden Chang, Taiwanese companies that moved to the mainland to take advantage of lower labour costs.

Pou Chen's plants, one in Zhuhai and one in Dongguan, employ 110 000 people and churn out 100m pairs of shoes a year for Nike, Adidas, Caterpillar, Timberland, Hush Puppy, Reebok, Puma and others. Production on this scale requires buildings that would have challenged the most ambitious Lancashire mill owner during Britain's industrial revolution. Tens of thousands of young women hired from all over rural China work on bustling production lines that snake through a series of long, five-storey buildings.

Dr Martens' Northampton factory uses small groups of workers assembling complete shoes to reduce inventory costs. Pou Chen uses mass production techniques little changed from Henry Ford's days. Dr Martens pays its 1100 UK workers about \$490 a week and has built a stadium for the local football club. Pou Chen pays about Rmn800 (\$100) a month, or 36 cents an hour, for up to 69 hours a week and provides dormitories for migrant workers who must obey strict curfews.

Yet the light, well ventilated working conditions are far better than many visitors expect. Stung by complaints of exploitation, Nike and other buyers have full-time local offices monitoring most aspects of employee life. Some of Pou Chen's older Taiwanese managers seem bemused by their customers' recent interest in workplace standards. 'In the past, it was all about whether you could hit the workers or slap them. Now we talk about how we celebrate their birthdays,' says Thomas Shih, deputy manager.

Nevertheless, older shoe factories are beginning to find it hard to attract and retain workers tempted by better-paid jobs in other plants. Pou Chen is opening a factory further inland where labour is more plentiful. Nearer the coast, the latest boom is in high-technology and capital-intensive industries such as petrochemicals and plastics. Although labour rates are creeping up, the economies of scale keep supply costs down and attract even more companies to relocate.

The 'great sucking sound' caused by this rush of inward investment can be heard throughout the world. While the rest of Asia has a glut of electronics factories, many plants in China are doubling output this year. During last year's global downturn, the port of Shenzhen leapfrogged both Rotterdam and Los Angeles to become the world's sixth largest container terminal. Last week, Rio Tinto, the global mining group, announced that Chinese consumption of raw materials such as steel and copper had overtaken that of the US, even though the American economy is eight times larger.

Few companies illustrate the Chinese boom as well as Flextronics, a Singapore electronics manufacturer, which acts as contract producer for Microsoft, Motorola, Dell, Palm and Sony Ericsson. Globally, the company has suffered from the bursting of the internet bubble; but its Chinese plant in Doumen has doubled its payroll to 12 000 in 12 months.

Unlike the neighbouring shoe factories, Flextronics uses modern techniques to make products such as Microsoft's Xbox computer game console. The proximity of suppliers is just as important as cheap labour. Four years ago, only 5–10 per cent of the plant's components came from local factories. Now it is between 50 and 70 per cent.

'This area has about the lowest direct labour cost we have found anywhere – at least 15 per cent less than Shanghai and about 30 per cent less than Malaysia – but well under 1 per cent of our costs are labour-related,' says Tim Dinwiddie, the Doumen manager. 'It is a myth that companies are coming here just for the cheap labour. It is the efficiency of the supply chain that drives them here, as more and more of worldwide demand is consolidated in this area.' This relentless competition among local suppliers keeps profit margins almost invisible for many companies, especially those manufacturing branded products for others. Flextronics competes with nearby contract manufacturers making Sony Play Station and Nintendo game consoles. Pou Chen has to worry about more than 800 other shoemakers in the Pearl river delta. Among Chinese companies, the price war is particularly

▶

101

intense because competitors are often chasing market share rather than trying to improve short-term profitability.

Tiny variations in commodity prices can wipe out profits almost entirely. 'Generally, our costs go down by 15 per cent every year but this year they have risen because of new Chinese tariffs on imported steel [in retaliation to US anti-dumping measures], which have increased the cost of an oven by Rmn40,' says Yu Yao Chang, deputy general manager of Galanz, a microwave oven manufacturer. He insists that his 13 000-man production line is still eight times more efficient than those of developed countries. 'In Europe, people work for five days a week, perhaps six hours a day. Here we have three shifts each working eight hours every day.'

Yet since the margin on a low-end oven can be as little as Rmn2–Rmn3, and domestic steel producers have failed to keep pace with demand from China's car factories, the new tariffs have caused Galanz's profits to collapse by Rmn1bn.

Some of the cost can be passed on to the 200 branded suppliers that purchase most of Galanz's 12m ovens – but attempts to reduce their power by producing own-brand substitutes for western markets have met with stiff resistance. Apart from General Electric, none is willing even to admit it uses the shabby Chinese factory.

Yet it would be a mistake to assume that the Pearl river delta is destined for a lifetime of servitude to global brands. Many Chinese companies are learning the tricks of today's virtual economy and launching their own brands aimed at China's rising middle class. Other foreign-owned factories are overturning the rule that developing countries make only low-end products already commodotised by more pioneering factories in the rich world. Japanese electronics groups such as Ricoh, which makes most of its photocopiers in Shenzhen, have traditionally used domestic factories to make newer models. But now it starts to make colour models in Shenzhen only months after they first roll off the production lines in Japan.

'There are high levels of engineers and college graduates and plenty of girls with good eyes and strong hands,' says Mitsuhiko Ikuno, managing director in Shenzhen. 'If we run out of people, we just go deeper into China.'

The flood of US and Japanese money is also pulling much-needed investment away from the rest of Asia's industrial heartlands. Foreign direct investment in South Korea fell 63.7 per cent last quarter. Indonesia's figure dropped 35 per cent in 2002.

Even countries that long ago gave up competing with Asia on the price of manufactured goods are not immune to the dramatic impact of China's integration with the global economy. In Britain, the trade deficit in physical goods rose in November to its highest level since records began in 1697. The US trade deficit with China climbed to a record $83bn last year.

From the banks of the Pearl river, workers look enviously at a western consumer boom partly fuelled by their falling costs of production. As Galanz's Yu Yao Chang says: 'People in the outside world should say "thank you" to China because we save them money which they can use to buy high value-added things.'

Official US perceptions of China have long been separated by a fundamental fault line: those who would engage economically with the world's most populous nation and those who, by limiting contacts, would restrain its ascending power.

Those committed to containment, represented mainly by the Republican party's right wing, insist that economic engagement does not foster changes to China's repressive political system. The engagement school holds that as the Chinese become more wealthy, so their demands for political representation increase. Former President Bill Clinton, for example, argued that China's accession to the World Trade Organisation in 2001 would result in significant political reform.

It is too early to make a definitive judgement but important changes now under way in China support the case for engagement. Not only is the southern boom town of Shenzhen about to be designated a test-bed for the boldest political reform since the 1949 revolution but cities in coastal China are also embarking on experiments to introduce checks and balances to single party rule.

Yu Youjun, mayor of Shenzhen, said in an interview that the wishes of multinational corporations were one motive for the city's experiment. Foreign companies, especially those establishing high-technology factories, are mindful of the need to protect intellectual property. For this, they need a fair local government. 'Every multinational company and investor is influenced by the investment environment created by governments,' said Mr Yu, whose city was chosen 22 years ago as a laboratory for China's first capitalist reforms and now leads the country in per capita income.

The 'hard environment' of roads, railways, ports and telecommunications was important for multinationals, Mr Yu said. But more crucial was the 'soft environment', meaning a government that is 'democratic' and transparent. 'We have made achievements in building our economic structural reform,' said Mr Yu. 'Now we need to make reforms to our political system to promote democratic politics.'

The crux of the reform was a strict separation of the roles of the Communist party, the executive government and the local legislature. As part of this, the powers of the Communist party, which currently resides 'above everything' in China, would be curtailed. The party would be responsible for setting the broad direction of policy but would be prevented from interfering in its execution. The local legislature would be charged with reviewing and supervising the government's work. Mr Yu said details of the plan would become clear once it is implemented in February or March.

The plan remains distinct from western-style democracy. There is no intention to permit opposition political parties or allow direct elections for senior government officials. The media, increasingly free to expose economic misdeeds, remain muzzled in the political arena.

But what distinguishes the Shenzhen experiment from other administrative reforms is its political nature; it represents a local variant of the 'separation of the three estates of power' that underlies western democracies and which was expressly forbidden by the late leader Deng Xiaoping. And what unites Shenzhen's ambitions with those of other cities in China is a desire to attract investment by creating an efficient and accountable government.

The rewards are high – $52.7bn in foreign investment entered China last year, meaning the country surpassed the US as a destination for foreign direct investment for the first time – and the competition is intense. Seizing on the trend for greater accountability, many cities last year opened themselves up to criticism from local and foreign companies. The practice, known as *wan ren ping zhengfu* or '10 000

people criticise the government', has become something of a phenomenon. 'We want to improve our "soft environment" to attract companies to invest here,' says one official in the Xicheng district of Beijing, an area locked in rivalry with Chaoyang to become the capital's central business district.

Chaoyang also sent questionnaires to companies – 40 per cent of them foreign – asking participants to rate the performance of local government departments. The top-rated departments will receive a bonus; the bottom ones will have their bonuses reduced.

The motivation for the strategy is much the same as in Shenzhen. China has decreed that local governments will have to survive purely from tax income, cutting them off from the dividends they used to collect from local state-owned enterprises.

Source: Financial Times, 4 February 2003. Reprinted with permission.

Question for exit case study 3.3

1 Discuss how the approaches to organisational behaviour discussed in this chapter could apply to the companies in the Pearl river delta and their development.

 For more case studies please visit www.booksites.net/capon

Short-answer questions

1 What was the basic assumption underpinning Taylor's approach to his studies on work and management?

2 Explain the Hawthorne effect.

3 State what, according to Drucker, are the tasks of tomorrow's manager.

4 What is McGregor's theory Y?

5 What did Rosabeth Moss Kanter study?

6 Identify the following as either terminal or instrumental values for a manufacturing company: world class, cleanliness, precision, customer satisfaction.

7 According to Herzberg, what are 'hygiene' factors?

8 Explain the term 'attribution theory'.

9 Name the different types of groups an individual working for an organisation may find themselves a member of.

10 Illustrate the five different stages of group development.

11 Identify the factors which can affect group performance.

12 Explain the different types of leaders which may be found in organisations.

Learning outcomes for assignment questions

While reading this chapter and engaging in the activities, you should have learned how to apply theory and models, analyse situations, and evaluate the application and analysis you undertake. The learning outcomes specified below outline what you should be able to do and the assignment questions provide an opportunity for you to test how well you have achieved the learning outcomes for this chapter.

Application	Check you have achieved this by	
1 Identify the key elements of McGregor and Herzberg's work	summarising the key points of McGregor and Herzberg's theories	answering assignment question 1
2 Understand why individuals join and participate in groups	explaining your own membership of a group	answering assignment question 2
Analysis	**Check you have achieved this by**	
1 Analyse the similarities and differences in McGregor and Herzberg's work	identifying and discussing the comparability of McGregor and Herzberg's work	answering assignment question 1
2 Analyse a group's activities and its performance (successful and unsuccessful)	differentiating factors which contribute to both successful and unsuccessful performance of groups	answering assignment question 2

Assignment questions

1   Undertaking relevant further research, compare and contrast the work of Douglas McGregor and Frederick Herzberg.

2   Choose a group of which you are or have recently been a member – it can be at work, college or outside of work or college. Identify the type of group it is and your reasons for joining it. Discuss the group's development and evaluate the success of its development and performance.

Weblinks   available online at www.booksites.net/capon

These weblinks look at unacceptable behaviour in organisations and how it can be dealt with.

1 This is the website of arbitration service ACAS.
   http://www.acas.org.uk/
   Click on 'employment topics'.
   Select 'Problems between individuals and employers'.
   Select 'Bullying and harassment' links.

2 This is the website of the Trade Union Congress.
   http://www.tuc.org.uk/tuc/rights_bullyatwork.cfm

3 This is an American website which looks at unacceptable behaviour in the workplace. http://www.workdoctor.com
Click on 'Tutorial on the phenomenon'.

Further reading

Ackroyd, S and Thompson, P (1999) *Organizational Misbehaviour*, London: Sage.

Francesco, A M and Gold B A (1997) *International Organizational Behaviour*, Englewood Cliffs, NJ: Prentice Hall.

Huczynski, A and Buchanan, D (2001) *Organizational Behaviour*, Harlow: Financial Times Prentice Hall.

Jones, G R (2001) *Organizational Theory*, Upper Saddle River, NJ: Prentice Hall.

Pettinger, R (2000) *Mastering Organisational Behaviour*, Basingstoke: Palgrave.

Robbins, S P (2000) *Essentials of Organizational Behavior*, New Jersey: Prentice Hall.

Tyson, S and Jackson, T (1992) *The Essence of Organizational Behaviour*, Hemel Hempstead: Prentice Hall.

Vecchio, R P (2000) *Organizational Behavior,* Fort Worth, TX: Dryden Press.

References

1 Clutterbuck, D and Crainer, S (1990) *Makers of Management*, London, Papermac Macmillian.
2 Ibid.
3 Ibid.
4 Ibid.
5 Jones, G R (2001) *Organizational Theory*, New Jersey: Prentice Hall.
6 Robbins, S P (2000) *Essentials of Organizational Behavior*, New Jersey: Prentice Hall.
7 Huczynski, A and Buchanan, D (2001) *Organizational Behaviour*, Harlow: Financial Times Prentice Hall.
8 Tyson, S and Jackson, T (1992) *The Essence of Organizational Behaviour*, Hemel Hempstead: Prentice Hall.
9 Vecchio, R P (2000) *Organizational Behavior,* New Jersey: Prentice Hall.
10 Robbins, op. cit.
11 Tuckman, B C (1965) 'Development sequence in small groups', *Psychological Bulletin*, 36 (6), pp 384–99 and Tuckman, B C and Jensen, M A C (1977) 'Stages of small group development revisited', *Group and Organization Studies*, 2 (4) pp 419–27 in Huczynski, A and Buchanan, D (2001) *Organizational Behaviour*, Harlow: Financial Times Prentice Hall.
12 Vecchio, op. cit.
13 Robbins, op. cit.
14 Robbins, op. cit.
15 Robbins, op. cit.

4

Marketing

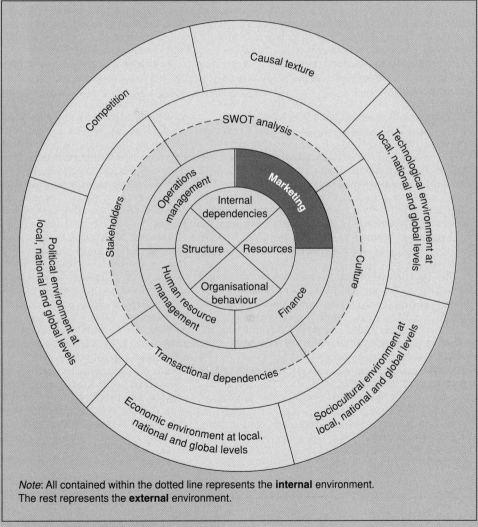

Note: All contained within the dotted line represents the **internal** environment.
The rest represents the **external** environment.

Figure 4.1 Organisational context model

ENTRY CASE STUDY 4.1

FT

China's urban cool develop a thirst for a cappuccino

By James Harding

'Coffee brings its own special atmosphere, its own sense of romance,' says Yang Qingqing, Shanghai's best-known fashion columnist and self-appointed style guru. 'The young generation drink coffee not because they prefer it to tea. The real reason is that coffee represents modern, western culture.'

In China's largest city, thousands of cafés have opened in the last couple of years and a taste for a cappuccino has become a badge of cool. Much more than a beverage, coffee has become a mark of cosmopolitan culture and a milestone on the path to prosperity.

Rural China, by contrast, remains a devoutly tea-drinking society. Instant coffee is practically non-existent in the poorer households of the Chinese countryside, but has become a regular feature of urban homes. According to a Gallup market survey, just 1 per cent of rural homes have a jar of coffee granules, but in Shanghai 51 per cent of houses do.

The fashion for coffee in more prosperous urban areas, though, has been enough to multiply the coffee business in China several times over.

Theo Klauser, managing director of Nestlé China, says sales of Nescafé, by far the best-selling brand of instant coffee, have 'increased five times in the last five years . . . although from a small base'. Sales from the Nescafé plant in Dongguan were worth RMB450m ($54.4m) last year, he says.

The International Coffee Organisation recently sent a delegation to Beijing and Shanghai to promote coffee consumption and provide support to China's coffee producers in Yunnan, in the country's south-west.

As with so many other consumer goods in China, the massive potential of the market can have a dizzying effect on the industry.

Coffee consumption in mainland China is one cup a person, a year, according to Nestlé, but wealth and greater integration with the west has tended to develop a thirst for coffee in Asia.

In Taiwan, people drink 38 cups each year, in Hong Kong 44 cups and in Japan 330 cups. This compares with 440 in the UK, 463 in the US and 1100 in Sweden.

Jonathan Eisenberg, who set up a gourmet coffee shop in Shanghai and a sister shop in Beijing called The Daily Grind, says: 'The Chinese will go for coffee. Look at what has happened in Japan, Korea and Hong Kong. But they will probably go for a US-style coffee, something that is diluted with milk.' Making a good cup of coffee in Shanghai, though, has its problems. 'To do Asian-style coffee you need foam,' which means buying a lot of good quality milk, notes Mr Eisenberg. For a take-away coffee shop, one of the chief headaches is cups and lids, he says: 'They are often more expensive than the beans.' Tariffs on coffee beans are also very high, prompting Mr Eisenberg to buy beans roasted in China.

The country's largest processing operation, the Yunnan Coffee Processing Plant, aims to increase annual production of 1500 tonnes last year to 5000 tonnes in 2000.

But the company expects the business environment to get tougher as more foreign brands and coffee importers target the market. 'We are trying to set up a sales network throughout China's major coastal cities, but we have a long way to go. Cheaper and more famous foreign coffee companies promise to be a big challenge.'

Mr Eisenberg cautions against excessive enthusiasm about the coffee market: 'Coffee for coffee's sake is still a novelty. The coffee market is still premature for serious growth.'

Likewise, Mr Klauser at Nestlé warns that while the potential of the Chinese market may be beguiling, it is a long way from being realized. 'Coffee drinking is still foreign to the Chinese, who are essentially tea drinkers and their habits are not so easily changed,' he says.

In large part, coffee producers and café owners say, this is because Chinese people are not yet convinced by the taste. After a lifetime of tea, coffee seems bitter and acrid, which helps explain the popularity of the sweeter and milkier cups of coffee such as latte, cappuccino or instant coffee ready-mixed with milk and sugar.

But, then, for the time being, the modish Ms Yang suggests that people drink coffee often for something more than the taste: 'Coffee has its own mood . . . for example, if a young man invites a young lady for a cup of coffee, this is a good way for him to express his feelings.'

Source: Financial Times, 21 May 1998. Reprinted with permission.

Introduction

This chapter examines the relationship between the **marketing** department and the external and internal environments of organisations. Conclusions will be drawn about the interactive nature of this relationship. Organisations and their context will be examined with the aim of assessing how the external environment dictates the activities of the marketing department, or whether marketers inside organisations are able to exercise their marketing talents to influence the external environment. In addition, how the marketing department relates to other departments in the effort to achieve organisational goals will be examined. Basic **marketing tools** will be presented and these will be applied to practical examples in order to facilitate an understanding of marketing and of how marketing tools play their part in this process.

Marketing

Marketing is the first of the departments to be considered for two reasons. First, the nature of its activities is such that marketing could be the activity best placed to interact with the external environment. Through its **market research** activities, the marketing department is the internal area of the organisation most explicitly required to scan, analyse, monitor and contend with what is going on in the outside world (*see* Chapters 8 and 9). It is therefore the role of marketers to understand the size and nature of the **marketplace**, to know the organisation's customers and to undertake market research into customer requirements. While scanning the external environment, the marketing department will be continually monitoring the activities of competitor organisations and the latest developments in the same or similar fields. These research and monitoring activities are the way in which the marketing department's efforts help ensure that the organisation is first into the market with the products or services to meet its customers' identified needs or wants. Therefore it could be argued that the marketing department is most aware of the external environment, and of the environmental linkages between the external and internal environments (*see* Chapter 9). Additionally it also follows that marketing is the department most aware of any changes in this relationship and of the effects that these changes may have on the strategic or operational management of the organisation.

Second, it is clear that the marketing department has several roles to play in the relationship between the external and internal environments. It has to identify changes in the external environment and predict the kinds of products or services the outside world requires. In addition, the causal effects of these changes mean that marketing has to manage closely the links between the marketing department and the other departments of the company in order to meet the organisational objectives of satisfying customer wants or needs. Without close collaboration and communication within the organisation, referred to here as **functional convergence**, the marketing department or function will not be able to marshal the tangible, intangible and human resources necessary to achieve organisational objectives. Without functional convergence, the organisation risks wasting organisational energy on internal tension and conflict and not being able to meet the goals it has set itself. Thus this chapter will look closely at the relationship between marketing and the other elements of the internal environment and will draw some conclusions about how the organisation's internal efficiency affects its ability to achieve its business goals.

The development of the marketing concept

■ Production era

From the industrial revolution onwards, the urbanisation of an ever larger part of previously rural populations in Britain resulted in a workforce able to produce large quantities of goods to supply mass markets. At the same time, lifestyle patterns altered, with the long hours of factory work instead of agricultural activity. Therefore urban workers had to buy products that they previously would have grown or made themselves, thus creating a demand for the goods that other workers produced. As technology advanced, labour-intensive activity gave way to mechanised mass production. The new range of products included mechanised products and labour-saving devices that had previously been unimaginable and unavailable to a wider public at prices they could afford. This meant that new markets for these new products were easily created and satisfied.

This is referred to as the **production era**, when organisations treated their customers as a plentiful and captive supply of people who were easily pleased with the new-fangled devices offered to them by manufacturers. In the production era, if organisations did not make it, customers could not buy it. Further, if organisations did not make it, customers could not conceive of it.

■ Sales era

As industrialisation progressed through the eighteenth, nineteenth and twentieth centuries, competition between manufacturers increased, and organisations were obliged to work harder to woo their customers away from competitors' products. The British Empire expanded all the while, driven and fuelled by trade imperatives. The Empire brought to British companies ever-expanding sources of raw materials and labour and endless captive markets for their goods. Like the production era, this **sales era** still did not consider the actual needs or wants of customers before deciding what products or services to provide. Rather, organisations concentrated on making the public and thereby potential customers aware of what was available from Company A so that they would be enticed to purchase Company A's products, rather than Company B's or C's.

Advertising focused on reliability and brand loyalty in its efforts to retain customers once hooked. Little was done to survey customers and find out if there were unfulfilled needs and wants that the company itself could work towards meeting. Services such as transport, health and education, particularly on the election of a Labour government after the Second World War, became more and more centralised and less responsive to need or want when nationalised by the government into monopolistic public providers. In the private sector, however, it became the prime focus of organisations to sell as much of what they could make as possible.

■ Marketing era

Given the ever-increasing rate and scale of the competitive environment in the twentieth century, the sales orientation gave way to the **marketing era** or marketing concept, which is the subject of this chapter.

Defining the marketing concept

In order to understand the activities of the marketing department, it is first important to define the marketing era or marketing concept that underpins its activities. At its most basic, a marketing orientation leads organisations to consider the needs and wants of their actual or potential customers before considering what services and/or products to offer. More than this, the marketing concept could be said to be a holistic approach to managing organisations.

Marketing-oriented organisations focus on gearing all their internal activities towards achieving their goals and objectives by satisfying customers' needs and wants. Marketing can be likened to a philosophy or a firm set of beliefs. There is a huge literature on and by marketers defining their role in the environment and within the organisation.

Peter Drucker[1] defines marketing as:

> **not only much broader than selling, it is not a specialised activity at all. It encompasses the entire business. It is the whole business seen from the point of view of its final result, that is from the customer's point of view. Concern and responsibility for marketing must therefore permeate all areas of the enterprise.**

This gives an idea of the holistic nature of the marketing concept, dealing as it does with the organisation's activities from the very beginning of product research and planning through to after-sales service and customer comments.

Kotler et al.[2] defined marketing as:

> **a social activity and managerial process by which individuals and groups obtain what they need and want through creating and exchanging products and value with others.**

This introduces the idea of the role of the marketing department as contributing to adding value to the organisation's inputs, an essential element of the resource conversion process (*see* Chapter 1). Kotler goes on to suggest that marketing is the area of a business that identifies and quantifies current unfilled needs and wants, before determining the markets that the organisation can best serve with its current and future products and services. Thus marketing links a society's needs and the organisation's response.

The professional body for marketers in the UK, the Institute of Marketing, in Lancaster and Massingham,[3] identifies the marketing department as 'the management process which identifies, anticipates and supplies customer requirements efficiently and profitably'. This introduces to the marketing concept the notion of prediction and anticipation of **customer needs and wants**. In the realms of innovation and technology, marketers have a role in providing for needs and wants before potential customers know that they could need or want the product or service on offer. Who, for example, in the heyday of the long-playing record could have known that they would have been updating their collection to compact disc before the end of the twentieth century?

According to the marketing concept, it is the *raison d'être* of the marketing-oriented organisation to allow the marketing department the power and resources to dictate what should be done, for whom and when, to the organisation's other departments. This focus is achieved through marketing's research activities, which are the mechanism for identifying customer needs and wants and competitor provision. Marketing can provide further evidence of how effective it has been in doing this through its customer service and feedback capabilities, closing a circular loop of information and data gathered from the outside world. This is clearly illustrated by the entry case study for this chapter, showing that companies such as Nestlé have identified China as a growth market for coffee.

☑ Check your understanding

Do you understand the development of marketing?

Check your understanding by explaining the move from the production era to sales era, to marketing. Use examples where appropriate.

The organisational context of marketing

The marketing concept demands not only that marketing should focus on meeting the wants and needs of customers but that nothing less than the full dedication of people and resources from all sections of the organisation to the marketing concept will ensure that the organisation can achieve business success. In order to achieve the customer satisfaction it heralds as the key to business success, the marketing concept dictates that any effort in the organisation is wasted if it is not directed towards customer satisfaction and providing the products and services that it says the customer wants or needs. In this, all the organisation's departments need to work together in harmony to achieve organisational objectives. This harmony is referred to as functional convergence, as the internal departments or functions of the organisation must converge their efforts to succeed.

Because the marketing concept deals with the satisfaction of customer needs and wants through organisational activities, it can be seen in organisations' in-house programmes that are focused on achieving 'customer orientation', 'customer satisfaction' or 'customer care'. Hence marketers hold as the tenets of their philosophy the consideration of three basic points:

1 What do customers need or want?
2 How can the organisation meet these needs or wants?
3 How does the organisation make money doing so?

This last is true not only of private-sector, profit-making enterprises but also of contemporary public-sector or voluntary-sector organisations. In the latter cases, the aim would be to make enough money from products or service to break even or increase activity level rather than making profit for redistribution to owners or shareholders.

This marketing concept demands that the only point of the organisation's existence is to try to make or do whatever market research has proved that customers need or want. The organisation must have whatever resources or technology are necessary in order to achieve this. Any organisational resources, whether tangible, intangible or human, that are not focused on meeting the needs and wants of customers are therefore redundant. Although to the business studies student this approach may seem obvious, the opposite attitude may still be found in some organisations, with their approach summed up in the more production- or sales-oriented phrase: 'We make this product because we know how to. Now, who can we find to sell it to?'

An example of this latter approach was the early mass-production pioneer Henry Ford, who famously offered his customers any colour Model 'T' Ford car, as long as it was black – the only colour of car his company made. In the early days of mass production this approach was successful due to the simpler nature of the competitive environment (*see* Chapter 10). This meant that customers and markets were more easily satisfied by the new products that technological advances brought, as the vast majority had never had access to such products before.

✓ Check your understanding

Do you understand the organisational concept of marketing?

Check your understanding by identifying the role of the marketing department in an organisation.

Marketing assumptions

Underpinning the marketing concept are three basic assumptions about the external environment, marketplace and customers. First, marketers must assume that their actual or potential customers have some element of free choice. In politico-economic systems containing free markets or a mixed economy with commercial competition supported and regulated by the politico-legal system, customers or consumers will have the opportunity to exercise free choice between products or services when spending money (*see* Chapter 9). Second, actual or potential customers have disposable income that can be spent on whatever product or service is being offered. This crucial financial aspect empowers customers to follow their needs or wants and make decisions about the deployment of spare income. Finally, if customers have both disposable income and the freedom to spend it as they wish, it is the job of marketers to attempt to persuade them to alter their choice and move from something to which they are loyal or with which they are familiar to something new in the same line. The entry case study to this chapter highlights the efforts that have been made by companies like Nestlé to tempt Chinese people to drink coffee instead of the tea with which they are familiar.

True marketing orientation could be renamed customer orientation. If organisations are truly marketing or customer oriented, they are achieving the necessary focus of all organisational activities on customer satisfaction. In achieving marketing orientation, the organisation has recognised that the only point of organisational effort is to try to satisfy customer needs and wants through the combination of marketing, finance, human resource and operations management activities. In order to do this, the organisation needs to aim to achieve a level of integration of the efforts of all departments. This is the concept of functional convergence: the co-operation and collaboration of all internal elements of the organisation towards its corporate mission of customer satisfaction. To achieve this, the organisation must understand the needs and wants of the customer.

■ Needs and wants

It is useful at this stage to consider the difference between customer needs and customer wants, as occasionally marketers will be appealing to a perceived need, but more often they will be focusing marketing activities on appealing to customers' wants or desires. A need is something that cannot be done without, like basic food and water. A want could be said to be something to which someone aspires or which they desire. People need grain and water to survive, but might want to have a variety of grains and vegetables and fruit juice or alcohol to drink.

This difference can be illustrated by using Maslow's hierarchy of needs.[4] This American psychologist defined need at various levels. People all have in common certain basic requirements for food, drink and sleep, referred to by

Maslow as 'physiological or basic needs'. In less well-developed countries these needs are the prime concerns of citizens. The family's income is spent on keeping enough food in their stomachs, whether that income be earned through economic activity or handed out in subsidy from the state or from private charity. Once basic physiological needs are met and satisfied, the next priority is to keep a roof over the family's head. Maslow refers to this as 'security or safety needs', which include self-defence and saving for future eventualities.

Once these needs are satisfied, essential life is not threatened by homelessness or hunger and the future is planned for in terms of the upbringing of children and social security for the elderly and sick in the family, less fundamental needs can emerge. Maslow's next level refers to the human proclivity for socialisation activities, e.g. going to the pub, cinema or theme park. Maslow refers to this as 'belonging or affection needs'. From this, natural ambition and aspiration lead to spending surplus income on more luxurious accommodation or better food, or improving social status through acquisition of possessions or land. Maslow calls this 'esteem or ego needs'.

Finally, the pinnacle of Maslow's hierarchy of needs is the stage of self-fulfilment, not only having achieved the fundaments needed for basic food and shelter but also being able to obtain things that are desirable for complete fulfilment. Thus the ultimate dream home with all modern conveniences, a top-of-the range sports car, designer-label clothes, regular five-star holidays and eating only in the best restaurants might be the height of aspiration for the successful entrepreneur or lottery winner. Maslow calls this 'self-actualisation'.

Therefore while organisations can never make customers actually need anything, the job of the marketing department is to tempt potential customers to deploy their financial resources to meet their needs by purchasing Company A's products or services instead of Company B's. For example, in the entry case study to this chapter, the International Coffee Organisation, in promoting coffee drinking in Beijing and Shanghai, is tempting urban people in China to forgo their traditional tea and on occasions drink coffee instead. Hence while marketers cannot create need, they can sometimes make customers want something through their marketing activities, activating the higher echelons of Maslow's hierarchical model. The marketing department therefore needs to focus its efforts on appealing to the various needs and wants of the target market. This is why market research (*see* later in this chapter) is important.

☑ Check your understanding

Do you understand the term 'needs and wants'?

Check your understanding by indicating specific needs and wants that customers may have.

■ The customer

'Customer care', 'customer orientation' and 'customer service' are very much part of the rhetoric of organisations striving for business success in Britain in the twenty-first century. To what extent this orientation is sincere or successful will be examined later in this chapter. In the private sector many truly customer-oriented examples can be cited. Car manufacturers have come a long way since the days of Henry Ford's Model 'T', largely under the influence of the Japanese car manufacturers whose post-war domination of global markets is legendary. Nissan UK Ltd is an example of a marketing-driven car manufacturer. No car going through the factory on the production line in Sunderland has not been ordered by a sales showroom for a customer. Therefore each car being made is bespoke, i.e. constructed with a particular customer's needs in mind.

In the UK public sector, service delivery has changed radically since the election of the Thatcher government in 1979. With the introduction of markets in the NHS, education and local government services, public-sector organisations have had to begin considering customer needs and wants in the provision of their services. The university sector also faced radical change in its markets with the expansion of higher education and the introduction of student loans and tuition fees directly payable by students instead of by their local education authority. However, despite having introduced marketing departments, managers and officers, universities have considerable work to do before they could be considered to have a marketing orientation. They are still more fixed in the production or sales era, expecting students to want to take the courses they already teach, rather than truly designing courses that meet identified customer needs or wants.

Marketing activities

If, put simply, marketing can be said to be the carrying out of business operations to steer the flow of goods and services from manufacturers to consumers, it is then useful to define exactly what it is that the marketing department does in order to achieve this goal. There is a temptation to associate marketing with **selling**, but sales is in fact just one of the activities that may be located within the marketing department – *see* Figure 4.2. Housed within the marketing

**Figure 4.2
Marketing activities**

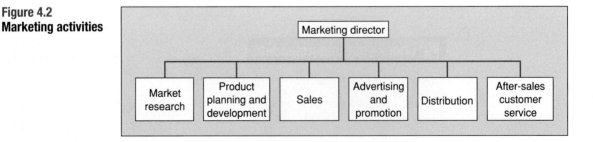

department are likely to be many individual subdepartments, including market research, **product planning and development**, advertising and **sales promotion**, sales, **distribution** and **after-sales customer service**.

This section will examine the marketing department's relationship to the external environment, its activities, and its relationship to other elements of the internal environment of the organisation. In its relationship with the organisation's external environment, the marketing department must seek to answer the following questions:

1 Who is in the marketplace and where is the market?
2 What are the changing needs and/or wants of the marketplace?
3 What resource inputs are necessary to meet those needs/wants?
4 How will the organisation make money doing this (even voluntary, public-sector or other not-for-profit organisations have to make their running costs)?

■ Market research

Having stated at length the importance that the marketing concept places on establishing customer needs or wants, a company will be only as successful as its market research activities. Through market research, organisations can identify who is in the marketplace, where they are located, what they need or want, and how products and services can be developed to meet these identified needs and wants.

Organisations can carry out market research in two basic ways: through generation of **primary data**, or through use of available **secondary data**. The generation of primary data requires the organisation to invest heavily in terms of time, money and people and in the execution of extensive and detailed surveys of current and potential customers through direct contact with them. This may take the form of postal or telephone surveys of a data-base of current customers. Alternatively, the organisation may purchase commercially produced marketing databases of potential customers who fulfil certain criteria in terms of location, income, profession or family composition and then survey them directly.

Examples of primary market research include Cable & Wireless's 1998 survey of households regarding the type of telephone and television services they wished to see developed in the future. After the privatisation of British Telecom, Cable & Wireless, a renowned international telecommunications player, had established the first private competition to BT, called Mercury Communications. Later it decided to relaunch Mercury under its own Cable & Wireless brand name. The customer survey, along with wide media advertising, was a way of conducting useful market research and introducing the new brand name to a wide audience.

The advance of technology has assisted organisations in knowing their customers better and contacting them more frequently, as well as increasing the amount and quality of primary data available to help organisations with their market research. The use of itemised bills and customer loyalty cards in supermarkets and shops enables those organisations to build exact customer profiles, and to target the marketing of various products and services at particular customer groups. This technique is called data warehousing and is a growing market research trend in many sectors. A customer identified from the checkout terminal as having begun to buy baby products might be sent details of the supermarket's discount scheme on baby products. Unlike Sainsbury's, Tesco does not offer its loyalty discounts directly at the checkout, but rather mails discount vouchers up to the amount 'saved' on the loyalty card directly to the customer's home address, thus enabling it to include details of other relevant products, services or offers.

Sainsbury's and Tesco have invested large sums in data warehousing to track customer preferences and behaviour, thus providing a rich seam of market research. The speed and sophistication of the technology allow millions of customer records to be searched and processed relatively quickly. This method enables supermarkets to break down their customer base by category of shopper, e.g. young families, thirty-something singles, elderly couples, elderly single people. Thus the supermarket can compare actual shopping habits with a perceived theoretical shopping basket that each average consumer type 'should' be purchasing. This then enables the retailer to tell which products customers do and do not buy from that particular store. This market research can then be used to promote certain products that the customer may be buying elsewhere outside the store. The supermarkets can also tell the frequency of visits and the impact this has on shopping habits. For example, families with young children may shop at the weekend, at which time supermarkets may promote economy brands, bulk-purchase discounts, baby and children's products, including clothes as well as foodstuffs. These efforts are based on information arising from the data and customer records that the supermarket has stored and collated in its data warehouse.

Organisations may also choose to use specialist market research firms to conduct market research for them, particularly when they may not have the skills or resources in house specifically to devote to carrying out the research themselves. The market research firm may carry out bespoke market research expressly and confidentially for its client, or it may carry out generic market research that is of use to and available to more than one customer. Alternatively, secondary data may be collected and compiled by private market research companies such as Mintel and Euromonitor. This will be topic specific, e.g. retailing of children's clothing, but not specific to any one company. The secondary data will be collected through mailshots to business customers or private households, through cold calling by telephone or in person to business or private addresses, or by in-person interviews on the street. It will then be sold to any interested companies or libraries. There are also publicly available forms of secondary data, including census data and information on social and demographic trends.

■ Product planning and development

Having gathered the required market research data on customer needs and wants, the next stage in the marketing process is to try to ensure that the organisation is in a position to introduce new products or services designed to meet the needs and wants it has identified. This may seem an obvious and simple stage to achieve, but there are in fact many complex factors to take into account. The organisation may first want to consider how it might meet those needs or wants with its existing product or service range, through utilising the marketing tools explained later in this chapter. However, if existing products or services are no longer suitable, the marketing department must clearly work closely with the other departments to achieve a balance between what is required and what can be provided. These internal relationships are dealt with more explicitly in the next section.

In terms of relationships with the external environment, product planning and development are responsible for a number of factors:

- identifying new technology that improves design or production capabilities;
- identifying suitable suppliers of necessary raw materials or components;
- liaising with customer or consumer focus groups at various stages to take into account changes in taste or design.

Product planning and development are included here as part of the marketing department, but considered under the banner of research and development (R&D) it could equally comfortably be located in the operations management department of an organisation. Without close liaison with the operations managers, the marketers' dreams remain dreams. The operations management department must realise the ambitions of the marketing department. Therefore in different organisations the responsibilities for R&D might be found in marketing or operations management. Whichever is the case, there must be close co-operation between marketing and operations management. This is the functional convergence mentioned before. Functional convergence could be defined as the situation where two or more departments or functions of an organisation work in harmony towards meeting organisational goals and objectives without rivalry or internal competition.

■ Sales

Once the new product is up and running, there then comes the task of selling it to the people who were identified as needing or wanting it by the market research. However, this is by no means a foregone conclusion. During the market research and product development stages, customers have had time to develop other wants or needs that may supersede those originally identified. Additionally, competitors have had time to enter the market with new products or services. At this stage it is vital to decide on appropriate pricing and marketing strategies to get the finished product or service delivered to the target market at a price it can afford and that also makes money for the organisation. There are different and conflicting approaches to costing and pricing that are covered in Chapter 6.

The marketing-oriented approach to pricing examines what prices the market might support through its market research. If potential customers find a certain price acceptable for certain products, marketers will want their new product's prices to fit in with the public's perception of 'normal' prices. For example, if the range of prices for a 1.5kg box of washing powder in the supermarket is between £4.89 and £5.29, then any new powder introduced has to be priced within or close to this range in order to be successful. For a higher than normal price to be acceptable to the marketplace, the product has to be differentiated (*see* Chapter 10). This is where the manufacturer relies on additional product features ('Now destroys grease'), quality reputation ('Still the market leader') or brand loyalty ('Your favourite washing powder') to be able to sell the new washing powder.

Therefore the organisation's challenge is to be able to produce the product and make a profit within this price range, ensuring that all inputs, costs and overheads are covered. This is one aspect where the idea of functional convergence might falter. While marketing is dictating to the organisation not only what products must be made but also what price the marketplace will stand, the operations management department's reaction can be to state what it is possible to produce and what the basic cost of this will be.

A production-oriented approach to pricing examines the costs of all inputs, including overheads and labour, and then adds profit to this to achieve a sales price. This appears to be a logical approach, even if the resulting price is higher than the market norm for a similar product or service. It is not logical, however, where the ultimate price of the good is higher than the customer is prepared to pay for such a product.

▪ Salesforce

From the manufacturer's point of view, the typical method for achieving sales is through a salesforce of representatives who are able to travel to existing or potential customers with a view to achieving new or continued sales. In addition to staff costs, there is the investment in a fleet of company cars and mobile phones to be considered. Managing the salesforce, with its quasi-independent status, cut off geographically from the internal culture of the organisation, is a complex issue. There are important concerns covering the quality of information passed between the salesforce in the field and the organisation, as orders must be processed correctly and quickly and organisational developments communicated to sales personnel. Salesforces work on salary-plus-commission contracts, adding a motivational incentive to encourage them to meet and/or exceed their targets.

■ Wholesalers

A large amount of goods are sold not directly to the consumer but through an intermediary such as a wholesaler. This is convenient for the manufacturer as, although reduced profits are made since wholesalers command discounts from manufacturers, they have a simpler task in only selling to centralised wholesalers rather than having to identify and target a variety of customers. Wholesalers need discounts from the manufacturers because they too wish to make a profit from the transactions of buying and selling on to retailers, and they have their own operational costs to consider. The wholesaler requires efficient distribution networks, including appropriate transportation. The wholesaler also removes the need for the manufacturer to keep a large amount of finished goods in stock, as it is the wholesaler who needs the large warehousing capacity, centrally positioned to service a network of retailers.

■ Retailers

The retail trade sells goods to the end user or consumer of the product. In order to be successful in retailing, it is crucial to make correct decisions about a number of factors. Location is a key issue, as the retailer must position itself in the place the consumer would expect or would like to find the goods on offer. Thus city-centre shops are faced with tough decisions when a new out-of-town shopping mall opens, taking trade away from the city-centre location. Do they remain loyal to the city centre? Do they move site into the new environment of the shopping mall? Or do they attempt to make both locations successful?

Department stores in Sheffield are an interesting case in point. Meadowhall opened outside the city in 1992. This had a further significant impact on city-centre shops, given that the economic situation of Sheffield as a whole has never fully recovered from the economic downturn in the 1970s. The department chain House of Fraser initially opened a second store in the Meadowhall complex and kept its city-centre store open. However, after five years of operating two stores, in 1997 it finally closed its town-centre store in favour of the Meadowhall location. Shoppers had demonstrated a preference for visiting the shopping centre-based store over the town-based one. John Lewis, however, remained loyal to the city-centre location with its Cole Brothers store. It resisted the challenge of Meadowhall and retained its band of loyal customers.

■ Direct selling

Many organisations are avoiding intermediaries such as wholesalers or agents in order to reduce costs and thus prices, hence passing on cost savings to the consumer. In this way, manufacturers or service providers can also increase profit margins by charging the end price directly to the customer rather than selling at a discount to a wholesaler or agent. Examples of organisations now dealing directly with their customers or consumers are home and car insurance services, which sell their services by telephone or via the internet instead of in a shop or office, hence reducing overheads and providing a more customer-oriented service. Customer service is also improved by giving customers access to services at a time convenient to them.

Remote shopping

There is a 'chicken and egg' link between customer orientation and customer demands. As organisations improve their products and services, customers become used to a high level of service and good-quality products. As they become accustomed to better services and products, they demand more and more from the organisations they patronise. One of the manifestations of this is longer opening hours in shops (late-night shopping in city centres, supermarkets opening 24 hours a day at busy periods, such as just before Christmas, and even year-round in some locations).

Another trend is the growing popularity of remote shopping. **Remote shopping** refers to shopping by customers in locations other than a retail or sales outlet. Many high street names offer remote shopping in addition to their high street stores. For example Marks and Spencer, Next, Debenhams and Currys all offer website shopping and/or catalogue shopping. The retailer Littlewoods, with its high street shops and successful catalogue shopping business, has developed its business to include the home shopping catalogue, the high street store catalogue (Index shops), and the all-inclusive catalogue. These catalogues can be used by customers in their hard-copy form or can be accessed via Littlewoods' website, where orders can be placed and paid for.

Many retailers now offer more than one way of shopping in an attempt to make it easy for customers to shop with them and to put their goods and services more widely on display, i.e. a website is accessible 24 hours a day, every day of the year. Additionally many other goods and services such as banking, insurance, holidays and cars can be purchased via the web, with companies often offering a good price if the ordering and payment are carried out online. There are also examples of internet shopping being used to promote associated services. For example, Barclaycard has promoted its credit card as being the ideal way to buy Christmas presents without leaving home, by shopping on the internet.

Advertising and promotion

In order to bring new products or services to the attention of the potential market, there has to be advertising and promotion. These, along with sales activities, are the subdepartments most easily associated in the public consciousness with the term 'marketing'. Advertising and promotion are not necessarily the same activities. They are the part of the marketing department responsible for planning strategies to retain existing customers and attract potential customers. Advertising and promotion are carried out in a variety of media appropriate to the product or service and to the target audience.

Advertising takes two forms: institutional or product. That is to say, advertisements either promote the company as a whole and do not focus on specific products; or they focus on particular products, irrespective of where they are sold. The advertising media most familiar to the general public are print media (newspapers and magazines), broadcast media (television, radio, cinema and the internet), and public spaces, such as roadside billboards and street furniture. The cost of advertising space varies according to the size of audience likely to be reached and the date or time of the advertisements placed.

Many advertisements take on a life of their own quite beyond or apart from the popularity of the product. An example of this is the Renault Clio advertisements which featured 'Nicole' and 'Papa', whose names became quite familiar to the British public. This was extended in such a manner that the 1998 advertisement for the Renault Clio, and thus the latest remodelling of the car, was announced well in advance of its first television broadcast, in the commercial break of *Coronation Street*, a popular soap opera, on a Friday evening. In a sense, this went beyond advertising and into the realm of promotion.

Promotion is the way in which the organisation attempts to manipulate the external environment by combining advertising with special offers and particular benefits or service packages intended to attract customers. There are many famous examples of organisations that have failed to match the demand created by special promotions and have come unstuck as a result. The Hoover promotion of free trips to America seriously underestimated the number of people prepared to purchase a new vacuum cleaner in order to benefit from the offer, and the company ended up in the courts having to justify why customers had not benefited from the promised holidays. Advertising and promotion constitute one part of the marketing department that is strictly regulated by law and the Advertising Standards Agency (ASA).

■ Distribution

Having whetted the customer's appetite with advertising and promotion, and potentially having made sales to them by remote methods, ensuring that products or services are physically available to customers who wish to purchase them is the next stage in the successful marketing process. The 1998 football World Cup was dogged by problems of ticket distribution. First of all there were the restrictions placed by the French organising authorities on ticket allocations to national football associations to be sold in participating countries. Then they announced that tickets could only be bought over the telephone by customers with an address in France, effectively debarring all non-residents. In order to remedy this situation, they offered an extra allocation of tickets by international telephone over a certain period, only to find the lines so over-subscribed that few callers could get through. This was obviously a clear case of demand outstripping supply, but also one of extremely poor distribution management.

Efficient distribution networks are particularly important for mail-order companies or companies moving towards direct selling to the customer at home rather than in the shop. Consumer protection organisations and radio and television programmes are kept particularly busy in the early part of each year investigating complaints from customers who have ordered and paid for goods as Christmas presents that were not delivered in time.

■ After-sales customer service

The final stage in the holistic customer-oriented package is how customers are dealt with once their purchase has been made. Dealing effectively with follow-up enquiries or complaints is a key indicator of the truly marketing-oriented organisation. This enables organisations to target customers for current or future alternative products or services. Organisations often include aspects of their after-sales service as part of the promotion package, offering money-back guarantees, 24-hour helplines, or free installation or home visits. The standard of this type of service is often the factor enabling customers to judge whether repeat business will be placed with the company or not. The cable communications company that keeps the complaining customer on hold for half an hour before putting them through to 'one of our service operatives' does not demonstrate excellent customer service or good telecommunications equipment.

Privatised utilities have invested heavily in this end of their customer service, which may be partly due to the fact that they have many dissatisfied customers who find service levels below par and prices rising. Partly due to customer service initiatives, and partly due to external regulation, utilities offer *per diem* refunds for any disruption of service in water, electricity or gas, as well as compensation schemes for complaints received.

☑ Check your understanding

Do you understand what each of the activities undertaken by the marketing department involves?

Check your understanding by summarising the key points of each activity carried out by the marketing department.

Relationship to the internal environment

As well as operating on a set of assumptions about potential or actual customers, the marketing concept makes some basic assumptions about the organisation for which the marketing effort is being made. The first of these assumptions is that the organisation is able to be flexible and alter its products and processes in order to meet newly identified customer needs and wants. Having identified customer needs and wants, in theory it should be a simple process for the organisation to plan the production or service delivery required to provide customers with the products or services that they have indicated, via market research, are a need or a want. However, as we will see later in this chapter, the internal culture or structure of the organisation could make this more difficult than might be anticipated.

The second assumption about the organisation is that it is able to react quickly enough to the consumer's perceived needs or wants and redirect the necessary resources away from their current focus towards meeting newly perceived needs and wants in the marketplace. Without the necessary financial resources to purchase new technology or recruit new people, and without the production flexibility to rearrange current production lines to produce the new product lines, the marketing effort is wasted. Again, the marketing department's effort is dependent on the other departments for support and implementation.

The marketers' internal challenge, therefore, is to ensure that their organisations produce only what they have identified as the customers' needs or wants and are flexible enough to react to perceived changes in customer requirements and other external environmental elements. The functional convergence mentioned before is the ultimate goal, i.e. all departments of the organisation work rationally towards meeting the ultimate goal of customer satisfaction. However, this is not always so easy to achieve. With the marketing department's specialist knowledge gained through its market research of the external environment, and with its philosophical conviction of the needs of marketers to take precedence within the organisation, departmental tension can replace functional convergence. Therefore the relationships that marketing has with the other departments are crucial not only to customer satisfaction but also to the cultural and structural survival of the organisation.

■ Marketing and operations management

As mentioned previously, the R&D stage is the point at which marketing clearly requires a close and supportive working relationship with operations management, to decide on product or service design and to agree the resource inputs needed. Once resource levels are agreed, operations management can decide costs and marketing the sales price, thus working towards deciding together how profits can be made within cost and price constraints. Operations management obviously also requires an input into the design of new products and services, to indicate from a practical point of view what can be manufactured technologically and physically.

■ Marketing and finance

The link between finance and marketing is crucial but is also dependent on the link between marketing and operations management. The finance department is responsible for ensuring that the organisation has enough money to perform all the organisation's activities. Operations management has the responsibility of manufacturing within cost constraints. Marketing must bring the products to market and sell enough of them at a sustainable price to make profits for the organisation.

■ Marketing and human resource management

If new products and services are being introduced, marketing must keep the human resource management (HRM) department fully informed of developments. The message concerning new products or services must be communicated, as the HRM department needs to know the type of skills and experience that current or new workers will have to possess to be able to deliver the new products or services. HRM will develop its own strategies in order to plan for recruitment and selection of any new staff or to formulate training programmes for existing staff who lack the necessary skills or expertise.

☑ Check your understanding

Do you understand the term 'functional convergence'?

Check your understanding by explaining how functional convergence can occur in organisations. Use examples where appropriate.

Marketing tools

So far this chapter has examined the relationships that the marketing department has with the external and internal environments of the organisation. We have looked at marketing in terms of its responsibility for monitoring changes in customer needs or wants. The marketing department must convince senior management and the other departments that the organisation should be producing new products or delivering new services to meet these perceived changes. Therefore the marketing department uses an array of tools to monitor elements of the external environment.

Marketing is not only about purely reacting to perceived changes in the external environment. It also has a responsibility to aim to be proactive in relation to the external environment. Thus marketing may aim not only to provide the products or services the customers know they want but also to attempt to influence customer choice by anticipating what customers are likely to need or want in the future and providing it ahead of competitors. This proactive stance is to a large degree reliant on assumptions about customers and the organisation. Marketing tools can thus be used both to react to and to influence the marketplace. Some of these basic tools are presented and applied here to a variety of products and services.

The marketing mix

Borden[5] developed the idea of a **marketing mix** to describe the marketing elements that could affect the way a product performed in the marketplace. McCarthy[6] summarised the marketing mix as the four Ps of marketing (*see* Figure 4.3). Today the marketing mix or 4Ps is one of the traditional tools used to manipulate the organisation's relationship with the external environment. The 4Ps are product, price, promotion and place. That is to say, there are four basic ways in which organisations can affect the relationship they have with their customers to increase sales and profitability.

■ Product

Once the initial investment in research and development has been paid back and resulted in a successfully launched product, it is in the manufacturer's financial interest to recoup as much profit on that investment as possible. Thus the manufacturer will want to make as much of the product for as long as possible with little new investment or alteration in order to keep sales high and reap profits. If sales do begin to decline after a certain time, it is not necessarily inevitable that a brand new product needs to be found straight away. In order to keep sales of the existing product buoyant, it is possible to manipulate certain aspects of that product at little cost in order to offer a newer, fresher and updated product. The clear aim is to continue to attract new customers and/or tempt existing customers to remain loyal and not be attracted by a competitor's product.

Product aspects that may be manipulated include style, performance, quality, branding, packaging and after-sales service. Examples of such product manipulation abound in the washing powder industry. Famous and familiar brands are often relaunched as 'new', 'improved' or as version two or three. While alterations to the basic washing powder have undoubtedly been made in order that trade description legislation is not infringed by the use of these words, the basic product is still washing powder, with additional features. Altering the

**Figure 4.3
The marketing mix**

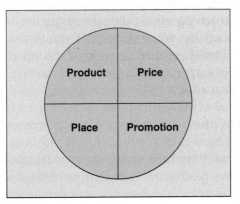

product slightly offers the manufacturer the opportunity to make a statement to the marketplace about continual innovation, improvement and customer orientation. Hence this type of manipulation of the product is a reasonably simple yet effective marketing tool. Product manipulation requires co-operation between the marketing and operations management departments.

■ Price

The second of the four Ps is price, and there are various ways in which organisations can use the price they charge to influence sales. The music industry has used pricing strategies aggressively to influence the positioning of new releases in the pop charts. Most singles on release are now sold at a discount price in the first few weeks to entice customers to purchase them. The national music charts are compiled out of sales figures at monitored outlets, and these subsidised sales cause new releases to have a high entry position in the pop charts in the first week, which encourages more radio play. This produces continued sales as radio listeners go out to buy the music they have heard.

Price can be used not only when introducing new products but also when products are perceived to be near the end of their natural life (*see* the discussion of **product life cycle** in the next section). Special offers and finance deals can be used to affect customers' buying habits. The mass television advertising by DFS/Northern Upholstery of its dining-room and lounge furniture is an excellent example of this. The frequent, prime-time advertisements offer cheaper prices, 'buy now, pay later' deals, 0 per cent finance on hire purchase and long payment terms of 4–5 years. All these are offered in special sales promotions that 'must end Sunday 5pm' and yet seem very similar from week to week. Price manipulation depends on co-operation between the marketing and finance departments.

■ Promotion

As well as manipulating price to influence customers, a product can be advertised and promoted with the aim of encouraging sales. Decisions have to be made concerning the advertising media to be used: press, magazines, television, radio or internet. Alongside the advertising decisions, the promotional activity for a product has to be decided. A combination of advertising and promotional activities is required to create and support a successful product. The combination of activities needs to create an awareness and interest in the product and acceptance of it by the marketplace.

The promotional activities that can be used are varied. In supermarkets with loyalty cards, the offer of extra bonus points on certain products or goods entices customers to switch loyalty from one brand to another or to buy products not normally on their shopping list. Magazines are frequently used to offer free samples of cosmetics, cassette recordings or even books to their readership, in the hope of capturing new and potentially loyal customers. The launch of new products can be heralded by the delivery to target households of free samples, discount vouchers or promotional literature. The sponsorship of television programmes is a relatively new activity in the UK following deregulation of broadcast advertising, and is an effective promotional method. Thus Cadbury, 'the nation's favourite' chocolate manufacturer, sponsors *Coronation Street*, one of the leading soap operas, and the holiday company Going Places sponsored *Blind Date*, where winning contestants are sent off on holiday dates around the world. Neither of these television programmes explicitly advertises the companies' products, but implicitly links their products with the programme in the viewers' minds.

The importance of an organisation's advertising and promotion activities is clear if a product is a leading brand and the organisation seeks to maintain that position. The importance of good advertising and promotion is heightened if a competing brand advertises heavily and is easily substituted (*see* Chapter 10). Also the advertising and promotion surrounding a product will remind consumers making frequent repeat purchases to buy the same brand of product as before, which is crucial if **customer loyalty** to a brand is low. A product's added value or low cost, which will be important to particular groups of customers as explained in Chapter 10, can be emphasised by the use of advertising and promotion.

■ Place

The fourth element of the traditional marketing mix is the location of the interface between customer or consumer and product or service. This links with the issue of distribution, and getting the right amount of product to the right place at the right time is essential. This is fundamental to each stage of the distribution process, whether from manufacturer to wholesaler, wholesaler to retailer, retailer to customer or manufacturer direct to the customer. This is particularly so for those organisations that are reacting to customer demand for more products that can be delivered direct to the home without the need to go out shopping, with for example mail-order or internet shopping.

The manipulation of the place element of the marketing mix can also take in shops themselves. For example, the simple positioning of sweets at a supermarket checkout constitutes the use of placement to attract customers or their children who might be tempted to buy that bar of chocolate for the journey home. Supermarkets also use place on a grander scale by frequently changing the position of everyday basket goods by locating them next to more unusual or aspirational goods that shoppers might not purchase on a regular basis. Placing products not normally associated with a particular location is also included. Thus being able to buy Häagen-Dazs ice cream at a Warner Brothers cinema links the two brands in the customer's mind. Similarly, many supermarkets have begun to offer a range of other goods and services, including petrol stations, pharmacies, dry cleaning and photo development, as part of their overall one-stop-shop package.

The extended marketing mix

The extended marketing mix or 5Ps (*see* Figure 4.4) is a development of the traditional marketing mix with the addition of a fifth element: people.

■ People

It is initially difficult to see how marketers could manipulate people in the same way as they could manipulate the other 4Ps, as the latter are internal elements within the direct control of the organisation, whereas people in terms of customers are not part of the organisation's internal environment. The people element inside an organisation is constituted by the employees. However, the consideration of people in the marketing mix reflects the importance to successful marketing of both the person who is the customer and the person doing the selling. Interpersonal skills play a large part in achieving a successful relationship between customer and organisation. Hence there is a crucial relationship between the marketing and human resource management departments in ensuring that appropriate staff are recruited to do the selling and marketing. In addition, recognising who customers are and what they want is an explicit part of the people element of the marketing mix.

**Figure 4.4
The extended
marketing mix**

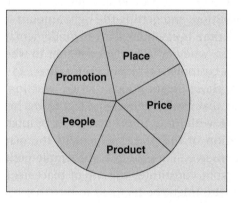

✓ Check your understanding

Do you understand the term 'marketing mix'?

Check your understanding by naming and illustrating the components of the marketing mix. Use examples where appropriate.

Product life cycle

The product life cycle is the 'natural' lifespan of a particular product or service and may last for a few short months or many years. For example, a *Harry Potter and the Philosopher's Stone* tee-shirt has a life cycle measurable in months or until the next big film hits the cinema screens and its associated merchandise the shops. In contrast, a product like a television set has a product life cycle of many years, due to continued **product development** in the field of television and broadcasting. These developments have included the very first black-and-white television sets that became available in the 1950s, through colour, stereo and digital television sets. The development of associated products such as satellite dishes, cable television and digital television has also helped to extend the product life cycle of television sets.

There are five stages in a product life cycle: introduction, growth, maturity, saturation and decline. Companies adopt different strategies for marketing products or services depending on the stage in the life cycle they identify that particular product as having reached. Various products and services will also need varying levels of financial and human resource investment according to the marketing strategy adopted.

■ Introduction

The introduction stage is self-evidently that stage when a new product or service is launched into the marketplace. The market research and product development have been completed and the product has been designed with its target market in mind. This has necessitated considerable investment on the part of the organisation with no attributable profit, since, until the product is sold, there is no income from it. Thus the sales and profit curves run together at the bottom of the profitability axis in Figure 4.5. It is clear that for new organisations this is the 'make or break' period, as the investment for new products or services is likely to have come from bank loans or other borrowings. For existing organisations the investment for research and development may come from profits earned by other products. This issue is examined under the **Boston Consulting Group matrix** later in this chapter. Research and development will have considered the product and price elements of the marketing mix for the new product or service.

A product in the introduction phase of the product life cycle will have relatively few buyers and those who do purchase the product will buy it to try it. Thus at the introduction stage, promotion of the product is crucial if it is to move on to the growth phase. The introduction of Dr Pepper's to the UK market was a case in point. The drink itself was a long-term successful soft drink in the US, as familiar as either Pepsi or Coca-Cola, but had never been sold in Britain. Therefore its introduction to the UK market relied on successful

**Figure 4.5
The product
life cycle**

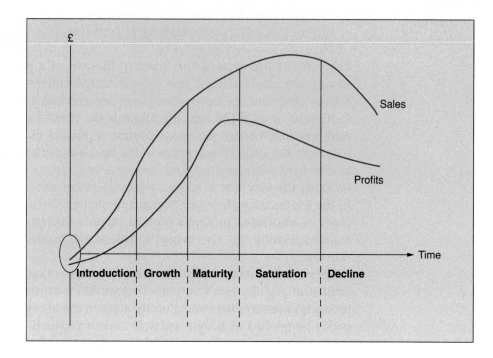

promotion, since the product, with a price comparable to other soft fizzy drinks, meant that product and price aspects of the marketing mix were to a large extent unalterable. In television advertisements, Dr Pepper's product was promoted as something that had arrived literally from another planet and was proven safe to a suspicious public by a risk taker wearing a silver suit in a sealed environment testing the drink.

■ Growth

If the research and development work has been done correctly, a newly launched product will sell well in the early period of its life cycle. Thus sales will rise quite dramatically. However, the profit curve remains relatively low due to the cost of the continued promotion needed to allow sales to grow. Nevertheless, profits are made and market share starts to be accumulated in the growth phase of the product life cycle. The marketing department will use a variety of promotional tools to achieve growth in sales, some of which will include manipulation of other elements of the marketing mix, such as place. For example, a new fragrance could be promoted through a number of locations: the distribution of free samples in fashion magazines; high-profile sales stands in up-market department stores; large advertisements on roadside billboards; as well as television and cinema advertisements. The unisex fragrance CK One achieved growth in sales through such a variety of promotional methods.

■ Maturity

The dramatic growth in sales of a product or service slows down when the maturity stage of the product life cycle is reached. Depending on the type of product and the type of market, the maturity stage may last a long or a short time. A product in the maturity stage still has limited growth, but rapid and significant progress such as that achieved in the growth phase of the product life cycle is unlikely. The maturity stage is where maximum profits are achieved and the outlay required to maintain sales is minimal compared with that in the growth stage – *see* Figure 4.5.

Advertising and promotion of a product in the maturity phase of the product life cycle are aimed at retaining existing customers and persuading others to switch from competitor products. The overall aim is to keep the product at the peak of the maturity stage of the product life cycle for as long as possible as this is when profits peak.

■ Saturation

The saturation stage of the product life cycle is reached when growth tails off and the market for a product is no longer growing. Nevertheless, sales volume may be kept buoyant and loyal customers retained by price competition and special offers, although this will mean reduced profits – *see* Figure 4.5. These are competitive options that are easy for rivals to replicate. An alternative would be for the marketing department to choose to implement an **extension strategy**. This is discussed briefly in the next section.

■ Decline

Following the saturation of the marketplace, products eventually lose sales volume through being replaced, in the customers' eyes, by new products introduced by the same organisation or by competitors. A product or service in decline may be withdrawn from the market if it is losing money. Alternatively, it may find a small, loyal, niche market that either breaks even or makes a limited profit for the organisation. An example here is the vinyl LP record. Most people today prefer their music to be on compact disc or mini disc, therefore most music produced today is in those formats. However, there exists a small group of consumers who still buy vinyl LP records, either vinyl buffs or DJs in clubs, so record companies continue to release a certain amount of material on vinyl. The decline of vinyl LPs is long and slow.

✓ Check your understanding

Do you understand the term 'product life cycle'?

Check your understanding by summarising the key attributes of product in the different stages of the product life cycle. Use examples where appropriate.

Extending the product life cycle

The initial research and development programme, the most costly part of the process, should be recouped by the organisation during the growth and maturity phases of the product life cycle. A product in the saturation phase will continue to generate profit, but profits will decline towards the end of the saturation phase. Therefore the majority of the profit that a product can expect to make in its life cycle will have been made by the end of the saturation phase – *see* Figure 4.6. Hence extension of the product life cycle should be considered before the product reaches the end of the saturation phase.

There are various methods for accomplishing this. Ansoff[7] summarises four different marketing strategies that organisations may follow and presents them in the Ansoff matrix. The first three strategies, **market penetration, market development** and **product development,** can all be used to extend a product's life cycle – *see* Figure 4.6. The fourth, **diversification,** involves changing to a significantly different product.

Figure 4.6
Product life cycle and extension strategies

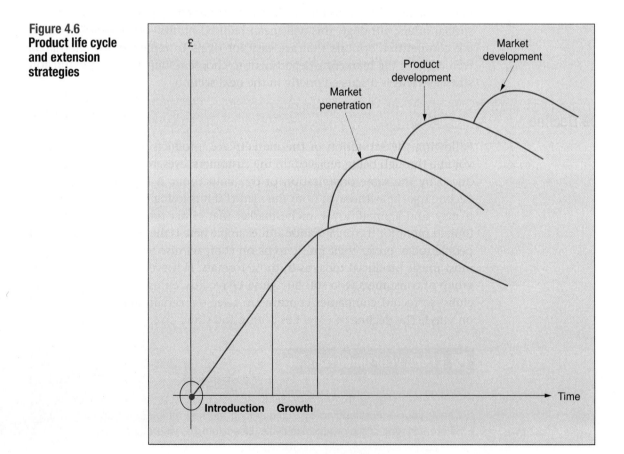

■ The customer growth matrix

In following Ansoff's marketing strategies, organisations are seeking to increase the number of sales and/or the number of customers. Jenkins[8] presents four different types of customer growth options that organisations may follow to achieve sales and customer growth – *see* Figure 4.7.

Customer loyalty

Customer loyalty is important and should be developed by organisations because it brings greater profitability.[9] Faithful customers will affect profit directly by purchasing products and services over an extended period of time, and indirectly by telling friends, neighbours and relatives about the benefits and satisfaction they derive from the company's products and services.

The supermarkets in the UK are examples of organisations which attempt to create customer loyalty via their use of so-called 'loyalty cards'. Loyalty to the service provided by the supermarket is created by offering money-off shopping when a certain number of 'loyalty' points have been collected by a customer. The development of loyalty to products involves manipulation of the marketing mix. Alterations may be made to the price at which products are being sold, or to promotional activities or distribution locations in order to try to increase sales to existing customers.

Customer extension

Customer extension is concerned with extending the range of products or services available for a customer to purchase from the organisation. Increasing sales in this way involves following strategies of product development and diversification.

Product development is likely to be the preferred choice of the organisation that is good at research and development and strong in the area of innovation. Other organisational features which will make product development the preferred choice for expanding sales include an organisation structured around product divisions and products with short product life cycles. Consumer electronics companies fit this profile very well. The original Sony Walkman, a

Figure 4.7
The customer growth matrix

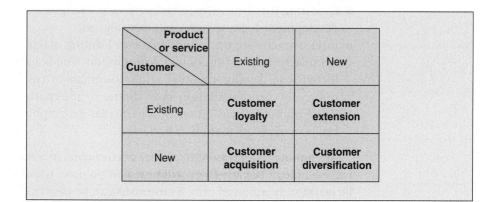

Source: Jenkins, M (1997), *The Customer Centred Strategy*, Prentice Hall. Reproduced with permission.

portable cassette player, was the result of product development by Sony and extended the range of entertainment products which customers traditionally purchased from Sony. In 2000 the launch of the DreamCast2 computer games console once again extended the range of Sony products.

Diversification is an alternative option for extending the organisation's range of products and services. Diversification is risky, as both organisational effort and capacity are stretched. There are two basic types of diversification: related and unrelated. Related diversification occurs when development is beyond current products and markets but still in the same broad industry. For example, if Sony were to diversify into producing other electronic goods for the home such as fridges, freezers and washing machines, this would be related diversification, extending the range of products available to include white goods but remaining in the broad industry of providing electrical consumer goods. In contrast, unrelated diversification for a company like Sony would be a move into running a rail franchise, which is completely unrelated to electrical consumer goods but still increases the range of products and services available to customers. Richard Branson's empire is a good example of an organisation which has expanded through unrelated diversification and currently offers customers a wide range of products and services including air travel, train travel, cola, cinemas, mobile phones, mega stores, financial services, holidays and cosmetics.

Customer acquisition

Customer acquisition is expanding the number of customers for existing products. This could involve expanding customer numbers in home markets, which will be easiest if home markets are growing in size. If home markets are mature, expansion into growing overseas markets may provide the best opportunity for increasing the number of customers. This was one of the reasons for expansion into China by Nescafé, which was seeking to increase the number of customers drinking and buying instant coffee – *see* the entry case study for this chapter.

Customer acquisition in overseas markets requires the organisation to engage in international business activities such as exporting or internationalising its operations.

- Exporting involves selling existing product ranges, which incur no further development costs, to new customers abroad.
- Internationalising operations involves locating activities overseas, such as manufacturing, distribution and promotion. The benefits of doing this can include overcoming import controls, lower labour costs and lower distribution costs. An organisation may choose to internationalise its operations if the number of customers in a particular geographic market is large and home markets are mature or in decline.

Attempting to increase the number of customers in a static or mature market will be difficult because there will be few or no new customers available – it can be realistically achieved only if customers can be persuaded to switch products or brands. This requires customer loyalty to a competing product or brand to be broken. The only other opportunity for attracting customers in a static or mature market will arise if the market leader becomes complacent and allows performance to slip. Increasing customers while operating in a declining market is possible only if competitors leave the marketplace early and their customers transfer their business to those remaining in the industry. However, it should be noted that seeking to increase customers while operating in a declining market is a short-term option with a limited lifespan.

Organisations may choose to follow a combination or hybrid of customer growth options. An organisation may expand its sales and customer base by following both customer loyalty and customer acquisition options.

Customer diversification

Expanding customer numbers by **customer diversification** is the riskiest of all of Jenkins' options. Customer diversification is achieved if sales are increased by selling a new product or service to new customers. The availability of a new technology or process is usually required if customer diversification is to occur.[10]

The best recent examples of customer diversification are those being achieved through e-commerce by many of the so-called dotcom companies offering products and services over the internet. It is the use of new technology (computers and the internet) which allows the provision of services to be offered in an entirely new way: for example, the provision of financial services by many of the high street banks via the internet, bookshop services by companies such as Amazon, and What Car? Online for researching and buying a new car over the internet. March 2000 saw the launch of the company lastminute.com, selling last-minute travel, trips and gifts via the internet. These dotcom companies are pursuing a risky strategy in hoping to sell to customers via the internet. The risk arises from the way such companies provide their service, which is largely untried and untested in the marketplace, so it is not known whether customer numbers will grow. The risk is also heightened as many of these dotcom companies have small sales revenues and have not yet made a profit.

☑ Check your understanding

Do you understand the term 'the customer growth matrix'?

Check your understanding by summarising the attributes of each customer growth option. Use examples where appropriate.

The Boston Consulting Group matrix

Bruce Henderson[11] of the Boston Consulting Group developed seminal work on categorising products in a useful way that then enables the marketing department to decide appropriate strategies for products in different stages of the life cycle. The categories are based on the rate of market growth identified

**Figure 4.8
The Boston
Consulting Group
matrix**

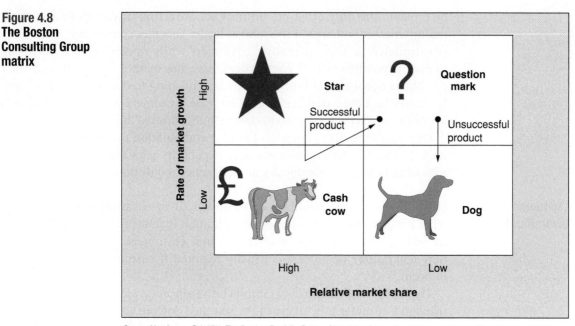

Source: Henderson, B (1970) *The Product Portfolio*, Boston Consulting Group. Used with permission of The Boston Consulting Group.

compared with the volume of market share the product has achieved in the marketplace – *see* Figure 4.8. It should be noted that large market share alone will not generate low costs and high margins. The relative comparison of costs and margins to those of competitors is also important (*see* Chapter 10).

■ Question marks

The question mark is a product located in the introduction stage of its product life cycle that is likely to achieve high market growth but currently holds low market share. If a question mark is to become a star, then high expenditure will be required to promote the product or service such that higher market share is achieved. The funding of a question mark will come from other successful products in the organisation's product range – *see* cash cows below. A product that is a question mark is not necessarily certain to be successful in the future.

■ Stars

The successful question mark will gain market share and become a star. The star product is located in the growth stage of its product life cycle. The market at this stage may still be small in terms of overall sales or size. However, the star has a sizeable portion of overall market share. It is likely that star products will be successful, based on predicted growth in sales and continued domination of the growing market. The successful star product will be on its way to being a cash cow of the future.

■ Cash cows

The cash cow will be in the maturity or saturation stage of its product life cycle. The rate of market growth will be low, but the volume of market share will be high, as shown in Figure 4.8. Hence sales of the product are at maximum levels, as are profits. Therefore the cash cow is the bread-and-butter product of the organisation, and its profits provide the finance for research and new product development. The organisation is thus reliant on cash cows and needs to maintain them in its product portfolio.

■ Dogs

Dogs are products that are definitely in the decline stage of the product life cycle and may have previously been successful cash cows. Dogs have no growth in terms of sales and do not have significant market share. Therefore the organisation has to decide what to do with its dogs. If the dog product is profitable and has a small but loyal band of consumers still willing to continue purchasing it, then keeping it in the product portfolio is a viable option. Alternatively, the organisation may decide to kill off the dog. This would be the more viable option if the dog product had become loss making or if the organisation had a substitute product that was a star.

✓ Check your understanding

Do you understand the term 'BCG'?

Check your understanding by summarising the key attributes of products in the different quadrants of the BCG. Use examples where appropriate.

■ Successful and unsuccessful products

A successful product will move around the Boston Consulting Group matrix in the following order: question mark, star, cash cow, dog. Hence a successful product will at times cost the organisation money and at other times make it money. A product that ceases to be successful may return to the right-hand side of the matrix, moving from being a star or cash cow to being a dog. A product that is never successful will stay on the right-hand side of the matrix (low cash generation) and go from being a question mark directly to being a dog and will never make significant profits for the organisation.

Summary

This chapter examined the concept of the marketing-oriented firm, the marketing activities that organisations carry out today, and some of the best-known marketing tools. The following summary covers all aspects of this chapter.

1 The marketing department of an organisation is that which is best placed to interact with the external environment. The marketing department has to understand and anticipate the products and services its customers require at the present time and in the future.

2 The marketing concept has developed over time. Initially there was the production era, when customers were easily pleased with whatever goods companies supplied. This was followed by the sales era, in which companies advertised products with the aim of attracting customers to purchase their products rather than those of a competitior. The sales era has been followed by the marketing era, which developed in the West in the period after the end of the Second World War and continues to develop today.

3 The marketing era or marketing concept acknowledges customer needs and wants, which will be identified by an organisation's market research activities. A need is defined as being something that cannot be done without; a want is something to which a customer aspires.

4 The marketing department in an organisation should ensure that it addresses the following three basic points:

(a) What do customers need or want?
(b) How can the organisation meet these needs or wants?
(c) How does the organisation make money doing so?

5 The marketing department is required to make three basic assumptions concerning its competitive arena. First, customers have disposable income to spend on goods and services. Second, customers have an element of choice when deciding how and where to spend their money. Finally, the marketing department needs to acknowledge that it is its job to persuade the customer to spend that disposable income on the goods and services offered by its company or organisation.

6 There are a number of different activities which the marketing department may undertake, which range from market research through to after-sales service. The marketing activities also include product planning, sales, advertising, promotion and distribution.

7 The organisation should be flexible enough to alter its products and processes to meet newly identified customer needs and wants. This involves the organisation directing resources away from the current focus towards meeting those new needs and wants. This requires functional convergence, i.e. all departments of the organisation working rationally towards meeting the ultimate goal of customer satisfaction.

8 The marketing mix or 4Ps is one of the traditional tools used to manipulate the organisation's relationship with the external environment. Aspects of product, price, promotion and place can all be altered to encourage customers to purchase a particular product.

9 The product life cycle has five stages: introduction, growth, maturity, saturation and decline. Introduction is where sales and profits are low and is the 'make or break' period for the product. In the growth phase sales will increase rapidly, market share starts to be accumulated and profits made. In the maturity phase sales growth still occurs but at a slower rate than in the growth phase and profits reach a peak. In the saturation phase the rate of sales growth starts to slow but sales volume remains buoyant. However, profits will decline as price competition and special offers abound. The decline phase is where a product loses sales volume, profits decline and losses may occur.

10 The customer growth matrix shows four different options that companies can follow to achieve sales and customer growth: establishing customer loyalty; customer extension by extending the range of products and services available to customers; customer acquisition, which involves expanding customer numbers for existing products; and customer diversification, which is selling new products or services to new customers.

11 The Boston Consulting Group matrix groups products based on the rate of market growth and volume of market share. The question mark is a product located in the introduction stage of its life cycle. In turn a successful question mark will gain market share and become a star, which is located in the growth stage of the product life cycle, while continued growth will see a star product become a cash cow. A cash cow product will be in the maturity or saturation stage of the life cycle. Finally, a dog is a product in the decline phase of the product life cycle and may be profitable due to a small band of loyal customers or can be a loss-making product which should be withdrawn from the marketplace.

Learning outcomes for case studies

While reading this chapter and engaging in the activities, you should have learned how to apply theory and models, analyse situations, and evaluate the application and analysis you undertake. The learning outcomes specified below outline the type of application, analysis and evaluation of which you should be capable in relation to organisations. The case studies and the questions which follow provide an opportunity for you to test how well you have achieved the learning outcomes for the ethical issues and exit case studies for this chapter.

Application	Check you have achieved this by	
1 Devise a marketing mix for a specified product or service	applying the marketing mix to a product or service of your choice	answering exit case study question 1
2 Place a range of products in the correct sections of the product life cycle curve	applying the product life cycle curve to a selection of products or sevices with which you are familiar.	answering exit case study question 2
3 Identify a range of products and categorise them according to their position on a BCG	applying the BCG to the products and services of an organisation that you know	answering exit case study question 2
Analysis	**Check you have achieved this by**	
1 Analyse the marketing mix of a product of your choice	comparing the marketing mix of your chosen product with one that is similar	answering exit case study question 1
2 Use the product life cycle to anticipate the future of a product or service of your choice	contrasting current performance with predicted future performance	answering exit case study question 3
3 Use Ansoff's strategies to show how the product life cycle for a product of your choice can be extended	generating possible future marketplace behaviour and position for your chosen product on the plc	answering exit case study question 3
4 Use the Jenkins customer growth matrix to show how a company may achieve growth in both sales and customers	showing how the growth options could be applied to an organisation of your choice	answering exit case study question 3
Evaluation	**Check you have achieved this by**	
1 Evaluate the accuracy and usefulness of a variety of marketing tools in anticipating a product's future behaviour in the marketplace	critically judging the relevance of marketing tools in organisations today	answering exit case study question 4
		answering ethical case study question 1
2 Evaluate the approaches different stakeholders may take to influence marketing strategies for a particular product or service	assessing the power and interests of different stakeholders in the marketing of a product or service	answering ethical case study questions 2 & 3

ETHICAL ISSUES CASE STUDY 4.2 FT

Tobacco Advertising

By Danny Rogers

The leaked internal memo reads: 'We can use the SMS (text messaging) service to bring consumers to specific outlets in which we will run our promotions.'

Nothing unusual in that, you may think. Text messaging is now a popular way of marketing to today's teenagers, obsessed as they are with their mobile phones. But this is not from a youth marketing agency in Clerkenwell.

It was written by a suited and booted executive at British American Tobacco, the multi-national cigarette giant of which Conservative party leadership candidate Ken Clarke is deputy chairman. The memo, which was leaked to anti-smoking group ASH, reveals a new clandestine marketing strategy aimed at young people and themed around bars and nightclubs.

The memo reveals that BAT, maker of the Lucky Strike and State Express 555 brands, is behind a new website called CityGobo.com.

It looks like an independent guide to nightlife in European cities and has no reference to BAT or tobacco. But a quick search confirms that its domain name was registered in July by CG Ventures, based at Globe House, BAT's headquarters.

Earlier in the year BAT registered a smaller-scale site called CityGorilla in Poland, but that name now seems to have been ditched.

The project has been codenamed HORECA, which is tobacco industry terminology for distributing cigarettes through hotels, restaurants and bars. BAT's idea is that it can use the ostensibly 'cool' site to attract young people to certain venues where it sells its cigarettes.

'Dance, drink, eat, chill out,' says the home page. 'Invite your friends, organise a party.'

At the moment the portal brings together guides on cities in Belgium and Poland, which offer information in English and native languages, but more country guides are expected to be added soon.

BAT says: 'This is not a tobacco marketing tool. Our aim is to create the best web-based nightlife guide to strengthen our relationships with the venues.'

But anti-smoking activists are concerned about what they consider to be the deceptive nature of the site.

The leaked memo continues: 'One perceived risk for the HORECA portal is the possible association with BAT and thus tobacco. A key success factor is developing a customer perception that the site is trendy and happening.'

Experts on tobacco marketing believe young people visiting the bars or nightclubs will be hit with heavy promotions for BAT's coolest brand, Lucky Strike.

'It is interesting that the first cities featured are in Belgium and Poland,' says Look Joossens, senior consultant to the European Union on anti-cancer initiatives.

'These are countries where a tobacco advertising ban is in place, but opportunities for point-of-sale promotion still exist. Trendy bars are the only place you can really target this audience.'

Joossens says he has encountered other bars in Europe where the logos of the bars are redesigned to resemble the Lucky Strike brand and where well-dressed girls approach punters with Lucky Strike-sponsored games and offers.

BAT claims that other brands will be on sale at the bars promoted on CityGobo.com but admits that it 'may run promotions'.

According to the small print on the website, the company intends to mail registered site users with special offers and other forms of marketing communication.

As well as the insidious nature of this 'invisible' marketing, anti-smoking groups are concerned that it is simply another way of making cigarettes appeal to kids.

BAT insists that cigarettes are sold legally in these establishments and points out that the 'average' age of a nightclubber is 18. However, observers argue that cigarette companies have a long track record of targeting a much younger audience than that.

'Promotions through bars and clubs makes smoking cool, and if you make something cool for an 18-year-old it becomes cool for younger kids as well,' says John Connolly, ASH's marketing specialist.

'Internal documents uncovered under the 1999 Master Settlement Agreement (a disclosure agreement between the US government and the domestic tobacco industry) show that tobacco companies, including BAT's US subsidiary Brown & Williamson, have long been using this technique to attract very young smokers,' he argues.

Sean Pillot de Chenecy, a brand development consultant who has spent 10 years working with governments on anti-smoking campaigns, agrees:

'All tobacco companies need young consumers to survive. They describe them as "replacement smokers" when the older smokers die. Lots of brands are heavily targeting teens.'

'Studies in the US have shown that 86 per cent of under-18 smokers smoke the most heavily advertised brands, but that these are not the most popular brands among adult smokers. Kids are vulnerable to such promotion and once they start smoking, they tend to be very brand loyal.'

Chenecy adds that the bar and cafe culture of central and eastern Europe tends to give tobacco companies access to a younger audience than in western Europe.

▶

Martin Brooks, managing director of Agency Republic, an Omnicom-owned digital marketing agency, says: 'A lot of youth brands are using this type of marketing technique which combines the internet, mobiles and venues.'

'It tries to borrow underworld community information to appear credible. On average young consumers receive and send around 200 text messages per week. Smirnoff does something similar but alcohol companies can be more upfront about it.'

'CityGobo.com looks like it was designed by older executives who aren't exactly on the money, but younger kids may find the site quite cool. Tobacco companies realize that their marketing dollar is much better spent on younger kids, who if they smoke a brand for the first 18 months, will tend to stick with it,' says Brooks.

David Hinchcliffe, chairman of the House of Commons Health Committee, urges the government to crack down on this type of marketing practice.

'This is an excellent example of how tobacco companies will seek to evade any advertising legislation,' he says. 'The government needs to anticipate their antics and set up a Tobacco Regulatory Authority which will monitor their marketing strategies.'

BAT says the CityGobo.com project is still in a 'pilot' stage.

The company adds: 'It's too early to say whether we will roll it out to the UK and other countries worldwide. We will evaluate that in the near future.'

www.CityGobo.com

Source: Financial Times, 1 September 2001. Reprinted with permission.

Questions for ethical issues case study 4.2

1 In your opinion is text messaging an acceptable tool for BAT to use to aid the promotion of cigarettes?

2 Do you agree with the BAT quote or the ASH quote from the case study? Explain and justify your answer.

   BAT quote
   'BAT insist that cigarettes are sold legally in these establishments and points out that the "average" age of a nightclubber is 18.'

   ASH quote
   'Promotions through bars and clubs makes smoking cool, and if you make something cool for an 18-year-old it becomes cool for younger kids as well,' says John Connolly, ASH's marketing specialist.

3 Is it acceptable for the UK government to establish a Tobacco Regulatory Authority to monitor the marketing strategies of tobacco companies like BAT, or would such a move be unnecessary interference in big business? Would the establishment of a Tobacco Regulatory Authority strengthen or weaken the position of the anti-smoking group ASH?

 For more case studies please visit www.booksites.net/capon

Coca-Cola in secret plans for vanilla-flavoured drink

By Richard Tomkins

Coca-Cola, the US soft drinks company, is secretly working on plans to launch a vanilla-flavoured version of its flagship Coke drink.

If the project goes ahead, the new drink – probably named Vanilla Coke – will be the biggest launch of a new Coca-Cola product since the disastrous introduction of New Coke 16 years ago.

Coca-Cola would not confirm or deny it was considering the launch, saying only that 'we've always got a number of things in development'. But the latest edition of Beverage Digest, a respected industry newsletter, will reach subscribers this week quoting one US bottler as saying: 'It's over 90 per cent (certain), and it's a great idea.'

John Sicher, Beverage Digest's publisher, said numerous people in the Coca-Cola system had led him to believe there was 'a strong chance' the company would launch a vanilla-flavoured cola in the US 'within the next few months'.

He said the plan was 'well beyond the idea stage' and some people had seen working versions of the label. Bottlers he had spoken to were 'very enthusiastic' about the project.

Coke is the world's most valuable brand and the Coca-Cola company has traditionally been extremely cautious about extending it to other drinks or products for fear of diluting it.

Although the company introduced a lemon-flavoured version of its Diet Coke last year, the only flavoured version of standard Coke it has ever made is Cherry Coke, launched in March 1985.

However, cola drinks are losing market share to other soft drinks in the US, putting manufacturers under pressure to reinvigorate sales with new products. Last year, according to Beverage Digest, Coke's volume declined 2 per cent in the US in spite of a big increase in advertising.

PepsiCo, maker of Pepsi-Cola, is also feeling the pressure. Pepsi's volume fell 2.8 per cent in the US last year, and the company last summer introduced Pepsi Twist, a lemon-flavoured variant of its flagship drink.

Vanilla Coke already has a popular following in the US. People make it by adding a shot of vanilla syrup – the sort used for flavouring coffee and pouring over desserts – to a glass of ordinary Coke.

It is widely sold in cafes, diners and restaurants, along with other locally flavoured variations of standard Coke such as raspberry, lemon and chocolate.

Coca-Cola's last big launch of a cola product was in April 1985, when the company changed the 99-year-old formula of traditional Coca-Cola and replaced the drink with New Coke. The move caused a national outcry in the US, where it was seen as akin to replacing the Stars and Stripes with a new, improved version.

Coca-Cola was eventually forced to bring back the old formula but ended up with an increased market share.

Douglas Daft, who became Coca-Cola's chairman and chief executive two years ago, is under intense pressure to revitalise the company's flagging growth by improving marketing and introducing new products. www.ft.com/consumer.

Source: *Financial Times*, 1 April 2002. Reprinted with permission.

Questions for exit case study 4.3

1 Devise a marketing mix for traditional Coca-Cola. How does the marketing mix for Vanilla Coke differ from that for traditional Coca-Cola?

2 Identify at least five 'Coca-Cola' products, e.g. Diet Coke, and place them on a product life cycle curve. State whether the 'Coca-Cola' products you have identified are question marks, stars, cash cows or dogs.

3 Consider the extension of the product life cycle and the Jenkins customer growth matrix. Identify and discuss how Coca-Cola may have applied these models to help ensure the continued success of 'Coca-Cola' products in the marketplace.

4 Evaluate the usefulness of marketing models in relation to a product like Coca-Cola.

Short-answer questions

1 Define the term 'production era'.

2 Define the term 'sales era'.

3 List three basic assumptions underpinning the marketing concept.

4 State the 4Ps of marketing.

5 Name the fifth P of marketing.

6 In which stage of the product life cycle does a product make most money?

7 In which stage of the product life cycle does a product sell most?

8 In which stage of the product life cycle does a product make virtually no profit and why?

9 Name three strategies that are used to extend the life cycle of a product.

10 In which stage of the product life cycle is a 'star' product located?

11 Name Jenkins' four different types of customer growth options.

12 Product development and diversification are methods for achieving which of Jenkins' customer growth options?

13 List the characteristics of a cash cow product.

14 In what circumstances should a company decide to keep a dog product?

15 Explain the path of an unsuccessful product around the Boston Consulting Group matrix.

Learning outcomes for assignment questions

While reading this chapter and engaging in the activities, you should have learned how to apply theory and models, analyse situations, and evaluate the application and analysis you undertake. The learning outcomes specified below outline what you should be able to do and the assignment questions provide an opportunity for you to test how well you have achieved the learning outcomes for this chapter.

Application	Check you have achieved this by	
1 Devise a marketing mix for a specified product or service	applying the marketing mix to a product or service of your choice	answering assignment questions 1, 2 & 4
2 Place a range of products in the correct sections of the product life cycle curve	applying the product life cycle curve to a selection of product or sevices with which you are familiar	answering assignment questions 1, 2 & 3
3 Identify a range of products and categorise them according to their position on a BCG	applying the BCG to the products and services of an organisation that you know	answering assignment questions 1, 2 & 3
Analysis	Check you have achieved this by	
1 Analyse the marketing mix of a product of your choice	comparing the marketing mix of your chosen product with one that is similar	answering assignment questions 1 & 2
2 Use the product life cycle to anticipate the future of a product or service of your choice	contrasting current performance with predicted future performance	answering assignment questions 1 & 2
3 Use Ansoff's strategies to show how the product life cycle for a product of your choice can be extended	generating possible future marketplace behaviour and position for your chosen product on the plc	answering assignment questions 1 & 2
4 Use the Jenkins customer growth matrix to show how a company may achieve growth in both sales and customers	show how the growth options could be applied to a organisation of your choice	answering assignment questions 1 & 2
Evaluation	Check you have achieved this by	
1 Evaluate the accuracy and usefulness of a variety of marketing tools in anticipating a product's future behaviour in the marketplace	critically judging the relevance of marketing tools in organisations today	answering assignment questions 3 & 4

147

Assignment questions

1 Consider your own organisation (employing organisation or university/college). Using the marketing tools discussed in this chapter, analyse the marketing that it undertakes. Use the findings of your analysis to recommend what the organisation should currently be doing in terms of market penetration, product development, market development and diversification. Present your findings in a 2000-word report.

2 You are setting up a small travel company that specialises in outdoor pursuits holidays in the UK. Write a 2000-word report outlining both the marketing and development plans for the venture.

3 Compare and contrast the product life cycle and Boston Consulting Group matrix as marketing tools. Comment on their relevance to marketing departments in the twenty-first century.

4 The 4Ps of marketing were discussed in 1964 by N H Borden in his paper 'The concept of the marketing mix', published in the June issue of the *Journal of Advertising Research*. Critically evaluate its usefulness to today's marketing practitioner.

Weblinks available online at www.booksites.net/capon

1 This site is a source of advertising and promotion resources.
http://adres.internet.com/

2 This site is a US site for marketing and e-business strategists.
http://www.netb2b.com/

3 This site is about starting marketing and promotion on the internet.
http://www.marketingtips.com/newsletter/issue11/page1.html

4 This site looks at how different types of businesses make money via the net.
http://www.marketingtips.com/newsletter/issue10/page1.html

5 This site is about how the market research company Gallup does its work.
http://www.gallup.com/

6 This page contains links to organisations which regulate and inform about marketing activities in different countries.
http://www.business.vu.edu.au/bho2250/regulation.htm

Further reading

Aaker, D A (1997) 'Should you take your brand to where the action is?', *Harvard Business Review*, September/October.

Abell, D F and Hammond, J S (1979) 'Portfolio analysis', an excerpt from *Strategic Marketing Planning*, Harlow: Prentice Hall, reprinted in Quinn, J B, Mintzberg, H and James, R M (1996) *The Strategy Process*, 3rd edn, Hemel Hempstead: Prentice Hall.

Blois, K J (1989) 'Marketing in five "simple" questions!', *Journal of Marketing Management*, 5 (2).

Burke, R R (1996) 'Virtual shopping breakthrough in marketing research', *Harvard Business Review*, March/April.

Christopher M and McDonald, M (1995) *Marketing: an Introductory Text*, Basingstoke: Macmillan.

Crush, P (2001) 'How small businesses can win the sponsoring game', *Management Today*, May.

Doyle, P (1976) 'The realities of the product life-cycle', *Quarterly Review of Marketing*, Summer.

Fisher, M L (1997) 'What is the right supply chain for your product?', *Harvard Business Review*, March/April.

Gwyther, M (1999) 'The big box office bet', *Management Today*, March.

Hofer, C and Schendel, D (1978) 'Portfolio analysis', adapted from *Strategy Formulation: Analytical Concepts*, West, reprinted in de Wit, B and Meyer, R (1994) *Strategy Process, Content, Context*, St Paul, MN: West.

Hoffman, D L and Novak, T P (2000) 'How to acquire customers on the web', *Harvard Business Review*, May/June.

Iansiti, M (1997) 'Developing product on Internet time', *Harvard Business Review*, September/October.

Keith, R J (1960) 'The marketing revolution', *Journal of Marketing*, January.

Kenny, D and Marshall, J F (2000) 'Contextual marketing: the real business of the internet', *Harvard Business Review*, November/December.

Kotler, P and Levey, S J (1969) 'Broadening the concept of marketing', *Journal of Marketing*, January.

Kotler, P, Armstrong, G, Saunders, J and Wong, V (2001) *Principles of Marketing: European Edition*, 3rd edn, Harlow: Financial Times Prentice Hall.

Lambert, R (2002) 'Taking the pink 'un across the pond', *Management Today*, August.

Levitt, T (1960) 'Marketing myopia', *Harvard Business Review*, July/August.

Levitt, T (1975) 'Marketing myopia 1975: retrospective commentary', *Harvard Business Review*, September/October.

Mitchell, A (1998) 'The dawn of a cultural revolution', *Management Today*, March.

Rigby, R (1998) 'Tutti-frutti capitalists', *Management Today*, February.

Surowiecki, J (1998) 'The billion dollar blade', *Management Today*, August.

Vishwanath, V and Mark, J (1997) 'Your brand's best strategy', *Harvard Business Review*, May/June.

References

1 Drucker, P (1954) *The Practice of Management*, New York: Harper & Row.

2 Kotler, P, Armstrong, G, Saunders, J and Wong, V (1996) *Principles of Marketing*, Hemel Hempstead: Prentice Hall.

3 Lancaster, G and Massingham, L (1988) *Essentials of Marketing*, Maidenhead: McGraw-Hill.

4 Maslow, A H (1943) 'A theory of human motivation', *Psychological Review*, 50.

5 Borden, N H (1964) 'The concept of the marketing mix', *Journal of Advertising Research*, June, reprinted in (1998) *Management Classics*, 6th edn, Harlow: Allyn & Bacon.

6 McCarthy, E J (1981) *Basic Marketing: A Managerial Approach*, Burr Ridge, Il: Irwin.

7 Ansoff, I (1987) *Corporate Strategy*, London: Penguin Business.

8 Jenkins, M (1997) *The Customer Centred Strategy*, Harlow: Prentice Hall.

9 Ibid.

10 Ibid.

11 Henderson, B (1970) *The Product Portfolio*, Boston: Boston Consulting Group.

5

Operations management

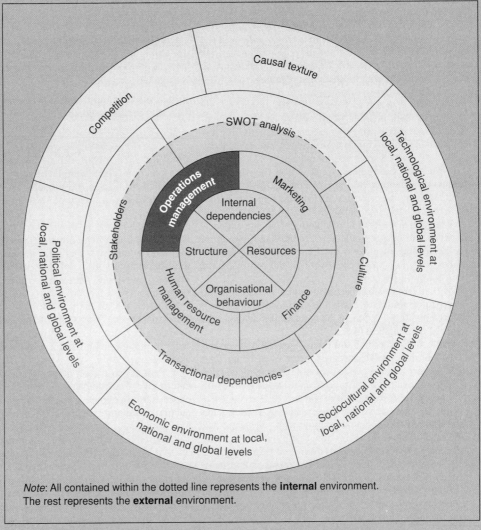

Note: All contained within the dotted line represents the **internal** environment. The rest represents the **external** environment.

Figure 5.1 Organisational context model

Lessons in improvement

By John Griffiths

Perkins Engines, the UK-based diesel engine maker sold for $1.3bn recently by Lucas Varity Corporation to Caterpillar of the US, invited in a few outsiders just before Christmas to help Perkins tear itself apart.

Large mobile cranes, forklift trucks and anything else that might be needed were placed to hand. Then the management stood back – well, almost – and let them get on with it.

The outsiders came from a diversity of companies; some to which it is a supplier of engines; others in the financial services and accountancy fields. They came from a variety of working backgrounds, with few having close connections with process engineering.

Yet just four days after they had first started walking purposefully towards key areas of Perkins' production lines, to embark on what was formally named a 'Shop-floor Kaizen Breakthrough', the transformations they had achieved in terms of improved efficiency and productivity could be described accurately as radical.

In the four production areas which the outsiders, formed into teams with a mix of Perkins' own workers, tackled, few of the processes in place just four days earlier were immediately recognisable.

A large area devoted to machining of engine connecting rods had been completely reconstructed, including the reshuffling of process machinery weighing several tonnes. The floor space needed for all the processes had been cut by 72 per cent.

Work in progress had been reduced by 93 per cent. The labour force required to carry out the processes had been reduced by 40 per cent, and the number of machine tools required from eight to five.

The results, according to Perkins' general manger and divisional director, Brian Amey, were even better than the company has come to expect from the ongoing series of 'kaizen breakthrough' taskforces it has now sent into action in some 150 areas of the plant.

Until the most recent four-day exercise in 'kaizen' – the Japanese term for continuous improvement – the teams had consisted always of Perkins' own employees, but from different areas of the company from that being targeted. The 'breakthrough' idea is that the teams, comprising usually a dozen or so, bring a fresh and critical eye to long-entrenched, but not necessarily efficient, production processes in the space of a short, highly concentrated exercise lasting just a few days.

This time round, however – an occasion regarded by Perkins as a big first – was to be a public kaizen, opening the company's doors and its processes to wider critical scrutiny.

The productivity and cost-saving gains were made by all teams involved in the exercise, with empirical evidence of the improvements when the four teams of the public kaizen made formal presentations to Perkins management at the end of the exercise.

Another team of a dozen or so which examined the core build area of Perkins' four-litre engine range made sweeping changes.

Much process plant was shifted around, with parts for assembly made to fall more easily to hand by opening up both sides of the assembly line and reducing radically the number of movements required of operators. Result:

- A 41 per cent improvement in operator productivity;
- A 79.5 per cent reduction in inventory;
- Floor space reduced by 45 per cent;
- Cycle time reduced by 25 per cent.

Total distance travelled by employees between process functions for a complete cycle reduced from 350 metres to 50 metres. Previously, the team had found 'workers hopping around the production line like rabbits'.

The process meets no apparent resistance from the shop floor. To the contrary, most of the company's several thousand employees, many of whom have themselves now been involved in internal kaizen breakthrough, say they have found the exercises stimulating as well as surprising.

However, part of the ground rules set down by North Carolina-based TBM Consulting Group, which has overseen Perkins' kaizen activities, is that employees receive pledges of no redundancies arising from the exercises.

In Perkins' case such assurances have not been difficult to give. The company has embarked on a number of expansion programmes expected to result in engine production doubling to around 500 000 units a year by early next decade.

Some of the public kaizen solutions were relatively obvious and clearly had been in the back of managers' minds as needing improvement even before it began.

For most of the teams, indeed, the pre-exercise discussions with plant managers gave some clear pointers as to where some improvements might come. Nonetheless, Perkins managers are adamant that the teams were not merely following up ideas for improvement planted by managers themselves.

Much of the teams' attention was taken up with dismantling 'pipeline' processes – so restricted and sequential that they can only move at the speed of the slowest operator or piece of equipment – and putting in their place a system which could flow around obstructions.

In all operations like this, says Anand Sharmah, TBM's president and chief executive, the idea is 'to lower the water around the process to make any efficiencies visual and painful. If you let people continue to hide problems then you cannot manage those problems'.

Mr Amey, who joined Perkins in late 1995 from Nissan, where he had been deeply involved in ongoing improvements of production systems, knew very substantial production increases were in prospect for Perkins when he joined, and one of his first acts was to start kaizen activities.

Factory floor space started appearing as if from nowhere. 'It proved time and time again that we already had the space capability to double production,' recalls Mr Amey.

But can kaizen breakthroughs work for everyone?

Mr Sharmah agrees that this is not the case, but says that what he would regard as companies failing to get a serious grip on kaizen-type improvements represent no more than 5 per cent of the more than 100 US and more than 20 UK companies with which TBM has worked.

Kaizen, stresses Mr Sharmah, is surprisingly easy to make gains initially. 'But it is much more difficult to sustain.'

Source: *Financial Times*, 23 February 1998. Reprinted with permission.

Introduction

Operations management is the term applied to the activities at the core of any organisation's business and is concerned with the way in which the organisation actually puts into practice what it has set out to do. An organisation will undertake operations to make a product, provide a service or perform a combination of the two. Hence Glaxo manufactures pharmaceuticals; BT provides telecommunications services; and Laura Ashley produces and sells clothes. Accordingly, operations management is concerned with managing the way products are made and/or service delivered, which has a direct connection with how the organisation achieves its objectives. The principles of operations management can be applied to any organisation.

Organisations and operations management

On comparing and contrasting two very different organisations, it would appear that their operations have few similarities. The operations of Glaxo, for example, would seem very unlike the operations of a chip shop run by its self-employed owner. However, closer examination will reveal surprising similarities. Both organisations have to choose the best location, buy raw materials, forecast demand for their products, calculate the required **capacity**, arrange resources to meet demand, use the raw materials to make products, sell the products to customers, manage cashflows and human resources, and seek out reliable suppliers. Both Glaxo and the chip shop want to run an efficient operation, with high **productivity**.

153

**Figure 5.2
Manufacturing and
service sectors**

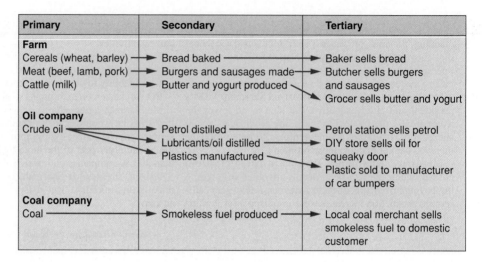

There are two basic ways of categorising organisations and the operations they undertake. The first is to consider organisations as belonging to different sectors: primary, secondary or tertiary – *see* Figure 5.2. **Primary-sector organisations** are concerned with producing raw materials and include oil extraction, coal mining, diamond mining and farming to produce food. **Secondary-sector organisations** manufacture and produce goods, often from raw materials produced by primary-sector organisations. **Tertiary-sector organisations** sell goods produced by primary and secondary organisations. The tertiary sector includes service-sector organisations such as banks and social services.

✓ Check your understanding

Do you understand the organisational context of operations management?

Check your understanding by explaining the role of the operations management department in an organisation.

An alternative way of viewing organisations is to consider whether the organisation produces goods, provides a service or delivers a mixture of both, and whether it is a private-sector organisation or not – *see* Figure 5.3 for more details. There are no public-sector/not-for-profit organisations that manufacture. If a public-sector or not-for-profit organisation is to provide a manufactured product, it is most likely that manufactured goods will be made by a subcontractor from the private sector. For example, local councils provide domestic and commercial council tax payers with wheelie bins which are not manufactured by the council but bought in bulk via a negotiated contract from a supplier in the private sector.

Figure 5.3
Manufacturing
and service
organisations

	Not-for-profit organisations	Public-sector organisations	Private-sector organisations
Manufacturing			• Pharmaceuticals (GlaxoSmithKline) • Cars (Vauxhall) • Food (Northern Foods)
Manufacturing and service	• Retailing (Oxfam shop/fair trade initiatives)	• Housing associations (build and let homes) • Provision of artificial limbs (NHS)	• Restaurant (Pizza Hut) • Retailing (Laura Ashley) • Carpet shop (supply and fit carpet)
Service	• Charities (Red Cross) • Religious organisations (Church of England)	• General practitioner (GP – NHS) • Refuse collection (local council) • Education – schools (LEA)	• Banking (Abbey National) • Telecommunications (BT) • Hotels (Hilton)

Operations management

Operations management can be considered from the perspective of the organisation as a resource converter – *see* Chapter 1. It is concerned with forecasting the output required and scheduling the conversion process such that customers' orders are delivered on time. The purchasing and **just-in-time** management of inputs are also crucial if the conversion or operation process is to happen efficiently and effectively. It is these activities, along with a few more, that will be examined in this chapter – *see* Figure 5.4.

The principles of operations management examined in this chapter can be applied to organisations providing a product, service or mixture of both. This section considers the characteristics of all three types of organisations: an organisation delivering a service, with the example of a bank providing financial advice to a customer; a product, with the example of a car company

Figure 5.4
Operations
management:
an overview

Location	Product development	Forecasting	Layout of facilities
Process and system performance	Inventory management	Material requirements planning	Just in time
Quality	Scheduling	Purchasing	Maintenance

producing a car that has been ordered by a garage for a customer; and a mixture of product and service, a pizza restaurant.

First, we consider the service and product organisations. The most basic difference between a service and a product is that a product is tangible – the car can be touched and driven by the customer – whereas a service is intangible – the financial advice cannot be seen and touched. The latter is delivered by the financial adviser and assimilated by the customer simultaneously and cannot be stored to be repeated another day. This contrasts with a product, which is able to be stored, highlighting the delay between manufacture and consumption. For example, the car is built in the factory and there will be a delay of at least a few days, maybe longer, before it finally reaches the customer who is going to own and drive the car.

The level of contact that occurs between a service provider and customer and a manufacturer and customer is also very different. In delivering a service there is significant contact between the service provider, the financial adviser, and the customer; in contrast, the buyer of a good, such as the purchaser of a car, and its manufacturer are very unlikely to have any contact at all. This is because in providing a service the customer is part of the process of its delivery: the customer has to be there to receive the financial advice. Therefore the facilities are located close to the customer, e.g. the bank's office will be on the local high street and accessible to the individual receiving the financial advice. In contrast, the customer will not participate in the manufacture of their car and the factory is likely to be located some distance from the end user, maybe even in another country. Finally, in general services are labour intensive and production is automated.

An organisation that both provides a service and delivers a product will assume characteristics of a service provider and/or a manufacturer. Taking the example of a pizza restaurant, the food is a **tangible product**, but cooking and serving the food are **intangible services**. The food may have been stored in the restaurant's fridge or freezer before being used to produce a pizza. Serving a meal is a service that cannot be stored and indicates the simultaneous nature of service provision: the food is served hot as soon as it has been cooked and is eaten as soon as it is served. Showing the diners where to sit, giving them menus, taking their orders, serving the food and taking payment are all service provision and will therefore involve contact between the waiting staff and customers in the restaurant. In contrast, there will be limited or no contact between diners and the kitchen and cooking staff who produce the pizza. Again, as a service is being provided, the location will be easily accessible to diners: pizza restaurants are on the high street in most towns in the UK. The dining area of the restaurant will be the section of the premises most accessible and used by diners; the storage areas, kitchens and bins will be towards the back of the premises and rarely accessible to customers. A restaurant is one example where providing the service, done by the waiting staff, and production, food preparation and cooking, are both labour intensive.

The examples discussed in the section illustrate that the scope of operations management is wide ranging and applicable to organisations undertaking different operations. The rest of this chapter goes on to examine the activities of operations management and how they apply to all types of organisations.

Location

An organisation deciding on a location will have to consider a number of alternatives. The best location for a manufacturing organisation may be one where the overall costs are minimised. In a service organisation the customer is directly involved in the supply process, therefore issues such as ease of access and speed of delivery have to be considered along with costs.

■ Location strategies

Naylor[1] identifies three location strategies. The first is **product-based location** and is commonly used by large organisations. A large organisation using this location strategy takes into account that it has different divisions, each responsible for their own product ranges. Therefore several divisions with similarities or differences can be in the same area or on neighbouring sites. This separation based on product range allows each division to adopt and utilise the appropriate resources for its business. Locating all divisions in a large organisation together is likely to cause problems of focus and control.

An alternative to the product-based location is the **market-based location**. This strategy reflects the geographic divisions of the organisation and locates facilities in a location convenient to its geographic markets. For example, new supermarkets are usually built close to residential areas in out-of-town locations, which means that they are close to the customers – most customers will not want to travel very far to do supermarket shopping, as it is something that is done fairly frequently, for example every week.

Finally, a **vertically differentiated location** strategy is when separate stages of the supply process are in different locations. Some industries have vertically integrated firms which combine several stages of the manufacturing cycle. Rather than locate the whole operation on one site, location decisions are made for each stage.

■ Push and pull factors

The decision to relocate is often made by small and medium-sized enterprises (SMEs) for a variety of reasons, which include the need for more space, increase in the scale of operations, and a reduction in unit costs. Larger organisations often relocate if more locations are required.[2] The factors causing organisations to relocate can be categorised as push or pull factors. **Push factors** result from dissatisfaction with existing locations, hence causing the organisation to consider changing location. Push factors originate from a wide variety of issues, some of which are presented below.

1 Current location is inconvenient for current customers and makes providing a good service cumbersome.
2 Competitors have locations that offer competitive advantage.
3 Different facilities are required for changing product/service range.
4 Regulatory authorities impose constraints related to health and safety, effluent disposal or noise.
5 There is a shortage of appropriately skilled labour.
6 The cost of the current site is increasing, for example due to rising rent.

In contrast, rather than pushing an organisation out of an old location, the **pull factors** attract or pull it towards a new location. For instance, an organisation may be pulled to locate in a particular region or country due to the availability of cheap skilled labour. Many consumer electronics companies have located assembly facilities in Malaysia as there are educated workers available, requiring wages that are a fraction of those paid in western economies. Sometimes a combination of factors will pull an organisation to a particular location. The Japanese car companies Nissan and Toyota located in Sunderland and Derby respectively as both labour and government grants were available. The location of the North of England also allowed both companies access to the European market and a location geographically close to mainland Europe, making selling cars in Europe much easier than importing directly from Japan.

☑ Check your understanding

Do you understand why an organisation may choose a particular location?

Check your understanding by explaining the choice of location strategies and indicate factors which may affect that choice.

Product development

Product development and forecasting are both activities that occur early in the operations management process. The commercial evaluation of a new product will include assessing or forecasting likely demand. The process of product development is discussed in this section and forecasting in the next section.

To be successful, an organisation has to manufacture the products that customers desire. Therefore it must discover the kind of products that customers require and continue to supply them. To do this an organisation has to introduce new products and update or withdraw old products from the market (*see* Chapter 4). The development and introduction of a new product are expensive activities, hence careful planning is essential. The development of the new Rover 75 will have taken several years and cost several million pounds before it was launched on the market in the summer of 1999. There are a number of steps in the product development process, shown in Figure 5.5.

■ Generation of ideas

The first step, the generation of ideas, relies on a number of sources of ideas for new products or services. The results of research and development may lead to a new product, for example the drug Viagra. Alternatively, sales staff out in the field may report customer demand for a new product and/or customers themselves may contact the organisation to suggest new products. The operations management department itself may come up with ideas for new or better products. Finally, the competition may be a source of ideas. Cadbury developed the textured chocolate bar Wispa in the 1980s to compete with the successful Aero bar produced by its main rival at that time, Rowntree.

■ Evaluation of ideas

The evaluation of all ideas is necessary to filter out those with obvious deficiencies and weaknesses. The sources of deficiency and weaknesses in

Figure 5.5
Product development process

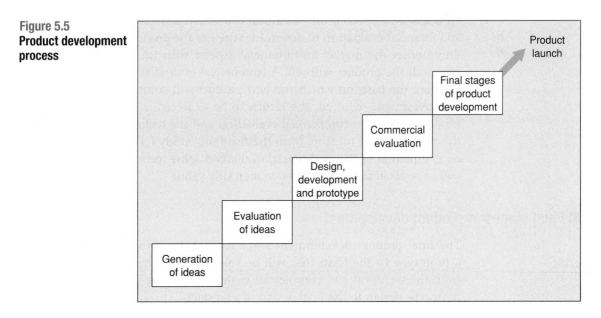

an idea for a new product or service can arise from a number of areas. For example, the manufacture of the product may be technically impossible at present. Alternatively, the manufacture of the product may require skills and abilities that the organisation does not possess or the product does not fit into the organisation's current product ranges.

This initial evaluation needs to be done by a team containing a range of people from different areas of the organisation, so that all relevant points of view are considered. Such a team includes representation from marketing, finance and operations. The ideas appraised as worthy of further considera- tion are taken forward to the next stage of the product development process, namely that of design, development and prototype. In that stage the tech- nical specification required to deliver a successful final version of the product is considered.

Design, development and prototype

Initial basic questions concern whether (a) it is possible to make the product; (b) there are any patent problems; (c) there are any competitors to consider; or (d) there are any current technical developments likely to overtake the product and render it obsolete by the time it arrives in the marketplace. Next, the following questions need to be addressed. Is the current design technic- ally feasible for the organisation to manufacture and does the organisation have the necessary technology and skills? Does the new product complement the organisation's current products? The production and testing of a prototype will often help answer such questions.

Commercial evaluation

Products with a satisfactory technical evaluation move on to undergo market and financial evaluation to determine whether the product will make a profit. This studies the market and financial aspects with the aim of determining how well the product will sell. A commercial evaluation will study the com- petition, the basis on which the new product will compete (*see* Chapter 10), the investment required, the return to be expected, and estimation of the expected sales. The commercial evaluation and the technical evaluation from the previous stage together form the feasibility study for a product. Therefore on completion of the commercial evaluation some technically valid products will be rejected as they are not commercially valid.

Final stages of product development

The final product development stage sees the feasible product move from a prototype to the form that will be sold to customers. The lessons arising from the technical and commercial evaluation will be used to move from a prototype design to the final design of a product.

For the final version of the product, the design has to be functional (to do the job it has been designed for), attractive (to appeal to customers) and easy to make (to keep down production costs).[3]

■ Product launch

Finally, the new product is launched onto the marketplace and its success depends on a number of factors that customers are likely to consider. First price: some customers are price sensitive, other are not (*see* Chapter 10). Next, the quality of the product or service: the quality of food purchased from Marks and Spencer is different from that sold in Netto; and a consumer's response to quality is often directly related to their response to price. Accordingly, consumers who are extremely price sensitive will shop at Netto and those who are very quality sensitive will shop at Marks and Spencer. Finally, ease of access for the customer: a home computer that can be taken home from the shop today will sell better than a model for which there is a 10-week waiting list.

The operations management department of an organisation will attempt to simplify and standardise the design of its products. This makes manufacture easier, as fewer components are used. In addition, the manufacturing process contains fewer steps, is cheaper and waste is minimised. The same principles can be applied to the delivery of a service. An organisation delivering a service will seek to reduce the number of steps a customer has to move through and to minimise queuing time.

☑ Check your understanding

Do you understand the different stages of the product development process?

Check your understanding by explaining and illustrating the product development process.

Use examples where appropriate.

Forecasting

Forecasts become effective at some point in the future when a decision is made concerning, for example, demand for a product. Hence forecasts need to be based on the likely conditions in the future. In the example of a company trying to predict demand for a product, conditions such as the amount of disposable income consumers will have and the competition's activity will affect the forecast. For instance, a company manufacturing ice cream making a forecast in December concerning demand for ice cream in the following June, July and August will consider the likely weather conditions and the new varieties of ice cream to be launched by its competitors for the summer.

There are a number of ways in which forecasting can be done. One key criterion for a forecast is the time period in the future that it covers. Long-term forecasting looks ahead over a number of years. The types of projects that will be affected and influenced by long-term forecasts are, for example, capital expenditure projects, such as the building of office blocks or shopping centres. The decision to build a new out-of-town shopping centre will have been influenced by forecasts covering factors such as the number of people likely to visit at different times of the year – Christmas, school holidays and wet Tuesday afternoons in February – the size of the surrounding population, and the distance people will be prepared to travel to get to the shopping centre.

Medium-term forecasts are defined as covering a number of months, from say 3 to 24 months. The types of decisions that will be influenced by medium-term forecasts are the launch of new products and fashions. Medium-term forecasts tell retailers and producers which toys will be popular with children in 12 to 18 months' time and what gifts will be in greatest demand from retailers next Christmas, for example. This will depend on what toys are likely to be made fashionable from the latest films, cartoons, TV programmes and bands. Toy manufacturers could easily predict that Harry Potter games, toys and figures would be popular for Christmas 2003, due to the publication of the fifth Harry Potter book, *The Order of the Phoenix*, in the preceding June.

In contrast to long- and medium-term forecasts, short-term forecasts cover a few weeks and often have a direct operational effect on the factory. Returning to the company producing ice cream and expecting a good summer in June, July and August, in the UK a wet summer and a forecast of more rain to come at the end of July, as the schools in England break up for the summer holiday, will have a rapid and direct effect on sales and the amount of ice cream that needs to be produced by the ice cream factory.

■ Quantitative forecasting

Forecasting can be either **qualitative** or **quantitative** in nature. Quantitative or numerical forecasting is feasible if the company is already producing the product or providing the service, as historical data already exists concerning the demand for a product or service and the factors affecting demand.

Quantitative data can be used in two ways to forecast future demand. First, **projective** methods examine the patterns of previous demand and extend the pattern into the future. For example, if a supermarket has purchased 100, 150, 200 and 250 tubs of ice cream over the four weeks of June, it could be projected that demand in the first week of July will be for around 300 tubs. Secondly, **causal** methods examine the impact of external influences and use them to forecast future demand or activity. The productivity of the ice-cream factory might depend on the bonus rate paid to employees over the busy summer months. In this situation it would be more accurate to use the bonus rate than demand from shops and supermarkets to forecast productivity.

Both projective and causal methods of forecasting depend on accurate data and figures being available. This will not be the case if the company is launching a new product for which no data exists. In this situation it is not possible to use quantitative methods of forecasting, therefore qualitative methods have to be used. Qualitative methods of forecasting rely on the views and opinions of different stakeholder groups.

■ Qualitative forecasting

There are five commonly used methods of qualitative forecasting:[4] personal insight, **panel consensus**, market surveys, **historical analogy**, and the **Delphi method**.

Personal insight

Personal insight is a frequently used method of forecasting and should be avoided by managers when making critical decisions. Personal insight is simply when a manager who is familiar with the situation produces a forecast based on their own views and opinions. This means the individual's views and opinions are taken into consideration along with their individual pre-judices and misconceptions concerning the situation. Hence personal insight is an unreliable method of forecasting.

Panel consensus

The panel consensus is an attempt to dilute the prejudices and misconceptions of an individual. The panel, assuming it is able to talk openly and freely, should produce a more credible agreement. The disadvantages of a panel will occur if the views of the panel members are too wide ranging to come to a consensus. Also some members of the panel may not perform well in a group and fail to get their views across, hence leaving those who are loudest and most forceful to win through and falsely represent the group.

Market surveys

Market surveys collect data and information from a sample of customers and potential customers. The data and information are analysed and inferences made about the population at large. However, market surveys can be expensive and time consuming and rely on the following being the case if they are to provide reliable information: a valid sample of customers accurately representing the population, unbiased questions being asked, customers giving honest answers, correct analyses of the answers, and valid conclusions being drawn from the results.

Historical analogy

The product life-cycle has periods of introduction, growth, maturity, saturation and decline (*see* Chapter 4). If a new product is being launched, it may be valid for the organisation to assume that demand for the new product will follow the same pattern as that for a similar product already on the market. For example, a publisher launching a new book is able to forecast demand based on the actual demand for a similar book that it published earlier. In the summer of 1999 the publishers of the popular *Harry Potter* children's books correctly forecast that demand for tales of Harry Potter's latest adventures would be very large. This was based on the fact that the previous two volumes of Harry Potter tales had sold extremely well.

Delphi method

This is more formal than the other qualitative methods that have been discussed. The Delphi method follows a well-defined set of procedures in which a number of experts are asked to complete and return a questionnaire by post. The replies from the experts are analysed, the results summarised and posted back to the experts. They are asked to amend their previous replies in light of the summarised results. The replies to the questionnaires are anonymous and the experts do not know who the other experts are. Therefore the problems of face-to-face discussion, mentioned in the section on panel consensus, are avoided. The amending of replies is repeated several times, up to about six occasions. This should allow a range of opinions to emerge that is narrow enough to aid the decision-making process.

☑ Check your understanding

Do you understand the different types of forecasting available to organisations?

Check your understanding by comparing and contrasting quantitative and qualitative forecasting.

Layout of facilities

Facility layout is concerned with the physical arrangement of resources in the organisation's premises. It covers all types of organisations, for example factories, offices, schools, shops and hospitals. The location of resources and their location with respect to other resources is important – if done well, the flow of work is smooth and efficient; in contrast, poorly laid-out facilities disrupt operations and reduce **efficiency**.

The layout of resources in an organisation therefore has two clearly linked aims: to organise the resources and facilities so that the desired output of product or throughput of customers is achieved using minimum resources, and to ensure that the physical arrangement of resources allows maximum output or throughput. Consequently the layout and design of an organisation's premises should allow operations to run efficiently.

Take the example of retail premises, such as a supermarket like Tesco or Sainsbury's, where the goods are organised in parallel aisles. The layout is designed to allow a steady throughput of customers, even on a busy Saturday morning, and to encourage shoppers to purchase particular items in addition to those they need. For example, staple products such as bread and milk are located around the outside of the store some distance from each other, so the shopper has to walk past aisles of other goods to get to them, hence providing an opportunity for other goods to be promoted to the customer in-store. This includes stocking particular goods on the ends of aisles that customers will see as they search for more staple products.

Layout policies for manufacturing

There are a number of layout policies that manufacturing organisations can follow: the process layout, the product layout, the hybrid layout and the fixed position layout.

Process layout

A **process layout** involves similar equipment and machinery being located together. In a factory manufacturing armchairs and sofas, the process layout would mean all sawing machines would be located in one area, all drilling machines in one area, all equipment used to assemble the frames in another area, and all equipment to upholster the chairs and sofas in another. The process layout works best when a range of products is manufactured on the same general-purpose equipment, as this is less expensive than specialised equipment.

One benefit of the process layout is the ease with which specific orders and variable demand can be met. However, this can mean low **utilisation** rates of the equipment and a high unit cost if the batch size for production is small. Nevertheless, the process layout does allow operations to continue if some equipment is unavailable because of breakdown or planned maintenance. For example, if the upholstery equipment is broken, the factory can continue producing frames. Consequently, the scheduling and controlling of the work in the process layout have to be carefully managed, otherwise queues and backlogs of work can occur, resulting in very large stocks of work in progress. Finally, in the process layout people are grouped together according to their work and skills, which can lead to high morale and productivity. Hence splitting up such groups can be difficult when reorganisation and changes occur.

Product layout

A **product layout** puts together in one location all the equipment required to manufacture one particular product. This forms the basis of a traditional production line, where all machinery is lined up and each unit passes from one piece of equipment to another. A good example of the product layout is the production line in a car plant. The car body moves down the production line, with different bits being added as the car moves along the assembly line, for example the engine, the doors, the seats, the brakes, the lights, the windscreen and windows and the wipers, so at the end of the production line the car is complete. The process uses dedicated equipment that is laid out so that the product can move through in a steady flow.

The production line layout results in a high rate of output and high levels of equipment utilisation and low unit cost. In most production lines the unit cost is further reduced by the use of automation and different methods of **inventory** control, such as JIT – *see* later in this chapter. The implementation of an appropriate system of inventory control will reduce levels of materials, components and work in progress. On a production line, scheduling and controlling operations are easy and it is possible to achieve high and consistent quality.

The disadvantages of the production line layout include the inflexible nature of the operations, as it is difficult to adapt a production line to make another product. For example, adapting a car production line to produce washing machines is impossible without a major refit of the premises. Hence production lines are dedicated and expensive, with failure in one part of the production likely to disrupt the whole line.

■ Hybrid layout

If neither a product nor process layout is suitable, it is possible to combine them in a **hybrid layout**. For example, this allows a product to be assembled from two components, one being manufactured on a production line and the other in another part of the factory in a job shop using the process layout.

■ Fixed position layout

A **fixed position layout** occurs when the product is too big or heavy to move, as in shipbuilding, airplane assembly and oil rig construction. All the operations are carried out on one site around the static product. The difficulties of the fixed position layout are that materials, components and workforce all have to be moved onto the site and this will be difficult if there is limited space on site. In the fixed position layout, careful management is required to ensure that the schedule of work is maintained, otherwise completion dates will be in jeopardy. Factors such as weather conditions may also affect operations and completion dates.

✓ Check your understanding

Do you understand why an organisation may choose a particular layout?

Check your understanding by explaining the choice of layouts available to an organisation and indicate factors which may affect that choice.

Process and system performance

All organisations have a finite capacity: a factory can manufacture only so many TV sets in a month, and a school can accept only a finite number of new pupils into Year 1 every September. Therefore consideration at the design stage of the process system is needed to determine the capacity required in order that products can be made, or services can be offered, to meet the demand of customers.

System capacity involves a significant capital investment, hence careful planning should be undertaken to optimise the utilisation of financial resources and meet demand. This can be crucial, as customers can be lost quickly if a firm's capacity is insufficient to meet demand. Alternatively, under-utilised capacity can be very costly. For example, a local education authority will close down a school if pupil numbers fall significantly, as maintaining school buildings and employing staff are costly activities.

Defining capacity and measuring performance

In theory, an organisation examines the forecast demand for a product and from this determines the capacity needed to satisfy that demand. However, in practice factors other than forecasted demand affect capacity, for example how hard people work, the number of disruptions, the quality of products manufactured and the effectiveness of equipment.

Capacity is a basic measure of performance. If a system is operating to capacity, it is producing the maximum amount of a product in a specified time. Decisions concerning capacity are made at the location and process design stage of an organisation's operations management activities. Ideally, an organisation should aim for the capacity of the process to match the forecast demand for products. Mismatches between capacity and demand will result in unsatisfied customers or under-utilised resources. If capacity is less than demand, the organisation cannot meet all the demand and it loses potential customers. Alternatively, if capacity is greater than demand, the demand is met but spare capacity and under-utilised resources result.

In contrast, if the capacity utilisation hovers around 100 per cent during certain time periods, then on those occasions bottlenecks or queues will occur. A common example of capacity being less than demand is when you are left standing in a long queue in a sandwich bar at lunchtime. You may exercise your consumer choice and go to another sandwich bar with no queues and many staff waiting to serve you. Here capacity is greater than demand, but the cost of paying these under-employed staff will be reflected in your bill.

Utilisation and productivity are directly related to capacity. Utilisation measures the percentage of available capacity that is actually used, and productivity is the quantity manufactured in relation to one or more of the resources used. Take the example of the lunchtime sandwich bar, which makes up sandwiches to order. It has five staff serving at lunchtime and its full capacity is 150 sandwiches per hour. If one member of staff phones in sick with food poisoning on Thursday morning, then utilisation of staff, a key resource in the sandwich bar business, is 4/5 or 80 per cent. If it takes on average two minutes to serve a customer and make up their sandwich to order, then one server has the productivity of 30 sandwiches per hour.

Another measure of how well operations are proceeding is efficiency. Efficiency is the ratio of actual output to possible output, usually expressed as a percentage. Returning to the sandwich shop, where a long-term member of staff and experienced sandwich maker has left and been replaced by a trainee 16-year-old school leaver with no catering experience, on their first day the new staff member can manage to make only 20 sandwiches an hour and is therefore operating at 20/30 or 67 per cent efficiency.

Efficiency should not be confused with effectiveness. Effectiveness is how well an organisation sets and achieves its goals. For example, the sandwich shop may not be 100 per cent efficient while the new member of staff is in training, but it can still remain effective if it achieves its goals of serving sandwiches made from fresh and organic ingredients.

In considering capacity, utilisation, productivity, efficiency and effectiveness, thought should be given to how these measures combine. For example, high productivity is of no use if the quality of products produced is poor or if the finished products remain in a warehouse because there is no demand for them.

✓ Check your understanding

Do you understand the different ways of measuring process and system performance?

Check your understanding by explaining and illustrating the methods for measuring process and system performance. Use examples where appropriate.

Process flow charts

The activities, their order and relationship between activities can be shown in a **process flow chart**. For example, the process a customer goes through when visiting the hairdresser is examined. The operations carried out at the hairdresser's might be described as:

- junior sweeps up hair clippings;
- pay receptionist;
- arrive on time and tell receptionist you've arrived for appointment;
- junior makes you a cup of tea or coffee;
- make next appointment;
- hair is cut by stylist;

- hair is washed by junior;
- you look in mirror and confirm you are happy with haircut;
- wait for stylist to finish cutting previous client's hair;
- sit down and read magazine until called;
- hair is dried by junior.

The following steps are gone through to complete a process flow chart form (*see* Figure 5.6).

Figure 5.6
A process flow chart

Symbol	Activity	Time	Cumulative time	No of occasions activity can occur in one hour
⬤ ⮕ ⬜ ◗ ▽				
⬤ ⮕ ⬜ ◗ ▽				
⬤ ⮕ ⬜ ◗ ▽				
⬤ ⮕ ⬜ ◗ ▽				
⬤ ⮕ ⬜ ◗ ▽				
⬤ ⮕ ⬜ ◗ ▽				
⬤ ⮕ ⬜ ◗ ▽				
⬤ ⮕ ⬜ ◗ ▽				
⬤ ⮕ ⬜ ◗ ▽				
⬤ ⮕ ⬜ ◗ ▽				

Key   ⬤ Operation   ⮕ Transport   ⬜ Inspection   ◗ Delay   ▽ Store

1 Look at the processes and list all the activities in their proper order on the process flow chart. This is shown in the column headed 'activity' in Figure 5.7.

Figure 5.7
A process flow chart:
visit to hairdressers

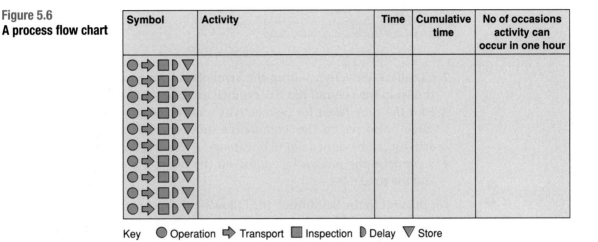

Symbol	Activity	Time (mins)	Cumulative time (mins)	No of occasions activity can occur in one hour
⬤ ⮕ ⬜ ◗ ▽	Arrive on time and tell receptionist you've arrived for appointment	0.5	00.5	120.0
⬤ ⮕ ⬜ ◗ ▽	Sit down and read magazine until called	20	20.5	003.0
⬤ ⮕ ⬜ ◗ ▽	Junior makes you a cup of coffee	1.5	22.0	040.0
⬤ ⮕ ⬜ ◗ ▽	Hair is washed by junior	8	30.0	007.5
⬤ ⮕ ⬜ ◗ ▽	Wait for stylist to finish cutting last client's hair	5	35.0	012.0
⬤ ⮕ ⬜ ◗ ▽	Hair is cut by stylist	14.5	49.5	004.1
⬤ ⮕ ⬜ ◗ ▽	Junior sweeps up hair clippings	1	50.5	060.0
⬤ ⮕ ⬜ ◗ ▽	Hair is dried by junior	10	60.5	006.0
⬤ ⮕ ⬜ ◗ ▽	You look in mirror and confirm you are happy with haircut	0.5	61.0	120.0
⬤ ⮕ ⬜ ◗ ▽	Pay receptionist	1	62.0	060.0
⬤ ⮕ ⬜ ◗ ▽	Make next appointment	1	63.0	060.0

Key   ⬤ Operation   ⮕ Transport   ⬜ Inspection   ◗ Delay   ▽ Store

Figure 5.8
Process flow
chart symbols

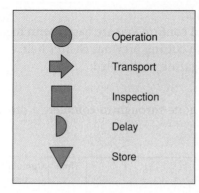

Operation	
Transport	
Inspection	
Delay	
Store	

2 Classify each activity using the symbols shown in Figure 5.8. These are shown in the column headed 'symbol' on the process flow chart.
3 Find the time taken for each activity and record it in the column headed 'time'. Also record the 'cumulative time' and the 'number of times an activity can be carried out in one hour'.
4 Summarise the process by adding up the number of each type of activity and the total time.

For the visit to the hairdresser, the following time is spent:

	No.	Time
Operations	7	37
Delay	2	25
Transport	1	0.5
Inspection	1	0.5

Drawing up a process flow chart will help answer the following questions:

■ What operations are performed?
■ What is the sequence of these?
■ Which operations cannot be started until others have finished?
■ How long does each operation take?
■ Is the system being used to full capacity?
■ Are products being moved?

Once the process flow chart for a product or service has been drawn up and the basic questions above answered, areas for improvement in the process can be looked for and examined.

In the example of the visit to the hairdresser, finishing the longest activity takes 20 minutes, therefore at the moment the maximum number of people that can be processed in one hour is three. However, the longest activity is waiting, therefore this indicates that the appointments system is one area for improvement. The activity that takes the next longest amount of time is cutting hair and up to four people can be processed by one stylist in one hour. If demand is greater than four haircuts per hour, the number of stylists will need to be increased. An increase in the number of stylists may be needed only on the busiest days, for example Friday and Saturday.

The first three steps give a description of the procedure for drawing up a process flow chart and step four provides some indication of the types of issues looked at if improvement is sought.

Operations management should aim for fewer operations and shorter times, while still ensuring that each operation gives the output required by the customer. If bottlenecks occur, the process and/or equipment need to be adjusted so that the process improves.

✓ Check your understanding

Do you understand how to draw up and use a process flow chart?

Check your understanding by drawing up a process flow chart for a visit to the doctor. Using the process flow chart you have drawn up, indicate where queries may occur in the system which is in place to consult the doctor. How may these realistically be overcome?

Inventory management

All organisations have to use raw materials, components and/or consumables to carry out their operations and meet forecast demand. Insurance companies and council offices use consumables such as paper, pens, computer discs and stock enough to ensure they do not run out of these items. In contrast, a shoe shop such as Clarks will hold stocks of finished goods in the form of pairs of men's, women's and children's shoes in different styles and sizes. Equally, organisations in the manufacturing sector hold **inventory** or stock of different types of items. The inventory can be raw materials, for example paper pulp, wheat, coal and crude oil. Inventory can also be components, for example a car production plant will buy in certain items of inventory in component form, such as tyres, lights and assorted engine parts.

■ Raw materials and component inventory

Raw materials and components are held as stock by manufacturing companies in case raw materials and components cannot be supplied on demand. Consequently, holding a certain level of inventory allows for production planning to continue. Anticipation of increases in the price of raw materials such as coal, cocoa, crude oil or wheat may mean that organisations choose to purchase larger than normal amounts, possibly via futures contracts. Alternatively, large quantities of raw materials or components may be purchased to take advantage of a lower unit price or reduced transportation costs. For example, coal-fired power stations negotiate rates for the coal they use based on the large amount purchased and its delivery by the trainload.

■ Work-in-progress inventory

Components and raw materials that have been partly processed by the manufacturing operation have a value to the company and hence are counted as inventory and referred to as work in progress or WIP. There are two points of view on work-in-progress inventory. The first is that if production rates are uneven, work-in-progress inventory ensures that the system always has work to carry out and provides flexibility. The opposite point of view is that work-in-progress inventory merely creates queues and bottlenecks. Consequently the production rate should be balanced, allowing a smooth flow of work right through the process, with no queues.

■ Finished goods inventory

The final type of inventory is goods that have completed the manufacturing process and are finished goods ready to be passed on to the customer. For many manufacturing organisations the customer is not the end consumer but a manufacturer buying components, for example the car manufacturer buying light fittings, or a distributor of goods, such as a car showroom, acquiring cars to sell.

Retailers such as Marks and Spencer, Next and Debenhams hold an inventory or stock of goods for a variety of reasons. Forecasts for goods are not always completely accurate and the extra inventory allows consumer satisfaction to be met rapidly, rather than the customer purchasing the goods at a competing shop. Alternatively, the distributor may offer a significant discount if finished products are purchased in bulk, hence making it more economic to take advantage of a lower unit price and store what is not needed immediately.

■ Types of inventory

Inventory can be categorised into two broad types of stock. **Independent demand inventory** is items that are not dependent on other components, i.e. they are finished goods, like cars or shoes. Demand for such goods is directly dependent on consumer demand and to manage this inventory requires the use of forecasts of consumer demand (*see* earlier section on forecasting).

The other category of inventory is **dependent demand inventory**, which covers items or components used in the assembly of a final product. For example, manufacturing a child's tricycle requires three wheels, one frame, one pair of pedals and one saddle. Hence demand for the component parts depends on the demand for the product. This is the dependency and it can be managed using materials requirement planning, discussed below. If 1000 tricycles are to be produced next month, 1000 frames are needed, which in turn means 1000 saddles, 2000 pedals and 3000 wheels.

■ The cost of holding inventory

Inventory is of value to an organisation and costs money to store. The costs associated with inventory are carrying costs, ordering costs and stockout costs. Inventory carrying costs are the expenses associated with storing stock, borrowing money to purchase the stock, the opportunity costs, the purchase or rental of warehouse premises (which can be expensive if the goods are perishable like food or cut flowers and require refrigerated facilities), insurance, obsolescence and security costs.

Inventory ordering costs

Inventory purchased from an external source incurs the cost of the salary of purchasing staff; preparation and dispatch of the order; salary of accounting staff involved in processing the necessary invoices and making payment; communication including postage, telephone, fax and electronic mail; expediting of the goods if they do not arrive on schedule; and receiving, handling, classifying and inspecting of incoming goods. In summary, inventory ordering costs are the expenses of procurement of the inventory and do not include the cost of purchasing the stock.

Inventory stockout costs

Inventory stockout costs are those costs incurred when inventory is too low to satisfy customer demand. These costs can be difficult to quantify, but include the profit lost on not making a sale and potentially the cost of a client moving all their business to another supplier.

☑ Check your understanding

Do you understand the different types of inventory an organisation may choose to hold and the costs involved?

Check your understanding by explaining the different types of stock an organisation may hold and the possible costs incurred.

Materials requirement planning

The dependent demand inventory system can be managed by use of **materials requirement planning** (MRP). MRP relies on production plans to propose a timetable for when materials orders are required. Consequently the resulting stocks of materials depend directly on a known demand. The alternative is an independent demand inventory system, which means that large enough stocks of materials to cover any probable demand are held.

A hotel coffee shop using an independent demand system would look at the ingredients used last week and ensure that there are enough of the same ingredients in stock to cover likely demand. In contrast, if an MRP system were in use, the number of meals and snacks to be served each day would be assessed and this information used to determine the food required and the time and day of delivery. Hence with an MRP system overall stocks are lower, as only the ingredients and goods needed are ordered and are delivered just before production commences – *see* Figure 5.9. In contrast, with independent demand systems the stocks are not related to production plans, so they are kept higher to cover any level of expected demand and are replenished to maintain levels to cover any demand – *see* Figure 5.10.

Figure 5.9
Stock levels
using MRP

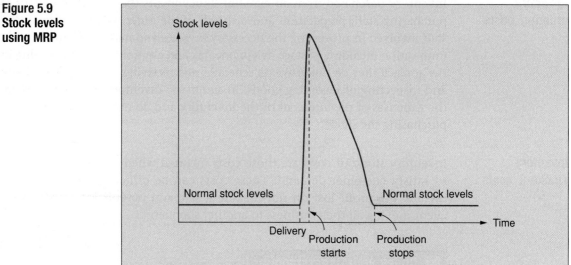

Figure 5.10
Stock levels for an
independent demand
inventory system

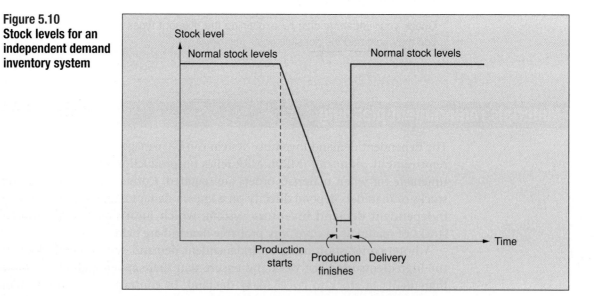

■ The MRP procedure

The MRP inventory control system requires a great deal of information about components and products and is therefore computerised. The main information comes from three files:

- master production schedule;
- bill of materials;
- inventory records.

The MRP procedure starts with the master production schedule, which indicates the number of each product to be made in each period. The bill of materials is prepared by the designer or production engineer and is the result of the MRP being broken down to show the materials and components needed to manufacture a product and the order in which they are used. The bill of materials for the desk shown in Figure 5.11 is shown in Figure 5.12. The figures shown in the circles are the numbers needed to make each desk and every item is given a level number that shows where it fits into the process. The finished product is always level 0, with level 1 items used directly to make the level 0 item, the level 2 items used to make the level 1 items and so on.

**Figure 5.11
Desk**

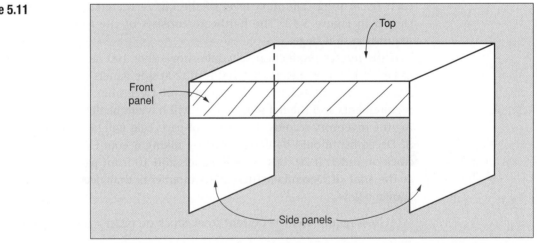

**Figure 5.12
Bill of materials
for a desk**

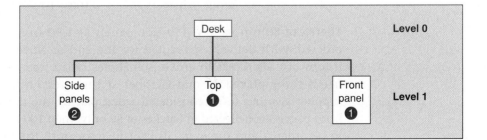

Figure 5.13
Bill of materials for a desk showing details of desktop

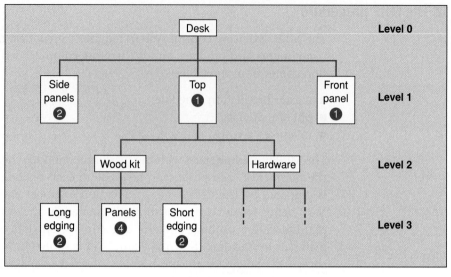

Closer examination shows that the desktop is made from a wood kit and hardware. The wood kit contains four panels 150cm long, 15cm wide and 2cm thick, two pieces of edging 150cm long, and two short pieces of edging each 60cm long. The next level of the bill of materials for the desktop is shown in Figure 5.13. The hardware consists of the tools and machinery required at that stage.

If the master production schedule shows that 100 desks have to be made in December, this means that 100 tops, 200 side panels and 100 front panels have to be available by the beginning of December. These are the gross requirements and the net requirement will have to be determined by examining the inventory records. The stocks of parts that will be available at the start of December should be determined by taking account of current stock and stock on order. If 20 tops, 50 side panels and 10 front panels will be in stock at the start of December, the net requirements that need to be ordered are shown below.

Gross requirements – current stock/stock on order = net requirements

Tops	100 − 20 = 80
Side panels	200 − 50 = 150
Front panels	100 − 10 = 90

Therefore 80 top panels, 150 side panels and 90 front panels need to be ordered, with delivery scheduled for the end of November. For example, if tops take six weeks to arrive (sometimes called lead time) then the order needs to be placed by mid-October at the latest. Information from the supplier also has to be considered when placing the orders, for example if front panels are delivered in batches of 50 only, then 100 front panels will have to be ordered and the extra 10 kept in stock until the next batch of desks is made. Alternatively, the supplier may offer a 15 per cent discount if side panels are purchased in batches of 100. Therefore careful calculation and consideration have to be given to deciding whether it is worthwhile buying 200 side panels instead of the 150 required. Once the stock and order situations have been clarified, a timetable for production in December can be produced.

Just in time

This chapter has looked at independent inventory demand systems and dependent demand inventory systems, both of which operate with the main aim of managing mismatches between supply and demand for stock. Independent demand inventory systems manage the mismatch by ensuring that stocks are high enough to cover any expected demand. In comparison, dependent demand inventory systems using MRP overcome the stock mismatch by using a master schedule to match the supply of materials approximately to demand. The closer the match of supply to demand, the lower the stock levels needed to cover any mismatches. The just-in-time (JIT) system takes things a stage further and attempts to eliminate the stock mismatch altogether. A just-in-time system is organised so that stock arrives just as it is needed. Accordingly, the immediate nature of JIT systems depends on suppliers and customers working together to achieve the common objective of supplies arriving on time.

JIT systems operate in car plants, such as the Nissan plant in Sunderland. The car body moves down the production line to a work station and the doors arrive at the same point at the same time and are fitted. This is repeated all the way down the production line for seats, engines, windows and other parts, until the finished car emerges from the end of the production line.

JIT is commonly seen as a way of reducing stock levels to zero in the organisation. However, it does influence other aspects of operations management. Traditionally, organisations have set arbitrary quality levels, such as a maximum of two defective items per 100 produced. However, the JIT system takes the view that any defect costs the organisation and it is cheaper in the long run to prevent defects happening in the first place than to pay to correct them later. Hence JIT supports the principles of **total quality management** (*see* later in this chapter). The principle of no defects also extends to the reliability of equipment. The JIT system of supply of materials and components works on the basis of operations being continuous. Hence if a piece of equipment is unreliable and breaks down, managers have to discover why this happened and take action to ensure that this failure does not re-occur. This may include reviewing maintenance procedures and policies (*see* later in this chapter).

Accordingly, JIT is not only a means of reducing inventories but a way of viewing the whole range of activities in which an operations management department is involved and minimising delays of all kinds, including stockouts, breakdowns and defects.

☑ Check your understanding

Do you understand the different systems for managing inventory?

Check your understanding by comparing and contrasting MRP and JIT. Use examples where appropriate.

Quality

Quality can be defined as the ability of a product or service to meet and preferably exceed customer expectations. For example, a breathable hill-walking jacket that keeps out the rain and wind and makes the wearer comfortable fulfils its quality expectation, as does a meal in a restaurant to celebrate your birthday if good food, wine and ambience are in evidence. This illustrates the importance of quality. Quality contributes to helping an organisation remain competitive by producing goods and services of the quality demanded by customers. If the quality fails to meet the quality needs and wants of customers, market share and profits will be lost. Hence managers and organisations invest significant effort into quality management, which is concerned with all aspects of product or service quality.

Quality management is affected and influenced by improvements in technology that ensure greater accuracy in the manufacturing processes, resulting in consistently high-quality products. This consistent quality is used by organisations as a competitive tool to gain competitive advantage (*see* Chapter 10). Therefore organisations have to pursue the manufacture of high-quality products, as consumers have come to expect them and have become reluctant to tolerate anything less. Hence if the demand for high-quality products is ignored, an organisation will lose out to competitors that can meet customers' quality demands.

Now you can see why organisations must make high-quality products. Any organisation that ignores the demand for high quality will lose out to competitors that can meet customer expectations. Although high quality will not guarantee success for a product, low quality will guarantee failure. There are clear benefits to an organisation from manufacturing high-quality products, such as improved reputation, competitiveness, sales and productivity, along with reduced costs.

The quality of an organisation's products or services can be viewed from two basic points, inside and outside the organisation. The inside or organisational viewpoint of quality is that the performance of a product or service meets its design specifications exactly. The external or customer viewpoint is defined as how well a product or service does the job for which it was purchased. Hence there are two types of quality. The first is designed quality, which is the level of quality designed into a product or service. For example, a Fiesta has a different level of designed quality to an Audi. Second is achieved quality, which illustrates how closely a product achieves the designed quality. For example, at most British mainline railway stations there is a board showing the targets or designed quality for trains running on time, say 97.5 per cent, and alongside these figures the achieved quality, i.e. the actual trains running on time, say 84 per cent. Accordingly, achieved quality is often lower than the designed quality.

■ Quality costs

The management of quality will both incur and save costs for an organisation. Suppose that a faulty computer games system is sold to a customer buying a Christmas present for their child. The customer complains and the manufacturer arranges for the system to be repaired. However, money could have been saved if the manufacturer had found the fault prior to the games system leaving the factory, and even more money could have been saved by producing a games system that was fault free in the first instance. These costs are known as external failure costs.

There are three other categories of costs associated with quality: design costs, appraisal costs and internal failure costs. Design costs cover the expense of designing a good-quality product. This involves employing appropriate design staff, considering the type and cost of materials, the number of components, the manufacturing time, the ease of production, the amount of automation used, and the skill level required by the workforce. Appraisal costs cover verifying that the designed quality is the same as the achieved quality, which includes quality control costs such as those for sampling and inspecting the goods and work in progress. Finally, internal failure costs cover the cost of any items not meeting the designed quality. This can cover scrapping the item or returning it to an earlier point in the process to be reworked. There is also the cost of the work carried out on the defective item before it was detected. Therefore defects should ideally be found as early as possible in the process.

Savings are made when a quality system eliminates defective items from the system. For example, if a manufacturer sells goods, 10 per cent of which are defective, and replaces them under guarantee when reported by customers, there is great inefficiency. The inefficiency arises as the manufacturer has to increase production by 10 per cent to cover the faulty goods. A system for dealing with complaining customers and faulty goods also has to be maintained, which incurs costs for the organisation. It is the removal of these inefficiencies that will save money. If the manufacturing process were to eliminate the manufacture of defective goods, productivity would rise by 10 per cent, unit costs would fall, there would be no more customer complaints, and the cost of dealing with them would no longer be incurred.

■ Total quality management

Total quality management is defined as the whole organisation working together to improve product or service quality. The aim of total quality management is zero defects.

Organisations typically had separate quality control and production departments. These two departments would often have conflicting objectives, with production departments aiming to manufacture products as quickly as possible, and quality control slowing down production by inspecting products, removing defective items and asking for them to be reworked. In this arrangement it is easy for quality control and production to forget that both departments have the overall common objective of customer satisfaction.

Throughout the 1980s and 1990s in the West, quality management and production became integrated into the operations management department. The role of quality staff is to help and ensure that quality is built in, not inspected out. The production and quality staff look for ways of working with each other, customers, marketing staff, engineers and anyone else with a role to play in ensuring high quality.

☑ Check your understanding

Do you understand the importance of quality to an organisation?

Check your understanding by explaining the benefits of 'good' quality and the impact of the costs of quality on the quality of the final product or service which is delivered to the customer. Use examples where appropriate.

Scheduling

Scheduling involves drawing up a timetable of work that will ensure that customer needs and wants are met. Scheduling is critical in making certain that the utilisation of labour and equipment is optimal and that bottlenecks in the process are avoided. Scheduling generally deals with activities that are normally repetitive and short term in nature. Examples of timetables or schedules are shown in Table 5.1.

Table 5.1 Examples of schedules

Railways: Railway timetables for trains, drivers, guards, ticket inspectors, catering staff and passengers
Hospitals: Hospital schedules for operations, patients, nurses, surgeons, beds and operating theatres
Chocolate manufacturer: Chocolate manufacturer producing handmade chocolates has a schedule for customer orders, employees, equipment, raw materials delivery (cocoa, butter, cream and flavourings) and delivery of completed orders

Scheduling aims to meet the master production schedule and achieve low costs and high utilisation of equipment. This may appear to be straightforward and easy, but schedules must take account of many different factors. Take the example of drawing up timetables for first-year university students. The availability and requirements of staff, students, subjects and rooms all have to be balanced. The availability of staff and students has to be considered, for instance, as they can be in only one class at a time, and rooms of the right size and type have to be allocated to a subject at a time when both staff member and students can attend. This will be difficult if the number of rooms is limited or if special facilities such as a computer lab, language lab or science lab are required for the class.

There are four different ways for scheduling of services[5] and these are discussed below. Scheduling jobs in services is essentially the same as scheduling in manufacturing, but there are some differences. In service industries the customer is personally involved in the process, often being asked to wait in a queue, so queuing times are critical. Services contrast with manufacturing in that they cannot be produced during quiet times and held in stock for busy times, they have to be provided as required. Hence the capacity of a service process has to be organised to meet peak-time demands and cope with uneven patterns of demand. If there are large differences between peak-time demand and the lowest level of demand, then equipment will have a relatively low utilisation rate. In this situation the employment of staff can be dealt with by employing extra part-timers during the busy period.

■ First come, first served

First come, first served scheduling is what most of us encounter on a daily basis, for example in the supermarket or queuing for our lunch. It is simple and straightforward: customers are served in the order they arrive.

■ Fixed schedule system

A **fixed schedule system** arises when a service is delivered to many customers at once. The timetable or schedules are generally known in advance by customers as the information has been made publicly available. Examples include bus, tram, train and airline timetables.

■ Appointment system

Appointment systems are commonly used by doctors, dentists, lawyers and hairdressers and require the customer to make an advance appointment. The aim of using an appointment system is to ensure the best utilisation of resources and good customer service, such that neither the customer nor practitioner is kept waiting. Problems arise if the appointment systems do not run to schedule, with customers kept waiting beyond their appointed time, or if the customer cancels and the practitioner has to wait for the next appointed customer.

■ Delayed delivery

The delivery is deliberately delayed in situations when the customer will not be significantly inconvenienced. Dry cleaners are good examples of organisations that delay the delivery to enable them to match capacity and workload. A dry cleaner's that has enough work to operate to full capacity today will still accept clothes for dry cleaning. However, they will not be dealt with until tomorrow and the owner will be told to return the following afternoon or the day after next to collect the clothes. Repair shops such as shoe repairers are also good examples of businesses that operate a **delayed delivery** scheduling system.

> ### ✓ Check your understanding
>
> *Do you understand the different ways in which an organisation may schedule work?*
>
> Check your understanding by explaining and illustrating different scheduling methods. Use examples where appropriate.

Purchasing

The purchasing activity for organisations can be centralised, decentralised or a combination of both.

■ Centralised purchasing

Centralised purchasing is when the procurement of all purchased items for the whole organisation is arranged and controlled via one department. This allows bulk buying, which usually means that better prices and service can be obtained from suppliers (*see* Chapter 10). Centralised purchasing also yields a consistent standard and quality of purchased products for the whole organisation, reduced administrative costs, streamlined relations with suppliers, and a reduction in transport costs, since orders are delivered in larger quantities.

■ Decentralised purchasing

Decentralised purchasing occurs when every division or department of the organisation makes its own purchasing decisions, which is less bureaucratic than a centralised purchasing system. In addition, if the divisions or departments of a large organisation are buying from local suppliers who are responsive to their individual needs, it may be more cost effective than centralised purchasing.

■ Combination of purchasing functions

If neither a centralised nor a decentralised purchasing system is completely appropriate for the organisation, a combination of centralised and decentralised purchasing may be more suitable. If a combination of systems is used, responsibility for certain items, often of a relatively low value, rests with the decentralised system, which is managed by the division or department. In contrast, the centralised part of the system is used for relatively expensive items and infrequent purchases, such as capital expenditure, which may have to be approved by the board of directors.

✓ Check your understanding

Do you understand the term 'purchasing'?

Check your understanding by explaining the different approaches an organisation may take to buying the resources and inputs it requires. Use examples where appropriate.

Distribution

Distribution is concerned with moving finished goods from the manufacturer to customers. A normal distribution system involves finished goods being moved from the manufacturer's premises to the distributor's warehouse until they are allocated to customers. This type of distribution system allows manufacturers to achieve economies of scale by concentrating operations in central locations, which in turn means that distribution costs are reduced as large orders are moved from manufacturer to wholesaler, rather than small orders being moved directly to retailers or consumers.

This also means that the manufacturer does not need to keep large stocks of finished goods. Wholesalers placing large orders with manufacturers will negotiate a reduced unit price and will also stock a range of goods from many suppliers, hence allowing the retailers a choice of goods. If wholesalers offer short lead times and reliable delivery in addition to a good range of stock, retailers can carry less stock and still offer the consumer a wide range of goods.

✓ Check your understanding

Do you understand the term 'distribution'?

Check your understanding by explaining what is meant by 'distribution'. Use examples where appropriate.

Maintenance

Maintenance activity supports the operations management department by helping ensure that its equipment and facilities are kept in working order. Therefore an organisation's policy on maintenance is integrated with operations policy. This is important as any unplanned shutdown can have a significant effect on production systems, particularly if other carefully planned systems also support operations, such as a JIT inventory management system, as discussed earlier in this chapter.

Maintenance has two key aims: to reduce both the frequency and impact of failures. The frequency of failure can be reduced by proper installation of the correct equipment along with a programme of preventive maintenance and replacement of items that are wearing out. The impact of maintenance can be lessened by its being planned for quiet times and/or minimising downtime and repair times.

There are two types of maintenance policy: run to breakdown and preventive maintenance. If the consequences of failure are limited and the equipment is easily replaceable, run to breakdown is the sensible option. There are two ways to respond to a breakdown: emergency action if the breakdown has serious effects, or corrective action at a point in the future if the impact is limited.

Preventive maintenance is carried out on a planned basis. The intervals between maintenance work are established by experience, manufacturers or external authorities. Inspection is an important part of maintenance, especially for items that are expensive to replace or repair.

☑ Check your understanding

Do you understand the term 'maintenance'?

Check your understanding by explaining the different approaches an organisation can take to keeping its equipment and facilities in working order. Use examples where appropriate.

Summary

This chapter gave an overview of the operations management department of any organisation, product or service, public or private, and examined how operations management activities relate to one another and the other major departments of any organisation. This should have furnished the reader with a broad general knowledge of operations management.

1 Operations management is concerned with managing the way products are made and/or services delivered, which in turn has a direct impact on how well the organisation achieves its objectives. The principles of operations management can be applied to both manufacturing and service organisations.

2 Organisations and operations can be categorised as primary, secondary or tertiary. Primary-sector organisations are concerned with producing raw materials. Secondary-sector organisations manufacture goods. Tertiary-sector organisations sell goods produced by primary and secondary organisations. Tertiary-sector organisations also include service-sector organisations.

3 There are three basic location strategies. First, product-based location, with a company choosing to locate divisions with product similarities close to each other. The next is market-based location, where the company locates its facilities such that they are conveniently placed for the customers. Finally, a vertically differentiated location strategy is when separate stages of the supply process are in different locations.

4 Successful product development helps ensure that an organisation manufactures products that customers desire. The first step is the product development process which covers the generation of ideas, which may come from the sales force, other staff, customers and competitors. Next the ideas should be evaluated such that those which are not possible due to technical or skill limitations are not taken forward. The design and development of a prototype should answer the following questions.

(a) Is it possible to make the product?
(b) Are there any patent problems?
(c) Are there any competitors to consider?
(d) Are there any technical developments which are going to render the product obsolete by the time it reaches the market?

Products which undergo a satisfactory technical evaluation move on to undergo commercial evaluation. The commercial evaluation studies the market and financial prospects for the product, with the aim of determining how well the product will sell and the amount of profit it will make. The lessons learned from the technical and commercial evaluations will then be used to move from a prototype product to the final version of the product which will be sold to customers. Finally the new product will be launched onto the marketplace. Its success will be influenced by a number of factors, including price, quality and ease of access to the product.

5 Forecasts become effective at some point in the future when a decision is made concerning, for example, demand for a product. Long-term forecasting looks ahead over a number of years, while medium-term forecasting covers periods from 3 to 24 months. In contrast, short-term forecasting covers a few weeks and has an immediate and direct effect on the organisation's operations. Forecasting can be quantitative or qualitative in nature. Quantitative forecasting can be used to forecast future demand for a product or it can be used to assess the impact of external influences on demand. Qualitative forecasting relies on the views and opinions of different stakeholder groups. The qualitative forecasting methods include personal insight, panel consensus, market surveys, historical analogy and the Delphi method.

6 The layout of resources or facilities in an organisation has two linked aims: first to organise resources or facilities such that output is achieved using minimum resources and second to ensure the maximum throughput is achieved, giving good overall efficiency. The process layout is the grouping together of all similar equipment and machinery, and this works best when a range of products is manufactured on the same general-purpose equipment. However, this can result in low utilisation rates of equipment and a high unit cost if the batch size for production is small. The product layout puts together in one location all the equipment required to manufacture one particular product, i.e. as in a traditional production line. The fixed position layout occurs when the product is too big or heavy to move, as in shipbuilding. All operations are carried out on one site around the static product.

7 The use of resources in an organisation can be assessed by a number of measures. Capacity is a basic measure of performance and a system is operating to capacity when it is producing the maximum amount of product in a specified time. If capacity is less than demand, the organisation cannot meet all the demand and loses potential customers. Alternatively if capacity is greater than demand, the demand is met but spare capacity and under-utilisation of resources results. In contrast, if the capacity utilisation hovers around the 100 per cent mark, bottlenecks or queues will occur on occasions. Capacity is related to utilisation and productivity. Utilisation measures the percentage of available capacity used, while productivity is the quantity manufactured in relation to one or more of the resources used. Efficiency is the ratio of actual output to possible output, usually expressed as a percentage. In contrast, effectiveness is how well an organisation sets and achieves its goals.

8 Process flow charts show the activities performed to manufacture a product or deliver a service, the order they occur in and their relationships. Once a process flow chart has been drawn up for a product or service, it can be used to answer questions concerning the activities, their order, how long they take, and the capacity of the process and its efficiency.

9 All organisations carry inventory in varying forms, including raw materials, components and consumables. Raw materials and component inventory are held by manufacturing organisations to ensure that if supplies of raw materials and components cannot be supplied on demand, production can continue. Components and raw materials which have been partly processed are referred to as work-in-progress inventory. Finished-goods inventory refers to the goods which have completed the manufacturing process and are ready to be passed onto the customer.

10 Inventory can be classified in two ways: independent demand inventory, which is not dependent on other components, i.e. inventory or stock of finished items, whose demand is directly dependent on consumer demand, and dependent demand inventory, which covers items or components used in the assembly of final products, i.e. if a factory is to produce 1000 coffee tables next month, the dependent demand will be for an inventory of 4000 coffee table legs. The costs associated with holding inventory or stock include the carrying costs, the ordering costs and the stockout costs. Dependent demand inventory can be managed by use of materials requirement planning. MRP relies on production plans to propose a timetable for when materials orders are required. Consequently the resulting stocks of materials depend on a known demand. The MRP inventory control system requires a great deal of information about components and products and is therefore computerised. The main information comes from three files: the master production schedule, the bill of materials and inventory records.

11 The just-in-time (JIT) inventory system attempts to eliminate stock mismatches between demand and supply. A just-in-time system is organised so that stock arrives just as it is needed. Hence the immediate nature of JIT systems depends on suppliers and customers working together to achieve the common objective of supplies arriving on time.

12 Quality is defined as the ability of a product or service to meet and preferably exceed customer expectations. There are two types of quality, the first being designed quality, which is the level of quality designed into a product or service. The other is achieved quality, which is how closely a product achieves its designed quality.

13 Scheduling involves drawing up a timetable of work which will ensure that customer needs and wants are met. Key aims of scheduling include meeting the master production schedule, along with achieving low costs and a high rate of equipment utilisation. A first come, first served schedule is more commonly known as a queue, with customers served in the order they arrive. A fixed schedule system occurs when a service is delivered to many customers at once, an example being a bus service. The appointment system is where customers are required to make an advance appointment, to enable the service provider to use resources and time efficiently to provide good customer service. The delayed delivery system is used when customers will not be significantly inconvenienced. This allows the service provider to delay service to closely match capacity and workload.

14 Purchasing in organisations can be centralised, decentralised or a combination of both. Centralised purchasing is when the purchase of all items for the whole organisation is controlled via one department. This allows for bulk buying, which usually means better deals can be obtained from suppliers. Decentralised purchasing occurs when each division or department in an organisation makes its own purchasing decisions, which can be less bureaucratic than centralised purchasing. A combination of purchasing systems is used when it is appropriate for the purchase of certain items, usually of low value, to rest with the decentralised system, and the centralised system is used for expensive items of capital expenditure.

15 Distribution is the moving of finished goods from manufacturer to distributor. The distributor stores the goods before moving them to the customer. This type of distribution system allows manufacturers to achieve economies of scale by concentrating operations in central locations.

16 Maintenance activities help ensure an organisation's equipment and facilities are kept in working order. Breakdown or unplanned maintenance can have a significant impact on operations and activities such as a JIT inventory system.

Learning outcomes for case studies

While reading this chapter and engaging in the activities, you should have learned how to apply theory and models, analyse situations, and evaluate the application and analysis you undertake. The learning outcomes specified below outline the type of application, analysis and evaluation of which you should be capable in relation to organisations. The case studies and the questions which follow provide an opportunity for you to test how well you have achieved the learning outcomes for the ethical issues and exit case studies for this chapter.

Application	Check you have achieved this by	
1 Explain the different operations management activities which Boeing needs to manage correctly for success	identifying the problems faced by Boeing and how it can resolve them	answering exit case study questions 1 & 2
Evaluation	Check you have achieved this by	
1 Assess possible arguments for the production of hemp beauty products	determining whether the Body Shop or the Drug Enforcement Administration has the stronger case	answering ethical case study question 1

ETHICAL ISSUES CASE STUDY 5.2

The war of the weeds

As the blazing summer revives the eternal quest for a cure for skin that looks like shoe leather, those who have relied on the beauty industry's growing array of hemp products may have to turn elsewhere.

The Body Shop, the ethically conscious purveyor of lotions and potions, is bracing for a battle to save products such as its Hemp Lip Protector and Hemp Lip Conditioner, which it believes are threatened by forthcoming US drug regulations.

Last November, the Drug Enforcement Administration said it would ban the use of industrial hemp in products that can be absorbed into the bloodstream.

The hemp plant, whose fibres and seed oil are used to make paper, cloth, food and beauty products, belongs to the cannabis family and contains tiny traces of tetrahydrocannabinol (THC), the psychoactive compound found in marijuana.

The cultivation (but not the use) of hemp is currently banned in the US, except in Hawaii – an apparently illogical restriction that has fuelled an impassioned debate over the spindly plant. David P. West, who has a doctorate in plant breeding, said in a recent paper that 'no member of the vegetable kingdom has been more misunderstood'.

The official position on hemp has been far from unwavering. During the second world war the US government rallied farmers to plant the now-taboo crop with a 'Hemp for Victory' campaign as supply dwindled following the Japanese occupation of the Philippines, a major source of the crop. (Hemp is used in canvas and military garb.)

While the DEA does not appear to believe that a person can become intoxicated from a slather of hemp body butter, it is concerned that human consumption of hemp products interferes with workplace drug tests.

Apparently alarmed that body balm may provide a screen for furtive marijuana smokers, the US Air Force in April banned hemp products in order to 'to ensure military readiness'.

But hemp advocates, who include Woody Harrelson, the actor in Natural Born Killers and so forth, say scientists should be able to tell the difference between drug-testing samples taken from someone who uses hemp body lotion and someone who habitually smokes marijuana.

'If you bathed in hempseed oil every day and soaked in it for hours is it possible (to test positive for drugs)? Yeah. But the likelihood is so negligible as to be irrelevant,' said Eric Seenstra, president of the advocacy group Vote Hemp.

Kim Burr, the Body Shop's US director of values and vision, doesn't see why people should be forced to change what they use simply because 'the DEA is not doing (its) research'.

The Body Shop has hit back at the DEA's looming action – the rules are to be published in October – with a petition. The company believes a ban would hurt its US hemp product sales of about $5m a year.

Burr believes there is more at stake than just Body Shop products. 'It's an environmentally friendly, cash-yield crop,' she said, before invoking the campaign's slogan: 'Hemp is the future. Hemp is hope.' And hemp is money.

Source: Financial Times, 4 July 2001. Reprinted with permission.

Question for ethical issues case study 5.2

1 Do you agree with the Body Shop or the Drug Enforcement Administration in the US? Give your reasons.

EXIT CASE STUDY 5.3

FT

Boeing, boeing, bong

By Michael Skapinker

Everett, where the company assembles the 747, 777 and 767 aircraft, is the largest building on earth. Viewed from the platform set up for the 130 000 annual visitors, the scene is one of bustling activity. Thousands of workers scurry to fit wings and cables to rows of glinting aircraft fuselages.

It looks like a boom time for Boeing. It is not. Last week, the group announced a net loss for 1997 of $178m, the company's first for 50 years. 'It's a big disappointment. No question,' said Philip Condit, Boeing's chairman in an interview. What is going wrong at the world's largest aircraft maker?

The problem is not that the aircraft-building business is turning down. Far from it. Boeing has never been busier. Airline orders have risen sharply and the company has had to increase production to keep pace.

By the second quarter of this year, its factories in Seattle and Long Beach, California, will be turning out 47 aircraft a month. In mid-1996, the monthly total was just 18.

Nor has the problem much to do with the vast acquisition that Boeing made last year when it took over McDonnell Douglas. That $16bn deal doubled Boeing's size, helped increase its revenues from $22.7bn in 1996 to $45.8bn last year, and boosted its workforce from 112 000 to 238 000. The acquisition turned the world's leading manufacturer of commercial jets into the biggest maker of military aircraft too. (Boeing is also a substantial manufacturer of space equipment, accounting for 60 per cent of Nasa's budget.)

True, some of last year's losses resulted from indigestion. Boeing made a $1.4bn pre-tax provision to take account of its decision to run down some of McDonnell Douglas's civil aircraft production. Boeing is to phase out the company's MD-80 and MD-90 aircraft.

Yet, given the scale of the task, the merger has gone reasonably well. Harry Stonecipher, former chief executive of McDonnell Douglas and now president of Boeing, says some employees initially found it difficult to make eye contact with people they had regarded as enemies. But soon, he says, the two sides realised how similar they really were.

Staff from both companies confirm this. Ignore the remaining McDonnell Douglas signs that have still to be removed at some Long Beach plants, and it is impossible to tell who came from which company.

Morale has been aided by the fact that the two companies' activities were largely complementary, rather than overlapping. This means few programmes will be discontinued, although some factories will close.

Even the McDonnell Douglas civil aircraft workers have been cheered by Boeing's decision to proceed with their planned 100-seat MD-95 aircraft, now renamed the Boeing 717. Boeing will also continue to make the trijet MD-11 as a freight aircraft. Many McDonnell Douglas workers had feared the MD-11 was doomed.

No, where Boeing stumbled last year was not in its execution of the merger. Rather, the problem has arisen in the activity in which the company has long believed it led the world: the manufacture of commercial aircraft. Faced with what it called 'the steepest production increases since the dawn of the jet age', Boeing's factories seized up under the strain.

For a month last year, the company had to halt the Boeing 747 and 737 assembly lines. This did not mean, as widely reported at the time, that all work on the jets ceased. But managers stopped moving the aircraft along the assembly lines, leaving them in place so that workers could find missing parts and catch up with uncompleted work. The company had to make an additional $1.6bn provision to pay for its production problems.

To add to Boeing's woes, the price of aircraft plunged, in spite of the high level of demand. Some analysts say Boeing's obsession with selling more aircraft than Airbus Industrie, its European rival, resulted in price cuts, as sales staff struggled to win customers.

Boeing will not comment on a statement last month by Manfred Bischoff, chief executive of Daimler-Benz Aerospace, an Airbus partner, that competition between the two manufacturers had forced aircraft prices down by a fifth over the past two years. But operating margins on Boeing's commercial aircraft business dropped to less than 3 per cent in 1997 from 10 per cent in the previous two years.

Mr Condit says the reason prices are low at a time of strong demand is that aircraft manufacturers have to think about how to retain customers over 10 to 15 years. He cites the example of Southwest Airlines. When Boeing was approached by the carrier in the 1970s it did not insist on Southwest paying high prices for its aircraft. Not only is Southwest today the world's most successful low-cost carrier, it is also the biggest buyer of Boeing 737s.

'The decision to support a rag-tag group which came and said we want to buy some used 737s and start an airline in Texas has produced a phenomenal number of sales,' Mr Condit says.

Mr Stonecipher says he does not expect the price competition with Airbus to ease. 'There's no dynamic that indicates that price is going to change any time soon,' he says. For Boeing to raise margins, it needs to cut costs. And to cut costs, Mr Stonecipher says, the company will have to change the way it makes aircraft. 'The hardest way to cut costs is by trying to do the same things better. You have to do them differently.'

Some of the changes have already been made. Boeing was half-way through a $1bn programme of updating its manufacturing when it was hit by the surge in orders. The reason it did not cope was because its system of ordering and handling parts, and the manufacture of several of its aircraft models, were still too inefficient and old fashioned.

'You put a tremendous strain on your own system and your suppliers' system when you order some parts that you don't need or you fail to order a part that you do need,' Mr Condit says. Had Boeing completed the transformation of its manufacturing systems by last year, he says, 'I think a lot of the problems would have been avoided.'

The transformation of Boeing's production goes by the ungainly title of Define and Control Airplane Configuration/Manufacturing Resource Management or DCAC/MRM for not-very-short. The overall aim is to bring Boeing up to the manufacturing standards of the motor industry.

Central to the programme is greater standardisation. Aircraft are hugely complex to make: the Boeing 747 has 6m parts. Boeing has traditionally allowed airlines to choose how they want many of those parts arranged. There are, for example, 20 different types of clipboard that pilots can order for their cockpits.

Boeing does not plan to deprive its customers of choice. But those choices will, in future, come from a Boeing menu. Airlines opting for greater variation will have to pay more for the privilege. Bob Dryden, executive vice-president for production, says he expects 85 per cent of aircraft parts to be standard, with airlines specifying the rest.

Boeing also wants to transform the way it handles aircraft components. Until it began changing its manufacturing processes, Boeing kept track of parts through a mass of papers and 400 separate computer systems. DCAC/MRM involves putting all those parts on a single computer system.

The changes should allow Boeing to cut down on the number of parts it holds as inventory. Boeing turns over its inventory 2.5 times a year. Mr Condit says that is higher than the US average but low compared with the Japanese car manufacturer Toyota or with competitors such as British Aerospace. Mr Dryden says he would like to see Boeing turn over its inventory 12 times a year by 2005. As the company has nearly $9bn tied up in inventory, the savings could be substantial.

Boeing has also begun asking its suppliers to design parts on computers so that its aircraft are easier to assemble.

The Boeing 777, which began service in 1995, and the new generation of 737 were computer designed. The 747 was not and the parts did not always fit together easily. 'We were shaving bits off or we had to reject them,' says Mr Dryden. Northrop Grumman, the US manufacturer which makes fuselage sections for the 747, has computerised its production process, which makes assembly easier.

Inspired by Japanese practice, workers now receive their parts in colour-coded boxes, packed, counted and ready for assembly, rather than having to fetch them when needed. Specialists who sort out production problems now sit on the factory floor, not in a separate building.

The DCAC/MRM programme should be completed by next year. Whether it will be enough to solve Boeing's problems is another matter. The company will make 550 aircraft in 1998, compared with 374 in 1997. Production problems will continue to depress earnings until the middle of the year.

Boeing will also continue to face fierce competition from Airbus. The European consortium raised its output by 44 per cent to 182 aircraft last year – without experiencing any production problems. It plans another 30 per cent increase this year.

Holding off Airbus, while keeping aircraft prices at competitive levels will be a difficult task. And getting through 1998 without another production breakdown will be the test of what Mr Condit has achieved so far.

Source: Financial Times, 6 February 1998. Reprinted with permission.

Questions for exit case study 5.3

1 Summarise the problems faced by Boeing in 1998.

2 Draw up an outline plan of the operations management activities that need to be dealt with if Boeing's problems are to be resolved.

For more case studies please visit www.booksites.net/capon

Short-answer questions

1 Define operations management.

2 Define primary, secondary and tertiary organisations and give examples of each.

3 Name and briefly describe three different location strategies.

4 Name six stages of the product development process.

5 List five measures of process and system performance.

6 Name two different types of forecasting.

7 Name four different types of layout.

8 Define inventory management.

9 Briefly explain the term 'JIT'.

10 Briefly explain the term 'MRP'.

11 Briefly explain the difference between JIT and MRP.

12 Name four different methods of scheduling.

13 Briefly state the difference between designed quality and achieved quality.

14 Define total quality management.

15 Name two different types of maintenance.

Learning outcomes for assignment questions

While reading this chapter and engaging in the activities, you should have learned how to apply theory and models, analyse situations, and evaluate the application and analysis you undertake. The learning outcomes specified below outline what you should be able to do and the assignment questions provide an opportunity for you to test how well you have achieved the learning outcomes for this chapter.

Application	Check you have achieved this by	
1 Demonstrate how operations management principle can apply to manufacturing and/or service organisations	identifying the operational areas/activities of an organisation with which you are familiar	answering assignment questions 1 & 2
2 Apply the process flow chart to an organisation's operational process	using a process flow chart to examine a business process with which you are familiar	answering assignment question 2
Analysis	**Check you have achieved this by**	
1 Analyse the operations management activities of an organisation	identifying any problems which occur in the operations of an organisation of which you have some knowledge	answering assignment question 1
2 Analyse the operational effectiveness of a business process of your choice	examining a completed process flow chart for a business process with which you are familiar, identifying problem areas and suggesting possible solutions	answering assignment question 2
Evaluation	**Check you have achieved this by**	
1 Evaluate the usefulness of examining an organisation's operational activities	critically evaluating the relevance of considering the operational activities in organisations today	answering assignment questions 1 & 2

Assignment questions

1 Choose a manufacturing and service organisation of your choice. Research your chosen organisations and compare and contrast the operations management procedures they undertake. Present your findings in a 2000-word report.

2 Complete the process flow chart for doing a business studies assignment (Figure 5.14). What mechanisms are there for you to monitor and improve the quality of your work and how effective do you think each one is? What constraints affect the way in which you plan and execute your work?

Figure 5.14
Process flow chart for doing a business studies assignment

Order	Activity	Done by whom?	Symbol
	Make rough notes		
	Draw up contingency plan		
	Type up final answers/report		
	Put in correct references		
	Hand report into school office		
	Write questions and assessment criteria/learning outcomes		
	Go to library		
	Collect information		
	Read questions carefully		
	Prepare draft answers to questions		
	Collect information		
	Return feedback and mark for report		
	Buy newspapers		
	Select organisation		
	Mark reports		

Key   ● Operation   ▷ Delay   Unit leaders
       ➡ Transport   ■ Inspection   Unit tutors
       ▼ Store   Students

Weblinks available online at **www.booksites.net/capon**

1 This web site is the Business Open Learning Archive, which give details and information on a wide range of operation management activities. Click on 'Operations Management – study material for'. For something to complement the contents of this chapter select Health and Safety.
http://sol.brunel.ac.uk/bola/

2 This is website of Health and Safety Executive which deals with the regulation of risk in the work place.
http://www.hse.gov.uk/

3 This website is concerned with the work of Deming. Click on Deming Electronic Network (DEN), enter the website, click on the Deming Philosophy webpage, click on the Deming's 14 points. This looks at methods for quality and improvement in organisations.
http://deming.ces.clemson.edu/

Further reading

Bank, J (1992) *The Essence of Total Quality Management*, Harlow: Prentice Hall.

Barclay, I and Dann, Z (2000) 'Improving product development performance: key management and organizational factors', *Journal of General Management*, 26 (1), Autumn.

Blattbery, P C and Deighton, J (1996) 'Manage marketing by the customer equity test', *Harvard Business Review*, July/August.

Caulkin, S (2000) 'How we manage to fail', *Management Today*, November.

Hargadon, A and Sutton, R I (2000) 'Building innovation factory', *Harvard Business Review*, May/June.

Harrison, M (1996) *Principles of Operations Management*, London: Financial Times Prentice Hall.

Naylor, J (2002) *Operations Management*, Harlow: Financial Times Prentice Hall.

Slack, N, Chambers, S and Johnson, R (2001) *Operations Management*, 3rd edn, Harlow: Financial Times Prentice Hall.

van Biema, M and Greenwood, B (1997) 'Managing our way to higher service-sector productivity', *Harvard Business Review*, July/August.

Waller, D L (2003) *Operations Management: A Supply Chain Approach*, 2nd edn, London: Thomson Learning.

Waters, D (2002) *Operations Management: Producing Goods and Services*, 2nd edn, Harlow: Financial Times Prentice Hall.

References

1 Naylor, J (1996) *Operations Management*, Financial Times Pitman Publishing.
2 Ibid.
3 Waters, D (1996) *Operations Management: Producing Goods and Services*, Addison-Wesley.
4 Ibid.
5 Ibid.

6

Finance

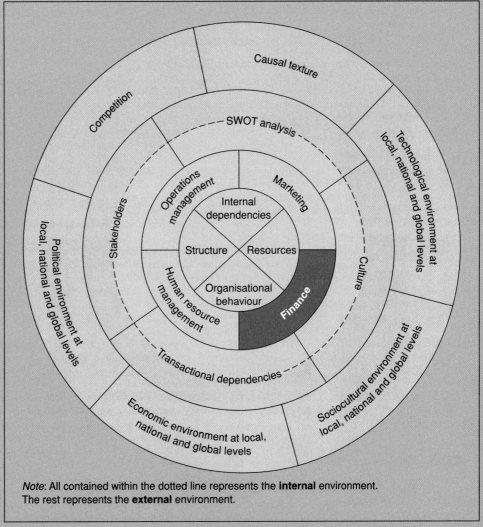

Note: All contained within the dotted line represents the **internal** environment. The rest represents the **external** environment.

Figure 6.1 Organisational context model

➡ ENTRY CASE STUDY 6.1 ⬛FT

SmithKline's well-sugared pill

By Daniel Green

Have you recently been on a tropical holiday? Given up smoking? Conquered depression? If so, you could have contributed to the record share price performance this week from SmithKline Beecham, Britain's second biggest drugs company.

Its 1996 results, published on Tuesday, showed sales and profits up 13 per cent and 14 per cent respectively. The company is rewarding its shareholders with a 25 per cent dividend increase.

Life was not so comfortable a year ago. SmithKline had been through 18 months of acquisitions and disposals and had to take restructuring charges and provisions for legal action against it.

Moreover, it was hit by the collapse in sales of its best selling product, Tagamet, an ulcer drug, following the expiry of its patents. And while most drug companies generate plenty of spare cash, debt was rising at SmithKline. Not surprisingly, the first half of 1996 was a period of poor share price performance.

The transformation of the company, run by charismatic former tennis star Jan Leschly, is due largely to the performance of the company's new product portfolio. Sales of Seroxat, an anti-depressant launched in 1992, reached £706m last year.

They will continue to grow rapidly as it chases Prozac, which made $2.4bn in sales for its maker Eli Lilly of the US. Indeed, SmithKline gleefully produced figures this week showing that Seroxat sales were growing three times as quickly as those of Prozac.

Sales of Havrix, a hepatitis A vaccine used by travellers which also was launched in 1992, may be more modest than Seroxat's. But any product showing a year-on-year growth of 29 per cent, with sales of £166m, is welcome.

Medications do not have to be high-tech to be money-spinners. Sales of SmithKline's newly launched nicotine chewing gum rose from £22m in the first quarter of last year to £78m in the last quarter.

Then, too, one of its most successful products is the toothpaste Aquafresh. Sales of this grew 24 per cent last year, to £258m, thanks to the launch of the brand in new markets.

Indeed, SmithKline now claims to be the market leader in oral health in western Europe, having overtaken Colgate and Unilever in the past three years.

Leschly also lifted the curtain a little this week on what some stock market analysts regard as the company's most serious mistake of recent years – the $2.3bn acquisition in 1993 of Diversified Pharmaceuticals Services.

Among other things, DPS manages drug purchasing in the US for clients such as hospital chains. Several related businesses were bought by other drug companies in 1994. Unfortunately, a few months later, the US Federal Trade Commission told them they could not use their new acquisitions to boost sales of their products.

In spite of this, DPS is turning into the cornerstone of Leschly's grand vision – which is for SmithKline to become a healthcare company, not just one selling specific products. SmithKline is using DPS to forge relationships with some of the most important healthcare buyers in the US and to gather data on patterns of drug consumption.

That, in turn, is helping what has for many years been SmithKline's weakest link: Clinical Laboratories, which conducts tests for hospitals. New technologies and heavy competition have helped to cut prices in this area of business but profits grew in 1996 for the first time since 1993.

The future for more conventional medications is promising. Leschly gave details of five drugs in the final stages of development. They range from Memric, for Alzheimer's disease, to one for irritable bowel syndrome, code-numbered SB207266. The launches are planned for 1999 to 2000, provided the clinical trials go well.

There is still plenty that could go wrong for SmithKline. The risks in drug development are exemplified by the company's decision to suspend work on Ultrair, an asthma drug, in the late stages of testing. Then, too, the US Food and Drug Administration is hesitating over Coreg, a drug for heart failure. A decision on whether to approve it is expected within weeks.

DPS remains a problem in financial terms. The business might be opening doors for SmithKline and sales are growing well, but Leschly is careful not to give profits figures away.

Nor are SmithKline's shares a bargain for investors. The price is now so high that even the company's own stock-broker, NatWest Markets, says Zeneca's are probably better value.

Even so, SmithKline embodies what has made the drugs sector an attractive investment for the past two decades. Good medicines give a company the security of a utility: the customers must buy its products even if times get hard.

At the same time, top-class research and development, plus the slice of luck that any research needs, make medicines into high-tech, high-growth products comparable with computer chips and software programs. Historically, pharmaceuticals is one of the world's most profitable industries. At the moment, SmithKline is living up to that reputation.

Source: Financial Times, 22 February 1997. Reprinted with permission.

Introduction

The resource of money is an important **asset** for nearly all organisations. The financial aims of private-sector organisations will include profit-making objectives. In contrast, for public-sector or charitable organisations the most efficient and effective use of often limited financial resources will be of primary importance.

Therefore the finance function of a business is concerned with the financing of the organisation, the use of finance by the organisation, and the explanation to interested parties or stakeholders of how the finance has been utilised. The detailed activities undertaken by the finance function will vary in nature from the operational to the strategic and will be influenced by changes in the organisation's external environment. Therefore the finance function is concerned with **financial management, management accounting and financial reporting**. We will look at these areas of activity later in this chapter.

External influences on the finance function

■ The single currency

The 1991 Maastricht Treaty set the timetable for the first round of monetary union to occur in Europe in 1999. The deadline for meeting the necessary economic targets to join the first wave of European monetary union, EMU, was the end of 1997. The key economic target that countries had to meet was the deficit:gdp (gross domestic product) ratio, which had to be 3 per cent or less. All member states except Greece met this target. However, along with Greece, Denmark, the UK and Sweden did not join the single European currency in the first wave in 1999.[1] In June 1998 Robin Cook, British Foreign Secretary, strongly indicated that Britain expected to join the single currency soon after the 2002 general election in the UK. The timing of a referendum on the UK joining the euro was still unclear in January 2003.

The single currency is called the euro and is managed by the European Central Bank, based in Frankfurt. The role of the European Central Bank is to maintain the euro as a stable currency, as it is hoped that this will stop price rises caused by devaluing currencies and produce a European economy that is built around low inflation and low interest rates. In the longer term it is expected that such a European economy will attract world trade and international investors keen to be less dependent on the US dollar.

The euro became legal currency for trade and financial markets on 1 January 1999. Coins and notes were introduced in participating countries on 1 January 2002, allowing individuals to be paid in euros, spend euros in shops and pay bills in euros. The two-stage changeover was aimed at allowing organisations to familiarise themselves with the euro and how it would operate. It also gave time for notes to be printed and coins minted. The notes are in denominations of 5, 10, 20, 50, 100, 200 and 500 euros, and the eight euro coins range from 1 cent to 2 euros (200 cents) in value. The circulation of old national currencies and the new euros occurred in parallel for several months after 1 January 2002. During this time organisations displayed the price of goods and services in both euros and a national currency, which along with charts and conversion tables helped the individual consumer to convert from their old national currency to the new euro.

The benefits of the euro for individual consumers include the greater ease with which the price of goods and services can be compared across participating EU member states. Purchasing goods or services from abroad via mail or the internet is less complex and the cost of foreign exchange and exchange rates when visiting different participating EU states no longer exists.

The benefits for organisations in participating countries include a decrease in the number of different-currency bank accounts held, a rationalisation of cash operations and an overall saving in operating costs due to the removal of cash conversion costs and cross-border payments. In contrast, the disadvantages of a single currency arise from the intrinsic risk of the euro as a new currency with no past form and the associated hesitancy which exists while exchange rates are finally established.

■ The minimum wage

The minimum wage was introduced in the UK in April 1999. The issues and debates surrounding its introduction centred around the level at which it should be set and whether that level should vary for particular groups of people.

The old Wages Councils that set minimum wages in a number of low-paying industries, including for example retailing, catering and textiles, were abolished by the Conservative government. It argued that the minimum wage levels set by Wages Councils made employing staff too expensive and hence jobs were lost; this same argument was directed by the Conservatives at the idea of a national minimum wage. However, the Conservatives never proved that discontinuing the Wages Councils *created* jobs. Hence it would appear that their termination had no effect on employment, so the minimum wages set by the Wages Councils could have been an appropriate starting point in establishing a minimum wage level. The minimum wage rates at the time the Wages Councils were disbanded ranged from £2.72 per hour to £3.18 per hour, with an average of about £3 per hour. Revising these rates in line with average earnings growth would have produced a minimum wage rate of £3.85 in October 1998.[2]

Various interested parties have had differing views on what level a minimum wage should have been set at and what should influence its level.

The TUC – representing the employees

The Trades Union Congress (TUC), which represents trade unions and employees, wanted the highest possible minimum wage and to get the best deal possible for workers. The TUC conference in 1997 voted in favour of a minimum wage of £4.26 per hour, the highest of all figures suggested. This figure was chosen because it was half male median hourly earnings. This may appear to be a simple and easy-to-apply method when deciding on the rate for a national minimum wage. However, there are different ways of calculating male median earnings. In the case of the TUC this was done by dividing weekly earnings, including overtime, by average hours excluding overtime. It is easy to see that if weekly earnings including overtime were divided by the number of hours worked including overtime, then a lower hourly rate would have been arrived at.[3,4]

The CBI – representing the employers

The Confederation of British Industry (CBI) expressed the view that a minimum wage level of around £3.50 could be acceptable. It views a high minimum wage rate as having the potential to harm businesses by increasing costs, leading to higher prices being charged and causing jobs to be terminated.

The academics – impartial

A group of academics (Richard Dickens, Stephen Machin and Alan Manning) advised the Low Pay Commission in October 1997 that a minimum wage of £3.85 would be the most appropriate, with lower rates for young people. A minimum wage at this level would have annoyed both the TUC and the CBI: the CBI wanted a lower minimum wage rate and the TUC a higher one. The figure of £3.85 per hour was arrived at on the basis of the average figure set by the different Wage Councils prior to their abolition of £3.07 per hour, which assuming average earnings growth would have stood at £3.85 in October 1998, when introduction of the minimum wage was expected. The academics recommended £2.50 per hour for 16–17-year-olds and £3 per hour for 18–20-year-olds. It was argued that the variation of minimum wage rates by age would have a noticeable effect on the pay packet of adults earning the minimum wage, without threatening the jobs of young people.[5,6] The gap in earnings between young and old workers was significant, with average pay before introduction of the minimum wage being around £7.80 per hour, while teenagers averaged only £3.10 per hour. The introduction of a minimum wage at a level of £3.50 or more, without age differentiation, would have affected over half of teenagers in work in contrast to about 10 per cent of the whole population.[7]

In contrast, the claim for changing the minimum wage according to regions was nebulous, as regional wage differentials in the UK are not generally significant. London and the South East of England clearly have higher wage rates and Northern Ireland lower wage rates, but there is meagre regional variation in the rest of the UK. Therefore, as expected, the minimum wage was introduced on a national and not a regional basis.[8]

It was estimated that the relative influence of a national minimum wage on the whole economy would be small even if it had been introduced at the high rate of £4.26 per hour. The effect on the wage bill would be smaller than the impact of the Equal Pay Act of 1970. However, the people affected by minimum wage legislation would be protected by law from the worst excesses and exploitation of the labour market and unfair employers.[9]

In the event, a minimum wage of £3.60 per hour for adults over 21 years old was announced in June 1998, along with a rate of £3.00 per hour for 18–21-year-olds, with no minimum for 16- and 17-year-olds. Both minimum wage rates came into operation in April 1999. By October 2002 the national minimum wage had increased to £4.20 for adults and £3.60 for 18–21-year-olds.

☑ Check your understanding

Do you understand the specific elements of the external environment that affect the finance function?

Check your understanding by discussing the impact of the external environment on the finance department of an organisation.

Financial management

Financial management involves raising capital to finance the organisation's operations and ensuring that sufficient revenue is generated to cover the cost of any finance raised, e.g. interest payments. In the UK there are four main sources of funding for businesses: reserves, loans, share issues and the government.

■ Reserves

Reserves are retained profits from previous years that have not been spent or distributed to **shareholders**. The use of reserves to fund expenditure means that the level of scrutiny to which the organisation's management is subjected is less exacting than if funds were raised from sources external to the company.

■ Loans

Loans are either **term loans** or **overdrafts** and are commonly provided by banks. Term loans are long term and provide the borrowing organisation with capital in return for repayment of the capital with interest over a number of years, e.g. five or ten. In contrast, overdrafts are short-term loans for 12 months or less and will vary from day to day depending on the amount by which the organisation's current account is overdrawn. However, for many organisations an overdraft will be a 'permanent' source of temporary finance.

Loans are for a definite period and repayable with interest. The amount of interest payable depends on the interest rate charged, which is driven by the base rate of interest set by the Bank of England. The level of risk taken by the lender in lending money to the borrower will be influenced by the security offered against the loan and what the money is to be used for. All these will in turn also influence the interest rate charged on the loan. It is common for long-term loans to be secured against company assets. Securing the loan reduces the risk for the lender and the interest rate for a secured loan will be lower than for an unsecured loan.

The interest payments come out of profits and cannot be reduced by the borrowing business if profits and trading conditions are unfavourable. This contrasts with **dividend payments**, which a company can alter depending on profits and trading conditions. A further characteristic of loans is that they do not carry ownership rights, which is in contrast to **ordinary shares** that do. If a company is unable to meet the loan and interest payments, then the bank or lender may decide to foreclose on the loan and appoint a **receiver** to take day-to-day control of the company. The receiver has to decide whether the business is able to continue trading under its guidance and generate enough cash to pay the bank and other **creditors**, or whether the business should be closed, the assets sold off and the cash generated used to pay the bank and other creditors.

In July 1991 Robert Maxwell used shares in the publicly quoted company Maxwell Communications Corporation (MCC) to secure loans to his own private companies of an estimated £300 million. Earlier in the same year, Maxwell had used shares owned by the pension fund of Mirror Group Newspapers to secure loans to MCC. Much of this was irregular and illegal and on 31 October 1991 the value of shares in MCC started to plummet. Shortly after this, on 5 November, Maxwell died from drowning by going overboard from his yacht near the Canary Islands. This example raises two key issues to bear in mind when accepting assets as security for a loan. First, are the assets being offered as security those the borrower is legally allowed to offer? Maxwell was not legally in a position to offer the shares belonging to the Mirror Group Newspaper pension fund as security, but he did so and they were accepted as security for loans to MCC. Second, will the assets offered as security be of a value equal to that of the loan should the lender have to foreclose on the loan and **liquidate** the security given? The value of MCC shares used as security for loans plummeted in October 1991, leaving the value of the loan security as minimal.

■ Ordinary shares

A company will issue ordinary shares to raise capital. Once issued shares can be traded on the **stock market** if the company is listed, where individuals or organisations may buy and sell them. Shareholders will usually fall into one of three categories: the individual investor, institutional shareholders and existing shareholders (**rights issues** are looked at in the next section). The value of a shareholder's investment in a company will rise or fall depending on how the company itself performs and on how the stock market as a whole performs.

SmithKline Beecham, the pharmaceutical company, saw the price of its shares rise from below 650p in April 1996 to nearly 950p in February 1997, slipping back to 720p in June 1998. The overall increase in the company's share price was in part due to the good performance of the company's products in the marketplace. In particular, SmithKline achieved a strong position in the market for oral health products, illustrated by the success of toothpaste brand Aquafresh. For further details see the introductory case study to this chapter.

Ordinary shares carry ownership rights entitling the holder of the shares to one vote per share owned at annual general meetings and extraordinary general meetings of the company and the right to receive a dividend if the company issues one. Dividends are a distribution of profits to the owners/shareholders of the company and can be raised or lowered as the company sees fit. They are usually expressed in the form of so many pence per share owned. For example, if a company announces a dividend of 17.5p per share, a shareholder owning 200 shares would receive a payment of £35. Most companies seek stability or a slight upward trend in their dividend payments with the aim of keeping shareholders satisfied.

Shareholders are either individual members of the public investing relatively small sums of money (thousands of pounds) in shares or corporate investors with large amounts of money to invest (millions of pounds) for the company or their clients. For the individual small investor, shares are a form of investment that is more risky than keeping savings in a building society or bank, but shares are highly likely to give a better return in the long term than a building society or bank. Corporate investors include insurance companies and pension funds, which invest money to enable them to pay pensions and attractive bonuses on insurance policies to their clients.

In the 1980s individuals were greatly encouraged to become shareholders by the Conservative government of Margaret Thatcher through privatisation offers. Many individuals were new to this type of investing. The companies in which they acquired shares included British Telecom, British Gas, electricity distributors, power generators, British Airways and Railtrack. These flotations were aimed at individual and corporate investors.

Margaret Thatcher's view of Britain's citizens as shareholders continued in the 1990s with privatisations in the financial services industry. In 1997 the insurance company Norwich Union floated on the stock market along with the Halifax, Alliance & Leicester, Woolwich and Northern Rock building societies. These flotations meant that the account and policy holders of those companies received shares in them, hence releasing many millions into the pockets of the individuals who sold the shares they received. Other shareholders viewed the Norwich Union and the building societies as good investments and kept their shares.

■ Rights issues

A rights issue is similar to a share issue but is for existing shareholders only. A rights issue is a way of raising capital that is viewed as less threatening than a share issue, as the shareholder breakdown remains the same. Hence there is no opportunity for another company to build up a stake in the business with the aim of mounting a **hostile takeover bid**. In a rights issue ordinary shareholders are offered new shares in proportion to those they already own. For example, if a shareholder owns 500 shares in a company and the rights issue is a one for ten offer, then the shareholder will be entitled to purchase one new share for every ten already owned, i.e. 50 new shares in total. Rights issue shares are usually offered at a price equal to or below the stock market price to make the investment appear attractive to the shareholders.

If shareholders take up the rights issue by purchasing the shares, the shareholder breakdown remains the same. If the existing shareholders do not buy the new shares and the rights issue is a failure, the shares are offered on the open market by the underwriters and the shareholder profile of the company is likely to change, offering the opportunity for a hostile takeover bid.

A failed rights issue may point to the possibility that the company is not doing well. Therefore investors should examine closely a company's reasons for undertaking a rights issue. A company using the money raised by a rights issue to expand the business, with the aim of seeing profits, share price and dividends rise in the future, will be a better investment than a company using the money raised via a rights issue to pay off old debts and avoid business failure.

In June 1991 Sainsbury's announced a £489 million rights issue, the first in its 18 years as a quoted company. The aim of this rights issue was clear: the cash was for building 160 new and replacement supermarkets, 70 Homebase stores and 10 Savacentre stores. Sainsbury's rights issue was a one for ten issue at £3.12 and shares were trading at £3.52 on the day of the announcement. The preferred source of finance was a rights issue as the market was receptive to the idea and Sainsbury's share price was strong.

■ Government

The Department of Trade and Industry (DTI) provides a gateway to information for businesses, including possible sources of funding, which can be accessed via the DTI website, the Business Link website or the Small Business Service (SBS) website, which are all listed in the weblinks section at the end of this chapter. The equivalent of Business Link in Scotland is Small Business Gateway, in Wales it is the Business Connect offices and in Northern Ireland it is EDnet. There are many organisations and funding schemes which target businesses which meet specific criteria. Examples include the loan guarantee scheme run by the Small Business Service, which guarantees loans for businesses that are unable to borrow capital from conventional sources due to a lack of appropriate security for the loan. Another scheme, in England, is the Enterprise Grants scheme, which is managed via Business Link and the Small Business Service, providing financial assistance to eligible small and medium-sized businesses in assisted areas in England. Under the Enterprise Grants scheme, sums of up to £75 000 are available for projects with a capital investment of up of £500 000, with preference given to high growth, maximum added value and high-quality projects which would not go ahead without the grant.[10]

Business start-ups by young people can seek funding and advice from the Prince's Trust, which seeks to help disadvantaged young people aged 14–30 achieve their goals. Financial help takes the form of low-cost loans of up to £5000, or in special cases grants are available to individuals or groups.[11]

Businesses which have good growth potential may seek investment from a venture capitalist, which are usually professional fund managers or informal investors, many of which are listed in the directory of the British Venture Capital Association. Venture capital funding is acquired by the business selling a stake in itself to a venture capitalist. In return the venture capitalist provides the business with an injection of cash, which will be viewed as a long-term investment and in return the venture capitalist expects to have a say in how the business is run, to share in the profits and to gain capital growth from the investment, which is realised when the venture capitalist sells the stake in the business, typically after 5–7 years.[12]

✓ Check your understanding

Do you understand the different ways in which a company can raise money?

Check your understanding by indicating how the following companies could raise money for expansion:

- an established public company, like Tesco;
- an established private company, like Clarks;
- an established small high-tech company;
- a new small business, like Tinytots nursery.

■ The use of capital raised and leasing assets

Organisations use the **capital** raised to acquire assets. Many organisations are more concerned with using assets than actually owning them and may make the decision to lease rather than purchase assets. The leasing of assets has become more common during the last 20 years. Leasing is one way of acquiring assets without paying the full price. The most commonly leased assets are cars, plant and machinery, and information technology and office equipment. The types of lease used to rent out a particular asset may vary. The common types of leasing arrangement are an operating lease, a finance lease and a sale and leaseback.

An operating lease is a short-term contract in which the supplier of equipment, for example information technology hardware, makes the equipment available to a business. The business will enter into an operating lease and make a series of lease payments to the provider of the equipment. The tax advantages of leasing assets accrue immediately rather than over a number of years, as would be the case with depreciation allowances on purchased assets.

A finance lease is used when suppliers of an expensive item of capital equipment are paid directly in full for the item they have supplied to the company by the financing organisation, e.g. bank, finance house or merchant bank. Therefore the financing organisation provides the finance and the company makes leasing payments to the financing organisation.

A sale and leaseback is used when a company is concerned with using rather than owning an asset. The key principle here is that the company sells the asset to release the capital tied up in the asset and leases it back. Organisations such as pension funds may purchase a large, expensive fixed asset, like a head office building, and lease it back to a company. Hence the capital is released in the form of cash for the company to spend on other projects, without the upheaval of moving office.

☑ Check your understanding

Do you understand the different types of lease available to companies?

Check your understanding by identifying the sort of lease suitable for:

- a company occupying a large corporate headquarters wishing to reduce the size of its HQ;
- a steel company purchasing a new furnace;
- a print and copy shop wanting to update its equipment.

Management accounting

Management accounting generates information for managers to use in planning and decision making relating to the allocation of an organisation's financial resources. The information generated is largely quantitative in nature and is generated by application of management accounting techniques. The type of management accounting techniques examined in this chapter are costing and investment appraisal.

Costing

Costing involves looking at and defining the costs involved in producing a product or service. How costs are defined influences their use in the techniques of absorption and marginal costing, which are looked at later in this chapter. The cost of producing a product or service has three elements to it: the costs of materials, labour and overheads. These costs will be direct or indirect and/or fixed or variable.

Material and labour costs can be either direct or indirect costs. Direct costs are the expenditure on elements that goes straight into producing the product or service. They include expenditure on raw materials and components and the wages of production staff or front-line service delivery staff. Indirect costs are often called overheads. **Overheads** or indirect costs are the expenses that do not contribute directly to the product or service being produced and therefore cannot be attributed to a particular job. Indirect costs or overheads include indirect labour costs, indirect material costs and indirect expenses. Office cleaners, catering staff and security staff are good examples of indirect labour costs for most organisations. Indirect material costs are the expenditure on cleaning materials, maintenance materials and subsidised food for employees. Indirect expenses are charges for items that have to be met, but that have no direct relationship to the cost of production. Indirect expenses include rent, heating and lighting bills and insurance.

Fixed costs do not change directly in relation to the level of activity or production, but have to be paid out, usually on a short-term basis such as monthly or quarterly. Fixed costs include many of the indirect costs just mentioned such as rent, insurance and maintenance contracts. Variable costs are sometimes called marginal costs. This is quite simply due to the marginal costing technique attributing variable costs only to the units of production/cost. Marginal costing is looked at later in this chapter. Hence variable costs are those that vary in relation to the level of activity or production and include direct labour costs and direct materials costs. **Prime costs** are the sum of direct wages and direct materials (prime costs = direct wages + direct materials).

■ Absorption costing

The use of absorption costing to provide quotes for jobs takes account of both fixed and variable costs. Absorption costing aims to ensure that all the overhead costs incurred by the business are covered by the revenues it receives. The data generated by absorption costing aims to provide information that can be used to give quotes for jobs. If an accurate quote for a job is to be provided, a correct amount has to be included in the quote to cover the portion of overheads incurred in carrying out the job. This requires a decision to be made on what basis the organisation is going to allocate overheads. Is it going to allocate them on the basis of materials used in jobs, the amount paid in direct wages to complete the job or merely the number of units produced?

There are six methods of absorbing production overheads. These overhead absorption rates (OAR) are outlined in the worked example below. Comment on the calculations being carried out is also provided.

Example question	**Absorption costing**
	(a) Calculate six different overhead absorption rates for Job 03/2014 and indicate the total overhead cost incurred for each OAR.
	(b) Using the most appropriate overhead absorption rate, calculate a quote for Job 03/2014.

Production Department – Monthly Costs Report – March 2003

Total cost centre overheads (TCCO)	£60 000
Number of cost units	1600 units
Direct labour hours	5000 hours
Machine hours	4000 hours
Direct wages	£50 000
Direct materials	£40 000

(Prime cost = direct wages + direct materials)

Job Number 03/2014

Direct material cost	£5000
Direct wages paid (£6.00 per hour)	£3750
Time taken on machine	500 hours
Number of units produced	250 units

Workings, answers and comments – part (a)

1 Cost unit OAR

$$\frac{\text{TCCO}}{\text{Number of cost units}} = \frac{£60\ 000}{1600} = £37.50 \text{ overhead per unit}$$

The use of the cost unit OAR means that overheads are charged at a rate of £37.50 per unit supplied. Therefore the use of the cost unit OAR for Job 03/2014 would result in an overhead charge of £9375 (£37.50 × 250 units produced).

The cost unit OAR is appropriate only if all units of production are the same.

2 Direct labour OAR

$$\frac{\text{TCCO}}{\text{Number of direct labour hours}} = \frac{£60\ 000}{5000}$$
$$= £12 \text{ overhead per direct labour hour (DLH)}$$

The use of the direct labour OAR means that overheads are charged at a rate of £12.00 per hour spent directly working on the job. The use of the direct labour OAR for Job 03/2014 is shown in the worked answer for Question (b). This method of absorbing or allocating overheads requires accurate records to be kept regarding the number of direct labour hours worked. However, this absorption rate is particularly suitable if the production department is labour intensive, as there will be a direct relationship between time spent on production and the overheads incurred.

3 Machine hour OAR

$$\frac{\text{TCCO}}{\text{Overhead per machine hour}} = \frac{£60\ 000}{4000} = £15 \text{ overhead per machine hour}$$

The use of the machine hour OAR means that overheads are charged at a rate of £15.00 per hour spent using machines to complete the job. Hence the use of the machine hour OAR for Job 03/2014 would result in an overhead charge of £7500 (£15 × 500 units produced). This method of absorbing or allocating overheads requires accurate records to be kept regarding the number of machine hours used. However, this absorption rate is particularly suitable if the production department is machine intensive, as there will be a direct relationship between machining time and the overheads incurred.

4 Direct wage percentage OAR

$$\frac{\text{TCCO}}{\text{Direct wages}} = \frac{£60\,000}{£50\,000} \times 100 = 120\%$$

The use of the direct wage percentage OAR will result in an overhead charge of £1.20 for every £1 of direct wages paid for completion of the job. Consequently, the use of the direct wage percentage OAR for Job 03/2014 results in an overhead charge of £4500 (£3750 × 120 per cent). This overhead absorption rate is in many cases an appropriate OAR as it takes account of rates of pay and the number of hours worked, which usually relate directly to the time a unit takes to produce. However, if there is considerable variation in the rates of pay workers receive, this method of overhead absorption or allocation is much less suitable.

5 Direct material cost percentage OAR

$$\frac{\text{TCCO}}{\text{Direct material cost}} = \frac{£60\,000}{£40\,000} \times 100 = 150\%$$

The use of the direct material cost percentage OAR will result in an overhead charge of £1.50 for every £1 of direct material used in the job. The overheads for Job 03/2014 resulting from the use of the direct material cost percentage are £7500 (£5000 × 150 per cent). This overhead absorption rate does not take account of time, i.e. if two jobs take the same amount of time to complete but one job uses more expensive materials, the overhead absorption rates will differ.

6 Prime cost percentage OAR

$$\frac{\text{TCCO}}{\text{Prime costs}} = \frac{£60\,000}{£90\,000} \times 100 = 66.7\%$$

The use of the prime cost percentage OAR will result in an overhead charge of £0.67 for every £1 of prime cost for the job. Hence the use of the prime cost percentage OAR will give an overhead charge of £5836.25 (£8750 × 66.7 per cent). This overhead absorption rate combines the downside of both the direct materials OAR and direct wages OAR, without having any benefits of its own.

Workings, answers and comments – part (b)

The next step is to apply one of the overhead absorption rates to Job 03/2014 and calculate a quote or total cost for Job 03/2014. There is considerable variation in the overheads to be charged depending on the overhead absorption rate used, from £9375 with the cost unit OAR down to £4500 with the direct wage OAR. In theory, any of the six overhead absorption rates can be used to provide a quote for a job. However, the company must choose one overhead absorption rate to use in its production department and use it consistently. In most instances the overheads incurred relate to the time a job spends in production, so it is usually best to choose a rate that takes account of time, such as the direct labour hours OAR or the direct machine hours OAR.

The production department in the example has marginally more labour hours (5000 hours) than machine hours (4000 hours), hence the company incurs overhead predominantly to provide labour. Therefore use of the direct labour hours OAR would be most appropriate and give a total cost of £97 500, as shown in the following calculation.

Job No 03/2014

1 Number of hours worked
   = Direct wages paid/hourly rate
   = £3750/£6 per hour
   = 625 hours worked on Job 03/2014

2 Calculation of overheads
   = Number of hours worked × Direct labour OAR
   = 625 × £12 (from answer to Q1)
   = £7500

3 Calculation of quote for job 03/2014

	£
Direct materials	40 000
Direct wages	50 000
Prime cost	90 000
Overheads	7 500
Total Cost	97 500

✓ Check your understanding

Do you understand the six different ways in which production overheads can be absorbed into the costs for a particular job?

Check your understanding by briefly explaining the six different absorption rates.

■ Marginal costing

Marginal costing is the technique of charging variable costs to the cost of production units. This is a direct contrast with absorption costing where, in addition to variable costs, fixed costs or overheads are charged to cost units by use of one of the overhead absorption rates examined in the previous section.

A key figure in marginal costing is the contribution. This is the difference between sales and variable costs and is a contribution towards fixed costs. Therefore fixed costs for a period are written off against the contribution for that period to give the final profit or loss for the period. The worked example below demonstrates the calculation of profit and contribution. Contribution can be calculated for one unit or any chosen level of sales.

Example question

Calculation of contribution

A product sells for £75 and has variable costs of £45. During the period ending 31 March 2003 the product sold 3500 units. Fixed costs for the period were £30 000. Calculate the total profit, contribution per unit and contribution for sales of 3500 units.

Working

	per unit	*3500 units*
Selling price	£75	£262 500
less Variable costs	£45	£157 500
Contribution	£30	£105 000
less Fixed cost		£30 000
Profit		£75 000

Answer

Total profit is £75 000, contribution per unit is £30, and contribution for 3500 units is £105 000.

■ Marginal costing and decision making

Marginal costing can assist in decision making, particularly when deciding:

- ■ which products to manufacture;
- ■ whether to stop production of one or more products;
- ■ whether to accept a special order or contract;
- ■ whether to make or buy a component.

Example question

Which products to manufacture

A company has a choice of manufacturing two out of three products. Indicate which products should be manufactured when each of the following ranking methods is applied to the information given below.

1 Ranking by contribution.
2 Ranking by profit/volume ratio.
3 Ranking by total contribution.

Information provided

	Product A	*Product B*	*Product C*
Selling price per unit	£35	£60	£45
Variable costs per unit			
Materials	£10	£24	£18
Labour	£6	£14	£8
Overheads	£4	£6	£6
Total cost	£20	£44	£32
Contribution per unit	£15	£16	£13

1 Ranking by contribution

Working and comment

This method of deciding which products to manufacture assumes that there are no limits on production resources or sales that can be achieved. Therefore the amount of the unit contribution can be the decision criterion.

Answer

Products A and B have the highest unit contributions, £15 and £16 respectively, and would therefore be the preferred products for manufacture.

2 Ranking by profit/volume ratio

Working and comment

If the products have a maximum sales income that can be achieved from any of the three products, then the profit/volume ratio can be used to rank the products. If maximum sales of £100 000 could be achieved for each of the three products, the calculation would be

$$\text{Profit/Volume ratio} = \frac{\text{Contribution}}{\text{Selling price per unit}} \times 100$$

$$\text{Product A} = \frac{£15}{£35} \times 100 = 42.9\%$$

$$\text{Product B} = \frac{£16}{£60} \times 100 = 26.7\%$$

$$\text{Product C} = \frac{£13}{£45} \times 100 = 28.9\%$$

With sales of £100 000 the contribution from Product A would be £42 900, 42.9 per cent of £100 000; for Product B the contribution would be £26 700, 26.7 per cent of £100 000; and for Product C the contribution would be £28 900, 28.9 per cent of £100 000.

Answer

In this instance the company should choose Products A and C as they make the biggest contributions to fixed costs.

3 Ranking by total contribution

Working and comment

If the maximum sales achievable for each product vary, ranking should be by the total contribution that each product makes to fixed costs. If maximum sales achievable are 5000 units of Product A, or 2500 units of Product B or 3500 of Product C, the following ranking exercise helps establish which products should be produced.

Total contribution = sales units × contribution per unit

Product A – Total contribution = 5000 units × £15 = £75 000
Product B – Total contribution = 2500 units × £16 = £40 000
Product C – Total contribution = 3500 units × £13 = £45 500

Answer

Products A and C have the highest total contribution and should therefore be the products manufactured.

Example question | **Ceasing manufacture of a product**

A company produces a range of three products. The profit and loss account for the period ending 31 March 2003 shows that Product B has made a loss. The managing director suggests that Product B should be dropped as this will not influence sales of the other products. Produce a marginal cost statement for the period ending 31 March 2003 and advise the managing director as regards dropping Product B.

Information provided

Profit and loss account, year ended 31 March 2003

	Product A	Product B	Product C
Sales	250 000	200 000	140 000
Direct materials	62 500	110 000	32 500
Direct labour	55 000	60 000	40 000
Variable overheads	35 000	12 000	29 000
Fixed overheads	50 000	65 000	30 000
Total costs	202 500	247 000	131 500
Profit/(Loss)	47 500	(47 000)	8 500

Working and comment – marginal cost statement

Marginal cost statement, year ended 31 March 2003

	Product A	Product B	Product C	Total
Sales	250 000	200 000	140 000	590 000
Direct materials	62 500	110 000	32 500	205 000
Direct labour	55 000	60 000	40 000	155 000
Variable overheads	35 000	12 000	29 000	76 000
Total variable costs	152 500	182 000	101 500	436 000
Contribution	97 500	18 000	38 500	154 000
Less total fixed costs				145 000
Profit				9 000

The marginal cost statement above shows that Product B makes a contribution of £18 000 to fixed costs. If the company ceased to manufacture Product B, the contribution of £18 000 would be lost and the company would make a total loss of £9000, calculated in the following way: profit £9000 – Product B contribution £18 000 = –£9000 loss. The general rule is that it is usually expedient to continue with a product that makes a contribution to fixed costs.

Answer

Advise the managing director to continue manufacturing Product B.

Example question | ## Acceptance of a special order or contract

A company manufactures a product that has variable costs of £15 per unit and a selling price of £19.50. A regular customer asks for an additional 3000 units as well as its normal order, but wants to negotiate a special price of £18 per unit for the additional units. Should the company agree?

Working and comment

In this situation there are clearly issues of customer relationships and the behaviour of competitors, particularly if the additional order is not accepted. However, the financial viewpoint is straightforward. The variable costs of the product are £15, hence any selling price above £15 will give a contribution. Accordingly for financial reasons it is worth accepting the order at the reduced price of £18 per unit. In this case the general rule applies that any product giving a contribution is worth manufacturing.

In contrast it would not make financial sense to sell the product at a price less than variable costs as this would result in a negative contribution. Similarly, if the company could supply the required additional 3000 units at £18 but to do so had to reduce its current sales at £19.50, accepting the additional order would reduce the total contribution and therefore it should not be accepted.

Answer

In this case accept the additional order at a price of £18.

Example question | ## Making or buying a product

Company CHC can make Component X itself and incur variable costs of £27 per unit or purchase the component from Company RBC for £30 per unit. Which is the best option for Company CHC?

Working and comment

If Company CHC has unused capacity, it makes sense for the component to be produced in-house as the variable cost of £27 per unit is lower than the buying-in price of £30 per unit. It should be noted that fixed costs are omitted from the comparison as they will continue to be paid even when none of the factory facilities is in use. If the company does not have unused capacity and in-house manufacture of the component requires manufacture of another product to be stopped, further analysis is required.

Answer

In this case Company CHC should manufacture the component in-house.

☑ Check your understanding

Do you understand how marginal costing can assist organisations in decision making concerning the purchase and manufacture of goods?

Check your understanding by explaining how marginal costing can be used to help a company decide:

- which products to manufacture;
- whether it should cease the manufacture of particular products;
- whether it should accept a detailed contract to manufacture and supply goods;
- whether it should make or buy in a component.

Investment appraisal

Investment appraisal techniques are used by management to help in making decisions concerning investment in long-term projects and spending capital finance. The application of the investment appraisal methods discussed in this chapter provides quantitative data for use in this type of management decision making. Quantitative data can be useful and pertinent when decisions are being made concerning the investment of capital that an organisation has raised. Hence there is a clear overlap between investment appraisal, an area of management accounting, and the use to which the funds or capital raised are put (*see* section on financial management earlier in this chapter). Capital will be invested in major projects such as the purchase of new equipment or machinery, the acquisition of another company or the development and launch of a new product or service.

Thorough and objective evaluation of an investment opportunity before capital is spent will include assessment of both quantitative and qualitative information. Assessment of any investment opportunity will also include estimating the risk involved in not making the investment and an evaluation of the risk if the project fails. The quantitative assessment of an investment opportunity can be carried out by using any of the investment appraisal methods discussed in this chapter: payback, accounting rate of return, net present value and internal rate of return. An investment represents the commitment of money now for gains or returns in the future, and the quantitative data generated by investment appraisal will help answer the following questions concerning an investment:

1 Will the investment provide an adequate financial return?
2 Is the investment the best alternative from the options the company has available?
3 What is the cost if the project fails?

■ Payback method

The **payback method** measures the length of time taken for the return on the investment exactly to equal the amount originally invested. Hence where two or more investment proposals are being considered, the one that recovers the original investment in the shortest time is the more acceptable.

Payback method

Consider each of the three investment opportunities outlined below. Apply the payback method and state which would be the preferred investment.

	Investment A	Investment B	Investment C
Year 0 original investment	(£20 000)	(£30 000)	(£40 000)
Year 1 net cashflow	£12 000	£8 000	£16 000
Year 2 net cashflow	£6 000	£8 000	£12 000
Year 3 net cashflow	£6 000	£6 000	£10 000
Year 4 net cashflow	£4 000	£6 000	£8 000
Year 5 net cashflow	£4 000	£6 000	£8 000

Example calculation – Payback method – Investment A

Investment A = £20 000

	Cashflow	Cumulative cashflow
Year 1 net cashflow	£12 000	£12 000
Year 2 net cashflow	£6 000	£18 000
Year 3 net cashflow	£6 000	£24 000
Year 4 net cashflow	£4 000	£28 000
Year 5 net cashflow	£4 000	£32 000

1 The investment has been paid back by the end of Year 3.
2 But exactly when in Year 3 does payback occur?
3 At the end of Year 2 £18 000 has been paid back, leaving £2000 of the original £20 000 investment still to be paid back.
4 The total payback in Year 3 is £6000, therefore the calculation below shows that the £2000 is paid back in the first four months of Year 3.

$$\frac{\text{£2000 (to payback after Year 2)}}{\text{£6000 (Year 3 net cashflow)}} \times 12 \text{ (months in a year)} = \frac{2000}{6000} \times 12 = 4 \text{ months}$$

Therefore the total payback period is 2 years 4 months.
The payback period for Investments B and C can be calculated in the same way.

	Investment A	Investment B	Investment C
Payback period	2 years 4 months	4 years 4 months	3 years 3 months

Answer

Hence the preferred investment is A, as this pays back in the shortest time.

Advantages and disadvantages of the payback method

The advantages of the payback method are that the **payback period** is simple to calculate and easy to understand. However, the payback method takes no account of profit, loss and depreciation from the sale of fixed assets, although it does recognise the uncertainty of the future. Therefore the payback method acknowledges that the sooner the investment is recovered, the smaller the risk involved, and thus uses the earliest cashflows first. If the money is to be invested in a project that is subject to rapid technological change, the project with the most rapid payback and turnaround will be the most favourable.

Further drawbacks of the payback method are that it ignores all cashflow after the payback period and the total life of the project. Other difficulties are that no allowances are made for the lower value of money paid back in the future. The value of money paid back today is more than that of money paid back in the future, i.e. £100 today is worth more than £100 in five years' time. An added problem with the payback method is that profits are disregarded and an investment with a shorter payback period may be selected even if it is less profitable overall than a project that takes longer to pay back. For example, an investment of £5000 will pay back quicker than a £50 000 investment, regardless of the fact that the £50 000 investment may be more profitable in the long run. Another disadvantage is that the payback method relies on estimates of net cash inflows and the timing of their receipt.

◼ Accounting rate of return

The **accounting rate of return (ARR)** expresses the profit generated by an investment or project as a percentage of the capital invested.

$$ARR = \frac{Profit}{Capital\ employed} \times 100$$

In the ARR calculation the net profit before interest and taxation figure is used and averaged over the lifetime of the project. The capital employed can be either the **initial capital employed** or the **average capital employed** over the lifetime of the project. The latter takes into account the residual value of the project at the end of its working life – *see* method 2 below.

Therefore two methods for carrying out ARR calculations exist:

Method 1

$$ARR = \frac{average\ net\ profit\ per\ annum}{initial\ capital\ employed} \times 100$$

Method 2

$$ARR = \frac{average\ net\ profit\ per\ annum}{average\ capital\ employed^*} \times 100$$

$$^*average\ capital\ employed = \frac{initial\ capital\ employed + residual\ value}{2}$$

The worked example below uses method 2, average capital employed.

Example question | **Accounting rate of return**

Consider each of the three investment opportunities outlined below. Apply the accounting rate of return (ARR) method and state which would be the preferred investment.

	Investment A	Investment B	Investment C
Year 0 original investment	(£20 000)	(£30 000)	(£40 000)
Year 1 net profit	£12 000	£8 000	£16 000
Year 2 net profit	£6 000	£8 000	£12 000
Year 3 net profit	£6 000	£6 000	£10 000
Year 4 net profit	£4 000	£6 000	£8 000
Year 5 net profit	£4 000	£6 000	£8 000

Example calculation – accounting rate of return – method 2

	Investment A	Investment B	Investment C
Total net return	£32 000	£34 000	£54 000
less original investment	£20 000	£30 000	£40 000
Net profit	£12 000	£4 000	£14 000
Years of life	5	5	5
Average profit per annum (profit/years of life)	£2400	£800	£2800
Residual value	£5000	£5000	£7000
Average capital employed	$\dfrac{£20\,000 + £5000}{2}$	$\dfrac{£30\,000 + £5000}{2}$	$\dfrac{£40\,000 + £7000}{2}$
	= £12 500	= £17 500	= £23 500
Average rate of return	$\dfrac{£2400}{£12\,500} \times 100$	$\dfrac{£800}{£17\,500} \times 100$	$\dfrac{£2800}{£23\,500} \times 100$
	= 19.2%	= 4.6%	= 11.9%

Answer

Hence the preferred investment is A, as this shows the highest return.

Advantages and disadvantages of the accounting rate of return method

The ARR encompasses the entire life of the project and all expected profits. Its other principal advantage is its comparative simplicity to calculate and understand. However, there are a number of disadvantages relating to this method of investment appraisal. These include the net profit being defined in different ways, for example should net profit before or after depreciation on the investment be used? Other difficulties include the ARR using profits as a key factor in the calculation, whereas in investment decisions cashflow is the crucial factor. Also the ARR does not make allowances for the different value of money over time, compared with **discounted cashflow methods** (see the next method of investment appraisal to be looked at, net present value). High returns in the early years of an investment have a greater net worth and are easier to predict, but these factors are not taken account in ARR calculations. Interpretation of the ARR results can be ambiguous as often there will be no indication of what an acceptable ARR would be for a specific project, and furthermore different ARRs will be acceptable in different situations.

Finally, the use of residual investment values can substantially affect the ARR calculated. The use of residual values and an average capital employed can make a notable difference in the ARR values for a project. Remember that residual values are difficult to estimate and the difference they can make is illustrated below. The higher the residual value, the lower the ARR.

Example	
	Average net profit per annum = £100 000
	Initial capital employed = £300 000
	Residual values = £10 000 and £50 000

1 Residual value = £10 000

$$\text{Average capital employed} = \frac{£300\ 000 + £10\ 000}{2} = £155\ 000$$

$$\text{ARR} = \frac{£100\ 000}{£155\ 000} \times 100$$

$$\text{ARR} = 64.5\%$$

2 Residual value = £50 000

$$\text{Average capital employed} = \frac{£300\ 000 + £50\ 000}{2} = £175\ 000$$

$$\text{ARR} = \frac{£100\ 000}{£175\ 000} \times 100$$

$$\text{ARR} = 57.1\%$$

Despite the disadvantages, the ARR method of investment appraisal is suitable if the project is short term and accurate estimates can be made for any residual values to be included in the calculations.

✓ Check your understanding

Do you understand the advantages and disadvantages of payback and accounting rate of return as methods of investment appraisal?

Check your understanding by comparing and contrasting the payback and accounting rate of return methods of investment appraisal.

■ Net present value

The **net present value (NPV)** method of investment appraisal makes allowances for money received in the future being worth less than if it were received today. Therefore the NPV method converts future net cashflows into present-day values by discounting the value of money that is expected to be received in the future.

If the discounted net cashflows exceed the original investment then the project could go ahead. When choosing between two or more projects, the project with the highest positive NPV exceeds its original investment by the greatest amount and is usually the preferred project. If the discounted net cashflows are less than the original investment, then the investment should not be allowed to proceed as money will be lost. An acceptable interest rate or rate of return has to be decided on and the discounting factors to be used in the NPV calculation need to be read from a discount table.

In selecting a discounting rate the following need to be considered:

- the rate of interest that the company could obtain if the money were invested outside the business;
- the cost of capital required to make the investment;
- the rate of return (internal) that the company expects to gain on investments.

If the company is to be profitable, then in the long run the rate of return (internal) needs to exceed the external rate that it can earn investing outside the business. The cashflows are multiplied by the discount cashflow value from the discount tables to give the discounted value of future net cashflows. The discounted net cashflows are added up and the original investment subtracted – if the total NPV is positive, the project is acceptable.

Example question	**Net present value method**

Consider each of the three investment opportunities outlined below. Apply the NPV method of investment appraisal and state which would be the preferred investment. The cost of capital is 8 per cent.

	Investment A	*Investment B*	*Investment C*
Year 0 original investment	(£20 000)	(£30 000)	(£40 000)
Year 1 net cashflows	£10 000	£6 000	£12 000
Year 2 net cashflows	£8 000	£6 000	£12 000
Year 3 net cashflows	£6 000	£6 000	£12 000
Year 4 net cashflows	£4 000	£8 000	£12 000
Year 5 net cashflows	£4 000	£12 000	£12 000

Calculation – net present value

	Investment A			*Investment B*			*Investment C*		
	Cashflow	*DCF 8%*	*Net Cashflow*	*Cashflow*	*DCF 8%*	*Net Cashflow*	*Cashflow*	*DCF 8%*	*Net Cashflow*
Yr 0	(20 000)	1.000	(20 000)	(30 000)	1.000	(30 000)	(40 000)	1.000	(40 000)
Yr 1	10 000	.926	9 260	6 000	.926	5 556	12 000	.926	11 112
Yr 2	8 000	.858	6 864	6 000	.858	5 148	12 000	.858	10 296
Yr 3	6 000	.794	4 764	6 000	.794	4 764	12 000	.794	9 528
Yr 4	4 000	.735	2 940	8 000	.735	5 880	12 000	.735	8 820
Yr 5	4 000	.681	2 724	12 000	.681	8 172	12 000	.681	8 172
			+6 652			−480			+7 928

Answer

Hence the preferred investment is C, as this has the highest positive NPV.

Advantages and disadvantages of the net present value method

The main advantage of the NPV method is that cashflows and hence the relevance of liquidity are both taken account of in the calculations. The other fundamental advantage is that it takes account of the time value of money, unlike the payback and ARR methods. The comparison between projects' NPV values is straightforward and it is easy to judge which is the most profitable project. The disadvantages of the NPV method lie in the difficulty of accurately estimating the initial cost of the project, cash in-flows and the time periods in which cash in-flows will occur.

■ Internal rate of return

The **internal rate of return (IRR)** method of investment appraisal is similar to the net present value method. The key difference between NPV and IRR is that IRR seeks a discount rate at which the net cash in-flows, when discounted, exactly equal the amount originally invested, i.e. NPV = 0. The initial pieces of information that have to be sought for an IRR calculation are a discount rate giving a positive return or positive NPV, and a discount rate giving a negative NPV. There is no easy way of ascertaining which discount rates will give a positive or negative NPV, except by trial and error coupled with careful judgement.

The IRR is determined by interpolation between the discount rate giving a positive NPV and that giving a negative NPV (*see* guidelines below). The interpolation between the two rates is done by use of the formula shown below. This is not an exact method and the closer together the two discount rates used in the calculation, the more accurate the answer will be.

The formula for calculating the IRR is as follows:

$$\text{IRR} = \text{Positive rate} + \frac{(\text{Positive NPV} \times \text{Difference between discount rates})}{(\text{Range of NPV values})}$$

Guidelines for choosing discounting cashflow rates for IRR calculations

1 You have to find two DCF rates:
   (a) one giving a positive NPV value;
   (b) one giving a negative NPV value.
2 Which DCF rates do you choose?
   (a) Start with a rate of around 10 per cent. If this gives you a *total negative NPV*, then you need to choose a rate that is less than 10 per cent to get a *total positive NPV*, say 5 per cent.
   (b) If the first DCF rate you choose, say 10 per cent, gives you a *positive total NPV*, then the second rate will have to be greater than 10 per cent: you could try 15 per cent.
   (c) The two DCF rates used do not want to be more than 5 per cent apart, although they can of course be less than 5 per cent apart.
3 An alternative to starting with, say, 10 per cent is to start with the DCF rate you may have used in a previous NPV calculation on the same data. To do this the NPV given must be fairly close to zero.

| Example question | **Internal rate of return method** |

The company considering each of the three investment opportunities shown below requires a return of at least 10 per cent on all the investments it makes. Using the IRR method of investment appraisal, state which of the three investment opportunities the company should seriously consider.

	Investment A	Investment B	Investment C
Year 0 original investment	(£20 000)	(£30 000)	(£40 000)
Year 1 net cashflow	£10 000	£6 000	£12 000
Year 2 net cashflow	£8 000	£6 000	£12 000
Year 3 net cashflow	£6 000	£6 000	£12 000
Year 4 net cashflow	£4 000	£8 000	£12 000
Year 5 net cashflow	£4 000	£12 000	£12 000

Example calculation – internal rate of return – investment A

	Cashflow	DCF 22%	Net Cashflow	Cashflow	DCF 23%	Net Cashflow
Year 0	(20 000)	1.000	(20 000)	(20 000)	1.000	(20 000)
Year 1	10 000	0.820	8 200	10 000	0.813	8 130
Year 2	8 000	0.672	5 376	8 000	0.661	5 288
Year 3	6 000	0.551	3 306	6 000	0.537	3 222
Year 4	4 000	0.451	1 804	4 000	0.437	1 748
Year 5	4 000	0.370	1 480	4 000	0.355	1 420
			+166			−192

Internal rate of return = 22% + (166/358 × 1) = 22.464%

Example calculation – internal rate of return – investment B

	Cashflow	DCF 7%	Net Cashflow	Cashflow	DCF 8%	Net Cashflow
Year 0	(30 000)	1.000	(30 000)	(30 000)	1.000	(30 000)
Year 1	6 000	0.935	5 610	6 000	0.926	5 556
Year 2	6 000	0.873	5 238	6 000	0.857	5 142
Year 3	6 000	0.816	4 896	6 000	0.794	4 764
Year 4	8 000	0.763	6 104	8 000	0.735	5 880
Year 5	12 000	0.713	8 556	12 000	0.681	8 172
			+404			−486

Internal rate of return = 7% + (404/890 × 1) = 7.454%

Example calculation – internal rate of return – investment C

	Cashflow	DCF 16%	Net Cashflow	Cashflow	DCF 15%	Net Cashflow
Year 0	(40 000)	1.000	(40 000)	(40 000)	1.000	(40 000)
Year 1	12 000	0.862	10 344	12 000	0.870	10 440
Year 2	12 000	0.743	8 916	12 000	0.756	9 072
Year 3	12 000	0.641	7 692	12 000	0.658	7 896
Year 4	12 000	0.552	6 624	12 000	0.572	6 864
Year 5	12 000	0.476	5 712	12 000	0.497	5 964
			−712			+236

Internal rate of return = 15% + (236/948 × 1) = 15.249%

Answer

The investments that should be seriously considered are investments A and C, as both have an IRR of greater than 10 per cent.

Advantages and disadvantages of the internal rate of return method

The two clear advantages of the IRR method are that emphasis is placed on liquidity in the calculation and it results in a clear percentage return required on investment. The IRR is a measure of the intensity of capital use and also gives a return for risks. In the worked example for Investment A, if the cost of capital is 15 per cent and the IRR is 22.464 per cent, the return for the risk is therefore 7.464 per cent, the difference between the two figures (22.464 − 15). In general IRR is a more difficult method to apply than NPV. In most cases IRR and NPV will give the same answer as to acceptance or rejection of an investment, but may vary in ranking, thus possibly leading to different choices.

The disadvantages of the IRR method are that the reasoning behind the calculation is not easy to understand and it is difficult to determine two interest rates to interpolate between. Careful judgement should be exercised when making decisions based on IRR calculations. For example, an IRR of 25 per cent may appear attractive, but if the original investment is only £500, then an IRR of 15 per cent on an original investment of £10 000 would be more sensible.

☑ Check your understanding

Do you understand the similarities and differences between NPV and IRR methods of investment appraisal?

Check your understanding by explaining the use of both NPV and IRR as methods of investment apprasial.

Financial reporting

In the UK companies are obliged by law to produce an annual report and accounts that relate to their financial and business performance. A company's annual report and accounts have to be audited and a copy filed with the Registrar of Companies at Companies House in London. The Companies Acts of 1981, 1985 and 1989 specify the layout and format of modern-day published accounts. The published accounts have to contain certain pieces of information to satisfy the legal requirements. The types of information required include information on the directors and their report, **financial statements**, information to clarify the details of the report and accounts, and an **auditor's report**.

The section of the published accounts giving information about the directors is often at the front. In the case of many large well-known companies, e.g. Marks and Spencer or British Aerospace, a photograph of each director is accompanied by a vignette on their career to date and their role on the board. These directors have to produce a report to be included in the published accounts. The report must provide fair comment on the company's performance over the financial year and important events that have occurred since the year end. Details of transactions involving its own shares by the company must also be included in the directors' report. Comment must also be included on probable future developments and on any research and development that the company is undertaking. In the introductory case study reporting on the publication of SmithKline Beecham's 1996 results, the company's share price clearly rose in late 1996 and early 1997. This linked directly with the company reporting promising results on the research and development of new drugs for illnesses such as Alzheimer's disease and migraines.

The financial statements that need to be included in published accounts are the profit and loss account, the balance sheet and a cashflow statement. The profit and loss account and the balance sheet are summary statements. The profit and loss account provides a summary of the company's income or sales revenue and expenditure, leaving a profit or loss on the bottom line. This is complemented by the balance sheet, which summarises the company's financial position at the end of the financial year, showing its assets and liabilities. In contrast, the cashflow statement shows in detail how the business has financed its operations. The details included in a cashflow statement are the particulars of how money has been raised – shares, loans or profits – and how the money has been spent – to acquire fixed assets such as buildings and machinery, or to buy current assets such as stock, raw materials and components.

The other sections that need to appear in published accounts are a statement of accounting policies, notes to accounts and statistical information. Notes to accounts provide a large amount of detail relating to the accounts and activities of the company. Some of the details included in the notes are how the operating profit and turnover figures are calculated, how individual asset and liability figures are calculated, loans and interest payments, tax details, paid and proposed dividends, and changes to accounting policies. A complete list can be found in Dyson listed in further reading for this chapter. The statistical information section of the published accounts may compare the current year's financial performance with results from previous years. This can be done by use of the financial ratios for the business over two or more years – *see* Michael Brett's book.[13]

A necessary item in any annual report and accounts is the auditor's report. The auditor should be independent of the directors of the company and a member of one of the chartered professional accounting bodies approved to perform audits. The auditor's report is addressed to the shareholders and should ideally state that the report and accounts provide a true and fair view of the company's activities for the financial year examined. To do this the auditor needs to satisfy him/herself that the reported assets exist and have been correctly valued in the accounts. The auditor also needs to ensure that the disclosure of liabilities is complete and thorough. The auditor may also inspect data and documents to confirm that entries in the books are genuine, as well as checking the accuracy of the books. Finally, the auditor should check that all benefits are accounted for and have been collected by the proper recipients.

However, the thoroughness of auditing processes has been called into question by the collapse of Enron, the energy trader, in the United States. Arthur Andersen, an 89-year-old company and one of the world's top five accounting firms, signed off Enron's annual report for 2001. Just a few months after this Enron admitted its accounts for 2001 and the previous three years were more or less a work of fiction. Andersen then lost most of its business and 20 000 of its 28 000 employees in the United States. In June 2002 a jury in the US found Andersen guilty of shredding documents relating to Enron. Andersen was considering an appeal.

The annual report and accounts need to give a true and fair view of a company's activities for the financial year examined, as they provide significant information on the company and its activities and will therefore be of interest to a variety of players who want to know about the business. This will allow concerned parties or financial stakeholders to make informed judgements regarding their role in relation to the company.

■ Financial stakeholders

The state

The financial information provided will determine the level and amount of taxation that a company will pay to the state. At the time of writing, in the UK the current level of corporation tax is 30 per cent and for small businesses it is 19 per cent.

Current and potential investors

The information provided in the annual report and accounts will allow current and potential investors to make informed judgements about future and current investments. For example, in February 1997 SmithKline Beecham's shareholders would have very likely decided to hold on to their shares in the company, as dividends rose by 25 per cent and the company was showing significant growth in a number of areas. For further details see the introductory case study at the start of this chapter.

Employees

Companies that choose to involve employees in the running of the business may see the disclosure of financial information as an important element of the employees' participation. This is especially so if a profit-sharing or an employee share ownership scheme operates.

Creditors and banks

These interested parties are concerned with the company's liquidity and need to assess the risk involved in offering credit or loans. The information disclosed in the annual report and accounts will be useful in assessing this risk.

Customers and debtors

Customers and debtors are stakeholders who purchase the company's products and services and may find the information disclosed in the annual report and accounts useful in assessing the risk of placing long-term or large orders.

Competitors   Competitors as stakeholders typically find the information provided by the annual report and accounts a practical yardstick against which to measure their own performance. Insights into which directions competitors could be heading may be offered in their annual reports and accounts.

> ### ☑ Check your understanding
>
> *Do you understand which information is available in a company's annual report and accounts and how different financial stakeholders could use this information?*
>
> Check your understanding by explaining how the following people and organisations might use Marks and Spencer's annual report and accounts:
>
> - the John Lewis partnership;
> - Mr John Jones who shops at M&S on Sauchiehall Street in Glasgow and is thinking of buying shares in the company;
> - the Inland Revenue;
> - Mrs Susan Atkin who works at M&S at Meadowhall in Sheffield and owns 1000 shares in the company.

Summary

This chapter examined financial external environmental factors which impact on organisations as well as examining some of the financial activities which organisations routinely undertake. The following summary covers all aspects of this chapter.

1 In recent years two of the financial external environmental factors which have influenced many businesses in the UK are the euro and the minimum wage. The euro was introduced for business transactions in most European countries on 1 January 1999 and coins and notes followed on 1 January 2002. The minimum wage was introduced in the UK in April 1999, when it was £3.60 for adults; by February 2003 it was £4.20.

2 Financial management involves the raising and spending of capital finance by an organisation. Sources of capital for a company include its reserves (profits from previous years), borrowing money from a bank, financial institution or, if eligible, an organisation like the Prince's Trust, issuing shares, having a rights issue or seeking government funding.

3 Costing involves looking at and defining the costs involved in producing a product or service. Costs can be defined as fixed or variable. The cost of producing a product or service has three elements to it: the cost of materials, labour and overheads.

4 Absorption costing takes account of both fixed and variable costs, with the aim of ensuring that all the overhead costs incurred are covered by revenues.

5 Marginal costing allocates variable costs only to the cost of production units. A key figure in marginal costing is the difference between sales and variable costs, which is called contribution. Fixed costs are written off against contribution to give a final profit or loss.

6 The payback method of investment appraisal measures the length of time taken for the return on the investment to exactly equal the amount originally invested.

7 The accounting rate of return (ARR) expresses the profit an investment makes as a percentage of the capital invested. Like the payback method of investment appraisal it is easy to calculate and understand.

8 The net present value (NPV) method of investment appraisal takes account of all returns over the life of the investment and of money received in the future being of less value than that received today.

9 The internal rate of return (IRR) is similar to the NPV method, but seeks a discount rate at which cash inflows, when discounted, exactly equal the amount originally invested, i.e. NPV = 0.

10 Financial reports and accounts contain information on directors and their statement, financial statements (profit and loss account, balance sheet and cash flow statement), information and notes on the financial statements and an auditor's report. The annual report and accounts of a company provide financial stakeholders with information about the company which allows them to make informed decisions concerning their involvement with the company.

Learning outcomes for case studies

While reading this chapter and engaging in the activities, you should have learned how to apply theory and models, analyse situations, and evaluate the application and analysis you undertake. The learning outcomes specified below outline the type of application, analysis and evaluation of which you should be capable in relation to organisations. The case studies and the questions which follow provide an opportunity for you to test how well you have achieved the learning outcomes for the ethical issues and exit case studies for this chapter.

Application	Check you have achieved this by	
1 Predict how financial environmental factors impact on organisations	summarising the likely impact of issues such as the euro, minimum wage and PFI on organisations	answering ethical case study questions 2 & 3 answering exit case study questions 1 & 2
Analysis	**Check you have achieved this by**	
1 Compare and contrast the different impacts a financial environmental factor may have on an organisation	identifying differing views on the impact of a financial environmental factor on an organisation	answering ethical case study questions 2 & 3 answering exit case study questions 1, 2 & 3
Evaluation	**Check you have achieved this by**	
1 Evaluate the usefulness and relevance of assessing the impact of financial-based environmental factors on organisations	selecting and considering the views that are relevant to the organisation at the current time	answering exit case study question 3

ETHICAL ISSUES CASE STUDY 6.2

FT

PFI vanishing trick

By Andrea Felsted and Michael Peel

Her Majesty's Prison Kilmarnock, off the A76 road to Dumfries, stands as a symbol of how government efforts to secure private finance for public services can lead to peculiar results.

The building, which occupies the site of an old ordnance factory and has room for 500 inmates, does not exist in the balance sheets of either the Scottish Prison Service or those of Kilmarnock Prison Services, the private sector operator.

'Neither party is recognising HMP Kilmarnock as a property asset,' noted Robert Black, Scotland's auditor-general, in a paper published in December. 'The purpose of this report is to bring the situation to public notice.'

Yet no one is doing anything wrong. The situation reflects inconsistencies in the rules on accounting for the government's fast-growing private finance initiative, known as PFI.

The result is that information about building projects such as roads, schools and prisons may be absent from the public record.

The non-existent assets are more than an arcane accounting oddity. By keeping PFI building work away from their balance sheets, government departments and private companies risk giving a less than full picture of their financial health.

The practice may come under increasing scrutiny after December's collapse of Enron, the US energy trader that foundered after it revealed it had kept liabilities off its balance sheet. 'It's a very interesting point,' says Andy Simmonds, technical partner at Deloitte & Touche, the professional services firm. 'If there's one area of UK accounting where there is a serious risk of stuff being off balance sheet, it's government accounting for PFI.'

PFI has been the subject of heated debate since it was launched by the Conservatives in 1992. It uses the private sector to design, build, operate and finance services that traditionally the public sector has paid for and provided itself, from hospitals and roads to defence equipment, prisons and government accommodation. The aim is to achieve greater efficiency and better value for money, but trade unions and the Labour-left call it privatisation by stealth.

Some 450 PFI schemes, with a capital value of more than £20bn, have been signed up to September 30 2001.

The financial reporting complexities arise because PFI deals are a mixture of asset-leasing and service provision. This means they are a blend of areas for which accounting rules traditionally diverge. The contrast reflects variations in the risks faced by each party involved.

If the government has a contract for someone to provide it purely with a service, it will typically have no liability to pay them until they have done what is agreed. This means payments for services generally appear as an operating cost each year in the profit and loss account, with no long-term asset or liability recorded on the balance sheet.

The twist is that the leasing element of a PFI contract adds to the risks faced by the purchaser. Contracts are often written so that the government is obliged to pay the private sector operator a minimum amount based on the level of interest payments on the loans used to finance the building work.

The government may also have a degree of ownership of the asset through an agreement to take it over after the PFI contract.

In other words, the government has both long-term liabilities and assets that arguably should be reflected on its balance sheet. 'Even though it's presented as a service contract, it still has some strings attached,' says Mr Simmonds.

The blurring of the boundaries between service provision and leasing provides scope for exploitation.

Accountants have complained of pressure to craft deals to allow assets to be kept off balance sheets. That way, private companies improve important financial ratios, while government departments score better on Treasury financial analyses that help to determine public spending. 'Government departments and agencies like these things accounted for off-balance sheet for public expenditure scoring reasons and budgetary reasons,' says one person involved in PFI accounting.

The situation alarmed the Accounting Standards Board, the body that makes reporting rules for the private sector, because it saw PFI as a threat to its attempts to clean up company accounting. The Treasury eventually agreed to revise its guidance to make clearer its approach to allocating risk.

This is seen as an improvement but it has failed to resolve all anomalies. The treatment of PFI contracts still depends on the opinions of the accountants. The auditors of the private company and the government department might legitimately decide that the rules do not require their clients to register building assets on their balance sheets.

'Symmetry is not a requirement in accounting,' says Isobel Sharp, technical partner at Andersen, the professional services firm. 'You have got two groups of people making their own judgements.'

▶

The battles over interpretation have taken place in private. Some departments and agencies are known to have changed accounting policies after discussions with the National Audit Office, the public-sector accounting watchdog – although the NAO has yet to make a public criticism. 'If we disagreed with an accounting treatment on PFI we would qualify the accounts and we haven't done so yet,' it says.

The Office of Government Commerce, which deals with PFI accounting, says projects where risk has been transferred to the private sector are likely to come off the balance sheet. In these instances, the capital spend will not appear on the balance sheet, but the payment for services will. Where a limited risk has been transferred, the project might appear on the balance sheet.

The debates and disagreements are likely to increase as the PFI programme continues to expand. Enron's demise has sensitised financial markets and analysts to any financial reporting that seems to lack transparency. The Accounting Standards Board is believed to be re-examining the issue of off-balance sheet accounting in the private sector.

Bob Kiley, London's transport commissioner, has attacked the public–private partnership structure plans for London Underground as an attempt 'to disguise massive expenditure by hiding it off the balance sheet'.

Examples such as Kilmarnock Prison may further bolster those who argue that PFI provides a means for both the government and the private sector to conceal spending and risks. 'For the companies, it is a hidden asset,' says one analyst. 'For the government, it is a hidden liability.'

Source: *Financial Times*, 8 March 2002. Reprinted with permission.

Questions for ethical issues case study 6.2	1 Read the case study and visit the website http://society.guardian.co.uk/. Find and read the article 'PFI: the basics' by Matt Weaver, Tuesday 15 January 2001.
	2 Explain the term 'PFI' and state whether you agree that it is an appropriate way of funding public-sector projects.
	3 Express your view and opinion on the last paragraph of the case study.

'Examples such as Kilmarnock Prison may further bolster those who argue that PFI provides a means for both the government and the private sector to conceal spending and risks. "For the companies, it is a hidden asset," says one analyst. "For the government, it is a hidden liability."'

◄◄ EXIT CASE STUDY 6.3   **FT**

TUC calls for up to 29% rise in minimum wage

By David Turner

The Trades Union Congress has called for a rise of up to 29 per cent in the national minimum wage, provoking warnings of possible job losses from business leaders.

The TUC says in a statement published today that the minimum wage should rise from £4.10 an hour to between £5 and £5.30 by autumn 2004.

The suggested increase dwarfs the government's planned rise of 10p an hour from October this year. But it reflects a new emphasis among unions on boosting the pay of the most poorly rewarded earners. Their efforts culminated earlier this month in a two-year settlement of almost 11 per cent for the lowest-paid council workers, bringing their hourly rate up from £4.80 to £5.32 an hour.

The TUC also says the lower minimum wage for 18 to 21-year-olds should be abolished, raising young people's wages to the same rate as older people's. It adds that there is 'a strong case for protection' for 16 and 17-year-olds, who enjoy no minimum rate.

John Monks, TUC general secretary, said: 'The introduction of the national minimum wage is one of the Labour government's major successes. It has made a real difference to more than a million workers and helped make Britain a fairer place.'

But the TUC's demands – which imply a rise of between 22 and 29 per cent – go far beyond simply increasing the rate in line with earnings growth across the whole economy. Economists are likely to warn that such a sharp rise in the rate would mean an unprecedented and risky experiment with Britain's labour market.

John Cridland, deputy director-general of the Confederation of British Industry, said: 'Other organisations can get easy headlines by naming higher national minimum wage levels. The CBI is concerned with making sure that low pay is tackled in a way that protects jobs and businesses.'

Source: Financial Times, 12 August 2002. Reprinted with permission.

Questions for exit case study 6.3

1   Summarise the situation the TUC would like to see as regards the minimum wage.

2   Imagine you were deputy director-general of the Confederation of British Industry, the employers organisation, and summarise the likely view of the CBI as regards the minimum wage.

3   Do you agree with the view of the TUC or the likely view of the CBI? Justify your answer. Should organisations consider the views of both the TUC and the CBI? Explain your answer.

 For more case studies please visit www.booksites.net/capon

Short-answer questions

1   Explain the role of the finance function.

2   Define financial accounting.

3   When did European monetary union occur?

4   When was the national minimum wage introduced in the UK and what level was it set at initially?

5   Name four sources of finance for a company.

6   State the key difference between a share issue and a rights issue.

7   What is a sale and leaseback and when do companies use one?

8   Define management accounting.

9   What is the key difference between absorption and marginal costing?

10   What is the payback method?

11   State the key advantages of the NPV method of investment appraisal.

12   Define financial reporting.

13   Why is an auditors' report necessary in published accounts?

14   Name the three financial statements that must be included in published accounts.

15   What use would a competitor have for a company's published accounts?

Learning outcomes for assignment questions

While reading this chapter and engaging in the activities, you should have learned how to apply theory and models, analyse situations, and evaluate the application and analysis you undertake. The learning outcomes specified below outline what you should be able to do and the assignment questions provide an opportunity for you to test how well you have achieved the learning outcomes for this chapter.

Application	Check you have achieved this by	
1 Demonstrate how financial factors impact on private and public organisations	identifying the impact of financial factors on an organisation with which you are familiar	answering assignment questions 1, 2 & 3
Analysis	**Check you have achieved this by**	
1 Discuss and evaluate the impact of financial factors on an organisation	summarising and judging the impact of financial factors on the organisation being examined	answering assignment questions 1, 2 & 3
Evaluation	**Check you have achieved this by**	
1 Evaluate the usefulness of assessing the impact of financial factors on an organisation	critically evaluating the usefulness of considering the impact of financial factors on organisations today	answering assignment questions 1 & 2

Assignment questions

1 Choose a private-sector organisation. Research and assess the impact of the euro on the organisation's activities. Should such an organisation routinely assess the impact of the euro on its commercial activities? Present your findings in a 2000-word report.

2 Choose a charity or public-sector organisation. Research and assess the impact of the minimum wage on the organisation's activities. In your opinion, is it relevant that a non-commercial organisation routinely assess the impact of financial matters, such as the minimum wage, on itself? Present your findings in a 2000-word report.

3 Evaluate the impact of the external environment and financial stakeholders on an organisation of your choice. Present your findings in a report, including an executive summary.

Weblinks available online at www.booksites.net/capon

1 This site contains more about the collapse of Enron and the role of Arthur Andersen. Generally the BBC website is a good source of information about news and business news.
http://news.bbc.co.uk/1/hi/business/1760107.stm
http://news.bbc.co.uk/1/hi/business/2047122.stm

2 The DTI website is a good source of information about all sorts of issues affecting organisations. The addresses below will connect you to the DTI website and its pages on help for small businesses and the national minimum wage respectively.
http://www.dti.gov.uk/for_business_small_business.html
http://www.dti.gov.uk/er/nmw/index.htm

3 The Treasury website contains information about influences on organisations, including the euro and the chancellor's annual budget statement.
http://www.hm-treasury.gov.uk/Documents/The_Euro/euro_index_index.cfm
http://www.hm-treasury.gov.uk/budget/bud_index.cfm

4 This is another government website which is about the euro.
http://www.euro.gov.uk/home.asp?f=1

5 Further information about financial help available for small and medium-sized businesses can be found at the websites below, for the Prince's Trust, British Venture Capitalist Association, Business Link Small Business Gateway, Business Connect and EDnet respectively.
http://www.princes-trust.org.uk/
http://www.bvca.co.uk/
http://www.businesslink.org
http://www.sbgateway.com/
http://www.businessconnect.org.uk/
http://www.ednet.ledu-ni.gov.uk

Further reading

Brett, M (2003) *How to Read the Financial Pages*, 6th edn, London: Random House Business Books.

Byers, S, Groth, J C, Richards, J C and Wiley, M K (1997) 'Capital investment analysis for managers', *Management Decision*, 35 (3&4).

Chadwick, L (2001) *Essential Finance and Accounts*, Harlow: Financial Times Prentice Hall.

Chadwick, L (2001) *Essential Management Accounting*, Harlow: Financial Times Prentice Hall.

Dyson, J R (2001) *Accounting for Non-Accounting Students*, 5th edn, London: Financial Times Prentice Hall.

Garrett, A (1999) 'Ready steady euro', *Management Today*, January.

Reid, W and Myddelton, D R (2000) *The Meaning of Company Accounts*, 7th edn, Aldershot: Gower.

Saunders, A (2000) 'Whose cash is king?', *Management Today*, June.

Taggart, J and Taggart, J (1999) 'International competitiveness and the single currency', *Business Strategy Review*, 10 (2), Summer.

Vernon, M (1998) 'Dangers of the short-term view (of the euro)', *Financial Times*, 5 November.

Wood, F and Sangster, A (2002) *Business Accounting: Volume 1*, 9th edn, London: Financial Times Prentice Hall.

Wood, F and Sangster, A (2002) *Business Accounting: Volume 2*, 9th edn, London: Financial Times Prentice Hall.

References

1 Helm, T (1998) 'Rome and Bonn clear the EMU hurdle', *Daily Telegraph*, 28 February.
2 Manning, A (1997) 'If it's good enough for everyone else, it's good enough for us', *Independent on Sunday*, 11 May.
3 Ibid.
4 Atkinson, M (1997) 'Experts press case for £3.85 minimum wage', *Observer*, 26 October.
5 Manning, op. cit.
6 Atkinson, op. cit.
7 Manning, op. cit.
8 Ibid.
9 Ibid.
10 http://www.dti.gov.uk/for_business_small_business.html.
11 http://www.princes-trust.org.uk/.
12 http://www.bvca.co.uk/.
13 Brett, M (1995) *How to Read the Financial Pages*, 4th edn, London: Century.

7

Human resource management

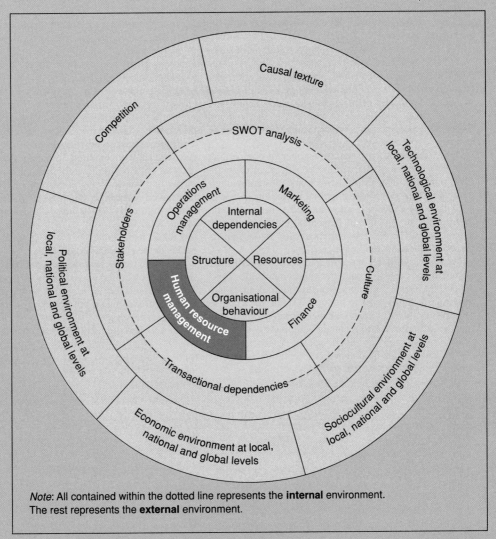

Causal texture

Competition

SWOT analysis

Technological environment at local, national and global levels

Stakeholders

Operations management

Marketing

Internal dependencies

Political environment at local, national and global levels

Structure

Resources

Culture

Human resource management

Organisational behaviour

Finance

Transactional dependencies

Economic environment at local, national and global levels

Sociocultural environment at local, national and global levels

Note: All contained within the dotted line represents the **internal** environment. The rest represents the **external** environment.

Figure 7.1 Organisational context model

ENTRY CASE STUDY 7.1

FT

Alternative to poaching

How companies can collaborate to beat skills shortages

By Vanessa Houlder

Competition in the Scottish electronics industry for skilled technicians is famously intense and in the early 1990s recruitment problems were getting out of hand. 'We were basically poaching from each other and pushing salaries up. It was becoming a vicious circle,' says Morag McKelvie, a personnel manager at NEC Semiconductors.

The idea then that managers from competing companies would start working together to solve the skills shortage would have seemed incredible, she says. Russell Pryde, manager of Lothian and Edinburgh Enterprise (LEEL), one of Scotland's local enterprise companies, the equivalent of the Training and Enterprise Councils in England and Wales, agrees. 'I don't think they would have sat in the same room together.'

But in a striking turnround, a number of competitors have embarked on an unprecedented degree of cooperation on training over the past two years. Yesterday, their innovative approach was recognised when, together with a local college and LEEL, they received a special training award from the Institute of Personnel and Development at the National Training Awards, organised by the Department for Education and Employment.

The initiative dates back to mid-1993, when LEEL made a proposal to the main electronics companies in its area – NEC Semiconductors, Seagate Microelectrics and Motorola. It volunteered to put up £100 000 for a course to be run by West Lothian College to train people in the specific skills needed to maintain equipment – the main skills shortage faced by the companies. It envisaged that the students would be drawn from declining industries such as shipbuilding, who needed to be retrained.

The companies would choose the candidates who were awarded places on the 40-week course; employ them for a six-week placement during the course and have the first chance to recruit them at the end of the course. If they took on one of the students, they would pay LEEL £3000 to reimburse it for the cost of that individual's training.

Pryde admits that the scheme 'seemed hare-brained at first'. The perception was that foreign-owned companies investing in Scotland were used to being wooed with generous grants and would baulk at being asked to pay training costs in full.

In fact, however, the companies felt that the £3000 charge was good value, compared with the fees charged by recruitment agencies. They were enthusiastic about the chance to choose the students selected for the course. They also welcomed the opportunity to design the course. The skills required by the equipment technicians drew on both electronics and mechanics.

The first course began in November 1994. Since then, four have run, training about 50 technicians who ranged in age from early 20s to early 40s. About three-quarters of the total found jobs with sponsoring companies; a few others have found work with suppliers or other companies in the electronics industry.

On its own, the Lothian scheme can only address a small part of the skills shortages in British electronics. The UK's success in attracting semiconductor-related investment will mean much more training is needed to fill labour market gaps.

But LEEL participants believe that their course is a valuable model for others. 'It is a prime example of a training and enterprise council and a college reacting to industry's needs,' says McKelvie.

Source: Financial Times, 13 February 1997. Reprinted with permission.

Introduction

Organisations all employ people to enable customer needs to be met. Hence this chapter aims to explain the role of **human resource management** in the organisational context model, Figure 7.1. This chapter focuses on human resource management at the national level, as global human resource management is covered in international business books, for example Daniels and Radebaugh.[1]

This chapter examines:

■ the role of the human resource management function in organisations;
■ the key legislation covering the recruitment and employment of human resources;
■ **demographics** and the human resource management function;
■ the **flexible firm** model;
■ the employee recruitment process.

Human resource management

Human resource management is an integrative general management activity that involves examining the organisation's demand for human resources with particular skills and abilities. This includes the recruitment of new staff along with the training and development of existing staff. Alternatively, if the organisation is over-staffed, the issues of redundancy, retirement and non-replacement of staff who leave will all have to be considered.

Therefore human resource management considers the whole picture of staffing in the organisation and takes a strategic and operational view of human resource requirements. The operational role of human resource specialists includes them in offering guidance and support to enable other managers in the organisation to handle their role as managers of human resources. This occurred because the activity of human resource management became more decentralised as organisations found a growing need for a more flexible workforce in order to respond more easily to influences and changes in the external environment.

In summary, the activity of human resource management includes recruitment and selection of appropriate staff, training and development of staff, and the management of the employment relationship, which includes contracts, collective bargaining, reward systems and employee involvement.

■ Human resource management and personnel management

Personnel management is a centralised and administrative function which focuses on the workforce. The activities covered by the personnel function include recruitment, training, pay administration, dealing with employees' work-related needs and problems, explanation of management expectations of the workforce, justification of management decisions, and negotiation regarding adaptation of management expectations and decisions if they are likely to produce a hostile reaction from the workforce.

In contrast HRM focuses on management needs for human resources to be utilised by the organisation. The main priority is planning, monitoring and adjusting the number and nature of the organisation's human resources. The issues relating to employees' work-related needs and management expectations of employees are discussed and dealt with as a management activity, with much less direct workforce involvement than in personnel management. The argument for this is that employees' interests are best served by effective overall management which takes account of their skills, abilities and career development needs.

In conclusion, personnel management is directed very much towards the personnel or workforce and the personnel department managing their work-related needs. In comparison, the HR department considers the strategic contribution that employees make to the organisation. Issues concerning the number of employees, the skills required and the cost to the organisation of employees with the required skills are of prime importance to the HR department.

■ External influences on human resource management

The human resource management function is influenced by the external environment. The main external influences currently include legislation, demographics and the move to a more adaptable workforce. Legislation that affects and influences the human resource management function falls into three categories, shown in Table 7.1, and is discussed later in this chapter. Additionally there are three bodies in the UK whose role is to tackle discrimination

Table 7.1 Employment legislation

Employment legislation	• Industrial Relations Act 1971 • Trade Union and Labour Relations (Consolidation) Act 1992 • Trade Union Reform and Employment Rights Act 1993 • Employment Rights Act 1996 • Employment Rights (Dispute Resolution) Act 1998 • Employment Relations Act 1999
Health and safety at work legislation	• Factories Act 1961 • Offices, Shops and Railway Premises Act 1963 • Fire Precautions Act 1971 • Health & Safety at Work Act 1974
Equalising employment legislation	• Equal Pay Act 1970 • Sex Discrimination Acts 1975 and 1986 • Race Relations Act 1976 • Disability Discrimination Act 1995

and promote equality in the workplace and they are discussed on page 243. Demographics and the flexible workforce are discussed later in this chapter. Sociocultural, economic and technological influences are discussed in Chapter 9.

☑ **Check your understanding**

Do you understand the role of HRM in organisations?

Check your understanding by outlining the activities an HR department could expect to be involved in.

Employment legislation

The **Contracts of Employment Act 1963** specified, for the first time, that employees should receive the main terms and conditions of their employment in writing. This Act covered the formation, changes to and the ending of the contract of employment. The **Industrial Relations Act 1971** allowed employees, again for the first time, to take their employer to an employment tribunal for unfair dismissal. Both Acts were assimilated in the **Employment Protection (Consolidation) Act 1978**. This Act put into place the condition that an employee must have been in full-time employment for two years or more with an employer before being able to go to an employment tribunal with a case of unfair dismissal.

The Conservatives were in power for a continuous period from 1979 to 1997. During the 1980s Margaret Thatcher and her government embarked on a methodical approach to legislation that reduced the power and rights of both the individual employee and the trade unions. The creation of an economic system that was increasingly free market was one of the aims of the Thatcher government. Consequently, it held the belief that the rights of the individual employee and unions, as established by the 1970s legislation, were obstructive to the establishment of a free-enterprise culture and job creation in the UK economy. Hence a significant amount of employment legislation was passed in the 1980s and some of the key acts are the **Employment Acts of 1980, 1982 and 1988 and the Trade Union Act 1984**. These four pieces of legislation all diminished the rights of individual employees and unions and expanded the legal regulation of industrial action and trade union activity. This meant there were changes to ballot requirements for calling a strike and nearly all types of secondary industrial action were outlawed – secondary industrial action occurs when employees in one workplace take industrial action in support of employees in another workplace who are in dispute with their employer.

In the 1990s, it was clear that the Tory governments of Margaret Thatcher and later of John Major had won their battle with the trade unions. The **Employment Act 1990** allowed those individuals refused employment due to their lack of membership of a trade union and hence of a closed shop to take the union involved to an employment tribunal, further curtailing the power of the trade unions. This Act also made all forms of secondary industrial action unlawful. The Trade Union and Labour Relations (Consolidation) Act 1992 and the Employment Rights Act 1996 (as amended by the Trade Union Reform and Employment Rights Act 1993 and the Employment Relations Act 1999) consolidated and replaced previous employment legislation.

Health and safety at work legislation

There are four key Health and Safety at Work Acts, outlined below. These deal with the health and safety of employees at work and were all passed between 1961 and 1974. These four key Acts were updated in the 1990s by EU Directives. These Directives include regulations covering the provision of rest and no-smoking areas, minimum standards for safe use of machines and equipment, provision and use of protective equipment, lifting heavy loads and provision of lifting equipment, provision of free eye tests, glasses, regular breaks and training for employees using visual display monitors, and increasing health safeguards for employees working with carcinogenic substances. Other health and safety regulations include the Control of Substances Hazardous to Health Regulations 1988, introduced under the 1974 Health and Safety at Work Act. The regulations place a requirement on employers to pay close attention to the manner and the extent to which substances hazardous to health are handled, used and controlled.

Factories Act 1961 and Office, Shops and Railways Act 1963

The Factories Act 1961 lays down minimum standards in factories regarding cleanliness, workspace, temperature, ventilation, lighting, toilet facilities, clothing, accommodation and first aid facilities. The Offices, Shops and Railway Premises Act 1963 extends the same general cover as outlined in the 1961 Act to other work premises. However, there are some small differences in the 1963 Act covering minimum workspace provision and temperature.

Fire Precautions Act 1971

Workplace premises require a fire certificate and the Fire Precautions Act 1971 allows the fire authorities to impose conditions on the certificate holder, including closure of a building if it does not comply with the conditions. These conditions can cover the means of escape and exit from the premises, instruction and training of employees on how to react in the event of a fire, and limits on the number of people on the premises at any one time.

Health and Safety at Work Act 1974

The Health and Safety at Work Act 1974 is a comprehensive piece of legislation covering people at work and those who may be at risk from the activities of those engaged in work. It created the Health and Safety Commission, whose six to nine members are selected by the Secretary of State to represent employers, employees and local authorities. The Health and Safety Commission has to ensure that the Act is implemented correctly and hence one of its roles is to provide advice to local authorities, employers and others to enable them to understand their responsibilities under the Act. The Health and Safety Commission has the power to carry out investigations and enquiries if it appears that the Act is not being adhered to in a workplace and the Commission may also issue codes of best practice and regulation.

The Health and Safety Commission and the Secretary of State select three people to form the Health and Safety Executive. This assists in the enforcement of the Health and Safety at Work Act 1974 by undertaking the daily administrative affairs relating to its implementation.

Discrimination commissions

There are three bodies in the UK whose role it is to tackle discrimination and promote equality in the workplace. They are the **Equal Opportunities Commission** (EOC), the **Commission for Racial Equality** (CRE) and the **Disability Rights Commission** (DRC).

The Equal Opportunities Commission was established by the 1975 Sex Discrimination Act, with the powers to work towards the elimination of discrimination on the grounds of sex or marital status, to promote equality of opportunity for women and men, to keep under review the Sex Discrimination Act (1975) and the **Equal Pay Act** (1970), and to provide legal advice and assistance to people who have been discriminated against.

Today in the early twenty-first century the EOC is actively working and campaigning on a number of issues impacting on people and the organisations they work for, including closure of the pay gap between men and women, an end to sexual harassment at work, an end to male and female stereotypes, making it easier for parents to balance family and work commitments, making public services relevant to the differing needs of men and women, and securing comprehensive equality legislation across the UK and Europe.

The Commission for Racial Equality was established by the Race Relations Act 1976 to tackle racial discrimination and promote racial equality. Additionally the CRE seeks to encourage good relations between people from different racial and ethnic backgrounds and monitors the way the Race Relations Act 1976 is working and advises on possible improvements.

The Disability Rights Commission was established in April 2000 by the Disability Rights Commission Act 1999. The role of the Disability Rights Commission is to work to eliminate discrimination against and promote equality of opportunity for disabled people and promote good practice in these areas. Additionally the DRC advises the government on disability legislation.

In October 2002 the government published a proposal to change the equality laws and to establish a single equality body incorporating the EOC, the CRE and the DRC, although at the time of writing no final decision had been made.

Equalising employment legislation

Equal Pay Act 1970   The Equal Pay Act 1970 came into force on 29 December 1975 and promotes equal pay for men and women. It stipulates that a man and woman should receive equal pay if either of the following types of circumstances applies:

- a man and a woman are doing like work; for example a male shop assistant and a female shop assistant would clearly both be entitled to the same pay;
- a woman can show that she is carrying out work rated as equivalent to that of a man, under the organisation's job evaluation scheme. The woman may have a clerical post in the organisation and the man a technical job; if both jobs score the same points under the job evaluation scheme, then the woman can claim pay equal to that of the man.

Proceedings against the British government by the European Commission resulted in the Equal Pay (Amendment) Regulation 1983, which came into force in 1984. This makes it possible to claim equal pay for work that is considered to be of equal value to that done by a member of the opposite sex. Equal value considers the skills, effort and decision-making responsibility involved in carrying out the job and requires no job evaluation scheme to be in operation.

In July 1995 the Conservative government's policy of compulsory competitive tendering was significantly undermined when the Law Lords ruled in favour of 1300 school meals staff employed by North Yorkshire Council. The council had sacked the school meals staff, then re-employed them and reduced their conditions of service by reducing pay from £3.40 to £3.00 per hour, cutting holiday entitlement and abolishing the sick pay scheme. The council carried out these cuts in order to defeat an outside tender for the school meals service. It did so regardless of a 1988 job evaluation scheme that found the work of the school meals staff to be of equal value to that of road sweepers, gardeners and refuse collectors, who were predominantly male. This meant that the school meals staff were discriminated against under the equal pay legislation and entitled to more than £2 million in lost pay and damages.[2]

The 1995 judgment by the Law Lords set a precedent and in July 1996 nearly 2000 school meals staff employed by the old Cleveland County Council won more than £1 million in lost wages and damages at an industrial tribunal. The compensation was for a pay cut introduced to aid the success of Cleveland County Council in compulsory competitive tendering against private firms.[3]

Race and sex discrimination

There are two types of race and sex discrimination: direct and indirect. Direct discrimination occurs when workers of a particular sex, race or ethnic origin are treated less favourably than other workers, for example specifying a female secretary in a job advert when the job could be done equally well by a man. Indirect discrimination arises when a requirement is applied equally to all workers but it is more difficult for one group of workers by virtue of their sex, race or ethnic origin to comply. For instance, a job advert requiring perfect written English for a manual labourer would discriminate against people of race, ethnic origin or nationality where English is not a first language.

Sex Discrimination Act 1975

The Sex Discrimination Act 1975 came into force at the same time as the Equal Pay Act 1970, at the end of 1975. This allowed organisations five years to achieve parity of pay between the sexes. The Sex Discrimination Act 1975 promotes the equal treatment of men and women in the areas of recruitment, training, promotion, benefits and dismissal. It also established the Equal Opportunities Commission, whose role is to eliminate discrimination on grounds of sex or marital status, promote equal opportunities between men and women, and monitor implementation of the Equal Pay Act 1970 and the Sex Discrimination Act 1975.

If a genuine occupational qualification applies to the post, then discrimination is allowed. Vacancies in the field of modelling or acting have a genuine occupational qualification, for example a woman to model female clothes.

Race Relations Act 1976

The Race Relations Act 1976 is similar to the Sex Discrimination Act 1975. It makes it unlawful to discriminate against someone on grounds of their race, colour, nationality or ethnic origin and established the Commission for Racial Equality.

The exceptions to the Race Relations Act are similar to those for the Sex Discrimination Act 1975 and include the areas of entertainment, acting, artistic or photographic modelling, specialised restaurants and community or social workers providing personal services to members of a particular racial group. However, discriminatory treatment in terms and conditions of employment is not allowed.

■ Examples of race and sex discrimination

The existence of race and sex discrimination legislation does not guarantee a complete lack of discrimination in the workplace and it is the role of the Commission for Racial Equality and the Equal Opportunities Commission to monitor and ensure effective implementation of the legislation.

In recent years clear examples of race discrimination have been found in the armed forces and the legal profession. For example, in December 1996 the Government Legal Service, which employs solicitors and barristers to work in government departments, was found guilty of breaking the laws relating to both race and sex discrimination with regard to its recruitment procedures. It was taken to an industrial tribunal by a black woman, Chineme Nwoke, who was supported by the Commission for Racial Equality.[4] When she was interviewed for a job by the Government Legal Service she was given a very low grade, which effectively precluded her from applying to the organisation again. She won her case and was awarded £2000 for injury to feelings and a very unusual exemplary payment of £1000 for 'aggravated damages'. In its ruling the tribunal reported that while Chineme Nwoke did not do sufficiently well to be recommended for appointment, her application was not sufficiently unsatisfactory to permit her exclusion from future shortlisting for interview. The tribunal also pointed out in its judgment that during the recruitment process for the Government Legal Service:

- all white candidates with local government experience received a C grade or above, while no applicant from the ethnic minorities with a corresponding background achieved such a rating;
- eight white candidates with a 2.2 degree or lower received a C grade, but no one from the ethnic minorities with the same qualification received such a grade;
- 2.4 per cent of black and Asian candidates gained a C grade or above, compared with 7.6 per cent of white men and 11.2 per cent of white women. Despite women gaining higher grades, they were less likely to be recommended for a vacancy and if recruited were paid less than men;
- 50 per cent of black and Asian shortlisted candidates were finally appointed, compared with 76.2 per cent of white men and 63 per cent of white women.[5]

Discrimination in the armed forces was highlighted in March 1997 when an independent report commissioned by the Ministry of Defence was published.[6] This report detailed widespread incidents of racial harassment in the armed forces. The existence of racial harassment and the low number of ethnic minorities in the armed forces, 1.4 per cent of personnel, led the Ministry of Defence to aim to improve its recruitment, training and appraisal systems to remove any racial discrimination and bias. This included the need to train and educate existing staff in the seriousness of racial inequality and the handling of racial issues. The report featured the example of the Navy, where good statements and policies on equal opportunities exist but implementation is unplanned, unco-ordinated and unmonitored.

Disability Discrimination Act 1995

The **Disability Discrimination Act 1995** defines disability as:

> a physical or mental impairment which has a substantial and long-term adverse effect on a person's ability to carry out normal day-to-day activities. People who have had a disability, but no longer have one, are covered by the Act.[7]

Discrimination happens when a disabled person is dealt with less favourably than an able-bodied person due to their disability and this cannot be justified. Employers are not allowed to justify unfavourable treatment of a disabled person if adjustment could be made to overcome the reasons for unfavourable treatment. For example, an employer could not refuse to promote a disabled person because the equipment they had to use could not be accessed, if by rearranging the equipment the disabled person could do the job.

Organisations employing more than 20 people must not discriminate against disabled employees in the areas of recruitment, working conditions or employee benefits – bonuses, promotion, training and dismissal. This covers permanent members of staff, temporary workers and contract workers. However, it does not cover the armed services, police officers, active members of a fire brigade and prison officers, or people working on ships, aircraft or hovercrafts.

The advertising of jobs must not indicate that a person might not get a job because of their disability or because the employer is unwilling to make adjustments. The selection process must not favour people who have no disability, offer jobs on less favourable terms to a disabled person, or refuse employment because of disability.

☑ Check your understanding

Do you understand the issues which employment legislation covers?

Check your understanding by naming the Act which:

- allows an employee to take their employer to an industrial tribunial for unfair dismissal;
- requires workplaces to hold a fire certificate;
- led to the establishment of the Disability Rights Commission.

Demographics and human resource management

Demography is the statistical study of changes in the nature of a population. The US, western Europe and Japan all experienced a growth in their working-age population from 1950 to 1980. In contrast, all expect to experience a decline in their working-age population between 2010 and 2050. In 1990 a quarter of the working-age population in OECD countries was less than 25 years old and about a third was 45–64 years old. It is anticipated that by 2040 less than a fifth of the working-age population will be under 25 years old and over two-fifths will be above 45 years old. This is significant as younger employees are viewed as more adaptable, with better and more up-to-date training. Moreover, not all people of working age choose to work: some will be in full-time higher or further education and others, mostly women, may choose to stay at home to care for young children or sick relatives.[8]

From the mid-1970s through to the mid-1990s early retirement was an accepted method of reducing the size of the workforce.[9] Older employees are seen as being more expensive and less flexible. The notion of early retirement has been particularly prevalent in the public sector. The combination of early retirement and reduced numbers of young people in the population means that there is a likelihood of labour shortages in western Europe, North America and Japan in the early part of the twenty-first century, from 2000 to 2020. The likely response of organisations to this is the active recruitment of older staff to do part-time and temporary jobs traditionally taken by younger people.

In the UK the supermarket chain Tesco and the DIY chain B&Q are examples of companies whose employment policies include the active recruitment of older staff. In the future, retaining and retraining older employees will be a more appealing option for organisations as the competition for skilled younger employees will be increasingly fierce.[10,11] The advantages of an older workforce include the tendency of older people to change jobs and move around the country less frequently than younger people, hence contributing to lower labour turnover.

To attract and retain the required level of skilled labour, lifetime or long-term employment contracts may have to be offered. This will contrast strongly with the period from the 1980s to the early part of the twenty-first century when flexible labour contracts[12] and workforces fashioned on the **flexible firm model**[13] were more common.

The flexible workforce and human resource management

The advent of the flexible workforce owes much to the popularity of downsizing in organisations and the general shift in the economy from manufacturing to service provision. A manufacturer can either employ extra staff to meet peak demand or stock goods produced in a quiet time to meet demand at peak times. However, a service provider is unable to stock products to meet peaks in demand and therefore meets that demand by employing extra part-time or temporary staff. This is less expensive than employing a larger number of permanent full-time staff, as during troughs in demand the extra full-time permanent staff would be inactive. Therefore downsizing occurs when organisations delayer, removing layers of employees, so that they become structurally flatter, or when organisations reduce the number of core employees and recruit more part-time or subcontracted employees as and when required. The concept of the flexible workforce means organisations operating flexible working patterns to cope with peaks and troughs in demand by redeploying staff across different activities and locations or employing and laying off staff as cheaply as possible.

Classic examples of flexibility in the labour market include retailers taking on extra staff over Christmas; frozen vegetable companies, like Bird's Eye, taking on extra staff during summer months when the vegetables are harvested; restaurants or pubs taking on extra staff on Friday and Saturday evenings when they are busiest; and universities taking on part-time lecturers during an academic year when student over-recruitment has occurred.

The idea of an organisation and its flexible workforce is best summed up by the flexible firm model.[14] This divides employees into three categories: core, peripheral and external. The **core permanent employees** have highly skilled jobs, with relatively good job security and career prospects. These employees are expected to be flexible in terms of their role in the organisation and working location.

The **first peripheral group** are those employees with full-time jobs, not careers. In this group labour turnover is higher than for core employees. Employees in this group often require more vocational skills than core employees. They include supervisors, secretaries, assemblers and administrators.

The **second peripheral group** provides the major component of flexibility in the workforce and includes employees on short-term contracts, part-time employees, job-sharing employees and subsidised trainees. Employees on short-term contracts will hold full-time skilled jobs, for example a software engineer may be employed on a short-term contract to work full time on developing a piece of software for an organisation. In contrast, part-time employees work on a permanent basis for the organisation but only for a fraction of the hours of a full-time employee. For example, a part-time employee may work only mornings or certain days of the week. Job sharing occurs when two people split a job, the pay and rewards between them. This type of arrangement is common among women who wish to work but not for the full working week. Subsidised trainees work for the organisation while learning a trade and/or gaining qualifications. A portion of the costs is covered by government funding. A good example of a subsidised training initiative is the Modern Apprenticeships Scheme. Launched in September 1995, a Modern Apprenticeship takes three years to complete and involves the apprentice studying for a National Vocational Qualification in an area of craft, technical or junior management skills. The government covers around 25 per cent of the cost to the organisation of employing and training the apprentice.[15]

The final category of staff in the flexible firm model is **external staff**. They can be brought in quickly to meet increased demand and include self-employed consultants, subcontractors and temporary agency staff. The latter may include secretarial staff, administrators and supervisors. The common subcontracted activities are those that are non-core and can be done more cheaply and satisfactorily by contracted staff, such as cleaning, catering, provision of IT support and running the payroll. In contrast, self-employed consultants are used on a project-by-project basis, particularly when the necessary skills are not available in-house.

Organisations have been able to develop and create further flexibility in the workforce with the use of technology. The arrival of faxes, mobile phones, laptop computers and modems has resulted in employees being able to work anywhere – in hotels, on trains, planes or at home. The ultimate use of technology is in the activity of teleworking or telecommuting. **Telecommuters** work at home, with technology that enables them to receive and send work and messages to their employing organisation. The potential advantages of telecommuting are that it saves commuting time, especially in the South East of England where traffic congestion is common; there are environmental benefits, such as reducing the 19.8 billion gallons of exhaust fumes produced each day by cars in the UK; it saves money, as estimates suggest that homeworkers spend less money on working clothes and there is no cost of commuting, resulting in a real pay rate 50 per cent higher than if they were commuting; and there are savings to companies estimated at between £1500 and £3000 per employee per year.

The potential disadvantages of telecommuting include homeworkers feeling isolated, lonely, overworked and neglected by their work colleagues and the organisation. The danger exists that home and the office are the same place and work takes over the home environment, hence home is no longer an escape from work. The telecommuter also loses the companionship and social side of office life, so augmenting feelings of isolation, loneliness and neglect. The potential benefit of being able to work at any time of the day or night may not materialise for telecommuters as their clients may work only from nine to five. Those involved with high-volume, low-margin work may be reluctant to take time off as they fear loss of business and earnings, leading to feelings of overwork.

The company DEC has developed a home-working scheme that involves employees working from home but includes regular contact with other tele-commuters via technology and occasionally in person at an office or telecentre, where telecommuters may drop in to meet other telecommuters. This provides a social focus for office life and helps to combat feelings of isolation, loneliness and neglect among teleworkers.[16]

✓ Check your understanding

Do you understand the different categories of employees in the flexible firm model?

Check your understanding by placing each of the employees in the appropriate category (core, first peripheral, second peripheral and external). Employees are a part-time university lecturer, an electrical subcontractor, a managing director and his/her secretary.

The employee recruitment process

The recruitment of employees to an organisation is crucial if the organisation is to acquire, retain and maintain the skills and abilities to provide customers with the products and services required in an efficient and effective manner. This also contributes directly to helping the organisation achieve its strategic goals. The development and use of a suitable recruitment procedure allows appropriate applicants to be matched to suitable posts. This should result in employees remaining with the organisation and making efficient and effect-ive contributions to its goals.

The lack of a suitable employee recruitment process or poor implementation of the process may result in initial low recruitment costs. However, a lack of forethought and planning is false economy, resulting in unsuitable employees being recruited. The appointment of over- or under-skilled and qualified employees leads to tasks and activities not being done effectively and employees leaving their jobs relatively soon after taking up employment. This rapid turnover of employees results in the recruitment process being repeated to find a replacement employee and incurring the associated costs: in the areas of defining the job and the type of applicant, reading and shortlisting completed applications, and interviewing shortlisted applicants. There will also be the costs of any advertising undertaken and employment agencies used.

Rapid turnover of employees and associated high recruitment costs can result from a shortage of appropriately skilled labour. The electronics companies in the entry case study for this chapter experienced a high turnover of skilled technicians due to a shortage of people with suitable skills in the labour market. They bore the costs normally associated with high labour turnover and paying increasing salaries to attract the required skilled technicians from competitor companies. These skilled technicians normally remained with their new employer for a relatively short period before moving on to another company offering higher pay and more perks. The electronics companies confronted the shortage of skilled technicians by collaborating with each other and with a local college to fund and develop a training course that produced technicians equipped with the required skills and abilities. The manner in which they sought to deal with the skills shortages is an excellent example of organisations managing, influencing and changing a key aspect of their external environment.

The shortage of skills can be addressed on a number of fronts: the recruitment of employees, the use of training and development, the redeployment of existing staff, and work patterns and practices.

The recruitment of employees is one area to consider and build on in any attempt to ease a skills shortage. The advertising of vacancies can be boosted by widening the geographic area of search and increasing the range of advertising media employed. In addition, the advertising effort could be directed towards non-traditional groups of potential employees, for example the nursing profession targeting men, the engineering or construction professions targeting women, or, as B&Q has done, targeting people over 50 to do jobs traditionally done by younger people. Other tactics involve requiring successful applicants recruited in one part of the country to relocate to the organisation's premises in another area where a skills shortage exists. The direct approach of offering higher pay and more perks is always available, but expensive. However, the danger of this lies in the vicious circle that can be created when organisations poach skilled staff from each other and drive pay ever upwards, as in the entry case study. The lowering of entry requirements, such as qualifications and relevant work experience, is another means of reducing a shortage of skills. For example, the Army has on occasion lowered the standard of physical fitness required of recruits and extended the basic training to allow new recruits to attain an acceptable level of physical fitness. Alternatively, for some organisations the use of consultants, subcontractors and agencies could be initiated or extended to reduce a skills shortage.

Another way of handling a shortage of skills is to train existing employees to the required skills level. This will help diminish the skills shortage, although training and acquiring skills can take time and this is not a short-term method. However, if the training is ongoing and developmental, it may well help in the retention and increased motivation of existing employees. The hazard of providing appropriate and good training is that well-trained and qualified employees leave for a better job elsewhere, with more pay and perks. One way of stemming a loss of recently skilled employees is to offer opportunities and promotion within the organisation.

An alternative to closing the skills gap by increasing the skills available in the organisation is to reduce the need for skills by altering work practices to accommodate existing skill levels. This includes reducing output, improving productivity, overtime working and adjusting shift patterns, which is particularly practical if it leads to increased productivity and reduced overtime. The skills gap could also be reduced by restructuring and reorganising the workforce and their jobs, which may entail multi-skilling, which in turn may necessitate further training.

Another option for dealing with a lack of skills is to find staff with the required skills from among those already in the organisation and second or promote them into the positions where the skills shortages exist for a temporary or permanent period.

The four stages of the employee recruitment process are looked at in theory (*see* Table 7.2) and in relation to a city-centre café/bar recruiting part-time staff.

Table 7.2 Employee recruitment process

Stage 1	**Assessment of the job** ● Job analysis ● Job description
Stage 2	**Assessment of the type of applicant required** ● Person specification ● Key results areas
Stage 3	**Attracting applicants** ● Placement of the advertisement ● The advertisement
Stage 4	**Assessing applicants** ● Assessment of application forms ● Assessment of applicants

✓ Check your understanding

Do you understand how an organisation may reduce a skills gap or shortage?

Check your understanding by identifying three ways to reduce a skills gap or shortage.

Stage 1 – Assessment of the job

■ Job analysis

This is the first step in the employee recruitment process and involves gaining the correct information relating to the vacant job, as this will allow an accurate **job description** and **person specification** to be drawn up. **Job analysis** normally starts when the current job holder hands in their notice. Information has to be collected in order that the job description for the vacant job is clear and up to date. This is crucial, as the job description and the person specification drawn up from it will be central to the employee recruitment process.

The information collected should cover the areas of the job and its position in the organisation, the tasks and activities the job involves, the responsibilities of the job, and the conditions under which the job is carried out. The current job description is a good initial source of information. Further and more up-to-date information can be gathered by interviewing the current job holder before they leave the organisation and key personnel who surround the vacant job. These key personnel include the manager or supervisor of the current job holder and the latter's peers and subordinates. The utilisation of these sources of information gives a good indication of the tasks that the job involves and the key reporting and working relationships that the job holder must maintain. This information, along with consideration of the organisation's current and future plans and strategy, permits an up-to-date and accurate job description to be compiled.

■ Job description

The job description defines and outlines the job and covers the areas of the job shown in Table 7.3. In the sections of the job description and personnel specification, all areas are examined and related to the part-time job of a server in a city-centre café-bar, the type of part-time job a full-time student might seek to supplement their student loan.

Identification of the job

This section of the job description sets the job in its organisational context by stating the job title and the location of the job in the organisation. The location is defined by stating which section, department or division the job is situated in and where it will be based. This is important if the organisation has

Table 7.3
Job description

1	Identification of the job
2	Summary of the job
3	Content of the job
4	Working conditions
5	Performance standards

253

several sites in different geographic locations. The role of the job should also be put in context by outlining which staff the new appointee will be responsible to and how many staff the appointee will be responsible for. Staff with whom the new appointee will be expected to work and liaise, both inside and outside the department, are also to be indicated. The city-centre café-bar seeking to recruit part-time staff must identify which position part-time staff are going to occupy. Is the vacancy for a part-time relief manager, part-time bar/serving staff or part-time kitchen staff?

Summary of the job This segment of the job description examines why the job is done. This is accomplished by stating the overall objectives and purpose of the job, as well as comparing and contrasting it with other jobs in the organisation that are close or similar to it. The resulting differences between the vacant job and any similar jobs must be clearly demonstrated. Finally, the overall objectives and purpose of the job are linked with the overall objectives of the department and organisation. The café-bar recruiting part-time bar/serving staff may summarise such a job as 'welcoming customers and ensuring they receive friendly and accurate service'.

Content of the job This portion of the job description depicts the content of the job in detail and indicates what is done and how it is done. In writing this, the objectives of the job and why the job is done are also considered closely (*see* previous section).

It is necessary to specify the tasks and activities constituting the job. The main tasks and activities are listed first, followed by those that are secondary. This allows outsiders to the organisation, such as potential applicants, to understand what is involved for the job holder. The people and equipment available and required for carrying out the job tasks and activities are also indicated in this portion of the job description. Issues to consider here are:

- whether the individual does the job single handed, as part of a team, or perhaps the job requires a mixture of individual and teamwork (the café-bar server is required to work as part of a team);
- whether the job requires physical strength, intelligence, application of individual judgement or a combination of these traits (the café-bar server needs to be of average intelligence);
- whether the organisation provides resources and equipment to enable the job holder to carry out the required tasks and activities (the café-bar server is provided with a uniform of black trousers and purple shirt, which must be kept clean and must always be worn on duty).

Resources provided by the organisation could include access to office equipment such as computers, photocopiers, telephones, faxes and e-mail. Other resources made available to employees to enable them to perform their jobs may include portable personal computers, mobile phones, corporate uniforms, protective clothing, company cars, hand tools, specialised technical equipment and interest-free loans for season tickets.

If the job is for part-time bar/serving staff, the tasks and activities involved would include showing customers to their table, taking orders for food and drinks, serving food and drinks, laying tables, clearing tables, collecting payment, ensuring the customer is happy with the food and drink they have ordered and serving behind the bar. Such part-time bar/serving staff would be responsible to the manager and have to work with the kitchen staff in ensuring that correct orders for food are taken, passed on to kitchen staff and served to the right customer.

Working conditions This category of the job description looks at the working environment and circumstances of the job. The physical working environment should be reliably portrayed, e.g. a noisy factory, a clean, hygienic factory or an open-plan office. The hours of work and circumstances in which the job is carried out should also be accurately portrayed, particularly if they are unusual, for example the job may require the job holder to work shifts or travel away from home regularly. The server in a café-bar faces the working conditions of a trendy city-centre café-bar catering for all types of customers. The job is part time, the hours being 12–5pm Wednesday afternoon and Thursday and Friday evenings, which are very busy, from 6–11.30pm.

Performance standards This part of the job description gives an indication of the normal level of performance or productivity expected from the job holder. This can be expressed in terms of number of hours of work and in terms of meeting the objectives of the job as laid out in the summary of the job. Examples of performance standards for different jobs, including a part-time server in a city-centre café-bar, are shown in Table 7.4.

The job description serves as the basis for the next logical stage in the job recruitment process, the production of a person specification. A person specification is a series of criteria outlining the ideal person for the job. All applicants for the job will be assessed against these criteria.

Table 7.4 Performance standards for different jobs

University lecturer in marketing	• 450 hours' class contact per year • Organise and run successful open days to attract potential applicants to the business school • Four publications per academic year
Shop assistant in newsagents	• 37.5 hours' work per week • Organise correct delivery of morning papers • Pleasant appearance and personality
Computer salesperson	• Generate £15 000 sales per month • Provide relevant customer demonstrations on request • Clean driving licence
Part-time server in café-bar	• 15 hours per week, 1–6pm on Wednesday, 6–11pm on Thursday and Friday • Clean, neat and tidy appearance • Provide friendly and accurate service to customers

> ### ☑ Check your understanding
>
> *Do you understand the importance of performance standards?*
>
> Check your understanding by outlining performance standards for a professional football player like David Beckham.

Stage 2 – Assessment of type of applicant required

■ Person specification

The person specification is derived from the job description by translating the job activities into the specific skills and abilities required to perform the job effectively. Hence the employee recruitment process needs to ensure that the organisation fills vacancies by attracting, recruiting and retaining ideal candidates, who possess the skills and abilities required.

The person specification can be drawn up by using a predetermined framework. Frequently used frameworks include **Rodger's seven-point plan** and **Fraser's five-fold grading** system. Both these frameworks are used to draw up criteria that can be employed to assess applicants' suitability for employment – *see* Tables 7.5 and 7.6 respectively. The criteria drawn up should be identified as either essential or desirable. The essential criteria are those that applicants must meet if they are to be considered competent to carry out the job. However, in addition to meeting essential criteria, applicants are usually expected to meet some, but not all, desirable criteria.

Table 7.5 Rodger's seven-point plan

1	Physical make-up
2	Attainment
3	General intelligence
4	Special aptitudes
5	Interests
6	Disposition
7	Circumstances

Source: Torrington, D and Hill, L (1995) *Personnel Management: HRM in Action* (3rd edn), Harlow: Prentice Hall.

Table 7.6 Fraser's five-fold grading

1	Impact on others
2	Qualifications or acquired knowledge
3	Innate abilities
4	Motivation
5	Adjustment or emotional balance

The benefits which accrue from the use of such criteria are that the areas that are important to the recruitment decision are clearly defined before the recruitment process takes place, hence ensuring that they are covered; that the areas to be covered in the interview are divided into focused chunks that can form the basis for the main part of the interview; and that there is more consistency in the recruitment process and thus a greater likelihood that all candidates will be treated and assessed fairly. Today many organisations use a diluted version of one of these frameworks. Organisations should use such frameworks carefully as some aspects, such as physical make-up, could be discriminatory and may potentially contravene legislation such as the **Disability Discrimination Act 1995**, while the category 'general intelligence' can be difficult to define.

■ Rodger's seven-point plan

Physical make-up The physical requirements for effective performance in a job may cover the areas of general health, physical fitness, appearance, manner and voice. For example, the emergency services and armed forces require higher-than-average standards of physical fitness, as do the jobs of physical education teacher and aerobics instructor. Positions in organisations that involve employees in making an impact on others (clients or members of the public) usually require them to be of smart appearance and to possess a pleasant disposition. Alternatively, if the job is in a national call centre and involves frequent contact with clients or customers over the telephone, a pleasant voice will be important. In the case of the student seeking a job as a server in a café-bar, a neat, clean and tidy appearance will be important.

Attainment This deals with the level of education and experience required for the job to be carried out successfully. The level of education is assessed by considering the qualifications that an applicant has gained. Many jobs will have minimum qualification expectations of applicants. The qualifications sought for particular jobs may include some of the following: minimum number of GCSEs (or equivalents), including English and mathematics, A-levels (or equivalents), a degree, a postgraduate qualification, professional, technical or vocational qualifications. For example, the post of marketing assistant in a publishing company specialising in scientific books and journals may require someone with a first degree in science, such as chemistry, biology or physics, and a postgraduate marketing qualification.

The experience required for a job relates to the previous type of employment that suitable applicants are likely to have held. Senior vacancies in most fields of employment will require significant relevant work experience in a similar or related job, whereas posts for new graduates require much less relevant work experience, with the experience limited to that which a new graduate could have acquired via work placement or holiday employment.

257

For example, the post of European sales manager for a chemical company may require a chemistry graduate with a proven track record in European sales and at least eight years' sales experience. In contrast, a vacancy for a graduate trainee systems analyst in one of the main high-street banks may specify a computing or mathematics graduate with six or twelve months' commercial experience in systems analysis in a banking environment, gained via a placement or holiday employment.

The student seeking a job as a server in a café-bar is likely to be considered for the job as they will have a good number of GCSEs and A-levels (or equivalent), which are the qualifications to get into university or college. The manager of the café-bar may also look for part-time staff who have previous experience in a similar type of job. This may include working in a bar or restaurant, or a job where the applicant has led to deal with members of the public, e.g. a Saturday job in a shop.

General intelligence Applicants with an appropriate level of general intelligence will be required if a job is to be undertaken properly, hence the relevant level of general intelligence needs to be looked for in applicants. Jobs requiring complicated work patterns and activities to be picked up quickly will demand a different level of general intelligence when compared with jobs that are repetitive and very routine. Therefore students seeking a job as a server in a café-bar are likely to be considered because they are expected to possess a good level of general intelligence, which is demonstrated by the fact that they are at university.

Special aptitudes Special aptitudes are knowledge and skills that are vital for effective performance in the job. Ideally, applicants who already possess or have the propensity to acquire the necessary special aptitudes should be sought. The acquisition of essential knowledge and skills could simply require an applicant to be prepared to adapt or update existing skills and knowledge. The types of knowledge and skills covered by this section of Rodger's seven-point plan are presentation skills, interpersonal skills, telephone skills, numeracy skills, report writing skills, information technology skills and knowledge, and specific job-related knowledge.

The manager of the café-bar may seek part-time employees who already possess some relevant skills. These skills could include waiting on tables, changing a barrel or optic, and working a computerised till.

Interests The issue being examined in this section of Rodger's seven-point plan is the requirement of the applicant to have any out-of-work activities that support the application for employment. For example, a person playing in a weekend football team could be viewed as more predisposed to being an active team participant who gets on well with colleagues at work.

The manager of the café-bar may look for students who have experience of teamwork from either a sporting or social activity or as part of their studies at university or college. Students undertaking a business studies or catering course at university or college may use this fact to support their application to work part-time in the café-bar.

Disposition

The personal characteristics relevant to the job are considered in this section. If the job requires the successful applicant to work as a member of a team, then the ability to work well with others will be important. Alternatively, if the job is a supervisory or managerial position, then leadership and responsibility will be integral. Other personal characteristics include the ability to cope with pressure and meet tight deadlines and the competence to work on one's own initiative.

The part-time server in the café-bar should be able to get on with customers, work as part of a team and cope with the pressure of a very full bar on Thursday and Friday evenings. Wednesday afternoons are less busy and involve less bar work, but more waiting on tables for people ordering lunch, teas and coffees.

Circumstances

In this section the applicant's ability to conform to the circumstances in which the job has to be undertaken are considered. The circumstances may include shift work, weekend work, working away from home or being on call during evenings, weekends and public holidays. Examples include bus and train drivers working shifts, security guards working during the night and hospital consultants being on call at weekends.

The part-time server in the café-bar has to be able to work Wednesday afternoon 12–5pm and Thursday and Friday evenings 6–11.30pm.

■ Key results areas

The person specification defines the ideal candidate for the job, but it is becoming more common also to define the **key results** areas expected of the ideal candidate. Therefore the key results areas are assembled at the same time as the person specification. They declare the important results expected of the job holder. Key results are the outputs and outcomes produced by the job holder and are assessed by use of explicit success criteria. Success criteria express the expected outcomes and outputs in terms of quality, quantity, cost and time. The use of key results areas provides goals for the job holder, with a strong emphasis on outputs and expected results, hence providing a clear basis for appraisal of the job holder.

✓ Check your understanding

Do you understand how to use Rodger's seven-point plan?

Check your understanding by drawing up a person specification for a professional footballer.

Stage 3 – Attracting applicants

■ Placement of the advertisement

Organisations have to be able to attract potential employees with the required qualifications, work experience, aptitudes and disposition for the vacancy being filled. The success of the organisation in attracting appropriate potential employees depends in part on its selection and use of suitable advertising media and third-party recruitment bodies.

Direct advertising The interests of the organisation lie in placing advertisements in publications that will circulate among the largest number of suitable potential applicants. The type of publication used will depend on the vacancy being filled. A vacancy for a shop assistant or office cleaner is best advertised in the local press, as these are jobs for which people are unlikely to move into the locality from a long way away. In contrast, suitably qualified applicants for the vacancy of a marketing manager for a multinational company or a university professor are more likely to be attracted from a larger geographic area and therefore such vacancies are advertised at least in the national press or even in international or overseas press.

The local press in the UK varies depending on the geographic area. For instance, the area of Sheffield and South Yorkshire is served by several local papers including the *Sheffield Star*, the *Yorkshire Post* and the *Barnsley Chronicle*. Large cities also have local papers, many of which are published as evening papers, including the *Evening Times* in Glasgow and the *Evening Standard* in London. The café-bar seeking serving staff would be most likely to use a local paper.

The UK has a number of national broadsheet newspapers published either daily during the week or on a Sunday. Sunday broadsheet newspapers include the *Independent on Sunday*, the *Observer*, the *Sunday Telegraph* and the *Sunday Times*. These advertise senior jobs in a variety of fields.

Daily broadsheet newspapers include *The Times*, the *Financial Times*, the *Independent*, the *Daily Telegraph* and the *Guardian*. A number of these devote a particular day of the week to certain types of jobs, for example legal jobs are advertised in *The Times* on a Tuesday and the *Guardian* advertises jobs in education on the same day. This approach to advertising vacancies means that a sizable selection of jobs in a particular field is advertised together on a specific day. The advantage is that individuals seeking employment in a particular field can be guaranteed a good variety of vacancies in that field if they purchase the newspaper on the relevant day. The advantage to the advertising organisation of such an approach is that their vacancy is advertised on a day when a considerable number of individuals seeking vacancies in a particular field are likely to purchase the newspaper.

The alternative to advertising in a broadsheet newspaper is to advertise in the industry or technical press, as nearly all professions have at least one such publication. Examples include the *New Scientist* for research scientists and technicians; the *Engineer* for different types of engineering jobs, civil and mechanical; and the *Bookseller* for vacancies in publishing. The key advantages in using the industry or technical press are similar to those for advertising in daily broadsheet newspapers on an appropriate day. In addition, however, interested applicants are perhaps more likely already to be employed in the industry. The industry or technical press is appropriate for unusual or very specific technical jobs, which are not normally advertised extensively in the local or national press. Many have internet sites listing vacancies.

Other methods of advertising vacancies are equally valid and may be used as an alternative to or in addition to press advertising. Advertising within the organisation itself is relevant if it is large enough that staff in one part of the organisation are unlikely to hear about a vacancy in another part by word of mouth. Such internal advertising also opens up opportunities for skills mixing and development for existing staff. The cost of advertising within the organisation is much less than press advertising, although it reaches a much smaller audience. However, recruiting an employee who already works for the organisation can have advantages in that the applicant will already know about the organisation and its business. Internal advertising is usually through a vacancies bulletin circulated throughout the organisation to employees, on paper, on a noticeboard or electronically. These media can be accessible to staff only or to staff and the general public. For example, vacancy noticeboards are sometimes located inside supermarkets close to the main public entrance and are used to advertise jobs such as a cashier, on a full- or part-time basis.

☑ Check your understanding

Do you understand the importance of using the correct advertising media?

Check your understanding by saying where you would place an advertisement for the following jobs:

- a shelf stacker at a Waitrose supermarket in London;
- a trainee manager for Waitrose, at various locations around the country;
- a store manager for Waitrose in Southampton.

■ Third-party advertising

An alternative to the direct advertising of vacancies is to use a third-party organisation to help attract applicants. Third-party organisations bring together applicants seeking work and organisations offering the type of employment sought. Therefore they often focus on particular types of employment or employees.

Commercial employment agencies

There are many commercial employment agencies, which either specialise in one particular type of employment, for example accountants or HGV drivers, or operate in a range of fields. The Advance employment agency covers a range of occupations, including office support staff, engineering and technical staff, sales and marketing staff, and hotel and catering staff. Payment is made to place a vacancy with a commercial employment agency and in return the agency advertises the vacancy to its clients, monitors responses to the vacancy and performs the preliminary interviews.

University employment agency

Universities may set up their own employment agency dealing in part-time jobs for students. This type of agency brings together students seeking part-time work and local employers seeking part-time staff. The university agency can refuse to 'advertise' jobs that are likely to result in students being exploited, by offering less than the minimum wage for example.

Management selection consultancy

Management selection consultancies advertise on behalf of organisations seeking to fill managerial posts. They advertise in the press, sometimes not revealing the name of the organisation on whose behalf they are acting. The management selection consultancy will carry out the first interviews and produce a shortlist for the client company to assess further. Alternatively, the consultancy may act on behalf of a client and approach an identified person to assess their interest in the vacancy, which is commonly known as headhunting.

Schools, colleges and universities

An organisation specifically seeking a school, college or university leaver may use the university, school or college careers service. Schools, colleges and universities employ careers advisers and run careers libraries where brochures, application forms and careers literature are kept for the use of those students about to leave. Organisations supply schools, colleges and universities with brochures, applications forms, industry literature and posters free of charge. If the organisation frequently employs school, college or university leavers, then developing and maintaining a close relationship with schools, colleges or universities may be an appropriate strategy. The schools, colleges or universities may also supply the opportunity for organisations to carry out initial interviews on their premises, hence allowing the visiting organisation to see a number of applicants in one visit.

Job centres

Job centres are free to advertise in and provide help with shortlisting. The use of job centres is practical when there is a considerable pool of available candidates.

■ The advertisement

The cost of advertising vacancies in the press or via a third party such as a recruitment agency varies according to the publication or third party used, length and size of the advert, and duration for which the advert is on display. The successful advertising of jobs requires the use of appropriate publications

**Table 7.7
Suggested outline
of job vacancy
advertisement**

Brief details	● Name of the organisation ● Line of business – main products/services
Job and duties	● Job title and main tasks – summarised from job description
Key requirements of successful applicant	● Key qualifications, work experience, skills and circumstances – summarised from personnel specification
Salary	● State the salary or salary scale for the job ● Tell applicants how to apply, e.g. CV and covering letter or application form

or third parties. This is important, as suitable applicants have to see the advertisement to be attracted to the vacancy. Failure to attract suitable applicants means that the organisation will have squandered time and money on advertising in the wrong place and on dealing with unsuitable applicants.

The information in job advertisements needs to be clear and reliable and to tell potential applicants, in brief terms, what the organisation does, what the job involves and the key requirements looked for in applicants. This allows suitable applicants to assess whether the vacancy is relevant to them and to make an informed judgement about whether to apply or not. It is also usual to indicate the expected salary and how potential applicants should apply for the vacancy. A suggested outline advertisement is shown in Table 7.7.

Stage 4 – Assessing applicants

The assessment of applicants occurs in two steps. The first is an assessment of the applications received, with some being rejected at this juncture. The second step is a further assessment of selected applicants by interviews and aptitude tests, before finally choosing the successful applicant.

■ Assessment of application forms

The initial sorting of application forms can be a difficult and tedious task, particularly if there has been a large response to the advertising. However, the initial sorting of application forms and shortlisting of candidates for interview needs to be methodically and rationally undertaken. If the sorting process is to be fair and accurate, the staff doing this initial sorting process need to be involved in the recruitment process and fully understand the relevance and use of job descriptions and personnel specifications. A thorough shortlisting process aids in ensuring the accuracy and fairness of the recruitment process and lessens the likelihood of inappropriate applicants being called for interview. Therefore this initial shortlisting process makes use of the criteria from the person specification, and applicants meeting the essential and some of the desirable criteria are those who will be called for a first interview. Applicants not meeting the essential criteria in the person specification are rejected.

Table 7.8
Interviewing
applicants

One-interview vacancies	• Interview • Select successful applicant • Check references • Confirm appointment
Two-interview vacancies	• Interview • Select successful applicants for second interviews • Aptitude tests and activities • Second interview • Select successful applicant • Check references • Confirm appointment

■ Assessment of applicants

The next step is to assess the shortlisted applicants by interview. There are variations in the interview process: with some vacancies only one interview is required and for other jobs the interview process is in two stages. It is unusual for a candidate to experience more than two interviews for a vacancy. Equally, the number of interviewers can also vary. There are generally two views governing the number of interviewers. One is that an effective interview and discussion can take place only on a one-to-one basis, so candidates meet one interviewer. The other view is that the interview process should be more open, so the interview is carried out and the appointment decision made by a panel of interviewers.

The sequence of events for one- and two-interview vacancies is shown in Table 7.8. In two-interview vacancies aptitude tests and activities are usually taken after the applicant has been selected for a second interview, but prior to that interview being conducted. References should be checked after the selection of the preferred candidate and prior to the confirmation of appointment, as references are used to confirm the interviewers' opinion of the successful applicant.

Interviewing

The job interview is a two-way communication process. It is an opportunity for the interviewer to get to know the candidate and further assess them against the criteria in the person specification. It is also an opportunity for the interviewee to gain a greater insight into the organisation and the work being offered. The interviewer should commence the interview by putting the candidate at ease and outlining the structure of the interview. A possible interview structure is shown in Table 7.9.

Table 7.9
Interview structure

1	Scene setting
2	Application form and person specification
3	Candidate's questions
4	Close the interview

Scene setting

The physical scene or location needs to be appropriate, usually a quiet room away from the disruption of telephones, noise and interruptions. The interviewer should set the scene at the start of the interview and recap on what the job involves and the type of person sought. Information from the job description and person specification can be used to do this.

Application form and person specification

The main body of the interview is structured around the completed application form and the person specification. This allows the information provided on the application form to be tied in with the relevant section of the person specification. For example, qualifications and work experience listed on the application form will link to the attainment section of the person specification. This allows the interviewer to ask the candidate questions about the information provided on their application, while also making sure that the candidate is assessed against the criteria in the person specification.

The questions used in interviews to assess a candidate need to be open ended, as this allows the candidate's reasons for wanting the job to be examined. Open-ended questions give applicants the opportunity to explain the knowledge, skills and experience they have gained and justify how these equip them as suitable for the vacancy. If the candidate provides incomplete answers to the questions, the interviewer should ask follow-up questions and dig for the information required to assess the candidate against the person specification.

Candidate's questions

As previously stated, the interview is an opportunity for the interviewee to gain a greater insight into the organisation and the work being offered. Although having to ask questions may be seen as a nightmare for the nervous applicant, the well-prepared candidate will have researched the company and have a few intelligent questions to ask. Alternatively, from the interviewer's point of view it is always appropriate to give applicants the opportunity to seek any further information they require, as even the best recruitment process may have forgotten something.

Close the interview

The candidate should be thanked for attending the interview and told how to claim any expenses to which they are entitled. Candidates also need to be advised of when they will know the outcome of the interview.

Informing candidates

All candidates who were interviewed need to be informed of the outcome of their interview. The unsuccessful candidates need to be told that they have not succeeded and, if appropriate, why they have not been successful. Equally, the successful candidate needs to be told that they have gained the job. This should be confirmed in writing, along with information on the salary and arrangements for the candidate to start work. A contract of employment should be drawn up and issued to the successful candidate.

☑ Check your understanding

Do you understand the importance of using the 'right' interview process?

Check your understanding by outlining the interview process for:

- a shelf stacker at a Waitrose supermarket in London;
- a trainee manager for Waitrose, at various locations around the country;
- a store manager for Waitrose in Southampton.

Summary

This chapter examined human resource management and some factors in the external environment which impact upon HR in organisations. The recruitment process was also discussed. The following summary covers all aspects of this chapter.

1 The activity of human resource management includes recruitment and selection of appropriate staff and management of the employment relationship, which includes contracts, collective bargaining, reward systems and employees' involvement. Therefore HRM considers the whole picture of staffing in the organisation and takes both the strategic and the operational view of human resource requirements.

2 Personnel management is a centralised and administrative function which focuses on the workforce and work-related needs at the operational level.

3 There is much in the external environment which impacts on organisations, with much coming from the legislation. Employment legislation covers employees' rights with respect to contracts of employment, trade unions membership and industrial relations. Health and safety legislation covers the minimum requirement of an employer to ensure the employees work in a safe and secure manner and location. The equalising employment legislation covers the outlawing of discrimination and the promotion of good practice with respect to gender, race and disability, covering all aspects of workplace activity.

4 In the UK, organisations are faced with drawing staff from a labour market which has decreasing numbers of younger people and increasing numbers of older people. This is part of the challenge organisations have to deal with in retaining an appropriate number of staff with the required skills and abilities.

5 The flexible firm model divides employees into three categories: core; peripheral and external. Core permanent employees hold the highly skilled jobs in organisations. The first peripheral group are employees with full-time jobs, not careers, and include supervisors, secretaries and assemblers. The second peripheral group provides a major component of flexibility for organisations and includes employees on short-term contracts, part-time employees, job-sharing employees and subsidised trainees. External staff can be brought in quickly to meet increased demand and include self-employed consultants, subcontractors and temporary staff.

6 The employee recruitment process can be broken down into four stages. 'Assessment of the job' covers job analysis and production of an up-to-date job description. The second stage is 'assessment of the type of applicant required' and covers drawing up a person specification and identifying key results or outcomes the job holder is expected to meet. The next stage is 'attracting applicants', which involves drawing up a suitable advertisement and placing it such that appropriate applicants are drawn to the job and organisation. The final stage is 'assessing applicants' and includes an assessment of the applications received and of some of the applicants themselves, via interviews.

Learning outcomes for case studies

While reading this chapter and engaging in the activities, you should have learned how to apply theory and models, analyse situations, and evaluate the application and analysis you undertake. The learning outcomes specified below outline the type of application, analysis and evaluation of which you should be capable in relation to organisations. The case studies and the questions which follow provide an opportunity for you to test how well you have achieved the learning outcomes for the ethical issues and exit case studies for this chapter.

Application	Check you have achieved this by	
1 Demonstrate the benefits and costs of investing in training	summarising the impact of appropriate training on an organisation	answering ethical case study question 3
Analysis	**Check you have achieved this by**	
1 Identify the pros and cons of an organisation employing part-time and temporary staff	specifying the impact on an organisation of hiring part-time and temporary staff	answering exit case study question 1
2 Suggest how an organisation should manage part-time and temporary staff	identifying possible actions and their likely impact on helping to manage a part-time and temporary workforce	answering exit case study question 2
Evaluation		
1 Evaluate the notion that staff are an asset on which organisations should place a monetary value	comparing and contrasting the valuation of tangible assets and staff	answering ethical case study questions 1 & 2

ETHICAL ISSUES CASE STUDY 7.2

FT

There's no accounting for magic

By Richard Donkin

There may be those who care little for sport. Some may even profess lack of interest in football. But few who saw Chris Waddle's spectacular side-footed chip over the goalkeeper's head from 40 yards, which helped secure victory for Bradford City against Everton in Saturday's FA cup tie, would deny they had witnessed something special.

How can you place a value on such goals? How can you place a value on Chris Waddle? Such questions must tax the minds of football managers, particularly since the 36-year-old Waddle, approaching the end of his playing career, was given a free transfer to one of the English league's less fashionable clubs.

Beyond football, the value of employees is beginning to attract increasing interest from business leaders, some of whom are showing signs of frustration at the failure of the accountancy profession to devise a satisfactory way of assessing the worth of human talent.

This is apparent in a survey of directors among 120 of the UK's top service sector companies carried out for Theodore Goddard, the London law firm.

Some two-thirds of the directors harboured frustrations, they said, because they believed that accountants placed more value on tangible assets, such as property and equipment, than on staff.

But recently the accountancy profession has been spending more time debating goodwill accounting, and if the proposals outlined in FRED (Financial Report Exposure Draft) 12 are adopted by the UK's Accounting Standards Board, its nature will change. One effect would be that the value of intangible assets – like footballers – with a limited useful life would be reduced year by year over their estimated life.

But this is a highly contentious issue – made more uncertain by the Bosman ruling in the European Court which allows football players to move between EU member states without a transfer fee once their contracts have expired.

The biggest difficulty in valuing company employees is that, unlike fixed assets, they are not owned by the business. They can and do walk out of the door.

Karen Moloney, of Moloney and Gealey, a human resource consultancy, says evaluations of football players could hold the key to finding a process for assessing the human or intellectual capital of a company.

Defining intellectual capital, she argues, is important if employees, the so-called human resources, are to be seen as an investment rather than as a cost.

Kate Olley, a human resources consultant at Arthur Andersen, says that if companies could work out the real costs of their employees they could measure the expected return and, where necessary, identify potential cost savings.

Some of these issues are beginning to attract the attention of the personnel profession as it attempts to quantify its contribution to business development.

It may, for example, be incumbent upon personnel to point out the need to reorganise a company's pay and management structure to give better rewards and recognition to technical staff whose value, under a flatter employment structure, has risen beyond that of many of the managers.

This would only be possible, however, if the business had an effective system of valuing the contribution of individual employees.

But most existing evaluations, including employee appraisals, are extremely subjective. Returning to the football field, David Myddelton, professor of finance and accounting at Cranfield School of Management, likes to cite the French national squad's rejection of Eric Cantona, the Manchester United midfield player, because the manager does not regard him as a team player.

Yet Cantona, under skilful club management, has shown that he is one of the finest players gracing the English football league. Such observations make Myddelton doubtful that any accounting system could deal with the vagaries of human ability.

It may indeed be a red herring to look towards accountancy for a solution. That, at any rate, is the belief of Skandia, the Swedish insurance and financial services company.

For the past five years Skandia has included a supplement to its annual accounts highlighting value creation through human development.

Leif Edvinsson, director of intellectual capital at Skandia, explains it as the difference between harvesting – the job of the chief financial officer who focuses on the profit and loss account – and that of looking after the roots of the organisation, the feeding and nurturing necessary to maintain healthy future growth.

The Skandia approach embraces a more holistic view of a company within society that recognizes there is a relationship between profit, sustainability, renewal and employment.

Accountancy, argues Edvinsson, tends to focus on the concerns of the stock market that concentrate on financial values, such as earnings per share – another view of harvesting.

▶

Skandia is seeking to free up what it calls its structural capital – what is left at the office when people go home.

In some ways this concept is similar to that employed by Ricardo Semler at Semco, the Brazilian industrial products manufacturer. Semler has become less concerned with who the company employs than how the fixed assets are best exploited for profit.

Skandia has developed a series of alliances, collaborative ventures and partnerships that generate profit from professionals not directly employed by the company. In Skandia AFS, its assurance and financial services business, the ratio of direct Skandia employees to those employed in the network of alliances is 1:30.

The company has developed an accounting-style format for displaying its intellectual capital, a table it calls the Skandia Navigator. This includes such measures as a satisfied customer index, an empowerment index, and training expenses per employee. But the company also attempts to set out the processes involved in developing employees.

Such processes are beginning to spin off into the overall business. This concept of renewal is driving negotiations with the Swedish government for an insurance-led scheme that will allow Swedish employees to take time off work to learn new skills or renew their expertise.

The scheme, called competency insurance, is based on the premise that employees will need to spend between 20 and 30 per cent of their time reinvesting in training and learning if they are to keep up with changes in the international marketplace.

Employees would invest 5 per cent of their salaries in an insurance policy which would fund leave of absence to undergo re-training. The company is hoping to make the insurance payments tax deductible.

The perception of the Theodore Goddard survey that, to quote the report, 'bean-counters value bricks and machines more than people' may give accountants some food for thought. In the meantime they will receive few complaints from Bradford City, where they will be talking about that goal for years.

Source: Financial Times, 29 January 1997. Reprinted with permission.

Questions for ethical issues case study 7.2

1 Do you agree that accountants should place 'more value on tangible assets, such as property and equipment, than on staff'? Explain your answer.

2 The accounting function is ill-equipped to value the human resources of an organisation. Do you agree or disagree? Write 100 words defending or criticising this statement.

3 Summarise the benefits and costs to the employees and the organisation of investing in training, as occurs in Skandia ASF. In your opinion, do the costs outweigh the benefits to the employees and the organisation? Explain your answer.

Flexible friends

By Vanessa Houlder

The increasing emphasis on part-time and temporary work has changed the job market beyond recognition. But while this trend has improved the productivity and flexibility of many businesses, it has raised difficult issues for managers.

How do companies find high-calibre staff prepared to work unconventional hours, often for relatively low pay? And how do they combat the widespread perception that these workers, who often have an important role in dealing with customers, are poorly trained and undervalued?

Recent research by the Roffey Park Management Institute in Sussex concluded that businesses that are successful at managing part-time and temporary employees have put more effort into meeting their needs.

Burton Group, which replaced 1000 full-time staff with 3000 part-time jobs in 1993, has responded to recruitment problems by allowing store managers to write contracts to suit individual employees. At one Topshop outlet a job is shared by a student who works in the vacation and a woman who works during the school term.

Asda, the retail group where 80 per cent of the workforce work part-time, has also felt the need to be more flexible towards part-time workers. Consultations showed that one reason for staff turnover reaching 30 per cent a year was that many wanted a longer working week.

'Employees who work very short hours, below the National Insurance threshold, are very cheap employees,' says David Smith, employee relations manager of Asda. 'But we found people were leaving. So we are going against the trend and offering longer hours.' With the help of longer contracts and other measures, such as improved maternity leave, career breaks and the ability to swap shifts, staff turnover fell by 2 percentage points.

The issues concerning flexible workers are nothing new for Oxfordshire County Council, where more than two-thirds of the 16 000-strong workforce work part-time. That partly reflects the need to cover round-the-clock services, such as in residential homes and fire fighting, but offering flexible working is also a way to attract professional employees, such as legal staff, who might be paid more in the private sector. Valued staff may want time off for childcare, further education and other part-time jobs or may want to continue part-time after taking early retirement.

But much of the debate about flexible working concerns the other end of the spectrum, the poorly paid and lowly valued employees who do not qualify for National Insurance, for employment protection or for statutory benefits. Attention has particularly focused on zero-hour

contracts, introduced by companies such as Burger King, in which individuals are only paid when dealing with customers. More than half the part-timers interviewed in a 1995 TUC study said employers regarded them as 'second-class staff'.

The tendency to treat flexible workers as poor relations is creating a dilemma for employers, according to Christina Evans, a research associate at Roffey Park Management Institute. 'In many organisations, it is those who work "flexibly" who have the most responsibility for customer service, at peak trading periods. In other words it is the "flexible" employees who are the ones who have the most impact on sales,' she says.

She says better use of flexible workforces would bring benefits including 'better customer service, lower staff turnover and a more motivated workforce'.

Her research uncovered many positive aspects of flexible working. Companies often commented that part-time workers were more disciplined in their time management and so more productive.

Nonetheless, the research highlighted a number of barriers to making the best use of flexible employees. Managers are often unenthusiastic about supervising them since it complicates scheduling and rota arrangements.

The assumption that part-time employees are less career-minded can be self-fulfilling. Unless companies examine their promotion policies, there may be unintended barriers to the promotion of part-time workers. For example, at First Direct, the telephone banking service, the Roffey Park study noted an assumption that an employee could not be rated 'very good' unless they worked a full shift and were exposed to all the trading activities.

Training is a particularly vexed issue for flexible workers. Most companies would agree that part-time staff need at least as much training as full-time staff, yet few provide that. The training of 80 per cent of those in full-time employment is funded by their employer, compared with 36 per cent of those working part-time, according to the Labour Market Quarterly Report.

The widespread practice of offering flexible workers worse pay, training and conditions than the full-time workforce could backfire, says the Institute of Management. It warns that the current attitude towards flexible workers could 'lead to the development of two-tier workforces – with all of the difficulties inherent in managing them.'

More effort is needed to integrate flexible employees with the company's core workforce: 'What is needed is a new approach to managing flexible workers, which acknowledges the needs of this group of employees to be valued, included and invested in,' she says.

Source: *Financial Times*, 29 January 1997. Reprinted with permission.

▶

Questions for exit case study 7.3	1	List the advantages and disadvantages to an organisation of employing part-time and temporary workers.
	2	*'What is needed is a new approach to managing flexible workers, which acknowledges the needs of this group of employees to be valued, included and invested in.'*
		You are an HR manager for a national cinema chain and have the task of drawing up a plan to ensure that flexible staff will be 'valued, included and invested in'. Identify the positions in which your flexible staff operate and draw up the required plan. How do you measure your plan's success and ensure that it works? (Your annual bonus depends on the success of your plan!)

For more case studies please visit www.booksites.net/capon

Short-answer questions

1 Define human resource management.

2 Explain the difference between human resource management and personnel management.

3 Name the three categories of legislation that most directly influence the human resource management function.

4 Name the piece of legislation which led to the establishment of the Commission for Racial Equality.

5 Which body did the Health and Safety at Work Act 1974 establish?

6 Why in most industrialised countries are population demographics likely to influence the human resource management function in the future?

7 Explain why the move to a more flexible labour force has occurred.

8 State the main advantages of telecommuting.

9 State the main disadvantages of telecommuting.

10 Indicate two ways in which an organisation may manage a skills shortage in a particular area.

11 List the four stages of the employee recruitment process.

12 Explain the purpose of the person specification.

13 Name the points in Rodger's seven-point plan for the person specification.

14 Identify one potential difficulty with Rodger's seven-point plan.

15 Give two examples of where each of the following can take place: third-party advertising and direct advertising.

Learning outcomes for assignment questions

While reading this chapter and engaging in the activities, you should have learned how to apply theory and models, analyse situations, and evaluate the application and analysis you undertake. The learning outcomes specified below outline what you should be able to do and the assignment questions provide an opportunity for you to test how well you have achieved the learning outcomes for this chapter.

Application	Check you have achieved this by	
1 Suggest how an organisation may overcome a skills shortage	identifying possible strategies for retaining and developing a workforce	answering assignment question 1
2 Demonstrate the use of the job recruitment process	explaining the different stages in the job recruitment process	answering assignment question 2
3 Apply the job description process to a specified job	developing a job description for a specified job	answering assignment question 3
4 Determine which information should be included in the advert for a specific job	drawing up a job advert	answering assignment question 3
Analysis	**Check you have achieved this by**	
1 Analyse a job description for a specific job and derive a person specification for the same job	developing a person specification using a recognised framework in an appropriate way	answering assignment question 3
Evaluation	**Check you have achieved this by**	
1 Evaluate which elements of the job recruitment process are key in ensuring equality of opportunity	identifying the stages of the job recruitment process where the equality of employment legislation applies	answering assignment question 2
2 Evaluate the usefulness of different advertising media for different jobs	determining which is the appropriate media to advertise a specific job	answering assignment question 3

Assignment questions

1 Summarise and illustrate how an organisation with a workforce that is too small and lacking in the required skills and abilities could remedy the situation.

2 Name and explain all the elements of the job recruitment process and discuss which of these elements you consider to be key in terms of ensuring equality of opportunity.

3 Produce a job description for a university lecturer in marketing. Use the job description you have produced to draw up a person specification. Indicate where the job could be advertised and state what information you would include in any advertisement used.

Weblinks available online at www.booksites.net/capon

1 This site is for the Equal Opportunities Commission and it looks at equality of employment in the workplace and the associated legislation.
http://www.eoc.org.uk

2 This site is for the Commission for Racial Equality and it looks at promoting racial equality and ending racial discrimination.
http://www.cre.gov.uk

3 This site is for the Disability Rights Commission and it looks at establishing equality of opportunity and access to work and training for those with disability.
http://www.drc-gb.org

4 This site is for the DTI and the following pages look at issues such as employment relations and life-work balance and the benefits to business of training and development.
http://www.dti.gov.uk/for_employees.html
http://www.dti.gov.uk/training_development/

Further reading

Apgar, M (1998) 'The alternative workplace: changing where and how people work', *Harvard Business Review*, May/June.

Braid, M (1995) 'Tomorrow belongs to them', *Independent*, 2 October.

Bratton, J and Gold, J (1994) *Human Resource Management: Theory and Practice*, Basingstoke: Macmillan.

Brown, M (1997) 'Design for working', *Management Today*, March.

Butcher, D (2002) 'It takes two to review', *Management Today*, November.

Clement, B (1999) 'Nice suit. Is that the union rep?', *Management Today*, March.

Fenby, J (2000) 'Your ticket to the boardroom', *Management Today*, July.

Gabb, A (1997) 'University challenge', *Management Today*, December.

Grundy, T (1997) 'Human resource management – a strategic approach', *Long Range Planning*, 30 (4), August.

Gwyther, M (1992) 'Britain bracing for the age bomb', *Independent on Sunday*, 29 March.

Handy, C (1995) *The Age of Unreason*, Arrow.

Jebb, F (1998) 'Flex appeal', *Management Today*, July.

Kirwan-Taylor, H (2000) 'Coaching chanpions', *Management Today*, November.

Lucas, E (1999) 'Virtual realities of candidate selection', *Professional Manager*, March.

Lynn, M (2000) 'Attracting the head-hunters', *Management Today*, December.

Lynn, M (2000) 'Your strategy for the talent war', *Management Today*, October.

McIntyre Brown, A (1997) 'The pay band wagon', *Management Today*, August.

Merrick, N (1999) 'The key shift', *People Management*, 11 March.

Merriden, T (1997) 'Vacancies in the skills department', *Management Today*, May.

Mitchell, A (1998) 'New model unions', *Management Today*, July.

Nicholson-Lord, D (1995) ' "Greys" take over from the young as big spenders', *Independent*, 27 January.

Olins, R and Gwyther, M (2001) 'Ageism at work has had its day', *Management Today*, April.

Smith, D (1997) 'Job insecurity and other myths', *Management Today*, May.

Smith, D (1998) 'Skills shortage – we're learning (at last)', *Management Today*, July.

Torrington, D, Hall, L and Taylor, S (2002) *Human Resource Management*, 5th edn, Harlow: Financial Times Prentice Hall.

Prentice Hall.

Ulrich, D (1998) 'A new mandate for human resources', *Harvard Business Review*, January/February.

Wheatley, M (1997) 'Open all hours', *Management Today*, September.

References

1 Daniels, J D and Radebaugh, L (1997) *International Business*, 8th edn, Reading, MA: Addison Wesley Longman.

2 Clement, B (1995) 'Dinner ladies' equal pay win undermines competition law', *Independent*, 7 July.

3 Clement, B (1996) 'Dinner ladies awarded £1m over council's unfair pay cut', *Independent*, 30 July.

4 Clement, B (1996) 'Legal service found guilty of race bias', *Independent*, 7 December.

5 Ibid.

6 Gary, B (1997) 'Armed forces under attack for racism', *Financial Times*, 21 March.

7 The Minister for Disabled People (1996) *The Disability Discrimination Act – Employment*, DL 70, October.

8 Johnson, P (1990) 'Our ageing population – the implications for business and government', *Long Range Planning* 23 (2), April.

9 Ibid.

10 Ibid.

11 *Independent on Sunday*, 29 March 1992.

12 Johnson, op. cit.

13 Atkinson, J (1984) 'Manpower strategies for flexible organisations', *Personnel Management*, August.

14 Ibid.

15 Bolger, A (1997) 'Thoroughly modern training', *Financial Times*, 24 March.

16 Penman, D (1994) 'No workplace like home', *Independent*, 6 June.

8

The external environment

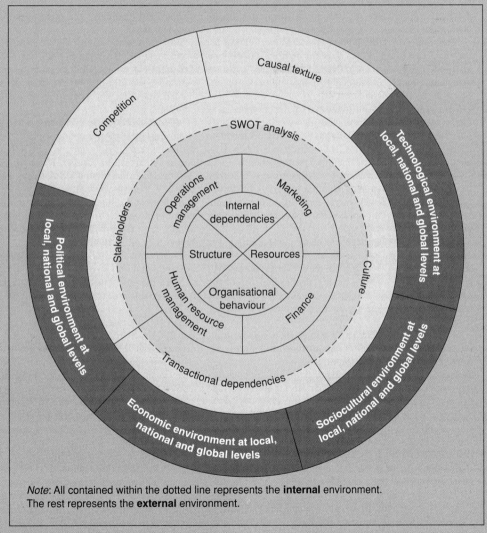

Note: All contained within the dotted line represents the **internal** environment. The rest represents the **external** environment.

Figure 8.1 Organisational context model

➡ ENTRY CASE STUDY 8.1   FT

US airlines: Big carriers unlikely to find much relief

By Paul Taylor

It has been a rough year for business travellers in the US, and the recent Chapter 11 bankruptcy filing by UAL, the Chicago-based parent of United Airlines, the world's second largest carrier, is likely to add to the uncertainty.

Over the past 12 months US business travellers have been forced to put up with upheaval in airport security systems in the wake of the September 11 terrorist attacks, the bankruptcy filings of two big airlines, and drastic changes in fares and frequent-flyer programmes.

Many are now complaining that airlines, fighting for survival in the midst of the one of the industry's worst-ever downturns, are 'nickel and diming' them with measures designed to squeeze additional revenues out of passengers or cut back on perks and benefits.

For example, many airlines have tightened up existing cabin baggage regulations and have begun to strictly enforce excess baggage charges – moves designed to garner additional revenues but which run the risk of alienating many business and other passengers.

Several recent newspaper articles have featured passengers who have been charged hundreds of dollars for an extra bag. Business travellers in particular complain that the premium prices they pay for their tickets are not reflected in standards of service.

Other airlines have begun to charge an additional fee of up to $25 if passengers insist on using paper tickets instead of electronic ones. Until they reversed themselves a few weeks ago, many of the big airlines had also begun to charge passengers $100 if they wanted to fly standby on flights on the same day as their originally scheduled flights.

Meanwhile, the Chapter 11 filings have left millions wondering whether their frequent-flyer miles are safe. Some airlines, including US Air, have already tried to add new restrictions to their frequent flyer programmes but have been forced to back down in the face of a barrage criticism from customers.

US passengers also face the prospect of fewer scheduled flights and a contraction in routes served by the main 'hub-and-spoke' carriers, including United. In the immediate wake of United's Chapter 11 filing, executives said there would be no immediate changes to the company's schedule of 1800 daily flights, providing service to 117 airports around the world.

Nevertheless, industry executives and analysts believe United will have to cut back its route system substantially and negotiate further substantial concessions from its employees if it is to survive.

They warn that if United manages to restructure and emerge from Chapter 11 by June 2004 as planned, it will be a very different airline to the globe-straddling carrier that profited handsomely, selling high-price last-minute tickets to business travellers during the economic boom of the late 1990s.

A more immediate concern is that the increasingly likely prospect of a war with Iraq could cause oil prices to spike, further undermining the shaky health of many US airlines and leading to the possibility that other carriers could go bust.

But even without an oil price spike, the traditional carriers in the US were already facing fierce competition from cut-price operators such as Southwest Airlines and three-year-old upstart, Jet Blue. Most have acknowledged that they will have to slash costs if they are to survive.

Overall, the US airline industry is in a parlous financial state. Last year alone, operators lost about $8bn on top of the more than $7bn they lost in 2001. The six biggest carriers – American, United, Delta Air Lines, Northwest Airlines, Continental and US Airways – have all suffered badly.

Southwest Airlines was the only significant carrier that did not cut back operations last year and its profitability, amid a sea of losses, has earned it a stock market value bigger than all its rivals' combined.

This is not the first time the US airline industry has been plunged into financial turmoil.

Since the government deregulated the industry in 1978, is has faced two serious recessions in the early 1980s and 1990s.

But the combination of the fear created by September 2001 terrorist attacks, competition from cut price airlines and the growing sophistication of travellers who now have access to comparative fare information via the internet makes this downturn different, say analysts.

The success of low cost 'no-frills' carriers in lucrative markets such as California and the east coast has destroyed the traditional carriers' profits on many routes that they once dominated.

For example, Southwest Airlines' share of the California market has jumped to more than 60 per cent in the 18 months while United's share has fallen to less than 20 per cent, in part because losses have forced the big carrier to cut back on its flights.

Other low-cost airlines, such as Spirit Airlines and Jet Blue, have begun cutting into the big carriers' business on longer routes.

▶

Faced with the success of the low price carriers and the underlying downturn in passenger traffic, most carriers have been forced to cut their already heavily discounted economy fares further.

According to estimates, the average price to fly a mile, adjusted for inflation, fell by 25 per cent in the 10 years to 2001.

Since they were unable to raise the prices they charged leisure travellers for fares booked well in advance, most big carriers have raised prices for last minute bookings and business fares. In some cases a business ticket is now almost six times as expensive as a discount ticket.

The widening gap between business and discounted economy fares has prompted many companies to re-examine their business travel policies, cancel trips and in some cases abandon the deals they had previously negotiated with big carriers.

At the same time, the internet has made it much easier for both business and leisure travellers to compare prices and tinker with itineraries in order to save money.

With the continuing uncertainty over the US economic recovery and geopolitics, the big carriers are unlikely to find much relief this year. For business travellers, that may translate into further uncertainty and turmoil.

Source: *Financial Times*, 30 January 2003. Reproduced with permission.

Introduction

This chapter introduces the idea of organisations analysing their external environment in order to make sense of the volatile world in which they operate, such that appropriate management and business decisions can be taken. In contemplating the complex and dynamic world in which they operate, organisations have to consider many influences and issues. The entry case study on the US airline industry is a good example of an industry in which companies have had to face a complex and turbulent environment, caused by competition, war, terrorism and bankruptcy.

Analysis of the external environment can be done at a broad general level by use of PEST and LoNGPEST analyses, which are covered in this chapter and Chapter 9. Further examination of other components of the external environment needs to occur for a full understanding of the external environment to be possible. These other components include competition, competitors, customers and other external stakeholders.

To be able to compete effectively, organisations need to understand who their competitors are and the best way to compete with them. The 'traditional' US airlines like Delta, Northwest and Continental all fared badly in 2001, due, in part, to competition from low-price airlines such as Southwest Airlines and Jet Blue. In response to this competition and in a bid to survive and compete effectively, big airlines such as Delta and US Airways have sought to trim costs and increase revenues by trying a variety of measures, with varying degrees of success, for example being more stringent about charging for excess baggage and even charging for issuing a paper ticket.

Organisations may choose to compete by offering low-priced, good-value products and services, such as airlines like easyJet and Southwest Airlines, or by offering a luxury product or service at a higher price, such as Concorde. We look at the issues of competition in Chapter 10. Equally, the understanding of competitors and their behaviour ties in directly with the need to understand the marketplace, who your customers are, where they are located, and how they can be persuaded to buy the products and services offered by your company rather than those of one of your competitors. This is explored in Chapter 4. For the US airlines, the access customers now have to information on flights and fares via the internet has resulted in airlines having to work harder to make their offering attractive and appealing to customers.

The tool of **PEST analysis** is examined and developed for the purpose of analysing the external environment or outside world. Analysis of the external environment is an ongoing process for organisations that take the dynamic and changing nature of the external environment seriously.

Hence, in summary, this chapter examines:

- the elements and levels of the external environment faced by organisations;
- the benefits of external environmental analysis;
- the guidelines for undertaking LoNGPEST analysis;
- in brief, the part that competition plays in the organisation's external environment.

The elements and levels of the external environment

The **external environment** is literally the big wide world in which organisations operate. Whatever the nature of their business, organisations do not and cannot exist in splendid isolation from the other organisations or individuals around them, be they customers, employees or suppliers. It is therefore clear that the external environment of any organisation is a large and complex place.

The term 'environment' in this case refers to much more than the ecological, 'green' issues that the word commonly evokes. 'Environment' here is more appropriately interpreted as the external context in which organisations find themselves undertaking their activities. Each organisation has a unique external environment that has unique impacts on the organisation, due to the fact that organisations are located in different places and are involved in different business activities, with different products, services, customers and so on. In addition to this unique context, individual organisations will all have their own distinctive view of the world surrounding them, leading them to interpret what is happening in the external environment correctly or incorrectly, depending on their ability to understand the external forces affecting them. This begins to suggest how crucial it is for organisations to undertake external environmental analysis and to aim to get it right.

Careful and accurate analysis of the external environment benefits organisations by providing overall greater understanding and an appreciation of the context in which the organisation operates. The key benefits of external environmental analysis are best realised if it is undertaken on a long-term, ongoing basis. These benefits can be summarised as follows:

- managers in the organisation achieve a greater understanding and appreciation of the external environment, leading to improvement in long-term and strategic planning;
- highlighting of the principal external environmental influences generating change;
- anticipation of threats and opportunities within a timescale of long enough duration to allow responses to be considered.[1]

☑ Check your understanding

Do you understand what is meant by the term 'external environment'?

Check your understanding by explaining what the external environment of an organisation is.

External environments can be defined and analysed using PEST analysis, examining political, economic, sociocultural and technological categories into which external influences on the organisation can be placed.

- *Political* influences on organisations encompass both those with a big and small letter 'p', i.e. politics in the conventional sense, with the rules and regulations imposed by government, as well as the **political influences** on organisations of various trade associations, trade unions and chambers of commerce.
- *Economic* influences on organisations include the impact of banks, stock markets, the world money markets, and trading blocs such as the European Union.
- *Sociocultural* influences on organisations include changes in the age and structure of populations, the manner in which populations behave, and the way in which the culture of a population or country changes and develops.
- *Technological* developments influence the magnitude and rate of change that organisations face, and how this affects their capacity to meet their customers' demands. Technological developments have included the development of increasingly sophisticated computer hardware and software. The development of media and communications technology covers electronics and telecommunications, including use of the internet. The ongoing development of the internet as a way of doing business and accessing information has meant a whole new 'media' which needs to be understood in terms of its potential use and reliability.

Basic analysis of an organisation's external environment can be done by breaking down the external influences on the organisation into the PEST categories and assessing the impact of the individual elements identified in each category.

However, there exists a second dimension to the external environment of organisations. This is the level at which the influences occur. There are three levels that will be considered alongside the PEST categories. The levels are local, national and global (LoNG).

- The *local* level can be said to be the immediate town, city or region in which the organisation operates.
- The *national* level is then the home country in which an organisation identifies its headquarters.
- The *global* level then becomes anything outside the local and national levels.

A company operating in and being influenced by the **global level** of the external environment will be trading in a foreign country, be it right next door or on the other side of the world. A company in this situation is subject not only to the laws and culture of its local and national environments but also to the laws and culture of the foreign country in which it is trading. In addition to national rules and regulations, there are the laws and procedures of both home and host countries specifically governing importing/exporting and foreign direct investment activity to consider.

The literature of international business clearly differentiates the terms 'international' and 'global'. Some of the issues considered here are 'international', i.e. they are issues that occur between nations. However, the third level will be described as 'global', i.e. affecting all parts of the world in similar and simultaneous ways. This is because many of the issues of globalisation at the start of the twenty-first century increasingly affect the local and national levels of organisations' external environments.

The traditional PEST analysis, then, is a short, one-dimensional view of the external environment. The two-dimensional analysis will be referred to in this text as a LoNG (local, national and global) PEST analysis. A generic LoNGPEST analysis could look like the grid shown in Table 8.1.

The grid represents the view that these external influential elements, whether political, economic, sociocultural or technological, all exist at local, national and global levels. The political, economic and **sociocultural influences** are easily identified at the three different levels. However, it could be argued that all types of technology affect and influence organisations at all levels of the environment.

It should be noted that not every organisation will identify strongly influential elements in all four PEST categories at all three levels all the time, but the possibility should be considered for any organisation when carrying out a LoNGPEST analysis because elements have to be identified before they can be evaluated and discounted.

The next section of this chapter offers some guidelines for use when carrying out external environmental analysis. The grid in Table 8.1 shows the possible different external environmental influences on an organisation. These external environmental influences are discussed in more detail in Chapter 9.

Table 8.1
Generic LoNGPEST
grid

	Political	Economic	Sociocultural	Technological

Local	• Local government
	• Local offices of
	  national government
	• Local associations
	  – Chambers of
	    commerce
	  – Business Link
		• Local bank
		  branches
		• Local economy
			• Local
			  community
			• Social capital
				• Communications
				  technology
				  – Mobile
				    phones
				    and faxes
				  – Video
				    conferencing
				  – Internet and
				    world wide
				    web
				
				• Organisations
				  and the
				  application of
				  technology
				  – The personal
				    computer
				  – The banking
				    and financial
				    services
				    industry

National	• National government
	• Devolution for
	  Scotland and Wales
	• National bodies
	  – Employers' bodies
	  – Employees' bodies
		• Central bank
		  – Bank of
		    England
		• Stock market
		  – London
			• Demographic
			  change
			• Social change	

Global	• Alliances and
	  agreements
	  – UK and USA
	  – UK and China
	  – EU
	  – Cold War
	  – CIS
	  – CBSS
	  – Eastern Europe
	• International bodies
	  – The Commonwealth
	  – NATO
		• Trading blocs
		  and bodies
		  – EU
		  – EFTA
		  – OECD
		  – NAFTA
		  – ASEAN
		• World money
		  markets
		• WTO
			• Global
			  demographics
			• Cross-cultural
			  issues
			  – Language
			  – Behaviour
			  – Culture shock	

✓ Check your understanding

Do you understand what is meant by LoNGPEST?

Check your understanding by naming one influence from each of the following categories: technology; local/political; national/economic; global/sociocultural.

Performing external environmental analysis

As has been stated previously, the external environment is an immensely complex and dynamic place. Therefore, performing an analysis of the external environment of an organisation requires access to a wide range of information. This information may already exist within the organisation or it may have to be sought, collected and collated from other sources. Sources of information within an organisation will encompass information from the four key functional areas of marketing, production, finance and human resource management. This will include sales reports, customer/client survey results, reports on staff skills and availability, and budgets and cashflow statements detailing the amount and availability of cash. In addition, information should be available on the systems in place in the organisation, including that on their capability and capacity, and efficiency and effectiveness. This type of information provided by internal sources, if it is up to date, will provide details of the resources available to deal with current influences in the external environment and indicate the level of resources needed to respond to possible future influences from the external environment.

External information sources are compiled by organisations other than that undertaking analysis of its external environment. The external information sources most widely available and accessible to everyone are the press, television and radio. In the UK the most familiar press includes the daily and Sunday broadsheet newspapers, which all contain business pages or sections in addition to reporting the general political and economic news. These are the *Independent*, the *Daily Telegraph*, *The Times*, the *Guardian*, the *Financial Times*, the *Sunday Times*, the *Sunday Telegraph*, the *Observer*, and the *Independent on Sunday*. Publications such as *The Economist* and *Management Today* supply more extensive coverage of the economy and the latest developments in the world of trade and commerce than that provided by the daily and Sunday press.

The annual report and accounts of a company also provide a summary of recent activities and may offer clues to or an indication of future activities. The annual report and accounts of publicly quoted companies are readily available from the companies themselves or via their website, so are easily obtainable by competitor companies. Specific information concerning an industry will be available from industry- or trade-specific publications.

Current affairs programmes on radio and television cover economic and political news as well as reporting company and industry news and events. For example, Radio 4's *Today* programme comprises items of economic, political and business news and is broadcast at breakfast time on weekday mornings. In addition, economic, political and business news is reported on television news programmes, for example on ITV and BBC1 at teatime and in the late evening. Daily news broadcasts, such as *Newsnight* on BBC2 and Channel 4 News, are longer news programmes than the broadcasts on BBC1 and ITV and consequently devote more time to economic, political and business news stories.

There are other television programmes devoted to business, economic and political stories and issues: for example, *Working Lunch* on BBC2 is broadcast every weekday at 12.30pm. Other weekly programmes include *Question Time* and *The Money Programme*, which focuses on political and economic issues. Programmes examining political, economic and business issues are broadcast in abundance on Sundays in the UK. These include BBC1's *Breakfast With Frost* programme, which has a political focus, followed by *The Politics Show* on BBC1 or *Jonathan Dimbleby* on ITV at lunchtime. Other television programmes that examine issues of relevance to business or organisations include documentary programmes such as *Panorama*.

The internet and electronic information are other sources of information which are widely available in organisations. An immense and extensive amount of information can be found on the internet, although one must be aware of

**Table 8.2
Blank grid for
LoNGPEST analysis**

	Political	Economic	Sociocultural	Technological
Local				
National				
Global				

who or which organisation originated the information, as this will affect its reliability and accuracy. Much printed and broadcast material can now be accessed via the internet, and many organisations have their own website.

The other method of accessing information electronically is via the use of subscription databases such as Lexis/Nexis, which gives access to the world's press. Other subscription databases which can be found in libraries include MINTEL, FAME and journal databases.

There is likely to be an increase in the number of websites available on a subscription-only basis. For example the FT internet archive is now subscription only.

The use of the LoNGPEST framework and information will allow analysis of the external environment of an organisation to be completed. The following guidelines will help in applying the LoNGPEST framework. It is suggested that a blank grid like the one in Table 8.2 is used when carrying out external environmental analysis.

■ Guidelines for external environmental analysis

1 Identify the influences affecting the organisation.
2 Categorise the influences by using the LoNGPEST grid.
  (a) First, decide whether the influence is political, economic, sociocultural or technological.
  (b) Second, decide whether the influence is local, national or global.
3 Make sure you can explain how and why a particular influence is affecting an organisation. Remember, elements in the external environment do not exist in isolation at any level and can impinge on and influence one another.
4 Select and judge which categories are most important to the company, for example **technological influences** at the global level or **economic influences** at the **national level**.

5 Select key individual influences from the important categories. For example, the important category economic influences at the national level may contain the crucial influence of falling interest rates.

6 Consider the important categories and influences you have identified. Do any of these pose threats or opportunities to which the company must react immediately or in the longer term, when anticipating and planning the future?

7 How should the organisation react to and deal with the opportunities and threats? Do short-term opportunities take priority over long-term threats or vice versa?

☑ Check your understanding

Do you understand the importance of information gathering and its reliability in undertaking external environmental analysis?

Check your understanding by stating where you would search for information on the following types of influences: political, economic, socio-cultural and technological.

Summary

This chapter examined the external environment influences (PEST) which impact on organisations and how those factors could also be assessed at the local, national and global levels of the external environment. The following summary covers all aspects of this chapter.

1 Organisations analyse their external environment in an effort to understand what it is that impacts upon them. In broad general terms, factors impacting on organisations arise from the PEST factors (political, economic, sociocultural and technological), competition and the marketplace.

2 Undertaking external environmental analysis allows managers to better understand the external environment and hence have an improved idea of how to respond to threats and opportunities in the external environment.

3 Political influences on organisations include legislation and industry regulations. Economic influences include the impact of banks, stock markets and trading blocs. Sociocultural influences cover age, structure and behaviour of populations. The impact of technology is wide reaching and includes computer hardware, computer software, communications technology and electronic media.

4 The second dimension to PEST analysis is that provided by consideration of the PEST categories at local, national and global levels, giving rise to LoNGPEST. The local level is the immediate town, city or region in which the company operates. The national level is the home country with which the organisation identifies. Hence the global level is anything beyond the local and national levels.

5 Information for performing a PEST or LoNGPEST analysis exists both inside and outside the organisation and takes the form of sales reports, budgets, press articles and TV programmes.

6 The guidelines for performing a LoNGPEST analysis cover identification of factors impacting on the organisation, their categorisation and an assessment of their impact on the organisation and its decision making.

Learning outcomes for case studies

While reading this chapter and engaging in the activities, you should have learned how to apply theory and models, analyse situations, and evaluate the application and analysis you undertake. The learning outcomes specified below outline the type of application, analysis and evaluation of which you should be capable in relation to organisations. The case studies and the questions which follow provide an opportunity for you to test how well you have achieved the learning outcomes for the ethical issues and exit case studies for this chapter.

Application	Check you have achieved this by	
1 Apply PEST analysis to specific situations	performing a specific PEST analysis for a real organisation	answering exit case study question 1
Analysis	**Check you have achieved this by**	
1 Identify and prioritise factors having the greatest impact on organisations	ensuring any PEST analysis you perform is complete and not just a series of lists	answering exit case study question 1
2 Decide how organisations could respond to external environmental factors	drawing up an organisational response to the external environment	answering ethical case study questions 1 & 2

ETHICAL ISSUES CASE STUDY 8.2

FT

Leading supermarket chains to ban 'alcopops'

By David Wighton, Liam Halligan and Robert Wright

Leading supermarket chains yesterday moved to ban 'alcopops' from their stores as Mr Tony Blair, the prime minister, underlined the government's determination to crack down on under-age drinking.

The Co-op and Iceland said they would stop selling the alcoholic soft drinks which critics claim are deliberately marketed to appeal to under-18s. Other large chains said they would end all promotions while reviewing their policy.

The moves follow this week's fierce attack on alcopop manufacturers by Mr Frank Dobson, the health secretary, who said the government would have to contemplate a ban.

Mr Blair yesterday used his first 'meet the people' question and answer session to back the tough stand. 'It is important that we enforce responsible behaviour in relation to this and you will find we will tackle this particularly clearly.'

The Co-op Retail Trading Group said its own ban on alcopops was prompted by concern over the popularity of the drinks among under-18s. 'We believe these drinks are designed specifically to appeal to young people and are, in fact, largely consumed by under-18s who cannot legally buy them,' it said.

Mr Malcolm Walker, chairman of Iceland, said the company was reacting to customer concerns. 'While commercially this decision will hurt, as a family company

we must act responsibly and reflect the views of our customers.'

There was clear evidence that alcopops were encouraging under-age drinking. But Bass, whose Hooper's Hooch is leader in the £250m-a-year market, denied the claim and insisted it took its social responsibilities seriously. 'There is no consistent, objective evidence that under-age drinking has increased since alcopops came on the market.'

Mr George Howarth, the Home office minister who is heading a government inquiry into alcopops, welcomed the Co-op's move. 'I am pleased to see that the Co-op shares ministers' concerns about alcopops and I welcome their readiness to address this serious issue.'

The Home Office said the review would consider all options, including an outright ban. However, the industry argues that this would be difficult without outlawing other drinks such as ready mixed gin and tonics.

The Portman Group, a voluntary watchdog funded by the drinks industry, has acknowledged the need for further restrictions, blaming problems on a few companies that have ignored its guidelines.

Tesco announced it would stop selling alcoholic milk drinks and the controversial sachets of alcohol, but stopped short of an outright ban.

Mr John Gildersleeve, a Tesco director, said: 'After listening to our customers, it is clear the majority do not favour a total ban. However, they do want further action.' Tesco joined other retailers in pressing for further packaging and labelling changes.

Source: Financial Times, 14 June 1997. Reprinted with permission.

Questions for ethical issues case study 8.2

1 Do you think that other large supermarket chains should follow the example of the Co-op and Iceland and stop selling alcoholic soft drinks or follow a policy of ending promotion of alcopops and press for additional packaging and labelling changes? Explain your answer.

2 Draw up a set of guidelines for manufacturers and retail outlets selling alcopops. The guidelines, if followed, should result in the retail outlets not selling alcopops to under-age drinkers.

For more case studies please visit **www.booksites.net/capon**

As annual sales near $270bn, can Wal-Mart conquer markets outside the US?

By Neil Buckley and Susanna Voyle

The sales figures flashing across Lee Scott's computer screen are the stuff of most chief executives' dreams. At least three times in recent weeks, they topped $1bn in a day. Within three years, they could average that every day.

Such numbers only hint at just how big Wal-Mart has become. It overtook Exxon Mobil as the world's largest company by revenues in 2001, with $218bn. In the coming year, sales should top $270bn. Its fleet of 20 aircraft, ferrying managers around the US and its growing overseas operations, clocks up as many passenger miles as a medium-sized commercial airline. It will spend $11bn this year on 48m square feet of new selling space – bigger than that of the UK's Tesco, itself one of the world's largest retailers.

Yet bulk brings challenges. As Mr Scott, Wal-Mart's chief executive since 2000, points out, for a $200bn company to grow by even 10 per cent means adding $20bn in sales.

Can Wal-Mart possibly maintain its extraordinary growth, which has averaged an annual 15 per cent in sales and earnings over 10 years? Put another way, having conquered America, can Wal-Mart conquer the world?

Some analysts have raised doubts about the sustainability of Wal-Mart's strategy. Competition in less-developed retail markets in Asia and Latin America is intensifying, while it continues to stir protests against expansion at home. 'We'd be silly to sit here and tell you it's not a challenge,' says Mr Scott.

'If you're looking from the outside it seems almost insurmountable. If you're looking from the inside, you're looking at the infrastructure that you have – and it all just moves forward. This year we opened a record number of stores, next year we will open a record number of stores. Our plans for the year after that are to open a record number of stores.'

Wal-Mart has hardly reinvented retailing. It sells a huge range of goods – 120 000 items, from bananas to books, from tropical fish to car tyres – in monstrous, edge-of-town superstores with a ruthless focus on price. Following principles laid down by Sam Walton, its mercurial founder, prices are set not slightly below competitors, as other retailers do, but at the lowest Wal-Mart can get away with and still make an adequate return. Its retail strategy is to ensure 'everyday low prices', eschewing temporary promotions.

Where Wal-Mart has really beaten its rivals is in paring costs and creating one of the most sophisticated supply chains of any retailer. Stores are non-unionised, keeping labour costs below competitors' – though staff benefit from profit-sharing and opportunities to buy company stock at a discount.

Indeed, its tightfistedness is legendary. Wal-Mart's headquarters in the southern US backwater of Bentonville, Arkansas, are in a converted warehouse. Mr Scott works from a cramped office with walls clad in cheap wood veneer. The international division is run from a single-storey, virtually windowless grey shed. Travelling executives share rooms in budget hotels.

Yet Wal-Mart does invest money to improve efficiency. Forced in the 1960s to set up its own distribution system because independent distributors did not serve the small rural towns where its first stores were located, Wal-Mart has been at the forefront of innovation in computers and barcode scanning to control its supply chain. By 1988, it had America's largest privately owned satellite communications network. Technology analysts claim Wal-Mart's central database is second in size only to the Pentagon's. It pioneered data sharing with suppliers, providing not just the previous day's sales but also sales forecasts. The policy has allowed manufacturers to fine-tune production. A McKinsey survey last year found Wal-Mart alone was responsible for a quarter of productivity increase in 1995–99 in the US economy. 'In the supply chain, they are head and shoulders better than anybody else in the US,' says Henry Vogel, a director at Boston Consulting Group.

Everything is bound together by a folksy corporate culture infused with Mr Walton's values. Employees, known as 'associates', pledge when they join to greet an customer who comes within 10ft. Managers and employees kick off weekly staff meetings with the Wal-Mart cheer: 'Give me a W! Give me an A! . . .' and so on. The hyphen in the store's name, which employees call the 'squiggly', is rendered by a shaking of the rear end – followed by a rousing 'Who's number one? The customer. Always!'

Having marched across all 50 states, however, Wal-Mart has faced increasing questions from analysts about whether it is approaching saturation in the US. Mr Scott says saturation is a lot further away than people think. 'Twenty years ago, we might have said we were 10 years from that. Ten years ago, we might have said we were 10 years from that. Today we might say we're 10 or 20 years away.'

The company is finding it can put its giant stores much closer together than it ever believed possible – as little as five miles apart – and still make the required return. New stores initially cannibalise sales from existing ones but the older stores can regain any lost sales within a year.

It also has growth prospects in big metropolitan markets, where its market share remains small. Getting sites for 200 000 sq ft stores in built-up areas such as central Philadelphia is impossible, concedes Mr Scott. But the company's international experience is teaching it to operate where land is scarce. In South Korea, for example, it runs stores eight storeys high. Wal-Mart is also trying its hand at convenience stores. Its Neighborhood Markets, a quarter the size of its traditional outlets, offer Wal-Mart prices on a select range of goods. These could eventually provide a way into urban markets.

Wal-Mart is also looking to expand into new product areas. The retailer began adding food to its traditional discount stores in 1988. By 2001, it was the biggest seller of food in the US, with sales of $53bn. Though it has only 15 per cent of the grocery market, analysts believe this could leap to 25 per cent by 2006.

On sale at Wal-Mart in Rogers, Arkansas, a stone's throw from where Sam Walton opened his first ramshackle discount store in 1962, are digital versatile disc players, personal computers and a plasma-screen television set for $5900 – items 'Mr Sam' could scarcely have conceived of.

But there is only so much growth to be had in the US; sooner or later, international expansion must become the growth engine. The retailer already expects overseas operations to provide a third of its sales and earnings growth in the next three to five years.

Analysts have, however, long raised doubts as to whether Wal-Mart can successfully export its downhome American culture and a formula that relies on vast stores and cheap land.

While its international operations notched up an estimated $40bn sales last year, results so far have been mixed. From a small joint venture in 1991, Wal-Mart has grown into Mexico's biggest retailer. After three years of heavy losses in Canada, it turned things round and achieved the same feat there. Its £6.7bn ($10.8bn) acquisition of Asda of the UK in 1999 has been hailed as a success. Expansion into China and Korea is proceeding well. But Wal-Mart is still making losses in Germany five years after its bungled entry – and can give no break-even date. Argentina and Brazil remain tough. It pulled out of Indonesia in the mid-1990s.

John Menzer, who took over as chief executive of Wal-Mart's international operations in 1999, is credited with injecting more sophistication into overseas stores. He gave more authority to country chiefs – now mostly non-Americans – and pushed headquarters staff out into the field. He set up a global sourcing unit to harness Wal-Mart's huge international buying power.

Mr Menzer says the company has learnt two lessons. First, no more 'flag-planting' – opening a handful of stores to test out a market. That approach backfired in

Argentina and Brazil when European retailers entered in force and took over the market while Wal-Mart was still toe-dipping. 'When we decide to go into a new market, we're going to go in with enough mass that we can use our core competences, which are our distribution and supply chain.'

Second, it hopes to be more realistic about the pace of change in acquisitions. The mistake in Germany was to rush the task of integrating two different chains with Wal-Mart, causing chaos.

Hence the softly-softly approach towards Japan, its latest foreign foray. It watched the market for five years before a possible partner came along – Seiyu, the fourth largest supermarket group – whose culture and management were a good fit. Wal-Mart took a small stake, with options to increase. It worked with other shareholders for nine months to agree a business plan and last month became the largest shareholder.

Wal-Mart is learning to spread lessons and experience from one country across the group. Asda's food expertise was exported to the US and elsewhere; so was a new approach to livening up sales through 'retail-tainment' learnt in China, where staff organised customer events such as catch-your-own-shrimp competitions.

As well as tailoring operations to national tastes, Mr Menzer says, it is learning to adapt its corporate culture. The key is to blend the US version – Sam Walton's three core values were 'respect for the individual, treat the customer as the boss and strive to improve every day' – with local values. 'I believe the culture really is transportable around the world. In fact that's the only reason I can do my job at all,' says Mr Menzer. 'But it becomes the Wal-Mart Asda culture, or the Wal-Mart Germany culture, or the Wal-Mart Brazil culture.'

The company evaluates potential markets using criteria including economic and political risk, growth potential, and property availability, revising its target list every two years. Where land is available, it will expand organically; where a market is saturated, it must rely on acquisitions.

On top of the complexities of international expansion, however, Wal-Mart will increasingly run up against other emerging global retailers such as France's Carrefour – with which it competes head-on in China – and Tesco. Neither has its size but both have systems and skills that approach Wal-Mart's.

Obstacles still loom at home. Wal-Mart has faced increasing attempts since the 1980s to block its expansion into new communities from campaigners who accuse it of destroying town centres. Political attempts to block a recent acquisition in Puerto Rico show it may not always be welcomed into every foreign market.

Perhaps the biggest danger, as with any successful retailer, is complacency. The Wal-Marts of their day 50 or 80 years ago, such as Woolworths and Montgomery Ward, have declined or disappeared as hungrier rivals emerged. Kmart, which opened its first discount store the same year as Wal-Mart and in 1989 was the world's biggest retailer, last year filed for bankruptcy.

But Shari Eberts, an analyst at JP Morgan, believes if any retailer can retain its dynamism, it is Wal-Mart. 'It's hard to find another retailer where two-thirds of annual growth in US retail space is coming at [its] own expense,' from relocating and expanding existing stores, she says. 'To me that's a testament to the company's foresight, their ability to destroy and recreate themselves.'

Wal-Mart's integration of Asda, the British supermarket chain, has been so successful that it has become a blueprint for other deals within the group.

John Menzer, who heads Wal-Mart's international division, says that Asda, bought for £6.7bn in 1999, has easily outperformed targets each year. 'What we learnt from Asda is now incorporated in our systems in Korea, the US, South America and everywhere,' he says.

Why has the Wal-Mart experience in the UK been so happy? And what has the entry of the discount retailer meant for Asda's rivals?

Wal-Mart's motive for buying Asda was two-fold. First, it wanted a good business in its own right. Second, it needed a firm foothold in Europe – one that might help sort out its troubled German business.

Wal-Mart's first foray into Europe was not successful. In 1997 it bought Wertkauf, a German hypermarket operator, before adding the distressed Interspar chain the following year. Yet, five years on, the German operations remain stubbornly loss-making.

Analysts say Wal-Mart tried to impose its way of doing business on Germany. It imported US managers and immediately stamped the Wal-Mart name above the doors. In addition, language differences and the peculiarities of the German market, dominated by hard discounters and private companies, made integration difficult. 'They bought bad assets, they haven't got enough critical mass and the German economy is all over the place,' says one rival retailer.

Inexperienced managers were a further hindrance, according to one old Asda hand. 'One of the surprises about Wal-Mart is how weak in conventional managers they are. They are very good at what they do in the Wal-Mart way. But you wouldn't put them in the same roles in other groups.'

The Asda deal has, however, helped strengthen Wal-Mart's European management, particularly in Germany. 'When they acquired Asda they had about 300 Americans in Germany. That has changed. Asda people have been able to help them,' says another former Asda executive.

Indeed, the Asda acquisition marked a contrast from the start. And the Wal-Mart management treated its new subsidiary very differently.

The key difference was that Asda was not a business in trouble; the turnround work had been done already. And, famously, the shake-up at Asda had been modelled on Wal-Mart. Asda has long had 'colleagues' not staff; shoppers are met by greeters; and the company has its own version of the Wal-Mart cheer chanted by employees before meetings.

Commercially, the two groups had the same strategy: to drive sales by wooing shoppers with 'everyday low prices'. Wal-Mart, therefore, adopted a much more gentle integration process with Asda. 'The Asda business has performed extraordinarily well since the deal,' says one former Asda executive. 'And to Wal-Mart's eternal credit . . . they did not send in the troops from Bentonville and change the way everything was done.'

At the time of the Asda deal, many predicted it would lead to immediate upheaval in the UK retail sector. In the event, little changed in the first year. But Asda has now started to reap the benefits, outperforming rivals and gobbling up market share. It is expected to overtake J. Sainsbury as number two behind Tesco this year.

Asda has been putting in Wal-Mart's information technology systems combined with an aggressive push into non-food business. 'Before the deal, Asda was growing at about 5 per cent – now that is closer to 10,' says one former food industry executive. 'There was a momentum there that is now beginning to snowball because of the greater investment levels from Wal-Mart.'

The result is that Asda and Tesco are pulling away from the pack. 'The lesson is that it is the big formats, where you can really do non-food, that are winning,' says the executive. 'Tesco and Asda are churning away at that and the smaller supermarket operators – Sainsbury and Safeway – are suffering.'

Tony DeNunzio, Asda's chief operating officer, says being part of Wal-Mart gives the chain incredible buying power. Prices have fallen accordingly, he says.

Before the Wal-Mart deal, Asda offered prices on average 7 per cent lower than its UK rivals. That, he says, has been improved by 6 percentage points, helping drive market share from 8.4 per cent to 10.5 per cent. But he adds: 'It has taken three years to convert the systems and we are still really learning how to use them, so there is more to come.'

Source: Financial Times, 8 January 2003. Reprinted with permission.

Question for exit case study 8.3

1 Using the guidelines for external environmental analysis in this chapter, the information in the Wal-Mart case study and your own general knowledge, perform a PEST analysis of the external environment faced by Wal-Mart.

Short-answer questions

1 Define the term 'external environment'.

2 Explain the term 'LoNGPEST'.

3 Explain the difference between 'international' and 'global'.

4 Name three economic factors which could impact on organisations.

5 Name three political factors which could impact on organisations.

6 Name three sociocultural factors which could impact on organisations.

7 Name three technological factors which could impact on organisations.

8 Name three trading blocs.

9 Where can organisations find the information which will allow them to analyse their external environment?

10 Write down the three key benefits to organisations of undertaking external environmental analysis.

Learning outcomes for assignment questions

While reading this chapter and engaging in the activities, you should have learned how to apply theory and models, analyse situations, and evaluate the application and analysis you undertake. The learning outcomes specified below outline what you should be able to do and the assignment questions provide an opportunity for you to test how well you have achieved the learning outcomes for this chapter.

Application	Check you have achieved this by	
1 Apply LoNGPEST analysis to specific situations	performing a specific LoNGPEST analysis for a real organisation	answering assignment questions 1a & 1b
2 Demonstrate understanding as regards the process of analysing the external environment	explaining the steps and stages which need to be undertaken to complete analysis of the external environment	answering assignment question 2
Analysis	Check you have achieved this by	
1 Choose information and data sources that best assist managers in organisations with scanning and understanding the external environment	comparing information and data sources and evaluating the most suitable medium and source	answering assignment question 3

Assignment questions

1 (a) Refer to the section 'Performing external environmental analysis' in this chapter. Identify and collect appropriate information to perform a LoNGPEST analysis of your own college, university or organisation. Your LoNGPEST analysis should contain a completed grid and relevant discussion and explanation.

or

(b) Refer to the section 'Performing external environmental analysis' in this chapter. Identify and collect appropriate information on a public- or private-sector organisation of your choice. Perform a LoNGPEST analysis on your chosen organisation. Your LoNGPEST analysis should contain a completed grid and relevant discussion and explanation.

2 External environmental analysis is an ongoing process for any organisation. Advise an organisation wishing to undertake external environmental analysis for the first time and seeking to set up a system to allow external environmental analysis to take place on an ongoing basis in the future. Present your advice in the form of a 2000-word report.

3 Identify and collect appropriate information from a variety of media sources that show how a particular organisation is evolving. Evaluate and analyse the general usefulness and reliability of the information sources you identify as currently available. Comment on the usefulness of the information to managers within the organisation that is being affected by changes in the external environment. Your answer should take the form of a 2000-word essay.

Weblinks available online at **www.booksites.net/capon**

The websites for this chapter are for some of the key bodies in the UK impacting on organisations. There are more websites, including those for international and global bodies, at the end of Chapter 9.

1 The following website is for British Chambers of Commerce.
   http://www.chamberonline.co.uk

2 The following website is for the House of Commons.
   http://www.parliament.uk/about_commons/about_commons.cfm

3 The following website is for the Bank of England.
   http://www.bankofengland.co.uk

4 The following website is for the London Stock Exchange.
   http://www.londonstockexchange.com/Default.asp

5 The following website is for the European Union.
   http://www.europa.eu.int

Further reading

Johnson, G and Scholes, K (2002) *Exploring Corporate Strategy*, 6th edn, Chapter 3, Harlow: Financial Times Prentice Hall.

Lynch, R (2003) *Corporate Strategy*, 3rd edn, Chapter 3, Harlow: Financial Times Prentice Hall.

Thompson, J L (2001) *Strategic Management: Awareness and Change*, 4th edn, Chapter 7, London: Thomson Learning.

Worthington, I and Britton, C (2000) *The Business Environment*, 3rd edn, Chapter 1, Harlow: Financial Times Prentice Hall.

Reference

1 Duncan, Peter M, and Ginter, W Jack (1990) 'Macro-environmental analysis for strategic management', *Long Range Planning*, 23 (6), December.

9

The composition of the external environment

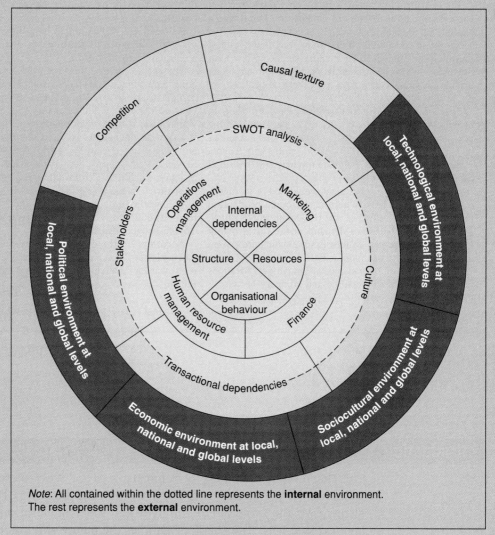

Note: All contained within the dotted line represents the **internal** environment. The rest represents the **external** environment.

Figure 9.1 Organisational context model

ENTRY CASE STUDY 9.1

FT

Peugeot to build new plant in Slovakia

By Robert Anderson in Prague, Martin Arnold in Paris, and John Reed in Warsaw

PSA Peugeot Citroën, the French carmaker, has chosen Slovakia as the site for a €700m ($738.9m) assembly plant, highlighting the ongoing shift of car manufacturing from western Europe to cheaper locations in the east.

The new plant in Trnava, western Slovakia, which will come on stream in 2006, will employ 3500 and have a capacity of 300 000 small vehicles a year.

The decision announced on Wednesday is the biggest greenfield investment in the country and a big boost for Slovakia – which has trailed its neighbours in attracting foreign investment. It is also a blow for Poland, whose Radomsko site was the main challenger.

Peugeot, Europe's second-largest carmaker, plans to increase worldwide vehicle sales by 22 per cent over the next three years to 4m despite a stagnant global market. It is already building a €1.5bn plant jointly with Toyota in Kolin in the Czech Republic to produce 300 000 small cars a year.

Peugeot said the Trnava plant would add to its manufacturing operations and help it overcome production limits at its plants in France, the UK, Spain and Portugal. The plant will also serve demand in the fast growing markets of central and eastern Europe which are poised to enter the European Union in 2004.

The company said it had chosen Trnava over locations in Poland, the Czech Republic and Hungary because it had good access to transport links and was 'in the centre of Europe'.

It also said the region's 'manufacturing tradition', the availability of well-educated labour and the possibility of building a supplier park next to the site had also influenced its decision.

Securing of the plant is also a triumph for the country's re-elected centre-right government, and the economy ministry hailed it as 'the investment of the decade for Slovakia'.

Before 1998 Slovakia had been ignored by foreign investors because of its international isolation and authoritarian government.

The auto sector has long been the country's brightest hope, employing 50 000 workers and making up a quarter of industrial exports. Volkswagen of Germany has led the way by ramping production at its Bratislava car plant, which made 180 000 vehicles last year.

Last year VW cut jobs in Spain after disappointing sales and concentrated manufacturing of the Polo model in Slovakia. Volkswagen's Seat operation has also shifted part of its production to Slovakia, blaming union inflexibility in Spain.

Wednesday's decision was another disappointment for Poland after losing out to the Czech Republic for the Toyota-Peugeot plant.

According to the Polish economy ministry, Peugeot had said that Poland's lack of highways and high-speed roads was the 'main barrier for siting such investments in Poland'.

Source: Financial Times, 15 January 2003. Reprinted with permission.

Introduction

This chapter follows on directly from Chapter 8 and seeks to examine in much greater detail the generic LoNGPEST model – *see* Table 9.1. The constituent elements of the external environment and their influence on organisations are discussed here. The chapter examines the nature and influence on organisation of politics, economics, society and culture and technology, all at the local, national and global levels.

Table 9.1 Generic LoNGPEST grid

	Political	Economic	Sociocultural	Technological

Local	• Local government
	• Local offices of national government
	• Local associations
	  – Chambers of commerce
	  – Business Link
		• Local bank branches
		• Local economy
			• Local community and social capital	• Communications technology
				  – Mobile phones and faxes
				  – Video conferencing
				  – Internet and world wide web

National	• National government
	• Devolution for Scotland and Wales
	• National bodies
	  – Employers' bodies
	  – Employees' bodies
		• Central bank
		  – Bank of England
		• Stock market
		  – London
			• Demographic change
			• Social change
			  – Inequality of income in UK society
			  – Family and household structure in UK society
				• Organisations and the application of technology
				  – The personal computer
				  – The banking and financial services industry

Global	• Alliances and agreements
	  – UK and US
	  – UK and China
	  – EU
	  – Cold War
	  – CIS
	  – CBSS
	  – Eastern Europe
	• International bodies
	  – The Commonwealth
	  – NATO
		• Trading blocs and bodies
		  – EU
		  – EFTA
		  – OECD
		  – NAFTA
		  – ASEAN
		• World money markets
		• WTO
			• Global demographics
			• Cross-cultural issues
			  – Language
			  – Behaviour
			  – Culture shock	

The political elements of the external environment

The political external environment comprises local and national government, local associations, trade unions and employers' bodies. All of these are likely to hold a political viewpoint. Countries and organisations that are the result of political agreement and co-operation are also considered in this section. Because national and global economies are largely organised and run by governments, there are many areas of overlap between the political and economic environments. In this chapter the use of separate sections attempts to clarify and analyse political and economic environments individually. There are many political elements in the external environment, so analysing political elements of the external environment is sometimes confusing. This section principally examines the effects that external environmental elements have on organisations, but inevitably it will become clear that organisations also affect the external environment around them. This is perhaps especially so for employers' organisations, as will be seen later.

The local political environment

At the local level, the political elements of the external environment are local government, local offices of national government and local associations – *see* Table 9.2.

■ Local government

Local government has a significant impact on the businesses within its boundaries. It has responsibilities for regulating private-sector business activity and for directly providing a wide range of services. Some of these responsibilities have a very direct effect on businesses and others a more minimal influence. Local authorities have a statutory responsibility, i.e. they are bound by law to uphold trading standards and environmental health. As such, they hold great powers over all organisations within their area, and have the authority to close them down if severe breaches of law are discovered.

The services provided by the local authority range from general social services such as care of the elderly or education to services used by private householders and organisations alike, such as refuse collection, street cleaning, transport and planning permission for new buildings or extensions to existing premises. Clearly, a local authority's policies on trade refuse collection, street cleaning and transport to and from the city centre are all going to affect local businesses and shops in the city centre. A congestion charge, such as that introduced in London by Ken Livingstone in early 2003, will be aimed

**Table 9.2
The local political
environment**

	Political	Economic	Sociocultural	Technological

Local	• Local government
	• Local offices of national government
	• Local associations
	  – Chambers of commerce
	  – Business Link			

National				
Global				

at reducing the amount of traffic in a particular area and is likely to have a detrimental effect on the amount of passing trade for shops in the area. The provision and promotion of effective and cheap public transport, however, ought to go some way to counterbalancing these detrimental effects.

Local government is also responsible for setting and collecting council tax from residents and business rates from commercial organisations. The money raised via council tax and business rates will partially fund the services that local authorities provide, although the main source of funding for local government is money provided by national government. For the purpose of environmental analysis, this illustrates neatly that the levels of the external environment are as interdependent as organisations and their external environments.

It is also important to remember that a local authority is a large public-sector organisation operating in its own external environment. In many UK regions, cities, towns and villages, the local authority is the biggest local employer and the largest organisation. It too has customers and suppliers, and with the introduction of Compulsory Competitive Tendering (CCT) by the Conservative governments of the 1980s, local authorities now also have competitors for the provision of services in the locality where previously they had the monopoly. Here we begin to observe one of the complexities of environmental analysis. Clearly demonstrated here are the interdependencies between different elements of the environment: one organisation has a complex external environment consisting of other organisations and individuals; it in turn is an element in each of these organisations' individual external environments.

Local offices of national government

As national government has responsibility for the direct provision of many welfare services, the local offices of national government departments play a key role in the lives of local organisations and the local people. There is a local interface between the Department for Work and Pensions, the local offices of the Inland Revenue, and the Department for Education and Skills local Jobcentre Plus service. The current Labour government introduced a review of welfare provision geared towards removing the disincentives to finding work that the welfare system can engender, and towards promoting the opportunities that unemployed people can offer organisations. The 1998 green paper 'A New Contract for Welfare' lays out proposals to introduce the first wholescale reform of the welfare state since its introduction in 1945. This will affect organisations in the local environment by providing funding for training and employment of those who are workless through various initiatives under what is called the 'New Deal'.

Local associations

For private-sector organisations in the model, local associations are defined as trade and business associations operating in the geographic vicinity.

■ Chambers of Commerce

The British Chambers of Commerce are a network of quality accredited chambers of commerce, which are independent, non-profit-making and non-political organisations which are funded via membership subscriptions. British Chambers of Commerce offer business training, and information on a range of issues, such as exporting, suppliers and saving on overheads. At local, regional and national levels the British Chambers of Commerce act to put forward views and opinions on matters affecting their member businesses with a view to influencing local and national government and other decision-making bodies. Chambers of commerce also offer a powerful voice in terms of comment in the media concerning businesses at the local, regional and national level.

■ Business Link

Business Links are privately led partnerships between Training and Enterprise Councils, Chambers of Commerce, Enterprise Agencies, local authorities and government. Business Link partnerships are involved in providing advice via a one-stop shop for small and medium-sized businesses. Business Link partnerships operate very much on a regional and local level; for example in South Yorkshire, Business Link services are available for Barnsley, Doncaster, Rotherham and Sheffield.

Business Link partnerships generally provide advice and expertise in the areas of raising finance, entering export markets, employee training and managing change. A Business Link partnership aims to provide advice and expertise at a price that small and medium-sized businesses can afford. The partnerships are funded by the Department of Trade and Industry, with the condition that by the fifth year of existence the partnership must be at least 25 per cent self-funding.[1]

The national political environment

The national government and national bodies constitute the national political environment – *see* Table 9.3.

■ National government

The ways in which the national government manages the economic environment are dealt with under the relevant section below. As a result of the UK's membership of the **European Union (EU)**, the distinction of a national political environment is becoming blurred. Acts that appear on the surface to have been the British Parliament making laws governing British businesses turn out to have originated in Brussels and required all member countries to

Table 9.3
The national political
environment

	Political	Economic	Sociocultural	Technological
Local				

National	• National government
	• Devolution for
	  Scotland and Wales
	• National bodies
	  – Employers' bodies
	  – Employees' bodies			

Global				

implement them. Examples of European decisions enacted by the national British government are the fitting of seatbelts to coaches, vans and lorries, adding costs to transport companies; the export ban on British beef in the wake of the BSE crisis and its effects on British beef farmers; and the abolition of duty-free goods within the European Union, meaning that tax-free shopping has come to an end except for inter-continental flights.

Examples of the purely national political environment affecting organisational activity are therefore increasingly hard to find, but focus largely on the legislation passed regarding permissible commercial activity, production and service functions and human resource strategies. This latter is dealt with in Chapter 7, but to give one example, the 1995 Disability Discrimination Act (DDA) made it illegal for organisations not to provide access for disabled workers or customers on their premises. The direct effect of this legislation, which was stronger than anything preceding it, caused many organisations to commission alterations to their existing facilities in order to comply with the new law. The DDA covers equal access to goods, facilities and services, and employment and education.

Although its effects could be said to be largely economic, the national government's political decision making affects most citizens directly through its annual budget. Government has to raise money to provide for its services. It does this via taxation revenue that it uses to pay for publicly funded services such as education, the National Health Service, public transport subsidies, and social and welfare services such as the state pension for those too old to be economically active. Some of the money raised by taxation is distributed via local government and some is distributed and spent directly by national government. This is covered in more detail under the national economic environment, later in this chapter.

Decisions with an economic effect on business, then, may be classified as political when taken by government. One such decision was made in November 1992 by Norman Lamont, then Chancellor of the Exchequer (Finance Minister) in the Conservative government. The pound sterling had been entered into the Exchange Rate Mechanism (ERM), the European Union's mechanism for preparing its member nations' currencies for European Monetary Union and eventual merger into a single European Currency Unit (ECU), now better known as the euro. The ERM was designed to bring all its currencies to a level value by setting a range of exchange rate limits beyond which a currency should not be allowed to rise or fall. Norman Lamont took the decision to withdraw the pound from the ERM and hence effectively took Britain out of the first group of countries to enter EMU. The pound was removed from the ERM because its value fell outside the exchange rate range within which it was supposed to remain. However, the decision was also taken for political reasons, as the Conservative party was showing early signs of the internal divisions over European policy that partially led to its defeat in the 1997 elections.

The withdrawal of the pound from the ERM resulted in what the City referred to subsequently as 'Black Wednesday', when there was an immediate 10–15 per cent devaluation of the pound in relation to other currencies. Consequently, businesses in Britain trading with overseas companies were affected. Companies importing goods, components or raw materials into the UK from overseas had to pay more for them. In 1992 the UK economy was depressed and importing companies faced the dilemma of whether to pass the increased costs on to consumers or to absorb the increased cost in whole or in part, via reduced profit margins. On the day the pound was removed from the ERM, Yorkshire Television news reported on a company based in Hull that was facing exactly this dilemma. The company imported high-quality, up-market German kitchens and kitchen appliances, manufactured by companies such as AEG, Siemens and Bosch. In contrast, companies exporting UK manufactured goods found it easier as the lower cost of production made UK goods more price competitive abroad. This partly contributed to the growth of the UK economy in 1993.

From this it can be seen that the link between the national political and economic environments is clear. Politicians are elected by the people and run the economy. In doing so, they decide the economic policy that affects both individuals and organisations operating at the national level of the environment.

■ Devolution in Scotland and Wales

The Labour government elected on 1 May 1997 had promised in its election manifesto to hold referendums on devolution in both Scotland and Wales. This was duly implemented. In Wales the referendum was held on 18 September 1997 and 50.1 per cent of the electorate turned out to vote, with 50.3 per cent voting for a Welsh Assembly and 49.7 per cent voting against. In Scotland the referendum on 11 September had a turnout of 60.4 per cent, with 74.3 per cent of those who voted supporting the creation of a Scottish Parliament and 63.5 per cent voting to give the Scottish Parliament limited tax-varying powers.[2]

The Scottish Parliament consists of a total of 129 seats, of which 73 are directly elected and 56 allocated to additional members. Directly elected members were elected by a constituency to represent them. The additional members were elected by the electorate voting for a party and the additional seats given to members of the party voted for. The allocation of additional seats is complex but is representative of the voting pattern in the electorate as a whole.[3]

The Scottish Parliament appointed a First Minister, Donald Dewar, who in turn appointed members to and headed the Scottish Executive. The First Minister and Scottish Executive are drawn from the party or group commanding the majority in the Scottish Parliament. The Scottish Parliament is able to pass laws in a number of areas for Scotland, including health, education, local government, housing, economic development, trade, transport, criminal and civil law, courts, prison, police and fire services, animals, the environment, agriculture, food standards, forestry, fisheries, sport and the arts. The Scottish Parliament also has powers to repeal legislation passed at Westminster as far as Scotland is affected.[4]

The Welsh Assembly contains 60 directly elected seats and 40 additional seats. In contrast to the Scottish Parliament, the Welsh Assembly does not have the same powers governing the establishment of legislation and the repeal of Westminster legislation. The areas of responsibility devolved to the Welsh Assembly include economic development, agriculture and food, industry and training, education, local government, health and personal social services, housing, environment, planning, transport and roads, arts and culture, the built heritage and sport and recreation. The Secretary of State for Wales has the power to make secondary legislation in these areas. For example, the Secretary of State for Wales is able to decide the school curriculum in Wales.[5]

■ National bodies

National bodies represent businesses and employees and present views on employment and trade issues to one another, and to the government and opposition parties. Both employer and employee organisations try to shape and influence events in the external environment for the benefit of their members. Employer and employee national bodies are often closely aligned themselves with the government or a particular political party. Employers' organisations traditionally support the Conservative Party, while the Labour Party is linked financially and in terms of membership to the trade unions. For the Labour Party to achieve victory at the 1997 general election, it was thus crucial for it to have gained support from both sides of the negotiation table.

Employers' bodies Examples of national employers' bodies include employers' organisations such as the Institute of Directors (IOD) and the Confederation of British Industry (CBI). The IOD was formed in 1903 and its members are individual company directors from large FTSE 100 companies through to smaller entrepreneurial start-up businesses. The IOD provides members with information, advice, training, conferences and publications. In addition the IOD seeks to be an influential organisation in representing the concerns of its members to government and does this via lobbying and the media. The CBI was founded in 1965, bringing together several other industry bodies. Members of the CBI are companies, including both multinationals and small and medium-sized enterprises as well as trade associations and employers' organisations. The CBI seeks to provide UK industry with a forum for developing and influencing policy on a host of areas which impact on business organisations, such as the economy, legislation and technology. Additionally the CBI seeks to encourage efficiency and competitiveness in UK industry and in doing so develop the contribution of UK industry to the economy.

These organisations provide a forum for employers or owners of businesses to put forward their views and be represented on issues affecting businesses, such as the national minimum wage and a single European currency. Both the IOD and CBI frequently use the printed and broadcast media to do this. At the time of the election of the Labour government, the CBI was contributing to the minimum wage debate via the media. Labour had made the introduction of a minimum wage in the UK a manifesto pledge, and the CBI was suggesting a minimum wage of £3.50 per hour as an acceptable amount. It pitched this figure between the £4.29 per hour favoured by the Trades Union Congress and the £3.00 per hour suggested by 'certain employers'.[6] The rate at which the minimum wage was initially set was £3.60 for workers aged over 21, and by October 2002 this had risen to £4.20, with the debate in early 2003 being about a minimum wage of £5.00 per hour.

Employees' bodies In contrast, trade unions are national bodies representing employees. Examples of trade unions are NATFHE, representing teachers in further and higher education, USDAW, representing shop workers, and UNISON, representing public-sector employees. Trade unions represent their members in negotiations with employers on issues concerning pay and conditions, whether in the private or public sector. They are linked to the Labour Party, although reforms made to party membership after Labour's 1992 election defeat attempted to reduce the unions' impact and promote the concept of 'one member, one vote'. Most trade unions are affiliated to the Trades Union Congress, which is the largest voluntary organisation and the largest pressure group in the UK. The TUC operates to represent its member unions collectively at a national level.

There has been a steady decline in trade union membership since 1979 – this is shown in Table 9.4. The reasons for this decline include a reduction in the number of jobs in manufacturing industries, which typically had high level of union membership among employees. This fall in union membership has

**Table 9.4
Trade union
membership**

Year	Membership	Percentage of workforce who are union members
1998	7.1 million	30%
1995	7.3 million	32%
1979	13.3 million	55%

Source: http://biznet.bris.ac.uk/compfact/tuc/tuc25.htm.

been consolidated by an increase in the percentage of people working for small companies where it is often more difficult for unions to organise themselves. Additionally larger numbers of unemployed people or people not working have helped to reduce the level of trade union membership. Finally, under the Conservative administrations led by Margaret Thatcher in the 1980s, trade union membership and the power of the unions were drastically curbed. This occurred as the view taken by the Thatcher governments was that Britain's industrial unrest of the 1970s and the cause of its industrial decline was due to the unions' rise to political power. In contrast, the Employment Relations Act 1999 established a new statutory procedure for recognition of independent trade unions in the workplace, although it did not include the adoption of European-style workers' councils. Union influence, however, is unlikely to rise to previous post-war levels.

The global political environment

■ Alliances and agreements

The global political environment (*see* Table 9.5) encompasses alliances and agreements between countries that have an effect on the international activities that each country's citizens may undertake. Two or more countries may come together to establish independent or semi-independent global bodies to oversee or regulate the conduct of international trade and commerce, as well as to work towards the improvement of social issues, such as health, poverty or human rights.

Alliances and agreements occur between two or more countries for mutual benefit. The countries involved concur to support each other in global politics or in bilateral or multilateral economic activity. In extreme cases, consent may be given to the merger of countries into a single entity, or one country may consent to divide into separate countries to fulfil ideals of cultural identity, national integrity or economic benefit.

The UK and the US A good example of an alliance in which two countries concur to support each other is the close and special relationship between the UK and the US. Although there are few formal bilateral treaties, a special relationship exists as a result of the two countries' historical and linguistic ties. In the 1980s the

Table 9.5
The global political environment

	Political	Economic	Sociocultural	Technological
Local				
National				

Global	● Alliances and agreements
	  – UK and USA
	  – UK and China
	  – EU
	  – Cold War
	  – CIS
	  – CBSS
	  – Eastern Europe
	● International bodies
	  – The Commonwealth
	  – NATO			

relationship between the UK and the US was personified by the close friendship and mutual support of Conservative Prime Minister Margaret Thatcher and US Republican President Ronald Reagan. Both headed conservative governments in their respective countries and combined radical free-market agendas with strong global politics. This caused some difficulty for President Reagan during the UK–Argentine Falklands War in 1982, as his special relationship with the UK required support of Britain's efforts, while US links with the rest of the American continent precluded actual aggression against Argentina. On a separate occasion in 1986, Margaret Thatcher approved the use of US airbases in the UK to launch bomb attacks against Libya.

The relationship and support continues, embodied in Labour Prime Minister Tony Blair and US Republican President George W Bush. In the 2003 Gulf War to liberate Iraq there was close agreement between the UK and the US, while France and Germany were in less agreement over the decision to go to war without a UN mandate. There had been greater global consensus over the 1991 Gulf War, where international forces, UK and US among them, liberated Kuwait from Iraqi invasion.

The UK and China

China is extremely important on the global political stage because of its sheer size, geographically, politically and economically. The Chinese market is an important part of Britain's overseas trade. UK exports to China totalled £117 million while imports topped £452 million in January 1998.[7] The return of

Hong Kong is an example of an agreement at the global level of the external environment, which was designed to promote business stability and minimise political and economic risk for British business in China. On 1 July 1997, the British colony of Hong Kong was handed back to China after 99 years of British rule under the terms of a lease forced from the Chinese at the height of Britain's imperial activity. This was unlike the fate of any of the UK's other colonial possessions, which all left the Empire to become independent countries in the Commonwealth – *see* Table 9.10 on page 310. Hong Kong, however, had not been independent before the colony was established but had always been part of China, so had to be returned to it at the end of the lease.

The negotiations governing the return of Hong Kong to China were started in the early 1980s by Margaret Thatcher and Deng Xiaoping, China's then paramount leader. In the late 1970s Deng Xiaoping engineered economic reforms in China and allowed the slow development of a more market-based economy, while retaining strict political control over personal liberty. He died on 19 February 1997 prior to the deadline for Hong Kong's return to China, which duly went ahead. China described itself as 'one country – two systems', referring to the promise to continue unchanged for a minimum of 50 years Hong Kong's capitalist free-market economy under Chinese communist rule. This free-market economy has long been the gateway to the Chinese market for foreign businesses and for Chinese exports to the world. Over half the value of China's foreign trade has been directed via Hong Kong, so it is greatly in China's interest to maintain the status quo.

China's lack of a democratic political system should not have been a cause for concern, as the British colony had been ruled without recourse to democracy. Nevertheless, following Britain's long-held policy of establishing democratic systems before withdrawing from colonial possessions, the last Governor of Hong Kong, former Conservative politician Chris Patten, attempted to introduce some last-minute democracy to the colony. In the 1990s Hong Kong people were allowed to vote for the first time for a minority of members of Hong Kong's governing body, the Legislative Council (Legco). However, the return of Hong Kong to China in 1997 saw the dismantling of the Legco and the appointment by Beijing of a replacement administration and a new Chief Executive of the Hong Kong Special Administrative Region, Tung Chee-hwa, a wealthy local businessman who had previously been ennobled by the Queen.

The European Union In 1957 the European Economic Community was established by the Treaty of Rome. There were six founding countries (*see* Table 9.6), with a further nine countries joining the European Union by 1995. In 1998 the EU's three main objectives were:[8]

- implementation of the Treaty of Amsterdam;
- expansion of the EU;
- the launching of the single currency.

**Table 9.6
European Union
member countries**

Year of entry	European Union member countries		
1957	● Belgium ● Italy	● France ● Luxembourg	● Germany ● Netherlands
1972	● UK	● Denmark	● Ireland
1981	● Greece		
1986	● Spain	● Portugal	
1995	● Austria	● Finland	● Sweden

Source: Financial Times, 25 March 1997.

The euro became legal currency for trade and financial markets on 1 January 1999 in all participating EU countries, and coins and notes were introduced on 1 January 2002. (See the other section on the European Union later in this chapter.)

The 1997 Treaty of Amsterdam covered new rights for EU subjects concerning issues such as freedom of movement and employment. The Agenda 2000 blueprint presented to the European Parliament in July 1997 allowed the EU to expand eastwards and for former Communist countries of Eastern Europe (*see* Table 9.7) to become members. Enlargement of the EU is viewed as an opportunity to unite Europe and extend and consolidate political stability and economic prosperity more widely. The criteria laid down by the European Council in Copenhagen in 1993 required potential member states to demonstrate democracy, human rights, a functioning market economy, and a commitment to the EU's aims covering political, economic and monetary union. The political and economic conditions of applicant countries have to be judged satisfactory by the EU before it allows their admittance. Negotiations to admit new members are complex and examine how the significant differences in economic and social development between member and potential members states can be tackled.[9]

In 2003 there were 13 countries awaiting or negotiating admittance to the EU (*see* Table 9.7). In October 2002 negotiations for admittance were concluded for 11 of these countries, giving a joining date of the start of 2004.[10] For two of these countries, Bulgaria and Romania, a membership date of 2007

**Table 9.7
European Union
membership sought**

EU deems political and economic conditions have been met, EU membership in 2004		
● Cyprus ● Slovak Republic ● Poland ● Slovenia	● Hungary ● Czech Republic ● Latvia ● Lithuania	● Estonia ● Malta ● Estonia
EU negotiations to be concluded, EU membership in 2007		
● Romania	● Bulgaria	
EU negotiations cannot begin, country needs to meet political criteria for membership		
● Turkey		

has been set, on condition that each country meets the entry criteria and successfully completes negotiations on membership with the EU. Turkey does not yet meet the EU's criteria on democracy and human rights and is still waiting to start negotiations despite officially being recognised as a candidate for membership in 1999.[11]

The Cold War

World political events result in alliances being created and demolished, hence altering the political map of the world. In order to understand events in the late 1990s, it is essential to consider some political background. After the Second World War in 1939–45, the world was plunged into the Cold War, an ideological battle between democratic and communist political systems backed up by the technology of nuclear warfare, bringing for the first time in history the constant threat of a Third World War that would annihilate millions of civilians and destroy entire countries. The two sides of the Cold War, put simplistically, consisted of the US and Western Europe – with its institutions such as NATO, EFTA and the EU – and the then Soviet Union (USSR or Union of Soviet Socialist Republics) and Eastern Europe, with its equivalent institutions – the Warsaw Pact was the mutual defence treaty signed by Communist countries in the USSR sphere of influence, and Comecon was the alliance of planned economies.

The division of East and West was never more starkly evident than in the division of Germany on its defeat by the victorious Allies into two states: the western, democratic, free-market Federal Republic of Germany (FRG), and the eastern, communist, **planned economy** of the German Democratic Republic (GDR). The former capital of Berlin, geographically inside the GDR, was itself split into two halves and a wall built down the centre between East and West. The Berlin Wall came to symbolise the Cold War.

The Cold War split was mirrored in the Far East during the Korean War (1950–53), where US forces supported the democratic South Korea against the Chinese-backed communist north. The country remains divided into two administrations and a state of civil war still exists officially. Similarly, the People's Republic of China (PRC) and the Republic of China on Taiwan both claim to be the legitimate government of China, after a similar civil war whose hostilities ended in 1949, but peace has never been negotiated. The US originally backed the Republic of China, and did not switch allegiances until president Nixon visited the PRC in 1973. In Vietnam, the American-backed south eventually fell to the communist north after many years of bloody war, uniting the country under a communist government in the early 1970s.

In Europe in the late 1980s and early 1990s, the geopolitical map altered considerably and unexpectedly, as a result of the collapse of strict controls over personal liberty in many communist-controlled countries. This had begun with the last ever President of the USSR, Mikhail Gorbachev, who introduced policies of *glasnost* (openness) and *perestroika* (economic restructuring) during his term in office. These alterations to the political map provided unprecedented opportunities for trade and commerce and began in the GDR, when the

Table 9.8
Members of the Commonwealth of Independent States (CIS)

● Armenia	● Azerbaijan	● Belarus
● Georgia	● Kazakhstan	● Kyrgyzstan
● Moldova	● Ukraine	● Uzbekistan

communist regime lost control over the population and the Berlin Wall was suddenly dismantled in a popular uprising that was not opposed by the police or military forces. By 3 October 1990 East and West Germany had officially reunified under the former FRG's government. As a result of reunification, the German government has moved its parliament from Bonn, capital of the FRG, back to Berlin.

Commonwealth of Independent States

The ending of the Cold War resulted in other changes to the geopolitical map of Eastern Europe. During the years 1989–91 the USSR collapsed as the Soviet government in Moscow went the way of the GDR government, and the Soviet Union dissolved the federation into its component independent states, which then came together under the auspices of a looser association called the Commonwealth of Independent States (CIS) – *see* Table 9.8.

Council of Baltic Sea States

The Council of Baltic Sea States (CBSS) was established in March 1992, when the foreign ministers of the member states met in Copenhagen at the invitation of the Danish and German foreign ministers – *see* Table 9.9. The foreign ministers were seeking to strengthen co-operation and co-ordination between Baltic sea states and viewed the creation of the CBSS as helping to achieve this aim, along with the promotion of democratic and economic development in the region.[12]

Eastern Europe

Countries such as Poland, Hungary, Czechoslovakia, Romania and Yugoslavia all experienced cataclysmic change after the dissolution of the USSR. In geographic terms Poland, Hungary and Romania remained unchanged, in contrast to Czechoslovakia and Yugoslavia, which altered significantly. Czechoslovakia, for reasons of national and economic identity, split into two countries, the Czech Republic and Slovakia. In the 1990s civil war split Yugoslavia into several independent countries: Croatia, Bosnia and Herzegovina, the former Yugoslav Republic of Macedonia and Slovenia, with Montenegro and Serbia remaining as a rump Yugoslavian Federation. A multinational peace-keeping force continues to administer Kosovo.

Table 9.9
Members of the Council of Baltic Sea States (CBSS)

● Denmark	● Estonia	● Finland
● Germany	● Iceland	● Latvia
● Lithuania	● Norway	● Poland
● Russia	● Sweden	● European Commission

Source: http://www.battinfo.org/CBSS.htm, 28 April 2000.

In January 2001 Zoran Djindijic was democratically elected as Prime Minister of Serbia, three months after toppling Slobodan Milosevic. Zoran Djindijic pushed for economic reform in Serbia and helped engineer the arrest and extradition of Slobodan Milosevic to the United Nations court in the Hague, where at the time of writing he was on trial for war crimes committed during the Balkan wars of the 1990s. However, in March 2003 Zoran Djindijic was assassinated. The worry for the international community is that extremists will take over in both Kosovo and Serbia.

All these former eastern bloc countries have seen major changes to their political and economic systems, with elections taking place in many countries and greater opportunities for international trade and commerce becoming available. Some of these opportunities allow western companies to invest and manufacture in countries such as Poland, Hungary, Slovakia and the Czech Republic, as illustrated in the entry case study for this chapter.

■ International bodies

The international bodies discussed here are bodies that have a global political influence on the world political order. This is important, as peace and political stability are key elements in allowing a country to have an active economy and stable trade with other countries.

The Commonwealth The Commonwealth derives from Britain's imperial past and comprises countries from all regions of the world, including Europe and the Pacific, Asia, Africa and the Caribbean. The countries belonging to the Commonwealth are shown in Table 9.10 and range from India, with a population of over 900 million people, to Naura in the Pacific, with 8000 people. The Commonwealth consists of 53 countries, 52 of which are former colonies or protectorates of the UK, the exception being Mozambique, a former Portuguese colony. Mozambique was admitted as a member in November 1995 due to its close association with the Commonwealth in opposing apartheid in South Africa and because it wanted to reap the benefits of membership. Apartheid was the official system of keeping the white minority population in South Africa in a position of power and wealth, while the black and coloured populations had no access to money or political decision making. South Africa withdrew from the Commonwealth in 1961 following pressure from other member countries over apartheid. It was readmitted only in 1994 after the promulgation of a new, democratic and multiracial constitution, with Nelson Mandela, a leading dissident of the old regime, released from imprisonment and elected president in the country's first ever democratic elections.

In contrast, Nigeria was suspended from the Commonwealth in November 1995 after its most recent military coup. The deteriorating relationship between Nigeria and the Commonwealth was caused by the Nigerian military cancelling the presidential elections in 1993 and in November 1995 executing nine minority rights leaders, including the author Ken Saro-Wiwa. The

Table 9.10
Members of the
Commonwealth

Year of entry	Countries			
1931	● Australia	● Canada	● New Zealand	
1947	● India			
1948	● Sri Lanka			
1957	● Malaysia	● Ghana		
1960	● Nigeria[1]			
1961	● Sierra Leone	● Cyprus	● Tanzania	
1962	● Uganda	● Jamaica	● Trinidad and Tobago	
1963	● Kenya			
1964	● Malawi	● Zambia	● Malta	
1965	● Singapore	● Gambia		
1966	● Lesotho	● Botswana	● Barbados	● Guyana
1968	● Nauru	● Mauritius	● Swaziland	
1970	● Tonga	● Western Samoa		
1972	● Bangladesh			
1973	● The Bahamas			
1974	● Grenada			
1975	● Papua New Guinea			
1976	● Seychelles			
1978	● Solomon Islands	● Tuvalu	● Dominica	
1979	● St Vincent and the Grenadines	● St Lucia	● Kiribati	
1980	● Zimbabwe	● Vanuatu		
1981	● Antigua and Barbuda	● Belize		
1982	● Maldives			
1983	● St Kitts and Nevis			
1984	● Brunei			
1989	● Pakistan[2]			
1990	● Namibia			
1994	● South Africa[3]			
1995	● Cameroon	● Mozambique		

Notes:
1   Suspended 1995, rejoined in 1999.
2   Rejoined, had withdrawn in 1972.
3   Rejoined, had withdrawn in 1961.
Source: http://www.thecommonwealth.org/about/general/general/1.htm1.

Commonwealth held a summit meeting in November 1995 in New Zealand and acted quickly and forcibly by suspending Nigeria from the Commonwealth.[13,14] Nigeria's suspension from the Commonwealth was finally lifted in April 1999, following the election of a civilian government led by President Olusegun Obasanjo.[15]

In 2003 the Commonwealth was discussing the suspension of Zimbabwe, due to President Mugabe's tyrannical regime, which has devastated its agriculture and economy. Australia has been outspoken in its criticism of President Mugabe and the ruling Zanu (PF) party and would like to see its suspension, in contrast to the African Commonwealth states, which favour a diplomatic solution.

The examples discussed above illustrate that the Commonwealth is an international body that can, along with other international bodies, affect and influence the status of a country with regard to participating in trade and commerce on a global level. Accordingly, the role of the Commonwealth is to further economic and social development, democracy and human rights in its member countries.[16]

The North Atlantic Treaty Organization

The North Atlantic Treaty Organization (NATO) was formed in April 1949 and consisted of 12 members, with a further four countries joining between 1952 and 1982 – *see* Table 9.11. NATO's primary role is to ensure the security of its member countries and in the first instance this largely involved countering the threat created by the Cold War until that came to an end in 1990/1. Since then NATO has reorganised and restructured to develop security arrangements for the whole of Europe and to allow 'peacekeeping and crisis management tasks undertaken in co-operation with countries which are not members of the Alliance and with other international organisations'.[17] The ending of the Cold War created an opportunity for the expansion of NATO and in July 1997 agreement was reached between member countries to allow the Czech Republic, Poland and Hungary to become members in 1999. Future likely members are Slovenia and Romania.[18]

Table 9.11
Members of NATO

Year of entry	Countries		
1949	Belgium, France, Luxembourg, Portugal	Canada, Iceland, Netherlands, UK	Denmark, Italy, Norway, USA
1952	Turkey	Greece	
1955	Germany		
1982	Spain		
1999	Czech Republic	Poland	Hungary

Source: http://www.nato.int/welcome/home.htm.

✓ Check your understanding

Do you understand the impact that political factors in the external environment can have on an organisation like Peugeot?

Check your understanding by referring to the entry case study, identifying and explaining the political factors which have made it possible for Peugeot to manufacture in Slovakia.

Political and economic links

The alliances and agreements between countries described in the previous section altered the political map and political systems for the countries involved. Alterations to their economic systems also occurred alongside the political changes. In terms of international business, the assessment of political and economic risks is a major factor when deciding which target market and mode of entry would be appropriate in various countries. Comparative analysis of various countries' political and economic stability, potential and future trends enables companies to take a judgement about whether or not to invest in or export to that destination.

■ Democracy

Democracy is the system of government most recognisable to those born and brought up in the West. Democracy comes from the Greek *demos*, 'the people', and *kratis*, 'power', and describes those systems where the people are able to choose, through a system of voting, those who represent them in the corridors of power and decision making. As it is impossible for every individual in society to be completely free and unfettered by the rules of the state, democratic systems are the mutual agreements under which people are able to live together collectively and yet express a collective opinion on periodic change via fair and proper elections. It would be understandable to think of all western governments as being equally democratic, yet not each country has the same system. Democratic systems divide broadly into those that have evolved and those that are the product of a sudden and cataclysmic change, e.g. popular revolution. The latter are those that have perhaps the greatest spread of democracy in their institutions.

For example, the UK is called a constitutional monarchy and has a parliamentary system. Despite a 40-year interruption under Oliver Cromwell, the UK's monarchy can be traced back a thousand years. The current system has evolved through a system of concessionary changes to the point where its system of hereditary figurehead monarch, popularly elected House of Commons and mix of hereditary and appointed second chamber, the House of Lords, is used as a blueprint of democratic government (there are now only 92 hereditary peers in the House of Lords, elected by their colleagues, pending further reform). Countries such as the US, France and Germany, in contrast, have all had occasion to invent their political systems from scratch after revolution or war. These systems are based on written constitutions and codes of conduct, and feature elected government at all levels, including both chambers and head of state (president).

■ Autocracy

The exact opposite of democracy, autocratic systems are those where one person retains all power in his or her hands. The historical embodiment of autocracy was the absolute monarchy, where the king held all political and economic power. During the Cold War, this lack of democratic process was most keenly observed under communism, where the people were unable to choose the political party to represent them and had little or no personal liberty (these systems are more appropriately called oligarchies, since they are dominated by a powerful elite).

■ The free market

Providing in-depth knowledge of economics is not the purpose of this text, but to be able to discuss a variety of political and economic contexts, it is necessary to define different economic systems. The free market is that situation in which there is little or no regulation of commercial activity on the part of political entities. In a free market, the market forces of demand and supply will lead to perfect competition, providing all that the people need or want at a price they can afford. If there is no demand for a product or service in a free market, that product will not sell, no matter how cheaply it is priced.

■ The planned economy

In communist countries, attempts were made to eradicate the free market and its differences between rich and poor, by planning and orchestrating all economic activity from central government. Thus people were not free to seek whatever job they wished, and organisations could not recruit whomever they wanted. All jobs, housing, production, services and food were organised by the state via its work units, or state-owned organisations. Market forces were denied, as consumers were able to purchase products or services only from the state-owned factories and companies, whether they were good or bad. No decision was left to the individual, no matter how small. Thus individuals' every need was catered for in a basic way, but individualism, innovation and creativity were stifled.

■ The mixed economy

Most western economies are a mixture of free and planned economic activity. Where there is no regulation on business, employees and consumers alike are at risk. Regulation in the UK protects employees at work through health and safety and employment protection legislation, while the consumer is protected by the Sale of Goods and Trades Descriptions Acts.

■ Links between countries' political and economic systems

When considering the global political environment (*see* Table 9.5) or the global economic environment (*see* Table 9.15), it is essential first to know something about the political and economic systems of various countries and regions in the world. Figure 9.2 is a matrix that plots various countries (*see* Table 9.12)

313

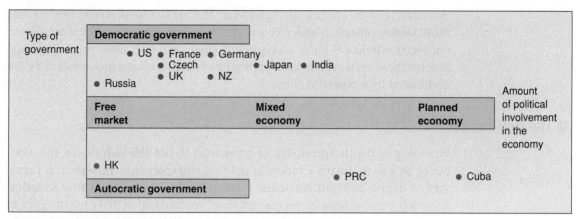

Figure 9.2 Government type and political involvement in the economy

Table 9.12
Country summaries

Cuba	After a communist revolution over 30 years ago, dictator Fidel Castro has presided over a decaying planned economy. Following the dissolution of the USSR, Cuba's main source of political and economic support, Cuba has found it increasingly difficult to survive under the US trade embargo.
Germany	A federal republic, united finally in 1991, its mixed economy is one of the post-war European success stories, despite the costs of integrating the former communist East.
Japan	Since the Second World War Japan has been a constitutional monarchy. However, the Liberal Democrats have been elected for most of those 50 years. The original successful Asian tiger economy, its success is also often attributed to the high levels of government intervention in the economy.
India	The largest democracy in the world, with a highly protectionist stance.
Hong Kong	Directly ruled from London for 99 years, Hong Kong reverted to the sovereignty of the People's Republic of China in 1997. A radical free market, it remains to be seen how this will continue under the 'one country, two systems' plan.
New Zealand	A Westminster system in the Commonwealth, it has seen a Labour government heavily interested in privatisation.
Russia	Since the collapse of the Soviet Union, the Russians have elected their leader for the first time in their history. The emergence of a mafia indicates a lack of regulation in the economy.
People's Republic of China	Controlled by the Chinese Communist Party following 'liberation' in 1949, China has liberalised its economy radically since the late 1980s without relinquishing any political power.
United Kingdom of Great Britain and Northern Ireland	Often called the 'Mother of Parliaments', the UK is a constitutional monarchy without a constitution, and only directly electing one of its two Houses of Parliament. There has been widescale privatisation since the early 1980s.
United States of America	With a written constitution, the Americans directly elect both Houses and their President. The federal system essentially allows for a variety in levels of free-market approach.

in relation to one another based on their level of democracy and the level of political interference in the economy. For the sake of this text, this matrix has been completed in a highly subjective and unsubstantiated manner, and indeed countries' positions will alter over time subject to political and economic change. In terms of assessing political and economic risk before entering new markets, organisations should invest in more objective forms of analysis, either done in-company or by external experts. The countries are plotted according to the background information given in Table 9.12.

> ### ✓ Check your understanding
>
> *Do you understand how the political and economic systems of countries in the former Eastern bloc, like Slovakia, have changed?*
>
> Check your understanding by placing Slovakia on the grid in Figure 9.2, both today and before the end of the Cold War.

The economic elements of the external environment

As has been stated, the economic environment faced by organisations is shaped and influenced by the political environment as well as by the economic bodies that are constituents of the external environment. The previous section examined the political elements of the external environment. In this section the role of economic bodies such as banks, stock markets, world money markets, **trading blocs** and bodies is considered.

The local economic environment

■ Local bank branches

Banks are a key local economic environmental player for companies, as the relationship between a company, big or small, and its bank is a local one between the two organisations. The relationship between a company and its bank is not normally one of national or global importance or influence. Hence a company's relationship with the bank with which it holds a business account will tend to be governed by issues concerning the amount of money in the account, overdraft and loan facilities. *See* Table 9.13.

■ The local economy

The general state of the local economy also exerts a direct influence on organisations. If the local economy is buoyant, the customer base for products and service will be wide and profitable. However, wages will be high and employees

Table 9.13
The local economic environment

	Political	Economic	Sociocultural	Technological
Local		• Local bank branches • Local economy		
National				
Global				

in short supply from among the local population. In areas with a depressed local economy, there will be little opportunity for selling products or services to people with little disposable income, but the workforce should be cheap and plentiful.

The national economic environment

The main influences on businesses at a national level come from the actions of the country's national bank and stock market (*see* Table 9.14). These two organisations together influence the value of investments held by businesses and individuals and hence affect the amount of cash available in the economy.

Government actions in relation to the economy also obviously have a great influence. The most common forms of taxation are income tax, corporation tax, value added tax (VAT) and duty on imports/exports. VAT is payable on many goods and services and at the time of writing stands at 17.5 per cent for most goods in the UK. The Conservative government increased the rate of VAT across the board from 8 to 17.5 per cent and also increased the number of items on which VAT is charged. The most opposed introduction of VAT was on domestic fuel, which had been zero rated and was to be charged at 8 per cent. This was not abolished but was reduced to 5 per cent by the Labour government in 1997. Basic food items and children's clothes are zero rated, i.e. VAT is chargeable but it stands at 0 per cent. Food items considered to be luxury items are subject to VAT at the standard rate.

The rate of taxation affects businesses as higher income tax lessens the amount of disposable income that people have available to spend on goods and services, and VAT makes goods and services more expensive to the consumer than the price set by the manufacturer or service deliverer. Therefore it is

Table 9.14
The national economic environment

	Political	Economic	Sociocultural	Technological
Local				

National		● Central bank
		  – Bank of
		    England
		● Stock market
		  – London		

Global				

crucial to the standard of living of the individual citizen, to the profitability of private-sector organisations, and to the standard of public services that a balance is achieved between taxation and public spending.

Businesses are affected by corporation tax as the higher the rate, the greater the amount of tax due on any profits made and hence the lower the amount of money available to pay dividends to shareholders and spend on activities such as marketing, product development, pay increases and updating equipment and facilities used to run the business.

Although much of the above is concerned with affecting the economic environment of the country, the decision making behind the management of the economy is essentially political, as it can be political parties' economic strategies that voters find key at the ballot box. Additionally, budgets from opposing political parties often show different approaches towards solving the same problems. Details of the latest budget can be found at the Treasury website – see the weblinks section at the end of this chapter.

■ The central bank – Bank of England

In the UK the central bank is the Bank of England. In May 1997 the new Labour Chancellor of the Exchequer, Gordon Brown, gave independence in the setting of the base rate of interest to the Bank of England and its Governor Eddie George. This separated out the economic and political decision-making processes concerning interest rates for the first time in the UK's history. Under the previous system, the Chancellor of the Exchequer and the Governor of the Bank of England would meet regularly and jointly agree changes to the base rate of interest. The base rate directly influences businesses and individuals as repayment of overdrafts, loans or mortgages will increase with higher interest rates, hence reducing the amount of activity in the economy. For example, when interest rates are high, businesses spend less on new equipment, advertising and product development and individuals spend less on the goods and services produced by businesses.

The effects of the government handing over decision making on base interest rates to the central bank should be that the influence of short-term political need on economic management is removed. Interest rates, a key economic management tool, should be decided from a purely economic perspective. When a government minister is deciding interest rates, they can be manipulated for political advantage before an election, as Nigel Lawson did when Chancellor of the Exchequer before the 1987 election. The so-called 'Lawson Boom' that he engendered led directly to the recession of the early 1990s. The Bank of England, in contrast, should take only rational, objective decisions about long-term economic strategy. This is in line with other European countries' practice and further prepares the UK for the possibility of entry to the euro at some date in the future.

■ The London Stock Market

The stock market is where shares of publicly quoted companies are traded. London is an international financial centre.

Company names and share prices are published in all the daily broadsheet newspapers. The shares of a company will trade on the stock market at a market price and the price will go up or down depending on the performance of the company and how it is viewed by the City. For example, a company that announces good profits is likely to see a rise in its share price and vice versa. However, good performance can be measured by factors other than profit. Manchester United, a profitable company, had a share price of £1.64 in February 1998; after being beaten 3–2 by Barnsley and knocked out of the FA cup on 25 February 1998, Manchester United shares fell 25p to £1.39. Continued good profits and better performance by the team on the pitch saw the share price climb steadily to £1.52 in June 1998, and to £2.30 in January 2000.

The value of shares will also be altered by overall movements in the stock market. If the economy is doing well and unemployment and inflation are low, trading conditions will be viewed as generally favourable. In this type of situation the stock market will be buoyant and overall share prices will rise. However, if share prices rise too much or the economy performs less well, share prices generally may fall.

The global economic environment

The global economic environment is shaped by how countries decide to behave economically in relation to each other, for example countries may decide to group together on a regional basis and confer trade benefits and support on each other. The other economic influence at a global level is the effect of the world money markets. *See* Table 9.15.

**Table 9.15
The global economic
environment**

	Political	Economic	Sociocultural	Technological
Local				
National				

Global		• Trading blocs
		  and bodies
		  – EU
		  – EFTA
		  – OECD
		  – NAFTA
		  – ASEAN
		• World money
		  markets
		• WTO		

■ Trading blocs and bodies

These are geographic blocs made up of a number of countries that agree to act together in some way with regard to trade and commerce. The countries may, for example, agree to allow special concessions on the taxing and movement of goods within the trading bloc or merely support each other with regard to economic issues.

The European Union Because of the close association between politics and the economy, it is necessary to mention the European Union again under trading blocs and bodies. The EU's Single European Market came into operation in 1993 and allows free movement of goods between member states. However, the issue of differing rates of taxation in different member states has yet to be dealt with fully. For example, the tax on wine, beer and cigarettes is much lower in France than in the UK and this is clearly shown by the popularity of day trips to France to stock up on cheap drink and cigarettes. The sale of drinks from pubs and retail outlets in the UK has been badly hit, particularly in the South East of England, with the closest and best access to France. There have been moves by the government to tackle the grievances of the UK drinks industry and this has included the abolition of duty-free sales within the EU. This led the government to face another fierce campaign, this time from the ferry companies, airports, travel companies, airlines, trade unions and the general public, all of which were in favour of retaining duty-free sales. However, abolition will only partly tackle the difficulties faced by the UK drinks industry, and day trips to France to stock up on cheaper goods will remain popular until duty rates throughout the EU are harmonised.

The 1991 **Maastricht Treaty on European Union** covers the issues of currency, **immigration** controls and defence policy. It set the timetable for the first round of European monetary union (EMU) that occurred in 1999. The deadline for meeting the necessary economic targets to join the first wave of European monetary union was the end of 1997. The key economic target that countries had to meet was the deficit:gdp (gross domestic product) ratio, which had to be 3 per cent or less. All member states except Greece met this target. However, along with Greece, Denmark, the UK and Sweden did not join the single European currency in the first wave.[19] The expectation is that the euro will generate an area of economic stability with low inflation and low interest rates.

European Free Trade Area

The European Free Trade Area (EFTA) was established in 1960 by the Stockholm Convention. Initially EFTA had seven member states: Austria, Denmark, Norway, Portugal, Sweden, Switzerland and the UK. Eventually some states left EFTA to join the European Union and new states joined EFTA. EFTA currently has four member states – Iceland, Liechtenstein, Norway and Switzerland[20] – and seeks to promote free trade and economic integration by managing the EFTA free trade area, participating in the European Economic Area (EEA), and developing a network of free trade agreements. The European Economic Area was created on 1 January 1994 when the three EFTA states, Iceland, Liechtenstein and Norway, and all EU states combined to create a large free-trade area. The EEA agreement allows free movement of people, goods and capital between participating nations.

Since the end of the Cold War, EFTA has sought to develop relationships with Central and Eastern European countries. This has led to the establishment of free-trade agreements with countries such as the Czech Republic, Poland, Latvia, Lithuania, Estonia, Bulgaria, Romania, Slovakia, Hungary and also around the same time, the early 1990s, Israel and Turkey. More recent free trade agreements have been with Macedonia, Jordan, Croatia, Morocco, the Palestinian Authority and Mexico.

Currently EFTA is focusing on developing links with other countries, some of which are beyond Europe. Hence EFTA has signed Declarations on Co-operation with countries such as Tunisia, Albania, Egypt, Cyprus and with MERCOSUR and the Gulf Co-operation Council (GCC). MERCOSUR's member states are Argentina, Brazil, Paraguay and Uruguay, while the Gulf Co-operation Council (GCC) has Bahrain, Kuwait, Oman, Qatar, Saudi Arabia and the United Arab Emirates as member states.[21,22]

Organisation for Economic Co-operation and Development

The Organisation for Economic Co-operation and Development (OECD) was established in 1961 and is based in Paris (*see* Table 9.16). On 5 June 1947 a speech by George C Marshall, US Secretary of State, gave rise to the post-war European Aid Program, commonly known as the Marshall plan. The view of the US government was that there had to be agreement among some or preferably all European countries as to the aid required and its use to reconstruct Western Europe. Therefore, European and North American countries came

**Table 9.16
Members of the
OECD**

Year of joining	Countries
1961	● Austria ● Belgium ● Canada ● Denmark ● France ● Germany ● Greece ● Iceland ● Ireland ● Italy ● Luxembourg ● Netherlands ● Norway ● Portugal ● Spain ● Sweden ● Switzerland ● Turkey ● UK ● USA
1964	● Japan
1969	● Finland
1971	● Australia
1973	● New Zealand
1994	● Mexico
1995	● Czech Republic
1996	● Hungary, Korea, Poland

Source: http://www.oecd.org/about/whats.htm, 28 April 2000.

together to establish the Organisation for European Economic Co-operation (OEEC). Its chief role was to facilitate the planning, allocation and implementation of post-war aid to Western Europe. However, in 1961 the OEEC decided that the reconstruction of post-war Western Europe was complete and sought to convert the OEEC into the OECD. The OECD did not focus on the giving and use of aid but on making the economies of the member countries involved prosper. To this end the policies of the OECD seek to:

- achieve the highest sustainable growth and employment and a rising standard of living in member countries, while maintaining financial stability, and thus contribute to the development of the world economy;
- contribute to sound economic expansion in member as well as non-member countries in the process of economic development; and
- contribute to the expansion of world trade on a multilateral, non-discriminatory basis in accordance with international obligations.[23]

**North American
Free Trade
Agreement**

In 1994 the **North American Free Trade Agreement** (NAFTA) between the governments of Canada, the US and Mexico was established. The principal strands of NAFTA relate to:

- encouraging goodwill and collaboration between NAFTA countries;
- establishment of a larger and more secure market for goods and services produced in NAFTA countries;
- strengthening and sharpening the competitiveness of companies from NAFTA countries in global markets;
- the generation of additional employment opportunities in NAFTA countries;
- the improvement of working conditions and living standards in NAFTA countries;
- the protection and implementation of workers' basic rights.[24]

Trade and the movement of jobs and goods between NAFTA countries are key issues for the countries involved. The setting up of NAFTA was rapidly followed by a devaluation of the Mexican peso in December 1994. This devaluation resulted in manufacturing wage rates in Mexico falling to 10 per cent of comparable US wage rates. Therefore cheap labour in Mexico, combined with weak environmental laws and rare health and safety inspections, usually with advance warning, meant that US companies found Mexico an attractive choice for relocation.[25] For example, in Mexico the hourly wage rate for workers in the motor industry has been estimated to be as little as 70 cents per hour. In 1997 union leaders in the US contended that low levels of pay in Mexico pushed down wage rates on both sides of the US/Mexico border.[26] However, by 2003 Mexico had become the world's ninth largest economy and seventh biggest exporter, since joining NAFTA in 1994. Mexico is now offering help and support to Central American countries seeking to join NAFTA.[27]

The Association of South East Asian Nations

The **Association of South East Asian Nations** (ASEAN) was formed in 1967 in Bangkok with five founding members and a further four members joining between 1984 and 1997 (*see* Table 9.17). In July 1997 Burma and Laos were admitted, but Cambodia's entry was postponed due to violence that threatened civil war.[28] Cambodia's entry finally occurred in 1999.

The three main objectives of ASEAN are:

- to promote the economic, social and cultural development of the region through co-operative programmes;
- to safeguard the political and economic stability of the region against big power rivalry;
- to serve as a forum for the resolution of intra-regional differences.[29]

■ The world money market

The world money market encompasses the world's stock markets and the exchange value of currencies against each other. The main stock markets that make up or have the biggest influence on the world money market are New York, London, Tokyo and Hong Kong. A collapse in one is quite likely to result in a drop in another, with the value of stocks falling and wiping value from the shares of companies.

**Table 9.17
Members of ASEAN**

Year of entry	Countries		
1967	• Indonesia • Singapore	• Malaysia • Thailand	• Philippines
1984	• Brunei		
1995	• Vietnam		
1997	• Laos	• Myanmar (Burma)	
1999	• Cambodia		

Source: http://www.aseansec.org/64.htm.

This was clearly evident in the Asian economic crises of late 1997/early 1998, which saw the stock markets of Japan, South Korea, Indonesia and Hong Kong all plummet. This also meant the key exchange rate to the American dollar for the Japanese yen, South Korean won and Indonesian rupiah fell. The Hong Kong dollar is pegged to the US dollar at a rate of HK$7.8 to US$1, and this peg remained in place.

The falling exchange rate against the US dollar for Far East currencies was mirrored in the latter currencies falling in value against other currencies. Hence, for example, the Malaysian dollar devalued very quickly against western currencies and halved in value, from around M$4 to £1 to M$8 to £1, hence making imported western goods in Malaysia twice as expensive. In contrast, overseas visitors from the West holidaying in Malaysia found hotels, restaurants, taxis and souvenirs, which had been reasonably priced before the currency crisis, halved in price. One other effect of the crisis was to slow economic activity in the Asian countries concerned. This meant that goods were more expensive, people felt poorer, and the prices of basic foodstuffs and fuel rose.

A further key effect was a rise in unemployment in an area of the world that had traditionally been viewed as having very low unemployment. As a result, immigrant workers were sent back to the neighbouring countries from which they had come. This happened in Malaysia, where many legal and illegal migrant workers were sent back to Indonesia by the authorities.

The chasm into which the economies in the Far East were plunging became deeper when student demonstrations and rioting in Indonesia eventually led to the downfall of President Suharto after many years in power as an authoritarian head of state. There was widespread rioting and looting in the capital city, Jakarta, as people vented their years of frustration of living in an authoritarian state with a poor economy. Foreign reserves in Indonesia were critically low and the rupiah virtually ceased trading, with little value to anyone. Interest rates rose to over 60 per cent and foreign debt was equivalent to £86 billion.

The full effects of the Asian economic crisis were felt in the West as Far East countries competed to export goods with falling prices to western countries. The other effect was that companies in western countries such as the UK which sold much produce to lucrative eastern markets faced a severe downturn in their export business. In May 1998 the CBI confirmed that British export orders were at their lowest levels since 1983.

The Asian economic crisis clearly demonstrates the effect that an economic crisis can have on its home markets and region as well as the knock-on effects on other parts of the world.

■ The World Trade Organisation

The **World Trade Organisation** (WTO) is located in Geneva, Switzerland, and officially came into existence on 1 January 1995, replacing its predecessor, the General Agreement on Tariffs and Trade (GATT). The WTO has

132 member countries and 34 observer governments, of which 33 have applied for membership.

The role of the WTO is summarised as:

- administering WTO trade agreements;
- forum for trade negotiations;
- handling trade disputes;
- monitoring national trade policies;
- technical assistance and training for developing countries;
- co-operation with other international organisations.[30]

The WTO handles trading complaints such as the formal complaint against India which was made in 1997 by the US, Canada, Australia and the European Union. The complaint objected to India's far-reaching import controls and payments on consumer goods and the slow speed at which these controls and payments were being phased out. India had offered to remove the import controls and payments over seven years, whereas the complainants wanted them phased out over three years. The complainants were supported by an International Monetary Fund (IMF) report concluding that India no longer had an acute balance of payments problem. Therefore the country's foreign exchange reserves were healthy and such import controls and payments could not be justified under WTO rules.[31]

The biggest change in the WTO in recent years has been the conclusion of China's long-term efforts and negotiations to become a member, from 1 January 2002. China's drive to join the WTO has been long and slow since it first applied to join GATT in 1987. Consequently in 1997 the thawing of previously frosty political relations between China and the US provided an opportunity for progress on China's entry to the WTO and negotiations took place in Geneva. Final agreement on the terms of China's entry to the WTO was reached on 15 November 1999.

Admittance to the WTO is a significant step towards allowing China's fast-growing economy to face more international competition and allowing foreign exporters and investors access to the country. However, membership requires China to adopt a thorough approach to many complicated issues that establish barriers to trade and commerce. These include the dismantling of investment restrictions, quotas, subsidies and tariffs. China agreed to accept WTO rules, open its economy to the rest of the world and to continue to engage in market-based reforms.

However, there was significant opposition in China itself, emanating from the state trading companies and the agricultural industry. The state trading companies will lose profitable monopolies and market share in the face of increased competition. There also exists the worry that more competition will lead to greater urban unemployment in China. Similarly, the agricultural industry in China receives substantial state subsidies, and membership of the WTO requires China to open up agricultural markets to greater competition, which will result in reduced state subsidies and more unemployment among agricultural workers. Consequently, the large agricultural exporters to China, including the US, Canada and Australia, were all able to influence China's application for WTO membership. China took up its membership of the WTO on 1 January 2002, giving it most favoured nation (MFN) trading status on an immediate and permanent basis.[32] MFN status ensures China's exporters access to US markets. Prior to membership of the WTO, China's MFN status was reviewed annually by the American Congress.

> ### ✓ Check your understanding
>
> *Do you understand the impact which economic factors in the external environment can have on an organisation like Peugeot?*
>
> Check your understanding by referring to the entry case study, identifying and explaining the economic factors which have made it possible for Peugeot to manufacture in Slovakia.

The sociocultural elements of the external environment

The sociocultural elements of the external environment include the age and structure of a national population, the way a population or society behaves, and elements determining how the culture of a population develops. This section will look at some of these and how businesses and organisations are affected. Greater detail on culture and organisational behaviour can be found in Chapters 2 and 3.

The local sociocultural environment

■ Local community and social capital

The local community is part of an organisation's external environment (*see* Table 9.18). The local community may be passive as regards the organisation or the local community and organisations can have an active influence on each other. For example, a local transport company regularly burns old and broken wooden pallets in its yard and produces a dense black smoke, making the atmosphere unpleasant for people who live in nearby houses with gardens overlooking the firm's yard. This local company has a very direct influence on the quality of life in the local community. The local people may act either individually or collectively and complain to the local council department dealing with pollution. If appropriate action is taken to stop the pollution, this is a very good example of a local firm, its local community and local government affecting and being affected by each other's actions.

**Table 9.18
The local
sociocultural
environment**

	Political	Economic	Sociocultural	Technological
Local			• Local community and social capital	
National				
Global				

There may be other local community influences to which the organisation is subject. A school is a public-sector organisation that interacts significantly with its local community. The community is greatly dependent on how well the school performs due to the personal nature of the service that the school provides. This kind of interdependence is considered in Chapter 10.

Social capital, which can be defined as community spirit and neighbourliness, increased in the 1990s, with more people feeling they helped others in their neighbourhood. Additionally membership of some voluntary groups such as the National Trust grew in the 1990s, while membership of other groups, for example the Women's Institute, fell significantly. However, strong social capital within community groups rather than between a number of community groups may lead to hostility towards those outside the group, as witnessed by riots in Burnley, Bradford and Oldham in the north of England during summer 2001.[33]

At the level of the family it is predicted that the role of older people, namely grandparents and great-grandparents, in the family will increase as the 'beanpole effect' is seen as families become smaller with fewer aunts, uncles and cousins. The result will be an increased reliance on grandparents and great-grandparents to help care for children as more women return to work, along with relationship break-down and divorce becoming more frequent.

The national sociocultural external environment

■ Demographic change

Demographic change is change in the age and structure of a population. This section considers demographic changes in the population of the UK (*see* Table 9.19). There are three fundamental demographic changes.

Table 9.19
The national sociocultural environment

	Political	Economic	Sociocultural	Technological
Local				

National			• Demographic change
			• Social change
			  – inequality of income in UK society
			  – family and household structure in UK society	

Global				

First, the number of people aged 35–50 in the population is increasing and these are those born in the post-war baby boom years of 1950–64. If people in this group have held good jobs and experienced the consumer boom of the 1980s, they are likely to continue to be generous consumers. These people will become the 50+ population of tomorrow. Second, there is a shrinking youth population, defined as those aged 15–24 years. The youth population is viewed, in general, as not being affluent as many young people are unemployed, in training or in tertiary education, none of which provides a large disposable income. This reducing youth population should mean the media's obsession with youth markets declines. However, youth programming has grown significantly on television and advertisers continue to be willing to pay for access to young people in their late teens and early twenties, who are perceived as being easier to persuade to switch between brands than older people, who are viewed as having established purchasing habits. The wisdom of this approach by advertising agencies has to be questioned, as in the UK only 5 per cent of advertising spending is aimed at the 20 million people over 50, who account for approximately one third of the UK's population but have access to over 45 per cent of disposable income.[34]

Finally, there is an increasing older population, those aged 50+, in the United Kingdom. In 1961 there were 16 million people aged over 50 in the UK; by 2021 there will be 22.5 million people, an increase of 40 per cent against an overall population increase of 15 per cent.[35] In 1995 people aged 50+ formed one-third of the UK's population; the number of people aged 75+ will have doubled by 2045.[36] The 2001 census showed, for the first time since the first census in 1801, that there are now more people aged over 60 than under 16 in the UK's population, with 1 million of those older people aged over 85 years, five times more than in 1951.[34] A significant number of these older people, 3–4 million, are white-collar workers of social class ABC1. This type of person will tend to have a good retirement income from an occupational pension scheme, will have savings and will own his or her home, with the mortgage paid off. Retired people in this situation are inclined to spend their relatively large disposable incomes on reading material (books, magazines and newspapers), gardening, visiting family and friends, eating out and drinking, insurance policies, home improvements and holidays. Consumers aged 50+ are the largest buyers of winter sun holidays and cruises.[37]

However, there is also a large group of less affluent older people, aged 60+, for whom the main source of income in old age is the state pension. These people, like the rest of the population, are likely to live longer and require medical treatment and a state pension during their longer life. The effect on the working population is an increase in their tax contributions. It is estimated that in the UK National Insurance contributions will have to rise from 12.5 per cent of the wage bill in 1990 to 18 per cent by 2030.[38] The increase in taxes paid by the employed and industry will prompt governments to alter the welfare system fundamentally to encourage more people to save for their own pension. Tony Blair's Labour government has targeted those currently in work but not contributing to an occupational pension scheme. This type of encouragement is crucial, as provision of retirement income needs to be boosted for the majority. This need is evidenced by the fact that, in 2001, 5.2 million pensioner couples and 4.1 million single pensioners had no income from an occupational pension scheme.[39]

This increasing difference in income between groups of older people is a reflection of what is happening more broadly in society, leading to an increasing income gap between rich and poor people. This is likely to continue as the proportion of pensioners in the UK's population is forecast to increase from 20 per cent in 2000 to 34 per cent in 2050,[34] and significant numbers of people, especially women, continue not to undertake financial planning for retirement.[33] This is also supported by the fact that public spending on pensions is not going to be a substitute for occupational pensions, as in the UK public spending on pensions was 5 per cent of gross domestic product in 2002 and this is set to fall to 4.8 per cent by 2052. This contrasts starkly with other European countries where public spending on pensions can be as high as 17 per cent.[40] There is further discussion of this income gap later in this section.

The effects of demographic changes on businesses

The effects of a decreasing youth population and an increasing older population can be seen in employment policies and products/services provided by organisations. In the mid-1980s the DIY company B&Q recognised that it would be affected by changing **demographics** and the declining number of young people in the population. Therefore it decided to utilise the opportunity presented by the growing number of older people. In 1988 it decided to open a B&Q store in Macclesfield staffed only by people aged 50+. Several years later the Macclesfield project was evaluated by an independent study, carried out by the American & Commonwealth Fund and Warwick University. The benefits identified were that, next to comparable stores, the Macclesfield store was 18 per cent more profitable, staff absenteeism was 39 per cent lower, staff theft was 59 per cent lower, and employee turnover was six times lower. This led to B&Q opening a similar store in Exmouth and seeking to have at least 15 per cent of the workforce aged over 50.[41] This is also an indication of organisations appreciating different attitudes towards work among different generations. B&Q has benefited from older people's stricter work ethic and high skill levels when engaging in work.

In the future Europe's economy is likely to fall further behind the US economy due to its ageing population, with the European Union's growth rate potentially shrinking to 1.25 per cent a year, half the US growth rate of 2.5 per cent. One view on tackling the issue of the decline of Europe's economy is to raise the retirement age by five years, significantly increase pension funding and also increase productivity, while reducing unemployment.[42] The alternative view to tackling this problem is for Europe to re-examine its current approach to immigration.

It is estimated that without significant policy changes in the EU, Europe's share of world output may decrease from its current 18 per cent to 10 per cent by 2050.[42] This trend is mirrored in Japan, whose share world output could fall from 8 per cent to 4 per cent. This is in stark contrast to the US, where it is estimated its share of world output could rise from 23 per cent to 26 per cent over the same period. This is attributed to the greater levels of immigration in the US, which brings more workers and increasing fertility rates, as immigrants tend to be young and of childbearing age. This argument that Europe's demographic problem may be helped by immigration is also echoed by the British Venture Capitalist Association (BVCA), which sees at least part of the solution to Europe's demographic problems lying in an enlightened approach to economic migration. The BVCA also points to the 'influx of South American economic migrants' into the US, who will contribute to the expected buoyancy in the US economy.[43]

■ Social change

Social change covers the development of and alteration in the way society behaves. The changes in society examined in this section are the developing inequality of income and the evolving family and household groups present in UK society. The role and influence of government are also considered.

Inequality of income in UK society

UK society is one of widening inequality: the well-off have got richer and the less well-off have become poorer. Income inequality has grown rapidly since 1977, fuelled to a large extent by the Conservative governments in power from

1979 to 1997. These governments introduced policies that led to large pay packets and rewards for successful people, in contrast to fewer and increasingly meagre social security benefits for the less well-off. Since 1981, state benefits have increased in line with prices and not average incomes. Hence the income distribution gap in the UK is one of the greatest among the industrialised countries of the world. This is confirmed by the statistics that 6 per cent of the population had an income less half the national average wage in 1970, while by 1990 over 20 per cent of the population had an income at this level.[44]

There are many ways in which government is reacting, as any organisation should, to these changes in the external environment. In terms of the ageing population, governments of both main parties take the view that more of the burden of social security, healthcare and pensions needs to be provided for privately as the population ages, since the workforce cannot keep up the level of provision offered in the 50 years after the welfare state was introduced. The Blair government also expressed concern about the widening gap in UK society, and established a Social Exclusion Unit to look at ways of bringing into the mainstream of opportunity and care those who had been excluded for social or systematic reasons, with a view to including more disadvantaged groups in mainstream provision.

This widening inequality is apparent when looking at different areas of the country. In England the problems of poverty, ill health and unemployment are mainly concentrated in cities in the South and the depressed industrial North, with pockets of rural poverty in Cornwall, Kent, Cumbria and Northumbria. In the South, outside of poor inner-city areas, there is generally a higher standard of living, with the problems of unemployment, poverty and ill health occurring less frequently than in impoverished areas. However, the stress of modern living is felt in both the city and the countryside, with fewer people working longer hours. This is illustrated by city workers attending working breakfasts and evening meetings and people in the countryside working longer hours on the land or in the holiday industry for minimal pay.[45]

Family and household structure in UK society

Further social change has occurred in the structure of the family. A significant development is the growing number of single-person households. There are various causes of this, discussed below.

Some 30 or 40 years ago a young person would have anticipated being single for a short time and remaining in the parental home, before marrying in their mid-twenties and settling down to a lifelong marriage and raising the average 2.4 children, being part of a traditional family unit. Society viewed being single as something undesirable that occurred as a result of misfortune and not an alternative that people chose. Being single was the result of being widowed or divorced because of an unfaithful spouse; indeed, both of these still occur today. The greater number of older people in the population and the higher life expectancy of both men and women now means that the number of older people living in single-person households will increase, usually due to the death of a spouse. The average lifetime is 79 years for a woman and 73 years for a man in the UK.

The UK has the highest divorce rate in the EU, with around 35 per cent of marriages ending in divorce, compared with a rate of around 10 per cent in the mid-1970s. Consequently, divorce is less shameful and more frequent than 30 or 40 years ago. Between 1970 and 1997 the increased divorce rate, coupled with a 50 per cent fall in the number of first-time marriages, added to the number of single-person households.

Further social changes have occurred with regard to the family. In 1996 married couples with children comprised 41 per cent of families, compared with 4 per cent of families composed of children living with cohabiting couples and 13 per cent of families consisting of lone parents with dependent children. The growth in lone-parent households results from the increase in divorce and fewer marriages. This is reflected in the statistic that in 1996 a third of all births were outside marriage, four times the 1971 figure. However, 80 per cent of the births outside marriage in 1996 were registered by both parents. Further social change in the family includes alterations in the role of parents. In 1985 both parents worked in half of all two-parent families with children; the figure was 62 per cent a decade later.

Today fewer people believe that it is a wife and mother's job to look after the home than did so in 1986. However, mothers still spend four times longer than fathers on cooking and housework.[46] The growth in the number of women in the workplace and the resulting greater financial independence of women are due to several factors. First, women are no longer expected to marry and be totally financially dependent on a husband. Since the 1960s there has been improved and increased access to higher and further education, which has meant greater access to better jobs and careers for women. This, coupled with the introduction of legislation in the 1970s covering equality of women in the workplace in terms of equal opportunities and equal pay, has contributed to women's greater role in the workplace.

There are some mixed messages to be observed in the political reactions to social change. In contrast to the moral rhetoric of family values that it espoused at the hustings, the Conservative government in the late 1980s introduced independent taxation for married women for the first time, thereby recognising both the earning potential and the legal status of married women. Nevertheless, in an effort to promote the responsibility of fathers in providing for their children beyond separation and divorce, it also established the Child Support Agency, whose job was to track down and make pay the errant fathers of children living in one-parent families with their mothers.

The last category of single people is, of course, those who choose to be single. A 1996 Mintel survey predicted a 17 per cent increase in single-person households by the year 2000. The greatest rise is expected in well-off men and women who have never married and are aged under 35. Approximately two-thirds of single women and over half of single men are in the ABC1 economic group, with three-quarters of single men and two-thirds of single women in full-time employment.

Examples of businesses that have gained from the expanding number of single-person households include supermarkets and cinemas. Supermarkets have reported an increase in the sale of single-person ready-cooked meals, and a considerable number of these will be purchased by single people who live alone. Cinema audiences more than doubled from 50 million a year in the mid-1980s to 120 million a year in the mid-1990s, and this was in part attributed to single people in the population spending their disposable income. In 1996 the government estimated that the number of households in the UK would increase by 18.5 per cent by the year 2011, with the greatest rise being in single-person households. This is one factor that will influence companies in the construction industry and the type and size of houses that will be built.[47]

The global sociocultural environment

Changes in populations at a global level impact on the opportunity for trade and economic development, hence some of the global demographic trends are examined in this section (*see* Table 9.20). In addition some of the sociocultural issues that affect organisations once they leave their home environment and operate overseas are also considered. Definitions of culture and how it affects individuals and national society are covered in detail in Chapter 2.

Table 9.20
The global sociocultural environment

	Political	Economic	Sociocultural	Technological
Local				
National				

Global			● Global demographics
			● Cross-cultural issues
			  – Language
			  – Behaviour
			  – Culture shock	

Global demographics

At a global level demographic changes will impact on the economic development of different countries and regions in the world. Significant reductions in fertility rates in Asia during the 1980s resulted in a sizable reduction in levels of absolute poverty, which is defined as the percentage of a population surviving on less than a dollar a day.[48] The impact of lower fertility rates and the resultant slower population growth is that there is faster economic expansion along with a reduction in poverty. Faster and improved economic expansion is logically due to smaller families having fewer expenses and being able to earn more, which in turn improves the opportunities people have to spend and save. However, it is estimated that around 50 per cent of improvement in economic growth in developing countries arises from a one-off 'demographic window' which occurs when large numbers of working adults support fewer children and older people.

In contrast, the demographics and populations of some countries and hence their economic development are affected by HIV and Aids. HIV and Aids are forecast to make the populations of the 53 most affected countries 480 million lower than expected by 2050. The total population of these countries is over 4 billion and the percentage reduction will be 8 per cent by 2050.[49] The impact of HIV and Aids is greatest in Africa, with the population of the 38 most affected countries being 16 million lower in 2000 than otherwise expected. This figure is expected to reach 320 million by 2050, which is 19 per cent or almost one-fifth reduction in the population. In most of these countries high fertility rates will likely result in growing populations; however, Botswana, Lesotho, South Africa and Swaziland are forecast to have lower populations in 2050 than today. This is supported by the projected life expectancy in these countries – in Botswana life expectancy in 2003 was 40 years, against the predicted 68 years without the impact of HIV and Aids; in South Africa, life expectancy was 48 years against the expected 67 years. By 2050, life expectancy in these countries is forecast to be only 56 years.

However, overall by 2050 the world's population is expected to age faster than ever before – *see* Table 9.21, which shows median ages (the age that divides a population into two halves). In the same period the world's population will grow at an annual rate of 1.2 per cent, giving a net increase of 77 million people every year, with 50 per cent of the increase arising from just six countries: India 21 per cent, China 12 per cent, Pakistan 5 per cent, Bangladesh, Nigeria and the US 4 per cent each.[49]

Cross-cultural issues

It has already been mentioned that organisations have to consider political and economic circumstances in other countries when contemplating international business operations. Culture plays just as important a part in governing international business at the global level of the external environment.

Table 9.21
Median ages

	2000 – median age	2050 – median age
Least developed countries	18.1 years	27.1 years
Developing countries	24.1 years	35.7 years
Developed countries	37.3 years	42.5 years
Overall	26.4 years	36.8 years

Source: Wolf, M (2003) 'People, plauges and posperity', *Financial Times*, 26 February.

Language

The most obvious illustration of culture is language. Investing in accurate language assistance when operating in another cultural context is a vital but largely underestimated consideration for organisations assessing the potential costs of international operations. The cost of getting it wrong is often much greater but is frequently ignored in short-term decision making. It is only necessary to consider how many misunderstandings occur between native speakers of English who originate from the UK, the US and Australia to begin to appreciate the difficulties of translating and interpreting other languages. The UK lecturer who asks an American colleague to invigilate an examination will be met with a blank look, as the American will be expecting to proctor it. The English tourist wanting to buy flipflops to wear on the beach in Australia will not be understood by the shop assistant, who will in turn shock the customer by offering thongs instead.

The back catalogue of language mistranslations and the choice of unfortunate words for products is huge. Volkswagen's multi-passenger vehicle (MPV) suffered when it was introduced to the UK from being called Sharon, a name not associated with the profile of customer to whom it was expected to be sold. Proton, Malaysia's national car manufacturer, did its market research and decided not to introduce its basic model to the UK under its Malaysian name, as 'Saga' is the brand name of products targeted at senior citizens, to whom Proton did not wish to limit sales. The Vauxhall Nova, General Motors' 1980s mini hatchback, was branded Opel Corsa in the rest of Europe as 'Nova', which was meant to have connotations of new, actually translates as 'does not go' in many European languages. The Rolls-Royce Silver Mist had to be renamed for the German-speaking market because *Mist* in German is a colloquial word for excrement.

Translation or the choice of words meaning other things in different languages is not the only skill required overseas. Interpreting – which is not translating the words but rather saying the right thing in the target language – is a crucial skill. At a business meeting between British and Chinese businesspeople, when the British host says 'We hope you have enjoyed your stay in the UK', a direct translation will sound arrogant and rude, so a skilled interpreter will replace this phrase with the customary 'We are sorry we did not look after you properly', and the courtesy requirements of both sides are fulfilled.

Behaviour

Other types of cross-cultural issues would relate to the consumption of alcohol in Muslim states and of beef in India, where the cow is sacred to Hindus

(McDonald's had to substitute a Hindu-friendly version of the burger). How much physical contact or personal space people are customarily allowed is also problematic, as some cultures remain physically very distant from each other, while in others regular touching is commonplace. Again, whether or not physical contact is permissible between the sexes or between people of the same sex is an issue. For example, in many Middle and Far Eastern cultures, any touching between the sexes is unacceptable, while man-to-man handholding and bodily contact are quite normal. This understandably becomes a minefield of danger to the foreign executive. In Japan, blowing one's nose in public is quite taboo, while in China the public expectoration of waste is unsurprising.

Therefore, the behaviour of foreign executives, the design of products and services, and the labelling, packaging and advertising of goods and services must all be subject to intense scrutiny.

Culture shock
The greater the distance between home and host culture, the more likely it is that the host culture will provide elements of everyday life that shock the individual travelling there. From language to food, from individual behaviour to collective customs, culture shock is a real and debilitating influence on the individual businessperson abroad. As it is based in experience, it is difficult to know how culture shock can be dealt with until it has been experienced, since there is still a huge difference between knowing something is going to happen (I have learned that China is crowded, so I expect that when I go there I will experience a lot of pushing and shoving on the streets) and actually experiencing it happening (everywhere I go in China people touch or push me – I come from a culture where touching strangers is almost taboo, so I hate it!). Nevertheless, organisations can invest in pre-departure orientation programmes, training people for overseas postings through contact with natives, visits and access to expatriates who have already lived in that culture. It is essential to consider not only the expatriate executive but also the relocation and comfort of family members.

☑ Check your understanding

Do you understand the sociocultural factors which could impact on an international company like Coca-Cola?

Check your understanding by identifying and explaining sociocultural factors which could impact on Coca-Cola.

The technological elements of the external environment

Technology has an influence on all aspects of business, from the very general to the very specific, at all different levels of the external environment: local, national and global.

■ Communications technology

The advent of technology has made it easier for people to communicate with each other, whether they operate in the political, economic, social or general business arena at a local, national or global level. The technology that has made communication easier takes the form of mobile phones, fax machines, video conferencing, the internet and the world wide web – *see* Table 9.22.

Mobile phones and faxes

Mobile phones have grown in popularity since the mid-1980s. Initially, mobile phones were large (therefore visible) and expensive. Hence in the 1980s they were very much the necessary executive accessory. The first mobile phones were also heavy and cumbersome to carry around. The technology improved throughout the 1980s and 1990s and the size and styling of mobile phones improved to give small and slim models that slip easily into a jacket pocket or handbag. In line with improved technology and styling, the price of mobile phones fell and connection is possible for under £50, which compares favourably with a cost of over several hundred pounds when they first came on the market. Recent developments include mobile phones which allow internet access and picture messaging. The key benefit to organisations that issue personnel with mobile phones is that staff can be contacted all the time (unless the mobile phone is switched off) and should be able to contact customers and clients without having to return to an office.

Table 9.22
The technological external environment: communications technology

	Political	Economic	Sociocultural	Technological
Local				● Communications technology – mobile phones and faxes – video conferencing – internet and world wide web
National				
Global				

Fax machines are another development of the 1980s that became common-place in the office of the 1990s, allowing letters or documents to be transmitted over a telephone line in a number of seconds or minutes. This compares favour-ably with the day or more it would take a letter or document to reach the same destination by post, hence making communication quicker.

If you look at Table 9.1, the generic LoNGPEST grid, you will see that P, E and S are clearly divided into local, national and global factors. With technological factors this is much less clearcut and the technological factor may apply at all levels (see also Chapter 8 for an explanation of this). Hence this is indicated by a lack of divisions in the technological section of the LoNGPEST model.

Video conferencing   Video conferencing is becoming increasingly popular among businesses. Large companies such as British Petroleum (BP) have been using video confer-encing since 1983 and have in-house studios in global locations. The greatest benefits of video conferencing are gained when it is used by people in two or more places in different parts of the world. For example, two teams of people based on opposite sides of the Atlantic in the UK and the US working on joint projects will need to meet regularly. The teams could meet by video conferen-cing rather than one team flying across the Atlantic for a meeting. Alternatively, a multinational that needs to have a meeting of senior managers, one based in Australia, one in Russia, one in Hong Kong and one in the UK, could all meet by video conferencing, assuming there are facilities in each location. SmithKline Beecham used to have over 30 video conferencing studios worldwide[50] and were able to carry out video conference meetings of the type described above. Organ-isations that do not have video conferencing studios are still able to participate if they book ahead and rent time in a video conferencing studio like the ones owned and run by Regus Management in London.[51] In 2003, it was possible that the increased threat of international terrorism and the spread of the SARS virus would result in an increased use of video conferencing by organisations seeking to reduce the risk to which their workforce might be exposed.

The most common form of video conferencing is the dedicated studio and people in the organisation wanting to video conference have to go from their desks to the studio to meet with their colleagues in a studio in another location. The obvious future development of video conferencing is to take it out of the studio and into the office. This is likely to happen as the technology and equipment develop. Portable video conferencing equipment that can be wheeled about, in the same way as televisions and videos on stands can be moved about offices, is cheaper and more flexible than the dedicated studio system of video conferencing. The portable system allows video meetings to take place from the desktop or from a meeting room, which may be more convenient than going to a central studio location.

The other development is PC-based video conferencing, which is popular with heavy users of video conferencing. However, a drawback of PC-based systems is that they are not particularly user-friendly as a shared resource. Consequently, organisations may be disinclined to install the necessary video conferencing board and software in every PC in the organisation. Also the current quality of the audio and video in PC-based systems is not as good as it is on portable video conferencing systems.[52] The cost of a video conferencing studio system will vary from £18 000 to £100 000, compared with about £5500 for a portable system and less than £700 for a PC-based system per computer.[53] Because the prices for portable systems have fallen and their operation and quality have improved, PC-based systems are unlikely to overtake portable systems in popularity until their price and quality similarly improve. The use of studio and portable video conferencing systems for internal communication in companies is the most likely continued use of video conferencing in the immediate future.

The extensive use of PC-based video conferencing systems for communication between different companies will not occur until there is a critical mass of users in different organisations all with the necessary technology in their PCs. Inter-company video conferencing will also require telephone companies to publish a video conferencing directory, hence allowing users to know who has a PC-based video conferencing unit.[54]

Be aware that if meetings have always been disorganised and unproductive in an organisation, video conferencing will not solve those problems, it will merely automate them.[55] The key benefits of video conferencing include the following:

- Less time is spent travelling to and from meetings, therefore reducing the cost and stress of travelling. The National Economic Research Council estimates that by 2007 video conferencing could replace 20 per cent of business travel.[56] A foreign business return trip can take from 8 to 55 hours depending on the distance involved: a door-to-door return trip from London to Frankfurt may take 8–10 hours' travelling time; at the other end of the scale a return trip to Australia from the UK will take over 50 hours.
- There is the possibility of more people attending the meeting, and technical experts can be called into the meeting at relatively short notice if their knowledge and expertise are required.
- Eye contact and body language are seen – a clear advantage over phone conferencing.
- There is enhancement of teamworking and communication among teams whose work is spread out across the globe.

The internet and the world wide web

The internet is an array of inter-connected networks to which millions of computers around the world are attached. There are a large number of internet sites that hold information, for example company sites or the *Financial Times* site. The world wide web (WWW) allows linking of internet sites and research and retrieval tools, meaning that the WWW and the internet are often seen as one and the same. Search engines such as Yahoo! and AltaVista allow searches to be carried out very easily, and it is equally easy to repeat and refine any searches that have been carried out previously.[57]

Electronic mail, commonly known as e-mail, is a frequently used application of the world wide web. The use of e-mail allows messages to be sent to anyone who has an e-mail address, whether an individual at home or someone in a company. Sending a message by e-mail is quicker than posting a letter, cheaper than faxing a message, and on occasions is more convenient than using the telephone. E-mail also has the advantage that the same message can be sent simultaneously to a large or small group of people.

Companies can take up a presence on the internet by setting up a website. This will give a company 24-hours-a-day, 365-days-a-year, worldwide exposure on the internet. Companies are able to use their internet presence to advertise their products and services and collect addresses and details from potential customers who visit the site, with a view to e-mailing or posting further information. The internet is equally accessible by both large and small companies, although large companies may have more money to spend on designing a site.

It is suggested that when designing a website the following are considered:

- The site should indicate the type of business the company is in early on.
- Do not make the pages over-elaborate or extensive as this can result in a lengthy wait when downloading individual pages.
- Do not use text that is too small and difficult for people to read on-screen.
- Decide whether the company wants to collect details of potential customers and/or create an awareness of products and services.
- Plan for how the company is going to deal with responses from actual and potential customers who visit the site, as a large amount of e-mail may be generated by an internet presence.[58]

A company that has set up an internet site also has to consider how it is going to persuade people to visit the site. Many companies advertise in the more traditional media, such as the television and press, and include their internet address in the advertisement. An additional method is to be included on search engines so that when users type in a keyword such as books or beer the relevant internet sites are listed. It is best if a company or its internet site is listed in the first ten, as potential visitors do not tend to scroll down the list and are therefore less likely to visit internet sites further down the list. Companies are also able to advertise on search engines by paying to have their logo appear, although costs are high.[59]

■ Organisations and the application of technology

In addition to the communications technology discussed above, organisations make use of other types of technology on a daily basis – *see* Table 9.23. For some organisations technology is increasingly the key to improved product or service delivery. Banking is such an industry and is looked at in detail in this respect later in this section.

Table 9.23
The technological external environment: organisations and the application of technology

	Political	Economic	Sociocultural	Technological
Local				
National				• Organisations and the application of technology – the personal computer – the banking and financial services industry
Global				

The personal computer

The manner in which organisations and the people in them operate has been radically altered by the advent and development of the personal computer (PC). When first introduced to organisations PCs were stand-alone machines and few people had a PC on their desk. At the start of the twenty-first century virtually all organisations are using PCs widely in carrying out their daily business. Accordingly, in many organisations everyone from the managing director to the most junior clerical assistant will have a PC on their desk. The other fundamental difference is that PCs are no longer always stand-alone machines but are at the very least networked together within the organisation, hence facilitating internal communication. It is also extremely common for an organisation's computer networks to be linked to the outside world via the WWW, hence allowing communication and information retrieval, as described in the previous section on communications technology.

The most familiar types of software developed and used on a daily basis by organisations are word-processing and spreadsheet packages, which are commonly used for producing letters and reports and for analysing data. The proper use of PCs and the appropriate software makes the storage, alteration and manipulation of data and information easier and less time consuming.

The banking and financial services industry

Banking and financial services is a good example of an industry where service delivery has been continually altered and modernised since the late 1970s. In banking the most obvious application of technology has occurred in the development of the cashpoint machine, now found on the high street, inside bank or building society branches, in supermarkets and in public buildings such as railway stations. The other main technological development has been in the use of central computer-based systems to hold customer details and account records. These applications of computer technology allow any customer with a passbook or cashpoint card to withdraw money from their bank or building society account anywhere in the country and even overseas. This contrasts to the 1970s, when withdrawing money from a bank account meant that you had to visit the branch at which the account was held before the bank shut at 3.30pm, but not during the 12.30–1.30pm lunch hour when the banks closed.

This greater reliance on technology to perform at least some routine tasks has been part of the reason why both banks and building societies have been able to use and train their staff to sell a much wider range of financial services. These include savings accounts, tax-free savings accounts such as PEPs and ISAs, pensions, insurance for cars, home buildings and contents, travel and health, a range of mortgages, and credit cards.

New ways of delivering banking and financial services have continued to develop and the clear preferred medium is via the internet, rendering redundant early trials with home banking via PC, private dial-up services, managed networks and TV-based services. Online banking allows customers to access their bank accounts via PCs and undertake a range of transactions, including looking at balances and statements on-screen, settling bills, moving money from one account to another, making arrangements to settle bills and move money, looking at standing orders and direct debits, observing transactions, including the use of a search-and-sort facility, ordering new cheque books and transferring information into other software, for example to be used by a personal financial adviser.[60]

> ## ✓ Check your understanding
>
> *Do you understand the technological factors which could impact on vacuum and washing machine manufacturer Dyson, which has moved production from the UK to the Far East?*
>
> Check your understanding by identifying and explaining technological factors which could impact on Dyson.

Summary

This chapter examined the composition of the external environment at the local, national and global levels. The following summary covers all aspects of this chapter.

1 The local political environment includes local government, national government operating at a local level and local business associations such as chambers of commerce. Local government is responsible for regulating private-sector business, for example via trading standards, and for providing a range of public services, e.g. refuse collection and schools. Chambers of commerce offers their business members access to training and business information on, for example, exporting goods.

2 The national political environment includes national government for the whole UK, Scotland and Wales and national bodies such as the CBI and trade unions. National governments pass legislation, which may impact on business, e.g. health and safety legislation. National governments are responsible for collecting taxation and deciding how it is to be allocated and spent to provide public-sector services such as healthcare and education. Employers' bodies like the CBI and employee organisations such as trade unions like UNISON seek to get the best deal for their members in the workplace environment and this may involve lobbying government to pass particular legislation or make a particular decision.

3 The global political environment includes alliances and agreements, such as the special relationship between the UK and the US. Other global factors include international bodies such as the Commonwealth and NATO, which, respectively, play a role in the world economy and the establishment of peace, which is needed to allow economies to flourish.

4 The local economic environment of an organisation will be shaped by its relationship with its bank, which is usually of local significance. The state of the local economy in which a business is located will influence the ease with which labour can be recruited and retained.

5 The national economic environment includes the Bank of England and the stock market. The Bank of England sets the base interest rate, which in turn determines the level of interest businesses and individuals pay on loans, which impacts on the amount of money consumers and industry have to spend, which clearly determines the level of economic activity experienced.

6 The global economic environment includes trading blocs such as the EU and NAFTA, world money markets and the WTO. Trading blocs confer free movement of goods between member states and significant tax concessions on goods imported from member states. For example, goods move freely between EU countries such as France, Germany and the UK. The WTO handles trade negotiations between countries, monitors trade policies and deals with trade disputes.

7 The local sociocultural environment includes the local community and social capital. An organisation's interactions with its local community may impact on the organisation's level of work, particularly if the organisation is, for example, a school. Social capital is defined as community spirit and neighbourliness, and this can either draw communities together or drive them apart by showing hostility to those outside the community.

8 The national sociocultural external environment includes demographic change and social change. Demographic changes are changes in the age and structure of a population. In the UK the key changes in the population are a shrinking youth population, increases in people aged 35–50 years and an increasing number of people aged 50+. Social change includes development and alterations in the way society behaves. This can include changes to income levels, family and **household structure**.

9 The global sociocultural external environment encompasses change in populations and their impact at a global level on the opportunities for trade and economic development. Such impacts include fertility rates, HIV/Aids, and age of populations, which is higher in the developed world than in the developing world. Also at a global level, the impact of cross-cultural issues, such as language, behaviour and culture shock, can be significant for companies.

10 The impact of technology on organisations occurs at all levels. Improved communications technology allows easier and faster communication between organisations, their employees, customers and potential customers. The use of the internet and the world wide web can allow customers access to an organisation and the products and services it offers all day every day.

Learning outcomes for case studies

While reading this chapter and engaging in the activities, you should have learned how to apply theory and models, analyse situations, and evaluate the application and analysis you undertake. The learning outcomes specified below outline the type of application, analysis and evaluation of which you should be capable in relation to organisations. The case studies and the questions which follow provide an opportunity for you to test how well you have achieved the learning outcomes for the ethical issues and exit case studies for this chapter.

Application	Check you have achieved this by	
1 Apply LoNGPEST analysis to specific situations	performing a PEST or LoNGPEST analysis for a real organisation or industry	answering ethical case study question 1 and exit case study question 1
Analysis	**Check you have achieved this by**	
1 Identify and prioritise factors having the greatest impact on organisations	ensuring any LoNGPEST analysis you perform is complete and not just a series of lists	answering ethical case study question 2 and exit case study question 2
Evaluation	**Check you have achieved this by**	
1 Choose information and data sources that best assist managers in organisations with scanning and understanding the external environment	ensuring any information recommended is relevant and any bias is recognised and taken into account	answering exit case study question 3
2 Evaluate LoNGPEST analysis as a management tool for understanding the external environment	assessing the benefits and limitations of the model when applied to real organisations	answering exit case study question 4

ETHICAL ISSUES CASE STUDY 9.2

FT

Nike weighs return to Cambodia

By Amy Kazmin

Nike, the US sportswear giant, may be about to make a comeback in Cambodia – two years after a television documentary on under age girl workers prompted the company to stop using factories in the country.

Nike's retreat was a serious blow to Cambodia's $1bn (£677m) garment industry, which accounts for more than 80 per cent of Cambodia's goods exports and employs nearly 180 000 young women and teenage girls – mostly migrants from impoverished villages who use their earnings to support their families.

Although Nike insisted its suppliers only employed girls over 16 – a year over the legal minimum working age – the embarrassing television documentary led the company to sever its ties with Cambodia as part of a damage control strategy.

Nike's possible change of heart has come about following the launch of independent monitoring in the country by the International Labour Organisation.

The ILO's first two reports, covering 70 factories, hardly paint a pretty picture. They said many factories routinely paid their workers less than the legal minimum wage and required them to work long overtime hours.

But the reports offer a degree of transparency unrivalled in the notoriously secretive garment industry, which companies like Nike believe could help them protect their brand image. 'It's appealing,' Nike spokesman Chris Helzer said. 'The ILO has a lot of credibility internationally.'

The new, more transparent conditions have been imposed on Cambodia's manufacturers by an unprecedented trade deal between Washington and Phnom Penh that promises the country an annual 18 per cent textile quota bonus if the local garment industry improves its respect for modern labour rights.

So far, Cambodian workers have gained little from the deal, says Jason Judd, a Phnom Penh-based representative of the AFL-CIO, the American trade union federation, which has long pushed for links between trade and labour standards.

ILO monitoring was slow to start, and in the interim Phnom Penh was rewarded simply for strengthening labour laws.

But with the monitoring process now gathering steam, Cambodian factories are coming under greater pressure to seriously adhere to the legislation.

Mr Judd, who is training Cambodian union organisers and workers, said: 'One of the things that makes this place attractive to them [manufacturers] is lax enforcement . . . But the ILO is getting deep into these factories and soon it will be apparent who the bad actors are.'

The scrutiny could be used to Cambodia's advantage. It has a unique opportunity to build a reputation as a 'manufacturing safe haven' for image-sensitive multinationals keen to protect their brands from the taint of the sweatshop.

It could help Cambodia survive fierce competition that will be unleashed in 2005, when textile quotas end for World Trade Organisation members and China is expected to unload low cost garments into the market.

'The only thing we can do is to build up our social responsibility, so American companies like Gap or Nike feel safe placing orders in Cambodia, knowing that factories comply with human rights, labour laws and good working conditions,' said Van Sou Ieng, president of the Garment Manufacturers Association of Cambodia.

However, success depends on whether government officials, who have long ignored blatant abuses of the law, are willing to crack down on factories that fail to clean up their act.

The ILO is to release a new report over the coming weeks that, for the first time, will name individual factories and detail both conditions inside and how managers have responded to suggestions for improvement.

Sok Siphana, Cambodia's commerce minister, insists authorities will get tough if they have evidence that laws have been violated. 'Whoever breaks the law has to pay the price,' he said.

Mr Van Sou Ieng says he is willing to protect the industry's reputation from the worst abusers by revoking membership in the manufacturer's association – a move that would in effect bar those factories from exporting from Cambodia.

Source: Financial Times, 18 June 2003. Reprinted with permission.

Questions for ethical issues case study 9.2

1 Identify the PEST/LoNGPEST factors which impact on Nike's presence in Cambodia.

2 Which factors are most critical if Nike is to secure a long-term presence in Cambodia?

◄◼ EXIT CASE STUDY 9.3   FT

The holiday package undone by the internet

By Michael Skapinker

Murderous attacks in Morocco. British Kenya-bound aircraft grounded for fear they will be shot down. War in Iraq. Sars. Tourists opting to stay home.

The travel industry has had its troubles before – notably during the last Gulf war – but it has never seen anything like this. These difficulties will eventually pass, but Goldman Sachs has declared that the industry as we know it will never recover.

In particular, the investment bank says, the giant European package tour operators have had their day. The companies that created a new industry, offering millions of northern Europeans holidays in the sun, are being undone by the internet.

In the past, tour operators used their buying power to purchase rooms, aircraft seats and car hire at knockdown rates. They then packaged these and sold them at prices far lower than holidaymakers could have achieved on their own. Now, says Goldman Sachs, holidaymakers can get better deals alone. Its London-based leisure analysts examined the tour operators' offerings, then attempted to book similar holidays themselves, largely relying on the internet.

In 70 per cent of cases, they were able to put together cheaper deals, with an average discount to tour operators' prices of 26 per cent. The traditional package holiday, they concluded, 'is in terminal decline'.

If true, it will be a significant event in internet history. In its 1990s heyday, the internet's champions claimed it would change everything. They said it would lead to 'disintermediation', a horrible word that meant consumers would be able to dispense with intermediaries such as bookshops, banks or supermarkets. They would go directly to the internet to get what they wanted. New online companies would be the beneficiaries.

It has not worked out that way. With the exception of Amazon.com, most companies that have succeeded on the internet have been established organisations, such as Tesco or the large banks. Like much else associated with the internet, disintermediation appeared to have been hyped.

So has it now finally arrived, and is it about to inflict significant damage on the package holiday companies? On the face of it, the idea makes no sense. Tour operators are not hugely profitable. They may bully hoteliers into cutting their rates, but the brutally competitive nature of the business means they have to pass much of the benefit on to consumers. Goldman Sachs estimates the margin on a mass market package holiday before interest and tax is little more than 3 per cent.

It is not as if tour operators are charging rip-off prices. How can individual travellers buy holidays 26 per cent cheaper? Why would a hotelier offer lower prices to a lone buyer than to a large operator offering to book his rooms for an entire season?

There are two explanations, one transient and one longer-lasting. The transient explanation is that, with so few tourists around, there are plenty of vacant rooms and empty aircraft seats. In normal times, hoteliers and airlines would charge the highest possible price for any rooms and flights that the tour operators had not snapped up, particularly at peak season. But these are not normal times. Rather than leave their facilities empty, the providers of tourist amenities prefer to offload them for whatever price they can get. Here, the internet does have an effect. Not only can individual travellers use it to compare prices; so can the hoteliers, driving prices down even further as they attempt to attract what little custom is available.

But longer-term trends are damaging tour operators – and these are only partly the result of the internet. The rise of Europe's low-cost airlines, led by Ryanair and EasyJet, has provided tour operators with stiff competition. The two airlines did not start out relying on the internet. Ryanair sold tickets through travel agents. EasyJet had its own telephone centre.

But they have now adopted the internet with enthusiasm, driving down costs for themselves and their customers. What is more, travellers who have booked their EasyJet air tickets can click on a neighbouring hotel site run by another company. Like the tour operators, these companies buy hotel accommodation in bulk. Travellers can take advantage of their lower prices, while assembling their own package holidays.

The potential problem for the traveller – and the cost advantage for the low-cost airlines – is that holidays bought in this way offer nothing like the consumer protection that Europe's tour operators have to provide by law. Paying for the bonds that protect package travellers adds to the tour operators' costs and makes their holidays that much more expensive.

What can the package tour operators do? They can offer reliability. Holidays are precious; time is short and paying for them takes a substantial slice out of most people's disposable income. But even prize-winning tour operators cut corners, not telling travellers that the sea view is obscured by an electricity pylon or forgetting to mention the motorway 200 metres from the villa. Brands matter more than ever when people buy online. Few holiday companies understand that.

▶

The upmarket specialist companies can offer something different, such as new destinations and activities. For mass market operators, the future looks grim. They should do better when travellers return, but they will not win back all the business they have lost. When times are bad, excess accommodation and flights will be dumped on the market, and the transparency of the internet will ensure they sell at ever-lower prices. Europe's tour operators have never been a great investment prospect. They look worse than ever.

Source: *Financial Times*, 21 May 2003. Reprinted with permission.

Questions for exit case study 9.3

1 Perform a LoNGPEST analysis of the external environment faced by the holiday industry.

2 Clearly identify and discuss the factors which have the greatest impact on the following type of organisations: a European package tour operator offering package holidays in Europe and to long-haul destinations; a low-cost airline operating in Europe only; a small family-run hotel in Torquay on the south coast of England.

3 Identify further sources of information which would enhance and improve your analysis in question 1.

4 Discuss the advantages and disadvantages of undertaking analysis of the external environment of an organisation or industry.

 For more case studies please visit **www.booksites.net/capon**

Short-answer questions

1 Name three influences from the political external environment, one each from the local, national and global levels.

2 Name three influences from the economic external environment, one each from the local, national and global levels.

3 Name three influences from the sociocultural external environment, one each from the local, national and global levels.

4 Explain why the influence of technology on an organisation is considered differently from the influence of economic, political and sociocultural factors.

5 Define autocracy.

6 Describe a democracy.

7 List the characteristics of a free market.

8 List the characteristics of a planned economy.

9 List the characteristics of a mixed economy.

10 Explain the function of chambers of commerce in the business community.

11 Summarise the role of the IOD and CBI in business.

12 Explain the role of trade unions.

13 Explain the role of NATO in the external environment.

14 Describe the role of the Commonwealth in the external environment.

15 Illustrate the role of the Bank of England in the economy of the UK.

16 Explain the role of the London stock market in the economy of the UK.

17 Indicate the role of the WTO in global trade.

18 Explain the role of NAFTA in North American trade.

19 Explain the role of ASEAN.

20 Explain the role of EFTA and how it differs from the EU.

21 Indicate by example what you understand alliances and agreements to be.

22 Define 'social capital'.

23 What is the main difference in public spending on pensions in the UK and other European countries?

24 Name the six countries with the fastest growing population over the next 50 years.

25 Why, by 2003, had life expectancy fallen in South Africa and Botswana to just 48 years and 40 years respectively?

Learning outcomes for assignment questions

While reading this chapter and engaging in the activities, you should have learned how to apply theory and models, analyse situations, and evaluate the application and analysis you undertake. The learning outcomes specified below outline what you should be able to do and the assignment questions provide an opportunity for you to test how well you have achieved the learning outcomes for this chapter.

Application	Check you have achieved this by	
1 Recognise the impact of technology on an organisation or industry	identifying the specific technologies which influence an organisation or sector	answering assignment question 2
Analysis	**Check you have achieved this by**	
1 Appraise the 'political' influence on the individual, workplace and economy	evaluating the impact of a 'political' organisation on the individual, workplace and economy	answering assignment question 1
2 Evaluate the relative impact of technology	examining the similarities and differences in the impact technology has on different organisations	answering assignment question 2
3 Assess the relative impact of global economic bodies	examining the similarities and differences in the roles of two trading blocs	answering assignment question 3
Evaluation	**Check you have achieved this by**	
1 Comment on the usefulness and relevance of information	appraising the relevance, accuracy and pertinence of information	answering assignment questions 1, 2 & 3

Assignment questions

1 Choose *one* of the following organisations: Institute of Directors (IOD), Confederation of British Industry (CBI) or Trades Union Congress (TUC). Identify and collect appropriate information and write an essay of 2000 words that demonstrates and evaluates the influence of your chosen organisation on the individual employee, the workplace and the economy. Comment on the sources of information used.

2 Select two organisations from different industries or sectors and collect relevant and appropriate information. Compare and contrast the impact of technology on your chosen organisations over the next three years and present your findings in a 2000-word report. Comment on the sources of information used.

3 Identify and collect appropriate information and write an essay of 2000 words comparing and contrasting the roles of ASEAN and NAFTA in their home geographic regions. Comment on the sources of information used.

Weblinks   available online at www.booksites.net/capon

The websites listed here are for international bodies which impact upon the external environment of organisations. Websites for UK-based bodies are listed at the end of Chapter 8.

1 The following website is for the European Union.
   http://www.europa.eu.int/

2 The website for the European Free Trade Area is shown below.
   http://www.efta.int/

3 The website of the European Bank Reconstruction and Development is shown below.
   http://www.ebrd.org/

4 The following website is for the Council of Baltic Sea States.
   http://www.baltinfo.org/

5 The following website is for the North America Free Trade Association.
   http://www.nafta-sec-alena.org/

6 The following website is for the Association of South East Asian Nations.
   http://www.aseansec.org/800x600.html

7 The website for the Commonwealth is shown below.
   http://www.thecommonwealth.org/

8 The website for NATO is shown below.
   http://www.nato.int/

9 The website of the World Trade Organisation is shown below.
   http://www.wto.org/

10 The website of the World Bank Group is shown below.
   http://www.worldbank.org/

11 The following website is for the International Monetary Fund.
   http://www.imf.org/

12 The website of the Organisation for Economic Co-operation and Development is shown below.
   http://www.oecd.org/

13 The Treasury website is shown below.
   http://www.hm-treasury.gov.uk

Further reading

Baer, W S (1998) 'Will the Internet bring electronic services to the home?', *Business Strategy Review*, 1 (1), Spring.

Bird, J (1996) 'Switching on intranets', *Management Today*, December.

Bird, J (1998) 'The great telephony shake-up', *Management Today*, January.

Ghosh, S (1998) 'Making business sense of the Internet', *Harvard Business Review*, March/April.

Griffith, M W and Taylor, B (1996) 'The future for multimedia – the battle for world dominance', *Long Range Planning*, 29 (5), October.

Gwyther, M (1999) 'Sold to the man on the internet', *Management Today*, June.

Hencke, D (2001) 'How lobbyist do the business', *Management Today*, April.

Mitchell, A (1998) 'New model unions', *Management Today*, July.

Molina, A H (1997) 'Newspapers: the slow walk to multimedia', *Long Range Planning*, 30 (2), April.

Pickard, J (1999) 'Grey areas', *People Management*, 29 July.

Smith, D (1998) 'How single is the single market?', *Management Today*, January.

Thomas, R (1999) 'The world is your office', *Management Today*, July.

van de Vliet, A (1996) 'Whatever happened to leisure', *Management Today*, May.

Wallace, P (1999) 'Agequake', *Management Today*, March.

Worthington, I and Britton, C (2000) *The Business Environment*, 3rd edn, Chapters 3–6, Harlow: Financial Times Prentice Hall.

References

1 http://www.businesslink.org.

2 http://www.bbc.co.uk/politics97/analysis/rozenberg2.shtm1.

3 Ibid.

4 Ibid.

5 Ibid.

6 Manning, A (1997) 'If it's good enough for everyone else, it's good enough for us', *Independent on Sunday*, 11 May.

7 *China-Britain Trade Review*, quoting HM Customs and British Trade Commission (Hong Kong).

8 http://www.europa.eu.int/abc-en.htm.

9 Barber, L (1997) 'No turning back from brave new Europe', *Financial Times*, 17 July.

10 http://europa.eu.int/comm/enlargement/faq/index.htm.

11 Reuters (2002) 'Giscard warns against Turkish EU entry', *FT.com* site, 8 November.

12 http://www.baltinfo.org/CBSS.htm.

13 http://www.priairienet.org/acas/96F23024.htm1; Ejime, P (1996) Panafrican News Agency (PANA), 'Reconciling Nigeria with the Commonwealth', 23 June.

14 http://www.africanews.org/west/nigeria/stories/19970821_feat1.htm1; Ejime, P (1997) Panafrican News Agency (PANA), 'Nigeria reassessing Commonwealth membership', 21 August.

15 http://www.thecommonwealth.org/.

16 http://www.thecommonwealth.org/about/general/general1.htm1.

17 http://www.nato.int/welcome/home.htm.

18 Buchan, D, Clark, B and White, D (1997) 'Nato expansion deal covers divide', *Financial Times*, 9 July.

19 *Daily Telegraph*, 28 February 1998.

20 http://www.efta.int/docs/EFTA/Gen . . . rmation/Informationsheet/221.htm1.

21 http://europa.eu.int/comm/external_relations/mercosur/intro/.

22 http://www.fatf-gafi.org/Ctry-orgpages/ctry-gc_en.htm.

23 http://www.oecd.org/about/works.htm.

24 http://www.nafta-sec-alena.org/english/nafta/preamble.htm.

25 Crawford, L (1997) 'Hazardous trades bring pollution and health fears down Mexico way', *Financial Times*, 6 June.

26 Dombey, D and Dunne, N (1997) 'Peso crisis turbo-charges revolution in motor trade', *Financial Times*, 11 June.

27 Silver, S (2002) 'Nafta plays down friction with success stories', *Financial Times*, 29 May.

28 Bardacke, T (1997) 'Cambodia rebuffed by Asean', *Financial Times*, 11 July.

29 http://www.aseansec.org/history/asn_his2htm.

30 http://www.wto.org/htbin/htimage/wto/map.map?8,33.

31 Williams, F (1997) 'India import curbs row goes to WTO', *Financial Times*, 17 July.

32 Jonquieres, G de and Walker, T (1997) 'New dawn in the east', *Financial Times*, 3 March.

33 Blitz, R (2003) 'Ageing population trend heightens pension fears', *Financial Times*, 30 January.

34 Brown, K (2002) 'A lost generation leaves Britain older and calmer', *Financial Times*, 5 October.

35 Nicholson-Lord, D (1995) '"Greys" take over from the young as big spenders', *Independent*, 27 January.

36 Braid, M (1995) 'Tomorrow belongs to them', *Independent*, 1 October.

37 Nicholson-Lord, op. cit.

38 Johnson, P (1990) 'Our ageing population – the implications for business and government', *Long Range Planning*, 23 (2), April.

39 Braid, op. cit.

40 Timmins, N (2002) 'Public spending on pensions set to fall despite ageing population', *Financial Times*, 28 November.

41 Gwyther, M (1992) 'Britain bracing for the age bomb', *Independent on Sunday*, 29 March.

42 Parker, G (2002) 'Brussels warns of ageing population crisis', *Financial Times*, 11 December.

43 Gimbel, F (2003) 'BVCA to call for immigration increase', *Financial Times*, 23 March.

44 Timmins, N (1995) 'A powerful indictment of the eighties', *Independent*, 10 February.

45 Mills, H (1995) 'Shift in wealth divides rich South and poor North', *Independent*, 1 February.

46 Jury, L (1998) 'Britons remain true to family values', *Independent*, 7 August.

47 Cooper, G (1996) 'The single society', *Independent*, 20 March.

48 Williams, F (2002) 'UN finds link between fertility rate and wealth', *Financial Times*, 3 December.

49 Wolf, M (2003) 'People, plagues and prosperity', *Financial Times*, 26 February.

50 Johnstone, V (1998) 'Companies switch on to virtues of global vision', *Daily Telegraph*, 30 April.

51 Ibid.

52 Baxter, A (1997) 'Face to face across borders', *Financial Times*, 26 March.

53 Johnstone, op. cit.

54 Baxter, op. cit.

55 Johnstone, op. cit.

56 Ibid.

57 Shankar, B and Sharda, R (1997) 'Obtaining business intelligence on the Internet', *Long Range Planning*, 30 (1), February.

58 Bird, J (1996) 'Untangling the Web', *Management Today*, March.

59 Ibid.

60 Daniel, E and Storey, C (1997) 'On-line banking: strategic and management challenges', *Long Range Planning*, 30 (6), December.

10

The competitive environment

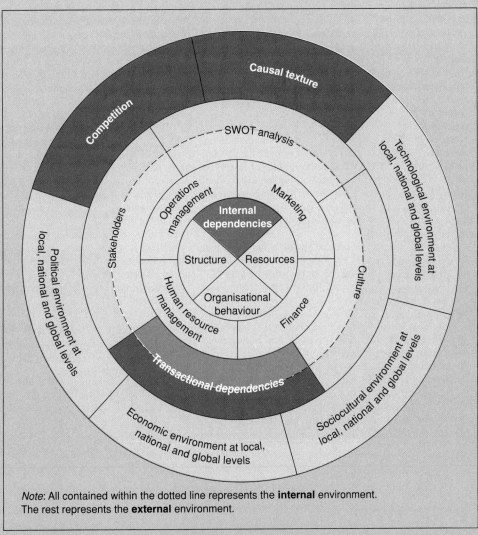

Note: All contained within the dotted line represents the **internal** environment.
The rest represents the **external** environment.

Figure 10.1 Organisational context model

Return to the wild frontier

Wrangler's European challenge to Levi's jeans bucks the campaign trend its rival has set

By Alison Smith

Jason Maddox and Trey King are used to riding tough animals as they compete on the rodeo circuit in Arkansas. Now Wrangler's hopes of breaking through to mount a serious challenge to Levi's in the European jeans market are riding on them.

The two rodeo riders are the stars of a television advertising campaign which breaks in the UK today and in Germany next week. 'We believe this is an opportunity to break out of the pack chasing Levi's and become a challenger for the number one position,' says David Smith, marketing director for Wrangler in Europe. Wrangler has earmarked £15m for spending on the European campaign this year.

Substantial sales are at stake. In the UK market alone, more than 39m pairs of jeans at a value of more than £900m were sold in the 12 months to the middle of last year. Levi's has more than 20 per cent of the branded market, while Wrangler has 8–9 per cent. The gap between the two brands is narrower in Germany, where each has a much smaller share of the market. In Ireland the two are broadly neck and neck.

The new Wrangler ads contrast sharply with the current Levi's campaign, already showing across Europe. Levi's ad, created by Bartle Bogle Hegarty, shows a man falling off a boat in a storm, and then escaping from three mermaids, who try to take his jeans off but fail because they fit too closely.

The down-to-earth Wrangler's ads from Abbott Mead Vickers show the rodeo riders in action, and talking about the extensive injuries they have received. The style is documentary, and the message is that Wranglers are worn by 99 out of 100 rodeo riders.

'A mistake a lot of brands have made is to forget their western roots and float off into something else. We are the authentic western jeans, and we have to take that positioning and make it aspirational and exciting,' says Smith.

Wrangler's strategy of moving outside the advertising genre of boy meets girl to chart topping soundtrack, created by Levi's since the mid-1980s, is seen by other advertising agencies as sensible for a number two brand. 'Unless you do something absolutely different, you will be seen as a "me too" Levi's ad,' says one. Levi's advertising is so dominant, however, that creating a significantly different approach is very hard, he adds.

Beyond that general difficulty, there lies a particular issue for Wrangler. The emphasis of its advertising is that real western values are epitomised by the riders who make their living by risking their lives in the arena. Yet they are taking that message to young European consumers, whose view of the west is likely to have been formed by Hollywood and American television. The gritty tone of the campaign may well not be what they expect to associate with the west.

Nigel Marsh, board account director at AMV, sees this as an advantage. 'If it is not what they expected, it will stick in the mind.'

Tom Blackett, deputy chairman of Interbrand, a brand consultancy, is not convinced about the campaign. 'It may appeal to the laddish tendency but I'm not certain it's an enduring image.'

Moreover, there is the risk inherent in any ad campaign based on real life that it ceases to be an unvarnished reality as soon as it appears in an advertisement. Wrangler is already talking about personal appearances by the two rodeo riders in the films. But the more the campaign makes them stars, the more it undermines their strength as real-life characters.

Wrangler has a strong start to the campaign, running with a mix of films instead of just one film as is more often the case. But it is by no means clear it will have an easy ride.

Source: Financial Times, 1 April 1997. Reprinted with permission.

Introduction

Earlier chapters have examined organisations and what they do. In addition the previous two chapters looked at the broad general external environment faced by organisations. This chapter deals with competition, which is an extremely important part of the external environment for organisations. Hence this chapter looks at the competitive environment, its regulation, its relationship to organisations, and strategies for operating in such a competitive environment.

Environmental linkages

Emery and Trist[1] suggest that understanding the environment of organisations depends on a firm grasp of the linkages within an organisation's environment. They identify three types of linkage: from within to within, from outside in and inside out, and outside linkages.

■ From within to within linkages

From within to within linkages are **internal dependencies** inside the organisation. These internal dependencies can be co-operative or confrontational in nature. A co-operative inter-dependency would be the marketing and production department agreeing to work closely together on developing a new product. A confrontational inter-dependency would occur if two divisions in an organisation were to disagree on the resources allocated to their divisions – *see* Figure 10.2, link number 1. This type of confrontational inter-dependency can usually be resolved by an appropriate third party, a more senior employee, for example a supervisor, senior manager or director, depending on the type of confrontation.

■ From outside in and inside out linkages

From outside in and inside out linkages are called **transactional dependencies**. Transactional dependencies are links in and out of the organisation. In any organisation there are a number of transactions that take place between organisations and elements of the external environments – *see* Figure 10.2, link number 2. These transactions can be simple or complex, frequent or rare, consistent or one-off. Depending on the kind of transaction, the level of dependence between the organisation and the environmental element will change. Obvious transactional dependencies are those between an organisation and its suppliers, buyers and competitors. The organisation manages such transactional dependencies by negotiation with the other parties involved.

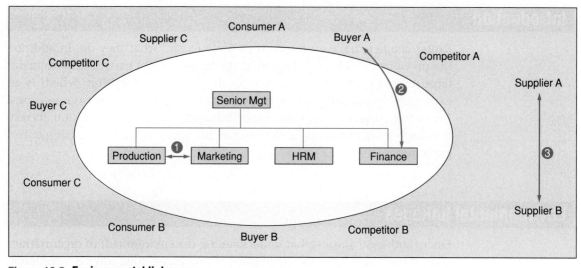

Figure 10.2 Environmental linkages

Source: Based on Emery, F E and Trist, E L (1965) 'The causal texture of organisational environments' in *Human Relations* 18: 21–32.

If a manufacturer, such as Nissan, operates a just-in-time production system (*see* Chapter 5), the manufacturer is not keeping stocks of raw materials or component parts. Therefore the manufacturer is hugely dependent on suppliers' abilities to provide the resource inputs in an accurate and timely fashion. If the right piece does not appear in the correct place on the assembly line at the proper time, the entire production process grinds to a halt. Thus there is a frequent and consistent transactional dependency between the manufacturer and the supplier, with the balance of the power resting with the supplier. Nevertheless, a collaborative, rather than combative, relationship is usually sought in such situations.

Complete independence is neither possible nor desirable for an organisation – not possible since organisations cannot provide all the resources or components they need internally, and not desirable since they must have customers to be in business, and *de facto* these customers are external to the organisation. Too much dependence on suppliers or customers, or other elements of the external environment, is also not desirable, as it leaves the organisation vulnerable. Thus senior managers need to attempt to tip the balance of power as much as possible in favour of their organisation to achieve at least inter-dependence and at most the upper hand.

■ Outside linkages

Outside linkages are referred to as **causal textures**. Causal textures are inter-dependencies outside the organisation in the external environment, which can have an effect on the organisation – *see* Figure 10.2, link number 3. The causal texture in which an organisation operates is called that because there is a cause-and-effect relationship between what elements of the external environment do and how this affects third-party organisations. The simplest example of causal texture would be two suppliers agreeing to fix prices to the detriment of retail buyers. This causes the cost of supplies to go up for buyers, who in turn increase prices charged to members of the public, which results in lower sales and reduced profits.

This type of linkage or causal texture is difficult for organisations to uncover and manage effectively, so responses to such linkages may be slow and apprehensive. This contributes to an organisation's doubt and uncertainty in managing the external environment. A very clear example of an organisation affected by causal texture is Clan Douglas. This is a manufacturer of luxury cashmere sweaters, based in the Borders area of Scotland, whose biggest market is the US.[2] In March 1999 the US government began a 'banana row' with the EU, with Britain being the most affected European country. The row centred around Britain's favouring of bananas produced by small farmers on Caribbean islands that are former British colonies, as opposed to bananas produced by US companies on plantations in South America. The US viewed this as unfair trade and therefore imposed a 100 per cent import tax on certain luxury goods imported by US companies from Britain and Europe. These goods included cashmere sweaters, which sell for $350, and fountain pens made by Mont Blanc and Watermans, which retail at $300.[3] The doubling of the price of these goods to over $600 would effectively kill the US retail market and hence put affected manufacturers out of business. Hence a company like Clan Douglas in the Borders would be severely affected by such outside linkages or causal texture. Such companies have absolutely no influence over the banana war, nor could they have been reasonably expected to have anticipated the disagreement.

> ### ☑ Check your understanding
>
> *Do you understand the three environmental linkages which can impact on an organisation?*
>
> Check your understanding giving one example of your own for each type of environmental linkage.

The competitive environment

The behaviour of competitors in the external environment, be they local, national or global, very often affects organisations. Therefore it is necessary to understand and analyse the nature and role of competition. Competition is readily recognisable in the private sector, and is a mainstay of the free market philosophy, as explained in Chapter 9. The analysis of competition is also applicable to the study of public-sector organisations. In the UK in particular, the rhetoric of the free market and competition have been introduced into the public sector through wholesale privatisation or the introduction of quasi-markets into public-sector services. This was clearly demonstrated by the privatisation of public utilities such as gas and electricity, which are still monitored by a regulator.

When examining an organisation's external environment, competition is considered an important element and is therefore analysed in addition to the general external environment, which is examined by LoNGPEST analysis. The importance of competitors and competition is further illustrated and reinforced in the entry case study, 'Return to the wild frontier', and the effort that Wrangler went to in 1997 to project a very different image from its competitor, Levi.

The regulation of competition in the UK

The UK economy is a mixed economy, which means that there is some influence and regulation of the competitive behaviour of firms. Some of the regulation of competition is by bodies that may intervene if there is a likelihood of anti-competitive behaviour occurring. These bodies are the **Office of Fair Trading**, the **Competition Commission** (formerly the **Monopolies and Mergers Commission**) and the **Restrictive Practices Court**.

■ Office of Fair Trading

The Office of Fair Trading (OFT) was established in 1973 and is an independent professional organisation which seeks to promote and protect consumer interests and ensure companies compete in a fair and competitive manner. The OFT is headed by the Director General of Fair Trading and is accountable to parliament.

The OFT's activities fall into three areas: enforcement of competition and consumer protection rules, investigation into how markets are working, and communication to explain the benefits of fair competition. The OFT aims to seek out and deter anti-competitive behaviour including cartels. Additionally the OFT will refer mergers and acquisitions that could significantly lessen competition to the Competition Commission. The OFT may investigate markets for specific products or services to ensure that they are working fairly for consumers. Investigations by the OFT can lead to enforcement of the competition rules and legislation or to recommendation to government. Finally the OFT seeks to ensure that all interested stakeholders, such as businesses and consumers, understand how the competition rules and laws apply to them.

Three key pieces of competition legislation are the Fair Trading Act 1973, the Competition Act 1998 and the Enterprise Act 2002. The Fair Trading Act 1973 was introduced to deal with complex and scale monopolies. A scale monopoly exists if one firm has a minimum of 25 per cent market share and a complex monopoly exists if two or more firms together account for more than 25 per cent market share and engage in similar behaviour. The Fair Trading Act is the piece of legislation under which the Director General of Fair Trading, the Utility Regulators and the Secretary of State can refer possible monopoly situations to the Competition Commission for investigation. If the Competition Commission finds that a monopoly situation exists and operates against the public interest, remedies may be imposed and can take the form of behavioural remedies, which is the stopping of particular practices, or structural remedies, which may include closing or divesting specified parts of the business.

The Competition Act 1998 makes anti-competitive agreements, cartels and abuses of a dominant position unlawful from the start and gives the Director General of Fair Trading new powers to stop anti-competitive behaviour from the outset. Competitors and customers who are victims of anti-competitive behaviour are able to seek damages, and perpetrators are liable to financial penalties of up to 10 per cent of UK turnover for up to three years.

The Enterprise Act 2002 came into force in summer 2003 and established the OFT as a corporate body and replaced the Director General of Fair Trading with two separate people, a chairman and chief executive. The main reforms of the Enterprise Act were in the areas of competition measures, consumer protection measures and insolvency reforms. The main changes to competition measures were an increase in criminal sanctions, with up to five years in prison for those convicted of dishonestly operating hardcore cartels, and greater opportunity for victims of cartels to gain redress, including allowing consumer bodies to make claims on behalf of individual consumers.

Consumer protection measures will be increased by the extension of Stop Now Orders to protect consumers from traders who fail to meet their obligations, for example failure to carry out building work to a satisfactory standard. This is complemented by the OFT approving codes of practice which should allow consumers to more easily identify trustworthy traders, for example an honest car repair business. Additionally consumer bodies will be able to make 'super-complaints' about features of a market which they feel harm consumers.

Insolvency reforms include reforming corporate insolvency law such that the process is simplified and streamlined, and the provision of an updated bankruptcy regime to encourage entrepreneurship, with limited restrictions of up to 12 months for those who failed through no fault of their own. In contrast, restrictions on bankrupts who abuse their creditors and the public will range from 2 to 15 years. Additionally the Crown's preferential right to recover unpaid taxes ahead of other creditors will benefit other unsecured creditors, such as small firms that have yet to receive payment for goods and service supplied.

■ Competition Commission

The Competition Commission (CC) was established by the Competition Act 1998 and replaced the Monopolies and Mergers Commission (MMC) on 1 April 1999. The Competition Commission has two distinct areas of activity.

The first is taking over the role of the MMC in carrying out inquiries referred to it by the other UK competition authorities, including the OFT and other industry regulators, for example OFGEM. This work is undertaken by the reporting panel at the Competition Commission. The second area of activity is the newly established Appeals Tribunals, which hear appeals against decisions of the Director General of Fair Trading and the Regulators concerning infringements of the competition legislation and abuse of a dominant market position. This work is undertaken by the appeals panel at the Competition Commission. Finally, the specialist panels for utilities (electricity and gas), telecommunications, water and newspapers assist in some of the regulatory inquiries, with newspaper panel members dealing only with newspaper inquiries.

■ Restrictive Practices Court

The Restrictive Practices Court was established in 1956 and controls practices that are presumed to be against the public interest. Restrictive practices can relate to the price of goods, conditions of supply, qualities or descriptions, processes or areas and persons supplied. A case in which the Restrictive Practices Court has recently ruled is that of over-the-counter medicines. The Office of Fair Trading launched a four-year investigation into the price-fixing agreement for over-the-counter medicines such as aspirin, vitamins and cough and cold remedies. In the 1970s this agreement guaranteed small chemists shops a reasonable profit and living by virtue of an assured profit margin on over-the-counter medicines. However, in the mid-1990s 40 per cent of the market for over-the-counter medicines was held by large supermarket chains. The Office of Fair Trading investigation began when one such supermarket chain, Asda, challenged the protected position of these medicines. In March 1999 the Restrictive Practices Court announced that it would allow the Office of Fair Trading to launch a full-scale hearing into the 30-year-old price-fixing agreement. In January 2003 the OFT recommended removing restrictions on entry to the community pharmacy market, which would include the abolition of the 1970 price-fixing agreement for over-the-counter medicines. This move should save consumers around £30 million a year.

Regulatory bodies for privatised utilities and industries

The privatised utilities in the UK, which immediately after privatisation were not subject to intense competition, are each monitored by a regulator. Regulators exist for telecommunications, gas, electricity, water and rail transport. Their responsibility is to encourage competition and see that customers are not unfairly exploited where there may be only one supplier of a service, such as the supply of water to domestic premises.

■ Office of Telecommunications

The Office of Telecommunications (OFTEL) was established by the Tele-communications Act 1984, the year that British Telecom was privatised. Like the Office of Fair Trading, OFTEL is a non-ministerial government department and is headed by a Director General who is appointed by the Secretary of State for Trade and Industry. OFTEL has three directorates: Regulatory Policy Direct-orate, which develops telecommunications policies; Compliance Directorate, which ensures phones companies comply with telecoms and competition regulations and legislation; and Business Support Directorate, which supports the whole OFTEL organisation. The key functions of OFTEL are:

- promoting the interests of consumers;
- maintaining and promoting effective competition;
- making sure that telecommunications services are provided in the UK to meet all reasonable demands including emergency services, public call boxes, directory information and services in rural areas.

■ Office of Communications

The Office of Communications (OFCOM) was expected to be operational by the end of 2003 and is the new regulator for the communications sector and will bring together five existing regulatory bodies: the Independent Television Commission (ITC), the Broadcasting Standards Commission (BSC), the Office of Telecommunications (OFTEL), the Radio Authority (RAu) and the Radio-communications Agency (RA). OFCOM's was established by the Office of Communications Act 2002, which defines OFCOM's duties as:

- furthering the interests of consumers in relevant markets;
- securing the optimal use of the radio spectrum;
- ensuring the availability of a wide range of television and radio services in the UK;
- protecting the public from offensive or potentially harmful effects of broadcast media;
- safeguarding people from being unfairly treated in television and radio programmes.

■ Office of Gas and Electricity Markets

The Office of Gas and Electricity Markets (OFGEM) replaces the Office of Gas Supply (OFGAS) and the Office of Electricity Regulation (OFFER). OFGEM's powers are provided under the Gas Act 1986, the Electricity Act 1989 and the Utilities Act 2000 and its main objective is to promote effective competition in the energy market for present and future customers. To achieve this OFGEM seeks to enforce licence obligations, competition and consumer law to protect customers, for example, from rogue doorstep salesmen. OFGEM also plays a major role in regulating the monopoly networks of fuel supply and does so by regulating the wholesale market and prices. OFGEM seeks to ensure that competitive supply arrangements mean competitive prices for customers as well as direct regulation of the prices customers pay for their fuel. Additionally OFGEM seeks to improve the quality of service to customers by encouraging effective long-term investment in the gas and electricity networks in the UK.

■ Office of Water Supply

The Office of Water Supply (OFWAT) is a government department led by the Director General of Water Services that regulates water supply and pricing to domestic and industrial customers. OFWAT checks that prices for different types of customers – metered or unmetered, large or small, urban or rural – are fair. Generally the prices charged by water companies should reflect the cost of supplying clean water and getting rid of dirty and draining water from homes and premises.[4]

The role of OFWAT is to:

- limit the amount companies can charge customers;
- make sure that companies can carry out their responsibilities under the Water Industry Act 1991;
- protect the standard of service customers receive;
- encourage companies to be more efficient;
- work to encourage competition where appropriate.

OFWAT works closely with two other water regulatory bodies: the Environment Agency, which implements water quality standards in inland waters, estuarial and coastal waters, and the Drinking Water Inspectorate, which regulates standards for drinking water.[5]

■ Strategic Rail Authority

The Transport Act 2000 saw the establishment of the **Strategic Rail Authority** (SRA) in February 2001. Shortly afterwards the Strategic Rail Authority unveiled its first strategic plan, which set out the strategic priorities for Britain's railway over the following ten years. The SRA is responsible for implementing the plan with the available resources. The government's key targets are a 50 per cent growth in passenger kilometres, an 80 per cent growth for rail freight, a reduction in London area overcrowding and an improvement in punctuality and reliability. In addition to developing and implementing strategy for Britain's railways, the SRA issues and manages passenger franchises, and deals with major infrastructure projects, freight grants and some aspects of consumer protection, and publishes an annual strategic review.

■ Office of the Rail Regulator

The **Office of the Rail Regulator** (ORR) was established under the Railways Act 1993 and is independent of ministerial control. The main functions of the Rail Regulator are to:

- regulate Network Rail, the owner of the UK's national rail network, including the setting of Network Rail's access charges, establishing its financial framework and ensuring its accountability to the public interest;
- issue modification and enforcement of licences to operate trains, networks, stations and light maintenance depots;
- approve the agreements for access to railway facilities, i.e. track, stations and light maintenance depots;
- exercise powers under the Competition Act 1998, concurrently with the Director General of Fair Trade, with respect to agreements, exemptions and anti-competitive behaviour.

✓ Check your understanding

Do you understand the reasons for regulation of the privatised utilities?

Check your understanding by naming one of the privatised utility regulators and briefly summarising its role and duties.

Assessing the nature of competition

Porter[6] presents a model for examining competition in an industry or sector – *see* Figure 10.3. He argues that five basic forces drive competition in an industry: **competitive rivalry**, **threat of new entrants**, threat of **substitute products or services**, **bargaining power of buyers**, and **bargaining power of suppliers**. These five forces need to be examined and understood if the nature of competition in an industry or sector is to be fully appreciated.

■ Competitive rivalry

The first of the five forces examines the nature of competitive rivalry within a particular sector or industry. There are a number of factors affecting how fierce competitive rivalry is in an industry or sector and consequently how difficult the market is for organisations operating there. The key questions to examine concern who the present and potential competitors are, and how intensive the competition is between them. In some industries there are numerous competitor companies, all of a similar size and capacity, all holding comparable market shares and all seeking to dominate the industry. There may be no dominant company or companies within the sector and little to distinguish

Figure 10.3
The five forces that determine industry profitability

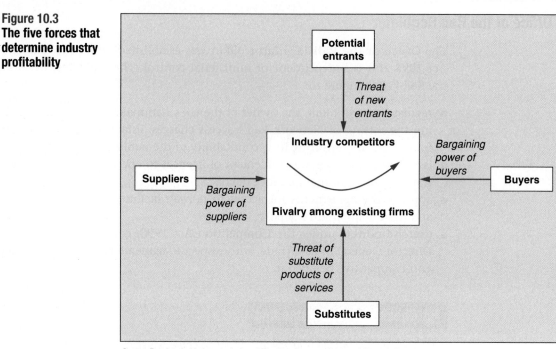

between the brands and products that are available to the customer. The market itself may be established or mature, with little prospect of major innovation or design surprises. In such an industry or sector, the intensity of competitive rivalry will be very high, as mature companies have to battle to retain market share, sustain **differentiation** and maintain their customer base.

The entry case study to this chapter discusses the competitive rivalry between jeans manufacturers Levi and Wrangler. Both are established companies seeking sustainable differentiation of their product, with the aim of maintaining market share and tempting customers away from the competitor's jeans. In the case of jeans, the role of advertising on television and in the cinema is key to promoting the appropriate image to attract jeans-wearing customers. The different approaches of Levi and Wrangler to image and advertising are discussed in the entry case study.

The supermarket industry in the UK is a good illustration of extremely fierce competitive rivalry. Tesco is dominant in terms of market share, but other players all have high profiles and similar market presence. For many customers there is little real difference between the big supermarket chains, with Tesco, Sainsbury's and Safeway all offering very similar ranges of products and services. Supermarkets compete ruthlessly and do so by offering an ever wider range of services, including those complementary to their core business. Supermarkets have opened banks to provide financial services, in addition to a range of ancillary services that are now standard, including dry cleaning, cafés, photo processing, clothes stores, recycling collection points and pharmacies.

■ Threat of new entrants

The second of Porter's five forces is the threat of new entrants to an industry or sector. It is necessary to identify which companies are likely to be able to enter the market in order to compete with existing operators, and to recognise the other markets in which these potential new entrants currently operate. The threat of new entrants will be greatest if an industry is attractive enough to entice them. The attractiveness of an industry depends on there being a sufficient customer base to support the new entrant's business along with existing organisations. High potential profits and low set-up costs make an industry attractive. This gives an attractive combination of low financial risk combined with high potential returns.

In the exit case study for this chapter, the move by Superdrug into the business of retailing up-market perfume and aftershave was undertaken in part as an opportunity for the company to make good profits. The standard profit margin made by an authorised retailer on a bottle of up-market perfume or aftershave is 40 per cent. Hence Superdrug was able to cut its profit margin to, say, 20 per cent and still make an attractive profit. This, combined with the relatively low set-up costs needed to exploit the opportunity, the cost of the perfume and securing supplies, meant it was too good an opportunity for Superdrug to miss.

■ Threat of substitute products or services

When considering the nature of competition, the alternative products or services available to be purchased require consideration. A substitute product or service provides the same function as the good for which it is a replacement. Straightforward examples of substitute products include tea as a substitute for coffee, or cans and cartons as substitute forms of packaging that have largely replaced glass bottles as containers for milk and soft drinks. In relation to the entry case study, trousers made from material other than denim would be a direct substitute for jeans.

Substitute products or services will be a threat if customers perceive that the alternatives perform a similar or equally good function. The threat from substitutes will be greater if the alternatives provide better value for money. This can be achieved by the substitute being equally good and cheaper or by being equal on price but offering a better product or more added value.

The consumer frenzy that is Christmas shopping provides a vivid example of the exercise of choice and decision making between alternatives or substitute products or services. For the man who is buying a gift for a wife or girlfriend, the initial decision between substitutes is perhaps a choice of a bottle of eau de toilette, a compact disc, a new sweater, or a piece of jewellery. If the customer decides on a compact disc, there are further decisions to be made. Which band or artist should they choose? Should it be their new Christmas album? Should it be an older album? Should it be a compilation of greatest hits? Where should it be brought: in a music superstore like HMV or Virgin, in WH Smith, by mail order from Britannia Music or online from Amazon.co.uk? The function of the merchandise purchased is to provide a good Christmas present, hence all of the possibilities mentioned are substitutes for each other and so pose a threat.

■ Bargaining power of buyers

Earlier in this chapter it was mentioned that organisations have varying degrees of dependence on their customers and suppliers. Porter's five forces of competition model refers to this as the 'bargaining power of buyers and suppliers'. There are two types of buyer: the industrial or commercial buyer who purchases goods on a large scale on behalf of the organisation for whom she or he works, and the individual consumer.

The bargaining power of a commercial buyer depends on a number of factors. If, for example, the threat of substitutes is strong, a number of choices exist and the buyer will shop around to find the best deal and most suitable choice. The bargaining power of the buyer is also strengthened if alternative sources for the supply of a product exist. In this situation the buyer will have the upper hand when negotiating supply and price. In the UK the supermarket sector is a good example of a group of organisations that have high bargaining power as buyers. In purchasing food to sell to the general public the supermarkets purchase in bulk and there are many substitutes and alternative sources of supply for them to capitalise on. Hence they can drive a hard bargain in terms of price and product.

In buying fruit and vegetables, supermarkets require suppliers of products like apples or tomatoes to grow a particular variety, supply fruit of uniform appearance and of a predetermined size. This allows for attractive in-store displays to tempt customers to buy the produce, which is aided by the uniform appearance of the fruit and vegetables, which also limits the amount of handling and rummaging though the goods by customers. If the size of a particular fruit or vegetable is important to the supermarket, that will be specified in the contract with the grower, along with the variety and delivery date. For round fruit and vegetables, size is specified as the circumference in millimetres. For example, in February 1999 Marks and Spencer sold pre-packaged South African plums, labelled as being of the Harry Pickstone variety, size 50/55mm. It should be noted that powerful buyers like supermarkets often work closely with their suppliers in developing new products and the systems for producing them.

The individual consumer is usually much less powerful as a buyer compared with large organisations. The bargaining power of an individual buyer is influenced by factors similar to those for commercial buyers. The strong threat of substitutes and the number of choices available will allow the individual consumer to shop around for the best deal. The city-centre office worker who goes out to buy his/her take-away lunch every day has a number of choices. They can buy a sandwich, drink and packet of crisps from a city centre store like Marks and Spencer or Boots, a bakery which is one of a chain of local bakeries, or a sandwich shop like Deli France. Other substitutes are available for the individual consumer to consider, such as a burger, fries and drink from a fast-food outlet like McDonald's or Burger King. Individual consumers are free to exercise choice but have no real power as individuals to negotiate over the price they pay for their lunch.

However, if individual consumers choose to act in unison they may be able to exercise power. For example, in the mid-1990s when the health scare over British beef and BSE erupted, McDonald's faced the prospect of large numbers of its customers acting together and refusing to buy and eat its hamburgers. Therefore it switched from supplies of British beef to supplies of Dutch beef.

■ Bargaining power of suppliers

The other side of the transactional relationship is the power exerted by suppliers. There are a number of different cases when the bargaining power of suppliers is high. In industries or sectors where there are few possible suppliers, they will be able to exert a good deal of influence on the organisations to which they supply raw materials, components or finished goods for retail. In the supply of highly specialist technology, of highly prized or rare materials where the quantity is low and price is high, the supplier is more powerful as it controls something that is greatly sought after. Thus oil-producing nations have the ability to bring the world to its knees since the most modern industrialised nations are entirely dependent on the supply of crude or refined oil. In some cases, suppliers may not be entirely satisfactory and alternatives may be available, but the cost of switching from one supplier to another is too high in the short term to be affordable, even if, in the long term, the savings would be greater. Hence where there are few suppliers who cannot be easily substituted, supplier power is high.

In contrast, the exit case study to this chapter provides an excellent illustration of suppliers with low bargaining power. The suppliers of fragrances to French perfume houses such as Yves Saint Laurent and Chanel are family-based firms located in the Grasse area of France. These firms are not paid for the research and product development work they undertake. They receive payment only if they win a contract with a fragrance house, which is issued once the fragrance house is satisfied with the fragrance that has been developed for them. The developers of the fragrances will be competing against other similar firms and they stand a one-in-ten chance of being successful and winning a contract with a perfume house like Chanel. Hence the bargaining power of the fragrance developers as suppliers to the fragrance houses is very low indeed.

✓ Check your understanding

Do you understand the forces driving competition in an industry?

Check your understanding by indicating what gives each of Porter's five forces of competition high power.

Guidelines for assessing competition

In assessing the competitive environment faced by an organisation in a particular industry or sector, it can be useful to consider the following areas in relation to the five forces driving competition.

■ Competitive rivalry

Identify present and potential competitors in the industry or sector. Assess the intensity of competition between the different organisations. Is this likely to change?

■ Threat of new entrants

Does a threat of new entry into the industry exist? From which organisations does it arise? Identify the industry in which potential entrants currently operate. Evaluate the likelihood of new entrants coming into the industry.

■ Threat of substitute products or services

Identify alternative products and services. In what industry are present and potential substitute products located? Assess the likely impact of substitute products and services on the organisation and industry being analysed.

■ Bargaining power of buyers

Name the buyers of the organisation's products and services. Identify and evaluate any sources of power the buyers have with regard to the organisation being analysed.

■ Bargaining power of suppliers

Name the suppliers of the organisation's key resources and inputs. Identify and evaluate any sources of power the suppliers have with regard to the organisation being analysed.

Competitive strategies and competitive advantage

In order to operate successfully in an industry or sector where substantial competition is created by the five forces of competition, organisations need to adopt a competitive strategy. They may choose to follow one of Porter's competitive strategies to gain competitive advantage – *see* Figure 10.4. Competitive advantage is gained when an organisation achieves a position in an industry due to cost or differentiation factors, which allows it to make

Figure 10.4
Generic strategies

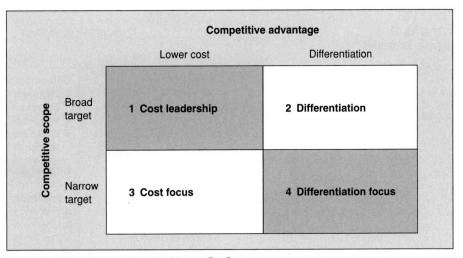

Source: Porter, Michael E (1985) *Competitive Advantage*, Free Press.

above-average or superior profits. When the supermarket chain Iceland started a home delivery service, which allowed customers to order food shopping from home and have goods delivered direct to their door, it was a source of differentiation that gave the company a competitive advantage over other food retailers, although this advantage has been eroded as its competitors have followed suit.

Porter[7] suggests that there are two decisions that organisations have to make to arrive at a suitable type of competitive strategy. The first is to decide whether competition is to be based on cost or added value. The second is to decide whether a broad target market (mass market) or a narrow target market (niche market) is to be served. Porter suggests that combinations of price and market type give rise to the following competitive strategies: **cost leadership**, selling a standard product to a mass market; differentiation, selling an added-value product to a mass market; **cost focus**, selling a low-cost product to a niche market; and **differentiation focus**, selling an added-value product to a niche market (*see* Figures 10.4 and 10.5).

■ Cost leadership

If an organisation serves or aims to serve a broad target or mass market, to be operationally efficient it will supply standard products or services to many consumers. If an organisation is following a cost leadership strategy, it will be seeking to be the lowest-cost producer in its industry or sector to supply a mass market. A successful cost leader will have achieved its position while offering products and services of a quality comparable to those offered by direct competitors. Hence in a mass market there are likely to be a number of key players, and the competitive rivalry could be fierce. However, because of the lack of specialism or high technology, costs for most organisations following a cost leadership strategy are likely to be average, as are profits.

369

**Figure 10.5
Examples of
generic strategies**

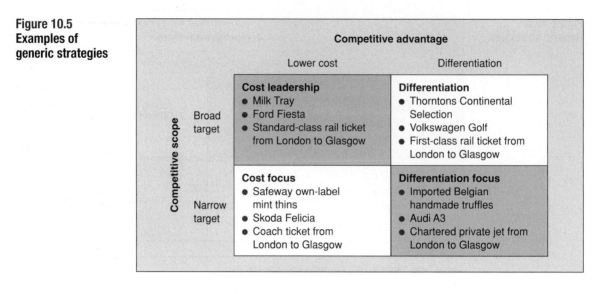

The successful cost leader who has achieved below-average costs but is sell-ing at an average price will make greater or superior profits – *see* Figure 10.6. It is difficult for any competitor serving a mass market with standard pro-ducts and services to charge above-average prices, as the competitive rivalry in the mass market prevents individual competitors from raising the price of standard products significantly. Figure 10.5 shows examples of organisations and products that follow a cost leadership strategy.

**Figure 10.6
Cost, profit and
price relationships
for cost-based
competitive
strategies**

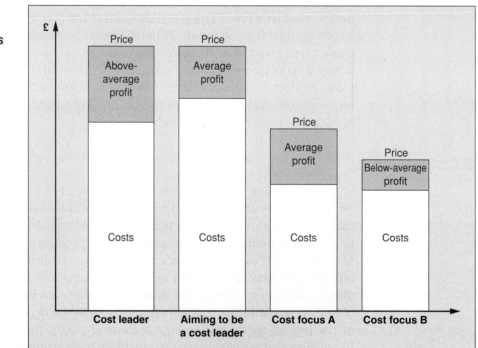

■ Differentiation

An organisation following a differentiation strategy perceives that it is still able to serve a broad target market, but by providing a product or service that is different and better – *see* Figure 10.4. A product or service is different and better due to its added value. Added value arises via the addition to the product or service of extra features, or from the better quality of the product or service. The customer needs to be prepared to pay extra for additional features or quality; if this is not the case, the organisation has wasted money in providing the added value. In this situation any superior profit that may have been made as a result of the added value is lost.

In an added-value or differentiated product, costs should be average in areas that do not add value and extra costs incurred only for added value, therefore overall costs are higher than average. This allows a higher or premium price to be charged, giving rise to superior profits – *see* Figure 10.7. This can be seen in department stores or supermarkets that have higher-than-average prices but still gain market share because their customers are willing to pay extra for goods they consider to be better.

Added value is not only located in the perceived quality of goods or services. People are prepared to pay extra for packaging and labelling, the image or reputation of the brand, or the lifestyle choices accompanying the use and purchase of certain goods – *see* Figure 10.5. This point is also illustrated by the fiercely pursued advertising strategies used by Wrangler and Levi, both anxious for their jeans to have the greater appeal and preferred image in the

**Figure 10.7
Cost, profit and price relationships for differentiation-based competitive strategies**

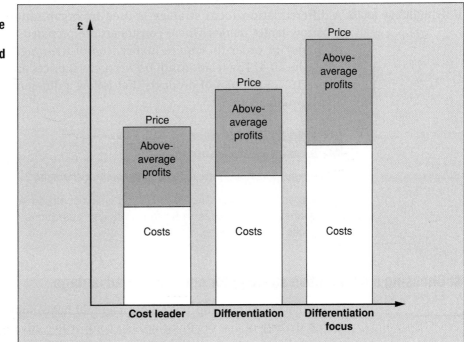

371

eye of the customer. This is important, as both companies produce basically the same product: good-quality casual-wear denim trousers. Without the image created around the jeans, they would not attract a higher-than-average price. Customers are willing to pay more for real or perceived added value, as outlined in Figure 10.7.

■ Focus strategies

An organisation employing a focus strategy will centre its efforts on a number of niche market sectors and serve only them, to the exclusion of other broad market segments – *see* Figures 10.4 and 10.6. The successful application of a focus strategy rests on there being clear and significant differences between the segments focused on and the other market segments in the industry and the market segments that are focused on being poorly attended to by the competitors serving the broad target market.

Cost focus

The cost focus strategy is followed by organisations aiming for a narrow target market, where customers are very price sensitive – *see* Figure 10.4. Organisations following a cost focus strategy will seek to deliver low cost and thus low-priced products and services to the market. In order to make profits, costs must be maintained at a minimum through using the lowest-priced raw materials, manufacturing processes, packaging, delivery and advertising. The cost focus strategy allows for average or below-average profits to be made, depending on how well costs are controlled and the level at which prices are set – *see* Figure 10.6.

Differentiation focus

A differentiation focus strategy is used by organisations wishing to serve a narrow target market where consumers are prepared to spend a great deal of money in order to acquire luxury, top-of-the-range goods or services – *see* Figure 10.4. The relationship between costs, prices and profits is shown in Figure 10.7. Examples of products that follow a differentiation focus strategy are shown in Figure 10.5.

> ### ✓ Check your understanding
>
> *Do you understand Porter's generic competitive strategies?*
>
> Check your understanding by indicating which competitive strategy each of the following shops pursues in its food retailing operations: Harrods, Marks and Spencer, Asda and Netto.

■ Choosing a competitive strategy for competitive advantage

The achievement of competitive advantage and hence superior profits is central to the strategy of any organisation. For competitive advantage to be achieved successfully, a company must be clear about which type of competitive strategy is being followed: cost leadership, differentiation, cost focus or differentiation focus. Porter argues that an organisation that tries to follow a combination of competitive strategies, i.e. cost leadership and differentiation, will achieve only average or below-average performance. Hence competitive advantage is not achieved, which Porter calls being 'stuck in the middle'.[8]

However, it is clear from looking at some organisations that it is possible to follow all of Porter's generic competitive strategies and still be successful. For example, British Airways pursues three of Porter's generic strategies by offering a range of different airline tickets: first class and Concorde (differentiation focus), business class (differentiation), and economy class (cost leadership). The supermarket chain Tesco also follows a variety of Porter's generic competitive strategies. In February 1999 the Tesco store on Abbeydale Road in Sheffield displayed, just inside the main entrance, a trolley of a typical selection of weekly groceries, with the slogan, 'All this for £14.52'. The groceries all came from Tesco's value line of products, with the distinctive blue-and-white striped packaging. Clearly a competitive strategy devised to tempt the price-sensitive customer into the store, this was, in Porter's parlance, a cost focus strategy. In contrast, Tesco also follows a differentiation focus strategy and sells a very up-market range of pre-prepared foods called 'Finest', which is clearly designed to appeal to a customer prepared to pay a great deal of money for a meal. Hence it is possible for organisations to follow both cost- and differentiation-based competitive strategies.

An alternative view of competitive strategies is presented by Gilbert and Strebel.[9] They argue that there are two constituents of competitive advantage: lower delivered cost and higher perceived value. However, unlike Porter, Gilbert and Strebel go on to argue that lower delivered cost and higher perceived value can be used together to give a company a superior position in an industry or sector. The essence of their argument is that to achieve competitive advantage a firm must strive to give the highest perceived value for the lowest delivered cost. Examples of organisations that strive to offer such a combination are IKEA and the John Lewis Partnership. IKEA, a chain of Swedish furniture stores, prides itself on offering 'good design at best ever prices'. It achieves this by seeking out and using good design, efficient suppliers, and innovative and rationalised global distribution systems.[10] The commitment of the John Lewis Partnership's retail stores to offering best quality at lowest prices is summarised in its own slogan: 'never knowingly undersold.' John Lewis offers to refund the difference if a customer finds the same item cheaper elsewhere.

Competitive advantage is achieved by creating 'disequilibrium' between the perceived value of the product and the asking price by increasing the perceived value or reducing the asking price. This alters the terms of competition and could drive competitors out of the market or influence them to offer more perceived value for the same price or the same value for less money. However, Gilbert and Strebel go on to argue that the number of competitive formulas is small, not large. They give two possible reasons for this, the first being that there is an 'internal logic to each business system' that dictates the possible combinations of perceived value and delivered cost that must exist for the whole business system. This number of combinations is clearly finite. The second somewhat obvious reason is that there are only two basic generic competitive strategies: high perceived added value and low delivered cost. Depending on a company's industry position and circumstances, there can exist only variations around these two themes, which must therefore limit the number of competitive formulas.

Further to this, Gilbert and Strebel proceed to suggest that strategic advantage is obtained by the implementation of generic competitive moves in a sequence, such that the implementation of one prepares for the implementation of another, which should of course result in high perceived value for low delivered cost.

✓ Check your understanding

Do you understand that companies may use lower cost and higher perceived value to compete effectively?

Check your understanding by indicating which businesses named below offers lower cost and higher perceived value: Amazon, easyJet, Poundstretcher, Tesco Metro.

Summary

This chapter examined the competitive environment, its regulation, its relationship to organisations and competitive strategies for operating in a competitive environment. The following summary covers all aspects of this chapter.

1 There are three types of environmental linkages: internal dependencies, transactional dependencies and causal texture. Internal dependencies are linkages between different parts of the organisation. Transactional dependencies are linkages between the organisation and its external environment. Causal texture are inter-dependencies, which are completely outside of the organisation and exist only in the external environment.

2 Competition in the UK is regulated by the Office of Fair Trading (OFT), the Competition Commission (CC), the Restrictive Practice Court (RPC) and a host of regulators for privatised utilities, industries and service sectors.

3 Porter's five forces of competition drive competition in an industry. Competitive rivalry is fierce if there are numerous competitors in an industry, markets are mature, with little differentiation and innovation. The threat of new entrants will be high if an industry is attractive, i.e. there are enough customers, profit margins are high and set-up costs low. Substitute products are a threat if they perform the same function as the product or service they replace. A substitute which provides more or is better value for money is a greater threat. Buyers generally are powerful if they have the opportunity to shop around for the best deal and they purchase a significant amount of a product. Suppliers are powerful if there are few suppliers of a good or service, as the buyer is denied the opportunity to shop around for a good deal.

4 According to Porter there are four competitive strategies: cost leadership, selling a standard product to a mass market; differentiation, selling an added-value product to a mass market; cost focus, selling a low-cost product to a niche market; and differentiation focus, selling an added-value product to a niche market.

5 Gilbert and Strebel argue that there are only two constituents of competitive advantage: lower delivered cost and higher perceived value, which can be used in combination to give a company a superior position in an industry or sector.

Learning outcomes for case studies

While reading this chapter and engaging in the activities, you should have learned how to apply theory and models, analyse situations, and evaluate the application and analysis you undertake. The learning outcomes specified below outline the type of application, analysis and evaluation of which you should be capable in relation to organisations. The case studies and the questions which follow provide an opportunity for you to test how well you have achieved the learning outcomes for the ethical issues and exit case studies for this chapter.

Application	Check you have achieved this by	
1 Identify the competitive strategies employed by an organisation to help it achieve success	applying Porter's generic competitive strategies to an organisation and its products	answering ethical case study question 2
Analysis	**Check you have achieved this by**	
1 Analyse the competitive environment of an organisation or industry	undertaking a five forces analysis of a competitive environment	answering exit case study question 1 and ethical case study question 1
Evaluation	**Check you have achieved this by**	
1 Evaluate the success of competitive strategy	critically judging the activities of an organisation	answering ethical case study question 3
2 Evaluate the effect of similar activities by companies operating in a fiercely competitive environment	assessing the impact of the same competitive moves by a number of companies in the same industry	answering exit case study question 2
3 Evaluate the impact of a reduction in regulation in a marketplace	explaining the likely outcome if regulation in an industry is significantly reduced	answering exit case study question 3

ETHICAL ISSUES CASE STUDY 10.2

FT

Ja! Organic wins fans

By Delia Meth-Cohn

There is little to praise about Austria's supermarkets. Aside from a few flagship stores, they are small, unfriendly and poorly stocked. But in one respect, the country's largest, the Billa chain, has long been the envy of Europe's food retail giants.

While they struggled to persuade people to pay extra for organic food, Billa launched an organic brand in 1994 that quickly became part of its standard range.

Ja! Natrlich (Yes! Naturally) was the brainchild of Werner Lampert, who started his working life as an importer of organic lemons His idea was to change people's image of organic food: instead of being something for wealthy muesli-eaters, he transformed it into good-quality food at reasonable prices.

Now, Ja! Natrlich has signed up almost 40 per cent of Austria's organic farmers, carries more than 300 products and is the most profitable part of Billa.

Part of Mr Lampert's success was down to clever marketing. But he faced a much easier task than his foreign rivals. Thanks to nature and government funding, Austria was the perfect place to source organic food.

Steep alpine pastures meant that intensive farming was never widespread, but farmers started converting to organic methods en masse in the mid-1990s, drawn by special subsidies and the promise of premium prices. In the 10 years to 1999, the number of organic farmers grew from fewer than 1000 to 20 000, putting over 10 per cent of Austrian farmland into organic hands. The EU average, despite massive growth, is around 2 per cent.

Ja! Natrlich has also played a significant role in making sure that organic farms stay in business. Its 7000 farmers are on five-year contracts, giving them a guaranteed market at a guaranteed price. The company has bought up dairies, mills and slaughterhouses to process organic products exclusively.

It has been particularly successful in the province of Salzburg, where it has 2000 farmers signed up. In Tirol, where it has not been active, the number of organic farms has fallen steeply over the past two years, largely because processors refused to pay premium prices.

Balancing supply and demand is a key to steady growth, says Alexandra Pohl, of Austria's Bio-Club, which represents most organic farm associations. If farmers cannot market their products properly they can't afford to stay organic.

In solving that problem, Ja! Natrlich has created enemies in the organic community. Some are opposed to mass marketing per se and mourn the demise of traditional health-food shops. Others worry that Billa's dominance is putting pressure on prices.

But Billa will not be a monopoly for long. Its main rival, Spar, has introduced its own 'natural' brand, ensuring that organic food will stay in the mainstream.

Source: *Financial Times*, 29 October 2001. Reprinted with permission.

Questions for ethical issues case study 10.2

1 Assess the competitive environment in which the organic food brand Ja! Natrlich competes.

2 Identify and explain the competitive strategies which Billa has employed to ensure the success of Ja! Natrlich.

3 Evaluate Billa's actions to date and assess whether they are adequate enough to stave off the competition from Spar.

The fragrance industry

By Claire Capon

The fragrance industry is one of France's largest and most well-known glamour image industries, along with champagne and fashion. Consequently France tops the table of perfume users, with French women splashing out an average annual spend of £36 on perfume, more than double that of her British counterpart.

The fine fragrances sold by companies like Chanel, Yves Saint Laurent and Givenchy are likely to begin life in Grasse in Provence in southern France. It is here that 30 member companies of the 70-strong Syndicat National des Fabricants de Produits Aromatiques are based. These companies specialise in raw material extraction, perfumery compounds and food flavourings. Some of them are owned by large multinationals such as Rhône-Poulenc or Bayer and others are family run and retain their independence. The companies extract essential oils from raw ingredients like jasmine, with the oils fitting into one of seven fragrance families: citrus, flower, fougere, chypre, wood, amber or leather.[11] The companies in Grasse develop fragrances for the perfume houses by blending the oils together. However, they undertake this product development work for free and only get paid if they win a contract with a fragrance house. The chances of winning a contract are one in ten.

A fragrance house will spend very large sums of money to develop and launch a perfume on the marketplace. Dior spent £40m on developing its Dolce Vita fragrance in the mid-1990s, with a £2.5m advertising campaign in the UK alone in its first year on the market.

The world's bestselling women's perfume is Chanel No 5, with retail sales of $130m in 1996. It is estimated that the sales of perfume and aftershave worldwide will top $21bn by the year 2000.[12] Therefore it is not surprising that relationships between the French government and France's fragrance industry are good, with the fragrance industry proving effective at lobbying the government on its own behalf. The French government is in turn effective at lobbying and influencing the European parliament and associated bodies on behalf of French industries, including the fragrance industry. As a result, the French fragrance industry is in a strong position and some of the large fragrance houses, like Givenchy and Yves Saint Laurent, have selective distribution arrangements that have been approved by the European Commission. The fragrance industry claims it sells images of glamour, passion, fantasy and exclusivity, which have taken the established fragrance houses 40 years to create and hence require selective distribution to protect the image that is being sold and to ensure that it remains up-market and exclusive.

These selective distribution agreements are implemented by the fragrance houses, who decide which retailers will stock and sell their brands of perfume and aftershave. A fragrance house will assess a retailer on a series of criteria covering staff training, lighting, ambience, location, size of windows, shelf arrangements and the quality of floor coverings. These are all considered to contribute to the image of the fine fragrance in the mind of the consumer.

In the UK up-market perfume and aftershave are typically sold by retailers such as Boots, House of Fraser, John Lewis and Debenhams. Boots is the market leader with 30–35 per cent market share. Fine fragrances are defined as perfume, eau de parfum, eau de toilette, eau de Cologne and aftershave lotion retailing at more than £15 per 50ml bottle.

However, in 1992 retailers such as Superdrug, Pound-strecher and What Everyone Wants started to sell fine perfume and aftershave like Chanel No 5, Aramis and Giorgio at lower prices. This was viewed as a threat to the profitability of both the fragrance houses and the usual high-street retailers. The costs and profit associated with the production of a bottle of perfume and aftershave costing £30 in the high street breaks down as follows: retailer – £12; tax – £5.13; fragrance house – £10.59 (to cover advertising, marketing, packaging and profits); perfume and aftershave – £2.28. The practice of department stores offering luxury gifts free when a purchase of a particular brand of perfume or aftershave is made also reinforces the existence of high profit margins for the retailers.

The major fragrance houses refused to supply retailers such as Superdrug on the basis that their shops, when assessed, failed to meet the criteria discussed above. The shops were thus defined as down-market and unsuitable for the retailing of fine perfume and aftershave. However, Superdrug was making considerable investment in modernising its stores and installing special fragrance counters with dedicated staff, and it continued to gain supplies of fine perfume and aftershave from the grey market; not illegal, just unauthorised. Supplies of an up-market fragrance are usually leaked on to the grey market at one of three points in the distribution chain. A manufacturer that has been commissioned to produce perfume or aftershave for a company like Chanel or Dior may over-produce and dispose of the surplus on the grey market, hence allowing an unapproved retailer or middleman to buy directly from the manufacturer. Over-production is difficult to police, particularly if there are several manufacturing sites spread across the world. Alternatively, the approved wholesaler may order too much stock and sell the surplus to an unapproved retailer or a grey market trader. The third possibility is that an approved retailer over-orders and is prepared to sell the surplus on the grey market. This allows companies like Superdrug or the supermarkets to acquire fine fragrances at a cut price and therefore to sell them at a price under-cutting the approved retailers.

The dispute between Superdrug and the fragrance houses centred on the selective distribution arrangements agreed with the European Commission. Therefore in late 1992 Superdrug complained to the Office of Fair Trading that it should be allowed to sell fine fragrances at dis-counted prices and as such should be supplied through the normal channels via the fragrance houses and their distributors. Superdrug submitted a 200-page report in support of its case, which outlined the alleged dis-crimination that it felt it was facing. This alleged dis-crimination related to two issues: the refusal of fragrance houses to supply Superdrug with perfume and aftershave, and the refusal of major newspapers (*Sunday Times* and *Observer*) and magazines (*Vogue*, *Marie Claire* and *Woman's Journal*) to carry Superdrug's advertisements for fear of losing lucrative advertising revenues from the fragrance houses.

The Office of Fair Trading, concerned that the selective distribution arrangements used by the fragrance houses might have been resulting in lack of competition and high retail prices, decided that there was a case to answer and referred it to the Monopolies and Mergers Commission for a full six- to nine-month investigation. The Monopolies and Mergers Commission issued its report in November 1993 and stated that a complex monopoly existed in the fine fragrance market, but that it was not acting against public interest.

The power of manufacturers of fine fragrances was reinforced in 1996 when the European Commission extended until 1999 the regulations allowing selective distribution of certain goods, including fine fragrances.[13] In December 1996 the European Court of First Instance also ruled in favour of Yves Saint Laurent and Givenchy against the French supermarket chain Leclerc. Leclerc argued that the criteria used by the fragrance houses for selecting outlets for its fine fragrances excluded all Leclerc stores and discriminated against new methods of distribution, i.e. multi-product stores. The court ruled that Yves Saint Laurent and Givenchy needed to be able to preserve the consumers perception of the product as one with the 'aura of luxury and exclusivity'.[14]

Questions for exit case study 10.3

1 By applying Porter's five forces of competition model, assess the nature of competition in:

- the fine fragrance industry (Chanel, Givenchy, Dior);
- the retailing of fine fragrance industry (Superdrug, Boots).

2 How does the launch of Glow by J. Lo and the use of celebrities by fine fragrance companies impact on the competitive environment they face? The use of celebrities includes Catherine Zeta-Jones as the face of ardenbeauty perfume, Sophie Dahl for Yves Saint Laurent's Opium perfume and Penelope Cruz for Ralph Lauren's Glamourous perfume.

3 If the selective distribution agreement for fine fragrances is abolished, what will be the likely effect on companies such as Chanel, Yves Saint Laurent, Dior and Givenchy?

For more case studies please visit www.booksites.net/capon

Short-answer questions

1   Define an internal dependency.

2   Define a transactional dependency.

3   Define causal texture.

4   Name three bodies regulating competition in the UK.

5   Name the two bodies which regulate the rail network in the UK.

6   Name the new regulatory body which becomes operational in late 2003.

7   Name the regulatory body which regulates the quality of drinking water.

8   Name Porter's five forces of competition.

9   Specify three factors making an industry attractive to new entrants.

10   List three factors making substitute products or services a threat.

11   Specify three factors strengthening a buyer's power.

12   List three factors strengthening a supplier's power.

13   Which of Porter's generic competitive strategies can be used to target a niche market?

14   Define competitive advantage.

15   According to Porter, how many competitive strategies does a firm need to follow to achieve competitive advantage?

Learning outcomes for assignment questions

While reading this chapter and engaging in the activities, you should have learned how to apply theory and models, analyse situations, and evaluate the application and analysis you undertake. The learning outcomes specified below outline what you should be able to do and the assignment questions provide an opportunity for you to test how well you have achieved the learning outcomes for this chapter.

Application	Check you have achieved this by	
1 Demonstrate the nature of competition faced by organisations	applying Porter's five forces of competition to a variety of organisations	answering assignment questions 1, 2 & 3
Analysis	**Check you have achieved this by**	
1 Analyse the competition faced by organisations	comparing and contrasting the nature of competition faced by different companies in the same industry	answering assignment questions 1, 2 & 3
Evaluation	**Check you have achieved this by**	
1 Evaluate the impact of environmental linkages on a selection of organisations	critically judging the effect of Emery and Trist's linkages on organisations	answering assignment question 2
2 Evaluate the effect of changes in competition on an industry	critically judging the relevance of competitive changes in an industry	answering assignment question 3

Assignment questions

1 Choose a private-sector industry that delivers a service to members of the public and analyse the competition in the industry by use of Porter's five force of competition. Select three companies in your chosen industry and discuss the competitive strategies they follow. Present your findings in a 2000-word report.

2 Consider the universities and colleges in the town or city nearest to where you live. Assess the nature of competition between these colleges and universities by use of Porter's five forces of competition. Determine whether the university or college that you attend is influenced or affected by Emery and Trist's linkages. Present your findings in a 2000-word report.

3 Research the deregulation of the domestic fuel market for gas and electricity from 1997 to 2003. Write a report that:

■ identifies changes in the regulation of the marketplace for domestic fuel that occurred between 1997 and 2003;

■ identifies changes in the companies providing domestic fuel which occurred between 1997 and 2003;

■ evaluates the effect of these changes on competition in the domestic fuel market.

Weblinks available online at www.booksites.net/capon

1 These are the weblinks for two important bodies in the regulation of the UK economy.
Office of Fair Trading (OFT) http://www.oft.gov.uk
Competition Commission (CC) http://www.competition-commission.org.uk

2 These are the weblinks for the regulatory authorities for some of the privatised sectors.
Office of Telecommunications (OFTEL) http://www.oftel.gov.uk
Office of Communications http://www.ofcom.org.uk/
Office of Gas and Electricity Markets (OFGEM) http://www.ofgem.gov.uk
Office of Water Services (OFWAT) http://www.ofwat.gov.uk
Strategic Rail Authority http://www.sra.gov.uk
Office of the Rail Regulator http://www.rail-reg.gov.uk

3 The following weblink to the Competition Commission's website provides the web addresses for other regulatory bodies in the UK and for overseas regulatory bodies in Europe, North America and Australasia.
http://www.competition-commission.org.uk/about/links1.htm

Further reading

Bell, E (1998) 'Winner takes all', *Management Today*, September.

Brown, K (1999) 'Competition policy could find it tougher to cut prices than win friendly headlines', *Financial Times*, 12 March.

Collis, D J and Montgomery, C A (1998) 'Creating corporate advantage', *Harvard Business Review*, May/June.

Johnson, G and Scholes, K (2002) *Exploring Corporate Strategy*, 6th edn, Chapter 3, Harlow: Financial Times Prentice Hall.

Jones, I W and Pollitt, M G (1998) 'Ethical and unethical competition: establishing the rules of engagement', *Long Range Planning*, 31 (5), October.

Lynch, R (2003) *Corporate Strategy*, 3rd edn, Chapter 4, Harlow: Financial Times Prentice Hall.

Lynn, M (1999) 'Can nice guys finish first?', *Management Today*, February.

Moore, K (1998) 'Power struggle', *Management Today*, February.

Porter, M E (1979) 'How competitive forces shape strategy', *Harvard Business Review*, March/April.

Rivette, K G and Kline, D (2000) 'Discovering new value in intellectual property', *Harvard Business Review*, January/February.

Rooney, B (2002) 'How to negotiate', *Management Today*, June.

Saunders, A (2002) 'The new skymasters', *Management Today*, September.

Thompson, J L (2001) *Strategic Management: Awareness and Change*, 4th edn, Chapter 8, London: Thomson Learning.

Thurlby, B (1998) 'Competitive forces are also subject to change', *Management Decision*, 36 (1).

Trueman, M and Jobber, D (1998) 'Competing through design', *Long Range Planning*, 31 (4), August.

Vickers, G (2000) 'The new music men', *Management Today*, June.

Wheatley, M (1998) 'Seven secrets of effective supply chains', *Management Today*, June.

References

1 Emery, F E and Trist, E L (1965) 'The causal texture of organisational environments', *Human Relations*, 18: 21–32.

2 BBC1, *Breakfast News*, 2 March 1999.

3 Edgecliffe-Johnson, A (1999) 'NY trade in luxuries becomes a victim', *Financial Times*, 6/7 March.

4 http://roof.ccta.gov.uk/ofwat/rolereg.htm.

5 Ibid.

6 Porter, M E (1985) *Competitive Advantage*, New York: Free Press.

7 Ibid.

8 Ibid.

9 Gilbert, D and Strebel, P (1988) 'Developing competitive advantage', in Quinn, J B, Mintzberg, H and James, R M (eds) *The Strategy Process*, Harlow: Prentice Hall.

10 IKEA catalogue 98, Inter IKEA Systems BV, 1997.

11 Harrington, C (1996) 'Heavenly scents', *Independent*, 20 July.

12 Rawsthorn, A (1997) 'Fragrant rival fails to outsell No 5', *Financial Times*, 25 January.

13 Pickard, S (1997) 'Message in a bottle', *Financial Times*, 11 February.

14 Tucker, E and Oram, R (1996) 'EU delays end of exclusive agreement', *Financial Times*, 15 October.

Stakeholder and SWOT analyses

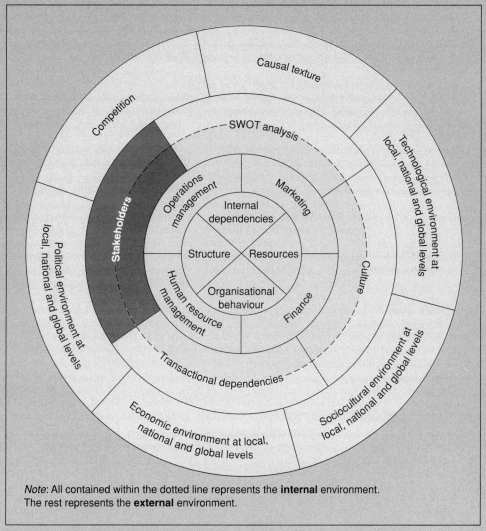

Note: All contained within the dotted line represents the **internal** environment. The rest represents the **external** environment.

Figure 11.1 Organisational context model

➡️ **ENTRY CASE STUDY 11.1**   **FT**

Business keeps rolling

By Nicholas Lander

Rolling out is the phrase employed at present by restaurateurs keen to exploit the growing interest in eating out.

Crucially, 'rolling out' involves finding a central – but not prime – location to attract a seven-day-a-week clientele; creating a friendly, unobtrusive interior design with a bar; and writing a medium-priced menu – say around £20 for three courses – that has a catch-all feel.

Once you decide to 'roll out' a restaurant, you can roll on. Oliver Peyton opened his micro-brewery and restaurant, Mash & Air, in Manchester last December and will open another in Great Portland Street, London W1, early next year.

Jean-Christophe Novelli opened his first restaurant in Clerkenwell, east London, and then moved west to open Novelli W8 in Notting Hill. He is branching out on a global scale next month when he opens a Maison Novelli in Constantia, South Africa.

Antony Worrall Thompson recently opened Woz, in Ladbroke Grove, where a five-course fixed dinner costs £22.50. Once the restaurant has been fine-tuned he hopes to open other sites around London.

However, in spite of a buoyant market, success is not guaranteed. When Cindy Pawlcyn and her partners in the successful Real Restaurants Group decided to move their style of California cooking to the midwest, they encountered insurmountable obstacles. 'We could not find the right ingredients, the right cooks or the right management,' Pawlcyn confessed.

Such is the confidence in London at present that two restaurant groups have opened prototype restaurants with a view to 'rolling them out' around the UK. The first, MPW, bears the initials of Marco Pierre White and is part of his joint venture company with Granada; the second, Zinc, is the mid-price offering from the Conran restaurant group.

The service at MPW left a lot to be desired. My colleague, a former chef, had already described it as 'minus two' by the time we had ordered. From the door we had spotted two waiters eating hurriedly behind the bar; the receptionist failed to explain that different menus were in operation – one on the terrace, the other in the main restaurant – and we had to ask for bread.

The cause, if not the explanation, was that MPW had served 140 customers during lunch. White has infused the chef, talented, peripatetic Gary Hollihead, and the kitchen staff with honourable intentions.

The menu offers a wide range of predominantly French classic dishes (one of which, pajarski of salmon, an up-market fishcake, my colleague had not seen on a menu for at least 10 years), at reasonable prices. But the delivery at MPW must get better.

There are 16 starters ranging from Escargot Chablis to a galantine of duck with Cumberland sauce; 12 fish dishes, including the rarely seen trout *au bleu* (sic) and a fresh shrimp omelette; and six meat main courses.

Our two starters, risotto of girolles and hot asparagus with a gleaming mousseline sauce, were well executed and proved far more enjoyable than the smoked haddock Monte Carlo and calves liver *à l'anglaise* which followed – after a considerable longueur.

The pleasure of sitting outside Zinc on almost pedestrianised Heddon Street on a bright sunny day proved transitory. We had just ordered our drinks as a truck crammed with scaffolding arrived to our left, while to our right came the joyful noise of hammers, saws and drills working on what will soon be a theme pub.

Unlike MPW's menu, Zinc's is written in designer-faded typewriter script, contains no surprises and is lacking in imagination. It is standard fare at standard prices. Starters include smoked salmon (£5), crab cake (£4.75) and *terrine de campagne* (£3.75). Middle courses include Caesar salad (£5.95), steak sandwich (£7.50) or a club sandwich at £6.95. Main courses range from fish and chips (£7.50) to rib of beef (£11.50) and sausage and mash (£6.50).

Zinc also serves its own version of a lobster club sandwich (£9.95), an idea created in New York by Anne Rosenzweig, chef/owner of Arcadia, where it became a great favourite of Sotheby's chairman, Alfred Taubman.

Source: Financial Times, 25 October 1997. Reprinted with permission.

Introduction

This chapter examines two further tools which can be used for analysing an organisation, namely stakeholder analysis and SWOT analysis.

Stakeholders are any individual or a collection of individuals with an **interest** in an organisation. Some stakeholders will be internal to an organisation and others will be external. Internal stakeholders include employees, managers, directors, trade unions and shareholders. External stakeholders include suppliers, customers, competitors, financiers, government and the general public. Various categories of stakeholder will affect or be affected by the organisation in diverse ways, hence stakeholders have different interests or stakes in the organisation. This is shown in Table 11.1.

Stakeholders are also able to influence an organisation to act in their best interests. However, the interests of different stakeholder groups will vary and

**Table 11.1
Stakeholders' power and interest**

Internal stakeholders	Stakeholder interests are:	Stakeholder power arises from:
Employees Managers Directors	• security of employment • wage levels • fringe benefits • responsibility • promotion prospects • working conditions	• job grade or title • position in organisational hierarchy • personal reputation • departmental reputation
Trade unions	• number of union members in the organisation • same as its members (*see* list in box above)	• number of union members • nature of bargaining (local or national)
Shareholders	• profit levels • size of dividend payments • capital growth in share price	• number of shares held
External stakeholders		
Suppliers	• size and value of contracts • speed of invoice payment	• location and availability of other suppliers
Customers	• quality of goods and services available • prices and payment terms	• location of other suppliers • quality of goods and services offered by other suppliers • prices and payment terms offered by other suppliers
Competition	• quality of goods and services available • prices and payment terms	• behaviour of other competitors
Financiers	• how promptly repayment of large and short-term loans occurs	• offering better deal (improved quality or better prices and payment terms)
Government	• payment of corporation tax • implementation of legislation (e.g. competition and employment legislation)	• enforcing the legislation via the legal system if necessary

may even conflict with each other. For example, employees may seek high wages and above-inflation pay rises, while customers would prefer lower prices and lower costs, which are not possible if labour costs are high. The interests of stakeholders in an organisation and the way in which **power** is exercised by stakeholders are shown in Table 11.1.

SWOT analysis, which we look at later in this chapter, provides an overview of the essential issues faced by an organisation and is concerned with identifying and evaluating:

- the ability of an organisation to use its **strengths** and **weaknesses** to operate successfully in its external environment;
- the influence of the external environment (**threats** and **opportunities**) on an organisation.

Stakeholders and the organisation

An organisation's stakeholders will be important for an assortment of reasons and to varying degrees, therefore different stakeholders will respond to the organisation and its behaviour in different ways. Stakeholders whose interests and expectations are met will tend to remain with the organisation. Unsatisfied stakeholders will leave or remain and use their sources of power in an attempt to persuade the organisation to meet their expectations or interests.

Stakeholders who experience a high level of satisfaction with an organisation will tend to demonstrate loyalty and choose to retain their position as stakeholders. For example, employees who feel that their well-paid jobs are secure and offer future prospects are likely to remain with that employer. In contrast, stakeholders who are disappointed with the organisation and its behaviour are more likely to relinquish their stake. The likelihood of an unhappy stakeholder withdrawing their stake in an organisation is increased if better opportunities and potentially greater satisfaction appear to be available by acquiring a similar stake in a different organisation. For example, shareholders in a company who feel that they are not gaining a good enough return on their investment may decide to sell their shares and invest the money in a company that will give a better level of return.

Alternatively, stakeholders who are unhappy with the organisation may decide to remain and attempt to change things. Unsatisfied shareholders may decide to try to influence changes to the organisation's leadership and strategies, with the aim of benefiting in the long run. To achieve this they will have to be able to exert the necessary amount of influence on planning and decision making within the organisation. This requires a suitable combination of authority, determination and ability. It is usually large institutional investors who stand the best chance of being successful with this type of approach, as they have greater power than smaller investors.

Analysing stakeholders

The analysis of stakeholders involves identifying who they are and considering their power and interest with regard to the organisation. Stakeholders can be identified by brainstorming and shown on a stakeholder diagram – *see* Figure 11.2. Once identified, the relative power and interest of the stakeholders can be mapped onto a power and interest matrix – *see* Figure 11.3.[1] Additionally this analysis can be extended to consider the reaction, behaviour and position of stakeholders if a particular strategy or plan were to be implemented by the organisation.

Stakeholders with high power and high interest (category D)

Stakeholders with high power and high interest are key players in the organisation and are often involved in managing the organisation and its future. If key players are not directly involved in managing the organisation, it is vital that they are given serious consideration in the development of long-term

Figure 11.2 Stakeholder diagram

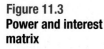

**Figure 11.3
Power and interest
matrix**

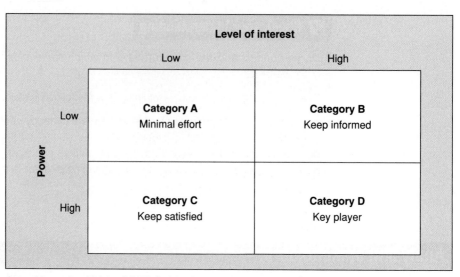

Source: Johnson, G and Scholes, K (1999) *Exploring Corporate Strategy*, 5th edition, Prentice Hall Europe. Reprinted with permission.

plans and the future direction of the organisation, as they have the power to block proposed plans and implement their own alternative agenda.

Stakeholders with high power and low interest (category C)

Stakeholders with high power and low interest are those who must be kept satisfied, for example institutional shareholders. Institutional shareholders will often remain compliant while they receive acceptable returns on their investment and are pleased with the organisation's management and activities. However, the ability of category C stakeholders to reposition themselves on the power and interest matrix into category D and become stakeholders with a continuing high degree of power and an increase in their level of interest should not be under-estimated. This occurs when category C stakeholders are not kept satisfied and feel that their interests are not being best served. Hence stakeholders with high power and low interest will increase their level of interest to make sure that their interests are met. The shift in position of unsatisfied category C stakeholders may impede an organisation's plans and prevent the expectations of key players or category D stakeholders from being met as expected.

Therefore a canny organisation will ensure that the expectations of category C stakeholders are well met and the necessary adjustments made to meet changing expectations arising as the current issues facing the organisation change. This helps ensure that category C stakeholders do not feel that their interests are being marginalised at the expense of the interests of key players, category D stakeholders. Hence the repositioning of category C stakeholders should not be an unexpected occurrence if they are managed appropriately. This requires a good working relationship and open channels of communication to be developed between category C stakeholders, the organisation and key players or category D stakeholders.

Stakeholders with low power and high interest (category B)

The stakeholders in category B are those with low power and high interest, who are able to exert relatively little power in influencing the organisation and its actions. However, these stakeholders have a high level of interest in the organisation and will voice their concerns if that interest is not being considered in a suitable manner. If category B stakeholders voice their concerns loudly enough and in the right way, e.g. via lobbying or petitions, they may be able to influence one of the powerful group of stakeholders in either category C or D and affect their behaviour. Therefore organisations need to keep category B stakeholders informed of the organisation's activities and decisions and in doing so convince them that their interests are being taken into account and considered seriously.

Stakeholders with low power and low interest (category A)

Stakeholders with low power and low interest are those in whom the organisation need invest only minimal effort. However, category A stakeholders should not be ignored as they may acquire a stake in the organisation by becoming, for example, a customer, supplier or competitor, which will mean an increased level of interest and/or power.

The Automobile Association and its stakeholders

It should be recognised that the position of stakeholders on the power and interest matrix is dynamic and will vary over time according to the current issues that the stakeholders are considering. The situation in which the Automobile Association (AA) found itself during April 1999 provides a good example of an organisation with groups of stakeholders who line up in a certain way due to a particular issue, in this case demutualisation.

The AA was founded in 1905 and by 1999 held around half the motor breakdown market, a market that was experiencing significant change. These changes included the acquisition of Green Flag by Cendant, the entry of the insurance company Direct Line into the market, and the RAC's expected trade sale or flotation. Therefore in April 1999 the AA considered its options with regard to retaining its mutual status or demutualising. It was rumoured that Ford had informally approached the AA with a takeover offer that would end the latter's mutual status. Other interested bidders were thought to include Centrica and a number of venture capitalists. The then Director-General of the AA, John Maxwell, initiated a strategic review to allow the AA to assess its options. The options available included demutualisation, a joint venture with a suitable partner or takeover by another company. The merchant bank Schroders was advising the AA.

In 1999 the AA had annual sales of around £600 million from its businesses, which included roadside service, publications and driving schools, and its value was estimated to be between £1 billion and £1.5 billion. Pursuit of the demutualisation option and stock-market flotation would give each full member of the AA a moderate windfall of £200–250. In 1999 the AA had 9.5 million members, of which 4.3 million were full-paying members who would receive the windfall payouts. However, excluded from the demutualisation windfall were the 1.7 million associate members, including the families of full-paying members who benefit from the association's services, and the 3.5 million members who are drivers of fleet cars with AA cover and drivers who received their AA membership as part of a package when purchasing a car.

The AA and stakeholders with high power and high interest (category D)

The key players were the Director-General of the AA and his immediate management team carrying out the strategic review, as well as the full members of the AA – *see* Figure 11.4. John Maxwell and his management team were key players with high power and high interest, as their planning and decision making would determine their future with the AA, the future of the AA, the future of those who worked for the AA, and the future of AA members. The full members would collectively decide whether the AA was to demutualise. They might have chosen to support any demutualisation recommendations made by John Maxwell and his team, or to reject them in favour of a bidder, such as Ford, buying the AA. The full members, for example, might have decided this if they were to lose confidence in John Maxwell and his management team and their ability to carry out the demutualisation successfully. Alternatively, full members might have taken the following view, expressed by one of their number in the press in April 1999:

> I got my membership when I bought a much-loved but temperamental MG Midget. If the AA does choose to demutualise, I would hope they would pay a differential for members who have been with the AA longer. I might vote in favour of the move if they were going to pay me a £300 windfall but the down-side could be that if they become a corporate commercial entity, the cost of its services could soar.[2]

Figure 11.4 Power and interest matrix for the Automobile Association (AA)

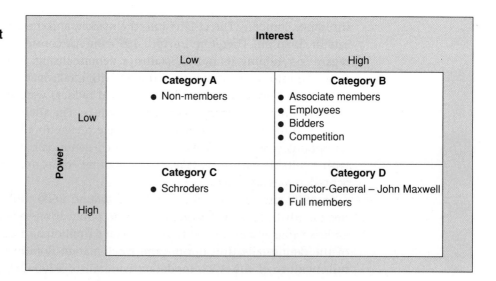

The AA and stakeholders with high power and low interest (category C)

The merchant bank Schroders was a category C stakeholder, as it had relatively little interest in whether the AA finally decided to demutualise. However, while in the position of corporate adviser to the AA, it was relatively powerful as it was able to advise and potentially influence John Maxwell and his management team.

The AA and stakeholders with low power and high interest (category B)

The category B stakeholders, those with high interest and low power in the demutualisation issue, included associate members and employees. The associate members clearly had a high interest in whether or not the AA decided to demutualise. The primary concerns for associate members were the effect of demutualisation on the services they received and the cost of associate membership. However, as non-voting members, associates had no direct power to influence the outcome of any ballot on demutualisation. Equally, employees had a high interest in the future of the AA and would be concerned as to the effects of demutualisation. Potential effects of demutualisation could have included the AA becoming more competitive and this being achieved via cost cutting and job losses. However, employees had no direct role in the ballot and would ultimately have to accept its outcome.

The **stakeholder matrix** suggests that category B stakeholders, high interest and low power, have to be kept informed, which is true of stakeholder groups such as associate members and employees. In April 1999, the AA kept its members and employees informed by issuing the following statement to the media and via answerphones in its own offices:

> The AA has always kept an open mind about its structure as it pursues its prime purpose: to serve the best interests of its members. No decisions have been made in this respect.

However, also with high interest and low power were other stakeholders like potential bidders such as Ford and competitors like Direct Line and Green Flag. These were external stakeholders with a great deal of interest in what the AA would eventually decide to do, as their business and the marketplace in which they operated would be directly influenced by that decision. Any organisation should be aware that any information it releases with the intention of keeping stakeholders such as employees and associate members informed will be in the public arena and therefore available to stakeholders such as competitors and potential bidders.

The AA and stakeholders with low power and low interest (category A)

The category A stakeholders are those with low power and low interest. For the AA, non-members fell into this category. They were unable to receive breakdown services from the organisation and had no influence over its demutualisation decision. However, it should be recognised that stakeholders' power and influence can alter over time. The opportunity of a £200–250 windfall might have encouraged some non-members to become members and move to category D, high interest and high power. This was perfectly possible, as the AA made it clear that it was not closing its doors to new members, nor was it expecting to distinguish between long-term and short-term full members:

> The AA has no intention of bringing the shutters down on membership. Everyone is as free to join the AA as they were before.[3]

> There is no distinction made among full members.[4]

If the number of new full members joining had been very large and there was no differentiation between new and longer-term members, the value of the windfall paid to full members could have decreased. This could have pushed longer-term full members to seek to lobby or influence John Maxwell and his management team to distinguish between long- and short-term members.

Stakeholder alliances and coalitions

When analysing stakeholders, two points should be noted. First, people and organisations may belong to more than one category of stakeholder. Second, stakeholders and organisations may depend on one another, with the nature of the dependency varying according to the amount of power and/or interest the stakeholder has in the organisation. For example, if the Director-General of the AA favoured demutualisation, he would have depended on the full-time members voting in large enough numbers for the demutualisation proposals. However, he would have needed to recognise that full members might have been subject to influence by associate members, who may have been related to full members, e.g. husband and wife. Similarly, some employees (category B) were also full members of the AA and how they were treated and informed as employees might have influenced their voting behaviour as full members. The employees might have felt that cost cutting and job losses were likely to result from demutualisation. Hence they might have lobbied and sought to influence the voting full members to vote against a change in the AA's structure or to vote for a takeover rather than demutualisation if they thought their best interests would be served in this way. Equally, if associate members were concerned about the service they received and its cost, they might have sought to influence full voting members, which would perhaps have been easy if the full voting members were family members. In addition, associate members and employees might have sought to influence John Maxwell and his management team directly, via letter-writing campaigns and petitions.

Therefore the arguments in favour of demutualisation had to focus on the benefits for full members (cash windfall and service levels at least maintained, preferably improved in some way), associate members (service levels at least maintained, preferably improved in some way), and employees, particularly those who were also full members (issues of job security and future operation of the AA for employees were crucial).

The members of the AA were balloted in August 1999 on the proposed sale of the AA to Centrica. The result of the ballot was announced in mid-September 1999 and showed 67 per cent of eligible members voted and 96 per cent of them voted in favour of the sale. The sale to Centrica was completed in July 2000 for £1.1 billion.

Do you understand the nature of stakeholders' power and interest?

Check your understanding by answering the following questions.

(a) A production operative has more power than a senior manager. True or false?

(b) A corporate investor is more powerful than an individual investor. True or false?

(c) The government is usually a stakeholder with low power and low interest in an organisation. True or false?

(d) The interest of a small individual customer is not high. True or false?

SWOT analysis and the organisation

SWOT stands for strengths, weaknesses, opportunities and threats, and analysis of these gives an overview of the position an organisation finds itself in, vis à via its external environment. The strengths and weaknesses of an organisation arise from its internal environment, namely resourses and their use, structure, culture and the tasks carried out by the four functions of business (marketing, operations management, finance and HRM) – refer to Chapters 4, 5, 6 and 7 respectively. Which strengths an organisation decides to build on and which weaknesses it seeks to minimise depends on the impact of opportunities and threats from the external environment. The identification of external influences on an organisation is aided by the use of PEST analysis, LoNGPEST analysis, competitor analysis and market analysis – refer to Chapters 8, 9, 10 and 4 respectively. Once the external influences on an organisation have been identified, they can then be judged to be either a threat or opportunity and be dealt with or taken advantage of as appropriate.

Strengths

A strength is a competence, valuable resource or attribute that an organisation uses to exploit opportunities in the external environment or to help it counter threats from the external environment. Strengths could include a resource such as a well-motivated and skilled workforce, with low turnover, or an attribute such as a strongly established brand image or reputation. Examples include Cadbury's Dairy Milk brand and Marks and Spencer's reputation for good quality.

■ Stakeholders and key success factors

Customers are stakeholders in an organisation and fulfilling **key success factors** involves the organisation in meeting the needs and expectations of its customers and other stakeholders (*see* earlier in this chapter). For example, a key success factor may be a good relationship with a reliable supplier. This will be especially true if the supplier is the only supplier or one of very few supplying a key component or part. Meeting the key success factors will require the organisation to meet the supplier's expectations, which will include regular orders of a certain minimum size, with little room for negotiation on price if the supplier is powerful.

In seeking to satisfy stakeholders, especially customers, while at the same time outperforming competitors, organisations should seek to:

- fulfil the key success factors for the industry or market;
- develop competencies that provide competitive advantage (*see* discussion on competitive advantage and premium prices);
- utilise competencies to meet the requirements of specific customers and aim to charge a premium price.

■ Competitive advantage and premium prices

Competitive advantage arises from the unique features or 'extras' that a product or service possesses and for which customers are prepared to pay a higher or premium price. For example, some dry cleaners offer a standard service and a gold service. The standard service includes dry cleaning the item of clothing, pressing it by machine and returning the item to its owner on a cheap hanger with a polythene cover over it. In contrast, the gold service includes dry cleaning the garment, hand pressing and finishing it before it is returned to its owner on a more robust hanger and in a more substantial plastic cover. There will be a small group of customers who will be prepared to pay a higher or premium price for the extras that the gold service provides. Being able to offer the gold service will give the dry cleaner a competitive advantage over nearby dry cleaners who do not offer this service.

Weaknesses

A weakness is defined as lacking a competence, resource or attribute that an organisation needs to perform better than its competitors in the external environment. A company producing tableware for the domestic and catering markets will rely in part on styling and designs to make products appealing to customers. If it relies on the designs that have always been used or occasionally on shopfloor staff coming up with new patterns, it is likely to lack competence in design, a key success factor for the tableware industry. The lack of a key resource, such as a new piece of technologically advanced equipment, is also a weakness, particularly if your competitors have access to that equipment.

Opportunities

Opportunities are openings or chances in the external environment or market-place that an organisation may pursue to obtain benefits. The identification of a new geographic market in North America for a firm's products is an opportunity. Such opportunities can be exploited by manufacturing the product in the firm's home country and exporting it to North America, or by forming a strategic alliance with a local US company and having the benefits of the greater understanding of the local and national external environment offered by that partner in the strategic alliance. This type of arrangement will also need to confer benefits on the alliance partner, otherwise it is unlikely to be successful in the long term. The third alternative is to manufacture the product locally, which is perhaps the most time and resource consuming of the three options as it involves setting up from scratch in a foreign country. This will be more difficult than operating in a home environment or with advice from an organisation for which the foreign market is a home environment.

■ Key success factors

The degree to which an organisation is successful depends on its ability to meet its key success factors (KSF). Key success factors are what an organisation must do well and better than its competitors if it is to succeed. They can arise from a number of sources.

First, key success factors may be established by the industry in which an organisation operates. For example, in the clothes mail-order business, being able to provide speedy delivery to the customer's home is a key success factor for all companies in the industry. Second, key success factors may be determined by the organisation itself. When the Midland Bank set up telephone banking with its subsidiary First Direct, the key success factors were to provide an accurate banking service that required a minimum amount of paperwork, could be accessed 24 hours a day, and did away with the need for high-street branches. Other banks have adopted these key success factors by providing their own telephone banking services and will continue to try to meet these key success factors by providing banking services in the home via the internet.

Finally, key success factors may be signified by customers indicating that they require products with particular features or services. One example is the demand from consumers for high-quality take-away coffee from coffee bars and sandwich shops. The demand from consumers is not only for high-quality coffee but also for a range of different types of coffee, from the familiar cappuccino and espresso to the more exotic sounding café latte, mocha and arabica. Therefore a key success factor for coffee and sandwich bars is the provision of a wider range of high-quality coffees.

Threats

Threats have the potential to damage an organisation's performance in the marketplace or external environment. Threats often arise from competitors or factors that are outside the control of the organisation. The competitor that cuts prices by 50 per cent today and the competitor that brings out a new generation of technologically advanced products both pose a clear threat to all other organisations operating in the same industry. Threats may also arise from changes in legislation or taxation relating to the industry in which an organisation operates. For example, the imposition of value added tax (VAT) on newspapers and books or children's clothes would affect both the manufacturers of such products and the amount of business done by retailers selling such products to members of the public.

Clearly, threats from the external environment may endanger an organisation. However, threats may also jeopardise good opportunities of which the organisation expects to take advantage. In 1997 the US company WorldCom tendered £19 billion for MCI, another US company. This offer outbid BT's proposal of £11 billion for MCI by over 70 per cent. The WorldCom offer became a realised threat that snatched an opportunity from under BT's nose and left a gap in the latter's strategy to secure a global partner.

Different types of SWOT analysis

The most basic SWOT analysis will examine how threats and opportunities can be dealt with while allowing the organisation to utilise its strengths and weaknesses to meet its key success factors. Merely producing long lists of threats, opportunities, weaknesses and strengths indicates a lack of thought and seriousness as regards the organisation. Lists should be brief and specific, indicating the key and important issues. The threats, opportunities, weaknesses and strengths should be judged and assessed in relative terms. For example, there is little merit in expressing the view that a particular strength or opportunity is 'good'. Its worth should be expressed relative to how a competitor fares with the same strength or opportunity. Organisations need to aim to be better than competitors when it comes to possessing strengths and exploiting opportunities. The same holds true for weaknesses and threats: organisations need to seek to minimise the effect of these to a greater extent than their competitors.

A basic SWOT analysis should discuss, illustrate and debate the threats, opportunities, weaknesses and strengths identified and how the organisation may build on the strengths, exploit the opportunities and minimise the weaknesses and threats to a greater extent than its competitors. This will include an assessment of where the company is at the current time and where it wishes to be at some point in the future. The organisation needs to decide how far away that future is – it will vary from a few months to many years depending on the organisation, the nature of its business and its current situation.

Guidelines for carrying out SWOT analysis

1 Identify key strengths, weaknesses, opportunities and threats. Do not produce a long list.
2 Once the key strengths, weaknesses, opportunities and threats have been identified, clear discussion and debate concerning them is required. The appropriate discussion and debate may be generated by considering the questions outlined below.

■ Strengths

Decide whether the organisation has the appropriate strengths on which to build and exploit its opportunities. How can it best exploit its strengths in relation to the opportunities available to it? Which strengths should the organisation seek to develop for the future?

■ Weaknesses

Decide whether remedying weaknesses is more urgent than building on strengths to exploit opportunities. Does ignoring important weaknesses make the organisation vulnerable to threats which could result in its going out of business or being taken over? How can critical weaknesses be offset or converted into strengths?

■ Opportunities

Identify new markets and market segments that might be suitable given the organisation's existing strengths and competencies. Identify changes that are occurring to existing customers and within existing markets. Consider using strategies of market penetration and market development to take advantage of any opportunities arising from existing and changing markets – *see* Chapter 4. Identify changes that need to be made to products and services. Consider strategies of product development and diversification to take advantage of any opportunities arising from changes to existing products – *see* Chapter 4.

■ Threats

Do threats need managing more urgently than the opportunities pursued? Which threats need to be dealt with immediately and in the short term? Which threats are issues for the organisation to consider when undertaking longer-term planning? How can critical threats be offset or turned into new opportunities?

> **☑ Check your understanding**
>
> *Do you understand why a good SWOT analysis is not a series of long lists?*
>
> Check your understanding by explaining the process which should be undertaken in doing a thorough SWOT analysis and the discussion points which should be raised.

Advanced SWOT analysis

A more **advanced SWOT analysis** involves developing a two-dimensional matrix. There are several forms that this two-dimensional matrix can take, and two are considered here.

■ SWOT analysis using external environmental factors, strengths and weaknesses[5]

First, key issues or factors from the organisation's external environment are identified. Again, this list should not be lengthy but should concentrate on the key issues in the external environment (*see* PEST analysis, LoNGPEST analysis, market analysis and competitor analysis in Chapters 8, 9, 10 and 4). A list containing a maximum of six to eight issues should be long enough in most situations. The same process needs to be undertaken for the organisation's strengths and weaknesses. These are then assessed and scored with + or – signs depending on how they are affected by the external factors or issues. This type of SWOT analysis is shown in Figure 11.5 for a new university in the UK at the start of the twenty-first century.

SWOT analysis – an example – the University Business School

The University Business School (UBS) is located in a new university in the centre of a large city in the middle of England. The UBS has a full-time academic staff of around 100, located in six subject groups: marketing, strategy, human resource management, computing and management sciences, international business, and public policy. All academic staff are qualified to at least master's degree level, with 46 staff also holding PhDs in a subject area relevant to their current job. A further 12 members of staff are currently undertaking PhDs by part-time study for which UBS pays the fees. UBS also employs around 30 part-time teaching staff, around 20 of whom are postgraduate students at UBS and 10 have taken early retirement from jobs in industry.

UBS has a portfolio of postgraduate taught programmes including a Master of Business Administration (MBA) and specialist master's courses in marketing, international marketing, international business, human resource management, management sciences and public-sector management. The under-graduate provision mirrors this with degree courses in BA Business Studies (BABS), BA Industrial Marketing (BAIM), BA Human Resource Management (BAHRM), BA Public Policy (BAPP), BA International Business (BAIB) and BSc

External factors ➡	Competitive market	Attractive to school leavers	Demographic trends	Introduction of tuition fees for f/t students	Reduced government funding per student	Abolition of grants for f/t students	Introduction of means-tested loans	Total +	Total –
Main strengths ⬇									
Capacity for developing vocational courses	++	++	+	+	– –	+	+	8	2
Good links with local FE college	+	0	+	+	–	+	+	5	1
Strong part-time courses	+	0	+	+	+	+	+	6	0
Research rating	++	0	+	0	– –	0	0	3	2
Well-qualified academic staff	++	++	++	++	– –	+	+	10	2
Main weaknesses ⬇									
Lack of staff accountability	– –	–	0	–	– –	–	–	0	8
High level of debt	–	0	0	–	– –	0	0	0	4
Inadequate student support systems	– –	– –	–	–	– –	–	–	0	10
Total of + from strengths and weaknesses	8	4	6	5	1	4	4		
Total of – from strengths and weaknesses	5	3	1	3	13	2	2		

Figure 11.5 SWOT analysis for UBS using external environmental factors, strengths and weaknesses

Management Sciences (BSMS). UBS also offers two BTEC courses, the Higher National Diploma in Business Studies (HND, full time) and Higher National Certificate in Business Studies (HNC, part time). The BABS, BAIM and BAHRM degree programmes are available on a part-time basis as well.

UBS has a strong reputation locally and regionally as a provider of top-quality business and management education, and many part-time postgraduate students will travel to UBS rather than attend the university in their home city. The average distance travelled by a part-time postgraduate student from outside the home city of UBS is a return trip of 63 miles. The part-time undergraduate courses attract students from a slightly more contained geographic area, with the average distance travelled by a part-time undergraduate from outside the home city of UBS being 48 miles.

A SWOT analysis of UBS is shown in Figure 11.5. If such an analysis is done carefully, it is possible to identify that the important strengths of the business school are its ability to develop vocational courses and its retention and development of a highly qualified academic staff. Therefore the business school's core competencies lie in course development and its HR policy. It is also clear that the biggest weaknesses and areas for development are student support systems and academic staff accountability. This may require the business school to develop a more extensive system of course leaders and personal tutoring, along with liaising more closely with the business school's administrative staff who are responsible for communication with the students regarding, for example, exam dates and results. This is currently a lengthy and time-consuming process that means students have to wait up to eight weeks after examination boards have met to receive written confirmation of exam results. The issue of staff accountability can be addressed only via the successful implementation of a suitable appraisal system, which is likely to require a change in culture among the academic staff concerned.

It is also clear that the biggest threat faced by the business school is the decreasing amount of government funding that each student attracts and there is little to counter this in what UBS is currently doing. The next main threat is to the business school's competitive position, with other universities and colleges possibly able to offer similar courses and perhaps lower fees. However, this threat is fairly well countered by the fact that the business school has vocational courses, which are well taught and are also available as on a part-time and full-time basis.

■ SWOT analysis using strengths, weaknesses, opportunities, threats and the four functions of business

The second method for undertaking a matrix-type SWOT analysis is to consider the strengths, weaknesses, opportunities and threats in relation to the four key functions of business: marketing, operations management, finance and human resource management. This type of SWOT analysis is shown in Table 11.2, which is an analysis of the restaurant MPW, named with the initials of the chef Marco Pierre White, who opened the restaurant with his joint-venture partner Granada. The information for this SWOT analysis is from the entry case study for this chapter.

Example question **SWOT analysis**

Undertake a matrix-type SWOT analysis of the MPW restaurant joint venture. Consider the strengths, weaknesses, opportunities and threats in relation to the four key business functions: marketing, operations management, finance and human resource management.

Workings, answers and comments

1 *SWOT analysis for MPW restaurant*

Table 11.2 SWOT analysis for MPW restaurant using strengths, weaknesses, opportunities and threats and the four functions

	Marketing	Operations	Human resources	Finance
Threats	● Other restaurants, particularly those that have a celebrity chef, like Anthony Worrall Thompson or Gary Rhodes	● The possible reducing number of locations available to expand into, particularly in London. This will be affected by the increasing number of similar restaurant chains seeking to expand in the same way and possibly drive up the cost of suitable locations that do exist	● Other restaurants opening in London and seeking to expand may seek to poach staff, particularly a talented chef who is a good cook and able to put together an imaginative menu	● If MPW is not very successful, Granada may choose to withdraw from the joint venture and cease to provide any expected financial resources
Opportunities	● Expansion around the UK, aim to have an MPW in every major city	● None mentioned in the case study	● None mentioned in the case study	● None mentioned in the case study
Weaknesses	● None mentioned in the case study	● Poor service from both waiting staff and the receptionist ● Some dishes served in the restaurant are not enjoyed by the diners	● Staff overworked during busy periods and offering poor service outside peak periods	● None mentioned in the case study
Strengths	● Marco Pierre White, MPW name ● Imaginative menu	● Some dishes served in the restaurant are greatly enjoyed by the diners	● Good chef, responsible for cooking and maybe putting together imaginative menu	● The MPW restaurant is the result of a joint venture with Granada, which will be an asset particularly if a chain of MPW restaurants is developed throughout the UK, as Granada has experience in managing chains of catering outlets ● Dishes on the menu are reasonably priced

It can be seen from Table 11.2 that the chief threats arise from other restaurants, particularly developing chains that may move into many of the locations in which MPW may be interested. Therefore MPW is going to have to be quick off the mark to obtain desirable locations into which to expand. MPW is also going to have to seek to retain good staff and prevent them from being poached by other expanding chains. It is going to have to ensure a good and stable relationship with its joint-venture partner the Granada group.

The key opportunity is expansion beyond London, via a strategy of market penetration and market development, which will involve offering the same type of reasonably priced food in cities around the UK.

The principal weaknesses arise from staff working flat out during peak periods and not being able to offer a high quality of service in the quieter times that directly follow those peak periods. This is likely to influence some customers' opinion of the restaurant.

The fundamental strengths of MPW undoubtedly rest with both its name and the imaginative and high-quality food offered at reasonable prices. These strengths are key factors for success in the restaurant business. Therefore these strengths, supported by a sound joint venture with Granada, put MPW in a convincing position to pursue an expansion or 'rollout' of MPW restaurants.

☑ Check your understanding

Do you understand the different types of SWOT analysis which can be performed?

Check your understanding by explaining the difference between a basic SWOT analysis and an advanced SWOT analysis.

Summary

This chapter examined two further types of organisational analysis, namely stakeholder analysis and SWOT analysis. The following summary covers all aspects of this chapter.

1 Stakeholders are individuals or groups who have an interest in an organisation. Different stakeholders have varying levels of power and interest in an organisation.

2 Stakeholders whose interests are satisfied by an organisation will remain with it. In contrast those stakeholders who are dissatisfied will seek to leave the organisation or they may chose to remain and try to change things.

3 Stakeholder relative power and interest can be mapped onto a power and interest matrix. Additionally this analysis can be extended to consider the reaction, behaviour and position of stakeholders if a particular strategy or plan were to be implemented.

4 Category D stakeholders, those with high power and high interest, are key players, such as the managing director. Category C stakeholders are those with high power and low interest, an example being a corporate shareholder in a company. Individual customers and employees often fall into category B, having low power and high interest. Those stakeholders in which the organisation has minimal interest are category A, low power and low interest.

5 Different categories of stakeholders may not always act individually – they may form coalitions with another category of stakeholders. For example individual employees (usually category B) may band together and try to influence category C stakeholders who have high power, unlike themselves.

6 SWOT analysis considers an organisation's strengths, weaknesses, opportunities and threats. Strengths and weaknesses are internal to an organisation, while opportunities and threats are external.

7 A basic SWOT analysis considers how an organisation can build on its strengths and take advantage of its opportunities, while minimising its weaknesses and avoiding threats. A more advanced SWOT analysis can evaluate the organisation's strengths and weaknesses against external environmental factors or evaluate strengths, weaknesses, opportunities and threats in relation to the four main areas of activity, namely marketing, finance, operations and human resource management.

Learning outcomes for case studies

While reading this chapter and engaging in the activities, you should have learned how to apply theory and models, analyse situations, and evaluate the application and analysis you undertake. The learning outcomes specified below outline the type of application, analysis and evaluation of which you should be capable in relation to organizations. The case studies and the questions which follow provide an opportunity for you to test how well you have achieved the learning outcomes for the ethical issues and exit case studies for this chapter.

Application	Check you have achieved this by	
1 Apply the power and interest matrix to an organisation and its stakeholders	demonstrating use of the power and interest matrix	answering ethical case study questions 1 & 2 and exit case study question 1
Analysis	**Check you have achieved this by**	
1 Perform comparative stakeholder analysis for an organisation of your choice	comparing and contrasting the stakeholder analysis of an organisation in different circumstances	answering ethical case study question 3 and exit case study question 2
Evaluation	**Check you have achieved this by**	
1 Explain how stakeholder analysis may aid in the analysis of an organisation's environment	formulating links between analysis of an organisation's environment and stakeholders in the organisation	answering exit case study question 3

ETHICAL ISSUES CASE STUDY 11.2

FT

How Monsanto got bruised in a food fight

By Michael Skapinker

When Monsanto brought its genetically modified food to Europe, Greenpeace was waiting. How did the US company respond? 'We sent over our American scientists and lawyers,' Kate Fish, Monsanto's vice-president for public policy, says witheringly.

In a speech to a conference on corporate citizenship in New York last month, Ms Fish mercilessly dissected her company's failure in the 1990s to deal with European fears about genetically modified foods. Monsanto's executives had become so caught up in the work done in their laboratories that they barely knew how to talk to non-scientists.

'For a company that believes in science, it's very difficult. When the Prince of Wales started talking about interfering with the realms of God, we weren't equipped to deal with that,' she told the conference.

Ms Fish was no stranger to environmentalism. In 1989 she founded EarthWays, an environmental group. Her first contact with Monsanto came soon afterwards, when it approached her about supporting Earth Day, which she was organising in St Louis, Missouri, the company's home town.

Monsanto's work on genetically modified foods – which, the company said, would lower pesticide use, increase crop yields and promote more efficient land use – appeared perfectly aligned with her belief in sustainable development.

She joined Monsanto's external advisory council in 1990 and when the company offered her a job in 1996, it seemed the perfect way to pursue her ideals. 'I had a sense of being employed doing something I wanted to do that could have some effect in the world,' she says.

Monsanto's promotion of genetically modified food enjoyed great success in the US. The products won regulatory approval and the amount of land under cultivation for such crops expanded rapidly. Taking the products to Europe seemed the natural next step. It did not occur to Ms Fish and her colleagues that European environmentalists would be anything other than enthusiastic. 'When I was an environmentalist and first started looking at these products, I thought this was exciting stuff. When you spend time in the labs, you get comfortable with it. It doesn't seem so scary,' she says.

Some Monsanto staff in Europe warned that genetically modified foods might not enjoy the easy ride they had had in the US. They were ignored. 'We heard the signals coming from Europe. Our people in Europe were saying: "There are some issues here." But they weren't loud enough. They were perceived as fringe signals. Until it starts to hurt, they're very hard to hear.'

The introduction of genetically modified foods into Europe was a fiasco. The environmental movement's campaign against them won huge public support. Supermarkets promised to banish such foods from their shelves. Crop trials were sabotaged. European governments imposed a moratorium on approval of genetically modified crops, which has been in force for more than three years.

This has given Ms Fish and Monsanto – which is now a subsidiary of Pharmacia, the pharmaceuticals group – plenty of time to consider the lessons. The first lesson is that what works in the US does not necessarily work anywhere else.

Americans, Ms Fish says, trust their regulators. Europeans do not – for good reason. Monsanto was attempting to introduce its products following the BSE (mad cow disease) crisis, where government assurances that beef was safe had turned out to be false.

Monsanto also appeared to be imposing genetically modified foods on Europe without consultation. 'You don't alter people's food without asking them first. It was as if their babies were being attacked,' Ms Fish says. 'There was a sense of outrage because it didn't appear that people had a choice. I think the whole industry didn't spend the time dealing with the consumer issues, talking about the technology. When consumers first heard about it, it was from Greenpeace, it wasn't from the industry.'

Is there any chance that, if Monsanto had spent more time listening and consulting, European consumers would have been willing to give genetically modified foods a try? 'It's so hard to say,' Ms Fish says. 'Certainly, we could have done it differently.'

Monsanto realises that winning Europe round will take years. In 2000, Hendrik Verfaillie, Monsanto's chief executive, announced a 'pledge' not to use genes from humans or animals in products intended for food or animal feed. Monsanto said it would never sell a product into which a known allergen had been introduced. Addressing an issue that has caused particular concern, it also promised 'not to pursue technologies that result in sterile seeds'.

Ms Fish now spends much of her time in Brussels. Mr Verfaillie believes the way forward is for Monsanto to attempt to find common ground with its critics rather than confront them. It has been holding meetings with European environmental groups. 'I can't give you names but we went to our most outspoken critics,' he says.

▶

Did he find these campaigners reasonable? 'It was absolutely amazing. We obviously had significant disagreements on certain points but they were very willing to engage. We may not agree with everything they say but they have a point of view that reflects at least a part of society. It's very difficult to get the most extreme critics to agree to anything but the middle-of-the-road organisations have as their objective improving the environment.'

Mr Verfaillie and Ms Fish are trying to convince those organisations that they and Monsanto have a common interest. Using genetically modified crops to reduce pesticide use is a line Monsanto continues to pursue. In Brazil, Mr Verfaillie says, planting of such crops has reduced leakage of pesticides into rivers. Increasing crop yields around the world would mean fewer forests and wetlands being taken over by agricultural production.

Monsanto is also talking to European farmers. 'How do we build and align what we're offering with the needs of European agriculture?' Ms Fish asks. 'Agriculture in the UK is very efficient but farmers' income is low. The UK's got one of the highest uses of pesticide in Europe, much higher than the US. Only the Netherlands' is higher.'

Mr Verfaillie sees signs that European public opinion is starting to turn. 'We do market research. We're still not where we need to be. But we see consumers in the UK and [the Netherlands] have gone from 20 per cent saying they would consume [GM] products to over 50 per cent,' he says.

The European Commission last year warned that the moratorium on approving new varieties of genetically modified crops was damaging the European Union's attempt to become the world's most dynamic economy. 'Europe cannot afford to miss the opportunity that these new sciences and technologies offer,' the Commission said. 'Biotechnology research efforts could and should be used to develop new GM varieties to improve yields and enable cultivation by small-scale and poor farmers.' It added that Europe risked losing more scientists to the US.

European ministers were unmoved, insisting last year that the moratorium could not be lifted until new rules on labelling and tracing genetically modified ingredients were in place. This could take another three years. Greenpeace's website continues to insist: 'Genetic scientists are altering life itself – artificially modifying genes to produce plants and animals which could never have evolved naturally.' It warns that such ingredients are still 'sneaking into the food chain through animal feed'.

Monsanto has admitted its mistakes in failing to take these fears seriously. It is likely to be living with them for a long time.

Source: Financial Times, 7 March 2002. Reprinted with permission.

Questions for ethical issues case study 11.2

1 Identify the stakeholders in Monsanto and their expectations.

2 Analyse the stakeholders in Monsanto using a power and interest matrix.

3 Identify the changes which will need to occur in your Monsanto power and interest matrix if genetically modified foods are to be accepted in Europe. How might Monsanto go about achieving these changes?

◀◼▶ EXIT CASE STUDY 11.3

Interflora

By Claire Capon

Interflora was founded in 1923 and is an association of florists owned by its members, which today is the largest UK flower delivery organisation, supplying four million bouquets annually, worth over £60m. The florists who belong to Interflora accept orders from around the world for flowers to be delivered in their local neighbourhood. Membership of Interflora allows co-ordination of flower deliveries and the organisation provides computer terminals for participating shops and clearing payments between its members. The updating proposals discussed in this case study proposed an increase in a florist's annual subscription charge for belonging to Interflora from £300 to £1750 and a reduction in the cost of each transaction from £2.99 to 60p.

Interflora and its affairs are managed by the members via an elected board of directors. Doug McGrath was identified by headhunters and in January 1996 was appointed chief executive of Interflora. He was recruited to update and overhaul the association, which was viewed by the board as a cosy trade organisation with traditional values. This was considered uncommercial and uncompetitive by Doug McGrath and the Interflora board. The updating was to take the form of the introduction of a corporate and commercial attitude to conducting business.

The updating of Interflora was announced at the organisation's 1996 Bournemouth conference. It was revealed by Doug McGrath and David Parry that Interflora was to have a mission statement and modern management thinking was to be introduced to the organisation to solve the problems faced by the organisation and the membership. The reasoning centred around the fierce competition faced by florists from garages and supermarkets, some of which offered home delivery of bouquets, e.g. Marks & Spencer and Waitrose. The view taken by Doug McGrath and the commercially minded chairman, Bristol florist David Parry, was that Interflora should ditch its traditional family values and act like a modern corporation.

Potentially, McGrath and Parry could have been a strong team that could have been of considerable benefit to Interflora, with McGrath's considerable business experience and Parry's extensive knowledge and experience of the florist trade. The view expressed by Caroline Marshall-Foster, editor of the trade publication the *Florist*, was that floristry was potentially a very profitable business and it is probably the opportunity for profit that McGrath and Parry saw.

If Interflora were to behave like a modern corporation, Doug McGrath saw opportunities for the centralisation of activities such as the purchase of flowers, which would produce economies of scale and make Interflora the largest purchaser of flowers in the UK. This would mean that all the flowers bought by Interflora would be purchased collectively on behalf of the members, giving it the power to negotiate better deals with suppliers than if members brought their flowers individually. The policy of centralised purchasing would be introduced along with standardisation of many other facets of the service provided by Interflora florists, such as opening times, service and corporate image, e.g. window displays.

David Parry and Doug McGrath left the Bournemouth conference convinced that their presentation of an updated and modern Interflora had been successful and that the conference delegates supported the proposed changes. However, they had not read the mood of the conference correctly. In fact, Interflora members saw the presentation of Interflora's image standardisation as dictatorial. This was illustrated by the views and actions of Bev Woods, an Interflora member and florist.

Bev Woods ran a florist shop in Leeds and did not view the mission statement and proposals on standardisation as suitable for her shop, as Interflora work comprised only a small proportion of the total amount of work undertaken by her business. A policy document was issued to all Interflora members outlining and reinforcing the conference proposals. The general view of the membership was that the proposals would be expensive for small florists, who make up a significant proportion of Interflora's members, and hence posed a financial threat to the long-term survival of small florist shops.

Realising that the proposals had not been as well received as he had initially thought, Doug McGrath decided to hold face-to-face meetings with Interflora members who were unhappy with proposals presented at Bournemouth and in the policy document. At one of these meetings, Bev Woods challenged the board over a small administrative change that she thought could be illegal. This challenge was met with a patronising reply, and in response the other Interflora members present displayed considerable anger at the manner in which Bev Woods was treated.

Hence Bev Woods and a fellow florist from London, Rose-Marie Watkins, joined forces and sought to gain the 250 signatures necessary to call an extraordinary general meeting (EGM) of Interflora. This involved the two women in stuffing and addressing 2600 envelopes by hand. The letters were posted so that they would arrive on the doormats of Interflora members the day after Valentine's Day and three weeks before Mother's Day in 1997, making use of a slight lull in the business calendar of busy florists.

Having realised that the proposals presented at Bournemouth had not been well received, Doug McGrath dropped plans for the centralised purchasing of flowers and other proposals that 50 per cent or more of Interflora's members disagreed with or felt neutral about. This was in line with a poll of members conducted by Interflora management. The poll was a telephone survey of a sample of 611 out of 2600 members. The results showed that 65 per cent of members agreed with the proposed changes. This was not accepted by Bev Woods and Rose-Marie Watkins, who thought that the views of all 2600 members should be taken into account.

The efforts and timing of Bev Woods and Rose-Marie Watkins paid off and by Mother's Day 1997 enough signatures had been gathered to force an EGM to be held in May 1997. This interrupted the programme of change that Doug McGrath and David Parry wanted in place by 1 June 1997. Bev Woods and Rose-Marie Watkins appointed a solicitor to help them prepare for the EGM, which was viewed as crucial if Interflora members were to retain their rights under the memorandum and articles of association, which were to have disappeared under the planned changes. Assistance in the battle against the board was forthcoming in the shape of Geoff Hughes, an ambitious Bristol-based florist, viewed by many as a political animal with a strategic outlook.

Geoff Hughes' primary aim was to remove Doug McGrath, David Parry and the rest of the Interflora board, as they were viewed as the drivers of the proposed change. This went beyond Bev Woods' original intention, which was to see the structure of Interflora change, as she thought that it allowed board members too much power. Despite being over-ruled, Bev Woods remained very much an active figurehead in the campaign to oust the Interflora board. The aims pursued by Bev Woods, Rose-Marie Watkins and Geoff Hughes were to diminish board support and appoint a caretaker board, a proposal which sent shockwaves through the organisation.

Bev Woods and Rose-Marie Watkins were determined to win and prepared very carefully for the EGM, rehearsing their speeches and actions. At the EGM they, Geoff Hughes and other Interflora members all had board members to mark. The turnout at the EGM was substantial, with 1200 florists coming to Warwick University, three times the expected number. In the electric and gladiatorial atmosphere of the EGM, Bev Woods spoke first and made an inspirational speech designed to get the support of non-committed Interflora members. The speech was even much admired by the opposition, Doug McGrath.

Rose-Marie Watkins employed cunning and laid a trap for David Parry to fall into. His role at the EGM was to chair the meeting and hence remain impartial. In her speech, Rose-Marie Watkins quoted from a recent *Daily Telegraph* article citing David Parry as stating that approximately 1000 Interflora members would cease to be members under the updating proposals. When this point was made, David Parry responded by rising to his feet to correct the remark by making a statement and in doing so breached his position as impartial chairman. This was raised as a point of order by Bev Woods, who indicated to him that by making a statement he was not being fair to both sides. The Interflora members present applauded. David Parry moved on to arguing with Geoff Hughes and the Interflora board continued to manage the meeting badly. A succession of Interflora members made speeches supporting the proposals of Bev Woods, Rose-Marie Watkins and Geoff Hughes.

There followed a much-needed lunch break. During lunch one Interflora member complained about the cold quiche buffet and in talking to the restaurant manager discovered that the amount paid for the lunch was £6 a head less than Interflora members had been charged. This was raised as a question in the afternoon session and it was suggested that the Interflora board was making money from its own members. This heightened the anger of the already hostile Interflora members and the meeting degenerated into an irate protest against the board. It was later clarified that the extra £6 a head was to cover the expenses of drinks, VAT and other extras.

The meeting was adjourned and voting took place, with board members waiting an anxious two hours for the results. These results removed all 13 board members, leaving Bev Woods, Rose-Marie Watkins and Geoff Hughes feeling ecstatic at their victory. However, a surprise was in store for the two women. The election of the new caretaker board saw their friend and ally Geoff Hughes moved into the role of chairman. It was from this position that he declared that he had never disagreed with business ideas of the previous board and he thought them appropriate.

In consequence, Geoff Hughes was not re-elected as chairman of Interflora in 1998. Interflora decided not to appoint a florist and Martin Redman, an accountant, was appointed chairman, not chief executive, of Interflora. There had been a radical change of personalities on the board of Interflora, but not of the aims that it was seeking to achieve.

Sources: Wolffe, R (1997) 'Interflora board ousted in protest over restructuring', *Financial Times*, 12 May 1998; 'Guns 'n' Posies', *Blood on the Carpet*, BBC2, 10 February 1999.

Questions for exit case study 11.3

1 Identify the stakeholders in Interflora before the 1996 Bournemouth conference and plot them on a power and interest matrix.

2 Consider the situation that Interflora was in by the time of the EGM in May 1997. Identify any additions or deletions to the Interflora stakeholders you identified in answering question 1. Plot all the stakeholders you have identified in Interflora as they would appear in May 1997, immediately after the EGM at Warwick University.

3 What lessons are to be learned from the Interflora experience with regard to identifying and managing stakeholders?

 For more case studies please visit www.booksites.net/capon

Short-answer questions

1 Define a stakeholder.

2 Define a key player.

3 Identify a stakeholder in an organisation and their source of interest.

4 Identify a stakeholder in an organisation and their source of power.

5 Briefly summarise the expected behaviour of satisfied stakeholders in an organisation.

6 Briefly summarise the expected behaviour of unsatisfied stakeholders in an organisation.

7 What should organisations seek to do with stakeholders who have high power and low interest?

8 What should organisations seek to do with stakeholders who have low power and high interest?

9 What should organisations seek to do with stakeholders who have low power and low interest?

10 Describe the key concerns of a SWOT analysis.

11 In the context of this chapter, define a threat.

12 In the context of this chapter, define an opportunity.

13 In the context of this chapter, define a weakness.

14 In the context of this chapter, define a strength.

15 Briefly outline the procedure for performing a basic SWOT analysis.

16 Explain the term 'key success factor'.

17 Explain the term 'competitive advantage'.

18 Explain the term 'premium price'.

Learning outcomes for assignment questions

While reading this chapter and engaging in the activities, you should have learned how to apply theory and models, analyse situations, and evaluate the application and analysis you undertake. The learning outcomes specified below outline what you should be able to do and the assignment questions provide an opportunity for you to test how well you have achieved the learning outcomes for this chapter.

Application	Check you have achieved this by	
1 Apply the power and interest matrix to an organisation and stakeholders with which you are familiar	demonstrating use of the power and interest matrix on an organisation you know	answering assignment question 1
2 Apply basic or advanced SWOT analysis to an organisation about which you have access to information	demonstrating use of SWOT on an organisation	answering assignment question 2
Analysis	**Check you have achieved this by**	
1 Perform comparative stakeholder analysis for an organisation of your choice	comparing and contrasting the stakeholder analysis of an organisation in different circumstances	answering assignment question 1
2 Reach appropriate conclusions from a SWOT analysis, including comment on the organisation's key success factors and sources of competitive advantage	identifying and communicating clearly the findings of a SWOT analysis	answering assignment question 2
Evaluation	**Check you have achieved this by**	
1 Explain how stakeholder analysis may aid in the analysis of an organisation's environment	formulating links between analysis of an organisation's environment and stakeholders in the organisation	answering assignment question 1
1 Evaluate the relevance of SWOT analysis to organisations today	evaluating the benefits and disadvantages of SWOT analysis to organisations	answering assignment question 2

Assignment questions

1 Choose and research an organisation. Identify all its stakeholders and plot them on a power and interest matrix. Comment on how and why you think the power and interest of the stakeholders will change in the next 12 months and the next five years. How does this analysis help you understand the organisation's environment?

2 Choose one of the categories listed below that you have not studied before, collect some information and identify the main companies operating in the category you have chosen.

    a Identify the key success factors and possible areas of competitive advantage for the category you have chosen.

    b Select one of the main companies you have identified and perform *one* of the following types of SWOT analysis:

- a basic SWOT analysis of the selected company;
- an advanced SWOT analysis of the selected company using external environmental factors, strengths and weaknesses;
- an advanced SWOT analysis of this company using strengths, weaknesses, opportunities, threats and the four functions of business.

    c Comment on the statement: 'SWOT analysis is overly simple and of no use to organisations.'

List of categories for SWOT analysis:

- Manufacturers of greeting cards.
- Manufacturers of pharmaceuticals.
- High-street financial institutions in the UK.
- Passenger road transport companies.
- Airlines operating on North Atlantic routes.
- Ferry companies operating out of English, Scottish and Welsh ports.
- Publishers of non-fiction books in the UK.
- Producers of frozen food in the UK.
- Footwear manufacturers whose goods sell in the UK.
- Furniture retailers in the UK.

Weblinks available online at www.booksites.net/capon

1 The website below looks at the National Grid and its stakeholders.
http://www.nationalgrid.com/uk/social&environment/stakeholders.asp

2 The website below is for the UK Shareholders Association – shareholders are important stakeholders in organisations.
http://www.uksa.org.uk/

3 The two websites listed below are for Monsanto, the ethical issues case study for this chapter.
http://www.monsanto.com/monsanto/
http://www.monsanto.co.uk/

4 The website below is for Interflora, the exit case study for this chapter.
http://www.interflora.co.uk/

Further reading

Ambrosini, V with Johnson, G and Scholes, K (1998) *Exploring Techniques of Analysis and Evaluation in Strategic Management*, Chapters 8 and 10, Harlow: Prentice Hall Europe.
Johnson, G and Scholes, K (2002) *Exploring Corporate Strategy*, 6th edn, Chapter 5, Harlow: Financial Prentice Hall.

References

1 Johnson, G and Scholes, K (2002) *Exploring Corporate Strategy*, 6th edn, Harlow: Financial Times Prentice Hall.
2 Jagger, S (1999) 'AA ponders its road to the future', *Daily Telegraph*, 24 April.
3 Ibid.
4 Ibid.
5 Johnson and Scholes, op. cit.

12

Managing a changing environment

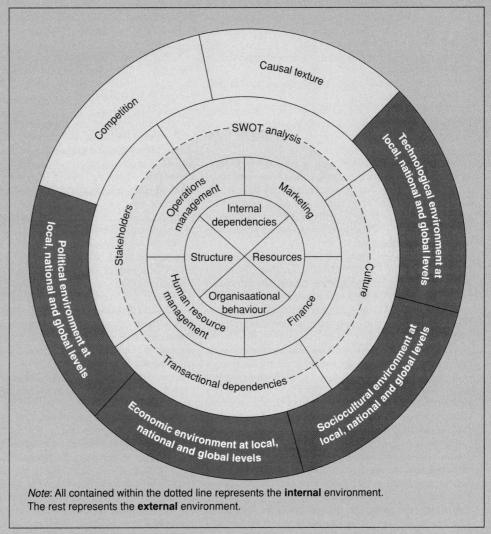

Note: All contained within the dotted line represents the **internal** environment.
The rest represents the **external** environment.

Figure 12.1 Organisational context model

The museum locked in the past

By Leslie Crawford

The Prado museum, Spain's top tourist attraction, has just under 12 months to get ready for the biggest expansion in its history, with the opening of three annexes that will double exhibition space for the world's finest collection of works by Goya, El Greco and Velazquez.

The expansion, which is long overdue, could turn out to be an unmitigated disaster. As things now stand, the Prado will have neither the budget nor the extra staff to run its bigger self. The looming crisis has triggered a heated debate about how Spain's leading museum should be managed and what degree of financial independence, if any, it should enjoy.

At the centre of the storm is Eduardo Serra, chairman of UBS Warburg in Spain and a former defence minister, who agreed to become the (unremunerated) chairman of the Prado's board of trustees 18 months ago. Mr Serra is candid about the museum's plight. The Prado, he says, 'is the great sick man of our culture'.

The catalogue of ills is as long as the Prado's history. In the early 19th century, the palace that houses the royal art collection was turned into a barracks by Napoleon's invading troops, who used statues and other works of art for target practice. More recently, a leaking roof forced the closure of the Velazquez rooms because rain was streaming down the walls.

Money is so tight that for several years the chief of security at the Prado has been 'on loan' from the police force. A government hiring freeze has also meant that the museum has not been allowed to fill 57 vacancies and must make do with only 350 staff – far fewer than at other European museums of similar size and importance.

Most frustrating of all is the fact that the Prado has no control over its finances. Its budget is set by the finance ministry and the museum must return any unspent money at the end of each year. The Prado is not allowed to operate a bank account and it cannot accept corporate sponsorship without the prior authorisation of Spain's finance ministry.

The museum last year turned down an offer of audio guides because the headsets bore the logo of a private telecommunications group. Only recently did it win special authorisation to publish a modest floor map for the 1.8m visitors it receives each year.

Few art-lovers would disagree with Mr Serra's diagnosis. The Prado, he says, is understaffed, underfunded and hamstrung by a legal framework that stifles all private initiative.

The remedy, however, is not straightforward. Mr Serra's plans for the modernisation of the Prado have clashed with the conservative views of Spain's art establishment. To them, Mr Serra is a merchant in their temple of high art; a philistine who would turn the Prado into a private playground for the rich.

Mr Serra's offence has been to argue that the Prado must be given more financial freedom and more control over its resources. He wants to treble the budget, to €45m (£28m), by 2005 and he wants to raise slightly more than half of this by the museum's own fundraising efforts.

Shrinking state subsidies mean that most museums in Europe have had to become active fundraisers. The Louvre in Paris now derives 40 per cent of its income from private sources, while the National Gallery in London meets a third of its running costs through donations, membership programmes and corporate sponsorship.

The Prado, however, has no such freedom. Mr Serra is campaigning for changes in the law, which limits private donations to the Prado to €300. As a result, the Foundation of the Friends of the Prado has only a few hundred members, who are offered no special privileges. 'I cannot send sponsors a magazine because we do not publish one,' Mr Serra laments. 'I cannot invite donors to special exhibitions because we stage so few of them.'

'Should we not make a greater effort to obtain private resources to make better use of public funds?' Mr Serra asked in a recent speech. 'This approach has been derided as a dangerous step towards the privatisation of the Prado. A dispassionate consideration of the problem would yield the very opposite conclusion.'

Few Spaniards, however, feel dispassionate about the Prado. As Mr Serra concedes: 'The Prado is the cultural symbol of Spain. To propose change is like laying your hands on the family silver. The very concept of modernising management is treated like a crime.'

At the heart of the debate is a tug-of-war between those who believe that the Prado's sole mission is to guard the national heritage and those, such as Mr Serra, who believe the museum should be more active in engaging the public, with a livelier educational programme and more frequent temporary exhibitions.

At present, a visit to the Prado is a dispiriting affair: there is little information for the layman, rooms are frequently closed to the public and there are only six guides for the thousands of tourists who arrive each day. The Prado knows little about its visitors: it keeps no records of their age or provenance, or how many of them have visited the museum before.

▶

The expansion, however, will require radical changes to the way the museum is managed. The Boston Consulting Group, which is advising the Prado on its modernisation programme, estimates that staff numbers will have to double to 700 and that the museum will require 'a new management model that is much more geared towards attending the public'.

Mr Serra believes the museum's staff should be better paid. He would like to introduce a proper career structure, with annual performance reviews and promotion for those who do well.

Change, however, does not come easily to a crusty, 18th-century institution whose bureaucracy is as dark and as impenetrable as any of Goya's Black Paintings. The Prado's staff are civil servants with life-long tenure and, although they are pitifully paid, they are suspicious of Mr Serra's attempts to drag them into the 21st century. They are particularly wary of his plans to circumvent the government hiring freeze by getting special dispensation to employ non-civil service staff on temporary contracts. In a letter to the board of trustees last year, the Prado's specialist staff rejected annual performance reviews and the carrot of better pay. They said they saw no reason for the Prado to change.

The clash between modernisers and traditionalists triggered the resignation last December of Fernando Checa, the Prado's director. Mr Checa, a mild-mannered art historian with a halo of fuzzy hair and large, tortoiseshell spectacles, accused Mr Serra of 'interfering too often in my relationship with the curators and with the museum's scientific staff'.

Mr Checa, a traditionalist, believed the scholarly integrity of the Prado was being undermined by Mr Serra's plans. His successor, Miguel Zugaza, who is credited with breathing new life into Bilbao's Museum of Fine Arts, is understood to be more in tune with the chairman's thinking.

Mr Zugaza and Mr Serra have only a few months to overcome the political, legal and bureaucratic obstacles that stand in the way of the Prado's modernisation. It will be a battle worthy of the great spectacles that are depicted in the halls of the museum, although it is to be hoped it will not be as bloody.

Source: Financial Times, 15 February 2002. Reprinted with permission.

Introduction

The first 11 chapters of this book have been concerned with understanding and analysing the tasks and activities which organisations undertake, along with the internal and external environments in which they operate. Hence this chapter examines how organisations cope with change from these environments and the tools and techniques that can aid organisations in planning for and managing change.

Sources of organisational change

The demand for change in organisations is caused by shifts in the external and internal environments in which they operate. External environmental factors were discussed in earlier chapters. The PEST issues – political, economic, sociocultural and technological – are drivers or sources of change that all organisations face. Additionally, the behaviour and demands of external stakeholders, including competitors, customers, financiers and shareholders, may drive change for an organisation. The influence an organisation has over these **drivers of change** is often limited, as they usually arise from another organisation or development over which the company has no or limited influence.

However, the actions of competitor companies or organisations which result in businesses having to change usually require a response. For example, the introduction of a price-cutting strategy by a competitor is clearly an event that requires an immediate reaction if a company is to retain market share.

The introduction of a new technology or technologically advanced product by a competitor will require a considered response that may take time to develop. Dyson's introduction of the bagless vacuum cleaner took the market by surprise and the company rapidly seized market share from other vacuum producers. Manufacturers of traditional vacuum cleaners took several years to develop a noticeable and competitive response to Dyson.

Internal sources or drivers of change include employees, trade unions and organisational departments. Demands from employees and trade unions for more pay and different wage and salary structures may mean that the rewards system operated by the organisation changes, although this is unlikely to happen in isolation. The likely outcome would be that a deal would be struck over working hours or productivity in return for improved wages and conditions of employment.

Therefore organisations have to assess the outcome of carrying on with current tasks and activities or decide to plan and implement change to allow the organisation to develop from its current position. The decision to implement change will depend on whether the organisation wants to maintain or increase market size. If an organisation is seeking to maintain market size, it should realise that this is a difficult task in declining markets and an easier task in stable or growing markets. Alternatively, if an organisation is aiming for market growth, it should recognise that this is most realistic if markets are growing, but still possible if markets are stable.

The decision to implement change requires an assessment of the resources available and those required. The difference between the two should be evaluated (*see* Chapter 1). Stakeholder behaviour, alongside current and changing expectations, should also be considered when planning for change (*see* Chapter 11). In the case of the Prado museum (see entry case study 12.1) it could be argued that the visitors, as stakeholders, expect enough guides, audio guides, maps, brochures and postcards, very little of which is currently provided by the Prado.

☑ Check your understanding

Do you understand the possible sources of change for organisations?

Check your understanding by identifying internal and external drivers of change and summarise how the drivers of change you have identified may impact on an organisation.

Types of organisational change

The changes that organisations choose to implement will cover many different aspects of organisational life. These changes can include alterations to organisational size, structure and culture, as well as changes to operational activities and the roles that people undertake in an organisation. Change is either reactive or proactive. Reactive change is where the organisation reacts to an event that has already occurred. This is the situation at the Prado museum (see entry case study 12.1). The chairman, Mr Serra, is seeking to make the Prado react to its current situation, which has been some time in the making, by seeking to tackle inadequate budgets, lack of devolved financial control and a leaking roof. In contrast, proactive change is where an organisation plans and prepares for expected and anticipated events and maybe even how to deal with unexpected events.

Unexpected events include shock occurrences, such as a chemical company experiencing a leak or explosion, or a food manufacturer suffering contamination of food or drink products with glass or poison. These types of events are rare and unpredictable, but organisations can plan for the steps they will take in such circumstances. The planning should cover what action should be taken and who in the organisation is responsible for taking it. The issues that should be covered include dealing with the event as soon as it happens, for example recalling all food or drink products that might be affected and offering a full refund, which is important if the dent to consumer confidence is to be minimised; liaising with the emergency services and investigating authorities, important in the example of the chemical company leak or explosion; dealing with those members of the public affected; and liaising with the media, the effectiveness of which is likely to affect public perception of the organisation and consumer confidence.

Major organisational changes in size and structure will affect hierarchical and reporting relationships, along with communication and decision-making systems. An organisation that decreases the number of middle managers it employs will also be reducing its size and that of its hierarchy. Hence the structure of the organisation will be flatter, and more communication will need to occur between those at the top and those further down. At the same time, decision making will have to be either decentralised to those further down the organisation or centralised with those at the top.

A change in organisational culture, which is difficult to achieve, is likely to involve changes in personalities and the position these people occupy in the organisation. This was demonstrated in the case of the Prado museum with the arrival of the new chairman Mr Serra, the departure of the director Mr Checa and the arrival of his successor Mr Zugaza. This means that leadership styles and the way in which people are motivated will change. Different organisational cultural styles are examined in Chapters 1 and 2. For employees of an organisation undergoing change, the changes will be felt in the tasks and activities they perform on a daily basis as part of their jobs. This may include changes in the way the job is carried out. The content of a particular job may change completely or only slightly. This will occur at the Prado museum if Mr Serra and Mr Zugaza succeed in driving through change, as the day-to-day activities will change to take account of the introduction of new staff on flexible employment contracts, better pay and performance reviews. Technology may alter the way someone's job is done and the way work is co-ordinated in the organisation, the obvious example being the introduction of audio guides at the Prado museum.

☑ Check your understanding

Do you understand the different types of change an organisation can experience?

Check your understanding by listing possible types of change an organisation may experience.

The process of change

In this section an overall view is taken of the process of change and the issues affecting the managers and stakeholders involved.

Lewin[1] suggests that change is the outcome of the impact of driving forces on restraining forces, more commonly known as **force field analysis** – *see* Figure 12.2. This can be thought of as the status quo that is under pressure to change. The resulting change is a direct outcome of either the driving forces or the restraining forces being more powerful. It is normal for the driving forces of change to have economic attributes. These economic attributes may arise from the external environment as a result of macroeconomic changes or because of internal issues, e.g. the need to cut costs and improve profit margins. One example of this is the shoe manufacturer and retailer Clarks reorganising and restructuring its US operations, when in the financial year ending 31 January 1996 trading profit was only £700 000, compared with £3.6 million in the previous year.

In most organisations undergoing change, at least part of the workforce will be dedicated and faithful to the existing work practices, as in the case of the Prado museum's life-long tenured civil service staff, who see no reason for

**Figure 12.2
Lewin's force
field analysis**

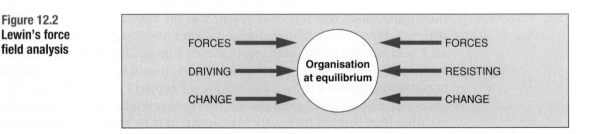

change. The news that these practices will have to change will leave staff feeling concerned about their jobs and future with the organisation. Their reluctance to accept and adopt suggested changes forms the restraining forces that contribute to the unbalancing of the status quo. The restraining forces will seek to persuade the organisation to discontinue or alter the recommended changes and counteract the driving forces of change.

Managers in organisations experiencing change obviously need to be aware of both driving and restraining forces. The managers involved should seek to communicate strong justification of the changes by offering a clear and unclouded explanation of the reasons for the changes and any advances in employee empowerment that will result. This was clearly so when Clarks reorganised and restructured its US operations, resulting in a change in the way shoes were produced for and sold to the US market. American staff were given the freedom to redesign and adapt UK designs for the US market. This resulted in selling US-designed shoes to American customers, instead of thrusting UK-designed shoes at them.

However, in planning such significant change a careful balance needs to be struck between providing too much information, which may raise fears and queries that cannot yet be dealt with, and providing inadequate information, which leaves people feeling that they have been told nothing and are being kept in the dark. Hence change requires strong and effective leadership from the managers involved, particularly if structural and cultural changes are to occur. The leadership in any new working teams or groups will have to be particularly strong and focused if the implemented change is to be successful.

A strong and effective change manager will disperse resistance to change by highlighting early achievements resulting from the change, which will also help maintain the momentum of the change programme and prevent it suffering from setbacks and periods of slow progress. Recognition that not everyone will support the change and that the feelings of those who are likely to be hurt by it require sensitive handling will help the change process to be managed successfully.

✓ Check your understanding

Do you understand what is meant by 'force field analysis'?

Check your understanding by explaining what a force field analysis demonstrates.

The change process model

The Lewin model[2] was developed to identify and examine the three stages of the change process. The first stage is unfreezing current attitudes and behaviour – *see* Figure 12.3. This unfreezing stage takes the view that if attitudes and behaviour are to change, then old behaviour must come to be regarded

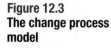

**Figure 12.3
The change process
model**

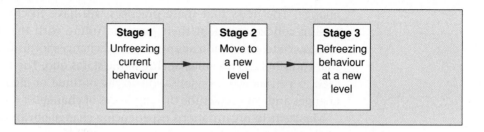

as unsuitable and must stop. Hence the requirement for change must be appreciated directly by the people to be affected by the change, as it cannot be imposed on them if the change process is to succeed. If Mr Serra and Mr Zugaza are to succeed at the Prado museum, they need to convince the civil service staff of the need for change, an extremely difficult task as they have rejected the 'carrot of better pay' (see entry case study 12.1). The **unfreezing process** may be achieved by realisation among the people involved that change is required for some reason. Common driving forces of change often result from commercial pressures, which include the need for increased sales or market share, better profitability or more efficient production. The unfreezing process requires employees affected by the change to understand and be clearly informed of the difficulties confronting the organisation. This involves information on the current problems being communicated to all employees. The current problems may include issues such as reducing market share, poor quality of product or service, or inefficient production levels when compared with competition. The civil servants at the Prado museum will need to understand the problems of the poor physical state of the building and its extention, the poor financial state of affairs, the demand for better services in terms of guidance and information which visitors expect, which will in return require more staff to be employed by the museum.

The second stage of Lewin's change process model is **moving to a new level**. A search for answers to the difficulties faced by the organisation has to occur. This involves reviewing alternative solutions, the examination of changing values and culture within the organisation, and an assessment of the organisational structure that would most suit the changing organisation. The people affected by the change should continue to receive regular updating communications about possible answers and solutions to the difficulties faced by the organisation. These informing and updating communications should be both verbal, via meetings, and written, for example via a newsletter. The use of meetings allows people's ideas and views on the proposed changes to be gathered and their questions, queries and fears to be addressed. Issuing a newsletter allows what has been discussed at meetings to be confirmed and is also a useful summary, particularly for anyone who was not able to be there. Meetings should be organised and structured so that all those affected by the change have the opportunity to be involved in the debate and discussions. If the change is significant and large numbers of people are involved, a series of meetings covering different departments, sections or divisions will be required throughout the period in which the change occurs.

Solutions and answers to the difficulties faced by the organisation need to be developed and the essential changes planned. Hence there is a need to continue communicating with those affected by the change. Once this has been achieved, the implementation of the planned changes can be arranged. Then the chosen solutions can start to be implemented, which may necessitate running in parallel new and current systems and methods of working. This allows the newly implemented solutions to be assessed as working satisfactorily, before the old method or system of working is withdrawn. There should then be a final review and tweaking of systems and methods of working to ensure that the required level of work and satisfaction is being achieved by the people involved.

The third stage of Lewin's change process model is **refreezing** attitudes and behaviour at the new level. This takes place once acceptable solutions have been found. The refreezing stage involves positive reinforcement and support for the implemented changes. This can be done by highlighting improvements in difficult areas that have occurred as a result of the changes, for example an upturn in sales or improvement in quality, which could include testimony from a satisfied customer reproduced in a company newsletter. People from other parts of the organisation not directly affected by the changes also need to be informed of what has been altered.

☑ Check your understanding

Do you understand Lewin's change process model?

Check your understanding by naming the three stages of Lewin's change process model and summarise what happens in organisations experiencing each of the three stages.

An alternative view of the change process is presented by Burnes.[3] He suggests that the change process consists of three interlinked elements: objectives and outcomes, planning the change, and people – *see* Figure 12.4.

Figure 12.4
The change process by Burnes

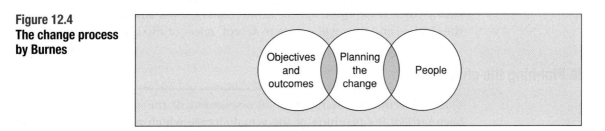

■ Objectives and outcomes

In assessing the objectives and outcomes, Burnes presents four phases that organisations should work through in deciding whether change is appropriate. First, a trigger for organisational change should exist and fall into one of the following broad categories: the requirement for change is core to organisational strategy; better performance is a core theme of competitive strategy; serious problems exist with current performance; or opportunities exist that will provide the organisation with a greater return than that currently achieved.

Once organisational change has been triggered, the second phase, the remit, is entered. Drawing up the remit is about establishing clear agreement concerning where the accountability and authority to instigate change exist in the organisation. This needs to be undertaken prior to proceeding further with the change process. The accountability and authority to instigate the change process rest with senior management in a bureaucratic and hierarchical organisation, but will be devolved in an organisation with a flatter structure and more modern approach to management. The remit also needs to outline the objectives of the change programme along with the time in which the change can be expected to be implemented and achieve its objectives and outcomes. Finally, it is very necessary for any remit concerning change to make crystal clear that a full range of options, not just one or two, needs to be examined and evaluated in deciding what change should take place.

Once the remit is established, an assessment team should be confirmed to explain the difficulty or opportunity facing the organisation, explore possible options, discuss the problems/opportunities and options with interested parties, and make recommendations about the way forward. The assessment team will usually contain representation from a wide range of people, for example those affected by the change, specialist staff (such as finance, personnel), senior management and in some cases a change agent – an outside consultant or facilitator who promotes and stimulates the change process.

The assessment team will seek to explain the difficulty or opportunity facing the organisation by gathering information and speaking to those directly and indirectly involved. This is followed by establishing possible options for dealing with the difficulty or opportunity. The options or solutions that offer the greatest benefit and are practical should be identified. The difficulties and possible solutions need to be discussed with the stakeholders affected by the change process. Finally, the assessment team should present its recommendations to those responsible for making the final decision on what change will occur. Those responsible may be senior management and/or those affected by the change, and they will decide to accept, reject or modify the proposals.

■ Planning the change

Once the remit for change and an assessment of the change required have been settled, the planning of the actual change which needs to occur and its implementation can be undertaken. The initial stage is to confirm the change management team, which will usually include many of the people who were members of the assessment team. Clarity, in terms of where and to whom the change management team reports, along with how it gains access to resources, is paramount, as during a period of change ambiguity can arise very easily.

The function of the change management team is to devise a schedule for change, specifying the tasks and activities that need to occur if successful change is to result. The tasks and activities should link directly to the objectives and outcomes of the change and be expressed in very focused terms if they are to be carried out accurately and within the desired timescale. This requires the support of those in favour of the change to be harnessed and used to progress the change programme. In a programme of major change it is important to review events periodically and assess whether the tasks and activities have been carried out correctly and are in fact achieving the objectives and outcomes of the change. In addition, such reviews are likely to yield lessons for future change programmes. Finally, most programmes of major change will require some form of training to allow those affected by the change to cope and perform well under the new working conditions. The training required can take many forms and may, for example, include skills development to cope with a new quality programme or technical training to allow staff to operate new equipment, machinery and computers.

■ People

The third and final element of Burnes's change process model is people. Whatever the change undertaken, people are normally part of the change process and therefore have to be given consideration. Burnes proposes that in implementing change there are three people-related issues that must be handled if the change is to succeed and the organisation flourish: people must be responsive to the need for change, they should be involved in the change process, and the impetus resulting from the change should be sustained.

Ensuring that people are responsive to organisational change is difficult, as it involves moving from the familiar to the unfamiliar. Therefore organisations need to ensure that the sources of resistance to change and how to deal with them are understood. This is exactly what Mr Serra and Mr Zugaza at the Prado museum are seeking to do (see entry case study 12.1). This can be done by making sure that employees are familiar with company plans and the pressures faced by the organisation from, for example, customers, competitors and suppliers. In this context, the focus of the information provided to employees should be to show that change is undertaken to secure, not jeopardise, the future of the organisation. Accordingly, the difference between current and desired future performance should be outlined in a manner that allows employees to relate the proposed change to themselves and their individual/group/section performance. This allows employees to think about how such improvement may be made and to contribute their own ideas to the change process. The successful achievement of change to meet the intended objectives and outcomes can be publicised to promote further change or change in a different part of the organisation, as required. In doing this mistakes do not have to be swept under the carpet, but should be regarded as a learning process for future change projects.

The management of a changing organisation also has to be responsive to change and understand the anxieties and apprehension felt by those affected directly by the changes. Significant concern about change in an organisation may indicate that all is not right with the proposed alterations, and further consideration of the suggested changes may be needed. The resistance to change that arises from anxiety and apprehension may be at least partly over-come by involving the people affected in the change process. Most change programmes are long and complex and if people are to be properly involved, they have to be so from beginning to end, in the development, planning and implementation of the changes.

Involvement should start with clear and regular communication with those affected. The communication process will involve the assessment team and the change management team and should seek to explain the context of the proposed change, its details and its consequences. The communication process should be two way. The people affected by the changes need to listen and take on board what is planned, and it is equally necessary for the change management team to listen to those affected and their views and ideas about what it is appropriate to change. This may result in the change management team reviewing their ideas and assumptions about what change is necessary. They should gain assistance in the change process rather than resistance to it. This can be encouraged by making every effort to involve those most closely affected and giving them responsibility for the change project.

Once the change has been developed, planned and implemented, the challenge for the organisation is to sustain its impetus. This is important, as if the impetus created by change is not sustained, there exists a danger that people will revert to old behaviour and past ways of doing things. In order to sustain the impetus, the organisation should consider several issues, starting with the provision of additional resources, both financial and human. These would provide clear support for staff striving to uphold previous levels of output for the duration of the turbulent period of change. The change man-agement team should also be given support and not be ignored, as they have been charged with motivating others and dealing with problems associated with the change process. If support for the change management team is not forthcoming, its members are likely to become disheartened and demotivated and will no longer be in a position to support and motivate others.

The development of new skills and knowledge among staff and leadership styles among managers is frequently required as part of the process of change. Backing for the process can also be provided by the organisation meeting the challenge of allowing staff and management to gain the required knowledge, skills and leadership style in a non-threatening and encouraging manner.

Sustaining the impetus of change can be reinforced by rewarding behaviour that supports the change and the new way of doing things. The rewards can be monetary or simply praise for achieving success in the changed organisation.

The process of change is an intricate blend of setting objectives, planning the change and managing the people involved, with all three areas involving gathering information and making decisions about what is most important. However, in many instances change will continue to occur long after the actual programme for change has been successfully implemented. This can become a pattern of continuous improvement and change.

> ### ✔ Check your understanding
>
> *Do you understand the Burnes view of organisational change?*
>
> Check your understanding by naming and explaining the areas in the Burnes model for organisational change.

Changing organisational structure

Structure and culture are the two most significant things that an organisation can change about itself. This section will look at changing structure and the next section at changing culture. The five basic organisational structures are identified and discussed in Chapter 1. Thompson[4] identifies four determinants of organisational structure: size, tasks, environment and ideology – *see* Figure 12.5.

■ Size

The size of an organisation will influence which structure is most suitable. The most suitable structure is that which allows the best and most effective communication and co-ordination within the organisation. A large organisation or one that has grown in size in terms of more and bigger markets, a greater range of products and services, an increasing number of employees or a greater number of factories or outlets will require a different structure from a small business that has just opened its first factory or outlet. The centralised

**Figure 12.5
Determinants of
organisational
structure**

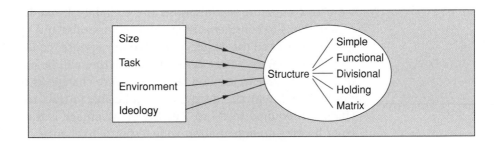

simple and functional structures are suitable for smaller organisations and offer a number of advantages and disadvantages, but these cease to be appropriate once an organisation has expanded significantly – *see* Chapter 1.

The question of structure can be illustrated by ICI and the dilemma the company faced in March 1998. It had just sold off its bulk chemicals businesses, retaining its paints business with the ICI Dulux brand, and had acquired other branded products such as Polyfilla. The debate centred around whether to keep the paints business together with the other branded goods or to separate it. ICI's view was that there were considerable benefits in keeping its paints business and the ICI Dulux brand together with its other branded products. However, one of its main rivals, Kalon, which specialised in paints, gained a much better profit margin than ICI from paint. The alternative view was that paint is a bulk chemicals business and there is no benefit in keeping it with branded goods, so it should be spun off into its own separate division. This was the approach of another of ICI's rivals in the paint business, Courtaulds, which had done just that. If ICI kept paints and branded chemicals together and the business did well, shareholders would be delighted; but if profits were not good and shares performed poorly, shareholders were likely to question the structure of the company.[5]

■ Tasks

A large and complex organisation with both interlinked and dissimilar tasks and activities will have a crucial need for effective co-ordination and communication. Where an organisation's tasks and activities are complex and interlinked, the most suitable structure will be decentralised such as the divisional or matrix structure. In contrast, if all the tasks and activities carried out by the organisation are dissimilar and unconnected, the holding company structure may be appropriate – *see* Chapter 1.

■ Environment

The external environment of an organisation exerts pressure on it to change. These external environmental pressures result from all areas of the external environment, typically including political, economic, sociocultural and technological pressures (*see* Chapters 8 and 9). Other external environmental pressures arise from changing customer demands and market size, as well as the behaviour of competing organisations (*see* Chapters 4 and 10). The key issue for organisations to consider is their ability to prioritise and select which pressures to respond to and the degree and speed of response required.

An organisation with a centralised structure will be much less flexible and therefore less able to respond rapidly to major change. In contrast, an organisation with a decentralised structure will be able to react more quickly to major change if required to do so, but the disadvantage is the greater difficulty in co-ordinating an organisation-wide response to change.

■ Ideology

The logical argument here is that the longer an organisation has operated with a particular structure, the more difficult it will be to change it. The difficulties will arise as people who are very familiar with their specific jobs and responsibilities are likely to be set in their ways and wary of change. This will have to be overcome, as described in the section on the process of change earlier in this chapter. A structure that allows the complexity, similarities and dissimilarities in the organisation's tasks and activities to be managed so that it operates both efficiently and effectively should be aimed for. This may mean that a new structure has to be designed that uses the best ideas from the five basic organisational structures.

> ### ☑ Check your understanding
>
> *Do you understand the determinants of structure?*
>
> Check your understanding by explaining how each determinant of structure may shape the structure of an organisation.

Greiner's model

The changes that an organisation's structure may undergo are summarised in Greiner's model – *see* Figure 12.6. This relates growth rate, age and size of the organisation to five phases of growth and development.[6] Each phase of growth consists of an **evolutionary stage** and a **revolutionary stage**. Hence it should be clearly understood that 'each phase is both an effect of the previous phase and a cause for the next phase'.[7] An evolutionary stage is one in which there is a dominant management style that is successful. In a revolutionary stage there is a dominant management problem that has to be resolved for the organisation to continue to grow and move on to the next evolutionary stage. The rate of growth is indicated by the steepness of the line on Greiner's model, a steep line indicating high growth and a gradual line indicating slow growth.

The key impact of an organisation's age is that the older an organisation, the more likely attitudes and behaviour are to be engrained, resulting in a potentially greater resistance to change. The larger the organisation, the more extensive the task of ensuring that communication, co-ordination and inter-dependence of the organisation's activities are achieved. An increase in both age and size of an organisation usually suggests that it has grown steadily over a number of years, which is termed a stage of evolution. During the stages of evolution (*see* Figure 12.6) the style of management behaviour continues to be more or less stable, with only minor adjustments required to ensure that the organisation is able to perform its tasks and activities effectively. In contrast,

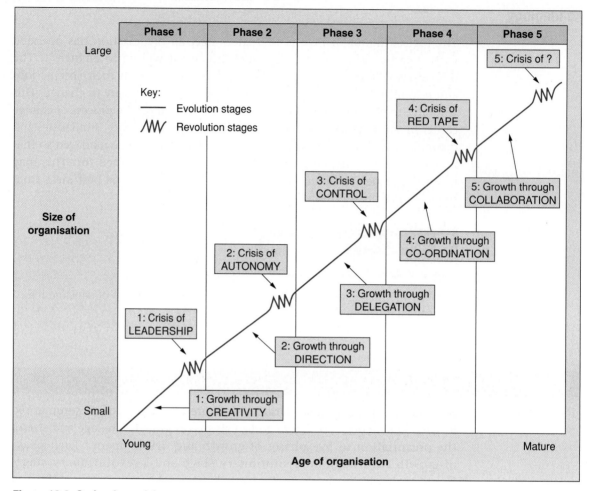

Figure 12.6 Greiner's model

periods of great flux and upheaval in an organisation's life are referred to as stages of revolution.

A stage of revolution is when old management and work practices are put under pressure from new requirements brought about by the increasing age and size of the organisation. The stages of revolution are shown on Greiner's model as crises with which the organisation has to cope if it is to pass successfully into the next stage of relative stability or evolution.

In the summer of 1999, the UK Passport Agency was in the midst of a period of revolution, with the installation of a new computer system and change in the law requiring all children under 16 who were not currently on a parent's passport to have their own passport. This created a crisis for the Passport Agency, as the number of applications for passports rose and waiting times for the issue of new passports also increased, from 6–8 weeks to as much as 15 weeks in some cases. This resulted in people panicking and believing that they were not going to receive their new passport in time to go on their summer holiday.

If an organisation is unable to deal successfully with a stage of revolution, it may be that it stagnates and eventually goes into decline, losing customers and market share, selling out-of-date products and services and having to make people redundant. The Passport Agency is the only issuer of British passports in the UK, therefore the government was anxious to ensure that the system worked. The crisis of the summer of 1999 was dealt with by the introduction of emergency measures enabling post offices to extend the expiry date of existing passports by two years.

Phase 1 – Growth through creativity and the crisis of leadership

In phase one of Greiner's model, an organisation's energies are directed towards developing and selling the product or service. Hence minimal energy goes into management activities and communication is regular and informal. The management of such an organisation reacts to feedback from customers and the marketplace. This type of organisation will typically adopt a simple structure (*see* Chapter 1). As the size and age of the organisation increase, a crisis of leadership will occur. The organisation's leader will be under considerable stress and unable to manage a growing organisation on their own via informal communication and co-ordination. There will be a clear need for greater management expertise in the organisation if the workforce and resources are to be handled effectively.

Phase 2 – Growth through direction and crisis of autonomy

The crisis of leadership is resolved through 'professionalising' the organisation. This involves any number of the following occurring: specialised managers being introduced to the organisation; restructuring, typically the functional structure being adopted; implementation of formal control and communication systems; and the development of a decision-making hierarchy. Professionalising of the organisation helps iron out the difficulties arising from running a growing organisation very informally and allows the organisation to continue to grow in age and size. After this further stage of evolution, 'growth through direction', another crisis occurs, this time the crisis of autonomy. The lack of autonomy results in employees feeling restricted by centralisation and the formal control systems that have been implemented. There is also a lack of opportunity for employees to act on their own initiative.

Phase 3 – Growth through delegation and crisis of control

The crisis of autonomy is handled by a move towards decentralisation, which gives more responsibility to plant and sales managers and provides an opportunity for employees to act on their own initiative. This is supported by implementing a structure such as the divisional structure, which uses profit centres and profit-sharing schemes or bonuses to motivate managers to perform well. Short- and medium-term planning is left to middle management and their workforce, while senior managers deal with long-term or strategic planning. The crisis in this phase is one of control. The move to decentralisation results in management feeling a loss of control over an organisation with a complex and diverse range of products and services in different and unrelated industries.

**Phase 4 –
Growth through
co-ordination and
crisis of red tape**

The crisis of control is tackled by the introduction of more formal planning procedures and an increase of staff in roles concerned with company-wide control and management of the workforce and resources. Critical functions in the organisation will be centralised, while decentralised units that show some relation or similarity will be merged into product groups. This should allow managers in the organisation to take a corporate-wide perspective rather than merely a local view of their own department or division.

The crisis arising from greater co-ordination is one of red tape. This is indicated by a lack of confidence in the relationship between staff in the organisation and headquarters, from where many of the co-ordination systems will have originated. The co-ordination systems may no longer support the local market conditions in which employees have to operate. In summary, there is an expansion of systems that is too extensive and rigid to allow an organisation still increasing in size and age to operate effectively. Innovation, which can aid organisational growth, will also be inhibited.

**Phase 5 –
Growth through
collaboration and
the ? crisis**

The red tape crisis is overcome by an increase in team and cross-functional activity, which usually involves the organisation restructuring to a matrix structure. The greater flexibility of the matrix structure allows team working and cross-functional activity to occur naturally. The strong co-ordinating management of the previous phase is replaced by social control and self-discipline of both individual workers and the teams in which they operate.

Greiner anticipates that Phase 5 may be concluded by a crisis of 'psychological saturation', where employees are exhausted by the demands of teamwork and the need for innovation. In conclusion, he suggests that organisations will adopt a dual structure. First, there will be a 'habit' structure within which employees carry out their routine, day-to-day work. Second, there will be a 'reflective' structure for 'stimulating perspectives and personal enrichment'.[8] This will be a structure that allows employees to refuel and may include things such as flexible working hours, revolving jobs and sabbaticals.

In conclusion, managers should be able to recognise the phase of Greiner's model at which their organisation starts currently and its associated organisational structure and features, and hence be able to identify the next phase of growth. This should encourage the development of the key skills and strengths required to get the organisation through the next crisis or stage of revolution and to continue success in the next stage of evolution. Moreover, progression from one phase to the next is not automatic and managers must consciously act to move the organisation through the rough revolutionary stage to the next higher evolutionary stage.

☑ Check your understanding

Do you understand the five phases of Greiner's model?

Check your understanding by naming and briefly describing the phases of Greiner's model.

Making cultural change successful

Deal and Kennedy[9] outline seven elements required for successful cultural change to be achieved.

Position a hero in charge of the process

Deal and Kennedy define a hero as a high achiever in the organisation and someone who personifies the organisation's cultural values and hence pro-avides an explicit role model for employees. **Heroes** 'show every employee "here's what you have to do to succeed around here."'[10] A hero put in charge of the change process will have to believe strongly in and be committed to the proposed changes. The person or hero in charge of the change process needs to inspire belief in and commitment to the change among the affected workforce.

Recognise a real threat from outside

Major cultural change in organisations requires sound reasoning before the change process can be initiated, as well as the appointment of a hero. An organisation's external environment may alter to such an extent that the culture of the organisation and the external environment no longer match one another. The more significant the threat posed to the organisation by the mismatch between its external environment and culture, the more likely it is that the culture can be successfully changed.

Make transition rituals the pivotal elements of change

The involvement of the people to be affected by change in the change process is a common recommendation of both academics and practitioners. Deal and Kennedy suggest a 'transitional ritual' or stage. This is where old ways of doing and organising things cease and new working relationships are established. This is a period of change in which people are encouraged to adopt new work patterns without rushing, while at the same time resisting the temptation to return to the old ways of working. Eventually the new working patterns and relationships become established as the norm.

Provide transition training in new values and behaviour patterns

New working practices and relationships need help to become established. Hence a programme of change will have to be available to all the employees affected. A culture change programme should focus on new values, new behaviour and new language if new working practices and new relationships are to become permanent and last in the long term.

Bringing in outside shamans

An organisation experiencing cultural change needs to drive the change from inside, hence the need for good management and clear direction. However, an outside 'shaman' or consultant can be useful in helping the people affected by the change span the gap between the two different organisational cultures. This can be done by defusing the friction and strife and helping those affected by the change see that the way forward suggested by the change in culture can work successfully.

Build tangible symbols of the new direction

People in an organisation affected by cultural change need to see and feel the effects of the change if they are to consider moving forward with the organisation and its cultural change. A good example of this would be a well-managed alteration to the structure of the organisation, as this would send a clear and tangible message concerning the direction in which the organisation was now heading.

Insist on the importance of security in transition

Proposed change in an organisation will always create uncertainty and as such needs to be minimised. The greatest uncertainty that people will feel is that surrounding the security of their jobs, and this needs to be made clear and dealt with swiftly. Those people who are staying with the organisation need to be informed that this is the case. Equally, those who are to be bought off or made redundant also need to be told. Dealing with the issue of job security in an unambiguous way is an crucial part of effective change.

Change is sometimes required in an organisation. Its result can be good or bad. The certainty of change is that it is usually risky, expensive and time consuming. However, if the managers involved are sensitive to the organisational culture, the change process can be managed successfully.

✓ Check your understanding

Do you understand Deal and Kennedy's seven elements for successful cultural change?

Check your understanding by briefly describing the seven elements for successful cultural change.

Summary

This chapter gave an overview of organisational change in its earlier sections. It then went on to examine two entities that are explored in earlier chapters and are also often changed by organisations, namely structure (Chapter 1) and culture (Chapter 2). The following summary covers all aspects of this chapter.

1 The causes of organisational change can arise from the external environment faced by a company, i.e. the PEST factors, competitors, markets and customers. Equally causes of change can arise from inside an organisation, namely the employees, trade unions, and individual departments or divisions.

2 The changes organisations experience may include alterations to size, structure and culture. Changes of this nature often result in changes to leadership, hierarchy and the decision-making process. Also the tasks and activities carried out by staff on a day-to-day basis may change.

3 The process of change is summed up by Lewin as being the outcome of the impact of driving forces upon restraining forces, which is commonly referred to as force field analysis. Certain stakeholders, e.g. employees, may be concerned about their future with the organisation and seek to resist change, while managers concerned about the long-term survival of the business seek to drive change.

4 Lewin also developed the change process model, which identifies three stages of the change process. First is the unfreezing stage, in which current behaviour has to become viewed as unsuitable. The second stage is moving to a new level, which involves finding and establishing new behaviours. The third stage is refreezing, when new behaviours become established and the accepted norm.

5 The Burnes model for organisational change identifies three areas which need to be tackled. The first, objectives and outcomes, involves identifying the trigger for organisational change, followed by agreement as to exactly who is responsible for instigating the change. Next an assessment team should be appointed to identify and recommend the changes which need to occur.

6 The second area in the Burnes model is planning the change, which initially includes confirming the change management team, who it reports to and the resources to which it has access. The function of the team is to devise a plan for undertaking and implementing change, which should link directly to the recommendations presented by the assessment team in the first stage, 'objectives and outcomes'.

7 The third area of the Burnes organisational change model is people. Implementing change needs to ensure people are responsive to change, involved in the change process and can sustain the change once it is implemented.

8 There are four determinants of organisational structure: size, task, environment and ideology. Changes to any of these for an organisation can be a driver for change in organisational structure.

9 Greiner's model is useful in looking at the different structures an organisation may adopt. Greiner argues that each phase or structure ultimately sows the seeds of its own decline and the move to a new structure needs to be actively managed for the period of revolution to be got through.

10 Deal and Kennedy identify seven elements required for successful cultural change. These are 'position a hero in charge of the process', 'recognise a real threat from outside', 'make transition rituals the pivotal elements of change', 'provide transition training in new values and behaviour patterns', 'bring in outside shamans', 'build tangible symbols of the new direction', and 'insist on the importance of security in transition'.

Learning outcomes for case studies

While reading this chapter and engaging in the activities, you should have learned how to apply theory and models, analyse situations, and evaluate the application and analysis you undertake. The learning outcomes specified below outline the type of application, analysis and evaluation of which you should be capable in relation to organisations. The case studies and the questions which follow provide an opportunity for you to test how well you have achieved the learning outcomes for the ethical issues and exit case studies for this chapter.

Application	Check you have achieved this by	
1 Demonstrate the use of force field analysis in a company or industry undergoing change	illustrating the forces driving and resisting change for an organisation or industry	answering exit case study question 1
2 Use the Lewin change process model to illustrate the nature of change in an organisation or industry	explaining the stages of change an organisation or industry experiences	answering exit case study question 2
3 Apply Burnes's model of change to an organisation or industry	summarising the decisions an organisation has to make when implementing change	answering ethical case study question 1
Evaluation	**Check you have achieved this by**	
1 Assess the relevance of managing change models	determining the potential usefulness of managing change models to managers in organisations experiencing change	answering ethical case study question 2

ETHICAL ISSUES CASE STUDY 12.2   **FT**

Cruising: sea change required on security

By Bill Glenton

With ever stricter security checks at airports, including the highly visible presence of armed guards, airline passengers can take heart that much effort is being expended to protect them from terrorism. But can the same be said for the millions using an even more tempting form of transport?

Is enough being done to safeguard the world's cruise fleets, which include 100 000-ton ships that can carry more than 3000 passengers at a time? Equally important, are the hundreds of ports worldwide properly protected?

Marine experts have little doubt that merchant vessels of many kinds are potential targets. The fact that terrorists successfully bombed a US warship anchored off Aden and planned an attack on a British ship in the Strait of Gibraltar recently gives more than pause for thought.

Cruise lines are certainly fully aware of the dangers. I can vouch for the much greater efforts many have made to reduce the risk of attack particularly since September 11. Most now use security aids similar to those at airports to check passengers and baggage.

Many have gone a stage further and introduced detector archways and X-ray machines that photograph passengers on boarding and issue them with a plastic identity card. These are checked every time anyone leaves or reboards. In addition, passengers are no longer allowed to bring guests on board ship in any port.

Virtually every cruise line employs trained security staff directed by a special security officer. Notable among these are former Gurkha soldiers employed by a specialist British security company. The use of CCTV to check onboard activity has also been much extended.

All of this is reassuring – so far as it goes. But protecting something as big and as complex as a cruise vessel,

▶

especially in an often loosely safeguarded port, is more difficult than doing so for an aircraft and an airport. There are obvious risks, for example, when loading hundreds of tons of stores on a busy quayside. Some lines check stores thoroughly but others are more casual.

Then there are the crews. They can number over 1000 in big ships and are often made up of several dozen different nationalities. Most lines check them for security risks but there are difficulties when so many nationalities are involved.

Of greatest concern, however, is the lack of tight security at many ports. Cruise ships often berth at cargo quays where there is a constant stream of vehicles and dock workers.

Given obvious dangers to such a global industry, one might have expected some determined internationally agreed action. Sadly, precautions are left to individual lines and port authorities. There is no unified policy – with one exception: the US Coastguard. Its 21-point policy for ensuring shipboard safety has already been made mandatory for lines using US ports.

It is mainly these rules that are expected to form the proposed International Ship and Port Facility Security Code, which has been discussed by the International Maritime Organisation for some time. If agreed by the IMO's 162 member-states at a top-level diplomatic conference this December, it should become international law worldwide around the middle of next year.

Many feel this is far from being soon enough and the IMO would have liked to move earlier. However, efforts by its safety committee to agree a code have been delayed by controversy over several of its suggested rules. While all agree the need for tighter security, some cruise lines feel that certain steps could seriously harm the essential, happy 'away-from-it-all' shipboard atmosphere.

A few lines were very slow to introduce gangway safeguards, fearing they would have a depressing counter-effect on passengers. My own impression is that most accept them gladly. But some cruise ship operators worry that too prominent a display of security might harm the relaxing atmosphere of their ships.

Brigadier Brian Parritt, whose Ashford, Kent, company International Maritime Security, supplies security officers to many of the leading lines, says safeguard standards have improved greatly but adds: 'It will be a real revolution when, for the first time ever, we will have mandatory international regulations agreed.'

The urgent need for an IMO agreed code is supported by Colonel Nigel Collett, whose Gurkha International Manpower Service in Newport, Shropshire, provides some 550 former Gurkhas as cruise security staff. 'Some countries need pushing to improve security in ports and ships,' he explains.

He also highlights the equal – if not greater – danger of terrorist attacks on merchant vessels such as container ships and oil and gas tankers. He adds: 'Some of these carry passengers and the checks on them are very rudimentary.'

One can be confident that much is being done and will be done to protect cruise ships from the more obvious forms of attack but, like the Twin Towers assault, it is the unpredictable that may pose the gravest danger.

As Jim Davis, experienced cruise executive and head of International Maritime Industries Forum, told me: 'Are we talking about hijacking, piracy, suicide attack or whatever? Identifying the likeliest risks is the problem that most needs tackling.'

Source: Financial Times, 6 Septemberl 2002. Reprinted with permission.

Questions for ethical issues case study 12.2

1 Apply the Burnes model of change to a cruise ship company which has introduced all the changes described in the case study.

2 How relevant is the Burnes model of change in helping organisations plan the introduction of change?

 For more case studies please visit www.booksites.net/capon

EXIT CASE STUDY 12.3

FT

Tata looks to MG Rover and the future

By John Griffiths

Tata, India's second-largest and longest established conglomerate, and Phoenix Venture Holdings, owner of British carmaker MG Rover, have signed a second co-operation agreement under which the British group will distribute some Tata vehicles in the UK and Ireland.

The move represents another step towards what Tata is now openly acknowledging as its goal of becoming the principal strategic partner for MG Rover.

Last year the two companies signed a deal under which Tata would provide MG Rover with a new small car, based on the Indica, so far sold only on the Indian market.

Tata is seeking a 'much deeper' relationship through which the two groups would develop new models jointly, along with major components such as engines and transmissions, Ratan Tata, chairman, said.

MG Rover is to start selling the Indica-based vehicle, badged as a Rover, in the UK in September, with a price tag of about £6,000 ($9,600). Planned volumes are higher than indicated previously. Under the agreement, Tata will provide up to 170,000 units over the next five years.

Phoenix has set up a new company, Phoenix Distribution, to handle distribution of Tata's Safari sports utility vehicle and Loadbeta pick-up, which will retain the Tata brand.

Tata also put on display at the recent Geneva motor show a new small estate car, the Indigo, as well as another utility vehicle, the Sumo, which Tata believes could fill further market niches.

Senior MG Rover executives are declining to be drawn on the prospects for a full strategic partnership with Tata, although they described the relationship so far as 'progressing positively'.

The current deal also gives MG Rover non-exclusive rights to sell vehicles in Europe, although Tata will retain its own existing sales networks.

It is clear that Tata regards itself as a potential replacement partner for China Brilliance, the Chinese automotive group with which MG Rover signed a partnership agreement more than a year ago. That pact provides for both market and model sharing, with its most important element

being the joint development and production of a lower-medium hatchback, one size up from the Indica, to replace MG Rover's current Rover 25 and MG ZR models.

Despite China's Liaoning provincial government seizing control of Brilliance in December – after its chairman, Yang Rong, was accused of economic crimes – MG Rover executives say the pact is still in place. Disclosure of Tata's partnership bid with MG Rover came as Mr Tata made clear that he was pressing ahead with a project to bring to market a '$2,000 car', which he believes could revolutionise personal transport in India and some other Asian countries.

He conceived the idea several years ago – to use components from the region's large scooter and motorcycle industries to create a basic four-seater, four-door car to which the region's millions of scooter and motorcycle riders, plus the many three-wheeler Tuk-Tuk users, could aspire. 'It is my greatest dream to make the car reality within my five years remaining as Tata's chairman,' Mr Tata said.

The project has become more ambitious as it has entered trial engineering phases, most notably with the cutting of the target retail price by one-third from the originally envisaged $3,000. Total material costs for the vehicle are claimed to have already been pared down towards the $1,200 mark. The vehicle might not be acceptable to Western consumers but 'it would not need to be a poor substitute for a car,' he said.

'It will look like a car and have proper seating – stretched canvas seats would not, for example, be acceptable. It would be all right for it to be a bit more noisy than an ordinary car, but it has to be both simple and safe.'

Despite the projected price being less than half that of the cheapest car on the Indian market – a basic Suzuki model – Mr Tata said it was not unrealistic and would not need to be subsidised. The vehicles would be produced primarily in kit form for assembly at several locations around India, to create local employment.

They have a potential market in other Asian states such as Vietnam, Malaysia and Indonesia, Mr Tata said, in addition to bridging the gap for 2m to 3m Indians between powered cycles and cars.

Source: Financial Times, 18 March 2003. Reprinted with permission.

Questions for exit case study 12.3

1 Apply Lewin's force field analysis to Tata to help identify the types of change Tata will have to face as it develops a 'much deeper' relationship with MG Rover.

2 How might Lewin's change process model be applied to Tata as it faces the changes discussed in your answer to question 1?

Short-answer questions

1 Name the external sources of change which may impact upon an organisation.

2 Name the internal sources of change which may impact upon an organisation.

3 Briefly summarise what is meant by 'force field analysis'.

4 Define 'unfreezing' as referred to in Lewin's change process model.

5 Name and define the second stage of Lewin's change process model.

6 Why is the 'refreezing' stage of Lewin's change process model important?

7 Name the three interlinked elements of the Burnes change process model.

8 Name Thompson's four determinants of organisational structure.

9 Which aspect of organisations does Greiner's model examine?

10 Name the five phases of Greiner's model.

11 Explain what a period of revolution is in Greiner's model.

12 Explain what a period of evolution is in Greiner's model.

13 According to Deal and Kennedy, why are 'outside shamans' useful in managing cultural change?

14 According to Deal and Kennedy, what is a 'hero'?

15 According to Deal and Kennedy, what is a 'transitional ritual or stage'?

Learning outcomes for assignment questions

While reading this chapter and engaging in the activities, you should have learned how to apply theory and models, analyse situations, and evaluate the application and analysis you undertake. The learning outcomes specified below outline what you should be able to do and the assignment questions provide an opportunity for you to test how well you have achieved the learning outcomes for this chapter.

Application	Check you have achieved this by	
1 Apply Greiner's model to an organisation with which you are familiar	stating which phase of Greiner's model the organisation is in and justifying your answer	answering assignment question 2
Analysis	**Check you have achieved this by**	
1 Analyse the change process that an organisation has experienced using the change process models	comparing and contrasting the analysis produced by different change process models	answering assignment question 1
2 Anticipate the future structure of an organisation using Greiner's model	assessing the organisation's ability to manage itself through periods of revolution	answering assignment question 2
3 Analyse, for an organisation you know, its ability to survive a period of cultural change	anticipating the likely outcomes of cultural change for the chosen organisation using different cultural change models	answering assignment question 3

Assignment questions

1 There are two models for change presented in Chapter 12: Lewin's change process model (Figure 12.3) and Burnes's change process (Figure 12.4). Choose *one* of the models of change. Compare and contrast your chosen model with another model of change from the literature (not Burnes or Lewin). Real-life examples should be used to illustrate the key points of your analysis. Present your findings in a 2000-word essay.

2 Apply Greiner's model to an organisation with which you are familiar and assess the organisation's ability to manage its potentially changing position on Greiner's model. Present your findings in a 2000-word essay.

3 The work of Deal and Kennedy identifies seven elements required for successful cultural change. Review the literature and present at least two alternative views on successful cultural change. Real-life examples should be used to illustrate the key points of your analysis. Present your findings in a 2000-word essay.

Weblinks available online at **www.booksites.net/capon**

1 This site contains articles and information about managing change.
http://www.change-management.com/

2 A site with 13 tips for managing change.
http://www.ncrel.org/skrs/areas/issues/educatrs/leadrshp/le5spark.htm

Further reading

Balogun, J and Hope Hailey, V with Johnson, G and Scholes, K (1999) *Exploring Strategic Change*, Harlow: Prentice Hall Europe.

Beer, M and Nohria, N (2000) 'Cracking the code of change', *Harvard Business Review*, May/June.

Burack, E H (1990) 'Changing the company culture – the role of human resource development', *Long Range Planning*, 24 (1), February.

Burnes, B (2000) *Managing Change*, 3rd edn, Harlow: Financial Times Prentice Hall.

Davidson, A (1999) 'The Andrew Davidson Interview', Christopher Bland/BBC, *Management Today*, June.

Johnson, G (1992) 'Managing strategic change – strategy, culture and action', *Long Range Planning*, 25 (1), February.

Kono, T (1990) 'Corporate culture and Long Range Planning, *Long Range Planning*, 23 (4), August.

Littlefield, D (1999) 'Kerry's heros', *People Management*, 6 May.

McCracken, D M (2000) 'Winning the talent war for women: Sometimes it takes a revolution', *Harvard Business Review*, November/December.

Parker, G (1998) 'Fear and loathing in Smith Square', *Management Today*, October.

Pascale, R and Millemann, M (1997) 'Changing the way we change', *Harvard Business Review*, November/December.

Senior, B (2002) *Organisational Change*, 2nd edn, London: Financial Times Prentice Hall.

Webster, G (1998) 'Changing places', *Management Today*, August.

Whitehead, M (1999) 'Hat trick', *People Management*, 29 July.

References

1 Lewin, K (1951) *Field Theory in Social Science*, Harper and Row, quoted in Thompson, J L (1997) *Strategic Management*, London: International Thomson Business Press.

2 Lewin, K (1947) 'Frontiers in group dynamics: concept, method and reality in social science', *Human Relations*, 1, quoted in Thompson, op. cit.

3 Burnes, B (2000) *Managing Change*, 3rd edn, Harlow: Financial Times Prentice Hall.

4 Thompson, op. cit.

5 Taylor, R (1998) 'ICI tries to get the right chemistry between old and new', Financial Times, 27 March.

6 Greiner, L (1972) 'Evolution and revolution as organizations grow', *Harvard Business Review*, July/August, reprinted May/June 1998.

7 Ibid.

8 Ibid.

9 Deal, T and Kennedy, A (1988) *Corporate Cultures*, London: Penguin Business.

10 Ibid.

Glossary

Absorption costing is a costing technique which ensures that all the overhead costs incurred by the business are covered by the revenues it receives.

Accounting rate of return (ARR) expresses the profit generated by an investment or project as a percentage of the capital invested.

Advanced SWOT analysis involves developing a two-dimensional matrix and assessing some or all of the strengths, weaknesses, opportunities and threats against external environmental factors or against the key functions of business.

Advertising is undertaken by organisations to attract new customers or retain existing customers. Advertising takes place in a variety of places: on TV, on radio, in the cinema, on the web, in the press. Firms usually have to pay to advertise in any of these media.

After-sales customer service is provided by organisations to support customers who have purchased and are using their products and services. Common examples include repair and maintenance services.

Appointment systems are schedules by which organisations see customers to enable resources to be used efficiently such that neither the customers nor practitioners are kept waiting.

Assets are things which companies own, such as buildings and stock.

Association of South East Asian Nations (ASEAN) is the trading bloc which encompasses many countries located in the Far East.

Auditor's reports appears in annual report and accounts and are addressed to the shareholders and should ideally state that the report and accounts, including the financial statements, provide a true and fair view of the company's activities.

Average capital employed over the lifetime of a project takes into account the residual value of the project at the end of its working life.

Bargaining power of buyers is where the industrial or commercial buyer is powerful if the threat of substitutes is strong, giving rise to a number of choices that allow the buyer to shop around. The individual consumer is usually much less powerful as a buyer compared with large organisations but is still influenced by factors similar to those for commercial buyers.

Bargaining power of suppliers is high in industries or sectors where there are few possible suppliers and they can exert a good deal of influence on the organisations to which they supply goods.

Behaviour defines things people do that can be observed.

Bet your company cultures occur in organisation which take high risks and wait a long time for the response to their decisions.

Boston Consulting Group matrix is one of the marketing tools which can be used to examine the range of products and product types an organisation offers. The idea is that a balanced portfolio is best.

Capacity is a measure of performance, and if a system is operating to capacity, it is producing the maximum amount of product over a specified time period.

Capital is money which a company raises to acquire assets and comes from sources such as bank loans, retained profits and shares.

Causal methods of forecasting examine the impact of external influences and use them to forecast future demand or activity.

Causal textures are outside linkages or interdependencies that are entirely in the organisation's external environment.

Centralisation is the concentration of decision-making responsibility in the hands of managers at the top of an organisation.

Commission for Racial Equality was established by the Race Relations Act 1976 to tackle racial discrimination and promote racial equality.

Competition Commission was established by the Competition Act 1998 and replaced the Monopolies and Mergers Commission (MMC) on 1 April 1999. The Competition Commission carries out inquiries referred to it by the other UK competition authorities and hears appeals against decisions of the Director General of Fair Trading and the Regulators.

Competitive rivalry in an industry or sector concerns who the present and potential competitors are, and how intensive the competition is between them.

Contract of Employment Act 1963 specified that employees should receive the main terms and conditions of their employment in writing.

Core permanent employees have highly skilled jobs, with relatively good job security and career prospects.

Cost focus is serving a narrow target market, where customers are very price sensitive and the company will deliver low-cost and thus low-priced products and services to the market.

Cost leadership is seeking to be the lowest-cost producer in the industry or sector to supply a mass market.

Costing involves looking at and defining the costs involved in producing a product or service.

Creditors are individuals or companies to which a firm owes money.

Culture – see local culture, national culture, global culture, organisational culture and personal cultural provenance.

Customer acquisition is expanding the number of customers for existing products.

Customer diversification is achieved by increasing sales of a new product or service to new customers.

Customer extension is concerned with extending the range of products or services available for a customer to purchase from the organisation.

Customer loyalty is the behaviour customers exhibit when they make frequent repeat purchases of a brand.

Customer needs and wants – the needs are those things customers must have, wants are those things which customers would like to have.

Debtors are individuals or other companies which owe a firm money.

Decentralisation is the dispersal of decision-making responsibility to operational managers.

Delayed delivery scheduling system occurs when the customer will not be inconvenienced by delivery of a service being delayed, e.g. a dry cleaners.

Delphi method follows a well-defined set of procedures in which experts are asked to complete and return a questionnaire. The results are summarised and the experts asked to amend their replies in light of the summarised results. This avoids problems of face-to-face discussion.

Demographic change is change in the age and structure of a population.

Demographics/Demography is the statistical study of changes in the nature of a population.

Dependent demand inventory covers items or components used in the assembly of a final product.

Differentiation is serving a broad target market, but by providing a product or service that is different and better due to its added value.

Differentiation focus is serving a narrow target market where consumers are prepared to spend a great deal of money in order to acquire luxury, top-of-the-range goods or services.

Direct costs are the expenditure on elements that go straight into producing the product or service, e.g. raw materials.

Disability Discrimination Act 1995 defines disability as a physical or mental impairment which has a substantial and long-term adverse effect on a person's ability to carry out normal day-to-day activities. People who have had a disability but no longer have one are covered by the Act.

Disability Rights Commission was established by the Disability Rights Commission Act 1999.

Discounted cashflow methods of investment appraisal take account of returns in later years being worth less than returns in the early years of a project.

Distribution is the method by which goods and services are delivered to customers.

Diversification is using new products to move into a new market, in which the company has not previously operated.

Dividend payments are the share of profits paid out to the shareholders of a business.

Divisional structures contain separate divisions based around individual product lines or based on the geographic areas of the markets served. The divisional structure is found in diversified organisations.

Drivers of change are influences inside or outside of the organisation that can be a source of change.

Economic influences on organisations include the impact of banks, stock markets and trading blocs.

Effectiveness is how well an organisation sets and achieves its goals.

Efficiency is the ratio of actual output to possible output, usually expressed as a percentage.

Egalitarian describes the principle of equal rights for all.

Employment Act 1990 allowed those individuals refused employment due to their lack of membership of a trade union and hence of a closed shop to take the union involved to an employment tribunal.

Employment Acts of 1980, 1982 and 1988 and the Trade Union Act 1984 all diminished the rights of individual employees and unions and expanded the legal regulation of industrial action and trade union activity.

Employment Protection (Consolidation) Act 1978 assimilated the Contract of Employment Act 1963 and the Industrial Relations Act 1971.

Equal Opportunities Commission was established by the 1975 Sex Discrimination Act, with the powers to work towards the elimination of discrimination on the grounds of sex or marital status.

Equal Pay Act 1970 came into force on 29 December 1975 and promotes equal pay for men and women.

European Union (EU) is a trading bloc which encompasses virtually all the countries of Western Europe, with countries from Eastern Europe due to start joining.

Evolution/evolutionary stage in Greiner's model occurs when there is one dominant management style that is successful.

Extension strategy is a plan for lengthening the life cycle of a product or service.

External environment is the big wide world in which organisations operate. It encompasses the broad general environment, the competitive environment and the marketplace.

External staff are those brought in quickly to meet increased demand and include self-employed consultants, subcontractors and temporary agency staff.

Factories Act 1961 lays down minimum standards in factories regarding cleanliness, workspace, temperature, ventilation, lighting, toilet facilities, clothing, accommodation and first aid facilities.

Financial management is the raising of capital to finance an organisation's operations and its careful use.

Financial reporting is allowing shareholders and other stakeholders in a company to know how it is performing. This is done by issuing an annual report and accounts.

Financial statements are found in a company's annual report and accounts and include balance sheets, profit and loss accounts and cashflow statements.

Fire Precautions Act 1971 requires work premises to hold a fire certificate and allows the fire authorities to impose conditions on the certificate holder.

First come, first served scheduling is simple and straightforward: customers are served in the order they arrive.

First peripheral group are those employees with full-time jobs, not careers. Employees in this group often require more vocational skills than core employees.

Fixed costs do not change directly in relation to the level of productivity, but have to be paid on a regular basis, e.g. rent and insurance.

Fixed position layouts are used when the product is too big or heavy to move, as in shipbuilding, airplane assembly and oil rig construction. All the operations are carried out on one site around the static product.

Fixed schedule system arises when a service is delivered to many customers at once. The timetable or schedules are generally known in advance by customers as the information has been made publicly available. Examples include bus, tram, train and airline timetables.

Flexible firm model divides employees into three categories: core, peripheral and external.

Force field analysis is the analysis of the impact of driving forces on restraining forces when an organisation is undergoing change.

Fraser's five-fold grading can be used to produce a person specification and covers the areas of impact on others, qualifications or acquired knowledge, innate abilities, motivation, adjustment or emotional balance.

Free market occurs where there is little or no regulation of commercial activity by government.

Functional convergence is the close collaboration and communication within and between departments in an organisation which helps ensure objectives are met.

Functional structures are common in both companies that have outgrown the simple structure and in well-established public-sector organisations. The organisation will be structured around the tasks and activities to be carried out.

Global culture emerges from the way in which national cultures interact with each other. The challenge for global organisations is to operate in a way which spans a variety of national cultures.

Global level is anything beyond the local and national levels of the external environment.

Health and Safety at Work Act 1974 covers people at work and those who may be at risk from the activities of those engaged in work. It created the Health and Safety Commission.

Heroes according to Deal and Kennedy are high achievers in organisations who personify the organisation's cultural values and hence provide an explicit role model for employees.

Historical analogy occurs when an organisation assumes that the sales pattern for a new product will be similar to that for a product already on the market.

Holding company structures are usually found in large industrial conglomerates with a parent company acting mainly as an investment company acquiring and divesting smaller subsidiary companies.

Hostile takeover bid is the buying of a majority shareholding in a company with the aim of becoming the new owners against the wishes of all or some of the current owners or shareholders.

Human resource management includes recruitment and selection of appropriate staff and management of the employment relationship, which includes contracts, collective bargaining, reward systems and employee involvement, and considers the strategic and operational view of human resource requirements.

Hybrid layout occurs when a product is assembled from two components, one being manufactured on a production line and the other in another part of the factory in a job shop using the process layout.

Immigration occurs when a person enters a new country with the intent of settling there on a permanent basis.

Independent demand inventory is items that are not dependent on other components, i.e. they are finished goods, like cars or shoes. Demand for such goods is directly dependent on consumer demand.

Indirect costs do not contribute directly to the product or service being produced, e.g. security staff. Indirect costs are often called overheads.

Industrial Relations Act 1971 allowed employees to take their employer to an employment tribunal for unfair dismissal.

Initial capital employed is the money available at the start of a project and takes no account of residual values at the end of the life of the project.

Intangible resources include things like brand image and information.

Intangible services are those things which organisations provide but which customers cannot see or touch, e.g. financial advice.

Interest is what stakeholders seek from an organisation, for example employees have an interest in the wages an organisation pays.

Internal dependencies are from within to within linkages or internal dependencies inside the organisation.

Internal rate of return measures the discount rate at which future net cash in-flows, when discounted, exactly equal the amount originally invested, i.e. NPV = 0.

Inventory or stock are different types of items held by an organisation and include raw materials, components, work in progress and finished goods.

Investment appraisal techniques are used by management to help in making decisions concerning investment in long-term projects and spending capital finance.

Job analysis is the first step in the employee recruitment process and involves gaining the correct information relating to the vacant job, to allow an accurate job description and person specification to be drawn up.

Job description defines and outlines the job. It includes identification of the job, summary of the job, content of the job, working conditions and performance standards.

Just-in-time systems attempt to eliminate stock mismatches and the system is organised so that stock arrives just as it is needed.

Key results are the outputs and outcomes produced by the job holder and declare the important results expected of the job holder. They are assessed by use of explicit success criteria. Success criteria express the expected outcomes and outputs in terms of quality, quantity, cost and time.

Key success factors are those things the organisation must do to satisfactorily meet the needs and expectations of its customers and other stakeholders.

Limited companies exist as individual legal entities, separate from the owners or managers. Therefore liability for debts is limited to the amount of issued share capital, whether the shares have been sold or not.

Liquidate is to turn into cash, usually done by selling assets.

Local culture could be defined as the type of place a village, town or city is, and the strength of identity that individuals from a place feel for it.

Local level of the external environment is the immediate town, city or region in which an organisation operates.

LoNGPEST is analysis of the PEST factors at the local, national and global levels of the external environment.

Maastricht Treaty on European Union covers the issues of currency, immigration controls and defence policy.

Management accounting generates information for managers to use in planning and decision making relating to the allocation of an organisation's financial resources.

Marginal costing is a costing technique of charging variable costs to the production units.

Market development occurs if an organisation manages to sell its existing products and services in new marketplaces.

Market penetration occurs if an organisation manages to sell more of its existing products and services to existing customers.

Market research is the way by which companies identify who is in the marketplace, their location, and their needs and wants.

Market survey is a collection of data and information from a sample of customers and potential customers. The data and information are analysed and inferences made about the population at large.

Market-based location is when an organisation locates its facilities in a place which is convenient for its geographic markets.

Marketing is the identification and meeting of customer needs and wants.

Marketing era for an organisation is when it gears all its activities towards achieving the goals and objective, associated with satisfying customer needs and wants.

Marketing mix describes the marketing elements that could affect the way a product performs in the marketplace. They are product, price, promotion and place.

Marketing tools are frameworks or models which can be used to conceptualise or think about a firm's markets, product and customers. Examples of marketing tools include the product life cycle and Boston Consulting Group matrix.

Marketplace is where the company's products are sold and can be defined by types of customers and/or location.

Materials requirement planning (MRP) relies on production plans to propose a timetable for when material orders are required. Consequently the resulting stocks of materials depend directly on a known demand.

Matrix structures attempt to merge the benefits of decentralisation with co-ordination across all areas of the business and are often used in organisations where there are two distinct and important areas of operation needing to be managed and co-ordinated in order to deliver the full product range.

Meritocratic describes government by persons selected according to merit in competition.

Mixed economy occur where there is some regulation to protect businesses, consumers and employees.

Monopolies and Mergers Commission (MMC) was replaced by the Competition Commission on 1 April 1999.

Moving to a new level involves finding solutions to the organisation's difficulties and implementing them successfully, such that old working practices are no longer followed.

National culture can result from one nation attributing characteristics to another, which can result in stereotyping and prejudice. National culture needs to take account of differences in the groups and communities which all contribute to national culture.

National level of the external environment is the home country with which an organisation identifies.

Net present value (NPV) method of investment appraisal converts future net cashflows into present-day values by discounting the value of money that is expected to be received in the future.

Norms are ways of behaving or attitudes that are considered to be normal.

North American Free Trade Agreement (NAFTA) is a trading bloc made up of Canada, the US and Mexico.

Office of Communications (OFCOM) is the new regulator for the communications sector and will bring together five existing regulatory bodies: the Independent Television Commission (ITC), the Broadcasting Standards Commission (BSC), the Office of Telecommunications (OFTEL), the Radio Authority (RAu) and the Radiocommunications Agency (RA) by the end of 2003.

Office of Fair Trading (OFT) seeks to ensure that all interested stakeholders, such as businesses and consumers, understand how the competition rules and laws apply to themselves and the competitive environment in which they trade.

Office of Gas and Electricity Markets (OFGEM) replaces the Office of Gas Supply (OFGAS) and the Office of Electricity Regulation (OFFER) and has powers provided under the Gas Act 1986, the Electricity Act 1989 and the Utilities Act 2000 to ensure effective competition in the energy market for present and future customers.

Office of Telecommunications (OFTEL) was established by the Telecommunications Acts 1984, the year that British Telecom was privatised, and regulates the telecommunications industry, including BT and other operators.

Office of the Rail Regulator (ORR) regulates Network Rail, the owner of the UK's national rail network, including the setting of Network Rail's access charges, establishing its financial framework and ensuring its accountability to the public interest.

Offices, Shops and Railway Premises Act 1963 extends the same general cover as outlined in the Factories Act 1961 to other work premises.

Opportunities exist in an organisation's external environment and often take the form of new markets or new chances for a firm to sell its products and services.

Ordinary shares are issued by companies to raise capital and are commonly traded on the stock market.

Organisational behaviour is the study of the performance of individuals and groups in different structures and cultures within the workplace.

Organisational culture results from the organisation's structure, employees and their behaviour, and the type of power and control present.

Overdrafts are short-term loans for 12 months or less and will vary from day to day depending on the amount by which the organisation's current account is overdrawn.

Overheads are costs which do not directly contribute to the product or service offered by the organisation.

Panel consensus is the gathering of consumer views on a product via groups, with the aim of reducing prejudices and misconceptions of the individual.

Partnerships are where two or more individuals join together in a business venture with each partner having unlimited liability.

Payback method measures the length of time taken for the return on an investment exactly to equal the amount originally invested.

Payback period is the length of time taken for the return on an investment exactly to equal the amount originally invested.

Person cultures are found in organisations where a set of professionals agree to collaborate to perform a specific service. These people could be self-employed, or at least would have little notion of being employees of an organisation in the traditional sense.

Person specification is derived from the job description by translating the job activities into the specific skills and abilities required to perform the job effectively.

Personal cultural provenance makes an individual the person they are and is determined by things such as name, gender, profession, icons, symbols, ceremonies, personal morality, norms and values.

PEST analysis is the examining of political, economic, sociocultural and technological categories into which external influences on the organisation can be placed.

Planned economies occur where production and other aspects of the economy are planned by central government.

Political influences on organisations encompass both legislation and industry regulations.

Power is the pressure a stakeholder is able to bring to bear to persuade an organisation to act in a particular way. For example, shareholders with many shares have greater power than those with only a few.

Power cultures are found in small, entrepreneurial organisations, where the owner works with few employees, with the centre of power, and all crucial decision making, resting with the owner/manager.

Power structures evolve in organisations over time and consist of individuals with power, who all share a common set of beliefs and values that underpins the way they work together.

Preventive maintenance is carried out on a planned basis, with the intervals between maintenance inspections established by experience, manufacturers or external authorities, and can be critical for items that are expensive to replace or repair.

Primary data is collected directly from people and organisations via questionnaires or surveys before being analysed to reach conclusions concerning the issues covered in the questionnaire or survey.

Primary-sector organisations are concerned with producing raw materials and include oil extraction, coal mining, diamond mining and farming to produce food.

Prime costs are the sum of direct wages and direct materials (prime costs = direct wages + direct materials).

Process cultures occur in organisations which take low-risk decisions, with feedback being slow.

Process flow charts show the order of and relationship between activities performed to make a product or deliver a service.

Process layout involves similar equipment and machinery being located together, as the processes they are use for are closely related.

Product-based location is used by large organisations with different divisions each responsible for their own product ranges located close to each other but separately, hence allowing each division to use appropriate resources for its own area of business.

Product development occurs when updated or new products and services are produced and sold to existing customers.

Product layout puts together in one location all the equipment required to manufacture one particular product and is the basis of a traditional production line.

Product life cycle is one of the marketing tools. The product life cycle can be used to examine the sales and profits a product or service is making, relative to the length of time in the marketplace.

Product planning and development covers identifying new technology which the company could use, new suppliers and opportunities to liaise with customers concerning new products.

Production era occurrs when organisations view their customers as a plentiful and captive supply of people who were happy to buy whatever firms produced.

Productivity is the quantity manufactured in relation to one or more resources used.

Projective methods of forecasting examine the patterns of previous demand and extend the pattern into the future.

Prototype is the first version of a new product, which will be tried with a few consumers as part of the market research process before being modified to give a final version which is launched onto the marketplace.

Public-sector organisations are owned and regulated by government at either local or national level.

Pull factors attract or pull an organisation towards a new location, e.g. the availability of cheap skilled labour.

Push factors result from dissatisfaction with existing locations, hence causing the organisation to consider changing location.

Qualitative forecasting is that which is non numerical and relies on people's views and opinions.

Quantitative forecasting is numerical and is feasible if the company is already producing the product or providing the service, as historical data will already exist concerning the demand for a product or service.

Receiver is a company or individual called in, often by the bank, to decide whether a failing business has any chance of survival and generating enough cash to pay its creditors or whether it should be shut down, assets sold off and as many creditors paid as possible.

Refreezing occurs in an organisation that has undergone change when the new behaviours are reinforced and become the norm.

Remote shopping occurs when customers purchase goods or service in a location other than a retail outlet, e.g. on the internet or via a catalogue.

Reserves are retained profits from previous years that have not been spent or distributed to shareholders.

Restrictive Practices Court was established in 1956 and controls practices that are presumed to be against the public interest. Restrictive practices can relate to the price of goods, conditions of supply, qualities or descriptions, processes or areas and persons supplied.

Revolution/revolutionary stage in Greiner's model occurs when there is one dominant management problem that has to be resolved for the organisation to continue to grow and move on to the next evolutionary stage.

Rights issues are share issues for existing shareholders only.

Rituals in organisational life are used to reinforce the routines and 'the way things are done around here'.

Rodger's seven-point plan can be used to produce a person specification and covers the areas of physical make-up, attainment, general intelligence, special aptitudes, interests, disposition and circumstances.

Role cultures are found in mature and large organisations with departments, in which everyone will have a specific job title and description and know how they are expected to contribute to the organisational mission.

Sales era was when firms did not consider the actual needs or wants of customers, but concentrated on persuading customers to buy their products rather than those of competitors.

Sales promotion is the activity firms undertake to persuade customers to buy their product or services. Examples include free samples and money-off vouchers.

Second peripheral group includes employees on short-term contracts, part-time employees, job-sharing employees and subsidised trainees.

Secondary data has already been collected and analysed and presented in written form, ready for people to use.

Secondary-sector organisations manufacture and produce goods, often from raw materials produced by primary-sector organisations.

Selling is part of the process by which organisations persuade customers to purchase their goods and services.

Shamans according to Deal and Kennedy are outside consultants who can be useful in helping the people affected by cultural change in an organisation span the gap between the two different organisational cultures.

Shareholders are the owners of a business as they hold or own shares.

Simple structures are adopted by small businesses in the private sector, which may be established businesses or in the very early stages of growth and development. The organisation is structured around the owner/manager.

Social change is change in the way people behave and live their lives, including the changing nature of decisions relating to marriage, divorce and children.

Sociocultural influences on organisations include changes in the age, structure and behaviour of populations.

Sole trader businesses are owned and administered by one person who is personally liable for all the debts of the business.

Stakeholder matrix is used to plot the varying levels of power and interest which stakeholders have in an organisation.

Stakeholders are any individual or a collection of individuals with an interest in an organisation and will hold varying degrees of power.

Stock market is where a company's shares are traded. The UK stock market is in London.

Stories in organisational life represent the organisation's history and typically highlight significant events and characters in its past.

Strategic Rail Authority (SRA) has responsibility for ensuring the implementation of an effective railway strategy for the UK.

Strengths are internal to an organisation and are the good things the organisation has or the things it is good at. Examples include a new up-to-date computer system or its good long-term supplier relationships.

Substitute products or services provide the same function as the goods they replace. A straightforward example is coach travel being a substitute for rail travel.

SWOT analysis is a way of looking at and evaluating an organisation's strengths and weaknesses (internal) and its opportunities and threats (external).

Symbols present in an organisation can be many and varied and often symbolise someone's position in the organisation or how much that individual is valued by the organisation.

Tangible products are those which customers can see and touch.

Tangible resources are physical resources and include things like machines and money.

Task cultures are flexible and often found in organisations that frequently undertake work for a variety of customers, which will involve a team with the required skills and knowledge undertaking very specific problem-solving or troubleshooting tasks as projects.

Technological influences include the impact of computers, software, communications technology and electronic media.

Telecommuters/teleworkers work at home, with technology that enables them to receive and send work and messages to their employing organisation.

Term loans are long term and provide the borrowing organisation with capital in return for repayment of the capital with interest over a number of years, e.g. five or ten.

Tertiary-sector organisations sell goods produced by primary and secondary organisations. The tertiary sector includes service-sector organisations such as banks and social services.

Threat of new entrants will be greatest if an industry is attractive enough to entice them. Attractive industries have high potential profits and low set-up costs.

Threats are in an organisation's external environment and can take the form of, for example, competition or tighter industry regulation.

Total quality management is defined as the whole organisation working together to improve product or service quality. The aim of total quality management is zero defects.

Tough-guy macho cultures occur in organisations which take high-risk decisions and receive rapid feedback on the effectiveness of their actions.

Trading blocs are made up of a number of countries that agree to co-operate with regard to trade and commerce.

Transactional dependencies are from outside in and inside out linkages or links in and out of the organisation, i.e. between the internal environment and the external environment.

Unfreezing process occurs when old behaviour in organisations becomes regarded as unsuitable and ceases, so that attitudes and behaviour can start to change.

Utilisation measures the percentage of available capacity that is actually used.

Values are things, people or attitudes that groups of individuals think are important or to be revered or respected.

Variable costs are those which vary in relation to the level of productivity and include direct labour costs and direct materials costs.

Vertically differentiated location strategy occurs when separate stages of the manufacturing and supply process are in different locations.

Weaknesses are in an organisation's internal environment and are things (e.g. resources or skills) the organisation needs but lacks.

Work hard/play hard cultures occur in organisations which take low-risk decisions and receive quick feedback on their performance.

World Trade Organisation (WTO) is the international organisation which deals with the rules and regulations of trade between nations.

Index